1 MONTH OF
FREE
READING

at

www.ForgottenBooks.com

By purchasing this book you are eligible for one month membership to ForgottenBooks.com, giving you unlimited access to our entire collection of over 1,000,000 titles via our web site and mobile apps.

To claim your free month visit:

www.forgottenbooks.com/free845751

ISBN 978-0-332-63399-2
PIBN 10845751

THE
MODERN PART
OF AN
Univerſal Hiſtory,
FROM THE
Earlieſt Account of Time.

Compiled from

ORIGINAL WRITERS.

By the AUTHORS of the ANTIENT PART.

VOL. XX.

IN RECTO DECVS

LONDON:

Printed for S. Richardson, T. Osborne, C. Hitch,
A. Millar, John Rivington, S. Crowder,
B. Law and Co. T. Longman, and C. Ware.

M.DCC.LX.

Modern History:

BEING A

CONTINUATION

OF THE

Univerſal Hiſtory.

BOOK XIX.

CHAP. I.

SECT. V.

The Hiſtory of Caſtile, *from the Time of its being recovered out of the Hands of the* Moors, *to the Time of its being erected into a Kingdom, in Favour of Don* Ferdinand, *the Son of Don* Sanchez, *King of* Navarre, *and who married Donna* Sancha, *Siſter and Heireſs of Don* Bermudo, *the third King of* Leon.

THE hiſtory of this country, and thoſe who governed it within this period, is exceedingly embarraſſed and perplexed, through the want of authentic records; the liberties that have been taken to ſupply theſe by fables and forgeries, and the unwillingneſs that ſome great men have ſhewn to have theſe coverings, bad as they are, taken away, and the naked and undiſguiſed truth brought to light. In order, however, to make things as eaſy and as evident to our readers as it is poſſible, to decline intricate or trivial diſputes as much as may be, and not to affect criticiſm

What is propoſed in order to the ſatisfying the reader's expectation on this ſubject.

to ſuch a degree of ſeverity as to hide from their knowlege thoſe marvellous traditions, which in early ages paſſed for undoubted truths, we will relate as briefly as may be both the falſe and the true, the fictitious and the real hiſtory of the old counts of *Caſtile*; after delivering ſomething previouſly, and that too as ſuccinctly as we can, of the etymology of the name and of the ſituation of this country; without the knowlege of which, what is to follow would be but imperfectly comprehended ; in the diſcuſſing of which point, if we ſhall appear to leave things ſomewhat looſe and indetermined, it muſt not be attributed to a want of diligence in our enquiries, or of a deſire to come at certainty, if it had been poſſible, but to that obſcurity, which, in ſpite of the endeavours of many learned men, ſtill hangs over this period, and hinders us from ſeeing ſo clearly as we could wiſh : a circumſtance which, how little credit ſoever it may bring us to confeſs, we nevertheleſs hold it our duty not to diſſemble.

Opinions concerning the origin of the name of this country and people. To begin then with the name of this country and people. Some have aſſerted, that it is to be referred to a certain old *Spaniſh* tribe, or nation, called by the *Romans Caſtellani*, who are ſuppoſed to have inhabited here as well as in *Catalonia* [a] ; but, perhaps, evidence would not be eaſily found to eſtabliſh this point, if it ſhould be controverted. There were, indeed, a people called *Callaici* in *Catalonia* [b] ; but if the beſt critics in antient geography are to be relied upon, the principal, if not the only nation in this part of *Spain*, were the *Vaccæi* [c] ; and it will ſurely be no eaſy matter to derive any thing for our purpoſe from them. Others imagine that the origin of this name is to be ſought no higher than the recovery of this country out of the hands of the *Moors* ; at which time, ſay they, there was a ſtrong caſtle built for the defence of the frontier, in which the count, or great officer of the province, reſided, from whence it took its name and its arms [d]. There is ſomething plauſible at leaſt, if not probable, in this, only the latter part of the argument ſeemed to be a little defective, if we may rely on the beſt judges of heraldry as to the antiquity of ſuch kind of bearings. However, as we are not like to meet with a better account than this, we may, perhaps, reconcile nicer critics to this notion, by obſerving, that if the name of the province was really derived from ſome ſuch caſtle, this may well be ſuppoſed to have been ſupported by tradition, as low as the times in which arms were aſſumed ; and then it will very well account for the aſſuming a caſtle by way

[a] HEYLIN's Coſmography, lib. i.   [b] CELLARII Geographi Antiq. lib. ii. cap. 1.   [c] CLUVER CELARII.   [d] HEYLIN's Coſmography, lib. i.

of

of allusion to that antient fortress [e].   But perhaps we may
have still a better account of this matter from what we are
going to relate, concerning the means by which this country
was rescued out of the hands of the infidels, and annexed to
that monarchy, which the Christians had formed in *Asturias*.
For in such enquiries one passage throws light upon another;
and if, taking all things together, they appear to have an easy
and natural connection, it is the best proof that can be had
that they are consistent with truth, or at least but a little removed from it; which, in such cases, is as much as can well
be desired, and more than can often be met with.

WE come next to describe the province of *Old Castile*, so *Situation*
called; because it was recovered from the *Moors* long before *of this pro-*
that which is stiled the *New*; as it stood in the times of which *vince, and*
we are writing, it was separated from the kingdom of *Leon* by *the manner*
the following little rivers, *Carrion*, *Pisuergo*, *Heva*, and *Re-* *of its being*
gamon; and, on the other side, it was bounded by the *Astu-* *recovered*
rias, *Biscay*, and the little province of *Rioja*; towards the *from the*
south it had for its limits the mountains of *Segovia* and *Avila*, *Moors.*
lying in the middle between the Christian kingdom of *Oviedo*
and *Leon*, and the *Moorish* sovereignty of *Cordova* [f].   As this
country was extremely fertile in corn and wine, abounded
with excellent pasture, and was consequently well stocked
with cattle, and the best watered of any province in *Spain*,
we need not wonder that both nations were desirous of being
its masters.   We are told by an eminent and elegant historian, that, even while it remained under the dominion of the
Moors, there were several great lords who maintained themselves in the possession of certain districts, and who, by degrees
increasing in wealth and power, at length shook off the yoke
of the infidels, and put themselves, as it was very natural
for them to do, under the protection of the kings of *Oviedo* [g].
If this account be true, as at least there is no authority to
prove it otherwise, we may very well believe, that these lords
had each of them a well fortified mansion, or castle; whence,
at the emancipation of this province from the yoke of the
Moors, it might well receive that name by which it has been
ever since known.   The same historian tells us, that these
lords, supported by their new protector, were not only able
to defend their frontier, but to extend their little territories
by their excursions against the *Moors*, as often as any favourable opportunity presented itself; and that from hence

[e] GUILLIM's Heraldry, p. 391.   [f] MARIANA Historia
general. de Espana, lib. viii. cap. ii.   [g] RODERIC TOLE-
TAN de reb. Hispan. lib. iv. MARIANA Hist. general de Espana,
lib. viii. cap. ii.

they

they affumed the title of counts ; and, being regarded as feudatories of the monarchs before-mentioned, were fummoned
in time of war to repair with their vaffals to attend the king's
ftandard, and in time of peace were called to the affemblies
of the eftates [h] (A).

[h] LUCÆ Tudenfis Chronicon, MORALES, MARIANA.

(A) We find counts diftinguifhed by the antient *Spanifh*
writers into thofe of the palace,
who had that title and dignity
in virtue of their offices about
the perfon of the king, and
counts who were appointed to
have the government of certain
provinces (1). The privileges
or prerogatives of both forts of
counts were precifely the fame ;
that is to fay, they had a vote
in the election of kings, a feat
in the affembly of the ftates,
and were not liable to any inferior jurifdiction. On the other
hand, thefe counts were bound
to perform their offices in the
palace, to raife the forces of
their provinces at the king's
command, and to repair to the
affembly of the ftates, when
and wherever it was fummoned
(2). We may eafily collect
from hence, that if a nobleman
affociated with, and fubmitted
himfelf to, a prince to whom he
was not born a fubject, he muft
take upon him the duties of fuch
an officer at the fame time that
he acquired the prerogatives ;
fo that, except the hereditary
poffeffion of eftate, and it may
be title, which, as the king did
not give, he could have no right
to take away, this affociated
count ftood in juft the fame point
of light with all other counts,

that is, did the like homage to
the king, and owed the fame
fervice to the crown. It muft
be acknowleged, that the cafe
would be very hard, if we were
obliged to make out every circumftance here advanced by in-
difputable authorities ; and yet
this does not in the leaft deftroy
either the force or the credit of
what is advanced, becaufe,
while it is in our power to fhew
the general form of this government, it concludes clearly as to
all that has been offered concerning this dignity. The kings
of *Oviedo* and *Leon* were elec-
tive and limited in their power,
and, therefore, fo muft their
companions be ; in which fenfe,
according to the natural meaning of the *Latin* word *Comes,*
the beft *Spanifh* lawyers have
underftood the import of this
title (3). But as the king was
no longer confidered in that capacity than while he governed
according to the laws, fo we
may be fure thefe counts were
under the like reftrictions ; and,
though they were the king's
companions, they were not his
mafters, or privileged to difobey
thofe orders, which, in virtue of
his dignity, the king, whom
themfelves had elected, had a
right to iffue for the benefit of
the ftate.

(1) *Las Partidas del rey Don Alonfo* II. tit. i lib. ii.   (2) *Petri Pantini de
dignitatibus et officiis regni a: c mus regiæ Goth rum commentarius.* tit. *Comit.*
(3) *Bobad. Polit. lib.* ii. *cap.* 16, *num.* 28.

DON

·DON *Rodriguez* is the firſt of thoſe counts mentioned by *Some par-*
name in the *Spaniſh* hiſtories, and he flouriſhed in the reign *ticulars of*
of Don *Alonſo el Caſto*, or the chaſte, whom he aſſiſted ·in his *true, much*
wars againſt the infidels.　Some antient writers ſay, that he *more of the*
was the father of Don *Diego Porcellos*, who is thought to be *fabulous*
the ſame that, as we have already ſhewn, received the king *hiſtory of*
of *Oviedo*'s orders to rebuild and and fortify *Burgos*.　There *the antient*
is, indeed, another account of this matter, which is, that one *counts.*
Nugno Belchides, a *German* lord, making a pilgrimage into *A.D. 884.*
Spain to the tomb of *St. James*, being kindly entertained by
this count, reſolved to remain with him, and to aſſiſt in defending the country againſt the infidels.　Don *Diego* was ſo
charmed with the generoſity of this ſtranger, that he gave
him in marriage his only daughter, Donna *Sulla-Bella*; and,
by his advice, collecting the people together out of the ſtrag-
gling villages, he brought them to live in a town, which he
ſurrounded with walls, and gave it the name of *Burgos*, from
the *German* word *Burgh* [1].　It muſt be admitted, that this has
ſo much the air of a fable as not to deſerve any credit; but
then to infer from hence, that the counts in *Caſtile* were not
hereditary, ſeems to be carrying the matter too far; ſince,
rejecting the fable, we may retain the hiſtory, and allow Don
Diego, the ſon of Don *Rodriguez*, to have built the city
of *Burgos*, not by the advice of this ſon-in-law, but by the
order of Don *Alonſo* the great [k].　What ſeems to render this
probable, and to give ſome degree of evidence to the before-
mentioned account of the origin of theſe nobles, is our finding that there were many of them at the ſame time; ſuch as
the count Don *Fernand Anſules*, Don *Almondar el Blanco*, or
the white, and Don *Nugno Fernandez*, which plainly inti-
mates, that they did not receive either their authority or titles
from the kings of *Oviedo*, but were indebted to them only for
their protection [1] (B).　　　　　　　　　　　　　　　　　　IN

---

[1] LUCÆ Tudenſis Chron. MARIANA.　　　[k] FERRERAS Hiſtoria de Eſpana, lib. iv.　　[1] MARIANA Hiſtoria general. de Eſpana, lib. viii.

(B) We may more clearly apprehend what is advanced in the
text, if we conſider the meaning
of the *Spaniſh* word *Caſtellania,*
which is derived from *Caſtillo,*
or, as it was antiently wrote,
Caſtil, which we find thus aſſerted in the dictionary of the
royal academy.　A ſeparate ter-

ritory, in the manner of a province, independent of any o-
ther; in which its particular
laws are obſerved, and which
has a juriſdiction over all the
places dependent on its capital
(4).　This clearly points out
what kind of authority theſe
lords had; who, upon the ge-

(4) *Diccionario d. la Lingua Caſtellana, tom. ii. p* 221.
　　　　　　· neral.

How a-
mongft the   In order to form a clearer idea of this, we are to confider,
great lords that the counts, to whom the grandees have fucceeded, were
one came to appointed by the king; and, in procefs of time, fuch as had
be ftiled the government of certain diftricts, difpofed things in fuch a
the count manner as their fons fucceeded them, yet always with the
of Caftile. confent of the crown m.   But, with refpect to the counts of
Caftile, we find no traces of their being appointed by the
kings of *Oviedo* or *Leon*; and if they had, there would, probably, have been but one count; and whenever that dignity
became hereditary, it would have been in his family; whereas
we have as much certainty as can be had of any thing in
thefe times, that it was not fo; but that, from the time of their
becoming a province to the kingdom of *Oviedo*, there were
feveral great lords, though it is not at all improbable that one
of thefe might have the precedency in virtue of the king's ap-

^m Morales, Mariana.

neral wreck of the Gothic monarchy, feized upon whatever
they were able to keep and to defend againft the common enemy.
It is, therefore, very probable,
that, as they were independent
of each other before they joined
themfelves to the kingdom of
Leon, they remained fo for fome
time afterwards; and that it
was not long before Don *Ferdinand Gonzalez*, who threw off
this yoke of homage, as he efteemed it, that any fingle perfon affumed the title of count
of *Caftile*, but at the time his
anceftors firft became eminent.
It is at leaft not repugnant to
probability to fuppofe, that they
might be intrufted with a fuperiority of power by the kings of
Leon, which, fetting them above
thofe who were as good as themfelves at home, made way for
their notion, that there could
be none better abroad; and
thus pride might eafily fuggeft

the defire of receiving, in
their own right, the refpect paid
them as reprefentatives of their
mafter (5). As to the city of
Burgos, it was raifed out of the
ruins of the antient town of *Au-
ca*, or *Occa*, from whence the
adjacent ridge of mountains is
ftiled *Sierras de Occa* (6). The
air of this capital is very fharp;
the inhabitants of that, and of
all the fifty towns, hamlets, and
villages, under its jurifdiction, are
hardy, induftrious, and robuft
(7); and it is univerfally allowed, that the *Spanifh* language, or, as called by themfelves, *Lengua Caftellana*, is
fpoken with greater purity here
than in any other part of his catholic majefty's dominions (8).
It contefts with *Toledo*, the capital of *New Caftile*, the pre-
cedence in the ftates, and upon
all public occafions; and it is
thought the difpute will not be
fpeedily ended.

(5) *Mayerne Turquet Hiftoire general d'Efpagne.*   (6) *Abbé Vayrac
etat prefent de l'Efpagne, liv.* i. *p.* 467.   (7) *Les Delices de l'Efpagne, par de
Juan Alvarez de Colmenar, vol.* i. *p.* 157.   (8) *A Tour through Spain and
Portugal, by Udal ap Rhys, p.* 40. *Lodovici Nonii Hifpania, cap.* lv.

pointment

pointment for the better government of the province; and also, that Don *Diego* might hold that dignity, when, by the command of Don *Alonso*, he built and fortified *Burgos*, which became afterwards the capital of the province, and the place where the king's count or governor resided [n].

If we consider things in this light, it seems highly probable, that *Nugno Fernandez* was the principal count and chief governor of *Castile*, at the time that Don *Alonso* the great consented to a match between his eldest son, the prince Don *Garcias*, and the count's daughter, which, as we have already shewn, was attended with unhappy circumstances, since that prince aspired to the crown in the life-time of his father, by which he drew upon himself the king's displeasure and a long imprisonment [o]. In these family quarrels the count of *Castile* not only countenanced his son-in-law, but also supported the queen *Ximena* and the prince Don *Ordogno*, governor of *Galicia*, and the younger brother of Don *Garcias*; so that at length, by their cabals, the good old king found it requisite to resign his crown to Don *Garcias*, who behaved more dutifully afterwards than he had done before; and it seems highly probable, that when, after the death of that prince, Don *Ordogno* came to be seated on the throne, he disapproved his brother's conduct and his own towards their father; and, on this account, retained a dislike to Don *Nugno Fernandez*, to whom he might impute those councils by which they were misled [p]. However that may be, it is certain that, having summoned that nobleman and the rest of the nobles at *Castile* to meet him at *Burgos*, in which they failed, he resolved to chastise them; but dissembling his intentions, and directing them once more to meet him at a little town called *Regular*, he caused them all to be arrested and carried prisoners to *Leon*, and there put to death. This Don *Roderic*, bishop of *Toledo*, represents as an act of tyranny, and a very foul stain on the administration of that king, who was otherwise a prince of great virtues [q]. Don *Lucas*, bishop of *Tuy*, barely relates the fact without any censure; and yet *Mariana*, and most of the modern historians, have followed the archbishop, and treated the king as a tyrant for this very act [r]; but *Sampiro*, bishop of *Astorga*, who had much better opportunities of knowing the truth, is directly on the other side, justifies king *Ordogno*'s severity, and speaks of these nobles as rebels [s]. But how just soever his motives might be, the manner of his

The king of Leon imprison'd, and puts to death some of these lords as rebels.

A.D.922.

---

[n] Chron. var. antiq.   [o] Roderic Santii Hist. Hispan. p. iii.   [p] Ferreras Historia de Espana, p. iv.   [q] De reb. Hispan. lib. iv.   [r] Luc. Tudens. Chron. Mariana, Ferreras.   [s] Sampir. Annal. reg. Hispan.

getting

getting these great men into his hands can never be defended ; and therefore we need not wonder that the people of *Castile* were generally disobliged, or that heats and heart-burnings were hereby kindled between the two nations.

Upon which, as is common-ly believed, the Casti-lians re-volt and set up judges,

ACCORDING to the general current of history, the sense which the *Castilians* had of this act of severity, joined to some new hardships they sustained under the reign of Don *Fraila*, who compelled them to resort to *Leon* for the decision of all disputes, provoked them to withdraw their allegiance from such tyrannical masters, and to set up a new form of government amongst themselves. This consisted in chusing two persons of quality, who were stiled judges, and in whom the supreme power was vested. The two first they say were Don *Nugno Rasura* and Don *Layn Calvo* ; the former of these was the son of Don *Nugno Belchides*, a man in years, of great experience, and of a mild and equitable temper : the latter younger, married to *Nuna Bella*, the daughter of his collegue, very brave and active. Don *Nugno*, therefore, was the legislator, and Don *Layn* the general of this new commonwealth [t]. They generally rendered justice together, seated on the same tribunal ; and, as a proof of this, they shew the remains of what they call the judgment-seat at the village of *Bijudico*, two leagues from *Medina de Pomar*, as a decisive evidence of the matter of fact, asserting, that it was built for their use [u]. We are also told, that the laws by which their sentences were regulated made the contents of an antient volume, entitled, *El Fuero de Castilla*, which continued in force to the reign of Don *Alphonso* the wise, by whom these laws were abolished, and a new code introduced [w]. It is, however, admitted, that nothing farther is known of the transactions of these magistrates ; how long they remained so, or who were their immediate successors. The truth seems to be, that the name of the village, and the ruins of something like a tribunal, together with the darkness of these times, inspired some fertile imagination with this history, that the birth of him who was really the founder of an independent sovereignty in *Castile*, might appear sufficiently noble : and to leave the reader in as little doubt as may be upon this head, let us intreat his patience for so much more of this story as will bring us down to this illustrious person, and we shall then dismiss these fabulous relations, which, however, he will find have passed for very good history with some very great men, as indeed what would not pass under an easy natural dress, which *Mariana* [x] gives to every story he tells.

[t] RODERIC SANTII Hist. Hispan. p. iii.	[u] Chron. var. antiq.	[w] LUCÆ Tudensis Chronicon. VASÆI Hispaniæ Chronicon.	[x] Historia general de Espana, lib. viii. cap. ii.

DON

Don *Gonzalez Nugno* was the ſon of Don *Nugno Raſura*, *The vul-* and ſome ſay that he alſo became one of the judges: but be *gar tradi-* that as it will, he is reported to have been a perſon of moſt *tion con-* extraordinary natural endowments, improved by more learn- *cerning the* ing than in that age laymen uſually acquired. He married *deſcent of* Donna *Ximena*, the daughter of the count *Nugno Fernandez*, *the firſt in-* who was put to death by Don *Ordogno*, and who was alſo a *dependent* lady of exemplary virtue and a moſt conſummate underſtand- *count of* ing. Theſe excellent perſons, having nothing ſo much at *Caſtile.* heart as the good of their country and the glory of the *Ca-ſtilian* nation, bred up moſt of the young nobles of *Caſtile* in their own family; by which they acquired, as no doubt they well deſerved, the univerſal eſteem and affection of all ranks and degrees of people. This illuſtrious couple were the parents of that great hero we mentioned, Don *Ferdinand Gonzalez*, of whom we are now to ſpeak, as of the real and indubitable founder of this principality, and whoſe actions were in themſelves too great, and his character in all reſpects too noble, to ſtand in need of any aſſiſtance of this kind; which, as it ever does, only obſcures what it ſhould illuſtrate, and renders that doubtful and ſuſpected that would be other-wiſe ſufficiently conſpicuous in its natural and proper point of light (C).

For, after all, it is morally certain, that no credit is to *Hiſtorical* be given to this genealogy, but that it is infinitely more *account of* probable this great man was the ſon of Don *Ferdinand Gon-* *the family* *zalez*, Lord of *Lara* in *Caſtile*, and who, from authentic *and firſt* records, appears to have been the founder of the monaſtery *eſtabliſh-* of *St. Peter de Alanca* [y], from whom his title and eſtate de- *ment of* ſcended to this ſon; who, by his excurſions againſt the *Don Ferdi-* *Moors*, by his hoſpitable and generous way of living, by his *nand Gon-* courage in war and conduct in peace, raiſed himſelf to ſuch *zalez.* an extent of power, and to ſo high a reputation, that he *A.D. 913.* married the Infanta Donna *Sancha* of *Navarre* [z], and go-verned *Caſtile* in the ſame abſolute manner almoſt as if he had been the legal maſter of it; but, notwithſtanding this,

[y] Morales, Ferreras.   [z] Roderic Toletan de reb. Hiſpan. lib. iv.

(C) When we attribute theſe ſtories in a very particular man-ner to *Mariana* (4), it is by no means to be underſtood, that he is chargeable with the mention of them, but that the honour he did them, by affording them a place in his hiſtory, has en-titled them to a credit with mo-dern hiſtorians; at which, with-out his aſſiſtance, they could never have arrived.

(4) *Hiſtoria general de Eſpana, lib.* viii. *cap.* 2.

he took care to preserve measures with the king of *Leon*,
whom himself, as well as his predecessors, depended ; th
highly probable, that as they increased in power the
deavoured to make that yoke as light they could ; as o
other hand, the great service they did, sometimes by rr
diversions, at others by joining their forces to the arm
Leon, made those monarchs less inclined to differ with

A.D. 938. than otherwise they would have been. At the famous
of *Simencas* [a] he was in the army of Don *Ramiro*, the f
king of *Leon*, and had a large share in obtaining that
rious victory, notwithstanding that *Mariana* [b] and
writers affirm, he did not bring up his troops till aft
battle was over, and that then pursuing the enemy wit
forces fresh and unfatigued he did prodigious execution.
it is sufficient to destroy the credit of all that laboured
tion, that he makes him found the monastery of *St. Pei
Alanca* in consequence of this victory, and of a vow that he
before it ; which monastery, as we remarked, was cert
founded many years before ; and, as there is just reasc
believe, by his father. However, by him, if any cred
due to the charters and privileges by them produced, it c
never be founded.

He disobeys IN the following year he thought fit to disobey that
the king of narch's orders, with respect to fortifying the frontier ;
Leon's or- as some writers say, entered into a confederacy against
ders ; who with the *Mohammedans*, which is not at all probable,
thereupon we find that the count *Ferdinand Gonzalez* and the count
seizes and ego *Nunez* were the next year reduced and brought to *l*
imprisons from whence the king sent them to two separate castles,
him, but kept them some time in captivity ; but at length, by the
afterwards terposition of the nobility, and very probably of the kin
releases *Navarre*, whose sister Don *Ferdinand* had married, he
and is re- set at liberty, reconciled to the king, and the prince Don
conciled to *dogno* married to his daughter [c]. At this time there is notl
him. clearer, than that Don *Ferdinand* and Don *Diego* both v
feudatories to the king of *Leon* ; for had it been otherv
no doubt but the king of *Navarre* would have sent them
siftance, and prevented his brother-in-law's disgrace ; bu
was too great and too wise a prince to protect him from
just resentment of his sovereign, otherwise than by an intei
sition of good offices in his favour, which we see had the
fired effect, and produced a reconciliation, at least for
present [d].

---

   [a] RODERIC SANTII Hist. Hispan. p. iii.   [b] Historia gé
de España, lib. viii.   [c] LUCÆ Tudensis Chronicon. Va!
Chronicon.   [d] RODERIC TOLETAN de reb. Hispan. lib. iv

BUT without all queſtion, Don *Ferdinand* was inclined to render himſelf independent; and there is nothing more probable, than that the king, by marrying his ſon to Donna Ur- the count's daughter, meant to divert him from that n, and to fix his and his ſucceſſor's fidelity to princes were of their own blood. Count *Ferdinand Gonzalez*, ſever, was too great a politician to be governed by ſuch a ſideration; and therefore the king was no ſooner dead he joined with his brother-in-law of *Navarre* to pre- ibe terms to Don *Ordogno*, who had married his daughter, d this with a view of making his brother Don *Sanchez* ng of *Galicia*, by which, the power of that monarchy being divided, he might with ſafety have ſet up for himſelf [e]. Yet when he ſaw that this ſcheme, though well contrived, was not eaſy to be executed, he did not care to run the hazard of a battle, though joined with the forces of *Navarre*; and this made a coldneſs between him and Don *Sanchez*, in whoſe favour he took or pretended at leaſt to take up arms [f]. He bore alſo the inſult offered him, by the ſending back the queen of *Leon*, with great ſeeming patience, which was purely the ef- fects of his policy, ſince it afterwards ſufficiently appeared that he was ſenſible enough of the affront [g]. His intereſt governed him then, and, indeed, upon every other occaſion, the great point he had in view was to render himſelf independent; and this he purſued indefatigably till at laſt he attained it, as we ſhall ſhew in its proper place. But this character of him, founded on facts, renders ſome ſtories of him by *Mariana* altogether incredible (D).

Marries his daugh- ter to the prince Don Ordogno, with whom he differed af- ter his ac- ceſſion, which oc- caſions his parting with his queen.

A.D. 951,

HE

---

[e] Chron. var. antiq.   [f] RODERIC SANTII Hiſt. Hiſpan.
p. iii.   [g] LUCÆ Tudenſis Chronicon. VASÆI Chronicon.

(D) Inſtead of troubling the reader with thoſe ſtrange and improbable exploits which are attributed by *Mariana* (1), and thoſe who have copied him, to this great man, we will content ourſelves with tranſcribing a very judicious remark from *Fer- reras*, which will give him more light than without his aſſiſtance we could have pretended to af- ford. The valiant actions of this brave man, ſays he (2), are ſo interlarded with fables and impoſtures, that it is very diffi- cult to diſtinguiſh between the true and the falſe, as is acknow- leged by *Sandoval*, with whom, in this point, all the critics a- gree. *Gonçales Arredondo* has written a hiſtory of this hero, which ſome perſons, for want of judgment, have conſidered as containing a detail of facts; whereas all that he intended was to afford proper inſtruction to a

(1) *Roderic Toletan de rebus Hiſpaniæ, lib.* v. *c.* 2. *Mariana* H *floris general* d *Eſpana, lib.* viii.   (2) *Ferreras Hiſtoria de Eſpana, p.* iv. *ſect.* x.

prince,

Don Ferdi
nand pro-
cures the
deposition
of Don
Sanchez,
king of
Leon, and
marries his
daughter
to Don Or-
dogno the
wicked,
who sup-
planted
him.
A. D. 954.

He pushed his dissimulation still farther ; and, upon Don Ordogno's making an irruption against the *Moors*, he likewise took a share in the war, and made a seeming diversion in the king's favour, though at the same time it answered a great purpose of his own ; for the infidels had built a strong fort at *Corazo*, on the frontiers of his country, which was a great thorn in his sides, and which he took this opportunity to remove [h]. Some writers say that he gained at the same time a great victory over the infidels, but that seems not a little doubtful, or rather it is confounded with another victory, of which we shall speak hereafter. It is, however, certain, that he took and demolished the fortress of *Corazo* ; and though by this he so apparently served his own turn, yet when, the year following, Don *Ordogno*, at the head of his numerous and victorious army, was on the point of entering *Castile*, he went boldly to that prince, pleaded the service he had done in the preceding campaign, and, by promising a steady adherence to his duty for the future, diverted that storm by which he must have been otherwise overwhelmed [i] ; and when the *Moors*, in revenge of that action, invaded his territories, he demanded and received such assistance from Don *Ordogno*, as enabled him to gain a victory at *St. Stephen de Gozmez* as entirely broke the force of the infidels, and left him nothing to fear on that side for many years to come [k]. The king of *Leon* he so much dreaded, dying soon after, he set on foot those intrigues against his brother and successor Don *Sanchez*, whose ally he had formerly been, as forced him to quit the throne, and retire for shelter into the territories of the king of *Navarre* [l]. Yet not satisfied with this, he took part with

[h] Chron. var. antiq.   [i] Roderic Toletan de reb. Hispan. lib. iv.   [k] Lucæ Tudensis Chron. Roderic Toletan Histor. Arabum.   [l] Vasæi Chronicon.

prince, under colour of writing the life of *Ferdinand Gonçalez*, which induced him to take the liberty of inserting therein whatever appeared requisite to inspire a monarch with heroic sentiments, in the same manner that *Xenophon* long ago composed his work of the education of *Cyrus*, as is well known to the learned. For this reason, continued he, I omit whatever

is mentioned in that book that is not supported by such authorities as manifest the truth of the history. We now see the true source of many of those strange things that have been already related, and it is also hoped sufficient reason for our declining to insert any more, as we would willingly inform without fatiguing our readers (3).

(3) *Mondejar, Noticia, y Juicio de los mas Principaly Hist. de España.*

Don

Don *Ordogno* the wicked, ſon to Don *Alphonſo* the blind, advanced him to the throne of *Leon*, and by that means reſtored his daughter to the title of queen [m]. In the quarrel of this prince, the worſt that ever ſate upon the throne, he broke with his brother-in-law Don *Garcias*, king of *Navarre*; and, being defeated and taken priſoner by him in the battle of *Aronia*, was carried by him to *Pampeluna*, where, it is highly pro- A.D. 960. bable, that monarch, in order to engage him to be quiet, prevailed upon his nephew Don *Sanchez*, king of *Leon*, to releaſe him from the homage due to him in that quality; and having by this means provided in the beſt manner poſſible for the ſecurity and good correſpondence of all the Chriſtian powers, he, at the requeſt of the counteſs of *Caſtile*, his ſiſter, ſet the count Don *Ferdinand* at liberty, and ſent him home [n].

ABOUT four years after he involved himſelf in a new war *Makes* with the infidels by fortifying *Sepulveda*, which ſo provoked *war upon* *Albacan*, king of *Cordova*, that he ſent *Mohammed*, his Alha- *the infidels* gib, or vizir, who afterwards acquired the ſurname of *Al-* *with va-* *mancor*, with a powerful army to demoliſh it [o]. The count *rious ſuc-* Don *Ferdinand*, knowing the extent of the place, ſuffered *ceſs.* them to inveſt it, by which their army occupied ſo great a ſpace of ground, that, by making a quick march, he fell upon them with an inferior body of troops with ſuch impetuoſity, that he forced the poſts he attacked, divided one part of the army from the other, which made way for a total defeat, wherein they loſt fifteen thouſand men and all their bag- A.D. 965. gage [p]. It is obſerved by *Ferreras* [q], as a circumſtance ſubject to ſome doubt, that at this time the infidels were at peace with Don *Sanchez*, king of *Leon*, who notwithſtanding took no umbrage at their invaſion of *Caſtile*; from whence we may collect with certainty of what has been before advanced, that Don *Sanchez* had relinquiſhed the ſovereignty, and no longer conſidered count *Ferdinand Gonzalez* as his vaſſal, which is a much better reaſon for his conduct than that which, in moſt of the general hiſtories of *Spain*, is very gravely aſſerted [r].

WE draw now towards the concluſion of this great man's *Deprives* life, who, as we obſerved more than once, ought to be re- *the family*

[m] RODERIC SANTII Hiſt. Hiſpan. p iii.   [n] RODERIC TO-LETAN de reb. Hiſpan. lib. iv.   [o] VASÆI Chron. RODERIC TOLETAN Hiſtor Arabum.   [p] LUCÆ Tudenſis Chronicon. RODERIC SANTII Hiſt. Hiſpan. p. iii.   [q] Hiſtoria de Eſpana, lib. viii.   [r] MARIANA, MAYERNE, TURQUET.

garded

of Vela *of* garded as the true author and founder of this principality; *the county* and though it cannot be denied, that, as well in point of *of* Alava; courage and military conduct as that kind of court-craft and *his great-* cunning which too often obtains the name of policy, he was *neſs and* one of the moſt diſtinguiſhed perſons in his time, yet many *death.* of his actions were ſuch as nothing but ambition could ſuggeſt; ſo nothing but a conſcience, rendered callous by a frequent repetition of crimes, could have borne. As for inſtance: at the time he projected the depoſition of Don *Sanchez*, king of *Leon*, amongſt other great lords whom he ſought to draw into a confederacy againſt that unfortunate prince, one was the count *de la Vela*, who ſeems to have poſſeſſed the little fruitful county of *Alava*, on the ſame terms that Don *Ferdinand Gonzalez* originally held his territories in *Caſtile* [t] (E). The count, however, reſiſted all his ſolicitations, and remained firm in the intereſts of Don *Sanchez*, even after he was conſtrained to abandon his kingdom and to retire into *Navarre*.

[t] RODERIC SANTII Hiſt. Hiſpan. p. iii. Chron. var. antiq.

(E) This little province, or county of *Alava*, has on the eaſt the kingdom of *Navarre*, Old *Caſtile* on the ſouth, and the country of *Biſcay* on the northweſt. It is in ſhape a long ſquare, extending one way about twenty-two miles and about eighteen the other. At different times it has been accounted part of each of the countries beforementioned; firſt of *Navarre*, on account of its being conquered from the *Moors* by Don *Sanchez*, with an intent to make it his frontier. As a part of *Biſcay*, the kings of *Oviedo* and *Leon* claim to be lords Paramount, as deſcendants from Don *Pedro*, duke of *Cantabria*, to whom the whole country belonged; and laſtly, count *Ferdinand Gonçalez* acquired it at this time by conqueſt (1). The

truth ſeems to be, that, with the aſſiſtance of their neighbours, the family of *la Vela* had induced the inhabitants to throw off the yoke of the infidels, and to live ſometimes under the protection of the crown of *Navarre*, and ſometimes under that of *Leon*. They ſeem to have been ſubjects of the laſt mentioned power at the time that the old count *de la Vela* and his three ſons were expelled by the count of *Caſtile*, to whom it is not impoſſible, that Don *Ordogno* the wicked, his ſon-in-law, might transfer his right to this country by way of compoſition for the great aſſiſtance that he had given him (2). But be that as it will, there can be nothing clearer than that, under ſome pretence or other, the count Don *Ferdinand* actually added this rich

(1) *Delices del Eſpagne, par Don Juan Alvarez de Colmenar, vol.* i. *p.* 93. (2) *Ferreras Hiſtoria de Eſpana, p.* iv. *ſect.* x.

varre [u]. The count Don *Ferdinand*, provoked at this, and at the same time perceiving how commodiously the country of *Alava* lay, if he could get it into his hands, resolved, as soon as Don *Ordogno* was placed on the throne of *Leon*, and had married his daughter, to make an expedition with all his forces against that excellent lord, and oblige him to pay for his loyalty no less a price than his whole dominions; in which, not without a great struggle, he prevailed, but could not get the person of the count into his power; who, with all his family, and the best part of his dependents, made their escape, and took refuge in the court of *Abderhaman*, king of *Cordova* [w]. He was there received and entertained in a manner suitable to his quality; and, at his intercession in

---

[u] LUCÆ Tudensis Chron. Arabum.	[w] RODERIC TOLETAN Hist.

---

country to his dominions. *Mariana* insinuates, it was in resentment of several irruptions made by the family of *Vela* into *Castile* (3); which if true, must have been in the reign of Don *Ordogno* the third, and by his orders, at the time of his repudiating Donna *Urraca* (4). This old count, taking shelter at *Cordova*, grew there into great intimacy with Don *Sanchez*, king of *Leon*, who was an exile as well as himself, and by the help of these unfortunate princes and their adherents, who were all determined enemies of the count of *Castile*, the infidels received so good intelligence of every thing in that country as rendered them infinitely more able to harrass the count *Ferdinand* than they had ever been; in most of which excursions, such is the force of implacable hatred, the counts, at the head of their followers, came in conjunction with their new allies, and were the chief instruments of the mischiefs done by them on all occasions (5). At length years infirmities, and vexations, absolutely broke the heart of the old count *de Vela*, but not before he had broke that of his enemy. For several historians say, and the fact is not at all improbable, that when, after all his labours, hazards, and victories, the great count of *Castile* saw his barrier destroyed, and his subjects in a manner ruined by this unnatural conjunction of Christians and *Moors* which he had brought upon himself, it affected him to such a degree that he died rather of grief than any other disease (6). A dreadful example of the inconstancy of human prosperity and the unexpected reverses of fortune, to which even the greatest politicians are always exposed.

---

(3) *Historia de Espana, lib.* viii.	(4) *Roderic de Toletan de rebus Hispan. lib.* v.	(5) *Lucæ Tudensis Chronicon. Joan. Vasæi Hispania Coronicon. Alphons. a Carthagena reg. Hispan. Anatephalæosis.*	(6) *Mariana Historia general de Espana, lib.* viii.

succeeding times, most of those dreadful incursions were made that sometimes reduced both *Leon* and *Castile* within a hair's breadth of ruin [x]. Notwithstanding this, and the repeated intercessions, as well of the kings of *Navarre* as of *Leon*, he never could be prevailed on to do that nobleman justice, but kept the county of *Alava* till the day of his death, which happened in the month of *July*, in the year of our lord 970 [y], when he left his territory free in all respects, very much extended, and the frontier well fortified, and a great corps of intrepid and well disciplined troops, to his son, a prince of great hopes, and highly esteemed by his neighbours.

Don Garcias Fernandez succeeds his father, and is victorious over the Moors.

THE name of this young count was Don *Garcias Fernandez*, who, from the time he became possessed of his father's dominions, turned his thoughts entirely upon the improvement of the country, and to the emolument of its inhabitants; by which he deservedly raised a very high reputation, and obtained not only the confidence of his own subjects, but of his neighbours [z]. He seems to have passed the first seven years of his government in peace, owing chiefly to the age and infirmities of one king of *Cordova*, and to the indolent temper of another; but this last having made choice of *Mohammed Abenanier* for his prime minister, who was a man of great abilities, and of an active and martial disposition, he readily listened to the repeated applications of the count *de la Vela*, and set on foot a numerous army, commanded by *Orduan*, one of the most experienced officers in his service, in order to restore him to his dominions, with whom went the count in person and most of his partisans [a]. As soon as count *Garcias* had intelligence of these formidable preparations, he strenuously sollicited the assistance of Don *Ramiro* the third, then king of *Leon*, but without effect; for that prince, being at peace with the *Moors*, refused to break with them upon his account. But his cousin Don *Sanchez Abarca*, king of *Navarre*, declared frankly in his favour, and began to arm immediately with the same zeal as if it had been in his own quarrel. *Orduan*, general of the *Moors*, entered *Castile* on the side of *Osma* and *St. Stephen*, *Gormez* wasting the country with fire and sword; but as soon as the troops of *Navarre* had joined Don *Garcias*, he attacked them with so much vivacity, that they were quickly routed, and with the loss of a

A.D 979.

[x] RODERIC TOLETAN de reb. Hispan. lib. iv. [y] VASÆI Chron. [z] MARIANA Historia general de Espana, lib. viii. FERRERAS Historia de Espana, p. iv. MAYERNE, TURQUET Histoire general d'Espagne, lib. vii. [a] RODERIC TOLETAN Hist. Arabum.

considerable

confiderable body of men, as well as of their baggage, were conftrained to make a precipitate retreat into the territories of *Cordova*, which gained count *Garcia Fernandez* great reputation [b].

As the infidels were highly provoked by this defeat, they levied the next year an army very far fuperior to that which had been beaten, and *Mohammed Abenamir*, furnamed after-wards *Almanzor*, took the refolution of commanding it in perfon [c]. The count of *Caftile* follicited as before both kings in his favour, but the one granted him none, and the other very fmall fuccours, under pretence that the former campaign had been very expenfive [d]. The count Don *Garcia*, therefore, found himfelf fo much inferior to the enemy that he durft not hazard a battle, yet he feemed often difpofed to hazard it, and by marches and counter-marches harraffed the *Moors* fo much that their general was exceffively provoked, and at length contented himfelf with befieging *St. Stephen de Gormez*. This place was fo well fortified, and defended by fo ftrong a garrifon, that his army fuffered exceedingly during the fiege, which induced him, when the place was taken, to put the garrifon to the fword, the rather becaufe his forces were fo much diminifhed and fatigued, that he found himfelf in no condition to undertake any thing farther, and was therefore obliged to defer the bloody vengeance he threatened to take till the next year [e]. The next campaign was notwithftanding lefs favourable to the infidels than the former, though Don *Garcia* had not a better army in the field; but his fortreffes were fo well provided, and the *Moors* had fo little ftomach to fieges, that, after moving up and down the open country which they ravaged, they found it expedient to retire; and the next year they either did nothing or employed their arms elfewhere [f].

ABOUT four years after *Almanzor* made a new irruption into *Caftile*, took *Sepulvida* after a long fiege, and feveral other places; from whence we may conclude, though there is no mention of it in the *Spanifh* hiftories, that he gained fome advantage over the count Don *Garcia*, who otherwife would not have been a tame fpectator of the miferies his people felt [g]. The refolution taken by the *Moors* next year to act with all their forces againft the king of *Leon* procured the *Caftilians* fome recefs, which the count employed in repairing his fortreffes and recruiting his troops. Three years after *Almanzor* made a new invafion, and brought with him

Marginal notes:
Baffles the Moors in feveral inwards vafions with inferior forces.

A.D. 980.

A.D. 981.

Carries on the war with great intrepidity, tho' with various fuccefs.

A.D. 986.

---

[b] RODERIC SANTII Hift. Hifpan. p. iii.　　[c] LUCÆ Tudenfis Chron. VASÆI Chron.　　[d] RODERIC TOLETAN de reb. Hifpan. lib. iv.　　[e] Chron. var. antiq.　　[f] RODERIC TOLETAN Hift. Arabum.　　[g] LUCÆ Tudenfis Chron.

the sons of the count *de la Vela* [h]. Don *Garcia* was now affisted by the kings of *Leon* and *Navarre*, but not in any proportion to the number of his enemies, who befieged and took *Alienca* ; which, however, put an end to their progrefs for

A.D. 989. that year [i]. The next was rather more unfortunate, for the count having but a very fmall army in the field, they ravaged and deftroyed the country at their pleafure, but without undertaking any fiege. The year following *Almanzor* invaded *Caftile*

990. again, and, after endeavouring to no purpofe to force Don *Garcia* to a battle, he, in the month of *Auguft*, befieged and

991. took *Ofma* after a long refiftance [k]. This war was in a good meafure fufpended for the three following years ; during which, however, the count Don *Garcias* was exceedingly perplexed with fome difputes that arofe between him and his coufin Don *Sanchez*, king of *Navarre*, which ended not but with the death of the latter.

Obtains   WHEN the infidels renewed the war, they made a greater
feveral ad- impreffion upon *Caftile* than they had ever done, and not
vantages only took but garrifoned *Corugna* and *St. Stephen de Gormez*,
over the which they held for feveral years [l] ; and it is highly probable,
infidels, that they might have pufhed their conquefts much farther, if
and recalls they had not at this time meditated the deftruction of *Leon*,
the family which they effected foon after. It was the lofs and ruin of
of Vela. that important place that faved the Chriftians in *Spain* from
being undone, by opening their eyes to the neceffity of
uniting, and produced that league between the kings of *Leon*
and *Navarre* and the count of *Caftile*. This firft gave a check
to the arms of the infidels, by the glorious victory [m] obtained
over them in the plains of *Ofma*, where all the three princes
acted in perfon ; and where, after the *Moors* were defeated,
the purfuit was committed to the count of *Caftile*, who executed it with fuch vigour, as drew upon him the particular
refentment of the infidels. As foon as they were able to gather
another army, they refolved to employ it folely againft his

A.D. 999. dominions ; but Don *Bermudo*, king of *Leon*, dying in the in-
terim, engaged them to alter their intention, and to make an
irruption into that kingdom, where the *Moorifh* army, under
the command of *Abdilmelech*, was thoroughly and fhamefully
beaten by the confederates, commanded by Don *Garcia*,

A. D. count of *Caftile* [n]. The year following died Don *Garcias*,
1000. king of *Navarre*, and was fucceeded by Don *Sanchez*, afterwards furnamed the Great ; and the fame year Don *Garcia*,

[h] VASÆI Chron.   [i] RODERIC·SANTII Hift Hifpan. lib. iv.
[k] RODERIC TOLETAN Hift. Arabum.   [l] Chron. var. antiq.
[m] LUCÆ Tudenfis Chron. VASÆI Chron.   [n] RODERIC TO-
LETAN Hift. Arabum.

count of *Caftile*, confented, that the fons of the count *de la Vela* fhould be reftored to their patrimony, and that a general pardon fhould be granted to them and all their adherents (F).

THE young king of *Navarre* being arrived at an age in *His fon* which it was fit for him to marry, caft his eyes upon Donna *raifes an*

(F) The propenfity of the *Spanifh* writers, to give place in their general hiftories unto the fictions contrived to raife the luftre of particular families, has diverted them from fuch enquiries as would have been of infinitely more ufe; fo that it is difficult to fay whether they deferve more blame for giving place to feigned hiftory, or for omitting fuch circumftances as might have illuftrated what is true (1). According to *Mariana's* account, there was a kind of war between *Leon* and *Caftile* during the beft part of Don *Garcia's* adminiftration, which he infers from the *Moors* continuing to infeft *Caftile* without any diverfion made, or any oppofition given, by the kings of *Leon* (2). This, however, feems to be carrying things too far, and yet there is a ground of truth at bottom. Don *Sanchez*, king of *Leon*, and his fon, were under fuch obligations to the king of *Cordova* as would not permit them to act againft the *Moors*, on account of their incurfions into *Caftile*, which was now become an independent principality, which was a great misfortune to Don *Garcia*. On the other hand, when the *Moors* attacked the kingdom of *Leon*, the people of *Caftile* were fo enfeebled by the long war which they had fuftained, that they were in no condition to yield affiftance to their neighbours, which brought deftruction upon the people of *Leon*; but at length all the Chriftian princes opened their eyes, and faw what they might have feen long before, that the diftrefs of one would very quickly become the deftruction of all, and they united but juft time enough to prevent it (3). All thefe mifchiefs were the effects of Don *Ferdinand Gonzalez's* ambition and falfe politics; and therefore his fon very wifely confented to recall the family of *Vela*; who, during their exile, had fufficiently revenged the injury done them of defpoiling them of their county of *Alava* (4); to which it is doubtful whether they were now reftored. But, however, the bringing back them and their partifans from the *Moors* proved of great confequence to all the Chriftian powers (5); who, from the beginning of the eleventh century, began to recover that fuperiority which they had loft for many years; and thus we have taken the liberty, by conjectures, to remove, in fome meafure, that obfcurity in which this period is involved (6).

(1) *Mondejar Noticia y Juicio de los mas principales Hiftoriadores de Efpana.* (2) *Hiftoria general de Efpana, lib.* viii.   (3) *Lucæ Tudenfis Chronicon. Roderic. Toletan de reb. Hifpaniæ, lib.* v.   (4) *Ferreras Hiftoria de Efpana, p.* iv. *fect.* x.   (5) *Mariana, Mayerne, Turquet, Ferreras.*   (6) *P. Moret inveftigationes biftoricas de los antiquitades del Reyno de Navarre, lib.* ii. *c.* viii.

insur-
rection a-
gainſt him,
but is re-
duced and
pardoned.
A. D.
1001.

Elvira, the daughter of Don *Sanchez*, and the grand daughter of Don *Garcia*, count of *Caſtile*, whom he ſoon after demanded in marriage by his embaſſadors, to whom the young lady being readily delivered, the marriage was ſoon after ſolemnized with great ſplendor at *Pampeluna* [p]. The great joy occaſioned by this event, which was indeed very favourable to the Chriſtian cauſe, was very ſoon damped by the ill conduct of this young queen's father, who, liſtening to the advice of count *Garcia Gomez*, and ſome other flatterers, began to form cabals againſt his parent and his prince. The count Don *Garcia* laboured all that was in his power to convince his ſon of the folly of his proceeding, but to no purpoſe, for the prince was as obſtinate as he was undutiful; ſo that at length the count of *Caſtile*, who was grown old in fighting againſt the infidels, was obliged once more to draw his ſword, in order to chaſtiſe his ſon [q]. Don *Sanchez* puſhed things to extremities, and would not ſuffer their differences to be any other way terminated than by a battle; in which, it is on all hands agreed, he was thoroughly beaten [r]; and though *Mariana* [s] and ſome other hiſtorians ſay, that he kept up the conteſt notwithſtanding till his father's death, yet authors [t], who lived nearer theſe times, aſſert, that he was wiſe enough to ſubmit to aſk pardon of Don *Garcia*, and not only to receive it, but by ſignal marks of repentance, and a ſincere return to his duty, effaced the very memory of his crime, which delivered the *Caſtilians* in time from a civil war, that might otherwiſe have rendered them an eaſy prey to the infidels, who, as it was very natural, began their preparations to invade *Caſtile* on the firſt news of this diſpute.

1003.

At length
taken pri-
ſoner by
the Moors,
and dies
of his
wounds.

ABDERAMA ſucceeded his brother *Abdilmelech* in the poſt of general, or commander in chief of the forces of *Cordova*; and being exceedingly deſirous to ſignalize his entrance on that great office, by revenging his father's death and his brother's diſgrace, he aſſembled a very numerous army, with which he invaded *Caſtile* [u]; and as ſeveral of the beſt fortreſſes had been ruined, and two of them were ſtill in the hands of the *Moors*, there ſeemed to be nothing more eaſy, than with ſuperior forces to ruin and deſtroy the country, if not to make an abſolute conqueſt. The count, Don *Garcia*, perceiving the enemy's deſign, and knowing no other way to preſerve his country from ruin, aſſembled as many troops

[p] RODERIC SANTII Hiſt. Hiſpan. p. iii.   [q] LUCÆ Tudenſis Chronicon.   [r] Chron. var. antiq.   [s] Hiſtoria general de Eſpana. lib. viii.   [t] VASÆI Chron. RODERIC SANTII Hiſt. Hiſpan. p. iii.   [u] RODERIC TOLETAN, Hiſt. Arabum.

as he could, and with them marched to give the enemy
battle.   The *Moors,* who looked upon this step as very favourable to their defign, did not at all decline an engagement; fo that, on the twenty-eighth of *July,* an action
enfued between the towns of *Alcocer* and *Berlanga,* in which
the *Cyftilians* had at firft the advantage [w]; but the count
Don *Garcia,* penetrating at the head of his cavalry too far,
was furrounded by the *Moors* before his infantry could come
up, and moft of his troops being killed, and himfelf dangeroufly wounded, was taken prifoner [x]; after which his
army made a precipitate retreat.   But by the defperate
charge made at the beginning, the infidels found themfelves
fo much weakened, that, except burning fome of the places
that were neareft them, they did nothing more that campaign.   As for the gallant Don *Garcia,* he died, partly of
his wounds, and partly of grief, two days after the lofs of
his liberty and of the battle, that is, on the thirtieth of
July, in the year of our Lord one thoufand and five, and
when he had governed *Caftile* thirty-five years complete [y].
The *Moorish* general *Abderama* fent his body in triumph to
Cordova, from whence being redeemed for a fum of money, it was brought back into his own dominions, and
buried in the monaftery of St. *Peter de Cardagna,* univerfally
regretted by his fubjects, and by the Chriftians in general.

   DON SANCHEZ GARCIAS fucceeded his father [a], the ran-   *Don San-*
fom of whofe body was the firft act of his adminiftration;   *chez Gar-*
and, as foon as he had paid his laft devoirs to it, he applied   *cias fuc-*
himfelf with inexpreffible diligence to recruit his forces, that   *ceeds his*
he might be in a condition to revenge his death upon the   *father, and*
infidels.   Several accidents contributed to facilitate his de-   *makes a*
fign; his neighbours, the kings of *Leon* and *Navarre,* fent   *glorious*
him confiderable fuccours, multitudes of his own people,   *expedition*
being afraid to till their lands, betook themfelves to arms,   *againft the*
and, before he could take the field, a civil war broke out   *Moors.*
in *Cordova* [b].   Don *Sanchez,* finding his army more numerous, and the conjuncture more favourable, than he expected, difpofed all things very wifely, in order to make the
moft of his advantage; for firft he blocked up the *Moorish*
garrifons in his own country, that they might give his fubjects no difturbance in his abfence, and then, paffing the
mountains that feparate the two *Caftiles* with the reft of his
troops, he fell into the open country behind them, and

---

   [w] Lucæ Tudenfis Chronicon.   [x] RODERIC SANTII Hift.
Hifpan. p. iii.   [y] VASÆI Chronicon.   [z] RODERIC
TOLETAN de reb. Hifpan. p. iv.   [a] MARIANA Hiftoria ge-
neral de Efpana. lib. viii.   [b] RODERIC TOLETAN Hift. Arabum.

having burnt three or four small places, he thereby so terrified the inhabitants of all the great cities and towns, that they immediately sent deputies to his camp, even from places at a great distance, and agreed to deliver him wine, provisions, and money, upon such terms as he thought fit to prescribe. Having thus spread terror throughout all the enemy's dominions, and fully indemnified his subjects for their want of a harvest that year, he repassed the mountains in the middle of autumn with his army, covered with glory and laden with riches [c].

Zuleiman a pretender to the crown of Cordova solicits his alliance.

His good fortune did not end here. Those who had revolted at *Cordova* from *Almahadi*, who then bore the title of king, could not agree amongst themselves whom they should place upon the throne in his stead; and at length dividing in favour of two persons, they came immediately to an action, in order to decide which of these competitors they should assist to dethrone the reigning prince. The name of him whose adherents were victorious in this action was *Zuleiman* [d], who becoming master of the person of his rival, kept him closely confined; but this success, which freed him from one opponent, rendered him much less able to contend with the other; for, notwithstanding those who revolted at first were strong enough to depose *Almahadi*, if they could have agreed, yet the remains of both parties found themselves manifestly too weak [e]. In this situation *Zuleiman* very wisely drew off his forces from the neighbourhood of the capital, that they might be less liable to be debauched; and having seized upon certain places, where for the present they might remain in safety, he sent his embassadors to count Don *Sanchez*, to propose a firm and constant alliance between them, promising him great advantages, if, by his assistance, a passage could be opened to the throne of *Cordova*, and accompanied these offers with presents of great value [f].

Don Sanchez assists him, and sets him on that throne by force of arms.

The count of *Castile* received these embassadors kindly; and having maturely weighed what they proposed, accepted the offers that were made him, and assured *Zuleiman*, that he would join him with his troops as soon as the season would permit them to take the field. Accordingly he not only assembled his own forces, but procured auxiliaries from the kings of *Leon* and *Navarre*, who saw with great pleasure so fair an opportunity offer of employing the *Moors* in the service of the *Christians*, and in weakening themselves. He passed the mountains with as good an army as he had led

[c] Lucæ Tudensis Chronicon. Vasæi Chronicon.   [d] Roderic Santii Hist. Hispan. p. iii.   [e] Lucæ Tudensis Chron.   [f] Roderic Toletan Hist. Arabum.

ⁱn his laſt expedition, and in conjunction with *Zuleiman*, who received him with great joy, advanced directly towards *Cordova* [g]. *Almahadi*, with the aſſiſtance of his Alhagib *Alhamer*, had drawn together a very numerous body of troops, with which he propoſed to defend the city, which, as it was extremely well fortified, he looked upon as very practicable, even if the enemy had been ſtronger than they were; but, upon the approach of the confederates, *Alhamer*, who had the confidence of the troops more than his maſter, formed a reſolution of marching out and giving them battle, in which he perſiſted, notwithſtanding all the reaſons *Almahadi* could offer. This deſign he executed with the ſame ſpirit in which it was formed, but had the misfortune, notwithſtanding, to be defeated by the confederates, and conſtrained to retire into another part of the kingdom, while they continued their march and inveſted *Cordova*, into the ſuburbs of which the count of *Caſtile* entered with his forces, whom he inriched with the plunder [l]. *Almahadi* found it impoſſible to defend himſelf, and therefore made his eſcape [k]; upon which *Zuleiman* was received without oppoſition, who, rewarding the count of *Caſtile* and his forces even beyond their expectation, ſent them home perfectly ſatisfied, and recommended to them the reduction of *Alhamer*, who had withdrawn himſelf to the frontiers of *Caſtile* [l].

A. D. 1008.

AT the return of the count Don *Sanchez*, his conſort was delivered of a ſon [m], who afterwards ſucceeded his father in his dominions. The next campaign the count made himſelf maſter of the fortreſs of *Alienca*, which was in the hands of *Alhamer*. Having diſmantled it, he ravaged the reſt of that country, and then returned into his own dominions, being perhaps unwilling to march again to the aſſiſtance of *Zuleiman*, becauſe the count of *Barcelona*, and other Chriſtian lords, had engaged themſelves on the part of his competitor, and he was unwilling to ſee Chriſtians deſtroy each other in fighting the battles of the *Moors* [n]. For want of his aſſiſtance *Zuleiman* was dethroned and expelled, which conſtrained him to retire into *Africa*; and this, in proceſs of time, afforded *Hiſſem*, the grandſon of *Abderhaman*, who was the lawful monarch of *Cordova*, and had been long kept in priſon by different uſurpers, an opportunity to mount the throne [o]. He found, however, very great difficulty to keep

Enters into a new league with Hiſſem king of Cordova, by which he obtains great advantages.

---

[g] Chron var. antiq. [h] VASÆI Chronicon. [i] RODERIC SANTII Hiſt. Hiſpan. p. iii. [k] RODERIC TOLETAN de reb. Hiſpan. lib. iv. [l] RODERIC TOLET. Hiſt. Arabum. [m] VASÆI Chronicon. p. iii. [n] RODERIC SANTII Hiſt. Hiſpan. [o] RODERIC TOLET. Hiſt. Arabum.

poſſeſſion

poffeffion of it; for *Abdalla*, the fon of *Almahadi*, who pe-
rifhed in thefe troubles, had got poffeffion of *To'edo*, where
he affumed the title of king P. On the other hand *Zuleiman*,
returned from *Africa*, and bringing with him confiderable
reinforcements, created new difturbances, and fent a frefh
embaffy to the count of *Caftile* to demand his affiftance once
more. But Don *Sanchez*, who made no fcruple of affifting
one tyrant againft another, made a fcruple of arming againft
Hiffem, whom he took to be a lawful prince q. He therefore fent an agent to *Cordova*, to propofe to the king, that,
if he would order the *Moorish* garrifon to evacuate *St. Stephen
de Gormez*, *Ofma*, *Corugna*, and other places, he would become his firm ally, and affift him with all his troops. Upon
mature deliberation *Hiffem* accepted this offer; in confequence of which the count of *Caftile* began to levy troops.
Hiffem, to fhew his confidence in the faith of that prince,

A. D.   honeftly performed his part of the agreement, and, having
1013.   given up to him all the places that he demanded, fummoned
the count of *Caftile* to the performance of his promife r.

Affifts him   DON SANCHEZ, equally ready to do what he had ftipu-
in befiege- lated, marched, at the requeft of his ally, to *Toledo*, where
ing and the troops of *Hiffem* were already arrived; and, as foon as
taking they had notice of the count's approach, invefted the place.
Toledo.   Don *Sanchez*, perceiving it to be very large and well fortified, and being alfo informed that it was very populous, advifed the *Moors* to blockade it very ftrictly, as not only the
fureft but the fhorteft method of becoming mafters of it.
They took his advice, and had no reafon to repent it; for
in a few days the inhabitants, finding themfelves oppreffed
by famine, feized upon the perfon of him whom they had
ftiled their prince, and furrendered the place s. After
which the count of *Caftile*, having fully made good what he
promifed, returned again into his own dominions. The
civil war ftill continued between *Hiffem* and *Zuleiman*, but
it does not appear that the count of *Caftile* took any farther
fhare therein on either fide, but remained quiet in his own
territories, where he governed his fubjects with great equity
and juftice. Yet a body of *Moors*, fuppofed to belong to
the garrifon of *Saragoffa*, made an irruption into his country,

A. D.   reduced *Cordagna*, and put the inhabitants there to the
1015.   fword; upon which Don *Sanchez* put himfelf in arms,
but found they had quitted his dominions, and retired

P Chron. var. antiq.   q Lucæ Tudenfis Chron.   r Ro-
DERIC TOLET. Hift. Arabum.   s Lucæ Tudenfis Chron.
VASÆI Chron.

to a place of safety, whither he held it improper to follow them [t] (G).

[t] RODERIC TOLET. Hist. Arabum.

(G) Among other privileges which this famous and fortunate count of *Castile* granted to his nobility, there is one that deserves to be particularly remembered, which is thus represented by *Mariana*; all the lords of that country, small and great, were obliged, as vassals to their count, to march, with such numbers of men as they could raise, whenever he summoned them to attend him in the field, without expecting any other recompence or satisfaction than what they were able to carve out for themselves at the expence of the enemy. This service, it is said, he took away, and engaged, for himself and his successors, that they should have a certain consideration proportionable to the number of men that each of them commanded, and the length of the campaign. Of the truth of this the *French* translator of *Mariana* seems to doubt, and we find not a word of it in *Ferreras*. As the military tenures in all the *Gothic* governments were much the same, it is not easy to conceive either how or why he should attempt to change them; more especially as there is nothing said of any equivalent, or of the method by which he was to raise that pay, which it is said he undertook to give them. Besides, it does not appear that he was ever in any such circumstances as could render it advisable or expedient for him to do this; or, indeed, that, upon the whole, such a privilege would have been advantageous to his nobility, since they were as much interested as he in the defence of their country, and had therefore no reason to desire, that the only effectual means of defending it should be laid aside. It is therefore highly probable, that the case was no more than this: He made two expeditions out of his own dominions as an auxiliary to *Moorish* princes; and it is very possible, as well as very reasonable, that he might exempt his nobility from attending him in such expeditions at their own expence, and engage to indemnify them out of the recompence or subsidy that he was to receive. It may indeed be said, that, while they were thus employed, they were in the service of their country as well as of their prince; but, at the same time, this was a kind of service to which they were not subjected by their tenures; and therefore it is very likely he would have found it difficult to comply with his engagements to the king of *Cordova*, if he had not by this concession cut off all grounds of dispute, and made these foreign expeditions a common concern (7).

(7) *Joannis Vasæi Hispaniæ Chronicon. Mariana Historia general de España, lib.* viii. *Petri Paulini de officiis regni Gothorum, tit. Dux & Comes. Ferreras Historia de España, p.* v. *sect.* xi.

Sends the family of Vela a second time into banishment.

ABOUT this time Don *Sanchez* found himself under an absolute necessity of doing what he took to be an act of justice. The three sons of the count *de Vela* had, from the time of their return, been treated with great kindness and respect, and the count of *Castile* had pushed this so far, as to make choice of the eldest, whose name was Don *Roderic de Vela*, to be the godfather of his son and heir apparent [u]. But whether these lords still retained their old resentment, or whether it proceeded from the natural fierceness of their disposition, so it was, that they behaved in such a manner to the *Castilians*, that the count received perpetual complaints of their excesses, which in the end provoked him to such a degree, that, forgetting how fatal their former exile had been to all the Christians in *Spain*, he drove them a second time out of his dominions [w]. Upon this Don *Alonso* the fifth, then king of *Leon*, apprehensive of the ill consequences that might ensue, if they should again take shelter among the infidels, offered them a retreat in his dominions, and actually gave them lands sufficient for their subsistence, at the foot of the mountains, with which for the present they seemed to be well contented [x]; but, as the reader hath seen in another place, these were very far from being the real sentiments, as clearly appeared after the death of the count Don *Sanchez*, when an opportunity offered of glutting their resentment by the murder of his son, and by the extinction of the male heirs of the counts of *Castile*. But at present our business is to continue the thread of our history, by relating the remaining atchievements of the count Don *Sanchez*.

Brings the affairs of Castile into perfect order during the short interval of peace.

A. D.
1016.

THE count Don *Sanchez*, having now an interval of peace, took great pains in correcting whatever errors had crept into his government during those stirring times, when justice is, generally speaking, silent. He repaired those fortresses that were proper to make a part of his frontier, and demolished others, that, either through an irruption of the *Moors*, or insurrections at home, might have proved nusances to his dominions. He took this opportunity also to regulate with the king of *Navarre* the boundaries of their respective territories, to prevent any disputes in succeeding times between their descendants [y]. He likewise facilitated the endeavours of Don *Alonso*, king of *Castile*, in repairing the places ruined by the *Moors*, and more especially in restoring such churches and convents as they had demolished [z].

[u] RODERIC SANTII Hist. Hispan. p. iii.   [w] Chron. var. antiq.   [x] LUCÆ Tudensis Chron. VASÆI Chron.   [y] RODERIC SANTII Hist. Hispan. p. iii.   [z] RODERIC TOLETAN de reb. Hispan. lib. iv.

Actions

Actions that shew him to have been a wise, active, and magnanimous prince, and therefore not likely to have proceeded with so much rigour, as is reported, against his mother. However, as the fact is related by more than one historian [a], and is represented as having given rise to more than one custom that still remains in general use in this country, it is not fit to hide it from the reader's knowlege, however improbable it may appear, as indeed there is hardly any thing that can wear an aspect more fabulous, or more incredible.

THE countess dowager of *Castile*, it is said, forgetting her birth, her honour, and her religion, cast her eyes upon a *Moorish* lord, with an inclination to have married him; but being apprehensive that this would have been displeasing to her son, who might have considered such a marriage as deriving discredit on himself, she resolved to remove that obstacle to the gratification of her passion by depriving him of life. With this view she prepared a violent poison, which she put into his drink, and which she afterwards offered him with her own hands; but the count, having received information of this black design, first desired, and then obliged her to drink it herself, and thereby turned the effects of this cruel project upon its author. But, says *Mariana* [a], how criminal soever the countess might be, her death, nevertheless, tarnished the reputation of her son, because gentler means might have been used to escape the intended evil, to punish the countess, and to put it out of her power to make any future attempts of the like kind. Some authors assert, that from hence arose the practice in *Spain* of the ladies drinking first [c]. It is also alleged, that the count himself, regretting the severity, built the noble monastery of *Ona* as an expiation of his crime. But, with much greater probability, others assert, that it was erected to gratify the desire of one of his daughters, who was inclined to quit the world, and became the abbess of this new foundation [d].

Improbable account of his obliging his mother to poison herself.

As the civil wars amongst the infidels still continued; when the count had adjusted all his domestic concerns, he was willing not to let slip so favourable an opportunity of extending his dominions; and therefore taking the field, with a complete corps of well disciplined troops, he presented himself before *Penafiel*, which, after a short siege, he reduced. After taking *Maderuelo* and *Montijo*, he at length invested *Sepulveda*, a place strong by nature, and even then somewhat assisted by art, with a good garrison,

Extends his frontiers by an expedition against the Moors, and dies soon after. A. D. 1019.

[a] Chron. var. antiq.   [b] Historia general de Espana, lib. viii.
[c] Chron. var. antiq.   [d] Lucæ Tudensis Chronicon, Vasæi Hispaniæ Chronicon.

which

which enabled it to make a great reſiſtance; however, being a place of conſequence, a mark of triumph in the infidels, and a thorn in the ſides of his ſubjects, he puſhed it ſo vigorouſly, that at length it fell into his hands [e], which enabled him to clear all that neighbourhood of the *Moors*, and to take ſuch precautions as might, for the future, put it out of their power to harraſs his ſubjects as in times paſt. He ſeems to have been thus employed, when he was ſeized with that diſtemper which brought him to the grave, to the great regret of his ſubjects, who loved him as he deſerved, ſince few princes have been either more fortunate or more indulgent. He deceaſed [f] *February* the fifth, in the year of our Lord 1022. *Mariana* [g], and indeed ſome other writers, place his death ſix years lower, but without any great appearance of reaſon, becauſe it is not reconcileable to the current even of their own narrations. His body was interred in the monaſtery of *Ona* (H) which he founded, and, at the time

---

[e] Rodéric Toletan Hiſt. Arabum.   [f] Rodéric Santii Hiſt. Hiſpan. p. iii.   [g] Hiſtoria general de Eſpana, lib. viii.

(H) This monaſtery of *Ona*, in which Don *Sanchez* and his family are interred, was of his own foundation, at the deſire of his daughter Donna *Frigida*, who choſe to quit the world and to embrace a monaſtic life, in the year of our Lord 1011, that is, about ſeven years after the deceaſe of his father (5). Some hiſtorians indeed are very poſitive that he founded this religious houſe upon a very different occaſion, and with an intention to atone for the putting of his mother to death, a circumſtance capable of putting that fact alſo out of doubt; for, if that monaſtery was not built till the time before-mentioned, and that he had a daughter of age to take the veil, we cannot but believe him near forty years of age, which does not very well agree with the wantonneſs aſcribed to his mother, who, loſing all the names by which ſhe was called in other parts of the hiſtory, is now ſaid to have no other name than *Ona* (6). The tomb of the count is near the high altar; not far from it ſtands that of his own wife Donna *Urraca*, who died three years after him (7); and, at no great diſtance, that of his ſon Don *Garcia*, whom the monumental inſcription is ſaid to make no more than thirteen (8); which agrees but very indifferently with the facts mentioned of him in hiſtory, and yet is far more reconcileable to them than the computation of a *French* hiſtorian, who makes him but nine. (9) It muſt be acknowleged, that even the beſt hiſtorians differ about the year in which

---

(5) *P. Marca, in Appendice.*   (6) *Mariana Hiſtoria general de Eſpana,* lib. viii. cap. 11.   (7) *Ferreras Hiſtoria de Eſpana, p. v. ſect. xi.*   (8) *Morales, Salazar.*   (9) *P. Orleans, Revolutions de l'Eſpagne.*

Don

of his deceafe, he left behind him four children, Don *Garcias Sanchez* his fucceffor, and three daughters, Donna *Nugno Elvira*, who married Don *Sanchez* king of *Navarre*, Donna *Urraca Therefa*, who became afterwards the confort of the king of *Leon*, and Donna *Frigida*, who was abbefs of the monaftery before-mentioned [h].

Don *Garcias Sanchez* [i] fucceeded his father under the tuition of Donna *Elvira* his mother, and the protection of Don *Sanchez*, king of *Navarre*, his uncle. There is a general concurrence of the *Spanifh* writers [k] to raife this young prince into a kind of miracle, with refpect both to his perfon, and his parts, but at the fame time they are very much divided about his years, fince. moft of them make them but nine, whereas we, following the other computation, efteem him then to have been about fourteen ; the rather, becaufe we find, that, on the 25th of *May* 1025, his mother died [l], and recommended him to the care of Don *Sanchez*, king of *Navarre*, who very foon after thought of marrying him. Befides, the perfon and the parts of a child of nine years old, though they may raife hopes, hardly excite admiration; whereas at fourteen, if he was really of fuch a fuperior genius, there is nothing abfurd in fuppofing, that it might be difcerned and diftinguifhed even by foreigners as well as his own fubjects; and as this was actually the cafe, it ferves greatly to fortify that notion. However, notwithftanding the pregnancy of his parts, and the refpect due to his father's memory, there wanted not fome among his fubjects, who were willing to take the advantage of his youth, and to difturb the peace of his dominions. The chief of thefe was Don *Ferdinand Guitterez*, who made himfelf mafter of the caftle of *Moncon*, and is reported to have had fome connection with the infidels [m].

marginal note: Don Garcias Sanchez fucceeds his father, and proves a prince of vaft hopes.

---

[h] Lucæ Tudenfis Chronicon, Vasæi Chronicon.   [i] Mariana Hiftoria general de Efpana, lib. viii. Ferreras Hiftoria de Efpana, p. iv. Mayerne, Turquet Hiftoire general d'Efpagne, lib. vii.   [k] Chron. var. antiq.   [l] Roderic Santii Hift. Hifpan. p. iii.   [m] Roderic Toletan Hift. Arabum.

Don *Sanchez* died (1), and about the time that his fon furvived him ; but the chronology of *Ferreras* being probable, free from all abfurdity, and at leaft as well fupported as any other, we thought ourfelves obliged to follow it for the fake of perfpicuity (2).

(1) R. *Toletan de rebus Hifponia. Lucæ Tudenfis Chronicon. Morales, Salazar.*   (2) *Hiftoria de Efpana, p. v. fect. xi.*

But

But Don *Sanchez*, king of *Navarre*, under colour of providing a proper match for his nephew, made a tour into *Caftile*, and brought with him, by way of efcorte, a confiderable number of troops, with which, and the forces about the perfon of Don *Garcias*, he quickly reduced Don *Ferdinand*, and fome other great men, to reafon [n]. This, and fome other affairs, requiring his prefence, Don *Garcias*, who was inclined to fhew his paffion for the princefs Donna *Sancha*, proceeded, with a few *Caftilian* noblemen that were about him, to *Leon*, which circumftance is omitted by *Ferreras*, though there is nothing in it improbable, and it feems to account for the abfence of Don *Bermudo* from his capital, which could hardly have happened, if his intended brother-in-law had not arrived there before he was expected. This eagernefs of his feems alfo to confirm our opinion as to his age, fince it is natural enough in a young man of twenty, but not altogether fo probable of a boy of fourteen. Upon his entrance into the kingdom of *Leon*, the three counts of the family of *Vela* made great demonftrations of joy; which had nothing in it ftrange, if we confider, that the eldeft of them was his godfather, and might very well pretend an inclination to be reconciled and to make his peace with a prince, whofe father he had acknowleged for his fovereign [o]. This will ftill be the more probable, if what fome hiftorians fay be true, that he gained the opportunity of ftabbing him, by pretending to kneel to kifs his hand [p]. The circumftances of the murder we have given before, on account of its being committed at *Leon*; but we are conftrained to mention it here again, as this unfortunate prince was the laft count of *Caftile* of his race. His corpfe was firft interred in the church of St. *John* at *Leon*, where a tomb was erected to his memory, but it was afterwards removed to the monaftery of *Ona*, where there is both a tomb and an infcription to his honour [q].

Don. *Sanchez*, king of *Navarre*, who had married his elder fifter, took poffeffion of *Caftile* in her right [r] (I). The reader

---

[n] Lucæ Tudenfis Chronicon. Vasæi Hifpaniæ Chronicon. [o] Roderic Toletan de reb. Hifpan. lib. iv. [p] Chron. var. antiq. [q] Roderic Santii Hift. Hifpan. p. iii. [r] Alfonsi Carthagana reg. Hifp. Anacephalæosis Francisci Taraphæ de reg. Hifpaniæ.

(I) As far as any thing can be known with certainty in relation to the antient form of government in thofe ftates, that rofe out of the ruins of the old *Gothic* monarchy, the rule in *Caftile* was that of fucceffion. The counts were originally equal

reader will perceive, from what has been related, the reason of Na-
why the affassins of Don *Garcias* made choice of the castle of varre, *in-*
Moncon for their retreat, because it belonged of right to Don *herits* Caf-
Ferdinand Guittierez, who might be inclined, upon the death tile, *and*
of the count, to excite new troubles; 'and lying near the *revenges*
territories of the *Moors*, might afford them an opportunity *Don* Gar-
of contributing by their affistance to raise new troubles [a]. In all cias' *death.*
probability this scheme might have succeeded, if Don *Sanchez*
had been in his own kingdom, and the malecontents in *Castile*
more at liberty; but, as it was, the king presently invested the
castle, and took it, before either the discontented *Castilians*

[a] RODERIC TOLETAN Hist. Arabum.

equal; and what were their pri- | count *Garcias*, was regular and
vate estates in the days of king | just (4). It may be, however,
Roderic, became so many lord- | that the troops he had brought
ships or principalities, when | with him into *Castile* might
themselves and their vassals de- | contribute to prevent any op-
fended them with their swords | position on the part of the no-
against the *Moors* (1). It is | bles, and that signal severity
also clear from their histories, | with which he had punished the
if any thing is so, that these | affassins of their late prince, re-
lordships descended to heirs fe- | commended him highly to the
male (2). As to the pre- | people (5). It is however af-
eminence of this family, not to | serted, that his queen, Donna
lay any weight on the fabulous | *Nugna*, insisted that she had a
history, it arose plainly from | power to dispose of this country
the active ambition of Don *Fer-* | which she brought, in favour of
dinand Gonzalez, who, as count | which of her sons she pleased;
of *Castile*, rendered himself in- | (6) and it was in virtue of this,
dependent; and the rest of the | that it was given to Don *Ferdi-*
lords by affisting, or at least ac- | *nand*; but as to the motives
quiescing, under what he did, | upon which it was thus be-
and which he could not have | stowed, as derived from the
done without them, from being | story told in the text, we ought
his equals became his vassals. | to consider them as false and
(3) In his line the succeffion was | feigned, and such as were never
without all doubt hereditary; | heard of till above one hundred
and in this light the claim of | years after the decease of that
the king of *Navarre*, in right of | great princefs, whose memory
his wife, the eldest daughter of | has been aspersed by them,
Don *Sanchez*, the grand daugh- | when, in fact, she was governed
ter of Don *Ferdinand Gonzales*, | in her choice merely by her ma-
and the sister of the young | ternal affection (7).

(1) *See the remarks of Mariana on this subject at the opening of the eighth
book of his History.*   (2) *Roderic Toletan, Lucæ Tudensis, Rol. Santii Hist.*
(3) *Mariana Historia general de Espana; lib.* viii.   (4) *Histoire genera e
d'Espagne, par Mayerne Turquet, lib* v.   (9) *Mariana, Ferreras, Vayrac.*
(6) *Chron. var. antiq.*   (7) *Compare Mariana's account with the rea-
soning of P. Moret.*

or the *Moors* had any time to difcover their inclinations. However, his vigour in purfuing, and his feverity in punifh-ing, the counts of *la Vela* and their adherents, of whom not one efcaped, could not but be pleafing to the bulk of the *Caftilians*, who retained a juft refpect for the memory of their young prince and his father, and might, very probably, contribute to that facility with which he was admitted to the poffeffion of that noble country, in which it does not ap-pear that he met with the leaft oppofition [t].

Sufpected of forming ambitious views foon after upon the kingdom of Leon.   DON *Sanchez*, king of *Navarre*, and count of *Caftile* in his wife's right, was very juftly furnamed the great [u], fince his prudence was at all times and in all refpects equal to his fortune. He was advanced in years when he made this great acquifition; and, that he might govern both countries with equal convenience, he fixed on the pleafant town of *Najara* [w] in *Old Caftile*, but near the frontiers of *Navarre*, for the place of his refidence, and applied himfelf with dili-gence to conciliate the love and efteem of his new fubjects; though *Mariana* [x] alleges, that his heart was intirely taken up with his ambition, and that, from the moment he had joined *Caftile* to *Navarre*, he had in his intention the an-nexing *Leon*, *Galicia*, and *Afturias*, likewife; and to this alone he attributes the war between him and Don *Bermudo* the third; whereas *Ferreras* [y] and other writers, feem to lay the blame of that affair upon the young king of *Leon*. In all probability the want of proper lights on both fides has occa-fioned this difference; though, to fay the truth, probability feems rather to be on the fide of *Mariana*. The fource of that war was the king of *Navarre*'s ordering the city of *Va-lentia* to be rebuilt, on account of a miracle [z] which hap-pened to him near that place; for as he was hunting the wild boar, the beaft ran fuddenly into the wood, and took fhelter in a fubterraneous place, to which the king imme-diately followed: but, as he lifted his arm to ftrike the boar, he found it without motion, and foon after perceived an altar and the ftatue of St. *Anthony*; upon which he made a vow, that if, through the interceffion of that faint, the ufe of his arm was reftored, he would build a church upon that fpot in honour of that faint; and being afterwards informed, that this fubterraneous place made part of the ruins of the antient *Palentia*, it made him fo much the more eager to perform his vow. But it feems Don *Bermudo* either did not

t Lucæ Tudenfis Chronicon.   u Chron. var. antiq.
w Roderic Santii Hift. Hifpan. p. iii.   x Hiftoria gene-ral de Efpana, lib. viii.   y Hiftoria de Efpana, p. iv.
z Roderic Toletan de reb. Hifpan. lib. iv. Lucæ Tudenfis Chronicon.

credit

credit the miracle, or did not apprehend the piety of introaching upon other peoples rights in order to perform a vow ; for *Palentia* now is, and it may be presumed was then, esteemed to lie within the dominions of *Leon*. *Mariana* [a] indeed cuts the matter short, and, without taking any notice of Don *Bermudo*'s resentment, ascribes the war to the king of *Navarre*'s invading *Leon* with a formidable army, and making the conquest of a confiderable tract of country, before Don *Bermudo*, who had no fuspicion of his defign, was in any condition to oppofe him. Be that as it will, it feems that the king of *Navarre* had a better intereft in the clergy than his antagonift ; for it was clearly by their influence over the peoples minds, that Don *Bermudo* was forced to make a peace, and to yield a confiderable diftrict by way of dowry to his fifter [b], who married Don *Ferdinand*, the fecond fon of Don *Sanchez*, who thereupon, with the confent of both monarchs, took the title of king [c], inftead of count of *Castile* ; and the ceffion made to him of this country by his father feems to be the only point of the treaty that was in reality acceptable to Don *Bermudo*, as it freed him in fome meafure from the apprehenfions he was under in having a monarch of *Navarre* for his neighbour.

WE, may collect, from what has been related, fo juft an idea of the motives which engaged the king of *Navarre* to beftow *Castile* upon Don *Ferdinand* his fecond fon, that there can be no reafon for having recourfe to that very ftrange and incredible ftory, which, moved by the credit of Don *Roderic* Archbifhop of *Toledo*, moft of the *Spanifh* writers [d] have inferted as truth. The fubftance of this ftory is, that while this great monarch was engaged in the war againft the *Moors*, his eldeft fon, Don *Garcias*, piqued at his mother's refufing him a horfe, upon Don *Pedro Seffa*'s reprefenting to her, that the king would be difpleafed with it, gave the king an account, that his mother and Don *Pedro* lived together in adultery ; upon this Don *Sanchez*, returned from his expedition, caufed the matter to be examined by the ftates ; who, upon the teftimony of Don *Garcias*, condemned the queen to be burned alive. Don *Ferdinand* it feems was paffive in this bufinefs ; but Don *Ramiro*, who was the king's natural fon by Donna *Caya* a lady of the court, undertook the queen's defence, and offered to fight with her fon in fupport of her innocence. But, before the day of trial could be fixed, a

The fabulous account of the motive on which Don Ferdinand was declared king of Castile.

---

[a] Hiftoria general de Efpana, lib. viii.   [b] RODERIC SANTII Hift. Hifpan. p. lii.   [c] RODERIC TOLET. de reb. Hifpan. lib. iv.   [d] Chron. var. antiq. MARIANA, MAYERNE, TURQUET.

certain hermit prevailed upon Don *Garcias* to own the accusation false, and to declare the true grounds of it. The queen, being upon this set at liberty, desired that *Castile;* which was her patrimony, might not be given to Don *Garcias,* but to her second son *Ferdinand;* and that *Ramiro,* who had so generously staked his life in her quarrel, might be rewarded with the kingdom of *Arragon;* which requests, say they, were complied with; and Don *Garcias* also made a pilgrimage to *Rome,* in order to obtain absolution from the holy father for becoming the false accuser of his mother. The whole has been so clearly refuted by a great writer [e], that we should not have mentioned it, but for the sake of giving the reader a hint whence many of these ridiculous fictions arose.

The last acts of Don Sanchez the great, and the manner of his death.
A. D.
1035.

THE truth is, that, after bestowing on his son Don *Ferdinand* the country of *Castile,* the good old king took care to make many regulations that were equally wise and popular, with a view of gaining to his sons the affections of his new subjects; such as directing, that a new road should be made through *Navarre* and *Castile,* for the conveniency of such pilgrims as went to St. *James* at *Compostella,* repairing the principal places on the frontiers, that the *Moors* might not be able to enter, as formerly they had done with impunity, and contriving to bring inhabitants into the places that he had either founded or rebuilt [f]; which accounts so well for the time he lived after this transaction, that we have no need of supposing a war with the infidels, of which there is nothing said in the best authors, purely to fill it up. Authors are very far from being agreed, either as to the time or manner of his death. *Ferreras* [g] seems to be in the right as to the former, and therefore we have followed him; but, with regard to the latter, he is silent; however, some writers affirm [h], that, going in pilgrimage to *Oviedo* with a small retinue, he fell into an ambuscade that was laid for him on the road; and, after so long and glorious a reign, was basely and barbarously murdered; which induced a suspicion, as supposing the fact true it very well might, that some of the neighbouring princes, who were afraid of his power, were concerned in this treacherous act.

Don Ferdinand without

IF we consider how soon after the death of this monarch, Don *Bermudo,* the third king of *Leon,* entered the country of *Castile* with an army so much superior to that of the king

[e] P. MORET Investigationes Históricas de las antiquitades del Reyno de Navarra.   [f] RODERIC SANTII Hist. Hispan. p. iii. LUCÆ Tudensis Chronicon.   [g] Historia de Espana, p. iv. [h] Chron. var. antiq.

Don

Don *Ferdinand*, that, though he was a prince of great cou- *difficulty* rage and spirit, he judged it not at all for his interest to *obtains the* hazard the whole of his dominions by a battle in the first *crown of* campaign, we may see some reason to suspect, that he was *Leon, as* not ignorant of that detestable design, or at least that he drew *well as of* the same advantages from it as if he had been in the secret; *Castile.* but if he was, he quickly received the just reward of so black a contrivance, as the reader has seen at the close of the last section; for being, as we have there shewn, killed in battle, Don *Ferdinand* not only recovered the country that he had taken from him, but succeeded likewise to the kingdom of *Leon* in right of his queen Donna *Sancha*, by which he became the most powerful of all the Christian princes in *Spain* [1]. It is true that the *Galicians* gave him some trouble when he first entered into the possession of that kingdom (K), but this was quickly over; and these people, as well

[1] RODERIC TOLETAN de reb. Hispan. lib. iv. MARIANA Historia general de Espana, lib. viii. FERRERAS, MAYERNE, TURQUET.

(K) It will, in all probability, afford the reader some satisfaction, if we enter a little into the reasons which induced the inhabitants of *Galicia* to be so much more untractable upon this occasion, than any of the other provinces of the kingdoms of *Oviedo* and *Leon*. It would appear rather an evasion than an answer, to allege that they were always mutinous, or to appeal to his own observation, that there were more insurrections here, than in any other country comprised within those realms (1). The real cause was, that they disliked their situation as a province, and were desirous of becoming a separate state. The source of this desire was, their being richer and in better circumstances; for *Galicia*, though but one hundred and fifty miles in length, has

near three hundred miles of coast, being washed by the ocean on the north, and on the west has more, and those too better, ports than any other part of *Spain*; which drew thither a very considerable trade even in those times (2). The country in itself is also fruitful, pleasant, populous, and exceedingly inriched by the resort of strangers from all parts of *Europe*; by land as well as sea, to the tomb of *St. James* at *Compostella*, the very bishops of which city lived in those days with the splendor, and in their power fell little short of princes. These circumstances rendered this country almost at all times a seat of faction, and inspired its inhabitants with a restless passion for a prince and court of their own; and, in all probability, it was a prospect of arriving

(1) *Mariana, Mayerne, Turquet, Ferreras. par D. Juan Alvarez de Colmenar, tom.* 1.

(2) *Delices de l'Epagne,*

at

well as the inhabitants of *Leon* and *Aſturias*, very ſoon ſaw
that it was their intereſt to ſubmit to a monarch by whom
Caſtile was again united to their crown ; and conſequently
their ſecurity as well as their grandeur viſibly increaſed [k].
On the other hand, if they had proceeded to a new election,
this muſt have produced a war, the event of which was uncertain, and a civil war too, of which this country muſt have
been the ſeat; beſides, when they came to conſider this,
they could find none more fit to wear the crown of *Leon*
than the huſband of Donna *Sancha*, the ſole heireſs of that
glorious race of kings, who, by their valour and virtue, had
preſerved the *Goths* from being extirpated, and were at leaſt
the principal authors of the progreſs which the Chriſtians had
already made towards the recovery of all *Spain*. We need
not wonder therefore that Don *Ferdinand* met with ſo little
reſiſtance, or that thoſe, who were inclined to oppoſe him,
were ſo ſlenderly ſupported.

The conſe-
quences of
civil diſ-
ſentions in
diminiſh-
ing the
power of
the Moors.

THE civil diſſentions, the violent commotions, and frequent revolutions, in the kingdom of *Cordova*, of which the
reader has had an account in its proper place, having ſhaken
that which was by far the moſt conſiderable monarchy of the
Moors to ſuch a degree, that, except an empty title of pre-
eminence, it ſcarce preſerved any thing more than the reſt ;
there aroſe almoſt as many ſovereignties as there remained
cities in their dominions ; ſo that, notwithſtanding ſuch as
held them aſſumed the title of kings, yet we cannot, with
any degree of juſtice, allow every little diſtrict they poſſeſſed
the ſtile of a kingdom. Amongſt thoſe of which we ſhal
have occaſion hereafter to ſpeak, the moſt conſiderable was
the king of *Seville*, next to him the king of *Toledo*, and in the
third rank we may reckon the king of *Huesca*, though perhaps the king of *Saragoſſa* might be thought to deſerve it as
well. As for the reſt it will be time enough to mention
them as occaſion requires.

[k] Chrón. var. antiq. MARIANA, FERRERAS, &c.

at this, whenever a favourable
opportunity ſhould offer, with
the aſſiſtance of the *Moors*, that
induced count *Siſenand* to take
ſhelter amongſt the infidels, rather than ſubmit himſelf to a
prince, who, independent of all
his different claims, had as
much perſonal merit as might
have intitled him to dominions

even ſuperior to thoſe which he
poſſeſſed. We ſhall ſee, that
this wiſe and prudent prince concluded it, at length, the moſt
effectual way to render theſe
people loyal to his poſterity, to
gratify them in this favour,
which expedient however was
not attended with ſucceſs (3).

(3) *See in the courſe of this hiſtory the fate of Don Garcia king of Galicia.*

                                                 AT

At this juncture, that is, at the opening of the eleventh century, we may conceive the spacious, rich, and beautiful continent of *Spain,* as divided into two unequal parts, by a strait line drawn from east to west, from the coasts of *Valentia* to a little below the mouth of the river *Duero* ; the country north of this line belonging to the Christians, who had the smallest and least valuable share ; and all to the south in the possession of the *Moors.* Both parties were happy in having allies of their own religion and tempers at their back ; but in this the Christians seemed to be more fortunate, as they had no sea between them, but might at any time receive whatever supplies were sent, or whatever auxiliaries were hired within the bounds of *France* ; whereas the *Moors* had the *Mediterranean* between them and their countrymen in *Africa.* The dependance of both upon these foreign succours was alike precarious, as being equally unwilling to invite, and equally inclined to grow jealous of such auxiliaries. In point of wealth, and real power by land and sea, the *Moors* were much superior ; but this was more than ballanced by the Christians being better connected. The kings of *Leon, Navarre, Sobrawa,* and *Arragon,* were all brothers, and the count of *Barcelona* nearly allied to them ; which, though it did not restrain them from quarrels, or even from wars, yet it hindered them from being pursued with rancour, or for any length of time. We may add to this another great advantage, which was the rough mountainous countries in their possession ; such as *Asturias, Biscay, Navarre, Guipuscoa,* and even part of *Old Castile* ; where a sharp clear air, a soil not over fertile, and the continual labour necessary to their subsistence, furnished them with constant supplies of men naturally hardy and robust, and consequently very capable of undergoing the fatigues of war. Whereas the *Moors,* though naturally more industrious, enjoying a warmer climate, provinces abundantly more fertile, and having likewise the benefit of foreign trade, were, generally speaking, rich, luxurious, and vehemently addicted to sensual pleasures ;. circumstances that gradually made way for their destruction, and had already brought most of their principalities to decline.

A prospect of the state of Spain at the beginning of the eleventh century.

These few general remarks will be of singular use towards understanding the following sections, in which we are to describe the contentions between these people, the ebbs and flows of their respective power, the uses both sides made of their advantages on certain occasions, and their neglect of them on others ; with those accidents that in a course of years made such defects irreparable on one side, as might have been easily corrected if they had been seen in time,

Conclusion.

and

and threw fo much weight into the fcale of the other, as enabled them at laft to opprefs their antagonifts with a fu- periority of force, that could be only refifted fo long as it was by defpair, and that fpirit of knight-errantry, which made men in love with danger, through an overweening fondnefs of praife ; and which did not long furvive thofe gallant infidels among whom it was bred and cherifhed, and of whofe vaft efforts it was the fole fupport.

S E C T. VI.

The Hiftory of the Kingdoms of Leon *and* Caftile, *from their firft Conjunction in the Perfon of* Ferdinand *the firft, to their perpetual Union in that of* Ferdinand *the fecond.*

The cha-   **A**LL the authors of *Spanifh* hiftory, antient and modern, *racter of*   agree, that few princes have been bleffed with greater Ferdinand talents, or the value of thefe lefs abated by vices, than him I. *and the* of whom we are going to fpeak, Don *Ferdinand* [a], the firft *firft feven* of *Leon*, and the fecond of *Caftile*. It may perhaps pafs for *years of* a kind of proof of this, that, for almoft feven years after he *his go-* came into the poffeffion of *Leon*, we find little or nothing *vernment.* undertaken by him, that could be properly the fubject of A. D. hiftory. He very well knew, that the acquifition of a king- 1037. dom was fometimes lefs difficult than the keeping of it. He perceived that the bulk of his fubjects were diffatisfied with the change of mafters ; and that though he had been very fparing of blood in the reduction of *Galicia*, yet he held that province rather by conqueft than any other title [b], than which nothing could be more difagreeable to a prince of his difpofition. He found it requifite therefore to fpend a great deal of time in correcting gradually thefe miftakes, and re- covering his fubjects from all their prejudices and prepof- feffions. He fpoke always with great clearnefs of the rights of the queen, and never permitted any claim to be men- tioned but that of her defcent [c]. He vifited all the pro- vinces, and indeed almoft every great town, careffed the no- bility exceedingly, paid a profound refpect to the clergy, but made it a part of that refpect to fee that fuch were feverely

---

[a] Mariana Hiftoria general de Efpana, lib. ix. Ferreras Hiftoria de Efpana, p. v. fect. xi. Hiftoire general d'Efpagne, par Mayerne, Turquet.   [b] Roderic Toletan de reb. Hifpan. lib. vi. Lucæ Tudenfis Chronicon.   [c] Chron. var. antiq.

punifhed

puniſhed as were a diſgrace to their order. He proſecuted his predeceſſor's plan of redreſſing grievances with indefatigable diligence; and, by inlarging the privileges of the people in *Galicia*, he in a great meaſure acquired their affection, and leſſened the power of their nobility by increaſing their number. He took leſs care of the frontiers of his hereditary crown of *Caſtile* than his predeceſſors had done; but he kept up greater garriſons, and by that means covered his territories in a great meaſure, and yet not ſo thoroughly, but that the *Moors* [d] had ſometimes opportunities of making incurſions, which they were ſure not to neglect, and which did not anſwer theirs better than it did the king's purpoſe.

WHEN he ſaw the interior of his dominions in perfect order, his ſubjects well united and unanimouſly well affected to his perſon and government, he began to applaud the conduct of his father-in-law Don *Alphonſo* the fifth, who had rightly diſtinguiſhed between the having no frontier, and the being obliged to defend one of a large extent; to avoid both which inconveniencies, the only method was to follow his plan, and, by recovering the beſt part of that country now called *Portugal*, to arrive at natural boundaries of mountains and rivers, with plains of ſmall extent between them, where the building two or three great towns, and fortifying them, would cover at once both his old dominions and his new conqueſts. The reſolution of making war being once taken, was immediately carried into execution, and he marched with a very numerous army directly towards *Zamora*. The fortreſs of *Xena* was the firſt place of ſtrength that lay in his way, which he cauſed to be carried by aſſault, in which the greateſt part of the garriſon were put to the ſword, and the reſt made ſlaves [e]. This had the effect he expected from it; all the little places in the neighbourhood ſurrendered on the firſt ſummons; ſo that he met with no farther oppoſition till he came to *Viſco*, which was naturally ſtrong, had been fortified with great care, was defended by a numerous garriſon, and had in it beſides almoſt all the rich people of the adjacent provinces, who had fled thither with their beſt effects. Don *Ferdinand* acted with caution; he cauſed the place to be battered by his engines, that threw ſtones of a vaſt weight, for three weeks, and then cauſed a general aſſault to be given, by which he carried the town [f], notwithſtanding an obſtinate defence. Here, amongſt other pri-

Invades the territories of the Moors, *and extends his conqueſts to the river* Malna.

A. D. 1047.

[d] RODERIC TOLETAN Hiſt. Arabum.	[e] RODERIC SANTII Hiſt. Hiſpan. p. iii. LUCÆ Tudenſis Chronicon.	[f] RODERIC TOLETAN Hiſt. Arabum.

soners, a crofs-bow man was taken, who difcharged the arrow by which Don *Alphonfo* the fifth was killed.   Don *Fer-*
dinand ordered his hands to be ftruck off, and fome fay his
feet alfo.[g]   He pufhed his conqueft this campaign as far
as the river *Malua*; and, having put good garrifons into
the beft places, he returned to *Lean*, and was received with
loud acclamations, after fuch a ferios of conquefts in fo
fmall a fpace[h] (A).

[g] Chron var. antiq.   [h] Roderic Toletan de reb.
Hifpan. lib. vi. Lucæ Tudenfis Chronicon.

(A) It is abfolutely neceffary
that we fhould give the reader
here fome account of the chronology that we follow; becaufe
it differs from almoft all the
writers of *Spanifh* hiftory, except *Ferreras*. Some of the beft
old hiftorians place the war between Don *Ferdinand*, king of
Caftile, and his brother Don
Garcias king of *Navarre*, before
the expeditions of the former
againft the infidels (1). But that
this is contrary to the order of
time in which thofe events happened is evident from authorities
more authentic than hiftory.
In the firft place it is evident,
from the canons made in the
council of *Coyanca*, that the war
with the infidels was then over;
and, as thefe are records, they
ought undoubtedly to be decifive as to this point (2). It is no
lefs clear from public monuments, mentioned in particular
hiftories of *Navarre*, that the
death of their king Don *Garcia*
did not happen till the fourth
year after that council (3). *Ma-*
riana, though he was far enough

from being exact in point of
chronology, was aware of this,
and has accordingly placed the
conquefts made from the *Moors*
before the difpute with the king
of *Navarre*; notwithftanding
which he has placed thofe conquefts fome years before they
happened; and this very probably, becaufe he did not think
it probable, that a prince (4) of
Don *Ferdinand's* active temper,
fhould, in the beginning of his
reign, fpend fo many years in
peace; and therefore he places
all thofe falutary regulations,
mentioned in the text, fome
years later than they really happened (5). But we hope the
reader fees them here in their
natural order, from whence many advantages arife; fince,
wherever chronology is either
doubtful or falfe, the facts related will appear either contra-
dictory or perplexed, though
ever fo elegantly related; fo
effential a thing is truth, and fo
impracticable it is to render hiftory pleafing without it.

(1) *Roderic Toletan de reb. Hifpan. lib. vi. cap. x. Lucæ Tudenfis Chronicon,*
Francifci Taraphæ de regibus Hifpan.   (2) *Card. d'Aguirre Concil. Hif-*
pan. tom. iii p. 209, 212.   (3) *P. Moret Invefligationes hiftoricas de las*
antiquitades del Reyno de Navarra, lib. iii. cap. iv. Diomis. Petac. ration. temp.
Succefs. LXIX.   (4) *Hiftoria general de Efpana, lib. ix. c. 2.*   (5) *Id.*
lib. c 4.

THE

THE very next year the king was in the field again. He had cast his eyes upon *Coimbra* or *Conimbra*, and considered it as a place of great consequence to his design of forming a strong barrier; for which reason he resolved to reduce it with as little prejudice to the place as possible. Instead therefore of investing the city with his army, he contented himself with posting his troops in such a manner as hindered them from receiving provisions; and, after some months, drew nearer, and threw up lines round the place. The besieged acted with great courage and constancy, and at length tired the king so much, that he had thoughts of raising the siege; but the monks, in a Christian convent at no great distance, prevailed upon him to proceed in his design, furnished him with provisions, and acquainted him with the enemy's distress, by which at last the *Moors* were brought to capitulate, and were allowed to quit the place [i]. All the *Spanish* writers, however, antient and modern, take the honour of so important a conquest, both from the king and from the monks, to bestow it upon *St. James* [k]. It seems that count *Sisenand* had quitted the party of the *Moors*, before the war began, and reconciled himself to the king; who, in reward of his services, and as a mark of his favour, made him governor of this city; in which office he acquitted himself with great reputation [l]. The following year he swept the frontiers of his hereditary kingdom of *Castile*, demolished all the little fortresses the *Moors* had erected, drove them beyond the mountains, and established strong garrisons to cover each of the passes; but adhered to the old policy of Don *Blayo*, erecting no fortresses on this side, that the martial disposition of the *Castilians* might not be abated.

IN his fourth campaign he ravaged all the country about *Medina Cœli*, visited all his conquests, and, having inriched his army with plunder and slaves, returned in triumph to the city of *Leon* [m]. The next spring, when he came to assemble his troops, he found them more numerous than they had been in any of his former expeditions, which induced him to invade the dominions of the king of *Toledo*, at this time one of the most powerful of the *Moorish* princes; and, after he had harrassed and destroyed the open country, he at length besieged *Alcala*; which, though a place of great strength, was at length reduced to such straits, that they sent

Marginal notes:
Besieges in another expedition the city of Conim-bra, *or* Coimbra, *and takes it.*
A. D. 1045.

A. D. 1046.

The Moorish monarchs of Toledo *and Sara-gossa become his tributaries and vassals.*

[i] RODERIC TOLETAN Hist. Arabum. ALPHONSI a Carthagena reg. Hisp. ANACEPHALÆOSIS FRANCISCI TARAPHÆ de reg. Hispaniæ.   [k] Chron. var. antiq.   [l] RODERIC TOLETAN de reb. Hispan. lib. vi.   [m] LUCÆ Tudensis Chronicon.

to *Almanon*, then king of *Toledo* [n], to inform him, that, if they were not speedily relieved, they must be obliged to surrender. That monarch, finding himself in no condition to oppose Don *Ferdinand* by force of arms, took the best part of the riches that were in his treasury, and, attended by a small guard, went directly to the Christian camp, and presented himself before the king, intreating him to desist from hostilities against his subjects, offered to become his vassal, and pay him an annual tribute, and at the same time threw himself and the treasures he had brought at the king's feet. The principal officers in the army were of opinion, that this was only done to gain time, but Don *Ferdinand* was so touched with that prince's distress, that he granted him all he desired, and retired with his troops into his own dominions [o]. He proposed the next year to have carried the war into the territories of the *Moorish* king of *Saragossa*, of which the latter no sooner received intelligence, than he sent embassadors to offer the like submission that had been accepted from the king of *Toledo*, and thereby diverted the intended expedition [p]. And of this vassalage he afterwards availed himself against another Christian potentate.

Sickness of the king of Navarre, deaths of queen El*vira and king* Ali Maymon.
A. D.
1050.
As the kingdoms of *Castile* and *Leon* enjoyed at this time a profound peace, the king thought no time so proper for holding a general council, which he summoned at *Cayanca*, in which there was no legate from the pope present; and in which thirteen canons were made, most with respect to ecclesiastical, but some of them likewise respecting civil affairs [q]. The year following his brother Don *Garcia*, king of *Navarre*, fell dangerously ill at *Najara* on the frontiers of *Castile*; of which Don *Ferdinand* was no sooner informed, than he resolved to pay him a visit. He went thither accordingly, and was received with all possible demonstrations of affection and respect. It seems, however, that two kings can never be long safe together in the same place; for, in a short space, he was informed, whether truly or not is a point historians have disputed, that his brother intended to secure his person; upon which, taking a hasty but civil leave, he retired into his own dominions, extremely nettled at this real or supposed injury [r]. On the fifth of *November*, in the year of our Lord 1052, died the queen dowager Donna *Elvira*, widow of Don *Alphonso* the fifth, and mother of the queen Donna *Sancha*; her body was interred in the dormi-

n R̨ODERIC TOLETAN Hist. Arabum.   o Chron. var. antiq.
p Rod. Tolet. Hist Arabum.   q Card. d'Aguirre Conc. Hispan. tom. iii. p. 212.   r P. Moret Investigationes Historicas de las antiquitades del reyno de Navarra, Roderic Toletan de reb. Hispan. lib. vi. Lucæ Tudensis Chronicon.

tory of the royal family at *Leon*[ſ]. The year following deceaſed the old king of *Toledo*, and was ſucceeded by *Ali*
Maymon[t], who ſeems to have remained tributary to Don
Ferdinand, as his power was not in the leaſt diminiſhed, and
as the *Mohammedan* princes were as far as ever from living
upon good terms among themſelves. Theſe ſhort ſcenes of
mourning ſeemed to be the preludes of more afflicting calamities which quickly enſued, and which proved extremely
fatal to the Chriſtians in *Spain*, who were generally the
authors of their own misfortunes.

Don *Ferdinand* falling dangerouſly ill in the ſucceeding
ſpring, his brother Don *Garcias*, to manifeſt an equal at-
fection, came to ſee him; but the king, who could not forget the informations, true or falſe, that had been given him
at *Najara*, though he received him at firſt with all the marks
of joy and fraternal kindneſs poſſible, yet cauſed him to be
ſoon after arreſted, and ſent priſoner to the caſtle of *Cea*[u], at
that time the ſtrongeſt place in his dominions. But notwithſtanding the ſtricteſt injunctions poſſible were given for
preventing either his eſcape, or his giving or receiving any
intelligence, ſo it was, that he found the means of conveying
an account of the uſage he had met with to ſome perſons
whom he could truſt in his own dominions, and whom he
directed to be at a place appointed at a certain time. They
came accordingly, and brought ſome of the fleeteſt horſes in
Navarre for the king's uſe; and he, by what contrivance is
unknown, was equally punctual, having found his way out
of the caſtle in ſpite of all the care that could be taken. His
flight was ſo ſudden and unexpected, that he was ſafe in his
own dominions by that time the news of it reached the ears
of Don *Ferdinand* at *Leon*[w]. The king foreſaw the miſchiefs that would attend this accident, and it may be, in his
own mind diſapproved that conduct he had purſued. However, when he heard that Don *Garcias*, with a great army,
was on the point of invading *Caſtile*, he went thither in
perſon and aſſembled another, ſuperior in troops as well as in
number; he was notwithſtanding very deſirous, if poſſible,
to avoid effuſion of blood; and, with this ſalutary view, ſent
ſome of the clergy, who were about him, to propoſe terms
of accommodation to Don *Garcias*, offering at the ſame
time whatever ſatisfaction he could deſire, explaining the
motives upon which he acted, and offering to bury in ſilence

The king of Navarre impriſoned, eſcapes and de-clares war againſt king Ferdinand.

ſ Roderic Santii Hiſt. Hiſpan. p. iii. Alphonsi a Carthagena reg. Hiſp. Anacephalæosis Francisci Taraphæ de
reg. Hiſpan. t Roderic Toletan Hiſt. Arabum. u Roderic Toletan de reb. Hiſpan. lib. vi. Lucæ Tudenſis Chronicon. w Chron. var. antiq.

all memory of either event [x]. The chief of the nobility
about Don *Garcias*, and fuch ecclefiaftics as were moft in his
efteem, concurred with the ambaffadors of *Caftile*, and laboured to reconcile him to his brother. All perfuafions were
vain; Don *Garcias's* breaft was wholly occupied by his refentment: he would hear no propofals, but obftinately perfifted, that all difputes between them fhould be decided by a
battle [y]. Don *Ferdinand* did all he could to decline it, acted
wholly on the defenfive, and refolved not to fight, unlefs his
brother was the aggreffor.

*Defeated
in a gene-
ral en-
gagement,
and killed
upon the
fpot.*

DON *Garcias* being informed of this, entered into the kingdom of *Caftile*, and advanced directly towards *Burgos*; and
notwithftanding Don *Fortuno Sanchez*, an antient nobleman,
who had been his governor, laboured all he could to divert
him, he fixed the firft of *September*, one thoufand and fifty-
four, for the day of battle [z], when the two armies appeared
in fight of each other between *Atupuerta* and *Ages*, about
nine miles from *Burgos*. Don *Ferdinand*, who was much the
better officer, ordered a corps of *Caftilian* cavalry to charge
the army of *Navarre* in flank, which they did with fuch fuccefs, that they penetrated to the poft where Don *Garcias*
commanded in perfon; and one *Sanchez*, a trooper, or, as
antient hiftory reports, an officer [a], to whom that monarch
had formerly offered fome infult, plunged his fpear into his
breaft. The nobility about his perfon prevented his being
taken, or wounded a fecond time; but that was of little confequence, fince the ftroke he had received was mortal. *Inigo*,
abbot of *Ona*, caught him in his arms, affifted him with his
prayers in his laft moments, and fupported him till he expired [b]. A column was afterwards erected in the place where
he fell [c]. As this misfortune could not be concealed from
the army, and as it affected the minds of the foldiers to fuch a
degree that they loft all courage, the difpute was foon at an
end, and the flight became general. Don *Ferdinand* would
not fuffer his troops to purfue; but, perceiving a large body
of *Mohammedan* auxiliaries, he caufed them to be furrounded
and cut to pieces, only their generals, being excellently well
mounted, made their efcape [d]. The king made no ufe of a

---

[x] RODERIC TOLETAN de reb. Hifpan. lib. vi. LUCÆ Tudenfis
Chronicon.   [y] Chron. var. antiq.   [z] RODERIC TOLETAN
de reb. Hifpan. lib. vi. LUCÆ Tudenfis Chronicon.   [a] Annal.
Complur. FERRERAS Hiftoria de Efpana, p. v. fect. xi.   [b] Chron.
var. antiq. RODERIC SANTII Hift. Hifpan. p. iii.   [c] AL-
PHONSI a Carthagena reg. Hifp. ANACEPHALÆOSIS FRANCISCI
TARAPHÆ de reg. Hifpaniæ.   [d] RODERIC TOLETAN Hiftor.
Arabum

victory

victory that he regretted; on the contrary, he suffered his brother's body to be interred in the monastery of *St. Mary* at *Najara*, which he had founded, with royal honours, and returned himself to *Leon*, not in triumph, but with all apparent marks of the most sincere grief [e].

WE find in some historians [f], that this war was continued, and that the king, Don *Ferdinand*, availed himself of his superior army, to the prejudice of his nephew, the king of *Navarre*; but this is not supported by any of the antient authors [g], and may be presumed from thence a gross misrepresentation. Indeed the king of *Leon* and *Castile* seems to have been a monarch of great mildness and moderation, and who made no other use of his superior power than for the benefit and protection of his subjects, by preserving peace on every side; and, while that subsisted, letting slip no opportunities of improving the great cities, and encouraging his people to cultivate to the best advantage their respective properties in all parts of his dominions. He removed the body of his father, Don *Sanchez*, from the monastery of *Ona* to the city of *Leon* [h]; where, having made choice of the church of *St. John Baptist*, in complaisance to his queen Donna *Sancha*, by whose father, Don *Alonso* the fifth, it was built for the place of his own sepulchre, he caused the old brick building to be pulled down, in order to rebuild it with stone [i], and with a degree of magnificence suitable to the power, and expressive of the piety of its founder. He caused a council [k] to be held the beginning of the year 1056, in the apostolic church (so the Spaniards stile it) of *St. James* of *Compostella*, in which some canons were made for the support of the discipline of the church. Yet, notwithstanding this prudent and pacific behaviour, which it might have been presumed would have given all his neighbours the utmost satisfaction, we find that Don *Garcias*, king of *Navarre*, and Don *Ramiro*, king of *Arragon*, had an interview at the monastery of *Leyra*, under pretence of the dedication of the church, where they made a defensive league [l] for the reciprocal protection of their territories, in case that either should be attacked by Don *Ferdinand*;

A general council held in the apostolic church of St. James at Compostella.

A. D. 1055.

---

[e] RODERIC TOLETAN de reb. Hispan. lib. vi. LUCÆ Tudensis Chron. [f] RODERIC TOLETAN, MARIANA, MAYERNE, TURQUET, P. d'ORLEANS. [g] Chron. var. antiq. [h] RODERIC TOLETAN de reb. Hispan. lib. vi. LUCÆ Tudensis Chronicon. [i] RODERIC SANTII Hist. Hispan. p. iii. ALPHONSI a Carthagena reg. Hisp. ANACEPHALÆOSIS. [k] Card. d'AGUIRRE Conc. Hisp. tom. iii. p. 199. [l] RODERIC TOLETAN de reb. Hispan. lib. vi. LUCÆ Tudensis Chronicon.

who,

who, it does not at all appear, meant them any disturbance, or took any umbrage at this precaution (B).

A legate ON the death of pope *Nicholas* the second there happened
from a schism; and one of the competitors, who took the title of
Rome, *Alexander* the second, sent a legate into *Spain*, in order to
who began derive all the help he could from that quarter. This may
the quar- seem an immaterial point, but it is really a thing of great con-

(B) We are assured by *Mariana*, that Don *Ferdinand* was not so disinterested a prince as no ways to avail himself of this victory (1); but that he made himself master of *Briviesca*, the mountains of *Occa*, and so much of the county of *Rioja* as lay on that side of the river *Oja* next to *Castile*; so that Don *Sanchez*, the son of Don *Garcias*, had only *Navarre*, *Biscay*, the remaining part of the county of *Rioja*, *Najara*, *Logrogno*, and some other places left; and which is still more singular, he speaks of the countries now taken by Don *Ferdinand* as if they had been the original cause of the differences between the two brothers, in which he not not only contradicts others but himself; and, indeed, the whole relation is incredible, because it is impossible. For if Don *Ferdinand* was desirous of possessing himself of these countries, he would have certainly been the aggressor, which all historians agree he was not; and, on the other hand, that Don *Garcias* did not take up arms to recover these from his brother is evident, from what *Mariana* says of their being taken from his son after his death. Upon the whole it is, perhaps, more than probable,

that not only *Mariana*, but an antient historian, in whom we also find something much to the same purpose, confound the death of Don *Garcias* with that of his son Don *Sanchez*, and speak of what certainly happened after the death of the latter, as if it had fallen out upon the demise of the former: for thus much of truth it must be acknowleged there is in the foregoing relation, that the countries therein - mentioned were taken from *Navarre*, and annexed to *Castile*; but this happened many years after (2), upon a compromise between the kings of *Leon* and *Arragon*, at which time the river *Ebro*, into which the *Oja* falls, was made the common boundary of their dominions (3). It is impossible, considering our plan, to discuss in this manner all the variations we have been obliged to make from the common manner in which the *Spanish* history has been stated in our language; but from a few instances we hope the candid reader will do us the justice to believe, that it is out of respect to proper authorities, and not out of an affectation of singularities, that we are led to the same conduct in other places.

(1) *Lucæ Tudensis Chronicon. Mariana Historia general de España, lib. ix.*
(2) *As the reader will find in the course of this history.* (3) *Ferreras Historia de España, p. v. sect. xi.*

sequence;

sequence; for this ecclesiastic was extremely offended with *rel as to* the old *Gothic* liturgy, and was for obtruding upon the *Spa-the Gothic niards* the *Roman* offices at once; with which, in their turn, *liturgy.* they were equally displeased.   At this juncture, indeed, there was nothing done in that matter, but it was this legate who laid the foundation of all that has been done since; for, upon his return to *Rome,* he reported, that the *Spaniards* could never be made good subjects to that see (and in that, no doubt, he was right) till the *Gothic* liturgy and their antient usages were removed out of the way: and this being thoroughly comprehended, the indefatigable spirit of the church of *Rome* never suffered the government of *Leon* and *Castile* to be at peace, till they had got the better in this respect; which was not, however, till some years after, as will be shewn in its proper place; and then it was in consequence of their having prevailed in other *Spanish* principalities before.   Let us now return from ecclesiastical to civil history, and observe what the strange consequences were of this legate's doctrine at the court of *Leon,* and how far, even under a wife and good prince, religious caprices operated upon the most important affairs of state.

THE church of *St. John* the *Baptist* being finished, the *Translati-* queen Donna *Sancha* was desirous of enriching it, according to *on of the* the superstitious humour of those times, with holy relics; and *body of St.* upon this there either came or was thrust into her head two vir- *Isidore,* gins, *St. Justa* and *St. Rufina,* who where martyred, and whose *bishop of* bodies were interred at *Seville.*   It was suggested, that the *Seville, to* surest way of obtaining them was by force of arms.   Upon *the city of* this, the ablest *Spanish* historians [r] boast of it to this day, Don *Leon.* *Ferdinand* made an irruption into the territories of *Mohammed Aben-Habet,* king of *Seville,* without provocation, and without any intimation of offence, murdered multitudes of *Moors,* drove vast numbers into slavery, and gave up the whole country to pillage, which brought the poor *Mohammedan* prince upon his knees [s] to *Ferdinand,* offering him all his treasures to ransom the bodies of his unhappy subjects, whom he wanted force to defend.   The king of *Leon* and *Castile* insisted upon having the body of *St. Justa* taken up and sent to *Leon,* and that the *Moorish* monarch should do him homage and become his vassal.   *Mohammed* submitted to all this very willingly and chearfully.   But when, some time after, three bishops and three counts came to *Seville* to demand the body of the saint, the poor king found himself in a very distressed

[r] MARIANA Historia general d'Espana, lib. ix. FERRERAS, MAYERNE, TURQUET.   [s] RODERIC TOLETAN Histor. Arabum.

condition,

condition, as not having the leaft knowlege where this fair
was to be found. The Chriftian inhabitants profeffed them
felves as ignorant as he [t]. In the midft of this perplexity
St. *Ifidore* very kindly appeared to *Alvitus*, bifhop of *Leon*
who was at the head of the embaffy, and told him, it was no
a proper time to remove the faints *Jufta* and *Rufina*, but
that they fhould take his body [u] with them, and pointed with
a crofs to the place were it lay. This was accordingly done,
and *Alvitus* himfelf dying in his return, both bodies were received with great reverence into *Leon*; the king, the queen,
and a great number of the nobility going out a confiderable
diftance to receive them; and the corpfe of St. *Ifidore* being
depofited in the new church of St. *John* the *Baptift*, has, in
fome meafure, changed its name [w].

Don Ra-
miro, king
of Arra-
gon, de-
feated and
killed be-
fore Sara-
goffa. WHILE the king Don *Ferdinand* was employed in the war
againft *Seville*, Don *Ramiro*, king of *Arragon*, with a formidable army, invaded the dominions of the *Moorifh* prince
of *Saragoffa*, who, being tributary to the king of *Leon*, immediately fent embaffadors to his capital to implore his affiftance: they finding him abfent, applied themfelves to Don
Sancho his fon, who fent them inftantly back to their mafter,
defiring him to affemble all the troops he was able; and affuring him, that he would forthwith march with a ftrong body
of forces to his relief, which he accordingly did. The Infant
Don *Sancho* having for his lieutenant the famous Don *Rod-*
rigo, furnamed the *Cid*, no fooner joined the *Moors* than he
propofed marching to give the king of *Arragon* battle, who,
on his fide, raifed the fiege of a town before which he lay,
and marched to meet them. The difpute was long and
bloody; but at length the victory [x] declared on the fide of the
Infant, the unfortunate Don *Ramiro* being killed upon the
fpot, as moft of the *Spanifh* writers agree; though there are
fome [y] who affirm, that he died fome time after in his bed;
and there are alfo others who affert, that he was not only
killed, but that his body fell into the hands of the infidels,
who caufed it to be flead; the probability of which will be
difcuffed in another place; at prefent it is fufficient to obferve, that the Infant Don *Sancho*, having relieved his father's vaffal, returned with his victorious troops to *Leon* [z] (C).

AT

[t] RODERIC TOLETAN de reb. Hifpan. lib. vi. LUCÆ Tedenfis
Chronicon.   [u] PELAG. OVETENS liber Chronic.   [w] Chron.
var. antiq.   [x] RODERIC TOLETAN Hift. Arabum.   [y] Chron.
var. antiq.   [z] PELAG. OVETENS liber Chronic.

(C) There is fomething very   of hiftory. *Mariana* (1), *Peta-*
dark and difficult in this piece   *vius* (2), and moft other writers

(1) *Hiftoria general de Efpana, lib. ix.*   (2) *Rat'on. Tempor. Succeff l. xix.*

place

At the time of the translation of St. *Isidore* (so the *Spa-* King Fer-
niards [a] stile it) the king Don *Ferdinand* held an assembly of dinand
the states at *Leon*, in which he opened to them his design *of proposes to*
dividing his dominions amongst his three sons; that is, to *an assembly*

[a] Mariana Historia general de Espana, lib. ix. Ferreras.

place the death of Don *Ramiro*
four years later, that is, in the
year 1067; and, upon that account, place the war not in the
reign of Don *Ferdinand* but of
Don *Sancho*, which is not easy
to comprehend, more especially
as it appears from the monument of this prince, in the monastery of St. *John de la Pegna*
(3), that he died on the 8th of
the ides of *May*, and also on the
fifth day of the week; but upon
examination this will be found
not to agree with the year 1067,
but with the year 1063, where
it is placed in the text (4). The
Infant Don *Sancho* therefore
must have commanded the troops
of his father, which joined those
of the *Mohammedan* prince of
Saragossa, and with him went
Don *Rodrigo*, surnamed the *Cid*,
to whom this remarkable victory is in a great measure ascribed (5). It is not a little
strange, that not only this particular fact of the king's death,
but the whole war has been represented as false and fictitious
by some very good criticks (6);
notwithstanding which we must,
if we agree with them, give up
those rules that have been hitherto looked upon as the safest
and best in judging of history,
since we have contemporary
writers who affirm it, and upon
their authority it has been re-

ceived by the best historians of
that country (7). *Mariana*, who,
as we have before observed,
places this event in the reign of
Don *Sancho*, acquaints us, that
it was looked on as an ill omen
to his administration, that it began with the death of his uncle
(8); but it is as proable, that
this omen might be applied as
well to his first campaign; for
we can scarce imagine, that the
Infant Don *Sancho* had commanded in person before this
time. There is little regard due
to omens; but without doubt
Don *Ferdinand* must conceive it
a great misfortune, that two of
his own brothers, and his wife's
brother, should fall in the field
by his arms: but, however, he
might comfort himself with this,
that in each of these actions they
were the aggressors, and his
forces only employed in the defence of his own subjects or of
his allies. It is an inexcusable
fault in *Mariana* notwithstanding, that he places the death of
Don *Ramiro* four years later,
to mention bulls directed to him
by pope *Gregory* the seventh,
who was not elevated to that
dignity till the year of our lord
1073, which shews how very
little attention he paid to chronology, which is indeed the capital fault in his history.

(3) *P. Moret Investigationes historicas de las antiquidades del Reyno de Navarro.*
(4) *Ferreras Historia de Espana, p. v. sect. xi.* (5) *Mariana Historia general
de Espana, lib. ix.* (6) *P. Moret.* (7) *Lucae Tudensis Chronicon. Roderic Toletan de rebus Hispaniae.* (8) *Historia general de Espana, lib. ix.*

of the give the kingdom of *Castile* to the eldest Don *Sancho*, upon
states the whom the *Moorish* king of *Saragossa* was to depend; th
division of crown of *Leon* and the *Asturias* of *Oviedo* to Don *Alonso*
his domi- and the kingdom of *Galicia*, with so much of *Portugal* as h
nions. had conquered, to Don *Garcia*, the youngest. We cannc
doubt but many of the nobility must foresee the mischiefs tha
would inevitably follow from this measure, so inconsisten
with all maxims of policy, as well as dictates of experience
But the majority complied with and applauded the king's pro
posal; upon which, at the breaking up of that assembly [b]
the Infants Don *Sancho* and Don *Garcia* were sent to tak
possession of *Castile* and *Galicia*. About the same time thre
Spanish prelates (which is the first instance of the kind) wer
sent to the council of *Mantua* [c], which was held by pope *Alex*
ander II. where they produced the *Gothic* offices; and, upo
perusal, the council unanimously declared, that they were or
thodox and pious; so that they have this testimony of :
learned council, with a pope at its head, in favour of thei
antient liturgy, if that could afford it any sanction. Some [d]
indeed, say, that the pope only approved the offices they sent
without suffering any to examine them but himself; and if so
then surely very little respect is paid to his decree, by those wh
speak so harshly of these venerable monuments of the doctrin
and discipline of the truly catholic Christian church among
the *Goths*.

Dies soon THE *Moorish* kings of *Toledo* and *Saragossa* were not long
after his before they took advantage of this impolitic division of th
return territories of the king Don *Ferdinand*, which, perhaps, they
from an might attribute to the weakness and infirmities of old age,
expedition and from thence incline to hope they might be able to shake
against the off the yoke and recover their independency. Yet how plau
kings of sible soever these notions might be, they drew them into a
Toledo hasty and fatal resolution. For having refused to pay their
and Sara- annual tribute [e], Don *Ferdinand* assembled a numerous and
gossa. well disciplined army, with which, before they suspected any
such thing, he swept the frontiers of both kingdoms, wasting
the country with fire and sword, and carrying multitudes into
slavery [f]. He advanced with his victorious army into the
neighbourhood of *Valentia*, the suburbs of which city he
burnt, and perhaps had done more, but finding himself indisposed, and his disorder increasing, he thought it time to retreat, and accordingly returned to *Leon* in the beginning of

[b] RODERIC TOLETAN de reb. Hispan. lib. vi.   [c] Concil.
tom. ix. p. 1179.   [d] Chron. var. antiq.   [e] RODERIC
TOLETAN Hist. Arabum.   [f] RODERIC TOLETAN de reb.
Hispan. lib. vi. LUCÆ Tudensis Chronicon.

winter.

winter. His health still declining, he caused himself to be carried into the church of St. *Isidore*, where he performed an act of public penance for his sins, and died the very next day[s], which was the twenty-seventh of *September*, one thousand sixty-five. Besides his sons before-mentioned, he left behind him two daughters, to the elder of whom, Donna *Urraca*, he gave the city of *Zamora*, which he had strongly fortified, with other lands, and to the younger, Donna *Elvira*, *Toro*, and some other places by way of appendages, that they might live in a manner suitable to their high birth, and without being dependant upon any of their brethren [h].

Don *Sancho*, king of *Castile*, though he submitted to the disposition which his father had made, looked upon himself as extremely injured thereby, from an opinion, that priority of birth gave him a just title to all the three kingdoms; but so long as his mother Donna *Sancha* lived, he did not suffer his discontent to appear, because her title to *Leon*, the *Asturias*, *Galicia*, and *Portugal*, seemed clearer than his own, and he was perfectly satisfied that what the late king had done was thro' her persuasion. He reigned therefore quietly at *Burgos*, and applied himself with indefatigable diligence to render the kingdom of *Castile* as flourishing as possible. But that princess dying [i] on the 7th of *November* in the following year, he found himself more at liberty, and perhaps would have discovered his real intention sooner, if he had not been involved in a war with the kings of *Arragon* and *Navarre*, both of his own name, which most writers place two years sooner; and in which, it is said, that he met with a total defeat. But as the causes and consequences of this war are very obscurely expressed, and as it is much more probable it happened after the death of Don *Ferdinand*, we have followed the example of *Ferreras* [k], and placed it here, though we are not able to acquaint the reader in what manner it ended. It may be the confederate princes, satisfied with their victory, and believing they had done enough for the security of their own dominions, were willing to give an example of moderation in their own conduct; or it may be they differed between themselves, which hindered them from pushing their success farther. But whatever the motive was, this war came to a very speedy conclusion; and for any thing that appears in authentic histo-

Marginal notes: Don Sancho, king of Castile, engaged in a war with the kings of Arragon and Navarre.

[s] RODERIC SANTII Hist. Hispan. p. lii. ALPHONSI a Carthagena reg. Hisp. ANACEPHALÆOSIS FRANCISCI TARAPHÆ, de reg. Hispaniæ. [h] RODERIC TOLETAN de reb. Hispan. lib. vi. LUC. Tudens. Chron. [i] RODERIC SANTII Hist. Hispan. p. iii. PELAG. OVETENS liber Chronic. [k] Historia de Espana, p. v. sect. xi.

rians, Don *Sancho* might have enjoyed the kingdom bestowed upon him by his father in quiet, if the turn of his own mind would have permitted it.

War be-
tween Don
Sancho,
king of
Castile,
and Don
Alonso
VI. his
brother.

DON *Alphonso*, king of *Leon*, was a prince of a very humane and gentle disposition, in consequence of which he had stood highest in his mother's favour, by whose counsels he was chiefly directed while she lived, and after her decease had great regard to the advice of his sisters, who were princesses of uncommon parts, and which was still more rare had nothing of jealousy or intrigue in their tempers. One of the first steps taken by this monarch after his accession was to conclude a treaty of marriage with a princess of *England*, whose name was *Aguda*, the daughter of *William* the first, surnamed the conqueror, whom he espoused by proxy, and who, in her pas-

A. D.
1067.

sage to *Spain*, died at sea. Her corpse was landed in *France*, and interred in a monastery there. This misfortune was succeeded by another; for Don *Sancho*, king of *Leon*, invaded his dominions with a formidable army, notwithstanding that the two princesses their sisters had laboured all that in them lay to prevent things from coming to extremities. Don *Alphonso* opposed him with troops superior in number, but not equal in courage, or at least in discipline. The battle was fought

A. D.
1068.

on the nineteenth of *July*, at a place called *Lantada*, in which Don *Alphonso*, being defeated [o], fled to *Leon*, and made the best disposition he could there for his defence; but, thro' the interposition of the princesses, a siege was prevented, and Don *Sancho* engaged to return for that year into his own dominions upon certain conditions; of which we have very indistinct accounts, and this probably because the agreement that was now concluded did not last long.

Disturb-
ances in
Galicia,
the king-
dom of Don
Garcia the
3d brother.

WHILE the realms of *Castile* and *Leon* were in such confusion, and the concerns of their inhabitants turned upon each other, the arms of Don *Garcia*, king of *Galicia*, were in very little better condition. He had a favourite, to whom he confided without reserve the management of all his affairs: the chief of his nobility had represented to him frequently the bad consequences of such a behaviour, and the bad use this man made of his unlimited authority; but as this had no effect, those great lords had recourse to rougher measures, and cut this insolent favourite to pieces [p], almost in the presence of his master; after which they thought fit to retire into the dominions of *Leon*, where they met with protection

[o] RODERIC TOLETAN de reb. Hispan. lib. vi. LUCÆ Tudensis Chronicon. PELAG. OVETENS liber Chronic. [p] Chron. var. antiq.

and

and favour. The reader has been informed, that the inhabitants of *Galicia* were of a very mutinous disposition; and
besides this, which is indeed a sufficient proof, there happened
another in that country within the compass of a few months;
for *Gudesto*, bishop of *Compostella*, having some disputes about
the rights of his church with Don *Froila*, a nobleman of
great authority, and his near relation, the latter found means
to enter the apartment of the prelate when in his bed and
fast asleep, and stabbed him to the heart with his dagger [q]; A. D.
notwithstanding which, the government was in such confusion, 1069.
that, for any thing that appears in history, he escaped with
impunity.

THE peace between Don *Sancho*, king of *Castile*, and his *Don* Alon-
brother Don *Alphonso*, king of *Leon*, had been with difficulty *so beats*
prolonged for somewhat more than a year, when Don *Sancho Don San-*
had again recourse to arms [r], without pretending any other *cho one*
motive than that of despoiling Don *Alphonso* of his territories. *day, and*
The latter had assembled a numerous and well disciplined *is totally*
army, towards which his brother Don *Garcia* [s] contributed, *defeated*
by sending him a considerable body of auxiliaries. The two *by him the*
armies met and fought on the fourteenth of *July*; when, after *next.*
a long and bloody dispute, Don *Alphonso* remained victorious [t]. A. D.
If he had pursued his advantage, he might very probably have 1070.
put an end to the war; but the mildness of his nature, and
his unwillingness to shed the blood of his father's subjects,
restrained him. Don *Sancho* had with him the *Cid*, who
rallied his army, and encamped not far from the field of
battle. He afterwards prevailed both upon the king and the
troops to fall upon the victorious army about an hour beyond
midnight; and taking them by surprise, it was rather a
slaughter than a fight, since they met with little or no resistance. The king Don *Alphonso* mounted the first horse he
could find, and fled to the first church, which was that of St.
Mary de Carrion; but Don *Sancho* pursued him with such
eagerness, that he was presently taken, and sent prisoner
under a strong guard of horse to *Burges* [u].

THE princesses, Donna *Urraça* and Donna *Elvira*, upon *Obliged to*
Don *Sancho*'s coming to *Leon*, interposed in behalf of their un- *abdicate*
fortunate brother, and were very earnest in persuading the *his throne*
conqueror to spare his life; to which with some difficulty he *by Don*
consented, upon condition that he should abdicate his domi- *Sancho,*
nions, consent to be shaved a monk, and retire to the abby of *who de-*

[q] RODERIC TOLETAN de reb. Hispan. lib. vi. LUCÆ Tudensis
Chronicon.   [r] Chron. var. antiq.   [s] LUCÆ Tudensis
Chronicon. PELAG. OVETENS liber Chronic.   [t] RODERIC
TOLETAN de reb. Hispan. lib. vi.   [u] Chron. var. antiq.

poſes Don
Garcia
likewiſe.

Sabagon ; which terms, however hard and inglorious, Don *Alphonſo* was forced to accept, and is ſaid to have taken a re-ligious habit in the houſe before-mentioned ; but an hiſto-rian [w], who lived near theſe times, tells us, that Don *Sancho* inſiſted only upon his quitting his dominions, and laying aſide the royal title (D). However that may be, Don *Sancho* found no great oppoſition in eſtabliſhing himſelf on the throne of *Leon*; and, indeed, in the ſituation things were then in, it is no great wonder. As ambition excludes content, ſo Don

[w] RODERIC TOLETAN de reb. Hiſpan. lib. vi. LUCÆ Tu-denſis Chronicon.

(D) As it contributes not a little to enlighten hiſtory, when we have the characters of the principal perſons mentioned in them drawn with fidelity and judgment, it may not be amiſs to obſerve here, that Don *Pe-layo,* biſhop of *Oviedo,* tells (1) us of Don *Sancho,* that in his father's life-time he drew the reſpect and veneration of the people, by the manly beauty of his perſon, which, though con-ſiderably beyond the common ſize, was perfectly well propor-tioned. His countenance was open and pleaſant, his air ma-jeſtic, active, and full of addreſs in martial exerciſes, and he had ſuch uncommon vigour, that he derived from thence the ſurname of Don *Sancho* the ſtrong. He was very brave, and in his own nature generous and beneficent; but he had one great foible, which was, that he loved praiſe, and them from whom he re-ceived it. *Mariana* (2) ſays, that quarrels had ariſen between Don *Alonſo* and Don *Garcia* be-fore Don *Sancho* made his firſt irruption into *Leon.* The arch-biſhop of *Toledo* (3) aſſerts po-ſitively, that Don *Sancho* ſpared

his brother's life upon no other terms than an abſolute renunci-ation, and taking the habit of a monk [y] to which he was per-ſuaded by Don *Pedro Aſſurez*; but the biſhop of *Tuy* (4) relates this matter otherwiſe, for he tells us, that at the requeſt of Donna *Urraca,* Don *Sancho* per-mitted his brother to retire to *Toledo,* on a promiſe that he would never return during his life without his leave, and that he alſo conſented, that Don *Pe-dro Aſſurez* and his two brothers ſhould attend him. But both writers agree, that Don *Alonſo* was undone by his clemency in forbidding the purſuit of his brother's army when broken, ſaying of the *Caſtilians* when he ſaw them fly, ſpare them; they are your brethren, and were my father's ſubjects; and they likewiſe attribute all that afterwards happen'd to the coun-cils given Don *Sancho* by the *Cid,* who ſeems to have held the ſame place in his favour that Don *Pedro Aſſurez* did in his brother's; and it may be there is a little exaggeration in one character as well as the other.

(1) *Pelag. Ovetens Chron.* (2) *Hiſtoria general de Eſpana, lib. ix.* (3) *De reb. Hiſpan. lib. vii.* (4) *Lucæ Tudenſis Chron. who very probably followed ſome more antient author.*

Sancho

Sancho could reap no joy in the possession of one brother's crown, while there was yet a diadem upon the head of another; and therefore as soon as the people of *Leon* had submitted and sworn allegiance to him, and he had received large reinforcements from *Castile*, he entered *Galicia* with his victorious army. If the people had been in any degree united, his conquest might have been at least disputed; but their want of a good understanding with their sovereign and each other, disabled them from making any considerable resistance, and the severity with which Don *Sancho* treated all who opposed him, was another circumstance that facilitated his conquest [y]. As for Don *Garcia*, his chief care was to avoid falling into his hands, and therefore, as soon as he found his affairs desperate, he threw himself, with such as remained firm to him under his misfortunes, who were but a few, into the dominions of the king of *Seville*; who, by the conquest of *Cordova* and *Murcia*, was become the most considerable of the *Mohammedan* monarchs in *Spain*, by whom he was very kindly received, and honourably protected [z].

WHILE Don *Sancho* was employed in the conquest of *Galicia*, Don *Alphonso* was contriving how to recover his liberty, and to escape out of the monastery in which he was confined into the dominions of some foreign prince. He found means to inform the princesses his sisters of his intentions; and Donna *Urraca* prevailed upon three lords, of the family of *Affurez*, to run the hazard of facilitating his escape. They accordingly supplied him with horses; and, having drawn him safely out of the monastery, conducted him with the utmost expedition to *Toledo* [a]. He acquainted *Ali-Maymon*, who was then king, with the situation of his affairs, and the reasons he had to have recourse to his protection. That monarch not only promised him all he asked, but provided for him, and those who resorted to him, with royal bounty; and, as he knew that he was extremely fond of hunting, he assigned him a district where he might enjoy that diversion, and where none were allowed to hunt but Christians. The sweetness of Don *Alphonso*'s temper prevailed so much upon his protector, that he visited him almost every day, and they lived together in the most strict and intimate friendship [b] (E).

Don Alonso withdraws into the kingdom of Toledo, and is well received.

Don

---

[y] *Chron. var. antiq.*   [z] RODERIC TOLETAN Hist. Arabum.   [a] RODERIC TOLETAN de reb. Hispan. lib. vi. LUCÆ Tudensis Chronicon.   [b] RODERIC TOLETAN Hist. Arabum.

(E) The reception met with by Don *Alonso* at the court of the king of *Toledo* was without doubt as good as he could desire

A. D.
1072.

Don *Sancho*, at his return to *Leon*, quickly gave his sisters reason to believe, that he resented in a very high degree their attachment to Don *Alphonso*, by signifying to them, that, having now united his father's dominions, it was no longer requisite that they should remain mistresses of the towns which he had given them ; but, upon their resigning these into his

sire, and much better than he could reasonably expect (1). But *Mariana*, in the method he has taken to make us sensible of this, has injured the elegancy of his description, by pushing it not only beyond probability, but beyond possibility also (2). He gives us the speeches of the two kings at their first interview, the conditions proposed and accepted, the disposition of the city and summer palace, the pensions settled upon such as followed the fortunes of this exiled prince, the services they rendered the king of *Toledo* in his wars with other *Moorish* princes, and abundance of other entertaining particulars; amongst the rest he acquaints us, that one day, when the two kings were together, with many of the *Moorish* nobility about them, in the royal garden, Don *Alonso* laid himself along by the side of a canal, and seemed to be asleep, while the king of *Toledo*, who attentively considered that city, of which they had a fair and full view from the spot where they were, desired their opinion of his new works, and whether they did not judge that the place was now in a manner impregnable ; to which one of his lords answered, that it was indeed much stronger than before, but that it might still be taken, by wasting for seven

years together all the country round, by which the magazines would be exhausted, and the recruiting them rendered impracticable ; after which a short siege would not fail of being attended with success. This discourse being over-heard, and treasured up in his mind by *Alonso*, furnished him in process of time with the means of becoming master of that capital. He adds, that there was such a resort of Christians to Don *Alonso*, that they built a town about his hunting seat, which is that now called *Bribuega*. But if he had adverted ever so little to the chronology of this history, it would have prevented, or at least have shortened, this description of the king's reception and manner of passing his time, since, by a comparison of circumstances, it is certain, he did not remain at *Toledo* a full year ; and an historian (3), who flourished in his grandson's reign, affirms, that his stay did not exceed nine months; which clearly demonstrates, that most of these stories are the pure effects of imagination, not in *Mariana*, but in the writers from whom he took them, and by whom he would have been in no danger of being misled, if he had attended to this circumstance, which will justify our omitting them.

(1) *Roderic Toletan. Hist. Arabum.* (2) *Historia general de Espana, lib.* ix.
(3) *Pelag. Ovetens Chron. very probably from some abby chronicle of that time.*

hands, he would affign them a maintenance fuitable to their rank. They reprefented to him in vain how unworthy it was of fo great a prince to think of oppreffing two feeble women, and thofe too of his own blood. However, they called together their vaffals, and acquainted them with the king's intention, whofe haughty, morofe, and cruel temper, having rendered him univerfally odious, thofe, who depended upon the princeffes, dreading nothing fo much as to become his fubjects, freely offered to defend the places of which they were poffeffed to the utmoft extremity; and this propofition being accepted, they took their meafures accordingly [c].

THE king was exceffively provoked at this conduct, which he did not expect; but, on the contrary fuppofed, that their vaffals would either have prevailed upon them to fubmit, or provided for their own fafety by fubmitting themfelves. As foon as he found himfelf deceived in that hope, he affembled a very numerous army, which he commanded in perfon [d], and had for his lieutenant general Don *Rodrigo*, furnamed the *Cid*. He firft attacked *Toro*, which belonged to Donna *Elvira*, and took it rather by the fhew than the force of his army [e], which pleafed him exceedingly, and gave him great reafon to hope, that he fhould find his next expedition attended with very little difficulty. But he very quickly found the contrary; Donna *Urraca* had fhut herfelf up in *Zamora*, which was very well fortified, and had a numerous garrifon, whom he could not intimidate by menaces, and by whom his troops were repulfed with great lofs in feveral affaults. There was a nobleman in the town, Don *Arias Gonzalez*, who acted as general and prime minifter for the princefs *Urraca*, and he acted fo well in both capacities, that the troops did their duty with fpirit, and were well fupplied from the magazines with every thing they wanted; fo that at length the king of *Leon*, notwithftanding the fuperiority of his forces, found himfelf obliged to retire to a greater diftance, and to turn his fiege into a blockade. This appeared to be a certain method of reducing the place; for as they had no fuccours to expect, fo famine within the town would quickly bring them into greater diftrefs than was in the power of an army without; and, indeed, all things confidered, Donna *Urraca* and her fubjects had great reafon to look upon their condition as defperate [f].

Don Sancho forms a defign to deprive his fifters of Toro and Zamora.

A. D. 1072.

---

[c] Chron. var. antiq.
Lucæ Tudenfis Chron.
[f] Chron. var. antiq.

[d] RODERIC TOLETAN de reb. Hifpan.
[e] PELAG. OVETENS liber Chron.

Besieges Zamora, *and is slain during the blockade by* Ataulphus.

It was not long before some in the town began to think it so, and to communicate their thoughts to their neighbours, which producing a kind of general murmur, a council [g] was called by the townsmen to know whether they should not demand a capitulation. After some very warm debates, one *Ataulphus* stood up, and assured them, that if they would have a little patience, he would undertake to deliver the place. Upon this the council broke up, and *Ataulphus*, at his own request, was permitted to go out of the city; he proceeded directly to the camp of the king of *Leon*, and having asked and obtained a private audience, he gave him an account of the council that had been held, assured him, that he was the only person who proposed a surrender; upon which they fairly turned him out of the town [h]. At this he expressed great resentment, telling him, that if he would advance with a party of horse near the place, he would discover to him a postern that might be easily forced, and the city taken by storm [i]. The king was extremely pleased with this intelligence, and at the request of him who gave it, kept it a secret from his officers. A few days after he advanced with a part of his cavalry, and when they were within sight of the walls, *Ataulphus* told the king, if he would dismount he would shew him the place, and him only. He readily complied with his request, but had not gone far before he found it necessary to ease himself; and while he was behind a bush for this purpose, *Ataulphus* struck him through the body with his javelin, and, leaving him swimming in his own blood, made his escape [k]. Thus fell the ambitious Don *Sancho*, king of *Leon*, *Castile*, and *Galicia*, on the fifth of *October*, one thousand seventy-two, when he had reigned almost seven years. The greatest part of his army separated immediately upon the news of the king's death; but the *Castilian* troops retired in good order, carrying his corpse with them, which they caused to be interred with royal honour in the monastery of *Ona* [l] (F).

The

[g] Roderic Santii Hist. Hispan. p. iii. Lucæ Tudensis Chron. [h] Roderic Toletan de reb. Hispan. lib. vi. [i] Lucæ Tudensis Chron. Pelag. Ovetens liber Chron. [k] Roderic Santii Hist. Hispan. p. iii. Alphonsi a Carthagena reg. Hispan. Anacephalæosis Francisci Taraphæ, de reg. Hispan. [l] Roderic Toletan de reb. Hispan. lib. vi. Lucæ Tudensis Chron.

(F) As singular and as extraordinary as the circumstances of Don *Sancho*'s death may appear in the text, they might have been rendered out of comparison more wonderful, if we had paid any regard to what modern historians have made no scruple

THE first care of Donna *Urraca*, when the blockade was raised, was to difpatch an exprefs to *Toledo*, to defire Don *Alphonfo* to make all the difpatch imaginable in repairing to *Zamora* [m]. When he communicated this intelligence to thofe who were about him, they unanimoufly diffuaded him from acquainting the *Moorifh* prince, from an apprehenfion that he would not fuffer him to depart. Their arguments had no effect upon Don *Alonfo*. He faid, that princes might indeed be juftified from policy in dealing artificially with each other, but that fuch a behaviour was inexcufable between friends. He went therefore to *Ali-Maymon*, prefented to him his fifter's letters, and defired his permiffion to return into his own dominions [n]. That monarch received him with all imaginable kindnefs, concealing his own intelligence which was very near as early as Don *Alphonfo*'s, he gave him the ftrongeft affurances, that his pleafure was not greater than his own, and, having gently put him in mind of the kindneffes he had done him, requefted a continuance of his friendfhip

(margin:) Don Alonfo VI. returns into his dominions upon the news of his brother's death.

---

[m] Chron. var. antiq.　　[n] RODERIC TOLETAN Hift. Arabum.

---

fcruple of inferting in their works upon this occafion (1). According to them, the name of the perfon who managed the fcheme of the king's death was *Vellido Dolfos*, which feems to be a corruption of *Ataulphus*. It is added, that the *Caftilians*, inftead of deferting the fiege, were fo enraged by the murder of the king, that Don *Diego Ordonez*, of the houfe of *Laura*, went up to the gates of *Zamora*, and threatened the inhabitants with the utter extirpation of every thing within their walls, if they did not purge themfelves of their having any fhare in the contrivance or execution of that affaffination; upon which, according to the cuftom then in ufe, Don *Arrias Gonzalez* and his three fons, Don *Pedro*, Don *Diego*, and Don *Rodrigo*, offered to maintain the innocence of the townfmen in fingle combat one by one againft Don *Diego Ordonez*, which was accepted; and in this fight Don *Diego* killed all the three young cavaliers; but the youngeft of them, Don *Rodrigo*, after he had received a mortal wound, aiming a ftroke at Don *Diego*, cut the reins of his horfe's bridle; upon which the beaft wheeled about, forced the barrier, and carried his mafter out of the field of battle; which, according to the laws of combat, was the fame thing as if he had been defeated. Upon this the judges refufed to give any decifion, and the *Caftilians* raifed the fiege and retired into their own country (2). The reader will know what credit is due to thefe relations, when he is told, that their moft authentic fupport are the ballads, fung time out of mind through all the provinces of *Spain* concerning thefe wonderful feats of arms.

(1) *Ferreras Hiftoria de Efpana, p. v. fect. xi. Mayerne, Turquet, Hiftoire generale de Efpagne, liv. viii.*　　(2) *Lucæ Tudenfis Chronicon.*

towards

towards himſelf and his eldeſt ſon *Hiſſem*; which Don *Alphonſo* having promiſed in the moſt ſolemn terms, he diſmiſſed
him with all imaginable marks of eſteem, and under the eſ-
corte of a ſtrong party of horſe, by whom he was ſafely conducted to *Zamora*, where he was received with all poſſible
teſtimonies of affection and duty, as well as with the greateſt
tenderneſs, by the princeſs Donna *Urraca*, to whoſe firmneſs
and fidelity he owed his reſtoration [o].

*Invited in-
to* Caſtile,
*but obliged
to purge
himſelf by
oath of the
murder of
Don* San-
cho.
THE principal nobility of *Leon* and *Galicia* repaired very
chearfully to *Zamora* to congratulate Don *Alphonſo* upon this
happy turn in his affairs, and to aſſure him of their fidelity [p].
The *Caſtilians*, however, were not altogether ſo haſty, but
they acted with as much prudence, and perhaps with more
dignity; for after ſome deliberation they ſent deputies to Don
Alphonſo, to acquaint him that they were willing to acknowlege him for their ſovereign, and were for this reaſon deſirous
of his preſence at *Burgos*; but knowing, as he did, that their
late king fell by the hand of a traytor, they expected he
ſhould purge himſelf by oath of all privity or participation in
that action [q]. Don *Alphonſo* readily accepted the crown on
this condition, and went to *Burgos* as he was deſired; but
when it came to the iſſue, none of the *Caſtilian* nobility had
courage enough to require the king's oath. At length *Rodrigo*, ſurnamed the *Cid*, adminiſtered it, which was certainly
very laudable; but not contented with this, he obliged the
king to repeat it twice more, which he did, but reſented it ſo
much, that Don *Rodrigo* could never after recover his good
graces [r]. This being over, the king took poſſeſſion of the
government, to the great joy and with the general ſatisfaction
of the *Caſtilians*.

Don Alon-
*ſo impri-
ſons Don*
Garcia,
*and de-
prives him
of his do-
minions.*
As ſoon as the news of Don *Sancho's* death, and Don *Alphonſo's* being quietly admitted to the ſucceſſion, reached *Seville*, Don *Garcia* requeſted the *Mooriſh* monarch, with
whom he had taken ſhelter, to permit him to return into his
own dominions, which he did with great readineſs [s]. What
reception he met with from his ſubjects, or how he behaved
towards them, we cannot with any certainty affirm. It is as
little in our power, and therefore as little in our will, to
ſuggeſt, that he meant to give his brother any diſturbance.
Ferreras [t], indeed, ſays it, but without proof; and we muſt
not ſupply facts to ſupport characters. Don *Alonſo*, being
informed of his reſuming the government in *Galicia*, invited

[o] LUCÆ Tudenſis Chron. PELAG. OVETENS liber Chron.
[p] Chron. var. antiq.   [q] RODERIC TOLETAN de reb. Hiſpan,
LUCÆ Tudenſis Chron.   [r] Chron. var. antiq.   [s] RO-
DERIC TOLETAN Hiſt. Arabum.   [t] Hiſtoria de Eſpana,
p. v. ſect. xi.

him

him to a conference; upon which he very readily came to *Leon*, and though at first received with all outward testimonies of kindness, was in a short time arrested by the advice of Donna *Urraca*, and sent prisoner to the castle of *Luna*, where he spent the remainder of his days [u]. It is alleged, that he was of a mutable and yet of a violent temper, which obliged his brother to have recourse to this method of treating him for his own security. We write the history and not the apologies of princes: the reader will judge of this action for himself; but certain it is, that the more antient historians are not so complaisant to the memory of Don *Alphonso* in this particular as the moderns [w]. We pretend not to determine the controversy, but we fairly report the facts. Their king being a prisoner, the *Galicians* readily and perhaps willingly submitted to Don *Alonso*, who thus united once more the dominions of his father, and became master of *Castile*, *Leon*, and *Galicia* [x].

A. D. 1073.

THE divisions among Christian princes were the true source of the papal power, which began now to extend itself in *Spain*. Don *Alphonso* found the *Roman* service introduced in the neighbouring kingdom of *Arragon*, and the emissaries of the pope used all their arts to engage the king's inclination to have it introduced also throughout his dominions. *Gregory* the seventh had succeeded *Alexander* the second; and having received some complaints of the behaviour of his legates in the other principalities of *Spain*, he made choice of cardinal *Hugo*, surnamed the *White*, to repair these mistakes, and sent him with special recommendations to the court of *Leon* [y], and with instructions no doubt to make himself as agreeable there as he possibly could. He proved an active and an able minister, as appeared from his success; for after a short stay he prevailed upon the king to suffer his ambassadors to accompany him to *Rome*, to assure the holy father of his obedience, and to sollicit the establishment of the *Roman* offices in all the churches throughout his territories; and this notwithstanding his predecessor had declared, that there was nothing in the *Gothic* liturgies but what was perfectly agreeable to the orthodox doctrines of the catholic church; so that what the king now asked as a favour to himself and subjects, was in reality a favour only to the *Roman* Pontif; and having thus explained from their own historians [z], and without the least exaggeration, the manner in which this objec-

The pope sends cardinal Hugo in quality of legate into Spain.

[u] Chron var. antiq.   [w] MARIANA, FERRERAS, MAYERNE, TURQUET.   [x] RODERIC TOLETAN de reb. Hispan. lib. vi. LUCÆ Tudensis Chron.   [y] Chron. var. antiq.   [z] MARIANA, FERRERAS, MAYERNE, TURQUET.

tion

tion of this church and state to the see of *Rome* was obtained, we will return to what is more immediately our province.

Don Alon- Don *Alphonso* had once been married without ever seeing his
so espouses wife, and believing that the safety of himself and subjects de-
Donna pended in a great measure upon his leaving posterity, he
Agnes, judged it high time to think of a second marriage; to which
daughter it may be he was instigated also by the legate. The lady
of the duke upon whom he cast his eyes, or rather who was recom-
of Guêne. mended to him, was Donna *Agnes*[a], the daughter of the duke
of *Guêne* and count of *Poitiers*, and their marriage was quickly
A. D. after concluded and celebrated. The rejoicings upon this
1074. occasion were interrupted by the news of a war, in which
Don *Alonso* thought himself obliged to take a part. Ambition
prompted *Mohammed Aben-Habet*, king of *Seville*, who had
already united three *Moorish* principalities, to attempt the
conquest of a fourth, and it was with this view that he af-
sembled the whole forces of his dominions; but as this could
not be done without Don *Alonso*'s knowlege, and as he knew
not where the storm would fall, he likewise assembled an
army; and upon receiving advice that the king of *Seville* had
entered the dominions of the king of *Toledo* on one side, he
without any ceremony entered them on the other[b]. *Ali-
Maymon*, as soon as he had intelligence of Don *Alonso*'s irruption, sent embassadors to put him in mind of the old
friendship that had passed between them. Don *Alonso* smiled
at the gravity of their harangue, and assured them, that it
was no other than the sense of that obligation that brought
him thither, and that *Ali-Maymon* might rest satisfied, that
his own subjects would not serve him more chearfully than
the forces under his command[c]. This made a speedy and
strange alteration. *Ali-Maymon*, who had fortified *Toledo*,
understanding the approach of Don *Alonso* and his intentions,
instead of expecting a siege, marched out and joined him with
all his forces; and, as some authors[d] say, attacked and
routed the king of *Seville* in a general engagement; though
others affirm, upon the junction of the armies, he thought
it expedient to retire into his own territories, and soon after
made a peace with the king of *Toledo* upon equitable conditions; but, however, it is on all hands agreed, that Don
Alonso had the honour of putting an end to this war, and of
expressing, in the most honourable manner, his gratitude and
affection towards his royal protector.

[a] Roderic Toletan de reb. Hispan. lib. vi. Pelag. Ovetens liber Chronic.   [b] Roderic Toletan Hist. Arabum.
[c] Lucæ Tudensis Chron. Pelag. Ovetens liber Chron.
[d] Chron. var. antiq.

WE

WE have more than once observed, that it is dangerous *Amazing* for the princes even in communion with *Rome* to shew any *assurance* extraordinary respect or deference for those who stile them- *in pope* selves the successors of St. *Peter*. We have a most amazing *Gregory* instance of this in the conduct of *Gregory* the seventh, who, VII. *to* having received the ambassadors of Don *Alonso*, king of *claim supe-* *Leon*, *Castile*, and *Galicia*, and the report of his legate car- *riority o-* dinal *Hugo*, who by the way has an extreme bad character in *king of* history, judged it proper to make him a suitable return; *Spain.* which, however, is thought and treated as a very extraordinary one even by the *Spanish* historians[f]. This return was claiming the supreme and absolute dominion of all his kingdoms, and not of his only, but of all the Christian princes in *Spain*; which strange title was suggested to stand upon as strange a foundation, that is, on a commission granted to *Eblon*, count of *Roussi*, to conquer countries in the hands of infidels, which he was to possess and enjoy for his pains, yielding an annual tribute, and acknowleging himself feudatory to the holy see of *Rome*. When or where this great conqueror lived does not at all appear, or what this commission to him had to do with the crowns of *Spain*. *Ferreras*[g] seems to suggest, that the argument drawn from hence was analogical. The count *de Roussi*, in case he conquered lands from the infidels, was to hold them from the see of *Rome*, and to pay an annual tribute: therefore, according to this precedent, all territories conquered from infidels were to be held from the see of *Rome* by an annual tribute. A very wild title this; and from an error in the date of the pope's letter one would be glad, for the credit of these bishops, to suppose it counterfeit; but even in this we shall not find ourselves much relieved: for this pope did not stop at a single letter, to which Don *Alphonso* and the other princes seem to have given no immediate answer, because they knew not well what answer to give, but repeated and insisted upon his demand, at the same time that he enjoined the kings of *Leon* and *Navarre* (for in *Arragon* it was already in use) to lay aside the *Gothic* service, and to receive that of the *Roman* church. This at last obliged Don *Alphonso* to answer plainly, as the other princes likewise did, that they were independent princes, and would own no superior upon earth. As to the other part of the injunction, the king of *Leon* was inclined to grant it, and did as much as he thought convenient to do; but some

[f] MARIANA Historia general de Espana, lib. ix. FERRERAS Historia de Espana, p. v. sect. xi. MAYERNE, TURQUET. [g] Historia de Espana, p. v. sect. xi.

of

of the bishops in his dominions peremptorily refused to quit their antient liturgy; and others, in obedience, or rather in complaisance to the king, introduced the *Roman* service.

Don Alonso *seizes a part of* Navarre, *and the king of* Arragon *the rest.* A. D. 1075.

BUT as much as the pope interfered in this, we find no traces of his interposition in another great affair, where it might have been more reasonably expected. Don *Sancho*, king of *Navarre*, being murdered by one of his brothers, and some others of his family being suspected of conniving at it, his subjects absolutely refused to obey any of his race or line. Upon this the Infant Don *Ramiro*, one of the brothers of the deceased king, called in Don *Alonso*, who possessed himself of *Biscay* and *Rioja*, while most of the nobility declared for Don *Sancho*, king of *Arragon*, who got possession of the rest [1]. Don *Alonso* took the Infant Don *Ramiro*, and the Infantas Donna *Urraca*, *Ximena*, and *Mayao* into his care; but what became of Don *Garcia*, the king's son, unless he died in his infancy, does not appear. If ever the interposition of *Rome* was necessary, it was in such a case as this, to prevent orphans and innocent persons from being injured; but of this we hear nothing. Yet the next year a council [m] was called at *Burgos* to force the *Roman* service upon the people; and upon this occasion, it is said, that the contest between the two offices was put upon the issue of a duel, and that the *Gothic* knight prevailed, and that both the services being thrown into the fire, the old book escaped without hurt; but notwithstanding this the king persuaded the major part of the ecclesiastics to make a canon, enjoining the use of the *Roman* service, which was attended with great murmurings and heart-burnings among the people (G).

THE

[1] RODERIC TOLETAN de reb. Hispan. lib. vi. LUCÆ Tudensis Chronicon.   [m] Cardinalis d'AGUIRRE Conc. Hisp. tom. iii. p. 258.

(G) We shall have occasion in another place to treat of this matter more at large (1), and to discuss the reasons which induced the people of *Navarre* to think themselves under the necessity of laying aside the reigning family, and calling in princes of the collateral line to govern them. At present we will confine ourselves to the matters of fact arising from this revolution. The great acquisition which Don *Alonso* made by these troubles might tempt one to believe, that he had some share in them; but when we consider that all the princes and princesses of the

(1) *In the history of the kingdom of Navarre.*

royal

THE year following came a legate from the pope, who *Pope's le-* found or made a great deal of business at court. The king it *gate di-* seems had a mind to part with his wife; and he had an ec- *vorces the* clesiastical favourite *Robert*, bishop of *Sahagon*, who had *king from* made himself some enemies by reforming that monastery, *one queen,* and who, being addicted to the old service-book, could find *and his* no passage there that would countenance kings parting with *chaplain* their wives when they had a mind to it. The legate was *finds an-* much an abler man; he did the king's business and his own *other.* with great facility; he found out that the queen Donna *Agnes* was some way related to the king's first queen *Agueda*; who, as the reader will remember, he never saw; and upon this pretence of consanguinity he dissolved the marriage. He **A. D.** likewise excommunicated abbot *Robert*, and sent him back **1080.** into *France* from whence he came: in his room came another *French* ecclesiastick, whose name was abbot *Barnard*, who, before the close of the year, negotiated a new marriage for the king with Donna *Constantia*, daughter of *Robert*, the first duke of *Burgundy* [r]. The poor repudiated queen like-

---

[r] RODERIC TOLETAN de reb. Hispan.   LUCÆ Tudensis Chron.

---

royal family of *Navarre* fled to him for shelter, and were the very persons that delivered up the countries they could not keep for themselves to him, in preference to the king of *Arragon*, we see all grounds of suspicion destroyed, and are obliged to own, that he acted with great generosity as well as like an able politician (2). Those of the deceased king of *Navarre's* family, for whom Don *Alonso* made provision, were his brother the Infant Don *Ramiro*, his sisters Donna *Ximena*, Donna *Urraca*, and Donna *Mayoa* (3). *Mariana* will have Don *Ramiro* to be the son of the deceased monarch, in which he is cer-

tainly mistaken; but, however, he is right in supposing that he married the daughter of Don *Rodrigo*, surnamed the *Cid*; Donna *Urraca* married Don *Garcia Ordonnez*, of the royal family of *Leon*, and Donna *Mayoa* the count *Macon* in *France* (4). By the treaty he made with the king of *Arragon* both crowns were great gainers. The noble country of *Biscay* was again annexed to the *Asturias*, and all the territories lying south and west of the river *Ebro* were incorporated into the kingdom of *Old Castile*; and all this without any effusion of blood (5).

---

(2) *Annal. Complut. Chron. Monach.* I. *Joan. Pezn. Roderic Toletan de rebus Hispaniæ.*   (3) *Sandoval, Moret, Ferreras.*   (4) *Roderic Toletan, Ferreras.*   (5) *Mariana Historia general d'Espana, lib. ix. P. Moret Investigationes historicas de las Antiquitades del Reyno de Navarre, lib. v. Mayerne, Turquet Histoire generale d'Espagne.*

wife found afterwards another husband [*] in the life-time of
the king; such was the purity that attended the new discipline, or rather such were the conveniencies that accompanied
the submission to the holy see, and such the arts by which the
pope's legates raised themselves into the favour of princes.

The king-dom and city of To-ledo con-quered, which be-comes the capital of Castile.
   THE good old king of *Toledo*, and *Hissem*, his eldest son,
being dead within little more than the compass of a year,
Hiaya, the younger son of the one, and brother to the other,
was seated on the throne, and proved, as the *Spaniards* [†] say,
a very great tyrant; insomuch that the people of *Toledo* solicited Don *Alphonso* to make himself master of that city and
kingdom; but if we advert to facts, we cannot help perceiving, that the conjuncture was extremely inviting. The
ambitious and all-grasping king of *Seville* had already attacked the unfortunate monarch of *Toledo*; the king of *Arragon* pressed hard upon other *Mohammedan* princes; so that
this unlucky king had not either an ally or a protector, when
Don *Alphonso* made his first irruption into that which is now
called *New Castile*. We have no very perfect account of this
war; but from the memorials still preserved, it is apparent,
that it lasted full four campaigns, during which Don *Alphonso* wasted all the country, and took every place of importance in the neighbourhood of *Toledo*; by which, having
prepared all things for the reduction of the place, he came
the fifth year with a very numerous army; and, having first
blockaded the city till the inhabitants began to be in want, he
at length turned that blockade into a siege. It is allowed,
that *Hiaya* defended himself with great courage and firmness,
and that Don *Alphonso* lost abundance of men before the
place, which induced some of the citizens to represent to
Hiaya, that it was better to capitulate in time than to expose
them to certain death by famine or the sword. That prince
clearly perceived, by the manner in which this advice was
given him, that he had nothing to do but to follow it; for
that otherwise the authors of it were like to treat for themselves. He therefore demanded terms from Don *Alphonso*,
and obtained such as would not have been given, if there
had been any great probability of *Toledo's* being taken by force.
In fine, it was agreed, that the king, and such as would
share his fortunes, should have leave to go where they
pleased; that the inhabitants should enjoy their religion and
laws, and not suffer the smallest injury either in their persons
or properties. The city being surrendered, *Hiaya* retired
with his followers to *Valentia*, where he established the seat
of his government, and passed the remainder of his days in

[*] PELAG OVETENS liber Chron.   [†] Chron. var. antiq.

the

the peaceable possession of a small principality; which seems to render it plain, that he might have reigned as quietly over his hereditary kingdom, if he had been happy in having better neighbours u (H).

THIS

u RODERIC TOLETAN Hist. Arabum.

(H) While Don *Alonso* was employed in the preparations for his great design of conquering *Toledo*, some of the detachments which he had sent to spoil the country advanced towards the frontiers of the territories held by the *Moorish* prince of *Saragossa*; and as he had not the least conception of the king's real intention, he judged his own dominions to be in the utmost danger; and as he had no forces capable of resisting those of the king of *Leon* and *Castile*, he had recourse to a stratagem that succeeded in part, and was very near being attended with all the success that he could expect from it. The stratagem was this: he ordered *Aben-Falax*, one of his principal commanders, to enter into a secret treaty with Don *Alonso*, in which he gave him to understand, that he had received such ill usage from his master as had determined him to quit his service, and at the same time to make himself master of the castle of *Rueda*, near the river *Xalon*, five miles from *Saragossa*, which, as he was apprehensive he could not defend with his own troops, he was willing to give it up to those of the king of *Castile*, provided he would come thither in person to accept of his homage. This was accordingly executed, with so much cunning and address, that Don *Alonso*

readily embraced it, and promised to do all that was expected or desired from him (1). Some, however, of the nobility were not so easily deceived, either because they knew the character of *Aben-Falax*, or had some secret reason for distrusting his insinuations. However that was, they prevailed upon the king not to go in person, but sent a body of troops, who summoned the *Moor* to the performance of his promise (2). *Aben-Falax* trifled for a time, and pretended that he would give up the place to none but the king. However, finding this would not do, he at length proposed to surrender it to such persons of distinction as the king should please to charge with his commission; upon which Don *Alonso*, desirous of having the place which was of great consequence, sent the Infant Don *Ramiro* of *Navarre*, the Infant Don *Sanchez* of *Navarre*, the count *Gonçales de Salvadores*, the count Don *Nunez de Lara*, and some other persons of great rank, with full powers to promise, in his name, what the *Moors* should require; who had no sooner prevailed upon them to enter his fortress than he caused them to be murdered. The king, upon hearing of this infamous act of treachery, came with all his forces, in hopes of reducing it, and of punishing

(1) *Annal. Complut. Annal. Toletan. niæ, lib. vi.*

(2) *Roderic Toletan de rebus Hispa-*

Aben-

Great pains taken by the king to secure and improve that city.

THIS city was furrendered to the Christians on the 25th of *May*, 1085, after it had been in the possession of the infidels three hundred and sevnty-two years [w]. Don *Alphonso*, who knew the importance of it, resolved to make it the capital of his dominions [x], and to people it as soon as possible with Christians, of whom he found many, and some illustrious families that had lived there from the time of the conquest by the *Moors*, and were for that reason, as we have shewn elsewhere, stiled *Mozarabians :* there were likewise abundance of *Jews*; and the number of *Mohammedans* who chose to remain under his protection was very considerable. There remained, however, room for many new inhabitants, and it was not long before they were supplied, the example of the king, and of the nobility attending upon his person, being a kind of irresistible motives. On the other hand, Don *Alphonso* omitted nothing that might render persons of different nations and different faiths easy under his government; and it very quickly appeared that he acted in this as a very wise and prudent prince, capable of foreseeing and providing against dangers that might otherwise have proved fatal to his interests. This shews that there are some natures that are improved by prosperity; and that as we frequently see men's understandings weakened and lost through unexpected success, so in the present case we cannot but discern, that the genius of Don *Alphonso* expanded itself with his fortune, and that no two princes can be produced in this history more different from each other in their characters, than this monarch from himself before his expulsion, and after his restoration. These remarks are so natural, that they may at least be thought excufable.

The Mohammedans are ex-

THE *Mohammedans* were astonished when they saw *Toledo* in the hands of the Christians, and the greatness of their loss was evident from the effects of that impression it made

---

[w] MARIANA Historia general de Espana, lib. ix. FERRERAS Historia de Espana, p. v. sect. xi.   [x] LUCÆ Tudensis Chron. PELAG. OVETENS liber Chronic.

Aben-Falax; but the place was so completely fortified, the garrison so numerous, and the magazines so well supplied, that, after several assaults to little or no purpose, he was obliged to retire, and to furnish the rela- tions of the noble persons that were slain with a sum of money to ransom their bodies, which were interred with great pomp in the monasteries of *Najara* and *Ona* (3).

---

(3) *Chron. Monachi Sancti Joannis, Annal. Toletan. Ferreras Historia de Espana, p. v. sect. xi.*

upon

upon them, since they immediately composed their differences, *ceedingly* and entered into a league against Don *Alphonso* z. The prin- *amazed at* cipal powers at the head of this confederacy were the kings of *the loss of* *Seville* and *Badajoz*, who at the same time sent ambassadors *this fa-* to the princes of their religion in *Africa*, imploring their im- *mous place.* mediate assistance; alleging, that they were now engaged in a religious war, and that Don *Alonso* had nothing less in view than to extirpate all who professed the faith of *Mohammed*. These preparations and intrigues were no secret to the victorious monarch of *Castile* and *Leon*; and that he might not appear wanting in his own defence, he assembled a numerous army in the spring, and at the same appointed a council to be held in his new capital the *Christmas* following, in order to the choice of an archbishop of that metropolitan see, which he had so fortunately restored to the Christians, and which he very justly regarded as the most considerable event of his reign, and it may be as the most glorious.

As soon as the season would permit, he marched with his *Don* Alon- forces into the territories of the king of *Badajoz*, that he *so takes* might convince him of his temerity in putting himself at the *Coria, and* head of a league against so powerful a prince, and with this *loses a bat-* view he ravaged the country of *Estremadura* with fire and *tle against* sword, and at length, meeting no resistance, besieged, and in *the* Moors. a short time made himself master of *Coria* ª. But the two A. D. *Mohammedan* kings, having by this time assembled a nu- 1086. merous army of hardy and well disciplined troops, advanced to give him battle; and accordingly, on the 23d of *October*, the armies met between *Merida* and *Badajoz*, where, after an obstinate and bloody engagement, Don *Alonso* was defeated ᵇ. Some authors say, that he was wounded in the leg, and that, having on his return to *Coria* reprimanded some of the nobility very sharply, they went over to the *Mohammedan*. Whatever truth there may be in these facts, we find the king in the beginning of *November* at *Toledo*, where he held a council, in which Don *Bernard*, abbot of *Sahagon*, was elected archbishop of *Toledo*, and the nobility gave the king their advice as to the most effectual means of raising a new army, numerous enough to repair the loss he had lately sustained, and prevent the infidels from acting, as it was evident they would otherwise do, offensively, as soon as the season would permit; and on this head gave him the strongest assurances of their fidelity and assistance.

ª RODERIC TOLETAN Hist. Arabum.　　ᵇ RODERIC TO-
LETAN de reb. Hispan. lib. vi, PELAG. OVETENS liber Chronic.
ᵇ RODERIC TOLETAN Hist. Arabum.

Count Raymond of Burgundy and Don Henry de Beſançon come into Spain.

THE king, though he relied much on theſe aſſurances, and not a little on the high rate at which the *Moors* had bought their late victory, yet he was reſolved not to truſt entirely to the ſtrength of his own dominions, extenſive as they were. On this account he wrote to *Philip* the firſt, king of *France*, deſiring his aſſiſtance, and to the great lords of his kingdom, amongſt whom count *Raymond* of *Burgundy* and count *Beſançon* went in perſon, at the head of a conſiderable body of troops, to the relief of the Chriſtians in *Spain* againſt the infidelᵉ. But before their arrival the war was at an end ; for Don *Alphonſo* having drawn together the whole force of his dominions, and marching towards his frontiers that the infidels might ſee that he meant not to decline another action, the two *Mooriſh* princes, apprehenſive of being overwhelmed by the foreign troops that they knew were raiſing, in order to paſs the *Pyrenees*, entered into a negotiation ; in which, as they were very ſincere, and as Don *Alonſo* found peace at that juncture very convenient to him, it was not long before terms were ſettled to their mutual ſatisfactionᶠ. Yet whether theſe *Mooriſh* princes became his vaſſals, and agreed to pay him an annual tribute, as ſome hiſtorians ᵍ ſay they did, is more than we can find ſufficient authority to aſſert, and think it a point of too great conſequence to be determined by bare conjecture.

The cathedral of Toledo taken from the Moors by the queen and the archbiſhop.

ACCORDING to the capitulation of *Toledo*, the cathedral, which the *Mohammedans* had converted into a moſque, was to remain in their hands, with which the king punctually complied. But the new metropolitan Don *Bernard* looked upon this a reproach to chriſtianity, and by his vehement declamations perſuaded the queen to be of the ſame opinion ; in conſequence of which, while the king was in the field, they diſpoſſeſſed the *Moors* by force of that noble ſtructure, reſtored it to its former condition, conſecrated and celebrated divine ſervice thereinʰ, not without great danger of raiſing an inſurrection. The *Moors*, however, reflected very prudently, that as this was done in the king's abſence, and without his knowlege, they ought, in juſtice to themſelves and him, to try firſt what might be done in the way of expoſtulation. They accordingly ſent deputies to meet Don *Alphonſo*, and to inform him of what had happened. The king, upon hearing of this flagrant breach of faith, which was at the ſame time the higheſt inſult upon his authority, though he was naturally of a calm and moderate diſpoſition,

---

ᶠ RODERIC TOLETAN Hiſt. Arabum.   ᵍ Chron. var. antiq.   ʰ RODERIC TOLETAN de reb. Hiſpan. lib. vi. LUCÆ Tudenſis Chronicon.

fell

fell into fuch a tranfport of rage againft the queen and the
archbifhop, as terrified the *Moorifh* deputies to fuch a degree,
that they left his camp, returned to *Toledo*, and made fuch a
report to their brethren as induced them to go in a body out
of the city to meet the king, and to befeech him to pardon
the authors of this injuftice, offering at the fame time to depart from their pretenfions to the cathedral, rather than become the inftruments of confufion in a ftate where they were
willing to live peaceably, and to enjoy the benefit of his royal
protection [i]. A very fingular inftance of prudence and felf-
denial, and which ought certainly to give us a very high opinion of their morals and good fenfe. The pacification thus
made, the king entered the city in triumph, with the univerfal
acclamations of all his fubjects; and on the 25th of *October*
following the cathedral was folemnly confecrated by the
archbifhop Don *Bernard*, in the prefence of the king and
queen, and with all the pomp and ceremony poffible [k].

As every thing was now quiet, Don *Alonfo* refolved to
take this opportunity of fortifying his dominions effectually,
by repairing the many cities that were deftroyed in the courfe
of the war, and to repeople them with Chriftians [l]. He
began with thofe of *Segovia*, *Avila*, and *Salamanca*, and committed the care of their reftitution to count *Raymond*, who,
in all probability, fettled a great part of his own people in
them [m]. The king likewife determined to repair all the great
towns between the river *Duero* and the mountains that feparate the two *Caftiles*; and by encouraging people to come and
fettle in them, he hoped to put the new kingdom he had
conquered into fuch a condition as, in cafe of frefh troubles,
it might be able to furnifh a ftrength fufficient to defend itfelf. In this likewife he was fo well feconded by count *Raymond*, that the feveral great towns of *Medina del Campo*, *Ara-
velo*, *Olmedo*, *Coca*, *Ifcar*, *Cuellar*, *Sepulveda*, and *Ofma*, were
reftored, and filled with Chriftian inhabitants in the fpace of
a few years [n]. In return for thefe and other eminent fervices,
as well as to attach him to the like for the future, the king
beftowed upon Don *Raymond* his only daughter Donna *Urraca*, whom he had by the reigning queen [o]. About this

A. D.
1087.

*Don Gar-
cia, the de-
pofed king
of Galicia,
dies in pri-
fon.*

[i] RODERIC TOLET. Hift. Arabum. PELAG. OVETENS liber
Chronic. [k] LUCÆ Tudenfis Chronicon. RODERIC SANTII
Hift. Hifpan. p. iii. [l] PELAG. OVETENS liber Chronicon,
LUCÆ Tudenfis Chronicon. [m] Chron. var. antiq. [n] RO-
DERIC TOLETAN de reb. Hifpan. lib. vi. LUCÆ Tudenfis Chron.
[o] RODERIC SANTII Hift. Hifpan. p. iii. ALPHONSI a Carthâ-
gena reg. Hifp. ANACEPHALÆOSIS FRANCISCI TARAPHÆ de
reg. Hifpaniæ.

A. D.
1090.
time, and chiefly through the mixture of foreigners that resorted into *Spain*, they quitted the old *Gothic* characters of
writing, and began to make use of those that were common
in other parts of *Europe* through all this monarch's dominions [q]. Don *Garcia*, king of *Galicia*, after having worn
out many years in captivity died in the castle of *Luna*, on the
22d of *May*, *Anno Domini* 1091; some say of disease; but
Mariana [r] asserts, of despair, and that he opened his veins
with his own hands. His corpse was transported to *Leon*,
and interred with those of his ancestors in the church of St.
Isidore; the king and queen, together with the Infantas Donna
Urraca and Donna *Elvira*, and most of the great lords and
bishops assisting thereat; and which is more remarkable, the
irons he had worn in prison were interred with him, according to his own directions [s]. The next year Donna *Constantia*, wife to Don *Alonso*, died, and he soon after married
Donna *Bertha*, the sister of his son-in-law Don *Raymond*, in
hopes of male issue; nor does it appear that consanguinity in
this case troubled the conscience of the king, or gave any
offence to *Rome*, though Don *Raymond*, and consequently his
sister, was nearly allied to the deceased queen [t].

Don Alon-
*so extends
his domi-
nions on the
side of* Por-
tugal *at
the expence
of the
Moors.*
THE interior of his dominions being in perfect order, Don
Alonso held it expedient to renew his excursions on the infidels; for he was sensible, that if his troops remained long
inactive they might degenerate in point of discipline, or become seditious and turbulent. To prevent this, he made an
irruption into the countries, since stiled *Portugal*, with a resolution not only to harrass and plunder it, as himself and his
predecessors had often done, but to make an absolute conquest
of it; very justly conceiving, that whatever he took from the
Moors was doubly beneficial to the Christians, as at the same
time that it weakened one interest, it added to the strength of

A. D.
1093.
another: his army took the field early in the spring, and began
their operations with the siege of *Coimbra*, which being
speedily reduced, he proceeded to *Santaren*, which having
subdued, he marched next to besiege *Lisbon*, and afterwards
took *Sintria* by capitulation on the ninth of *May* [u]. At this
very time he was also engaged in a war against Don *Sancho*,
king of *Arragon*, as an auxiliary to the *Moors*. The case was
this: the king of *Huesca* had become his tributary, and insisted upon his protection, in case he was attacked by the king

[q] Chron. var. antiq.   [r] Historia general de Espana,
lib. ix.   [s] Roderic Toletan de reb. Hispan. Lucæ Tudensis Chronicon. Pelag. Ovetens liber Chronic: [t] Chron.
var. antiq.   [u] Pelag. Ovetens liber Chronic. Roderic
Tolet. Hist. Arabum.

of *Arragon*, who was raising, as he apprehended, an army for that purpose; and it was the dread of that army that hindered Don *Alonso* from meeting with any resistance in his conquests. The next year this war broke out, and most of the *Moorish* princes entered into a league for the support of the king of *Huesca*, whose capital was quickly besieged. To this confederate army Don *Alonso* joined a body of auxiliaries, under the command of Don *Garcia*, count of *Najara*; but Don *Sancho*, king of *Navarre*, being wounded at this siege, and dying [x] soon after, suspended the operations of that war for the present.

A. D. 1094.

In the succeeding year died Donna *Bertha*, and Don *Alphonso* gave his natural daughter Donna *Theresa*, whom he had by Donna *Ximena Nugnez*, to *Henry Besançon*, who had accompanied his son-in-law Don *Raymond* into *Spain*; and, as an establishment for his daughter, bestowed upon him all that he conquered in *Portugal*, with the title of count, to be enjoyed by him after his decease, with a reservation only of homage to his successors, as the *Spaniards* say; but, as the *Portuguese* writers affirm, without any such reservation at all. The next year the war broke out again between Don *Pedro*, the son of Don *Sancho*, king of *Arragon*, and the infidels, which called Don *Alonso*'s troops into the field as auxiliaries of his vassal, the king of *Huesca*; but Don *Pedro*, tho' his army was inferior in number to the confederates, gave them battle notwithstanding, on the 18th of *November*, in the plain of *Alcoraz*, and, after a sharp and long engagement, totally defeated them, with vast loss on the side of the *Moors*; and as to Don *Garcia*, and the troops under his command, they were made prisoners [y]. By this glorious success the conquest of *Huesca* was secured, and an end put to that *Moorish* principality.

His forces, in quality of auxiliaries, made prisoners before Huesca.

A. D. 1096.

Don *Alonso*, either desirous of male issue, or weary of being longer a widower, and having heard wonders of *Zaide*, the daughter of *Mohammed Aben-Habet*, king of *Seville*, esteemed the most beautiful and accomplished princess of that age, he resolved to espouse her, in case she would change her religion. The proposition was very agreeable to her father, and the princess making no difficulty as to the condition, the marriage was quickly concluded and celebrated [z]; by which Don *Alphonso* acquired several places that were very convenient; and, on the other hand, restored, as a mark of his

Marries the daughter of the king of Seville, and enters into an alliance with him.

---

[x] Lucæ Tudensis Chron. Pelag. Ovetens liber Chronicon. [y] Roderic Toletan Hist. Arabum. Lucæ Tudensis Chronicon. [z] Roderic Toletan de reb. Hispan. lib. vi. Pelag. Ovetens liber Chronicon. Roderic Santii Hist. Hispan. p. iii.

friend-

friendſhip, *Sanctaren, Cintria,* and *Liſbon,* to the king of *Seville* ; who, upon the whole, was no gainer by this marriage. Some writers ſpeak of *Zaide* as the concubine only of Don *Alphonſo,* and a contemporary writer ſpeaks of her in this light ; but as he afterwards retracts this opinion, and acknowleges her for the lawful wife of Don *Alphonſo,* there ſeems to be no reaſon to queſtion this fact. It was in conſequence of this alliance that, by the perſuaſion of his father-in-law, Don *Alphonſo* entered into a negotiation with *Joſeph,* king of the weſt part of *Afric,* that is, of the kingdoms now known by the name of *Fez* and *Morocco.* The deſign of this negotiation was a very ſtrange one. The kings of *Leon* and *Seville* meditated the deſtruction of all the *Moorish* principalities in *Spain,* in order to divide their territories between them; and to effect this they demanded theſe auxiliaries upon certain conditions from this *African* monarch, who entered very readily into the treaty, and promiſed to furniſh troops for the deſtruction of his brethren with all the readineſs that the confederates could wiſh [b].

Joſeph, *king of* Fez, Tremecen, *and* Morocco, *conquers* Seville.

BUT king *Joſeph* had very different deſigns in his head. He aſſembled a very numerous army and a large fleet for their embarkation, and landed them without any difficulty or oppoſition at *Malaga.* There he received embaſſadors from the little *Moorish* princes, who were to be the victims of this alliance, who repreſented to him, that *Mohammed Aben-Habet* was a Chriſtian in his heart, and intended nothing leſs than the total deſtruction of the *Moors* and the *Mohammedan* religion in *Spain,* which in all probability he would accompliſh, unleſs, accepting of their aſſiſtance, the king would deprive him, as he deſerved, of his dominions, and condeſcend to become the protector of the faithful in *Spain* [c]. This was in a great meaſure what king *Joſeph* deſigned. He accepted their offer without the leaſt heſitation; and, marching directly to *Seville,* became maſter of the place and of the perſon of king *Mohammed* without difficulty or diſpute [d]. Having thus acquired a great kingdom, he began to look about him, and to conſider of the proper means of executing his own project in its full extent; and this it was that led him to affect a kind of neutrality towards Don *Alonſo,* and to carry on

A. D. 1097.

the war againſt his own nation till he had reduced *Granada, Almeria,* and *Murcia,* and had forced ſome other leſſer lords to acknowlege him for their ſovereign ; and, in the end, made

[b] Chron. var. antiq. [c] RODERIC TOLETAN Hiſt. Arabum. PELAG. OVETENS liber Chronic. LUCÆ Tudenſis Chronicon. [d] RODERIC TOLETAN de reb. Hiſpan. lib. vi. RODERIC TOLETAN Hiſt. Arabum,

himſelf

himself master of the best part of the rich country of *Anda-*
lusia with little or no resistance [e].

IT is necessary to say something here of the origin of this new
people with respect to *Spain*, whom the historians of that
country call *Almovarides* [f]. They were part of an *Arab* tribe
that entered that district of *Afric*, which they now possessed,
near half a century before, that they might live more at their
ease and in a state of retirement, as pretending to follow the
dictates of their *Khoran* more closely than others of their sect,
from whence they took the name of *Morabites*; from which,
as we observed, the *Spaniards* borrowed their appellation of
Almovarides. The first prince or chief of this nation was *Abu-*
beker-ben-Omar, who, in *Spanish* authors, is commonly called
Abu-Texifien [g]; and to him this *Joseph* had succeeded, under
whose administration their affairs had prospered exceedingly.
Whatever, therefore, he might pretend upon his first invitation, his real project was to make himself master of as much
of *Spain* as possible, both at the expence of *Christians* and
Moors; and the reason that he first fell upon the latter was,
that his power might acquire a suitable augmentation before
he run the hazard of contending with Don *Alonso*, whose reputation was very great, and of whose power all the *Moorish*
princes were very apprehensive. But the king of *Leon* and
Castile penetrating his design, sent an army, commanded by
Don *Rodrigo* and Don *Garcia de Cabra*, to insult *Seville*;
while *Joseph* was with his troops in the kingdom of *Murcia*.
He marched, however, to intercept this body of forces, and
obliged them to fight in the neighbourhood of *Rueda*, in *La*
Mancha; where, after a brisk engagement, the *Christian*
army, through the bad behaviour of Don *Garcia Ordonnez*,
was defeated, and a great number slain, and a still greater
number made prisoners [h]; which threw all the country adjacent into consternation.

THE *African* monarch would, in all probability, have entertained a much higher notion of his victory, if Don *Gar-*
cias Ordonnez, and some of his adherents who went over to
him, had not given him such intelligence as left him no room
to doubt, that this would prove a matter of very little consequence with regard to the fate of the war, since Don *Alonso*
would soon be at the head of another army, and, by com-

*A short ac-
count of the
Almova-
rides, who,
under this
monarch,
invaded
Spain.*

A. D.
1097.

*Don Alon-
so ad-
vances to-
wards Se-
ville, and
offers the
Moham-*

e Chron. var. antiq.   f MARIANA Historia general de
Espana, lib. ix. FERRERAS Historia de Espana, p. v. sect. xi.
MAYERNE, TURQUET Histoire general d'Espagne, liv. viii.
g RODERIC TOLETAN de reb. Hispan. lib. vi. LUCÆ Tudensis
Chronicon. FERRERAS Hist. de Espana, p. v. sect. xi.   h Ro-
DERIC TOLETAN Hist. Arabum. PELAG. OVETENS liber Chronic.

medans
battle.
A. D.
1098.

manding in perſon, prevent ſuch accidents [1] as that to which he owed his victory. The truth of this information quickly appeared; for Don *Alonſo* was indefatigable in raiſing forces through all his dominions, and defiling them as faſt as poſſible to the frontiers of *New Caſtile*; and, as ſoon as the ſeaſon would permit, he took the field, and marched directly towards *Seville*, though he was informed, that his antagoniſt was at the head of a more numerous army. *Joſeph*, however, taking the advice of Don *Garcia*, acted wholly on the defenſive. He ſaw clearly, that if he loſt the battle, it could never be repaired; and that, as things ſtood, he had not a force ſufficient to deal with the king of *Caſtile* and *Leon*, and at the ſame time keep the *Spaniſh Moors* in awe; for this reaſon he took a reſolution of returning to *Africa*, and ſending over a freſh army, which he accordingly executed; while Don *Alonſo*, finding it impoſſible to force the enemy to a battle, after he had ravaged the country about *Seville*, and inriched his army with booty and ſlaves, returned into his own dominions [k], much leſs ſatisfied with the ſucceſs of his expedition than thoſe who attended him, as he had received certain information, that *Joſeph* had in a manner extirpated Chriſtianity in *Andaluzia*, by tranſporting into *Africa* ſuch of the *Mozarabians* as had not an opportunity of making their eſcape [l]. An act of policy, or rather of violence, which proved afterwards a fatal precedent for the *Moors*, as will be ſeen in the courſe of this hiſtory.

King Jo-
ſeph finds
it expe-
dient to re-
turn to
Morocco.

THE orders and perſuaſions of the *African* monarch were ſo chearfully obeyed, and had ſo great an influence over his ſubjects, that, before the cloſe of the year, he ſent over incredible reinforcements to *Spain*, with orders to *Almohait Hiaya*, his lieutenant-general, to puſh the war with vigour, and to make all the uſe poſſible of his ſuperiority. He executed theſe orders with great punctuality, and took the field early with ſo great an army, that Don *Alonſo* was forced in his turn to retire into his hereditary dominions, and to ſummon all his nobility to join him under the higheſt penalties; yet, before this could be done, the *Mooriſh* general had actually inveſted *Toledo*, which ſiege he carried on with the utmoſt vigour, and even made ſeveral aſſaults, in which he was not only repulſed, but ſuffered great loſs [m]. On the approach therefore of Don *Alonſo*, at the head of all his

[1] Chron. var. antiq. [k] PELAG. OVETENS, lib. Chron. LUCÆ Tudenſis Chron. RODERIC TOLETAN, de reb. Hiſpan. l. vi. [l] RODERIC TOLETAN, Hiſt. Arabum. PELAG. OVET. lib. Chron. [m] LUCÆ Tudenſis Chron. RODERIC TOLETAN Hiſt. Arabum. PELAG. OVET. lib. Chron.

forces,

forces, he found himself in no condition to venture a battle, and therefore retired in his turn, and contented himself with taking a place on the frontiers, that he might have a passage open to renew his excursions whenever a favourable opportunity should offer [n]. About this time died the Infanta Donna *Elvira*, the king's sister; and this year was also fatal to that famous hero Don *Rodrigo*, surnamed the *Cid*; who with his own troops, and some assistance from Don *Alonso*, had taken *Valentia* from the infidels, and had gallantly maintained his conquest against several vigorous efforts that had been made to recover it [o], though far inferior in strength to the assailants (I).

A. D. 1099.

IN

[n] RODERIC TOLETAN de reb. Hispan. RODERIC TOLETAN Hist. Arabum. LUCÆ Tudensis Chron.   [o] PELAG. OVET. lib. Chron. RODERIC TOLETAN Hist. Arabum. LUCÆ Tudensis Chronicon.

(I) In the compass of this note we intend a succinct account of that celebrated hero in *Spanish* histories, as well as romance, Don *Rodrigo Diaz de Bivar*, surnamed the *Cid*, which in *Arabic* signifies lord (1). He was undoubtedly a person of very high quality in *Old Castile*; but we dare not pretend to give his genealogy, or even to warrant that found in *Mariana* and other historians (2): what we aim at is to represent fairly those great actions of his life which have been the objects of authentic history; and as for that fabulous legend of incredible, and even impossible adventures, which have obscured, and consequently diminished, his true fame, which they were intended to illustrate, we leave them to be found in a multitude of histories; and we are sorry that we cannot refer to the *Latin* life of this celebrated person, composed in the reign of the emperor *Charles* the fifth by *Ramiro Nugnez de Guzman*, and by him dedicated to the prince Don *Philip*, afterwards *Philip* the second, which has not, however, been published. The first time we find the *Cid* mentioned in the more antient authors (3), is in the year 1063, when he assisted the prince Don *Sancho*, who marched with a body of auxiliaries to the assistance of a *Moorish* prince, when he had a large share in the battle of *Grao*, where Don *Ramiro*, the first king of *Arragon*, was defeated and slain. In 1068 and 1070, he commanded under Don *Sancho*, king of *Castile*, against his brother Don *Alonso*, as is very certain; but that he attended that monarch into *Galicia*, rescued him when taken in battle, and afterwards brought Don *Garcia* prisoner, though related by some modern historians, is not so well established as to deserve intire cre-

(1) *Ferreras Historia de Espana, p. v. sect. 11.*   (2) *Historia general de Espana, lib. ix.*   (3) *Chron. war. antiq.*

dit.

The city of   IN the first year of the twelfth century deceased Donna
Valentia *Urraca,* who, as well as her sister the Infanta Donna *El-
gloriously*   *vira,*

dit. In 1072 he commanded, under his master Don *Sancho,* at the siege of *Zamora,* retired from thence in good order with the *Castilian* forces, carrying with him the royal corpse, which he caused to be interred in the monastery of *Ona.* We have remarked in the text, that he alone, of all the *Castilian* nobility, was so hardy as to administer the oath of exculpation to Don *Alonso* at *Burgos,* and, by the manner in which he did it, incurred his displeasure. Two years after, perceiving that the king's resentment continued, he resolved to retire out of his dominions, notwithstanding he had married a little before Donna *Ximena Diaz,* daughter to Don *Diego Alvarez de las Asturias;* and accordingly, followed by all his friends and dependants, and by many of his relations, he went into *Arragon;* where, after ravaging and plundering the country adjacent, he at length made himself master of the castle of *Alcocer,* situated at a very small distance from *Cala-tagud.* Thither resorted to him a multitude of malecontents from *Castile* and *Leon,* which enabled him to continue his inroads upon the *Moors* with great success. As he extended his conquest gradually, he penetrated at length into the district of *Teruel,* or, as some write it, *Teruel,* twenty-seven leagues south of *Saragossa,* where he fixed his residence in a strong

fortress, called to this day *Pena de el Cid,* that is, the rock of the *Cid* (4). It may not be amiss to observe, that there is not in all *Spain,* perhaps hardly in *Europe,* a more pleasant country than this, where the air is so pure, and withal so soft, that there is a kind of eternal spring; every little copse being enamelled with odoriferous flowers, that blow, flourish, and decay, in all the months of the year. It was during his residence here, that he had intelligence of the execrable murder of the unfortunate *Hiaya,* formerly king of *Toledo,* and then lord of *Valentia,* traiterously slain by *Aben Japhet,* who usurped his little principality. Upon this the *Cid* sent to the king, Don *Alonso,* to put him in mind of the obligations he was under to revenge that poor prince's death, and to desire, that he would send him a small detachment of troops, with which, joined to his own, he would try his fortune before *Valentia.* The king applauded his design, granted him all and even more than he asked; and the *Cid,* in 1094, after a long siege, took the city, and defended it against the whole force of the *Moors,* who attempted to recover it. There he continued the remaining part of his life; and there, full of years and of glory, he died in 1099 (5), leaving his widow Donna *Ximena* in possession of *Valentia,*

(4) *Lucæ Tudensis Chronicon. Roderic. Toletan de reb. Hispania, lib. vii.*
(5) *Mariana Historia general de Espana, lib. ix. Ferreras Historia de Espana, p. v. sect. 11. Mayerne, Turquet, Histoire general d'Espagne, lib. viii.*

which

vira, preferved her virginity during her whole life, and was *defended* buried with great magnificence in the church of St. *Ifidore* [P]. *againft the* The city of *Jerufalem* being at this time taken from the in- Moors *by* fidels by the forces of the Chriftian princes, under the com- Ximena, mand of *Godfrey* of *Bouillon*, feveral *Spanifh* noblemen pro- *widow to* ceeded to *Rome*, with an intention of joining the fuccours *the* Cid. that were about to pafs into the holy land; but Pope *Pafchal* the fecond very prudently interpofed, and advifed them to return home and deliver their own country from the infidels firft.   The *Moors*, as foon as they had intelligence of the death of the *Cid*, made very little doubt of their recovering *Valentia*; and therefore bent all their forces that way.   Don *Alonfo* oppofed to them a very numerous army, under the command of his fon-in-law the count Don *Henry*; who, endeavouring to ftop their paffage, gave them battle at *Malagon*, where, however, he met with a fignal defeat [q]; notwithftanding which Donna *Ximena*, the widow of the *Cid*, affifted by Don *Alvaro Fanez* the governor, defended the place with fuch fpirit and obftinacy, that after lying before it a long time, and fuffering great lofs, the infidels were at laft obliged to retire.   This was a very feafonable check, and prevented the *Moors* from harraffing *New Caftile*, which gave Don *Alonfo* time to regulate his domeftic affairs, and to put the city of *Toledo* into a ftate of defence, by repairing the walls from the church of St. *Stephen* to the river [r].

THE very next year the *Moors*, with a great army, ap- *Several* peared again before *Valentia*, which was preferved by the *alterations* fuccours fent by Don *Alonfo* over the mountains with very *by deaths,* great difficulty, and with fuch expence, as determined him *births, and* *marriages,*

[P] RODERIC SANTII Hift. Hifpan. p. iii. ALPHONSI a Carth. reg. Hifp. ANACEPHALÆOSIS, RODERIC TOLETAN de reb. Hifpan. lib. vi.   [q] RODERIC TOLET. Hift. Arabum. PELAG. OVET. liber Chronic. LUCÆ Tudenfis Chron.   [r] Chron. var. antiq.

which fhe alfo defended with more than mafculine bravery, till, in obedience to the king's orders, for reafons that are mentioned in the text, fhe thought fit to abandon it.   As to his wars with the kings of *Arragon*, and the counts of *Barcelona*, they appear to be but fabulous; and the fame thing may

be faid of many of his expeditions againft the *Moors*, at leaft as they are commonly reprefented; and as to the marriage of his daughters with the counts of *Carrion*, they have been already, by the judicious pen of *Sandoval*, fhewn (6) in their proper light, that is, of foolifh and inconfiftent falfhoods.

(6) *Hift. reyes de Caftilla y Leon.*

to quit that place; which, lying at so great a distance from the rest of his dominions, he believed would fall, sooner or later, into the hands of the infidels, with all the Christians who were in it, and who, at his command, withdrew [t]. Soon after this Don *Alonso* lost his fifth wife Donna *Isabella*, who was buried in the church of St. *Isidore* with great solemnity, leaving behind her a son, Don *Sancho*, who was considered as the heir apparent of all his father's extensive dominions [u] (K). But, notwithstanding he had now an heir male, the king resolved to marry again; and *Bernard*, archbishop of *Toledo*, whom he had sent to the Pope, negotiated a match with the princess *Beatrix*, of the house of *Este* [x]; very little to the satisfaction of the Infanta *Urraca*, and her

1105. husband Don *Raymond*. Soon after this he had the mis-

[t] Lucæ Tudensis Chronicon. Roderig Toletan, Hist. Arabum. Pelag. Ovet. liber Chronic. [u] Roderic Tolet. de reb. Hispan. lib. vi. Pelag. Ovet. liber Chronicon. Lucæ Tudensis Chronicon.

(K) We have already acquainted the reader, that this *Moorish* princess, to facilitate her marriage with Don *Alonso*, at the time of her baptism, took the name of *Maria Izabella*, or *Elizabeth*, for they are the same name; and yet a strange mistake happened very early in relation to this princess, occasioned by some obscurity in the inscription to her memory; whence Don *Pelayo*, bishop of *Oviedo*, has made her both the king's queen and concubine. His queen, by the title of *Izabella*, daughter to *Lewis* king of *France*, and his concubine, by the *Moorish* name of *Zaide* (1). *Mariana* corrects half this mistake, since he acknowleges her to have been the lawful wife of Don *Alonso*, but still this *Izabella* of *France* runs in his head also (2). Another inquisitive

and judicious writer (3) seems to have untied this knot effectually, for he has produced the inscription, which has given rise to this dispute; and which, notwithstanding, is as decisive as one could wish, and being very concise, we will transcribe it: *Hic R. Regina* Elizabeth, *uxor Regis* Alfonsi, *filia* Benavit *Regis* Siviliæ, *quæ prius* Zaïda *fuit vocata*; that is, Here reposes queen *Elizabeth*, wife of king *Alphonso*, daughter to *Benavet*, king of *Seville*, who was formerly called *Zaide*. The old writers many of them (4) bestow upon her two daughters by the king, which, however, she had not; but, as his family is very clearly represented to the view of the reader in the text, it would be needless and impertinent to repeat any thing upon that subject here.

(1) *Pelag. Ovet. Chron.*   (2) *Historia general de España, lib. x.*
(3) *P. Moret investigationes historicas de las antiquitades del reyno de Navarra. lib. iii.*   (4) *Chron. var. antiq.*

fortune

fortune to lofe a great battle againft the *Moors*, in which, however, he did not command in perfon; but notwith-ftanding it is acknowleged, that great numbers were flain, and many taken prifoners, yet by his prudence he had foon fo formidable an army on foot, that the *Moors* were not able to draw any great advantage from their victory [x]. The royal family was increafed on the firft of *March* 1106, by the birth of the infant Don *Alonfo*, fon to Don *Raymond* count of *Galicia*, by the infanta Donna *Urraca*, who was baptized in the apoftolic church of St. *James* at *Compoftella*; with re-fpect to the birth of which prince, the annals of thofe times unanimoufly report, that a new and bright ftar was obferved for thirty days together, before that in which he was brought into the world [y]; which in thofe days was regarded as a very favourable prefage, and will be defervedly exploded in thefe; fince, fuppofing the fact to be true, it could have no more relation to *Spain* than to any other country where that ftar was vifible.

JOSEPH, king of the *Almovarides*, thought it now high time to return into *Spain*, having fully atchieved all that he propofed in *Africa*, bringing over with him on board a nu-merous fleet, a much more powerful army of *Mohammedans* and *Moors* than had hitherto ever landed in that kingdom [z]. As foon as he had incorporated them with thofe which he had already on foot in that country, he judged his power fufficient to undertake at once the conqueft of the dominions of the king of *Caftile* and *Leon*, with which view he af-fembled two great armies, and all the remaining princes of the *Moors*, to which he deftined a third [a]. Don *Alonfo* was not a little alarmed at the news of thefe preparations; and, being too old to command an army in perfon, he fent for Don *Raymond*, his fon-in-law, out of *Galicia*, who fell ill of a fever in his journey, and died upon the road; but the good old king had the fatisfaction of vifiting, and affording him all the confolation in his power in his laft moments [b]. He then made a progrefs through the kingdoms of *Leon* and *Caftile*, in order to quicken the nobility in marching with

Invafion of the Al-movarides and the fatal bat-tle of Uclea.

---

[x] RODERIC TOLETAN. Hiftor. Arabum. LUCÆ Tudenfis Chro-nicon. RODERIC TOLETAN de reb. Hifpan. lib. vi. - [y] Chron. var. antiq. [z] PELAG. OVET. lib. Chron. LUCÆ Tudenfis Chronicon. RODERIC TOLETAN Hift. Arabum. [a] RODERIC TOLETAN de reb. Hifpan. lib. vi. RODERIC TOLETAN Hift. Arabum. LUCÆ Tudenfis Chronicon. [b] RODERIC SANTII Hift. Hifpan. p. iii. ALPHONSI a Carthagena reg. Hifp. ANA-CEPHALÆOSIS, PELAG. OVET. lib. Chron. LUCÆ Tudenfis Chronicon. RODERIC TOLETAN Hift. Arabum.

their vassals to form an army in the neighbourhood of *Toledo*, towards which city he foresaw the enemy would not fail to advance as soon as the season would permit. He was not mistaken in his conjecture; for king *Joseph*, having united his troops on the frontiers, bent his route directly towards the capital [c]. Don *Alonso*, in hopes that it would give fresh courage to his army, which was composed of almost all the force of his dominions, sent the infant Don *Sancho*, though a child but of eleven years old at most, with his governor Don *Garcia de Cabra*; but who had the chief command does not appear [d]. On the arrival of the infant the Christians advanced to *Ucles*, where they met the infidels ranged in order of battle; the dispute was very obstinate, and they fought on both sides with the utmost intrepidity, till at length the *Mohammedans* pierced into the center of the Christians, and surrounded that body of troops where the young infant was, whose horse being killed he stood on foot, and his governor Don *Garcia* covered him with his buckler, fighting with incredible bravery, though he was far advanced in years, till at length he fell, and bore down his pupil with him; when the *Moors* massacred all that body of troops; and the army being intitely broken, gained a complete victory, no less than seven counts dying in the field [e], This fatal battle was fought on the 29th of *May* 1108, and was the most heavy reverse of fortune the Christians had sustained since the loss of the city of *Leon*; but, however, the *Moors* bought this victory so dearly, that they were in no condition to reap any immediate advantage from it [f]. The infanta Donna *Urraca*, with the assistance of the bishop of *Compostella*, having assembled all the forces in *Galicia*, advanced immediately into *New Castile*, received the scattered remains of the defeated army, and marched with so good a countenance towards the *Moors*, that they did not judge it convenient to venture another battle, but contented themselves with the reputation they had acquired, and retreated into their own dominions. The Christians took this opportunity of putting a strong garrison into *Toledo*, while the old king brought out of

[c] RODERIC TOLET. de reb. Hispan. LUCÆ Tudensis Chron. RODERIC TOLETAN Hist. Arabum. [d] PELAG. OVETENS liber Chronic. RODERIC TOLETAN Hist. Arabum. LUCÆ Tudensis Chronicon. [e] Chron. var. antiq. [f] MARIANA, Historia general de Espana, lib. ix. FERRERAS Historia de Espana, p. v. sect. xi. MAYERNE, TURQUET, Histoire general d'Espagne, liv. viii.

Castile a fresh body of troops, which enabled him to cover that city with a good army in the field [g] (L).

THE king Don *Alphonso* was, as we may well suppose, extremely mortified to find himself in this sad situation in his declining years, and when his bodily infirmities, as well as his great age, disabled him from doing what his prudence dictated in favour of his subjects. He did not, however, omit

The death of Don Alonso VI. the greatest Christian monarch in Spain.

[g] PELAG. OVETENS liber Chronicon. RODERIC TOLETAN Hist. Arabum. LUCÆ Tudensis Chronicon.

(L) There can be nothing more evident, from the account given us of this fatal battle, than that the infant Don *Sanchez* was the legitimate son and heir apparent of Don *Alonso*; for otherwise it would have been an act of extreme cruelty, to have exposed a child of eleven years of age, to no purpose whatever. The heir of all was, or ought to be, the care of all; so that, in this desperate state of things, the king may be said to have acted wisely, in sending that young prince to the army; for, by this action, he plainly shewed, that the safety of his people was dearer to him than the safety of his children. He shewed also his courage and firmness of mind, in assembling fresh troops, and providing, notwithstanding this severe blow, for the future security of his dominions; which, in a prince so broken with age and diseases, was so much the more laudable, as it was less to be expected (1). Some historians tell us, that he did still more, and they report the occasion of it thus: They say, that, after this battle, discoursing with those who were most in his confidence, he expressed a strong persuasion, that

this was a severe visitation from heaven for some particular sins; and that they had little hopes of a change of fortune, till the necessary change was made in their manners; and how this might be effected he was at a loss to know, and would be glad to learn. One of his nobility took occasion from thence to observe, that heaven punished them by the *Moors*, for his having suffered too great an intercourse between them and his subjects, which had produced a great depravity of morals, and the fatal introduction of foreign luxuries, to which in former times the *Castilians* were utter strangers (2). The king received this admonition thankfully, and immediately published a prohibition (3) of public baths, and of all kinds of spectacles and diversions, which, in imitation of the *Moors*, had been introduced at first amongst persons of distinction, and by degrees diffused through all ranks of people, which had a very good effect, and banished for a season that propensity to idleness, vanity, and pleasure, which are always both the causes and the symptoms of a declining state.

(1) *Roderic Toletan de reb. Hispan. lib.* vii. *Lucæ Tudensis Chronicon, Roderic Toletan, Hist. Arabum.* (2) *Chron. var. antiq.* (3) *Mariana, Ferreras, Mayerne, Turquet.*

any

any thing that was yet within the reach of his abilities. *Guido*, archbishop of *Vienne* in *France*, brother to the deceased Don *Raymond*, coming into *Spain* to see his nephew Don *Alphonso*, the king caused the young prince to be brought to *Leon*; to which city he directed all the nobility of *Galicia* should repair; and in his presence, as well as of the French archbishop, take an oath of fidelity to their infant sovereign, whom he appointed his sole successor [h] in all his dominions, in case his daughter Donna *Urraca* should have no other male issue, having, in compliance with the desires of the nobility, consented to her marriage with Don *Alphonso* king of *Arragon* and *Navarre* [i]. He disposed the troops under the command of the several counts, who brought them into the field so judiciously on his frontiers, and gave his orders so properly for assembling a numerous army, in case the *Moors* should make any attempt, that they chose to carry their arms into *Catalonia* and elsewhere, rather than attempt to purchase any more victories at so dear a rate as the *Castilians* were accustomed to sell them [k]. It does great honour to the memory of this prince, that, though for the space of eighteen months he lay in a weak and languishing condition, the civil and military affairs of his kingdom were preserved in so good order, that there neither happened any invasion from foreign enemies, or any tumult or commotion among the people; and in his capital city of *Toledo* Don *Alvaro Fanez* whom he had appointed governor, disposed every thing to such advantage, that the inhabitants were not under the least apprehension, though they had every day fresh advices of the increasing strength of the *Moors* [l]. At length the king worn out with age, care, and sickness, departed this life *June* the thirtieth, in the year of our Lord 1109, when he had enjoyed the regal dignity thirty-seven years from the time of his restoration, and forty-four from the death of his father [m]. His sixth and last wife Donna *Beatrix* returned into *Italy* after his decease [n].

Disputes arise between the king Alonso of
THE demise of this prudent and potent monarch was indeed the epocha from whence might be dated the miseries of his subjects. Don *Alphonso*, king of *Arragon* and *Navarre*, believing it impossible to acquire kingdoms without an army,

[h] Chron. var. antiq. [i] RODERIC TOLETAN de reb. Hispan. lib. vi. PELAG. OVET. lib. Chron. [k] RODERIC TOLETAN Hist. Arabum. LUCÆ Tudensis Chron. [l] PELAG. OVET. liber Chronic. RODERIC SANTII Hist. Hispan. p. iii. [m] LUCÆ Tudensis Chronicon. ALPHONSI à Carthagena reg. Hisp. ANACEPHALÆOSIS, PELAG. OVET. lib. Chron. [n] RODERIC TOLETAN de reb. Hispan. lib. vi.

entered

entered *Caftile* at the head of a numerous body of troops, to Arragon, fupport his claim of the government in right of his queen; *and when* the ftates quickly put an end to the troubles that this might Urraca. have occafioned, by informing him, that they were not accuftomed to fee their fovereign at the head of foreign troops; that his army therefore might be better employed in his own dominions, fince there was no need of force, where the right of the queen was not at all difputed. Don *Alphonfo* received this meffage with the fpirit it deferved, he faid, he knew not the intentions of his people when he entered *Caftile* in arms; but that he was ready to difmifs his army, which he did immediately, and to rely on their loyalty which had been ever confpicuous [o]. He found it much more eafy to deal with the ftates than with their queen, who was fo very fond of fovereignty, that fhe would willingly have reckoned her hufband only the firft of her fubjects. The paffion of her firft hufband count *Raymond* had made him really fo; the dignity, and it may be faid the difpofition of the king of *Arragon* forbad it. He laboured to make her fenfible by reafon of the duty fhe owed to him, and fhe difcovered by her behaviour, that fhe underftood nothing of duty, but as others were bound by it to obey her will [p]. An old *Caftilian* nobleman, Don *Pedro Affurez*, the companion of her father's exile, the favourite of his whole life, and who had been intrufted with her education, took the liberty of expoftulating with her, and of fetting her conduct in a true light; which provoked her to fuch a degree, that fhe banifhed him the court, ftripped him of his employments, and confifcated his eftate [q]. The king could not bear this; he took Don *Pedro* into his immediate fervice, he reftored him to his honours, his employments, and his eftate; declaring, that whatever injury was offered to him, from whatever hand it came, he would regard it as done to himfelf [r]. This naturally increafed the diforder; which at length rofe fo high, that the king fecured the perfon of his confort, and made her prifoner in the fortrefs of *Caftellar* [s], from which fhe was fpeedily delivered by fome of the nobles of *Caftile*, and began to feel great trouble of mind on account of the relation between her and her hufband, for they were fecond coufins; fo that, to quiet her confcience, fhe was defirous the marriage fhould be diffolved [t].

---

[o] Chron. var. antiq.   [p] Lucæ Tudenfis Chronicon.
[q] Roderic Toletan de reb. Hifpan. lib. vi.   [r] Pelag.
Ovet. liber Chronicon. Roderic Toletan Hift. Arabum.
[s] Chron. var. antiq.   [t] Lucæ Tudenfis Chron.

A civil war breaks out in Galicia, where the rebels seize the young prince.
A. D.
1110.

IN the midst of these disturbances a civil war broke out in Galicia; Don *Pedro Frolaz de Traba* had been charged with the education of the young Infant Don *Alonso* by his father, and confirmed in it by his grandfather; his conduct was irreproachable; and this was the source of the war. Some of the nobility, headed by two brothers, Don *Arias Perez* and Don *Pedro Arias,* men of a most turbulent spirit, invested the castle where the young prince was; and, contrary to their faith given, tore him out of the arms of the countess Don *Pedro's* wife, and imprisoned for a time the archbishop of *Compostella,* who reproved them for their rudeness [w]. But the inhabitants of that city taking arms in behalf of their prelate, they thought proper to set him at liberty, retaining still the young prince in their custody, and pretending to colour all the violences they committed, with the specious pretence of loyalty to the child they kept a prisoner [x]; a sort of proceeding that put an end to the regular administration of affairs in that province, and threw all things into the utmost disorder and confusion. Such was the disastrous train of events that fell out in the first year after the demise of that great king, who had raised the power of the Christians in *Spain* to so formidable a point of elevation.

Ali Joseph, king of the Almovarides, besieges Toledo with out success.

JOSEPH king of *Morocco,* and of the *Almovarides* in *Spain,* died much about the same time with Don *Alphonso* the sixth, and was succeeded by his son *Ali Joseph* [y], who, for the sake of distinction, we shall call only *Ali,* and who had been for some years his father's viceroy in *Spain;* but at the time of his demise he was in *Africa,* from whence he speedily returned with a numerous army, and a potent fleet. He had no sooner debarked his forces, than he marched directly to *Seville;* and, having examined and given the necessary directions for repairing and augmenting this capital of his dominions, he issued his orders for a general rendezvous of all his forces at *Cordova,* to which city he repaired in person. Having made a general review, he concluded himself well able to accomplish what his father had only contrived; and, under a strong persuasion of this, grounded probably on the present state of the Christians, he proceeded directly towards *Toledo,* wasting all the country with fire and sword, and utterly demolishing two beautiful monasteries in his passage [z]. The city being completely invested, and no fear of disturbance

[w] PELAG OVET. liber Chron. RODERIC TOLETAN de reb. Hispaniæ, lib. vi.   [w] MARIANA, FERRERAS, MAYERNE, TURQUET.   [x] Chron. var. antiq.   [y] RODERIC TOLETAN Hist. Arabum.   [z] LUCÆ Tudensis Chronicon.

from

from any army in the field, he proceeded vigorously in his siege; and, by the help of the best machines then in use, actually made a breach in the walls sufficiently practicable. He intended to have stormed upon the eighth; but on the seventh day of the siege, Don *Alvaro Fanez*, with the best part of the garrison, passed, by the help of wooden bridges, over the breach into his camp a little before the break of day, levelled his works, burnt his machines, and gave his troops such an earnest of the reception they were like to expect, that the king of *Morocco*, finding they had no stomach to the attack, very prudently raised the siege the next day, with a resolution to insult *Madrid* [a].

THERE was but a small garrison in the place, but the inhabitants were very numerous, and they defended themselves so gallantly, that he was obliged to retire from thence also; but, to make himself amends, he took another route into his own dominions; and, sweeping all the country before him, amassed a prodigious booty, and carried many thousands of people into slavery [b]. All these, together with the remains of the Christians who still lived peaceably in his territories, he caused to be shipped on board his fleet, with which he returned to *Africa*; and having carried his miserable captives up to *Morocco*, dispersed them in the country adjoining to that capital, to replace, in some measure, the inhabitants whom he had carried to *Spain* [c]. Thus the Christians of *New Castile* were left to supply the vast loss they had sustained in the best manner they could, by their private endeavours, as they had received very little assistance, and could scarce expect more from the condition of their government, which was so extremely unsettled, that it scarce deserved that name, as appears from no efforts being made, either upon the irruption or retreat of the infidels, when they might have been attacked with the greatest probability of advantage.

Fails in the conduct of the whole expedition, and returns again to Morocco.

THE nobility of *Leon* and *Castile* saw with inexpressible concern how low they were fallen, and how much lower they might fall; they therefore solicited the queen to consent to a reconciliation with her husband; and to this, to satisfy their importunity, she at last agreed [d]. That it might appear an act of her own, she went to him, and was received, and they lived together again for some little time [e]. But the coldness and contempt of Don *Alphonso* was too apparent to be borne by a princess of so high a spirit; and therefore she

Quarrels continue between the king and queen, notwithstanding the interposition of the nobility.

[a] RODERIC TOLETAN Hist. Arabum. [b] RODERIC TOLETAN de reb. Hispan. lib. vi. [c] LUCÆ Tudensis Chron. ROD. TOLET. Hist Arabum. [d] RODERIC TOLETAN de reb. Hispan. lib. vi. [e] LUCÆ Tudensis Chron.

queen,

queen, believing that she had now given her nobility all the satisfaction they could expect, left him again, with a full refolution never to be reconciled to him more, which naturally increafed thofe diforders, that were but too many and too great already [f]. The king, on the other hand, depended upon the *Arragonian* lords, whom he had placed as governors in fome of the beft towns in both the *Caftiles*, and upon many of the *Caftilian* nobility, who were alfo in his intereft; for though he had conceived an implacable averfion to the queen, he was by no means willing to part with her dominions [g].

Don Alon-fo, *king of* Arragon, *determines to keep* Caftile, Leon, *and* Toledo, *by force.* THE queen, though her affairs wore fo indifferent an afpect, did not fuffer her fpirits to fink at all; but by her affability to all the lords of *Caftile* who came to pay their refpects to her, and by her gracious deportment towards the commons, drew over multitudes of all ranks to her party; and thefe at length came to entertain fo good an opinion of her caufe and their own force, that they fummoned the *Caftilians*, to whom the king had committed caftles, to furrender them; which, generally fpeaking, they did, and threatened to reduce the *Arragonians* by force [h]. Among the reft Don *Pedro de Affurez* furrendered thofe which the queen had taken from him, and to which he was reftored by the king's favour; but, as foon as he had done it, he went directly to *Toledo*, and having obtained an audience of the king, told him, that as for the fortreffes they undoubtedly belonged to the queen his mafter's daughter, who having demanded he had yielded them, as he conceived it his duty; but that, if his majefty confidered the thing in another light, he had brought his body to anfwer for the offence. At firft the king was in fo great a rage, that, if fome of his favourites had not interpofed, Don *Pedro's* life would hardly been fafe; but, as foon as that tranfport of paffion was over, the king embraced him, and teftified the higheft admiration of his loyalty and virtue [i]. From this moment the king difcerned, that his authority could no longer depend on any thing but fuccefs; and therefore, having recommended the kingdom and capital of *Toledo* to Don *Alvaro Fanez*, who had fhewn himfelf firmly attached to his fervice, he marched with a fmall body of excellent troops directly into *Caftile*, where he found the whole force of that kingdom affembled

[f] Chron. var. antiq.   [g] RODERIC TOLETAN de reb. Hifpan. lib. vi.   [h] RODERIC TOLETAN de reb. Hifpan. lib. vii.   [i] Chron. var. antiq.

to

to impede his paſſage, which put him under a neceſſity of beginning the war with what had very much the appearance of a deciſive battle ; and as things were come to this extremity, he was a prince of too much courage to decline it ; though without queſtion he could not avoid diſcerning of how dangerous conſequence theſe diſputes were to the Chriſtian cauſe.

THE queen's army was encamped in the neighbourhood *The battle* of *Sepulveda*, and, upon the king's troops advancing towards *of* Campo them, a battle enſued, which was fought on the 28th *of* de Eſpina, *October* 1111, in a large plain called *Campo de Eſpina*, which *in which* in *Engliſh* we ſhould call *Thornfield.* The vanguard of the *be totally* queen's army was commanded by Don *Pedro de Lara*, which *routs the* was quickly broke by the ſquare battalion of the *Arragoneſe queen's* infantry, commanded by the king in perſon; upon which *troops.* Don *Pedro* fled to *Burgos.* The ſecond line, commanded by the count Don *Gomez*, made a gallant and obſtinate reſiſtance ; and when they were at laſt broken, the count had the honour to die upon the ſpot, covered with glory and wounds. There fell likewiſe many other perſons of great diſtinction, and a great number of private men. In conſequence of this victory the king became maſter of *Burgos, Valentia, Carrion, Sahagon,* and the royal city of *Leon;* all which he gave up to be pillaged by his ſoldiers, who plundered even the monaſtery of *Sahagon,* and the church of *St. Iſidore* at *Leon,* the ſacred dormitory of their kings ; which filled all the adjacent countries with ſuch terror, that ſome places in *Galicia*, ſeduced by his emiſſaries, declared for the king °.

THE queen, who was retired to a place of ſafety, publiſh- *Galicia* ed, to repair this loſs, a proclamation, requiring all her ſub- *declares* jects, capable of carrying arms, to take the field P. In the *for the* mean time, however, the archbiſhop of *Compoſtella*, and *young* Don *Pedro Trolas de Traba,* prevailed upon *Pedro Arriaz* and *prince Don* his accomplices, to compromiſe their diſputes, and to ſur- *Alonſo* render the perſon of the young prince Don *Alonſo Raymond,* *Ray-* whom the archbiſhop crowned ¶ with great ſolemnity before *mond,* the high altar in the cathedral church of *St. James,* and *who is* quickly after carried him, at the head of the beſt army they *crowned* could raiſe, to join the queen his mother ; but were attacked *by the* in their paſſage by the king of *Arragon:* and though the *archbiſhop.* army was defeated, yet the archbiſhop found means to con-

° LUCÆ Tudenſis Chronicon.	P RODERIC SANTII Hiſt. Hiſpan. p. iii. LUCÆ Tudenſis Chronicon.	¶ MARIANA Hiſtoria general de Eſpana, lib. x. FERRERAS Hiſtoria de Eſpana, p. v. ſect. xi. Hiſtoire general d'Eſpagne, MAYERNE, TURQUET, liv. ix.

vey the young prince fafely to the queen, who, as foon as
it was in her power, retired with him back again into *Galicia*, where fhe immediately began to raife a new army;
while the king of *Arragon*, with his victorious' troops, befieged the city of *Aftorga*, in which were the remains of the
archbifhop's army, who made a gallant and a long defence[r].
The queen applied herfelf to count *Henry* of *Portugal*, who
had married her fifter, and intreated him to affift her, and
the fon of his friend, in this danger and diftrefs. Count
Henry advifed her to march immediately to the relief of
Aftorga, and promifed to join her with a confiderable body
of troops, which he did. The great lords of *Afturias* likewife joined her with the flower of their militia; and the nobility of *Caftile* about the fame time attacked and defeated a
body of *Arragonefe* troops that were in full march to join
their king; and that prince found himfelf in fuch circumftances, that he raifed the fiege of *Aftorga* in the night, and
retired precipitately to *Carrion* [s]. The queen followed him
fo clofe, that her forces invefted the city almoft as foon as he
entered it; and in all probability he had fallen into her
hands, if the Pope's legate, who was lately arrived in *Spain*,
and who appointed a council to be held in *Palentia* to judge
finally of the queen's marriage, had not prevailed upon her to
fuffer him to retire, upon his promife to deliver up all the
places in her dominions that were in his poffeffion; which,
however, he abfolutely refufed to perform [t]. The count
Don *Henry*, of *Portugal*, had fcarce the pleafure of feeing
the queen in *Aftorga*, before he died there [u], and was carried
from thence to *Braga*, where he lies under a fplendid tomb.
Mariana feems to have afperfed his memory by miftake, in
afcribing the lofs of the former battle to his deferting the
queen after it began [w].

A. D.
1112.

*The war
continued
between
the king
and queen,
of which
the* Moors
*take ad-
vantage.*

THE queen, Donna *Urraca*, finding herfelf deceived in her
expectations, and under a neceffity of having recourfe to
arms, in order to recover the city of *Burgos*, into which the
king her hufband had put a ftrong garrifon, and caufed a new
caftle to be erected for its defence, marched thither. She
found this enterprize, however, embarraffed with far greater
difficulties than fhe expected; for, on one hand, the lords
of *Caftile* were fo difpleafed with her conduct towards Don
Pedro de Lara, that they abated much of their zeal for her

---

[r] RODERIC TOLETAN de reb. Hifpan. lib. vii.   [s] LUCÆ
Tudenfis Chron.   [t] Chron. var. antiq.   [u] RODERIC
SANTII Hift. Hifpan. p. iii. FRANCISCI TARAPHÆ de reg. Hif-
paniæ.   [w] Hiftoria general de Efpana, lib. x.

service; and, on the other hand, the *Galicians* had their suspicions likewise, arising from their affection to the young king; so that, if the archbishop of *Compostella* had not been indefatigable in his endeavours, the army could never have been brought before *Burgos*; which city soon opened its gates, but the garrison held out a siege of several weeks, but at length was obliged to surrender on the feast of *St. John the Baptist* [x]. About this time the *Moors* made an irruption into the kingdom of *Toledo*, and advanced from thence towards the frontiers of *Galicia*; but, at the pressing instances of the queen and archbishop, a numerous army marched, against them; upon which they thought it more adviseable to retire with the plunder they had acquired [y], than to hazard a battle against troops that would otherwise be employed in their service, that is, in weakening the king of *Arragon*.

A. D. 1113.

THE queen, to put an end to these troubles, that had so long disturbed and distracted her subjects, called a general assembly of the states at *Burgos*; to which, at her request, resorted Don *Bernard* archbishop of *Toledo*, and Don *Diego* archbishop of *Compostella*. The debates in that assembly ran quickly very high; for most of the *Castilian* nobility, and more especially the deputies of the city of *Burgos*, declared roundly for the queen's being reconciled to her husband; and, upon the archbishop of *Compostella*'s insisting on the invalidity of the marriage, they were so exasperated, that he thought it prudent to withdraw; soon after which the assembly broke up, referring the decision of this difficult point to the council that was to be held at *Palentia* [z]. This council [a], held in the beginning of the succeeding year, and in which the Pope's legate presided, declared the marriage null; by which an end was put to all the king of *Arragon*'s pretensions; who, notwithstanding, raised by his emissaries a formidable rebellion in *Galicia*, which, but for the prudence and spirit of the archbishop of *Compostella*, might have been attended with very fatal consequences (M). About this time Don

A council held at Palentia, in which the queen's marriage is declared void.

A. D. 1114.

---

[x] LUCÆ Tudensis Chron.   [y] RODERIC TOLETAN Hist.
Arabum.   [z] Chron. var. antiq.   [a] Card. d' AGUIRRE
Conc. Hisp. tom. iii. p. 319.

(M) Those of the nobility, who now took up arms in *Galicia*, were *Pedro Gudesteo, Rodrigo Nugnez, Arias Perez,* and *Pedro Arias*; against whom the bishop of *Compostella* quickly marched with forces so considerable, that the malecontents thought fit to separate. *Pedro Gudesteo* and *Rodrigo Nugnez* retired to their castles, which lay by the sea-side, and invited an *English*

Don *Alvaro Fanez,* going on some occasion from *Toledo* to *Segovia,* an insurrection happened in the last-mentioned place, in which he was unfortunately killed. He was succeeded in the government of *Toledo* by Don *Rodrigo Nunez;* whether by the appointment of the king of *Arragon,* or by the choice of the inhabitants, does not appear; but by that time he was well fixed in his office, the city was invested by a numerous army of infidels, under the command of *Amazaldi;* but the place was so well defended, that he was obliged to retire [b]. To make himself some amends he ravaged all the adjacent country, and Don *Rodrigo Nugnez,* with the best part of his garrison, attacking him in his retreat near *Pulgar,* in hopes of recovering the booty, were thoroughly beaten for their pains. The next year *Amazaldi* returned with a great army of *Moors* into the neighbourhood of *Toledo,* when Don *Rodrigo Nugnez* had his revenge; for drawing his whole force out of the city, he gave the infidels battle in the field, and, after a long and bloody engagement, cut the greatest part of them to pieces, and their general *Amazaldi* among the rest [c].

A. D.
1115.

[b] RODERIC TOLETAN Hist. Arabum.   [c] LUCÆ Tudensis Chron. RODERIC TOLETAN Hist. Arabum.

English body of troops on shore, who happened to pass at this critical juncture along the coasts of *Galicia,* on board their own vessels, and had sent to desire leave to purchase provisions. They complied readily with this invitation; and were no sooner on shore, than they began to spoil and lay waste the country on every side. The bishop of *Compostella* had no sooner notice of this, than he directed some gallies, which had been built at his own expence, to act against the *Moorish* pirates, and which were laid up in the port of *Padron,* to be equipped, and embarked on board them some of his best troops, with orders to find out and engage the *English.*

They executed his instructions very punctually, and made themselves quickly masters of the whole squadron, including some vessels belonging to the *Galician* rebels, the best part of the men being on shore. At their return, the bishop purchased all their prisoners, that he might have an opportunity of setting the *English* at liberty; practising the like generosity upon the reduction of the castles, which very quickly followed. As for *Arias Perez* and *Pedro Arias,* they were no sooner informed of the fate of their companions, than they quitted *Galicia,* and retired to Don *Alonso* of *Arragon* (1).

(1) *Histor. Compostel. lib. i. which is a proper and sufficient authority to a fact of this nature, though not supported by any other, as probably lying out of the way of other historians.* --

DONNA

Donna *Urraca,* desirous of reducing the places that still *Fresh trou-* remained in the hands of the king of *Arragon,* went to *Com-* *bles arise* postella, in order to procure the assistance of the *Galician* nobi- *in* Galicia, lity; and conceiving some jealousy of the bishop, who had *where the* done her so many services, would have seized upon his per- *nobility de-* son, if she had not been prevented by some of the lords who *clare for* were his friends; after which a reconciliation was brought *the young* about, which enabled her to oblige Don *Alonso* to retire into *king.* his own dominions, who was upon the point of making a A.D. fresh irruption into *Castile* [d]. To this singular mark of his 1116. credit with the people, and loyalty to his sovereign, that pre- late speedily added another, by causing a small squadron of gallies to be built and equipped at his own expence, which not only freed the coasts of *Galicia* and *Asturias* from the in- sults of the *Moorish* pirates, who had pillaged and destroyed all the sea-coasts, but likewise made reprisals, by plundering their territories. Notwithstanding all this, the queen be- came again out of humour with him to such a degree, that she directed his friend Don *Pedro Frolaz* to secure his person; instead of which he gave him notice of his danger; and, after maturely weighing the many inconveniencies to which they were exposed from the mutability of this princess's tem- per, they judged it most expedient to put the government into the hands of her son, at least the kingdom of *Galicia,* to which his right seemed unquestionable, even in the life-time of his mother; which proposition was well received by all the nobility, and the design was put in execution, which occasioned new disturbances; for the queen assembled all the forces of *Leon* and *Castile,* and pretended to treat the bishop and his adherents as rebels, notwithstanding her son was with him, and approved of all he did [e]. At length, however, by the interposition of some of the principal nobi- lity, things were compromised; when the queen had visibly the advantage, and might have treated those who adhered to her son with great severity, or at least have obliged them to abandon their country [f]. But as there was nothing cordial in this reconciliation, so it did not last long, both parties retaining a deep resentment of what had passed; the queen looking upon the bishop and Don *Pedro Frolaz,* as men who had seduced her son into a rebellion; and they regarding her as a princess besieged by flatterers, inordinately fond of power, and far from having those abilities that were necessary to go- vern so many kingdoms, in so critical and perilous a con- juncture.

[d] Roderic Toletan de reb. Hispan. lib. vii. [e] Chron. var. antiq. [f] Lucæ Tudensis Chron. Roderic Toletan de reb. Hispan. lib. vii.

The

Several attempts made by the Moors against Toledo, without success.

THE *Moors* were so tempted by these intestine disturbances, to hope the recovery of *Toledo*, that they scarce failed either besieging or attempting to besiege it, every year. In this we are told, that *Ali* sent one of his generals, whom an antient *Spanish* chronicle calls *Acredelia*, with a numerous army, to ruin the country round about. But the Christian governor, whom the same author calls *Abbacil*, foreseeing the consequences of such expeditions would be distressing the place by famine, marched out with his forces, engaged and beat the enemy, and killed their general upon the spot. The *Moors*, provoked at this defeat, and still anxious to avail themselves of the troubles among the Christians, speedily drew together a fresh army, and under *Aben Haret*, a celebrated general of theirs, took the field, and marched directly towards *Toledo*. They found, however, their passage speedily stopped by the governor, and the whole force of the garrison, who immediately gave them battle, and this with success not inferior to the former; since the *Moors* were intirely vanquished, and *Aben Haret*, being taken prisoner, was sent to the castle of *Toledo*; while the governor, with his victorious army, ravaged the *Moorish* frontiers, and swept the places where he came so thoroughly of provisions, that it was impossible to assemble any third army there for that year, which, at that juncture, was indubitably a thing of infinite consequence to the cause of the Christians [h].

The queen and the bishop of Compostella in great danger of being burnt in a commotion.

THE compromise between Donna *Urraca* and those who declared for her son, was quickly violated by the queen's besieging *Gomez Nugnez* in the castle of *Turon*, which he held for Don *Alonso Raymond*, and she was soon after besieged herself in *Soberosa* by Don *Pedro Frolaz*, at the head of the *Galician* army, assisted by the troops of *Portugal*, though that country was governed at that time by her sister Donna *Theresa*; but the great lords of *Castile* and *Leon* came with a potent army to deliver the queen, and clapped up another pacification; soon after which she returned to the royal city of *Leon* [i]. Some new disputes arising in *Galicia*, the enemies of the bishop of *Compostella* took advantage of them, and were on the point of securing his person; for, being a moderate and an honest man, this prelate had the honour to be very heartily hated by the bigots of both parties; so that, to provide for his own security, he was obliged to retire to *Leon*. The queen received him with equal kindness and respect, desired him to write to those worthy men, who were his friends in

[h] RODERIC TOLETAN Hist. Arabum.   [i] LUCÆ Tudensis Chronicon.

Galicia,

Galicia, to compose these disturbances, and to put things into such a situation, as she might with safety visit her son; which in a little time was brought about, and the bishop first, and the queen not long after, went to *Compostella* [k]. The populace, surmising that there was a secret intention to punish them for the insults they had offered to their prelate, surprised him with the queen and the principal nobility in the cathedral, and, failing in their attempt to force it, set that noble structure on fire, crying vehemently, let the queen come out, and let the bishop and his adherents perish in the flames [l]. The bishop, more concerned for her safety than his own, obliged the queen to quit the cathedral, which she did, and retired to the church of *St. Mary*, loaded, in her passage, with all the foul language that an inraged mob could bestow; and, after her departure, the bishop, not without great difficulty, made his escape in disguise [m]. In the midst of these disorders, the inhabitants of *Toledo* took a very laudable resolution of recalling their natural prince; and accordingly Don *Alonso Raymond* made his publick entry into that city, 1117 [n],

AT this juncture there was a schism in the church of *Rome*; one party adhering to cardinal *de Gayette*, by the name of *Gelasus* the second; the other supported by the emperor *Henry* the fifth, to *Maurice Burdin*, archbishop of *Braga*, who assumed the name of *Gregory* the eighth, but was soon after deposed, and ended his days in prison (N). The prelates

A. D. 1118. Don Bernard, archbishop of Toledo, reduces Alcala de

---

[k] RODERIC TOLETAN de reb. Hispan. lib. vii.   [l] Chron. var. antiq.   [m] LUCÆ Tudensis Cron.   [n] RODERIC TOLETAN de reb. Hispan. lib. vii.

(N) We have as hideous a picture of this *Maurice Bourdin*, or *Burdin*, in various histories, as it was almost in the power of men to invent (1). Amongst other things it is said, that, being sent to *Rome* to solicit on behalf of *Bernard* archbishop of *Toledo*, he most ungratefully traduced that prelate, to whom he had the highest obligations; and laboured assiduously to get himself raised to that dignity; which, upon the whole, however, does not appear to be true. He was a native of *Limoges* in *France*, and was carried from *Rome* into *Spain* by the archbishop of *Toledo*, with whom he was in great favour. In the year 1108, he became bishop of *Coimbra*, or *Conimbra*; after which he made a tour to the holy land, and in his return staid some time at *Constantinople*, where he was very much ca-

---

(1) *Mariana Historia general de Espana, lib.* x. *Maimbourg, decad. de l'Empire, lib.* iv. *p.* 391. *Mayerne, Turquet, &c.*

ressed

Henarez
by *fiege*.

lates of this age in general were certainly very extraordinary perfons; for we find, that Don *Bernard*, archbifhop of *Toledo*, whofe gratitude to the memory of his protector had kept him firm to the interefts of his family, and who therefore, while the place was in the hands of the king of *Arragon*, remained under a cloud, no fooner regained his own authority, than he perfuaded the people to make an attempt upon the ftrong town of *Alecla de Henares*, the fame which the antients ftiled *Complutum*, and to which, from a

reffed by the emperor *Alexis.* (2) Upon his coming back to *Portugal* he was, in 1110, elected archbifhop of *Braga*. It was in confequence of this, that he came to differ with his old patron the archbifhop of *Toledo*, who, as the Pope's legate and primate of *Spain*, required fuch fubmiffion from him, as he thought inconfiftent with the rights of his fee, which had always contefted the primacy with that of *Toledo*. In reference to this difpute he went to *Rome*, and Pope *Pafcal* the fecond thought him fo far in the right, that by his letter to the archbifhop of *Toledo*, dated *November* the third 1115, he difcharged him from the exercife of his legantine power within the province of *Braga* (3). As a farther mark of his confidence in this archbifhop, the fame Pope fent him with the character of his legate, to treat with the emperor *Henry*, whom the archbifhop ventured to crown in his abfence; for which the Pope excommunicated him in the council of *Beneventum* (4). *Gelafus* the fecond, his fucceffor, was exactly of his fentiments; and

the emperor, hearing that he had affumed the Popedom without his leave, caufed the archbifhop of *Braga* to be elected by thofe of his party, *March* the 14th, 1114, who thereupon affumed the name of *Gregory* the eighth, and was fo acknowleged in fome parts of *Germany* and *England*; whereas in *France* and in *Spain* they acknowleged *Gelafus*, and in many countries they would own neither. *Calixtus* the fecond fucceeded *Gelafus*, made peace with the emperor, and then proceeded to *Rome*; upon which *Gregory* retired to *Sutri*, whither *Calixtus* followed him with an army, and made him prifoner in the month of *April* 1121. His foldiers mounted him upon a camel with his face towards the tail, with a fheep's fkin new flead and bloody about his fhoulders. He fent him prifoner to the monaftery of *Cava*, and from thence removed him to *Janula*, from whence his fucceffor, *Honorius* the fecond, transferred him to *Fuman* near *Alatri*, where he wote out the remainder of his days, and died in fuch mifery and contempt, (5) that the time is not known.

(2) *Vita Mauritii Burdini, archiepifcopi Bracarenfis, fcriptore Stephano Balnzio in Mifcellan. tom. iii. p. 471.*   (3) *Rod. a Cumba in tractatu de Primatu Bracarenfis Ecclefiæ.*   (4) *Hiftoire de Papes, tom. ii. p. 598.* (5) *Conftant. Caict. in not. ad vitam Gelaf. lib. ii. p. 68. Will. Tyr. lib. xii. cap. 8.*

conflux of waters, the *Moors* gave the name of *Alcala*, and distinguished it farther by the adjunction of *Henares*, the river upon which it stands; it was in all respects very considerable, but particularly in commanding a large district of country, well fortified, and had a numerous garrison; notwithstanding which, and that the *Moors* defended themselves gallantly, the archbishop reduced it, and immediately put it into the king's hands, who made a grant [o] of it to the archbishops of *Toledo*, from which place it is distant about 18 miles.

At the opening of the ensuing year died Pope *Gelasius*, who was succeeded by the archbishop of *Vienne*, uncle to Don *Alonso Raymond*, by the title of *Calixtus* the second, for which reason we mention it [p]. The queen, who at this time was upon good terms with her son, desired his assistance for recovering the places that were still held by the king of *Arragon*; and Don *Alonso* joined her with a considerable body of troops at *Segovia*, to which city she came with a numerous army, attended by most of the nobility of *Leon*, *Castile*, and *Asturias*. In a short time, however, after the king's arrival, disputes arose; for the nobility could not bear, that Don *Pedro de Lara* should put on airs of state and dignity in the presence both of his and their master, which excited murmurs in the army; till two of the principal lords cut things short, by seizing upon the person of Don *Pedro*, and carrying him prisoner to the castle of *Mancilla*; upon which the queen, in great discontent, retired to *Leon* [q]. After her departure, the king, with the forces under his command, entered upon the proper business of the campaign, and reduced most of the places that were held by the king of *Arragon*, while those two lords of the queen's army, who had seized Don *Pedro*, followed her to *Leon*, reduced that city, besieged her in the castle, which they constrained her to deliver up, and to be reconciled to her son [r]. The new Pope, at the request of a prelate who had deserved so well by his strict adherence to his nephew, raised the see of *Compostella* to the rank of an archbishoprick, of which dignity Don *Diego Gelmirez* took possession *July* the 25th, on the feast of *St. James*, in the year 1120; and in the succeeding year he held a council there, in which he presided as the Pope's legate, which gave no small offence to the archbishop of *Toledo*.

Discontents against the queen rise so high, that the nobles seize Don Pedro de Lara.

His cares were, however, unsuccessful, in respect to the preservation of the public tranquillity; some of the nobility

She is prevailed on

[o] Chron. var. antiq. [p] Lucæ Tudensis Chronicon.
[q] Chron. var. antiq. [r] Hist. Compostell. lib. ii.

by flatter-
ers to seize
the arch-
bishop of
Compo-
stella.

A. D.
1121.

in *Galicia* remaining in arms under slight pretences, but with high protestations of their fidelity to the king ; which brought Donna *Urraca* thither, who had again drawn together a considerable army, by the assistance of the lords of her party in *Castile.* The archbishop of *Compostella* received her with all imaginable marks of duty and respect, and, in obedience to her commands, endeavoured to reduce those of the nobility who were, in arms ; which, with some difficulty, he performed ᵘ. The queen then declared her intention to act against her sister Donna *Theresa,* on account of her having taken *Tuy,* and some other places which belonged to *Galicia.* The archbishop did all he could to prevent this war ; but finding this out of his power, he passed the river *Minho* with his forces, and the rest of the queen's army ; but when Donna *Theresa,* after having abandoned all the places in question, was besieged by the queen in the castle of *Laniosa,* the archbishop was desirous of retiring with his forces into his own diocese, which revived the queen's old resentments against that prelate, to whom she ascribed most of the disappointments she had met with in her violent projects. She dissembled, however, her disposition for the present, and gave him leave to send back his troops ; but, under pretence of relying wholly upon his advice, would not suffer him to retire from about her person. She could not, however, take her measures so secretly, but that her sister Donna *Theresa* gained intelligence of them, and gave notice to the archbishop of his danger, who was so much deceived by the queen's behaviour, that he considered this as an artifice to detach him from her service. He was very quickly convinced of his error ; for, upon raising the siege, and the army's repassing the *Minho,* the queen caused this prelate and his three brothers to be arrested, and sent to different prisons ʷ, without the king's consent, though he was in the army ; and at the same time seized upon several castles and lands that belonged

The people
of Galicia,
supported
by her son
Don Alon-
so, *force*
her to set
him at li-
berty.

to the archbishoprick of *Compostella.* The queen's politics deceived her extremely upon this occasion ; she imagined, from what had formerly happened, that this would have been pleasing to numbers of the *Galicians* ; whereas it proved quite otherwise. The enemies of the archbishop were only so on account of his attachment to the queen ; and therefore the news of his imprisonment was no sooner divulged, than they were the loudest in their clamours ; and those who would have burnt him in his church, now took up arms, or would have taken up arms, for his deliverance. It was

ᵘ 'Roderic Toletan de reb. Hispan. lib. vii.   ʷ Chron. var. antiq.

thought

thought more adviseable to try fair means first; and therefore four prebendaries of the cathedral, and four deputies
from the city of *Compostella*, were sent to know the reason
why the queen had confined their archbishop, and met with
a very ill reception. The queen went, however, in person
to that city; and, on *St. James's* day, proceeded in pomp to
the cathedral, which she found intirely hung with black; and
was met at the entrance by the principal persons of the city
in mourning, who very respectfully desired, that she would
lay hold of this opportunity to set their archbishop at liberty:
but the queen was inexorable; upon which her son Don
Alonso left her, and went and incamped with his forces on
the other side of the river, which raised the spirits of the
people, and intimidated the queen, who at length perceiving
her person in danger, and that the people had seized *John
Diaz*, in whose custody the archbishop was, she pretended
suddenly to change her mind, ordered the archbishop to be
released, declared she was satisfied of his innocence, and
that she meant with the utmost severity to punish his accu-
sers; but this had no effect; neither the populace thanked
her for the archbishop's deliverance, nor could that prelate
be ever afterwards brought to trust her [x]. So low, even
princes fall, when their artifices are discovered.

In a short time after this, things were on the point of *The death
coming to an open rupture; the queen and her Castilian of Donna
lords remaining in the field with one army, and the king Don Urraca,
Alonso*, with the archbishop, Don *Pedro Frolaz*, and most of *the cause
the nobles of *Galicia*, at the head of another; but, through of which is
the indefatigable pains of the prelate, things were at length differently
accommodated; and sixty lords of the queen's party bound reported.
themselves for the due performance of articles [y]. But soon A. D.
after all was in confusion again; Don *Alonso*, or at least the 1126.
nobility about him, would have *Galicia* taken for a separate
and independent kingdom, within which the queen should
have no power; whereas the queen pretended, that her son
held it in homage of her; and therefore very frequently committed therein most exorbitant acts of power. Some writers
[a] say, that, wearied out with these disputes and their consequences, Don *Alonso* confined her; but the contrary is
much more probable. At length on the sixth, as some [a] say,
on the eighth, as others [b] affirm, and, as some [c] again assert,
on the tenth of *March*, in the year of our Lord 1126, she

---

[x] Lucæ Tudensis Chronicon.   [y] Roderic Toletan de
reb. Hispan. lib. vi.   [z] Lucæ Tudensis Chron. Mariana,
Mayerne.   [a] Hist. Compostell. lib. ii.   [b] Annal Tolet.
[c] Chron. Adef. Imperat.

H 2   died

died at *Saldagna*, not far from *Carrion*, of the consequences of a miscarriage, as certain historians [d] allege; though there want not those [e] who affirm, that, having plundered the church of *St. Isidore*, she died suddenly as she came out, and was buried in the royal dormitory there, among the princes her ancestors, little regretted by her subjects [f].

Don Alon-
so VII.
succeeds in
Castile,
Leon, and
Asturias,
being be-
fore king
of Galicia
and To-
ledo.

THE king Don *Alonso* came to *Leon* within two days after the death of the queen his mother, and was received with all possible testimonies of affection and loyalty by the nobility of *Leon*, *Castile*, and *Asturias*, who there swore allegiance to him; only the citadel of that place, being in the possession of the adherents of Don *Pedro Lares*, and his brother Don *Roderic Gonzales*, were hardy enough to refuse giving up that fortress to the king, surrounded by his nobility [g]. They were quickly made sensible of their fault; for many of the great lords, and more especially the archbishop of *Compostella*, had brought troops; so that, with the assistance of the townsmen, the place was presently invested, and in a few days carried by storm; when the king might have put the rebels to death, as well by the rules of war, as by the laws of the land; but he contented himself with banishing them his dominions [h]. He next made a progress to *Zamora*, in order to receive the homage of the nobility in that neighbourhood; and this over, he went to *Ricorado*, which stands at the conflux of the rivers *Orbigo* and *Duero*, where he had a conference with his aunt Donna *Theresa*, and concluded a truce with her for a certain time; after which he returned to *Zamora*, to meet such of the *Galician* and *Castilian* nobility

A. D.
1126.

as had not hitherto sworn allegiance [i]. But some there were, who, hardened by that spirit of anarchy that prevailed during the late troubles, absolutely refused to acknowlege him for their prince. These were Don *Pedro Gonzales de Lara*, and his brother Don *Roderic*, who kept, with their adherents, in the mountains of *Santillana*; Don *Ximenes Iniquez*, who held the town now called *Valentia*; Don *Juan* and Don *Arias Perez* in *Galicia*, where they had seized *Castro*, *Luparia*, *de Pena*, *de Cornaria*, and other places [k].

Concludes
a peace

THERE were, besides these, some much more considerable places, that still held for the king of *Arragon*; such as *Car-*

[d] MARIANA Historia general de Espana, lib. x.   [e] MA-
YERNE TURQUET, Histoire general d'Espagne; liv. ix.
[f] FERRERAS Historia de Espana, p. v. sect. 11.   [g] MARI-
ANA Historia general de Espana, lib. x. FERRERA's Historia de Espana, p. v. sect. 11. MAYERNE TURQUET, Histoire general
d'Espagne, liv. ix.   [h] LUCÆ Tudensis Chron.   [i] RODERIC
TOLETAN de reb. Hispan. lib. vii.   [k] Chron. var. antiq.

rion, Burgos, Villa Franca, among the mountains of *Occa,* with Don
Najara, and some others; but this seems to have been Alonfo,
chiefly out of pique to Donna *Urraca;* for, as foon as the king of
king's acceffion was publiſhed, they moſt of them opened Arragon
their gates, and the people of *Burgos,* particularly, com- and Na-
pelled the king of *Arragon*'s governor to retire into the ci- varre.
tadel, which they reduced without any affiſtance, and then
put both the city and fortreſs into the king's hands ¹. In
Galicia the archbiſhop of *Compoſtella* humbled *Arias Perez,*
though not without effuſion of blood. Don *Ximenes* was
conſtrained to furrender *Valentia,* though he would not do it
but to the king in perfon; fo that, before the end of the
year, the king found himſelf in full poffeffion of all the dominions of his grandfather, except fome few diſtricts on the
frontiers of *Old Caſtile,* which, however, troubled him more
than all the reſt, as the king of *Arragon* had fome colour of
title to them, which he appeared determined to maintain
and make good by his fword. In the beginning of the fucceeding year he marched with a numerous army, refolved to
recover as much as poffible, or at leaſt to protect what was
ſtill left; the king of *Caſtile* and *Leon* advanced towards him
with the flower of both nations, and furrounded by the principal nobility and prelates of his dominions. When the armies drew near each other, neither of thofe princes difcovered any great eagernefs to fight. The king of *Caſtile* fpoke
very refpectfully of his antagoniſt, and the king of *Arragon*
could not help having a tendernefs for a prince he had been
accuſtomed to call his fon. The prelates and nobility on   A. D.
both fides faw this with great fatisfaction; and the king of   1127.
Arragon having been prevailed upon to fend a meffage, importing, that in forty days he would order all the places in
difpute to be evacuated, Don *Alonfo Raymond* demanded a
perfonal interview, where all their differences were amicably
determined, and the two kings parted perfectly good
friends ᵐ.

While the king Don *Alonfo Raymond* was at a diſtance Donna
from the frontiers of *Galicia,* Donna *Therefa,* who made no Therefa
doubt that the war in *Arragon* would find him full employ- depofed and
ment, caufed the troops of *Portugal* to pafs the *Minho,* in imprifoned
hopes of recovering *Tuy,* to which ſhe pretended a right. by her fon
Don *Alonfo* had no fooner notice of this, than he marched and her
thither with the utmoſt diligence; and having obliged the fubjects.
enemy to repafs the river, followed them into *Portugal,*

¹ Chron. ADEF. Imperat.   ᵐ ROD. TOL. de reb. Hifpan.
lib. vii. Chron. ADEF. Imperat.

H 3   where

where he began to lay the country waste with fire and
sword; but at length, through the persuasions of the archbishop of *Compostella*, who accompanied him, he was prevailed upon to listen to an accommodation, and things were
speedily adjusted between him and his aunt [n]. This was
quickly followed by an alteration of government in that
country, where the people were extremely dissatisfied with
Donna *Theresa's* administration, and her too great regard
for Don *Ferdinand Perez*, the son of Don *Pedro Frolaz*; and
therefore proposed to Don *Alonso Henriquez*, her son, that,
laying aside his mother, he should take the government into
his own hands; to which that high-spirited young prince
readily consented, and caused himself immediately to be proclaimed sovereign of *Portugal* [o]. His mother, however, who
was not of an humour to part with her right so easily, and
who had a good body of troops, under the command of her
favourite, about her person, marched directly to reduce the
prince and his adherents; but having the misfortune to lose
a battle, and being soon after obliged to surrender a fortress,
into which she had fled for shelter, she was constrained to do
as her subjects would have her, and to leave the administration in the hands of her son [p]; and as for Don *Ferdinand
Perez* he retired into *Galicia* (O).

A. D.
1128.

DON

[n] LucÆ Tudensis Chronicon.   [o] Mariana Historia ge-
general de Espana, lib. x. Ferreras, Mayerne Turquet.
[p] Rod. Tol. de reb. Hispan. lib. vi. LucÆ Tudensis Chron.

(O). The usage which Donna
Theresa has met with from the
generality of historians, is yet
harder than that of her sister.
It is reported, that she had an
intrigue with Don *Veramond*, the
son of Don *Pedro Frolaz*; but
being better pleased afterwards
with his brother Don *Ferdinand*,
whom she seems to have made
earl of *Traslamara*, she consented that Don *Veramond* should
marry the princess Donna *Elvira* her eldest daughter, and
then secretly espoused the earl
his brother; which excited, as
it very well might, a general
clamour amongst her subjects;
and produced that offer which
was made to the prince *Alonso*,
mentioned in the text (1). Whatever truth or falshood there may
be in the former of these facts,
the latter has such a concurrence of evidence, that it may
be regarded as certain; and
from thence we may easily account for the conduct of this
princess in respect to her sister
and nephew, as well as for that
intelligence which she seems always to have had with the malecontents in *Galicia*; and which
she knew very well how to turn

(1) *Manuel de Faria y Sousa, Epitome de las Historias Portuguesas, lib. iii.
cap. 1.*

DON *Alonso*, king of *Leon*, having at this time peace on every side, and being full two and twenty years of age, thought it time to provide for the succession by a prudent marriage; and with this view cast his eyes upon Donna *Berengara*, the daughter of Don *Raymond*, count of *Barcelona*, a young princess of great beauty and distinguished merit; which marriage was concluded by the interposition of the king of *Arragon*, to the great satisfaction of all parties ⁹. The year following he held a council ʳ at *Valentia*, in which Don *Raymond*, who succeeded Don *Bernard* in the archbishoprick of *Toledo*, presided; and in which many wholsome canons were made. Soon after this the king of *Arragon*, who had not been very punctual in fulfilling his promise, formed some pretensions upon *Medina Cœli* and *Moran*, the latter of which he besieged; but the king of *Leon* marching with a numerous army to its relief, the king of *Arragon* raised the siege, and retired into his own dominions. The appearance of this war raised another rebellion; for Don *Pedro*, count *de Lara*, and his brothers, attempted to engage the city of *Valentia* in a revolt, and not succeeding in that design, fortified several places in the mountains of *Santillana*. The king followed them hither sooner than they expected, invested the fort where Don *Roderic Gonzales* was, took it by storm, and made Don *Roderic* prisoner, who, knowing he deserved no mercy, did not expect it; but the king, having degraded and stripped him of his estates, gave him his life and liberty, but banished him his dominions; and not long after Don *Pedro* died of infirmities and a broken heart. His brother was no sooner informed of this, than he returned privately into *Castile*, threw himself at the king's feet, and desired leave to live obscurely in his own country, assuring

ᵠ Chron. ADEF. Imperat. MARIANA, FERREBAS. ʳ Chron. var. antiq.

to her own advantage. We are told, that at the time she was deprived of her administration and liberty by her son, he ordered two small chains to be put upon her legs, to prevent her escape, which she resented so much, that she prayed earnestly to God his legs might not continue whole as long as he lived; and it is added, that, being defeat- ed by the king of *Leon* he broke his leg in endeavouring to make his escape, by which accident he became a prisoner. It is also reported, that he remained ever after so lame, that, being unable to mount a horse, he travelled always in a kind of carriage (2), of which we shall have occasion to speak hereafter.

(2) *Mayerne Turquet, Histoire generale de l'Espagne, lib.* ix.

him

him, that he had not in his dominions a more faithful fubject. The king, touched with his repentance and humility,
reftored him to his honours, his eftates, and his employments, which he more than merited by his future fervices [t].
The king, perceiving that his forbearance would never procure the places that were ftill in the hands of the king of
Arragon, took the advantage of that monarch's abfence in
France, to reduce them by force; but he contented himfelf
with this, and did not offer any infult to that prince's frontiers, or to his fubjects. It is very poffible he might have
fome political motive to this moderation in his conduct.

lant beha-
viour of
Don Ro-
deric Gon-
zalez,
whom the
king par-
doned.

A. D.
1130.

ALL this time a prædatory war was carried on between
the Chriftians in the kingdom of *Toledo,* and the *Moors* fubject to the king of *Seville;* in which Don *Roderic Gonzalez,*
now reftored to the king's favour, had his fhare; and, tho'
he behaved very bravely, had the misfortune to be beat;
but, upon the arrival of *Texefin-ben-Ali* king of *Morocco,*
things began to have a more ferious afpect; for he privately
iffued his orders to his principal officers, to affemble a numerous army in the plain of *Lucena,* on the fide of *Cordova,*
looking towards *Toledo,* intending to have deftroyed all the
towns in the neighbourhood of that city. In the mean time
the Chriftians, vexed at their late defeat, formed a body of
a thoufand excellent horfe, and three or four thoufand foot,
paffed the *Tagus* on the fide of *Talavera,* and after that the
Guadiana and *Siera Morena,* with all the fpeed and fecrefy
poffible, and at length threw themfelves into the territory of
Cordova; with no other intent than to plunder, and make a
hafty retreat. There they received the firft intelligence of
the king of *Morocco's* being on the other fide of the city with a
large army; upon which, giving themfelves over for loft, they
took a fudden and generous refolution; and, after a fhort
repofe, began their march in the afternoon, continued it all
night, and, before break of day, fell into the *Moorish* camp,
where they made a horrible carnage; for the troops having
not the leaft expectation of an enemy, more efpecially on
that fide, and, being attacked in the night, were fo thunder-
ftruck, that they could make no refiftance; the king himfelf
wounded in the thigh got on horfeback, and fled to *Cordova,*
to which place as many followed him as efcaped; the victorious Chriftians plundered the camp, mounted all their infantry on horfeback, and, with immenfe riches, returned in
triumph to *Toledo* [u], where the people were equally rejoiced
at their fuccefs, and at their own happy efcape from a dan-

A. D.
1131.

[t] Lucæ Tudenfis Chron. Rod. Tol. de reb. Hifpan. lib. vii.
[u] Rod. Tol. Hift. Arabum. Chron. var. antiq.

ger,

ger, of which they had not the least notice, till it came, attended with that of their deliverance. A circumstance that rendered their transports the greater, and did not recommend their governor the less.

THE next year afforded the king of *Castile* and *Leon* troubles sufficient to exercise his courage and conduct. In the spring a rebellion broke out in the *Asturias*, at the head of which were the counts Don *Gonçales Pelaez* and Don *Roderic Gomez*: he marched immediately thither, and had the good fortune to make Don *Roderic* prisoner, whom he degraded from his honours and banished; but Don *Gonçalez*, retiring into the city of *Tudela*, made there a long and vigorous defence; but, finding it impossible to escape, he submitted to the king's mercy, who pardoned him freely; but by that time he returned to *Leon* had intelligence he had revolted again, and had made himself master of several strong places [w]. His attention to this misfortune was called off by a greater, which was was the news, that Don *Alonso* of *Portugal* had invaded *Galicia*. He was therefore obliged to march thither with his army, where he not only expelled the *Portuguese*, but took from them the country of *Limmia* [x]. While he was thus employed, advice was brought him, that the king of *Morocco* was on the point of invading the kingdom of *Toledo* with a numerous army; upon which he declared Don *Roderic Gonçales* governor of that city and kingdom. That nobleman raised a considerable body of forces; and having secured the capital, and heard that his master was advancing towards the king of *Morocco*, he threw himself into the kingdom of *Seville*, where he had the good fortune to defeat the *Moors* in a general engagement; and, having ravaged the country to the very gates of *Seville*, returned with his victorious army laden with plunder, and driving with them a multitude of slaves in triumph to *Toledo* [y]. The king of *Morocco*, on the approach of Don *Alonso*, after he had spoiled the open country, and taken and ruined some places of strength, thought proper to retire into his own dominions; where, meeting with a small body of Christians returning from an expedition, he surrounded them in the night, and the next day cut most of them into pieces [z].

THE *Moorish* monarch *Texefin-ben-Ali*, bearing still in his mind the importance of *Toledo*, and that the recovery of this place was absolutely necessary to restore the credit and power of his nation, resolved to make yet another attempt, with an army more numerous than any he had before employed; but

Marginal notes:
An insurrection in Asturias, *a war in* Galicia, *and an irruption of the* Moors.

A. D. 1132.

Don Alonso's glorious expedition against the

---

[w] Chron. ADEFONS Imperat. LUCÆ Tudensis Chron.   [x] RoDERIC TOLETAN de reb. Hispan. lib. vii.   [y] RODERIC TOLETAN Hist. Arabum. Chron. ADEFONS Imperat.   [z] RODERIC TOLETAN Hist. Arabum.

Moors, and triumphant return.

the king of *Castile* and *Leon,* being as early in the field as he marched directly towards that city which the *Moors* had scarce time to invest, who thereupon raised their siege, and withdrew into their own country [a]. Don *Alonso,* having reviewed the garrison of *Toledo,* and considering that the city could be in no danger while they were in the enemy's country,

A. D.
1133.

resolved to proceed forthwith into the territory of *Cordova,* by one passage, while Don *Roderic,* with the troops under his command, did the same by another, appointing the castle of *Gallelo* for the place of junction. There the armies being united, the king advanced into the neighbourhood of *Cordova,* wasting all the country before him, destroying their harvest, cutting down their fruit trees, tearing up their olives by the roots, carrying off their cattle, burning their villages, ruining their mosques, killing their priests, and driving their people into slavery; which, unless it was done from a principle of retaliation, and to prevent the continuance of such a method, was certainly extreme cruelty. He advanced in this manner to *Seville,* beyond it, and even to the sea coast: a his return, however, with an immense booty, he met the van-guard of the *Moorish* army; but being at the head of his own, composed of *Castilian* cavalry, he charged them so briskly, and with such success, that the gross of the army thought proper to retire into *Seville*; so that without any farther interruption he returned in triumph into his own dominions, and at *Taravera* dismissed his troops. [b]

Solemnly crowned, and invested with the title of emperor at Leon.

THE brave old king of *Arragon* was far from being so fortunate; his army being defeated by the infidels, and himself killed [c] before *Fraga.* As he died without heirs of his body, it produced great disturbances; the people of *Arragon* electing his brother Don *Ramiro,* though a monk, and the people of *Navarre* Don *Garcia Ramirez,* a descendent from their antient princes, for their king [d]. In the midst of these confusions, Don *Alonso* marched with a numerous army towards *Rioja,* where the inhabitants of *Najara* and *Callahorra* opened their gates to him, as did all the places of any consequence on the south of the *Ebro,* till he came to *Saragossa,* where he was met by Don *Ramiro,* king of *Arragon,* and the chief prelates and nobility of his dominions, to whom Don *Alonso* declared, that it was not through any motive of ambition, or with any views of conquest, that he came thither with his troops, but purely to protect them from the infidels [e]. While

[a] RODERIC TOLETAN de reb. Hispan. lib. vii. RODERIC TOLETAN Hist. Arabum. [b] LUCÆ Tudensis Chronicon. Chron. ADEFONS Imperat. [c] Chron. var. antiq. [d] MARIANA Historia general de Espana, lib. x. FERRERAS Historia de Espana, p. v. sect. xi. MAYERNE TURQUET. [e] RODERIC TOLETAN de reb. Hispan. lib. viii. LUCÆ Tudensis Chron.

he

he remained here, his brother-in-law, count *Raymond*, of *Barcelona*, repaired thither, and did him homage as his vassal; and his cousin Don *Alonso* of *Thoulouse* did the like. The king of *Arragon*, with the consent of his prelates and peers, yielded to him the city of *Saragassa*; and the bishops having, in great ceremony, bestowed upon him their benedictions in the church of our lady of the pillar, he returned with his army into his own dominions [f]. The new king of *Navarre* met him in his passage, and, being desirous to obtain his protection, did him voluntary homage [g]; after which he proceeded to *Leon* to keep his *Whitsuntide*, at which season he proposed to solemnize his coronation. There were present together at this high feast the king and queen of *Castile*, the Infanta Donna *Sancha*, the king's sister, Don *Garcia*, king of *Navarre*, with all the prelates, abbès, counts, and great lords of the kingdom. They met the first day in the cathedral church of that city, where they consulted of ecclesiastical affairs only, and of the means of restoring ecclesiastical discipline. The day following it was resolved to proclaim the king Don *Alonso* emperor; and, accordingly, a deputation was sent to bring him from his palace to the church, where Don *Raymond*, archbishop of *Toledo*, assisted by the bishops, abbots, and clergy, waited for him. As soon as he entered, the imperial mantle was thrown upon his shoulders, he was conducted up to the high altar, where, the crown being placed upon his head, and the scepter in his hand, supported on the right by Don *Garcia*, king of *Navarre*, and on the left by Don *Arias*, bishop of *Leon*, the clergy sung a solemn *Te Deum*; after which followed divine service; and, as soon as this was over, he was proclaimed emperor, all the assistants crying with a loud voice, Long live his imperial majesty [h] Don *Alonso*. This ceremony concluded, the emperor, with all who were present returned to his palace, where a sumptuous feast was prepared (P). WE

[f] Chron. var. antiq. [g] Chron. ADEFONS Imperat. [h] MARIANA Historia general de Espana, lib. x. FERRERAS Historia de Espana, p. v. sect. xi. MAYERNE TURQUET Histoire general d'Espagne, liv. ix.

(P) In the assembly of the lords and prelates, which, upon this occasion, is not stiled a council, probably because religious matters were not the subject of their deliberations, the following laws were made, or rather declared, for most of them seem to have been laws before, and to have received only on this occasion the sanction of the emperor, that his subjects might have the greater reverence for his new title (1).

(1) *Ferreras Historia de Espana, p. v. sect. xii. Chron. Adefons Imperat.*

1. The

*The mo-
narchs of
Navarre
and Por-
tugal enter
into a
league a-
gainst the
emperor.*
WE might reasonably, from the number of his vassals, and the good-will expressed to him on all sides, more especially in regard to the last mentioned action, conclude, that no prince had less to fear from his Christian neighbours : but such is the nature of men, and too frequently of princes, that they oppress those that are weaker, and envy such as are stronger. Upon this principle it was that Don *Garcia Ramirez,* king of *Navarre,* and Don *Alonso Enriquez,* sovereign of *Portugal,* entered into a league against the emperor; the cause of which was, that the former was desirous of recovering the country of *Rioja,* and the latter was unwilling to render homage to the emperor for his dominions, by whom it was required. In virtue of this league, Don *Alonso* made an irruption into *Galicia,* where he made himself master of *Tuy* [1], and some other places, partly by force and partly by corrupting the governors, who were entrusted with *Turon*

[1] RODERIC TOLETAN de reb. Hispan. lib. vii. Chron. ADEFONS Imperat.

1. The people shall henceforward be governed in the same manner, and enjoy the same privileges, as in the reign of Don *Alonso* VI. grandfather to the reigning emperor. 2. Churches and private persons shall be restored to whatever estates they can prove any legal title to. 3. All towns and villages that have been destroyed during the late troubles shall be rebuilt, and repeopled, and the country round them cultivated, by planting vines and fruit-trees. 4. The judges shall every where punish, with such severity as the law requires, malefactors of all kinds, without respect of persons. 5. Sorcerers and magicians shall be punished with death. 6. The alcaydes of *Toledo,* and other frontier provinces, shall annually make excursions into the enemy's territories, and waste the country with fire and sword. These

were all the laws they passed; and it appears to have been the meaning of this last to oblige the *Moors* to put themselves under the king's protection, or at least it had this consequence; for we find that, upon an expedition of this nature, about five years before, a certain *Moor* of great quality, whose name was *Zafadola,* descended from the antient kings of *Cordova,* and lord of *Rhoda,* in the province of *La Mancha,* submitted himself to Don *Alonso,* put that place into his hands with its dependencies, and, retiring with his family into the kingdom of *Toledo,* had very considerable grants of castles, houses, and arable lands, for his support ; and as his castle of *Rhoda* was given by the king to his new born son, it fixes the birth of the Infant Don *Sancho* to *Anno Domini* 1131 (2), which is of some importance.

(2) *Annal Toletan. Chron. Adefons Imperat. Roderic Toletan Hist. Arabum.*

and

and *Limmia.* The emperor sent an army into *Galicia,* commanded by some of the prime nobility, to expel the enemy, but they were unfortunately defeated. As for the king of *Navarre,* the emperor was no sooner informed of his behaviour, than he entered his dominions in person, at the head of a numerous army, and wasted his country, without being able to bring him to a battle [k]. In this expedition he had a conference with the king of *Arragon,* to whom he restored the city of *Saragossa,* upon condition that he should hold it as his feudatory, and do him homage, which he very willingly accepted [l].

ABOUT this time the emperor, upon some recollection of old distaste, dismissed Don *Roderic Gonçales* from his employments [m], who thereupon went to the *Holy Land* (Q), and

Don Alón-
so Enri-
ques of
ques of

---

[k] LUCÆ Tudensis Chron.   [l] Chron. ADEFONS Imperat.
[m] RODERIC TOLETAN de reb. Hispan. lib. vii.

(Q) There does not appear the least trace of the motives which induced the emperor to entertain fresh suspicions of Don *Roderic Gonçales.* All we know of the matter is, that this great man no sooner perceived it, than he demanded leave to take the cross, as was common in those days, in order to make an expedition into the *Holy Land,* which was willingly granted him; and he went accordingly, accompanied by such as were either desirous of making that expedition, or inclined to follow his fortunes. He behaved in the wars against the *Saracens* with the same courage and conduct as against the *Moors;* built a fort near *Ascalon,* which he fortified, and provided with every thing necessary for its defence; but being seized with a desire of seeing his native country, he made a present of it to the knights templars. On his return to *Spain,* he went first to the court of Don *Raymond,* count of *Barcelona,* afterwards to that of Don *Garcia,* king of *Navarre;* but it does not appear that he ever thought of entering *Castile;* from whence we may conclude, that he remained still under the emperor's displeasure. We have a farther proof of this, from his withdrawing out of *Navarre,* in order to put himself under the protection of *Aben Gama,* viceroy for the king of *Morocco,* in *Spain,* who resided at *Valentia,* where he was received with all possible testimonies of kindness and respect. Yet he did not continue long in this place; for the *Moors,* for what reason it is impossible to guess, gave him a poisonous draught, which threw him into a leprosy; and being by this means convinced that he could be no where safe in *Spain,* he returned again into the *Holy Land,* and there ended his days. A memorable instance of the danger in digressing once from the right path, which it is extreme difficult, if not impossible, to recover (1).

---

(1) *Chron. Adefons Imperat.*

appointed

Portugal *appointed Don* Roderic Fernandez *to the government of* To-
demands *ledo* in his stead; who, at the first entrance into his govern-
peace of ment, had the good fortune not only to make a successful in-
the empe- road in the territory of *Cordova*, but likewise to beat the
ror, which king *Texefin-ben-Ali,* who attacked him in his return to *To-*
is granted. *ledo*, which gained him great reputation [n]. The next year
A. D. the emperor went in person against the *Portuguese*, and sent
1137. three of his principal nobility, with a numerous army, to
make head against the king of *Navarre*. As his army was
more numerous than that of his antagonist, he entered the
kingdom of *Portugal*, and wasted the country with fire and
sword [o]. On the other hand, Don *Alonso Enriquez*, who
acted on the defensive, being extremely chagrined to see his
dominions ruined, and his subjects oppressed, fought, with
the utmost diligence, how he might be revenged; and perceiving that Don *Ramiro*, who commanded a great detachment of the emperor's army, was at too great a distance to
be succoured, he threw himself and his forces between him
and the emperor, and, attacking him with great fury, destroyed most of his troops, and made him prisoner [p]. This
check served only to irritate the emperor, who endeavoured
to force his cousin Don *Alonso* to a battle; who, upon intelligence received, that the *Moors* had made an irruption on
the other side of *Portugal*, was prevailed upon by his nobility
to send a deputation to the emperor, who received them very
obligingly; telling the ambassadors there would not be much
difficulty in making a peace; towards which there required
no more than restoring the places and setting the prisoners
at liberty taken on both sides. This was done on the part
of the *Portuguese* at the return of their deputies, and immediately after by the emperor, who then had an interview
with his cousin, and parted so good friends, that Don *Alonso
Enriquez* thought proper to order the counts Don *Gomez
Nugnez* and Don *Rodrigo Velloso*, who had given rise to the
war, by betraying their master, to quit his dominions [q];
the common reward of traitors; which affected the former
so much, that he retired into *France*, and became a monk;
as for the second, he went to the emperor, and expressed
so much sorrow for his offence, that he forgave him,
and restored him to his employments [r]. Don *Roderic Fer-*
nandez made another successful expedition against the *Moors*
this year; and the emperor's brother-in-law, Don *Raymand,*

---

[n] Roderic Toletan Hist. Arabum.   [o] Chron var. antiq.
[p] Lucæ Tudensis Chron. Chron. Adefons Imperat.   [r] Roderic Toletan de reb. Hispan. lib. viii.   [r] Chron. Adef.
Imperat.

obtaining

obtaining the crown of *Arragon* by the marriage of the heirefs, prevailed upon the emperor to reftore the places he had taken from that kingdom [s].

THE war on the fide of *Toledo* continued with pretty equal fortune on both fides; but the emperor, finding himfelf at eafe from his neighbours, refolved to make a brifk effort with all his forces againft the infidels, which he accordingly did, by entering *Andaluzia* with a numerous army. A confiderable detachment having paffed the river without the emperor's leave, out of a defire to pillage, there fell fo heavy a rain in the night, that they found the ftream altogether impaffable; and the very next day were furrounded by the enemy, and cut to pieces in fight of the emperor and his army, only one efcaping by his great fkill in fwimming [t]. This accident fo difgufted the emperor, that he returned into his own dominions, refolving to conclude the campaign with reducing *Coria*, a place of importance, and which, being in the hands of the *Moors*, gave him a great deal of trouble. He befieged it accordingly; but the place being very well defended, and Don *Roderic Martinez*, governor of *Leon*, and one of the emperor's principal generals, being killed upon the fpot, the emperor caufed the fiege to be raifed; and having beftowed upon Don *Oforio*, the fon of Don *Roderic*, his father's employments, he returned to *Leon* [n], by no means pleafed with the operations of the year, and refolved to employ the winter in preparing for a new expedition in the fpring; to which he was not a little excited, by having advice, that *Texefin-ben-Ali* had caufed the beft part of the Chriftians, inhabiting in his dominions, to be tranfported to *Africa* [w], where he employed them as foldiers, being well acquainted with their valour, and having no reafon to diftruft their fidelity, when fighting againft us well as for infidels; which afflicted the emperor exceedingly; who knew well enough, that the principal motive to this ill ufage was the inclination they had fhewn of becoming his fubjects. He took pains, therefore, to fettle, in the beft manner he was able, all difputes with his neighbours, and even to terminate fuch as had broke out between themfelves; from a perfuafion, that when they had no other quarrel on their hands, they would naturally employ their arms againft the *Moors*; and that, whether defigned or not, thefe would be in effect fo many diverfions in his favour. His fcheme, as it was well laid, was prudently and happily executed; fo that in the fpring he found himfelf at full liberty

The emperor turns his arms upon the Moors, but with indifferent fuccefs.

A. D. 1138.

---

[s] Chron. var. antiq. [t] RODERIC TOLETAN Hift. Arabum. [u] LUCÆ Tudenfis Chronicon. RODERIC TOLET. de reb. Hifpan. lib. vii. [w] RODERIC TOLET. Hift. Arabum.

to purfue the plan of operation he had laid down, without any apprehenfion of being compelled by new difturbances to alter his meafures, which had hitherto been the principal caufe that his arms had not made fo great an impreffion upon the infidels, as, from the fuperiority of his power, in comparifon with that of his predeceffors, he had juft reafon to expect. He certainly reafoned very right upon this head ; and if he could have prevailed upon the fovereigns of *Navarre,* *Arragon,* and *Portugal,* to have adopted the fame principles, and to have purfued them fteadily, the *Moors* had been much fooner driven out of *Spain* than they were.

He deter-
mines to
reduce the
caftle of
Oreja on
the fron-
tiers of
Caftile.

THE infidels had a very ftrong fortrefs at *Oreja,* which lay to the eaft of *Toledo,* from whence they made frequent irruptions into the territories of that city ; and the year before, the Chriftians, not without great difficulty, had erected the caftle of *Azeca,* in order to be a check upon this place; but it feems this did not prove fo effectual a remedy as the nature of the cafe required : the emperor, therefore, refolved to open the campaign with the reduction of *Oreja* [x], that his fubjects might be once for all delivered from this thorn in their fides, with which hitherto they had been continually troubled. Accordingly, Don *Roderic Fernandez* invefted it with the forces under his command, in the month of *April,* and the emperor joined him foon after with a very numerous and well appointed army. The alcayd of *Oreja* was *Ali,* efteemed the beft officer in the *Moorifh* fervice ; he had a very powerful garrifon, and the place was well fupplied with every thing neceffary ; fo that, as his countrymen expected, he made a very brave and well conducted defence [y]. At length he gave notice to the alcayds of *Cordova* and *Seville,* that their out-works were ruined, his garrifon much diminifhed, his magazines almoft exhaufted, and that, therefore, they muft fend him an effectual and fpeedy relief, if they expected he fhould keep the place. The alcaydes began to amafs provifions, and to raife forces, at the fame time that they gave intelligence to *Texefin-ben-Ali,* who was at *Marocco,* of the fituation things were in, and the apprehenfions they were under ; upon which he fent over a frefh body of troops, and ordered them to leave nothing untried to force the emperor to raife the fiege [z]. Upon the junction of their forces, the alcaydes found themfelves at the head of thirty thoufand good troops, with a vaft train of waggons, laden with provifions and other neceffaries. They refolved to march di-

[x] RODERIC TOLETAN de reb. Hifpan. lib. vii. LUCÆ Tudenfis Chronicon. [y] RODERIC TOLET. Hift. Arabum. [z] Chron. var. antiq.

rectly towards *Oreja,* and were so confident of success, that they sent instructions to *Ali* to make a vigorous sally upon the Christians when they should begin to raise the siege [a]. The emperor, who had perfect intelligence of all their measures, determined to wait for them, and to give them battle, if they persisted in their design, or to suffer them to besiege *Toledo,* if they proposed by that method to divert him from his enterprize.

IN their march, the *Moors* took a small fort or two, and at length insulted the castle of *Azeca,* where the empress lay with the ladies of her court [b]. She sent a message to the alcaydes, that the emperor waited for them at *Oreja,* which was the proper place for men of their birth and breeding to signalize themselves, and that little honour was to be got by disturbing a number of helpless women [c]. The *Moorish* generals excused themselves for their ignorance, and desired to have the honour of paying their respects to her imperial majesty. The empress, to gratify them, appeared upon the ramparts with all her ladies, richly dressed; and the alcaydes, at the head of their troops, in order of battle, having paid her their military salute, retired without giving her any farther disturbance. They tried every method they could devise to draw the emperor out of his lines, or to force a passage for their succours, but to no purpose. At last *Ali* sent to the emperor, and offered to surrender, if he was not relieved in a month, upon condition that his garrison marched out with the honours of war, and was escorted safely to *Calatrava.* The emperor accepted the proposal, and gave him leave to send to the king his master, who returned for answer, that he might surrender when he would, for that it was not in his power to relieve him [d]. When they came to march out, himself and garrison were perfect skeletons; the emperor received them very kindly, entertained *Ali* at his own expence, and ordered the garrison to be distributed through the camp. The alcayde expressed his surprise, and desired he might march to *Calatrava.* The emperor bid him be in no pain, that the articles should be punctually executed, but that he could not part with so many brave men in such a condition; and, after feasting them for a month, sent them back very well satisfied with their usage [e]. The fortress of *Oreja* was surrendered in the month of *October;* and, after the castle was thoroughly

Reduces it after an obstinate resistance, in spite of all the power of the Moors.

[a] LUCÆ Tudensis Chron. Chron. ADEFONSI Imperat. [b] MARIANA Historia general de España, lib. x. FERRERAS Historia de España, p. v. sect. xi. [c] RODERIC TOLETAN de reb. Hispan. lib. vii. Chron. ADEFONSI Imperat. [d] RODERIC TOLETAN Hist. Arabum. [e] Chron. var. antiq.

repaired, and a good garrison put into it, the emperor marched
in triumph to *Toledo*; where, after singing *Te Deum*, and receiving the benediction of the archbishop, he went to his palace, and sent for the empress and her court, extremely well
satisfied with the success of this campaign [f] (R).

Don Gar-
cia, king
of Na-
varre, de-
fends him-
self from
the empe-
ror and the
king of
Arragon.

RAYMOND, prince of *Arragon*, and count of *Barcelona*,
relying on his near relation to the emperor, endeavoured to
engage him in a league against the king of *Navarre*, against
whom the emperor wanted not some just causes of complaint ;
and, therefore, what the prince of *Arragon* desired was easily
brought about, who made no question now that he should be
able to reunite the kingdoms of *Navarre* and *Arragon*, giving
some places that lay convenient to the emperor for his af-
sistance [s]. But Don *Garcia* very judiciously set on foot a
negotiation with the young king of *Portugal*, by which he
was brought to discern how great his danger must be by any
accession of power to the emperor, which engaged him to
enter into a defensive alliance with Don *Garcia*. As soon,
therefore, as the season would permit, the emperor and the
prince of *Arragon* took the field ; Don *Garcia* was sensible,
that his forces were by no means sufficient to act against those
of the two princes joined together; from whence he very
wisely concluded, that it was his business to fight them separately, or rather to fight the weakest. Accordingly, having
put a strong garrison into *Pampeluna* [h], he left the rest of his
dominions to the emperor's mercy, marching with the best
body of troops he could assemble against the prince of *Arra-*

[f] LUCÆ Tudensis Chronicon. RODERIC TOLETAN Hist. Arabum. [s] Chron. var. antiq. [h] RODERIC TOLETAN de
reb. Hispan. lib. vii. Chron. ADEFONS Imperat.

(R) The emperor, after the
taking the fortress of *Oreja*, returned, as we have said in the
text, in triumph to *Toledo*;
where, as soon as the rejoicings
for his success were over, he
applied himself during the winter to regulate the concerns of
his civil government, to redress
grievances, to determine difputes amongst his nobility, and
to make the proper provisions
for settling and securing his conquests. We mention this once
for all in a note, that the reader
may form some notion of this
monarch's administration, who,
at the three great feasts, but
more especially in the winter,
caused his prelates and nobility
to resort to his court ; where, by
his authority always, and very
often in his presence, they heard
and decided differences of every
kind ; and, when this was over,
took the emperor's instructions
with regard to the particular
trusts reposed in them, as to
their respective governments (1).

(1) *Chron. Adefons. Imperat.*

gon.

gon. The emperor, meeting with no refiftance at *Navarre*, advanced to *Pampeluna*, and befieged it; but the place was fcarce invefted, before he had the news of Don *Garcia*'s having beat the prince of *Arragon* [1]; and this induced him to raife the fiege to give battle to the victorious army. Don *Garcia*, however, with his ufual prudence, quitted the field, and threw his troops into the adjacent fortreffes; upon which the emperor faw himfelf obliged to retire into his own dominions, and to defer the profecution of the war to the next feafon [k]. In the mean time Don *Garcia* took pains to recruit and ftrengthen his army in fuch a manner, that he quickly found it in his power to give the emperor battle; but upon that monarch's entering his dominions, the nobility and prelates on both fides interpofed fo effectually, that a peace was concluded [l]. The emperor's eldeft fon, Don *Sancho*, efpoufed the Infanta Donna *Blanca*, daughter to the king of *Navarre*; and, as this princefs was very young, fhe was fent to be educated at the court of *Caftile* [m]. The king of *Portugal* alfo, who had been extremely rudely handled in his invafion of *Galicia*, judged it expedient to make peace likewife; and by this means the ambitious fcheme of the prince of *Arragon* was entirely defeated, and the peace of the Chriftians in *Spain* reftored [n].

A. D. 1140.

THE war with the *Moors* continued all this time as hot as ever, and the alcaydes, *Aben-Azuel*, of *Cordova*, and *Aben-Çeta*, of *Seville*, having united their forces, refolved to undertake an expedition of importance; the confequences of which might prove more favourable to their nation than thofe prædatory excurfions that were commonly the bufinefs of their fummers. Accordingly, having taken all the precautions that they thought neceffary, and affembled the utmoft force of their refpective governments, they directed their march, with as much fecrefy as poffible, towards the fortrefs of *Mora*, between the rivers *Guadiana* and *Tayo*, and at no great diftance from *Toledo*; a place of infinite importance, as it covered the Chriftian frontier on one fide, and opened a paffage into the *Moorifh* territories on the other; where the Chriftian governor, *Muna Alonfo*, through an inexcufable indolence, was fo ill provided, that the place was eafily furprifed, and himfelf, with fome difficulty, made his efcape to *Toledo* [o]. The

The Moors, by a well executed expedition, take the fortrefs of Mora.

[i] Lucæ Tudenfis Chron. Ferreras Hift. de Efpana, p. v. fect. xi. [k] Chron. var. antiq. [l] Roderic Toletan de reb. Hifpan. lib. vii. Lucæ Tudenfis Chron. [m] Mariana Hiftoria general de Efpana, lib. x. Ferreras Hiftoria de Efpana, p. v. fect. xi. Mayerne Turquet Hiftoire general d'Efpagne, liv. ix. [n] Lucæ Tudenfis Chron. Chron. Adefons Imperat. [o] Roderic Toletan Hift. Arabum.

Moors inftantly furnifhed it with all things neceffary, and a numerous garrifon; and, having recommended the fupport of it to the alcayde of *Calatrava*, to whom it ferved as a barrier, returned home in triumph [p]. The emperor was very much affected at this news, and therefore fent immediate orders to build a new fortrefs over-againft that of *Mora*, and to place in it a good garrifon, under the command of Don *Martin Fernandez*, to which new caftle they gave the name

A. D. of *Piedra Negra*, or the Black Stone [q]. As for *Muna Alonfo*
1141. he was fo much afhamed of his late difgrace, that, putting himfelf at the head of fuch forces as his friends were content to furnifh him with, he made repeated inroads, in order to recover his reputation; and the emperor, who was naturally of a mild difpofition, did not fend for him to reprimand him as he expected for fo capital an omiffion, but willingly allowed him leifure to repair his fortune [r].

Coria, *af-* As the *Moors* had lately received great reinforcements,
ter a fhort and feemed to threaten fome expedition of importance, the
fiege, is re- emperor, being firft well apprifed of the ftrength of his fron-
covered tiers, ordered Don *Roderic Fernandez* to make an excurfion
from the from *Toledo*, and with a good body of troops that were under
Moors *by* his own command, and were intended for the war in *Portu-*
the empe- *gal*, fuddenly invefted *Coria*, which hitherto had defended it-
ror. felf againft all attempts by the ftrength of its fituation, and the care taken to keep the garrifon always complete, and in good order. It was for this reafon, perhaps, that they were lefs alarmed than otherwife they would have been at the news of this fiege, which the emperor profecuted with great judgment; for, having made a breach on one fide of the place, and finding the enemy numerous, and bent upon an obftinate defence, he remained quiet till famine had brought the *Moors* fo low, that they offered to capitulate, in cafe they were not relieved in thirty days; to which he confented [s]. But the governor of *Toledo*, being informed of the fituation that things were in, made his irruption juft at this juncture, which put it out of the power of the alcaydes of *Cordova* and *Seville* to fuccour the place; which, at the clofe therefore of the thirty days, furrendered; upon which the emperor caufed the breach to be immediately repaired, filled the magazines with provifions of all forts, and, leaving a ftrong gar-

A. D. rifon, returned to *Salamanca*; and then fending for *Muna*
1142. *Alonfo*, commended his fervices highly, and declared him

[p] Chron. var. antiq. [q] RODERIC TOLETAN de reb. Hifpan. lib. vii. Chron. ADEFONS Imperat. [r] RODERIC TOLETAN Hift. Arabum. LUCÆ Tudenfis Chron. [s] Chron. var. antiq.

lieutenant

lieutenant to Don *Roderic Fernandez* in the government of
the city and kingdom of *Toledo* [t], rewarding his good, and
passing by the ill consequences that had attended his imprudent behaviour.

THIS promotion inspired Don *Muna Alonso* with so warm *Irruption*
a desire of signalizing his gratitude, as well as his courage, *into the*
that, on the first of *March*, in the ensuing year, he made an *Moorish*
incursion, with nine hundred horse and a thousand foot, into *territories*,
the territory of *Cordova*, where his troops acquired a great *by Don*
booty [u]. But the alcaydes, *Aben-Azuel* and *Aben Ceta*, in- *Muna A-*
tending an expedition of the same kind, had just joined their *lonso*,
forces, when they had intelligence of Don *Muna Alonso's* re- *with great*
treat, whom they followed with such diligence, that they *success.*
quickly came up with him, and surrounded his troops, laden
with booty, with forces far superior to those which he commanded. Don *Muna* divided his forces into two battalions,
and, having recommended themselves to the protection of
God, began the fight with great courage, which they prosecuted with such intrepidity, that the *Moors* were not only
beaten, but both the alcaydes slain, and their heads carried
in triumph to *Toledo*; where, after they had for some time
been placed on the palace, the empress caused them to be
taken down, and sent to *Cordova* in a silver box, that they
might be restored to their wives, in remembrance of the civility she had received from those alcaydes in their life-time [w].

THE emperor, having assembled a numerous army, and *He is in-*
being on the point of making an irruption into the enemies *trusted*
country, sent orders to *Muna Alonso* and to *Martin Fernandez* *with Mar-*
to put themselves, with a strong corps of troops, into the *tin Fer-*
fortress of *Piedra Negra*, with strict injunctions to cover his *nandez to*
own territory from the incursions of the enemy, and to hinder *block up*
them from making any additions to the castle of *Mora*. On *the Moors*
the other hand, *Texefin-ben-Ali*, monarch of the *Moors* in *in the cas-*
Africa and *Spain*, had sent express orders for providing the *tle of Mo-*
fortress of *Mora* with every thing necessary, and for augment- *ra.*
ing the works of that place; with the performance of which
service, his viceroy charged *Farax-Adali*, alcayde of *Calatrava*, who, after making all the preparations necessary for
that purpose, marched towards *Mora* with a numerous body
of troops. *Muna Alonso*, in pursuance of the emperor's instructions, issued with a small troop of horse from the fortress
of *Piedra Negra* to scour the country, and by accident picked

---

[t] RODERIC TOLETAN, Hist. Arabum. Chron. ADEFONS Im-
perat.   [u] RODERIC TOLETAN, de reb. Hispan. l vii. LUCÆ
Tudenfis Chron.   [w] RODERIC TOLETAN Hist. Arabum.
Chron. ADEFONS Imperat.

up a ftraggling *Moor*, who gave him intelligence of the alcayde's approach.   Upon this, advancing to an eminence,
he met the van of the *Moorifh* troops, and charged them fo
brifkly, that he drove them back in confufion upon their
main body; of which, when he had taken view, he returned
to the fortrefs to confult with his collegue.   On his report,
Martin Fernandez propofed marching out and meeting them
in the field; to which *Muna Alonfo* readily confented.   When
they had proceeded as far as the wells of *Agador*, they found
the *Moors* drawn up in good order, whom they attacked with
great fpirit, and were received with much firmnefs.   The
difpute was fharp, and by no means decifive, both parties
finding it requifite to retire in order to gain a little repofe.
But *Muna Alonfo*, perceiving that his collegue was wounded,
advifed him to retire to *Piedra Negra*, with fuch as were in
the fame condition, or had loft their horfes, to take the neceffary meafures for the fecurity of the place; while he,
with the remainder of their forces, fhould endeavour to give
a check to the *Moors*, in cafe they attempted to attack it by
furprife [x].

After a
moft gal-
lant de-
fence is
killed in an
action by
the infidels.
A D.
1143.

FARAX ADALI, having received a reinforcement, marched
fpeedily to find out the Chriftians; who, perceiving their
great inequality in number, marched to an eminence, called
Pegna de el Zeirbo, where they might have fome advantage
of ground.   The *Moors* quickly invefted them; and, after
harraffing them with diftant attacks, at length charged them
on all fides with fuch fury, that, being already weakened and
fatigued, they were quickly broken and cut to pieces; which,
however, had not happened fo foon, if their gallant leader
had not been flain at the beginning of the general attack.
The alcayde, as foon as his body was found, caufed his head,
his left arm, and his right leg, to be cut off, and fent to the
widow of *Aben-Azuel* at *Cordova*, who was to tranfmit them
to the widow of *Aben-Ceta* at *Seville*, by whom they were to
be conducted to the king of *Morocco*; the reft of the dif-
membered body he reftored to the Chriftians; who, with
forrowful folemnity, caufed it to be buried at *Toledo*.   The
emperor received this unwelcome news at *Talavera*, to which
city he was returned after a glorious campaign; which, however, did not confole him for the lofs of this gallant commander, which he refolved to revenge, and repair the enfuing year, and gave orders that all his forces fhould affemble
for that purpofe early in the fpring [y].

The king
of Na-

AT the time Don *Alonfo* deliberated on the proper object
of this expedition, his fubjects complained to him fo loudly

[x] Annal. TOLETAN.   [y] Chron. APELON. Imperat.

of the disturbance given them by the *Moorish* garrison in the varre*m.r-*
fortress of *Mora*, that he determined with himself to pluck *ries Donna*
that thorn from their sides before he made an irruption into Urraca,
the enemies country; and, having accordingly invested the *natural*
place. he proceeded to the siege in form; but the garrison, *daughter*
perceiving little or no hopes of relief, thought proper, by an *to the em-*
early capitulation, to procure for themselves the best terms they *peror.*
could; by which means this place came again into the hands
of the Christians [z]. It was, in all probability, some intelligence
that the emperor received during the time he was in camp
before *Mora*, which induced him to alter his plan, and to assemble all the forces of *Castile* and *Leon* towards the middle of
the month of *May*, in the neighbourhood of *Najara*, with a
full resolution to reduce the monarch of *Navarre* so low, that
it should not be in his power to disturb him, and his brother
the prince of *Arragon* in haste. But when he was on the point
of entering that king's dominions, Don *Garcia* sent some of
his prelates and nobility to inform him of his great respect for
his person, his sincere desire to live with him upon good
terms for the future, and his inclination to marry Donna
Urraca, the emperor's natural daughter [a]. This proposition
disarmed the emperor, who, as he had nothing in view but
to be quiet on that side, readily granted all he asked; and,
having dismissed his troops, returned to *Leon*; to which city
came the empress Donna *Berengara*, with most of the nobility of the two kingdoms of *Castile* and *Leon*; thither also
came the princess Donna *Sancha*, the emperor's sister, bringing with her her beautiful niece Donna *Urraca*; and soon
after arrived Don *Garcia*, attended by the flower of his nobility [b]. The marriage was celebrated with all imaginable
pomp and magnificence, on the 24th of *June*; the emperor
gave his daughter a large sum of money, made very rich
presents to the king of *Navarre* and his nobility at their departure, and sent several persons of the first quality to accompany them to *Pampeluna* [c]. These rejoicings over, the emperor returned to *Toledo*; and, in the month of *September*,
made an irruption with all his forces into the *Moorish* territories, ravaged the country as far as *Granada* and the sea
coast, and returned with an immense booty, and a prodigious number of slaves, to his capital, in the beginning of
winter [d].

A. D.
1144.

[z] RODERIC TOLETAN Hist. Arabum.   [a] RODERIC TOLETAN
de reb. Hisp. lib. vii. Chron. ADEFONS Imperat. [b] LUCÆ Tudensis
Chron. Annal. TOLETAN. RODERIC TOLETAN de reb. Hispan.
lib. vii.   [c] Chron. ADEFONS Imperat. LUCÆ Tudensi Chron.
[d] RODERIC TOLETAN Hist. Arabum.

THE

Civil
wars, and
great re-
volutions,
amongst
the Moors
settled in
Spain.

THE affairs of the *Moors* at this time were in the utmost confusion ; for *Texesin-ben-Ali* found himself so distressed in *Africa*, that instead of yielding his subjects in *Spain* any assistance, he was continually requiring such supplies from thence as exhausted them; insomuch that the *Spanish Moors* determined at length to throw off the yoke, and to render themselves once more independent. It was with this view that they demanded of the emperor Don *Alonso*, *Zafadola* his vassal, on account of his being descended from their antient kings of *Cordova*, to whom they joined *Mohammed*, who was sprung from the same blood, and put them in possession of a great part of the country [e] ; while the viceroy, *Aben-Gama*, could only preserve the castle of *Cordova*, the city of *Seville*, and two or three other places ; and soon after one *Haben-Fandi*, a pretended saint, seized *Cordova* and *Calatrava* ; while *Jaen*, *Granada*, and *Mercia*, remained to *Zafadola* ; *Seville*, and the rest of *Andaluzia*, to *Aben-Gama* ; *Mortala*, *Valentia*, *Merida*, and *Tortosa*, to *Mohammed* [f]. *Zafadola*, not contented with his share, requested assistance from the emperor, who sent three of his generals with a considerable body of forces to his aid, with whom, after they had done him much service, he quarrelled, and attacked them with his *Moorish* troops, but was quickly beaten and taken prisoner ; and the soldiers, not being able to agree whose prisoner he was, killed him to put an end to the dispute [g]. *Aben-Gama* took this opportunity to recover *Cordova*, which he did, and obliged *Haben-Fandi* to fly to *Andujar*, and soon after delivered it up to the emperor Don *Alonso*, from whom he received it again as his feudatory. That monarch also took the advantage of these troubles to besiege and render himself master of *Calatrava*, a place of great importance ; and by which he acquired the command of the best part of *La Mancha*, which removed the *Moors* so much farther from *Toledo*.

A. D.
1147.

By the as-
sistance of
the
French,
Genoese,
and Pisans,
the empe-
ror takes
Almeria.

THE distractions of the *Moors* induced the emperor to hope for success in an expedition of still greater importance, which was the reduction of the city, fortress, and port of *Almeria*, at that time by much the strongest place the *Moors* had in *Spain* ; from whence their privateers, which were exceedingly numerous, not only troubled the coasts inhabited by their Christian neighbours, but gave equal disturbance to the maritime provinces of *France*, *Italy*, and the adjacent islands. But for the reduction of this place a maritime force, superior to that of the enemy, was absolutely necessary,

[e] LUCÆ Tudensis Chronicon. RODERIC TOLETAN Hist. Arabum. [f] Chron. var. antiq. [g] RODERIC TOLETAN Hist. Arabum.

which

which induced him to negotiate fupplies from his brother-in-law the prince of *Arragon*, the duke of *Montpellier*, the republic of *Genoa* and *Pifa*, who gave him the ftrongeft affurances, that if he took the proper meafures for invefting the place by land, their fquadron fhould not fail to block up the port by the firft of *Auguft* [h]; and Don *Alonfo*, relying on this engagement, was no fooner reinforced by the troops of *Navarre*, than he entered upon this great undertaking with all the forces of his dominions, and invaded *Andaluzia* in the beginning of the month of *May* (S). He firft of all reduced *Banos* and *Cazlona*, and then proceeded to inveft *Baeca*, which made a vigorous defence, and did not furrender before the middle of *June*. He put into the place a ftrong garrifon, commanded by Don *Manrique de Lara*, and, marching thro' the territories of the *Moors*, invefted *Almeria* on the land fide completely by the firft of *Auguft*, his confederates, with four

[h] Chron. var. antiq.

(S) It is fuppofed by fome, that the place, fince called *Almeria*, rofe upon the ruins of the antient town of *Abdera*; though others conceive, that *Abdera* lay fomewhat farther to the eaft (1). It lies within a fine bay, at the mouth of a pleafant river, clofe by the fea fhore, and was in thofe days all that it is faid to be in the text; and, upon its reduction under the power of the Chriftians, became a bifhoprick; whereas at prefent it is very little better than a village, but indifferently inhabited, and has nothing to teftify fo much as the probability of its former greatnefs, except it be certain circumftances that cannot be loft or effaced even by the indolence of the *Spaniards*. What thefe are, an ingenious countryman of our own thus elegantly defcribes (2): "Its climate," fays he, "is fo peculiarly bleffed, "that one really wants words "to exprefs its charms and ex-"cellence. Its fields and meads "are covered with flowers all "the year round; they are a-"dorned alfo with palms, myr-"tles, plane trees, oranges, and "olives; and the mountains "and promontories near it are "as noted for their producing a "great variety of precious "ftones, infomuch that the next "promontory to it is called the "*Cape of Gates*, which is a cor-"ruption from the word agates, "the hills thereabouts abound-"ing in that fort of precious "ftones, as well as in emeralds "and amethyfts, granates, or "coarfe rubies, and extreme curi-"ous alabafter in the mountain "of *Filaures*. And what is alfo "very fingular, there is a con-"fiderable river that runs di-"rectly under the town, and "then immediately difcharges "itfelf into the fea." Such is the fcite of *Almeria*, which was once fo ftrong and magnificent a place.

(1) *Indic. Rer. ab Aragon. Regib. geft. lib. i. Portugal, by Udal ap Rhys, p. 172.*

(2) *Tour through Spain and*

fine

fine squadrons, lying before the bay. The city being strongly fortified, having a noble castle, a numerous garrison, and being excellently provided with every thing necessary, made a gallant and glorious defence; but at length the emperor took it by storm, on the 17th of *October* [l], putting all the inhabitants to the sword who were found in arms; after which the victor distributed the best part of the plunder amongst his allies, whom he sent away thoroughly satisfied; and the *Genoese* particularly, who acquired here that emerald vessel [k], which still remains in their treasury, and is esteemed invaluable; yet the emperor, who remained master of the place, and delivered his subjects from the continual apprehensions they were under from this nest of corsairs, was by much the greatest gainer, and very wisely looked upon this campaign as the most glorious, as well as the most advantageous, with which Providence had favoured his arms.

Aben-Gama, the Moorish viceroy, forms a conspiracy against the emperor's life,

THE joy which this important acquisition gave to the Christians, however great, did not at all exceed the sorrow, vexation, and terror, with which the infidels were affected by so great a loss, but more especially *Aben-Gama*, who felt so sensible a regret on this account, that from the apprehension of the consequences that might, or rather must attend it, and despairing of any other method to ballance it, he projected, contrary to his faith and duty, as he was his vassal, against the dictates of honour and the principles of religion, the murder of the emperor [l]. In order to effect this, he threw himself into the strong city of *Jaen*, and sent Don *Alonso* a message with great secresy, that if he would advance towards him with a small body of chosen troops, with as much privacy as possible, he would open the gates, and admit him into the city, as he had done into *Cordova* [m]. The emperor was very near falling into the snare; but some of his nobility, to whom he communicated this proposition, dissuaded him earnestly; so that he sent Don *Manrique de Lara*, with part of his garrison, to demand of the *Moorish* chief the performance of his promise; and he had no sooner admitted that nobleman into *Jaen* than he attempted to secure him, and those who attended him; but the populace, either not understanding his scheme, or fearing the resentment of the emperor, raised a tumult, in which *Aben-Gama* was stabbed [n], and Don *Manrique*, and those who were to have been the

[l] Annal. TOLETAN. Chron. ADEFONS Imperat. [k] RODERIC TOLETAN Hist. Arabum. LUCÆ Tudensis Chron. [l] RODERIC TOLETAN de reb. Hispan. lib. vii. Chron. ADEFONS Imperat. [m] Chron. var. antiq. [n] RODERIC TOLETAN Hist. Arabum.

victims

victims of his treachery, were either permitted to withdraw by the inhabitants, or found means in the midst of this confusion to open a passage for their escape [o]; by which disappointment, and the death of the *Moorish* governor, the disturbances amongst the infidels were very much increased, as in some places there was scarce any form of government left (T).

The death of the empress Berengara, *or* Berenguela, *and disturbances among the* Moors.

The year following began with mourning; for on the third of *February* died the empress Donna *Berengara*, extremely regretted by Don *Alonso* and all his subjects, and her body was interred with all the pomp and ceremony due to her high rank in the apostolic church of *St. James* at *Compostella* [p]. In the beginning of *March* the emperor held the great assembly of estates at *Leon*, where he declared his sons Don *Sancho* and Don *Ferdinand* kings [q], the former of *Castile*, the mountains of *Burgos*, *Biscay*, and *Toledo*; the latter of *Leon*, *Asturias*, and *Galicia*, according to their an-

[o] Chron. Adefons Imperat. Roderic Toletan Hist. Arabum. [p] Roderic Santii Hist. Hispan. Alphonsi a Carthagena reg. Hisp. Anacephalæosis Francisci Taraphæ de reg. Hispaniæ. [q] Chron. var. antiq.

(T) We are assured by some eminent historians, amongst whom we may reckon *Mariana*, that the emperor had received a former specimen of the temper and fidelity of *Aben-Gama*, who, at the time he surrendered *Cordova* into the hands of that prince, suffered him at the instance of Don *Raymond*, archbishop of *Toledo*, to reconsecrate the cathedral, esteemed the largest and finest in the whole kingdom; and this only with a view that he might not leave a garrison behind him, which might have put him under great difficulties. But when the emperor had once lost this opportunity, *Aben-Gama* took care he should not recover it, by repairing the fortifications, and placing there the best part of his forces (1). He had, therefore, good reason to doubt his sincerity at *Jaen*; but as that also was of much importance, the emperor was exceedingly desirous of making the most of these confusions while they lasted: he was very near being made the victim of his own ambition. It is very uncertain how Don *Manuel de Lara*, and those who were with him, escaped, which, the nature of this adventure considered, we cannot think strange. Amongst the singular events, however, attending this enterprize, we may discern, in the death of *Aben-Gama*, that sooner or later fraud becomes fatal to itself; and that he, who is intent upon over-reaching his neighbour, finds himself, when he least expects it, the miserable contriver of his own destruction (2).

(1) *Mariana, Historia general de Espana, lib. x. Imperat. Ferreras, &c.* (2) *Chron. Adefons.*

tient

tient limits; which remarkable event some historians place earlier, and some later; but public inscriptions, and their signatures to privileges and charters by this new title, are the circumstances which have determined us to this date [r]. The new dynasty of *Almohades*, which, after overturning that of the *Almovarides* in *Africa*, had likewise gained most of the places they possessed in *Spain*, and particularly *Cordova*,

A. D.
1149.

treated the few remaining Christians in *Andalusia* according to their bigotted maxims, with unrelenting severity; so that, in a very short space of time, all who worshipped God according to the lights of the Gospel, were either transported to *Africa*, or utterly extirpated; which cruelty, joined with the sending over several bodies of *Moors*, and the known ambition of the new conqueror of *Morocco*, obliged the emperor not to wait till the *Mohammedans* were in a condition to attack him, but to prosecute those expeditions, by which he had hitherto so successfully weakened these implacable enemies [s].

A glorious victory obtained over them by the emperor and Don Garcia.

As soon, therefore, as the assembly of the estates was over, he gave instructions to his principal nobility to make their levies in the winter, and to bring their respective quotas into the neigbourhood of *Toledo* early in the ensuing spring. Count *Manrique*, who commanded the forces of that kingdom, in obedience to the emperor's command, took the field in the beginning of the month of *March*, and was very speedily joined by the king Don *Garcia*, at the head of a chosen body of his forces; the count *Ferdinand Perez de Trava* appeared at the head of the *Galicians*, those of *Asturias* and *Leon* were led by Don *Ramiro Frolaz*, Don *Guitterez Fernandez* was at the head of the *Castilians*, and Don *Ponce* brought the whole strength of the country of *Estremadura* [t]. The emperor put himself at the head of the army as soon as it was assembled, entered the enemy's territories, and proposed to besiege *Cordova*, but received intelligence in his march, that the enemy had formed the like design against *Toledo*; and, upon news of his invasion, were in full march to attack him. Don *Alonso* immediately made the proper dispositions to receive them; and it was not long before the *Moorish* army appeared, and charged the Christians with great fury. Their impetuosity at first occasioned some disorder; but as the troops of Don *Alonso* and Don *Garcia* were men accustomed to service, they quickly repaired this disaster; and perceiving that the enemy began to

[r] Ferreras Historia de Espana, P. v. §. 12.   [s] Roderic Toletan Hist, Arabum.   Annal. Toletan.   [t] Chron. Adefons Imperat.

relent,

relent, attacked them in their turn on all sides with such firmness and intrepidity, that the *Moors* were quickly broke, and those in the rear began a precipitate retreat towards *Cordova* [u]. The emperor and the king of *Navarre* pursued them so vigorously, that the whole army was obliged to have recourse to the same measure, and, not without very great loss, retired into that city, which the Christians quickly invested. But the emperor, perceiving that the siege would be long and bloody, and that when it was over his forces would not be in a condition to undertake any thing of importance, and perhaps find it no easy matter to preserve the place, he very prudently raised the siege [w]. He then marched to *Jaen*, which was in no condition to resist so great a force, plundered it [x], and would have proceeded to *Seville*, if the *French*, who had promised to send him a fleet to assist him in the reduction of that city, had not obliged him to put an end to a campaign already sufficiently glorious. At his return to *Toledo*, he found the archbishop, Don *Raymond*, dead, who was succeeded by Don *John*; and on the 21st of *November*, the same year, Don *Garcia*, king of *Navarre*, ended his life at *Pampeluna*, soon after his return thither, to the great regret of his father-in-law [y].

A. D. 1150.

In the beginning of the ensuing year the emperor caused great preparations to be made for solemnizing the marriage, long before concluded, of his son the Infant Don *Sancho* with the Infanta Donna *Blanca*, daughter to the deceased, and sister to the reigning, king of *Navarre*; which was accordingly performed at *Najara* on the twenty-fourth of *February* [z], with very great magnificence. At the same time this marriage was celebrated, Donna *Urraca*, queen dowager of *Navarre*, returned to her father's court, and received from him the principality of *Asturias*, the government of which she was to hold by way of appennage from the crown, for her subsistence, in a manner suitable to her birth; from whence we find her commonly styled by the antient *Spanish* writers, Donna *Urraca* the *Asturian* [a]. There was the same year an interview between the emperor and the prince of *Arragon*; but those who infer from thence, that a league was then made between these princes for the destruction, or at least the conquest, of the kingdom of *Navarre*, seem to

The infant Don San-cho *of Ar-ragon married to Donna* Blanca.

A. D. 1151.

[u] Roderic Toletan de reb. Hispan. lib. vii. Lucæ Tudensis Chronicon. [w] Roderic Toletan Hist. Arabum. [x] Chron. var. antiq. [y] Annal. Toletan, Mayerne Turquet Histoire general d'Espagne. liv. ix. [z] Lucæ Tudensis Chronicon, Adefons Imperat. [a] Ferreras Historia de España, p. v. §. 12.

be

be miſtaken; ſince, on the one hand, it is highly improbable that the emperor ſhould meditate the ruin of a prince
ſo nearly and lately allied to him; and, on the other, it is
not conſiſtent with facts, ſince we find nothing of the execution of this league, either within the compaſs of this or
the next year. It is indeed true, that the emperor left the
Mohammedans undiſturbed for about eighteen months, and
then made an irruption into *Andaluſia,* where the Infant Don
Alonſo gained great reputation, by defeating a body of *Moors* [b],
who attempted to diſturb the emperor in his ſiege of *Jaen*;

A. D.
1152.

which, however, he found ſo ſtrongly fortified, and ſo well
defended, that he was obliged to raiſe it; and, leaving the
army, returned to *Toledo,* while his troops continued to harraſs the *Moors,* though without any remarkable ſucceſs, even
in the depth of winter, which diſabled them from making
incurſions in the ſpring, according to cuſtom.

*Other
marriages
of the em-
peror, and
in the im-
perial fa-
mily.*

THE emperor having judged it expedient to marry a ſecond wife, and the king Don *Sancho,* of *Navarre,* having
ſignified his deſire of eſpouſing the Infanta Donna *Sancha,*
the emperor's daughter, the town of *Soria* was made choice
of as the moſt convenient for the celebration of both their
nuptials. The princeſs, of whom the emperor had made
choice, was named *Rica,* the daughter of *Ladiſlaus* the ſecond, king of *Poland,* and the princeſs *Inez* of *Auſtria,* who,
being conducted thither, the emperor eſpouſed her on the
fourth of *June,* in the preſence of the kings of *Arragon* and
Navarre; the king Don *Sancho,* when he married the Infanta, was, according to the cuſtom of thoſe times, made a
knight by his father-in-law, and reconciled to Don *Raymond*
of *Arragon,* at leaſt for the preſent [c]. Some time after *Louis*

A. D.
1153.

the ſeventh, king of *France,* concluded a marriage with
Donna *Conſtança* the emperor's daughter, having been a little
before divorced from his firſt queen *Eleonora,* ducheſs of
Aquitaine [d]. Theſe marriages ſeem to have occupied the
attention of the court, and to have prevented the war from
being carried on againſt the *Moors* with the ſame vigour as

A. D.
1154.

in the former years. However it was ſtill kept on foot, and
ſerved to hinder thoſe infidels from undertaking any thing of
conſequence againſt the Chriſtians, in conjunction with their
inteſtine diſputes, which at this time were as high and
fierce as ever; and perhaps the not attacking them might
increaſe them.

[b] RODERIC TOLETAN Hiſt. Arabum.   [c] LUCÆ Tudenſis
Chronicon, Chron. ADEFONS Imperat.   [d] RODERIC TOLETAN
de reb. Hiſpan. lib. vii. FRANCISCI TARAPHÆ de reg. Hiſpaniæ.

BUT,

BUT, as soon as the situation of his affairs would give him *The ar-* leave, the emperor, with a numerous army, passing through *rival of* that part of *La Mancha* which belonged to the *Moors*, and *Louis* VII. traversing the *Sierra Morena*, after taking several places of *king of* small force, set down before *Andujar*, which was so well *France, at* fortified, that it had escaped hitherto, though besieged by *Toledo,* numerous armies. Yet this monarch took his measures so *and his* well, and his reputation was so great, that, after a gallant de- *reception* fence, the besieged judged it expedient to provide for their *by the em-* own safety by a timely capitulation, which was granted *peror.* them [e]. We have good reason to believe, that the emperor had set his heart very much upon this conquest, since, while he lay before the place, he had the news, that his son-in-law king *Louis*, and his daughter Donna *Constança*, were arrived in *Spain* with a design of visiting the tomb of the apostle *St. James* at *Compostella*. He sent to compliment them, and to desire, that, after they had performed their devotions, they would repair to *Toledo*, where he promised to meet them; which he did after the conclusion of the campaign, and en- tertained them with great magnificence, and caused them to be accompanied at their return by the two kings his sons, and by Don *Sancho* king of *Navarre* [f]. On the eleventh of *November*, the same year, the king Don *Sancho*, of *Castile*, had a son born to him, who was named *Alonso*, and in pro- cess of time became one of the greatest princes that ever reigned in *Spain*; but the queen Donna *Blanca*, his mother, died a few months after [g]. This, as it created great grief in the imperial family, so it seems to have been fatal to her own; for the emperor having consented to a match be- tween Don *Alonso*, son to Don *Raymond* of *Arragon*, and his A. D. daughter Donna *Sancha*, who was hardly out of her cradle, 1056. was prevailed upon, in consequence of this alliance, to in- vade the kingdom of *Navarre* [h].

WE know little of the progress of that war, at least with *The death* regard to the emperor, who seems to have been diverted *of Alonso* from it by the news of a powerful invasion meditated by the VII. *who* *Moors*. He resolved to prevent this by marching with all *alone wore* his forces into *Andalusia*, accompanied by his son Don *San-* *the glori-* *cho* king of *Castile*, and by the principal lords and prelates *ous title of* of his court, amongst whom was the archbishop of *Toledo*. *emperor.* He advanced directly towards the enemy, whom he attacked with the utmost vigour, and, after an obstinate and bloody resistance, totally defeated them with great slaughter [i]. But,

[e] RODERIC TOLETAN, Hist. Arabum.   [f] Chron. var. antiq.
[g] FERRERAS Historia de España, p. v. §. 12.   [h] Chron.
ADEFONS Imperat.   [i] RODERIC TOLETAN Hist. Arabum.

before

before he had time to profecute this glorious victory, he
found himfelf attacked by a difeafe, which made him fenfible
that his end was quickly approaching. He quitted therefore
the command of the army to his fon Don *Sancho*, and fet
out on his return towards *Toledo*. His diftemper, however,
continually increafing, he ftopped at a little place called
Frefneda on the frontiers, where, on the twenty-firft day of
Auguft in the year 1157, he refigned his foul to his creator,
being affifted in his laft moments by the archbifhop of *Toledo* [k]. He was indifputably one of the greateft monarchs
Spain ever had to boaft of. He extended his dominions from
the mountians of *Bifcay* to thofe of the *Sierra Morena*, had
the fingular honour of receiving the homage of the kings of
Navarre and *Arragon*, and of acquiring, in confequence
of that, the glorious title of emperor [l], which has indeed
been afcribed to fome of his predeceffors, but without due
proof. He loved, and was beloved by, his nobility; but at
the fame time he juftly acquired, by his paternal care and
ftrict maintenance of the laws, the title of the father of the
commons, whom he protected from all oppreffion, and rendered far more happy and eafy in their circumftances, than
they had formerly been. He was a confummate and fuccefsful general, and withal the ableft politician of his time;
and did more towards the recovery of *Spain* out of the hands
of the infidels, than any of the princes who had reigned before him, his grandfather of the fame name only excepted.
He was highly refpected by his neighbours, and even by the
Moorifh princes, amongft whom *Mohammed Abenzel*, king
of *Murcia*, became his vaffal but a few years before his
death [m]. His fon, Don *Sancho*, no fooner underftood that
he had breathed his laft, than he quitted the army to attend
his corpfe to *Toledo*, where it was interred in the royal chapel of the cathedral, with a pomp fuitable to the melancholy
occafion [n]. In one refpect this great prince may be efteemed
more happy than his anceftors, that all his great actions
were both fairly and fully recorded, in a *Latin* chronicle that
bears his name, and was written in or near his time, which
is that we have cited after *Ferreras*, and has fupplied us
with many particulars, and rectified many dates, that muft
otherwife have remained perplexed or doubtful.

[k] Chron ADEFONS Imperat. MAYERNE TURQUET Hiftoire
general d'Efpagne, liv. ix.   [l] FERRERAS Hiftoria de Efpana,
p. v. §. 12.   [m] RODERIC TOLETAN Hift. Arabum.   [n] Ro-
DERIC SANTII Hift. Hifpan. ALPHONSI a Carthagena *de reg.*
Hifp. Anacephalæofis FRANCISI TARAPHÆ de reg. Hifpaniæ.

As soon as the funeral of the emperor was over, Don *Several* Sancho repaired to *Burgos*, where he was unanimously ac- *advan-* knowleged and received as king of *Castile*, his brother, Don *tages gain-* *Ferdinand*, being with equal unanimity admitted to the so- *ed by the* vereignty of the kingdom of *Leon*, *Asturias*, and *Galicia* o. *Moors* But, like young princes, they were more attentive to the *upon his* ceremony and pomp of their inaugurations, than to the high *demise.* and arduous functions of kings. In consequence of this, though the death of Don *Alonso* did not affect the civil go- vernment, yet it had a very great influence on their military affairs. The *Moors* were no sooner acquainted with it, than they flattered themselves the fortune of *Spain* was de- parted, the terror impressed by his name wore away, and, assembling in crouds, they offered themselves to their com- manders; who, making a proper use of this alacrity, fell upon *Pedraches*, *Andujar*, *Baeza*, and all the places they had lately lost, which they recovered with great facility, and drove the Christians in one autumn campaign out of all that the emperor had acquired in *Andalusia*; upon which happy success, they addressed themselves to *Abdulmenon*, king of *Morocco*, beseeching him not to let slip this favourable op- portunity of retrieving the honour and the dominions of the *Moors*. He received this application so favourably, and pro- mised such speedy and prodigious succours, that the *Knights Templars*, who held the town of *Calatrava* as a fief from the crown, resigned it as a place they should not be able to de- fend; upon which Don *Sancho* published an edict, in which he offered to give that place to any of his nobility, who would undertake to maintain and support it; the conse- quences of which will be hereafter seen at large P.

Don *Ferdinand* was hardly seated on the throne of *Leon*, *Generous* before he found, like most young kings, his person be- *and pru-* sieged by flatterers, to whom he was but too accessible; so *dent be-* that the first acts of his government were such as had an *haviour* evident tendency to overturn it; for, in consequence of the *of Don* bad advices given him, he discarded Don *Ponce de Minerva*, *Sancho,* and most of the old officers and statesmen that had been the *king of* friends and favourites of his father; who, finding them- *Castile, to* selves removed from all their employments, retired to the *his bro-* court of *Burgos*, and were received with extraordinary re- *ther* spect and kindness by the king of *Castile* q. Don *Sancho* was no sooner acquainted with the motives which had induced

---

• MARIANA Historia general de Espana, lib. xi. FERRERAS Historia de Espana, p. v. §. 12. MAYERNE TURQUET Histoire generale d'Espagne, liv. ix.   P Chron. var. antiq.   q Ro- DERIC TOLETAN de reb. Hispan. lib. vii. LUCÆ Tudens. Chron.

them to take shelter under his protection, than he marched with a considerable army into his brother's dominions; of which Don *Ferdinand* no sooner received intelligence, than he set out to meet his brother with a small retinue; for they had hitherto lived together with so much friendship and affection, that he could not apprehend any danger in the presence of one to whom he had been always dear. He met him at the abbey of *Sahagon* just as he was going to dinner, and the brothers, as soon as they had embraced, sat down to table [r]. After they had done, Don *Sancho* told him, " that he was glad to see him in that condition; for that, " finding his principal nobility retired out of his domi- " nions, he apprehended he stood in need of his assistance; " he added, that their father was a wise man, as well as a " great prince; that the former enabled him to make choice " of such officers and counsellors, as raised him into the " latter condition; and that he had given him little in giving " a kingdom, if he had not likewise left him these; that " he must therefore take them home with him, listen to " their advice, discard his flatterers, and rely upon it, that, " if his own forces were not sufficient, himself and his " *Castilians* were ready to assist him upon any proper occa- " sion." Don *Ferdinand* taking all this in good part, Don *Sancho* left him his old servants, and returned into *Castile* with his army [s]. The king of *Navarre* conceived this a fit time to recover the province of *Riaja*, which he looked upon as with-held from him by force, and which therefore he had a right to reduce, whenever it was in his power; but Don *Sancho* had intelligence of his design before he marched against his brother, and therefore appointed the count Don *Ponce* to command the troops intended for the defence of that province; in which command he behaved in such a manner, that the king of *Navarre* thought proper to retire into his own dominions, without coming to action.

He com-
poses all
differences
with the
king of
Arragon,
and con-
cludes
with him
a treaty.

UPON his return into his own territories, the first thing the king of *Castile* did, was to put the monarchs of *Arragon* and *Navarre* in mind, that the former was his uncle, the latter his brother-in-law; that, besides this, he had never offended either; and that it would not recommend them in the sight of God or of man, to take advantage of that invasion with which the *Moors* threatened his dominions; but that, if they conceived any injustice on his side, he was ready to meet them either together or apart, and to give

[r] Chron. var. antiq.   [s] FERRERAS Historia de España, p.
v. §. 12.

them

them any reasonable satisfaction. Both monarchs accepted this proposal; in consequence of which he had an interview with the king of *Navarre* at *Almazan*, where a peace and defensive alliance was concluded between them [t]. He went thence to *Osma*, where he met his uncle Don *Raymond*, who, expostulated freely with him on the acquisitions made by his father, at the expence of the crown of *Arragon*, alleging, that the emperor ought to have been content with his homage, which he rendered him freely, and not have curtailed his dominions. Don *Sancho* told him, that what he liked he would keep, and what he disliked he would restore; and accordingly consented by a treaty, that all the country on the right of the river *Ebro* should belong to the king of *Arragon* as in times past, upon condition that he did homage to the king of *Castile*, and assisted him with his sword drawn at his coronation; which conditions were readily accepted, and Don *Raymond* promised him a choice body of his troops [u]. About this time *St. Raymond*, abbot of *Vitero*, undertook the defence of *Calatrava*, without any other force than that of another monk, whose name was *Diego Velasquez*, who, as well as himself, had borne arms many years before they wore frocks; and without any other fund than that of their zeal and piety. The king granted the fortress without scruple; and, in the space of a few weeks they by their sermons raised twenty thousand men, and the means of subsisting them; upon which *St. Raymond* gave the rule of the *Cistercian* order a military turn, from whence arose that order of religious chivalry, which has been since distinguished by the name of *Calatrava* [w] (U).

ABEN-

[t] Chron. var. antiq. [u] MARIANA Historia general de Espana, lib. xi. Chron. var. antiq. [w] FERRERAS Historia de Espana, p. v. §. 12.

(U) In respect to points that depend upon records, there is a degree of certainty superior to most others; and therefore we find almost all the historians agree in placing the institution of this order *anno* 1158. This whole transaction is very fully and very elegantly related by *Mariana*, who observes, that the Knights Templars dishonoured themselves extremely by so base a proceeding; which however so far discouraged the nobility, that notwithstanding the offers made, and the temptation of so rich and noble a seignory, there was not one of them who had the courage to accept the king's offer, and undertake the defence of the place; which reduced that monarch to the necessity of promising it to any who would engage to keep it. Don *Diego Velasquez*, an old experienced officer, who had taken the *Cistercian* order, framed in his own mind a scheme for compound-

ing

ABEN-JACOB, the son of *Abdulmenon* king of *Morocco*, having brought over a great number of *Moors* from *Africa*, began to make vast preparations for attacking the kingdom of *Toledo*; upon which the inhabitants of *Avila* and the *Estremadurians*, with the consent of Don *Sancho*, assembled a great body of troops, with which they fell into the district about *Seville*. *Aben-Jacob*, as soon as he received intelligence of this, joined his forces with those of *Dalegen* and *Aben-Gamar*, and marched immediately to attack the Christians. The action was obstinate and bloody, but at length victory declared on the side of the Christians, and the *Moors* were not only beaten with great slaughter, but lost also their

ing the two professions he had himself sustained; and being strongly persuaded the thing might be accomplished, importuned Don *Raymond*, abbot of *Vitero*, to challenge the king's promise, which at length he did. *Diego Velasquez* procured from *John* archbishop of *Toledo*, in whose diocese *Calatrava* lay, a large sum of money; which enabled him to repair the fortifications. He then preached to the young nobility, that instead of retiring into convents, to pass an idle and inactive life, it would be far more glorious in the sight of God and man to dedicate themselves to the service and defence of their faith and country, in a manner suitable to their birth and breeding; and having by this means drawn eight or nine thousand men together, he insinuated to the common people the great strength and happy situation of *Calatrava*, now so well fortified, and provided with such a garrison, as afforded them a prospect of greater security than in most other places; adding, that the delightful villages along the *Guadiana*, under its jurisdiction, might be easily repaired, and be held from the knights upon very

moderate terms; by which he brought together ten or twelve thousand citizens and peasants; and in the course of a few years so fully executed his plan, that the order had an ample revenue, and the people from whom it arose thought themselves happy. In this juncture, therefore, a better expedient could not have been desired; and pope *Alexander* the third, by his bull in 1164, declared as much: but, as *Mariana* well observes, by degrees this noble institution has degenerated, the commanderies, which were formerly the reward of military merit, being frequently bestowed upon minions and favourites. Modern writers assure us, that the order has at present thirty-four commanderies and eight priories, which produce an annual revenue of 120,000 ducats. The knights wear on their upper garment a red cross, to distinguish them from other orders: and as that of *St. James* is distinguished by the epithet of the *rich*, and that of *Alcantara* is stiled the *noble*, so this of *Calatrava* is entitled the *gallant*, which, how it accords with its original institution, is not easy to discern.

two

two generals *Dalegen* and *Aben-Gamar*, so that the victory was equally glorious and compleat ˣ. But the joy they received from thence was of short continuance, since, on the last day of *August* 1158, Don *Sancho*, king of *Castile*, breathed his last at *Toledo*, when he had worn the crown but one year and ten days ʸ. His body was interred by that of the emperor his father; his loss was sincerely deplored by all his subjects, and by his allies; his actions, even in so short a space, having raised such hopes as could not have been easily satisfied; so that, how immature soever his death might appear to his people, it came at a juncture favourable to his glory (X).

THE crown of *Castile*, devolved on his son Don *Alonso*, then but three years of age, whom his father left to the care of Don *Guitterez de Castro*, whom he declared sole regent ᶻ, and forbid the removing any of his father's governors or officers before his son was at full age, unless from some indispensible cause. This appointment excited the envy of many of the most puissant nobility, but more especially of the house of *Lara*, of which Don *Manrique* was the chief, and who perhaps had not forgot the misfortunes of Don *Pedro*, at the beginning of the emperor's reign ᵃ. Don *Guitterez* however, deserved all the confidence his master had reposed in him: he was a nobleman far advanced in years, but not infirm; of great prudence, and of untainted probity. He committed the education of the king to Don *Garcia de Aza*, the son of Don *Garcia de Cabra*, who was killed at the battle of

Don Alonso III. succeeds him under the tuition of Don Guitterez de Castro.

ˣ RODERIC TOLETAN. Hist. Arabum.   ʸ RODERIC SANTII Hist. Hispan. ALPHONSI a Carthagena reg. Hisp. Anacephalæosis FRANCISCI TARAPHÆ de reg. Hispan.   ᶻ FERRERAS Historia de Espana, p. v. §. xii.   ᵃ Chronic. var. antiq.

(X) This young monarch was surnamed *el Deseado*, or the *Desired*, and is justly allowed to have the most unspotted character in the whole *Spanish* history. It is given us in few words, by the archbishop of *Toledo* and the bishop of *Tuy*; the latter tells us, that in religion he was sincere, and gallant in the field, distinguished by the sweetness of his temper, and adorned with every royal virtue. He adds, that he was alike dear to the populace and to the nobility, because he made it the whole study of his life to please God and good men. *Mariana* assures us that he died of grief for the loss of his wife, queen *Blanch*, and at the very time when he should have marched against the infidels, having assembled for that purpose a numerous army, better provided in all respects than any body of troops had been by most of his predecessors.

Ucles with the infant Don *Sancho,* and this notwithstanding he was brother by the mother's side to Don *Manrique de Lara,* who from the beginning had declared himself his enemy, and who quickly corrupted Don *Garcia,* and engaged him to put the person of the young king into his hands, contrary to his honour, and in breach of that trust which had been reposed in him [b]. Don *Guitterez* laboured all that was in his power to have this matter compromised, and the person of the young king restored; but finding this impracticable, he was about to have recourse to arms, when providence withdrew him from all these troubles to eternal rest [c], though his competitor would not allow his corpse peace in the grave.

His uncle the king of Leon claims the regency, but at length compromises the dispute. Don *Manrique de Lara,* and the lords of his family and faction, thought themselves now in a good measure secure, from having the sole government of the kingdom, during a long minority, disputed with them; and in order to make this absolutely sure, they took the only step that could render it precarious, which was breaking through the king's will, and depriving Don *Ferdinand,* and all his brothers, of their respective employments [d], merely because they were of the family of *Castro,* and the nephew of the deceased regent, who thereupon applied himself to Don *Ferdinand,* king of *Leon,* who at their request declared himself tutor and regent of his nephew, and with a numerous army entered the kingdom of *Toledo,* where the people very readily submitted, and even the inhabitants of the capital upon the first summons opened their gates [e]. The king, encouraged by this success, entered *Castile,* and Don *Manrique,* and the lords of *Lara,* perceiving an unwillingness in the people to fight against the uncle of their sovereign, retired to the fortress of *Soria,* carrying the young prince with them. At length finding themselves menaced with a siege, they entered into a negotiation with the king, and offered to deliver up the person of their young king to his uncle upon certain terms; but this was pure amusement; since, as soon as king *Ferdinand* listened to their request, they sent the king out privately, and carried him from place to place with such secrecy, that Don *Ferdinand* was at last obliged to come to their terms, which was to keep the best part of the kingdom, as well as the king, in their possession, and to leave the rest to be administred by him. A compromise that was by no means acceptable, either to the populace or to the nobility [f].

A. D. 1159.

[b] RODERIC TOLETAN de reb. Hispan. lib. vii. LUCÆ Tudensis Chronicon.   [c] MAYERNE TURQUET, Historia general de Espana liv. ix.   [d] Chron. var. antiq.   [e] Annal. Toletan.   [f] FERRERAS Historia de España, p. v. §. xii.

THOUGH,

Though this agreement was more in favour of the faction than they could either desire or expect, yet they were so
far from being contented with it, that Don *Ferdinand* was
no sooner retired into his own dominions than they attempted
to dispossess him by force of those places which they had put
into his hands. But though the king of *Leon* was in all respects a good-natured prince, yet he resented this behaviour
so much, that in the month of *March* following, he advanced with an army against them, gave them battle, and
defeated them, which threw their affairs into great confusion [g] ; and towards the close of the year the *Moors* entered
Castile, and gained some advantages. On the other hand,
Don *Sancho,* king of *Navarre,* judging no time so proper to
revive his pretensions to the country of *Riaja,* entered it
with a powerful army, and reduced the best part of it, before Don *Manrique,* and his associates, were in any condition to provide for its defence [h]. But as soon as they were
able to draw a competent number of troops together, and
found that he was engaged in a war with the *Mahommedans,*
they entered that country in their turn, and recovered it again
in as little time as it was lost. Other expeditions of the like
kind happened in succeeding years with various fortune; but
upon the whole Don *Sancho* of *Navarre* kept almost all the
places that he claimed [i].

It might be naturally apprehended, that the *Moors* would
not fail to lay hold of so favourable an opportunity to repair
the losses they had sustained, and to recover at least some of
the important places that had been taken from them by the
Christians; more especially, as they were sure of constant and
considerable supplies from their countrymen in *Africa,* and
saw the power of the Christians as much divided, depressed,
and distracted, as they could wish; and yet it does not appear,
that they made any great advantage of so favourable a juncture. The *Spanish* historians have not given us a very clear
account of this matter [k]; but as far as we can judge from a
comparison of facts, it may be ascribed, at least in a great measure, to three different causes. The first was, that though
the Christian princes were not well agreed amongst themselves, yet they did not employ their arms against each other,
so that the forces destined for the protection of the frontiers of
the kingdoms of *Castile* and *Toledo,* were not withdrawn;
and though they seldom acted offensively, yet being com-

[g] Lucæ Tudensis Chronicon, Roderic Toletan Hist. Arabum.   [h] Chron. var. antiq.   [i] Roderic Toletan de reb. Hispan. lib. vii. Ferreras, Mayerne Turquet.   [k] Chron. var. antiq.

manded

manded by able officers, it is likely they would have defended themselves with spirit, if attacked. A second cause was the new militia established on purpose to act continually either offensively, or defensively, against the infidels, by which we mean the new orders of chivalry; for, besides those already mentioned, there started up at this time another, which proved of double advantage to the Christians.   There was in the kingdoms of *Leon* and *Castile* a considerable number of wild debauched young gentlemen, who, by indulging their passions, had rendered themselves so obnoxious to the law, that they had no security but what they derived from their swords. These people had lived long in the mountains, and had been gradually brought under the command of Don *Pedro Fernandes*, who being both older and wiser than when he took up this dangerous trade, bethought himself of an expedient to set things right again, and to reconcile himself and his dependants to the civil government. The method he took was this; he bound all who submitted to his authority by oath never to injure any Christian, but to devote themselves to the protection of their country against the *Moors*; and having converted the rule of St. *Augustine* into a military institution, he made it that of his new order, which, with the licence and under the protection of the king Don *Ferdinand*, assumed the apostle St. *James* for their patron, and had lands given them by the crown [1] for their support (Y). Another cause was
the

---

[1] FERRERAS Historia de Espana, p. v. sect. xii.

(Y) It is true, that some writers carry the institution of this order much higher, *viz.* to *A.D.* 827; and it is also true that many who have rejected this date as fabulous, are nevertheless persuaded that there is evidence sufficient to prove this order of chivalry actually subsisted *A.D.* 1030, and must have been instituted some time, tho' they cannot say how long before it. But notwithstanding these authorities we agree with *Ferreras*, and in good measure also with *Mariana*, that the true and genuine origin of this order of knighthood ought to be placed

where it is in the text; and that Don *Pedro Fernandes*, called also from the place of his birth. Don *Pedro de Fuente-Enclalada*, which is a town in the diocese of *Astorga*, was its founder and first grand-master.   In order to give the reader some satisfaction upon this head, it will be requisite to represent to him, though very succinctly, the true state of the case. When the tomb of St. *James* at *Compostella* first became famous, and from the spirit of devotion that reigned in those times drew gradually a vast resort of pilgrims thither, it was found requisite to erect a
kind

the civil wars amongst themselves, in which some of the Christian princes wisely took part, and by constantly assisting the weaker side, without enquiring into the merits of the dispute, kept their quarrels on foot, and contributed not a little to weaken both. To all which we may add, that Don *Alonso*, king of *Portugal*, employed his arms against them all this time, and not without success, the king of *Arragon* also making occasionally some prædatory incursions.

kind of hospitals or public places of reception for these pilgrims at every proper stage, from the borders of *France* to the city of *Compostella*. This was *Fornò*, taken by the canons of St. *Eloy*, who likewise took care of these hospitals, and of such as lodged in them, by which they acquired the good will of the neighbouring nobility, who furnished them liberally with money for so pious and prudent a work. But amongst all these hospitals, that in the suburb of the city of *Leon*, dedicated to St. *Mark*, was by far the largest and best endowed. In these troublesome times, however, the pilgrims, in spite of all the charitable pains taken for their relief and support, were liable to great inconveniencies from the excursions of the *Moors*, and from the robberies that were frequently committed on the road; and this it was that induced Don *Pedro Fernandes de Fuente-Enclalada*, when he had formed his companions into some degree of order, to make a tender of his services to the canons of St. *Eloy*, to cover and protect these pilgrims in their passage: as this again induced the pope upon granting his bull of confirmation to assign the hospital of St. *Mark*, in the suburbs of *Leon*, for the capital residence of the grand master and his knights; and it is

from confounding these knights with the old canons that those difficulties have arisen as to the original of this institution. The ensign of this order is a cross, terminating like the blade of a sword, the hilt crosleted and fashioned after the ancient manner; whereupon it was called *La Orden de Sanctiago de la Espada*, as also *Ordo militaris Sancti Jacobi ensigeri à qualitate insignium*. And the reason why this ensign is always painted red rather than any other colour, is thus given by Don *Rodrigo Ximenes*, archbishop of *Toledo*. *Rubet ensis sanguine Arabum*. But these knights assumed not only the sword in form of a cross, but also the symbol of St. *James*, which, though it cannot be directly determined what it is, yet it seems to be the Escallop shell: For that the Escallop is generally among the *Spaniards* taken for the badge of St. *James*, and worn by pilgrims in their voyages to his sepulchre at *Compostella*. At present there are eighty-seven commanderies of the order of St. *James* in the kingdoms of *Castile* and *Leon*, which yield an annual revenue of two hundred and seventy thousand ducats, and about three score commanderies in the kingdom of *Portugal*, which are also of great value.

DON

Don Ferdinand of Leon marries the infanta Donna Urraca of Portugal.

A. D. 1463.

DON *Ferdinand* king of *Leon*, finding himself exceedingly disturbed by the intrigues of the family of *Lara*, and that he was in continual danger of losing the places he held in the name of his nephew, caused a negotiation to be set on foot with Don *Manrique*, in which he shewed so strong an inclination to compromise their differences, that this nobleman at length invited him to *Soria*, where he had a conference with his nephew, and adjusted every thing with Don *Manrique* [m] He took advantage of this calm, in order to repair and settle several great towns in the heart of his dominions, as well as on the frontiers, which were either fallen through time to decay, or else were but indifferently built and peopled at first; and to this he attended with so much care and vigilance, that they were very soon in as good a condition as he could wish. He granted also new privileges to the people, and neglected no means that could be devised to make his dominions flourish, and his people happy. Amongst other methods that were thought necessary for this purpose, one that was held of the greatest consequence by his father's old ministers, was his speedy marriage; that by allying himself with some powerful prince, he might the better secure assistance in case of foreign invasion, and defend his people from the miseries that might be apprehended from an unsettled succession. Don *Ferdinand*, moved by these suggestions, cast his eyes upon the princess Donna *Urraca*, daughter to Don *Alonso*, king of *Portugal*,

A. D. 1164.

and accordingly demanded her in marriage. Don *Alonso* very readily consented to the match, and soon after sent the princess to *Leon* with a splendid retinue, where she was espoused by the king Don *Ferdinand* with great solemnity, and to the universal joy of the people of both nations, who concluded that this must of necessity keep the two kingdoms in friendship and peace [n].

Rebuilds the city of Merobriga and Bletisa, which occasions an insurrection.

As soon as the ceremonies of the marriage were over, the king Don *Ferdinand* resumed the cares of government with his usual application, and casting his eyes upon *Merobriga* and *Bletisa*, places large and considerable in ancient times, though they were then little better than heaps of ruins, he gave orders that they should be rebuilt and fortified; it is evident enough, that he meant this to strengthen his territories on that side against *Portugal*, and took a very convenient time to do it. But the people of *Salamanca*, who considered these places as lying within their jurisdiction, and not at all de-

---

[m] RODERIC TOLET. de reb. Hispan. lib. vii. LUCÆ Tudensis Chronicon.   [n] EMANUEL DE FARIA Y SOUSA *epitome* las Historias Portuguesas. MAYERNE TURQUET, Histoire general d'Espagne, liv. x.

sirous of seeing them in a better state than they were, assembled several thousand men, with an intention to prevent by force the execution of the king's project. The king Don *Ferdinand* had acquired more experience, and was upon better terms with his nobility, than in the first part of this reign, and would not therefore submit to the dictates of the populace; but drawing out the forces of *Leon, Zamora,* and *Astorga,* marched against the rebels, defeated them in a bloody engagement, and then proceeding to *Salamanca,* chastised those who had been the authors of these troubles; after which things remained very quiet [o]. As soon as these places were restored and in some measure peopled, the king laid the plan of taking several others from the *Moors*; but first of all thought proper to conclude an alliance with the king of *Navarre,* that, in case his nephew, whom he discerned to be of a very brisk and active temper, should give him any disturbance, he might not be without an ally capable of making a diversion in his favour; and this precaution being taken, he added *Alcantara, Albuquerque,* and *Elvas,* to his dominions, without meeting with any great resistance from the enemy, or disturbance from his neighbours [p]. But let us now return to the affairs of *Castile* (Z).

Don *Manrique de Lara* paid so little regard to the soft counsels given him by the king of *Leon,* that instead of endeavouring to compose amicably those disputes that had been so fatal to the interests of the young king his pupil, he bent all his endeavours to inflame the mind of the young prince against the family of *Castro,* and at length raised an army, with which he marched to dispossess Don *Ferdinand de Castro*

The young king of Castile, by the advice of Don Manrique seizes Toledo.

[o] Chron, var. antiq.   [p] RODERIC TOLETAN Hist. Arabum. RODERIC TOLETAN de reb. Hispan. lib. viii.

(Z) The town of *Bletisa,* which, after it was rebuilt, as the reader has seen in the text, received the name of *Ledesma,* stood upon the river of *Tormes,* and was so happy in point of situation, that ever since the time of which we are now writing, it has been looked upon as a place of great consequence, and its fortifications kept in good repair. *Merobriga* lies south from thence and within four leagues of the frontiers of *Portugal* upon the little river *Agujar,* in the midst of a spacious plain, equally fertile and pleasant. It received the name of *Ciudad Rodrigo* from the nobleman under whose direction it was repaired, and very quickly became so populous as to be made the seat of a prelate as well as a garrison. It has continued to flourish ever since, and has been always a principal rendezvous or a place of arms for the *Spanish* forces, when that crown has been engaged in a war with *Portugal.*

of

of the government of *Toledo*, and his friends of the place
they poſſeſſed ; and to give the better colour to this he carri
the prince with him ⁹.   On the other hand, Don *Ferdinai*
de Caſtro oppoſed force to force ; and marching with a num
rous and well appointed army, met that of his competitor be
tween *Garcinarro* and *Huete*, where, after an obſtinate an
bloody action, Don *Manrique* being killed, his forces fled an
left Don *Ferdinand* maſter of the field of battle ʳ.   Yet not
withſtanding this great blow, Don *Nugnez de Lara*, broth
to the late count *Manrique*, chiefly by the influence of t
royal perſon, ſoon raiſed another army, and laid ſiege to
caſtle of *Zurita*, which was very gallantly defended by
de Arenas, placed therein by the *Caſtro's*, and had not bee
taken at laſt, if one of the governor's domeſticks had not, for a
ſum of money, baſely undertaken, and as barbarouſly executed,
the murder of his maſter ˢ.   The pecuniary reward in all
probability came from the miniſter ; but the young king Don
Alonſo thought ſo eminent a ſervice ſhould be accompanied
alſo with a royal reward, for which reaſon he ordered his eyes
A. D.
1166. to be put out ᵗ(A). This method having ſucceeded in a place of

---

⁹ Lucæ Tudenſis Chronicon. Annal Toletan.   ʳ Chron.
var. antiq.   ˢ Roderic Toletan de reb. Hiſpan. lib. vii.
ᵗ Ferreras Hiſtoria de Eſpana, p. v: ſec: xii.

(A) We have a large account
of this ſiege, and of the moſt remarkable paſſages therein, by
Mariana, who gives us amongſt
other particulars this, that the
governor Don *Lopez*, being
driven to extremity, offered to
treat ; and that Don *Nugnez de*
Lara, and another great general
of the king's, went into the place
upon his parole, and were immediately arreſted ; upon which
recourſe was had to that expedient, by which, as we have
ſhewn in the text, the place was
taken.   The traitor ſtabbed
his maſter while he was ſhaving
him, and made his eſcape out
of the town, before the death of
the governor was known.   By
laying all theſe circumſtances together, there ſeems to be good
reaſon to ſuſpect that this con-

ſpiracy was both formed and
executed, during a ceſſation of
arms ; and perhaps ſome inci-
dents forged in order to ſave the
reputation of Don *Nugnez de*
Lara, and his aſſociates ; for, if
it had been as *Mariana* repreſents
it, one cannot eaſily account for
the beſieged ſuffering theſe perſons, who were in their hands at
the time this treacherous murder was committed, to eſcape
unhurt ; to which we may add,
that there was evidently in this
tranſaction, ſomething that ſo
much wounded the king's honour, as induced him to hazard
the imputation of cruelty, rather
than not teſtify to his ſubjects
that it was a meaſure which,
though he might adopt, he could
by no means approve.

lefs confequence, it was judged expedient to practife the fame arts with regard to *Toledo* ; and a perfon of diftinction in that city having been prevailed upon to let in the king's troops fecretly, Don *Ferdinand Ruyz de Caftro* had the firft notice of this treachery from the acclamations of the people, at the fight of their young king : upon which having no other refource left, he mounted his horfe immediately, and, attended by a few friends, made his efcape into the territory of the *Moors* [u]. The capital thus taken by furprize, the reft of the cities, caftles and towns, in the kingdom of *Toledo*, opened their gates, and fubmitted to the king, or rather to Don *Nugnez de Lara*, who governed all things with almoft royal authority [w]. About this time deceafed *John*, archbifhop of *Toledo*, and was fucceeded in that high dignity by *Cenebruno*, who had been tutor to the young king *Alonfo*, a perfon eminent for his learning and great abilities [x]. *Mohammed*, king of *Valencia*, became at this time vaffal to the king of *Caftile* [y].

IT quickly appeared that Don *Ferdinand*, king of *Leon*, had formed a right judgment when he fortified his frontiers on the fide of *Portugal*, for notwithftanding he had married the daughter of Don *Alonfo*, that monarch made a fudden irruption into *Galicia*, and poffeffed himfelf of *Limmia* and *Turon*, into which he put ftrong garrifons [z]. The next year, elated with this fuccefs, he marched with a numerous army and invefted *Badajoz*, upon the news of which Don *Ferdinand*, who had affembled a good army at *Ciudad Rodrigo*, marched to its relief. It is neceffary to obferve, that this city was in the hands of the *Moors*, but in all probability was a feignory held by homage from the king of *Leon*, who therefore found himfelf, from principles of juftice as well as policy, interefted in its defence. Yet before he could arrive within fight of the place it was furrendered; upon which Don *Ferdinand* took a refolution of befieging the king of *Portugal* in his new conqueft, which Don *Alonfo* no fooner perceived than he endeavoured to draw out his forces into the field. Though he was then between feventy and four-fcore, he was himfelf on horfeback, and pufhing forward at the head of his guards to get out at the gate, ftruck his leg with fuch vehemence againft one of the bolts as fhattered it to pieces. This accident occafioned fuch confufion, that the troops of *Portugal* were eafily beaten, and Don *Alonfo* taken prifoner [a]. He was ex-

King of Portugal invades Leon, and is taken prifoner by king Ferdinand.

A. D. 1167.

---

[u] RODERIC TOLETAN Hiftor. Arabum. LUCÆ Tudenfis Chron.
[w] Annal Toletan. RODERIC TOLETAN de reb. Hifpan. lib. vii.
[x] Annal Toletan. [y] RODERIC TOLETAN Hiftoria Arabum.
[z] LUCÆ Tudenfis Chron. RODERIC TOLETAN de reb. Hifpaniæ, lib. vii. [a] EMANUEL DE FARIA Y SOUSA, epitome de las Hift. Portuguefas.

ceedingly

ceedingly mortified by this difgrace, and had no reafon to expect very kind treatment from his fon-in-law, after the ufage
he had given him, and therefore made him large offers to
procure his liberty. The king of *Leon* behaved towards him
with the moft profound refpect, and the greateft affection poffible; he defired him to lay afide thoughts of bufinefs and attend to his cure; but finding him reftlefs and impatient, he
affured him that he expected nothing more than to have things
put into the fame condition as before the war, and that they
might live in peace and friendfhip for the future, to which the
king of *Portugal* moft willingly affented, and before his cure
was perfected returned to his own dominions, which was the
reafon that he remained lame during the reft of his life [b].
As foon as the *Portuguefe* had evacuated the place, Don *Ferdinand* ordered his troops to quit it likewife, and receiving the homage of the *Mohammedan* governor, he left it
in the fame fituation as before the war begun. He then
returned to his capital of *Leon*, and applied himfelf affidu-
duoufly to the affairs of his civil government, which he
brought into better order than they had ever been in the times
of his predeceffors, who by having more extenfive territories
were lefs at leifure to look into things of this nature for the
eafe and benefit of their fubjects [c].

*Don Alon-
fo of Caf-
tile mar-
ries the
king of
England's
daughter
Eleonora.*

THE difputes between the *Almohades* and the independant
Moors of *Spain*, if thefe could be properly fo ftiled, who were
the fubjects of *Mohammed*, king of *Valencia*, who was the
vaffal of Don *Alonfo* of *Caftile*, ftill continued [d]. The king
of *Morocco* judged it impoffible for him to profecute the war
againft the Chriftians with any great effect; while any of the
Moors difputed his authority; and on the other hand, the
Chriftians judged it infinitely more expedient for them to act
againft the *Moors* as auxiliaries of *Moors* than as direct enemies, till it fhould be in their power to crufh them effectually
by a general confederacy. The people of *Caftile*, and more
efpecially the partizans of the houfe of *Lara*, were very defirous that the young king fhould marry, though he was not
at this time above fourteen; and as this was a point of great
concern to the nation, an affembly of the ftates was called at
Burgos to fettle this and other weighty affairs [e]. In confequence of their deliberations, embaffadors were fent to *Henry*
the fecond, king of *England*, at that time in *Guienne*, to de-

A. D.
1169.

[b] Chron. var. antiq. EMANUEL DE FARIA Y SOUSA epitome de
las Hiftorias Portuguefas. [c] RODERIC TOLETAN Hift. Arabum,
MARIANA, FERRERAS, MAYERNE TURQUET. [d] RODERIC
TOLETAN Hiftor. Arabum. [e] LUCÆ Tudenfis Chronicon,
RODERIC TOLETAN de reb. Hifpan. lib. vii.

mend

mand in the name of Don *Alonso* the princess *Eleanora* his daughter, by the duchess of *Aquitaine* of the same name [f]. While this treaty was on the carpet, the young king had an interview with the king of *Arragon* upon the frontiers, in which all old disputes were settled, and a new treaty offensive and defensive made between the two crowns, with an exchange of fortresses on both sides, for the better security of its being punctually performed [g]. At the same time, the king of *Castile*, as he was not at this juncture upon very good terms with the king of *Navarre*, stipulated with the monarch of *Arragon* for the safe passage of his queen, which was chearfully granted and performed [h]. The king, as soon as he heard of her arrival in *Arragon*, sent the archbishop of *Toledo*, the count of *Lara*, and several persons of the first distinction to receive her, met her in person at *Terrazona*, where their marriage was solemnized in the presence of the king of *Arragon* and the prime nobility of both nations; after which the king and queen of *Castile* proceeded to *Burgos*, being every where welcomed by the loud acclamations of their subjects [i]; and in the month of *August* in the succeeding year the queen was brought to bed of an infanta, who was named Donna *Berengara*, after her great grandmother [k].

A. D. 1170.

IN order to give a new turn to his affairs in *Spain*, *Joseph* king of *Morocco* sent over a very numerous body of troops, which, joined to those he had before, were put under the command of *Omar*, esteemed one of the ablest officers that had in this age commanded the *Moorish* armies. He marched with them against the king of *Valentia* in person, and at the same time sent a strong detachment to besiege *Santaren*, which had been many years in the possession of the king of *Portugal*; but against the former he was able to do little through the assistance that he received from the king of *Castile*; and the forces before *Santaren* were attacked and defeated by the *Portuguese* monarch, who obliged them to raise the siege and retire in great disorder [l]. This advantage was no sooner obtained, than Don *Ferdinand*, king of *Leon*, appeared in sight of the city with a numerous army, which alarmed the king of *Portugal* much more than the former invaders. He was however, soon out of his pain, upon receiving a message from

The Moors *invade Portugal, and the king of* Leon *assists in driving them out.*

[f] ROGER HOVEDEN, GERVASE TILBUR, &c. [g] Chron. var. antiq. [h] FERRERAS Hist. de Espana, p. v. sect. xii. [i] RODERIC SANTII Hist. Hispan. ALPHONSI a Carthagena, reg. Hispan. Anacephalæosis FRANCISCI TARAPHÆ de reg. Hispaniæ. [k] RODERIC TOLETAN de reb. Hispan. lib. xii. [l] EMANUEL DE FARIA Y SOUSA epitome de las Historias Portuguesas.

his

his fon-in-law, to compliment him on his victory, and to affure him, that he came with no other view than to lend him
his affiftance; upon which under the like circumftances he
might always depend. This was fo acceptable to the Portuguefe, that they could not help teftifying their fatisfaction in
the warmeft terms poffible, and it likewife made a very favourable impreffion upon the Chriftians throughout *Spain* in
general [m].

A. D.
1171.

THESE misfortunes, however, irritated *Jofeph*, king of *Morocco*, to fuch a degree, that he took a refolution of carrying
on the war in perfon; and in the fummer of the enfuing year
invaded the territories of Don *Alonfo* of *Caftile*, and befieged
Huete, which he reduced to the laft extremity; but upon
the approach of the king Don *Alonfo* with the whole force of
his dominions, he thought proper to retire into his own territories; where, having intelligence of the death of his old
enemy *Mohammed*, king of *Valentia*, he made himfelf fome
amends for his former difappointment, by an irruption into his
countries; where, without much difficulty, he conquered the
kingdom of *Murcia*, and added it to his empire [n]. He might
have done more if the fituation of his affairs in *Africa* had not
obliged him to return thither; and he might have been prevented from doing fo much, if the kings of *Arragon* and *Caftile*
had not turned their arms againft the king of *Navarre*, tho'
with little fuccefs, except harraffing his dominions, out of
which they were, at length, obliged to retire, without making
themfelves mafters of one confiderable place, or coming to any
action [o].

*Jofeph,
king of
Morocco,
makes him-
felf mafter
of Murcia.*

A. D.
1172.

UPON the return of *Jofeph*, king of *Morocco*, into *Africa*,
Aben-Jacob was appointed his lieutenant, and commander in
chief in *Spain*; who, to fignalize the firft year of his government, made an irruption into *Portugal*, where he befieged
Torres Novas, and took it by affault [p]. He then fuddenly entered the territories of *Leon*, of which the king, Don *Ferdinand*,
no fooner received intelligence, than he marched with a body
of troops he intended to have fent to the affiftance of his father-
in-law, and threw himfelf into *Ciudad Rodrigo*, juft time
enough to prevent that place from being invefted. He was
quickly convinced that the army of *Aben-Jacob* was much
more formidable than he imagined; and what chagrined him
moft, was, that Don *Ferdinand Ruyz de Caftro* had a fhare in
this expedition, with a very confiderable corps of brave men,
who had followed his fortune. The king apprehended his

*Don Fer-
dinand of
Leon
gains a
great vic-
tory over
the Moors.*

[m] Chron. var. antiq. [n] RODERIC TOLETAN Hift. Arabum.
[o] LUCÆ Tudenfis Chronicon. RODERIC TOLETAN de reb. Hifpan.
lib. vii. [p] RODERIC TOLETAN Hift. Arabum.

condition

condition to be very dangerous if he should be shut up in a
place scarce able to contain his troops; and therefore took a
wife, as well as generous resolution, of first trying his fortune
in the field [q]. The enemy were much embarrassed with the
spoil they had taken in *Portugal*, and had separated their army
into several bodies, with a view to prevent any relief from
being given to the place; so that being suddenly attacked by
Don *Ferdinand*, they were quickly thrown into confusion,
which, in a short time, produced a total defeat [r]. The king
improved this victory, by making such offers to Don *Ferdinand Ruyz de Castro*, as induced him to quit the party of the
Moors, and to depend upon the protection of the king of *Leon*,
who received him with great affability and kindness, and
assigned him lands sufficient for the subsistence of himself and
all his dependants [s].

A. D.
1173.

THE kings of *Castile* and *Arragon* were still busied in their
war against the king of *Navarre*, a prince far inferior to them
in force, but superior in his knowlege of the art of war; by
which he kept them from making any conquests that were
worth maintaining, and still preserved those places which had
given birth to these disputes, in spite of repeated invasions; in
which, though the confederates promised themselves much,
they were able to effect little. At length, as he wisely foresaw, they grew dissatisfied with each other, and from secret
murmurs and complaints broke at length into open hostilities,
begun by the king of *Castile*, who retook one of the castles
which he had yielded as a pledge for the due performance of
treaties, but continued by the king of *Arragon*, who at length
declared he would have nothing farther to do with the *Castilian*.
As the highest proof of his resentment, he refused to celebrate
his marriage with the Infanta Donna *Sancha*, daughter to the
emperor *Alonso*, aunt to the king of *Castile*, and sister to the
king of *Leon*; and, to shew how much he was in earnest, sent
embassadors to *Constantinopla*, to obtain the princess *Eudoxia*,
daughter to the emperor *Emanuel* [t]. This not only alarmed
the court of *Castile*, but that of *Leon* also; Don *Ferdinand*
making no secret that he could not be a tame spectator of such
an insult offered to his sister; so that the king of *Arragon* had
now the war with *Navarre* still open, and himself upon bad
terms with the kings of *Castile* and *Leon*; the consideration of
which, soon brought him to alter his measures, though even
then with some degree of reluctance and discredit.

An high
difference
arises be-
tween the
kings of
Arragon
and Cas-
tile.

---

[q] FERRERAS Historia de España, p. v. sect. xii. MAYERNE
TURQUET.   [r] LUCÆ Tudensis Chronicon. RODERIC TO-
LETAN Hist. Arabum.   [s] RODERIC TULET. de reb. Hispan.
lib. vii.   [t] Chron. var. antiq.

The houses of de Castro and Lara, bring their disputes to the decision of a battle.

In the mean time, the old quarrel between the families of Castro and *Lara* revived, and that to such a degree as to disturb the peace of the kingdoms of *Castile* and *Leon*, almost all the noble families in both taking part either on one side or the other; but, which was thought very extraordinary, the Count Don *Osorio*, though Don *Ferdinand Ruyz de Castro* had married his daughter, took part with the house of *Lara*, and actually joined himself with his vassals to the friends of that family, when a resolution was taken to determine, once for all, these implacable resentments by a general action, at a place assigned in the province of *Tiero de Campos* u. It is true that *Mariana* w represents this war, as if it had been between the uncle and the nephew; but all the ancient historians consider it in quite another light x. It may be, that a great part of those who attended Don *Ferdinand de Castro*, might be subjects of the king of *Leon*; and it is very probable they were; but this might be out of respect to his person, or from a liking to his cause, which, from the beginning, the king Don *Ferdinand* had espoused. However this may be, the battle was fought on the spot assigned, and at the day appointed, not only with great vivacity and spirit, but with all the rage and fury that inveterate hatred could inspire. In the end, Don *Ferdinand de Castro* gained a compleat victory y, the count Don *Alvaro* and the count Don *Osorio* being killed upon the spot, and the count Don *Nugnez de Lara* and the count Don *Rodrigo Guitterez* were made prisoners, whom Don *Ferdinand* generously dismissed, that they might take care of the funerals of their friends (B). He shewed not long after, that his resentment

was

---

u Ferreras Historia de España, p. v. sec. xii.　　w Historia general de España, lib. xi.　　x Chron. var. antiq.　　y Roderic Toletan de reb. Hisp. lib. vii.

(B) This passage in the *Spanish* history, shews us the true temper of the *Gothic* nation; and it would be no difficult matter to prove, that this method of determining great quarrels by combat was in general use, under the notion of an appeal to God. It is true, that the relation given us by *Mariana* is certainly inconsistent with this notion, since he makes it a war between the two kings, and speaks of Don *Ferdinand de Castro* as acting only in quality of governor and commander in chief of the king of *Leon*'s forces; who, he asserts, gave him his sister in marriage, as the only suitable reward for so great a service. We have observed in the text, that this is against the authority of all the old historians, some of whom must have been perfectly acquainted with every circumstance that attended this fact, and could be under no temptation to misrepresent it, though this alone suffi-

was not at all abated, by repudiating his wife for her father's offence [z], notwithſtanding he had paid for it with his blood; and the king of *Leon*, that he might attach him the more ſtrongly to his ſervice, gave him in marriage Donna *Tiennetta*, the natural daughter of the emperor, and his own ſiſter [a]. A circumſtance which, compared with that monarch's own match, will ſhew he was no deſpicable politician.

THE king of *Arragon*, perceiving that his own ſubjects *Kings of* were extremely offended at his breaking off the match with Caſtile, the Infanta Donna *Sancha*, and being informed that the courts Arragon, of *Leon* and *Caſtile* meditated an invaſion of his dominions, *and* Na-ſuddenly altered his purpoſe, and demanded that princeſs varre, *re*-as his wife, to which Don *Alonſo* readily aſſented, and the *fer their* marriage was ſolemnized on the eighteenth of *January*, at *differences* *Saragoſſa* [b], in the preſence of the Pope's legate, and of all *to* Henry the prelates and nobility of that kingdom. This naturally *the Second* engaged them to return to their former meaſures, in reſpect *king of* to the king of *Navarre*, upon whom they continued to make *England.* war for ſeveral years, but with as little ſucceſs as before; till at laſt, upon the repeated interpoſitions of the clergy and no-bility, all the three kings were prevailed upon to ſuſpend hoſ-tilities, and to refer the matters in diſpute, once for all, to the deciſion of the king of *England*, to whom each of the kings ſent embaſſadors, properly inſtructed to ſupport their reſpective pretenſions; and the king accordingly, after a ſolemn hearing

---

[z] Lucæ Tudenſis Chronicon. MAYERNE TURQUET. [a] Ro-DERIC SANTII Hiſt. Hiſpan. ALPHONSI a Carthagena reg. Hiſp. Anacephalæoſis FRANCISCI TARAPHÆ de reg. Hiſpaniæ. [b] MA-RIANA Hiſtoria general de Eſpana, lib. xi. FERRERAS Hiſtoria de Eſpana, p. v. ſec. xii. MAYERNE TURQUET.

ſufficiently juſtifies the preference we have given them: yet it may not be amiſs to obſerve, for the reader's ſatisfaction, that *Mari-ana* does not contradict them more than he contradicts him-ſelf; for had this been a war be-tween the two kings, how come we to have no account of its cauſes, commencement, and of its concluſion? How came Don *Ferdinand* to reſent ſo much his father in law's being in the field, when that was his duty? and laſtly, which is indeed the ſtrong-eſt of all, both in point of fact

and becauſe it is related by *Ma-riana* himſelf, how came Don *Ferdinand de Caſtro* to ſet Don *Nugnez de Lara* at liberty, after exacting from him an oath that all former quarrels ſhould be bu-ried in oblivion? Theſe are cir-cumſtances that evidently prove it was not a public, but a pri-vate quarrel; and therefore Don *Ferdinand de Caſtro*, after ſo glorious a victory, thought him-ſelf at full liberty to put an end to it, for which he is very juſtly commended by this hiſtorian.

of all parties, pronounced a very equitable award, with which however none of them were fatisfied [c]; though, after fome new difturbances, they were at length content to determine things amongft themfelves, upon pretty near the fame conditions which the king had prefcribed, after wafting much of the blood and treafure of their fubjects to no purpofe, unlefs it was to ferve the interefts of the *Moors* (C).

Don Ferdinand of Leon compelled by the Pope's cenfure to part with his queen.

THE king Don *Ferdinand* of *Leon* had lived for many years in the greateft harmony with his queen, and, for all that appears to the contrary, was inclined to live with her according to the laws of God and of his kingdom during his life; but the Pope's cardinal legate at his court, having found out that the king and the queen ftood in an equal degree of relation, or in other words, were both of them great grand children to the king Don *Alphonfo* the Sixth, he gave notice of it to his mafter, who thereupon enjoined the king to put away his wife, though he had by her a fon, the Infant Don *Alonfo*, who

A. D. 1175.

was to be the heir of his dominions [d]. It is faid that the king demurred a little to this, and that, he even went fo far as to keep his wife a year, notwithftanding all the exhortations and even menaces of the Pope; nay, it is even afferted that he was not brought to a compliance till his fubjects felt the thunder and lightning of *Rome*, by the kingdom's being put under

[c] ROGER HOVEDEN. RODERIC TOLETAN de reb. Hifpan. lib. vii. FERRERAS Hiftoria de Efpana, p. v. fec. xii. [d] RODERIC TOLETAN de reb. Hifpan. lib. vii. LUCÆ Tudenfis Chronicon.

(C) This remarkable embaffy and reference is taken notice of by our ancient hiftorians, particularly *Roger Hoveden*, who affures us, that there were feveral lords fent by each of the kings to fupport their pretenfions. The king of *England* having called together his prelates and peers, appointed the firft *Sunday* in Lent, A. D. 1177, to have this matter fully difcuffed before them; and after having heard all that could be alleged on either fide, and collected the opinion of the bifhops and nobility, met together for that purpofe, he decreed that the king of *Navarre* fhould reftore to the monarch of *Caftile* certain places which he had taken from him; and that the king of *Caftile* fhould make the like reftitution, and fhould alfo pay, for ten years together, the fum of three thoufand marvadies in gold, in compenfation for the expences of the war. This judgment of award appeared very equitable to the embaffadors on both fides, who figned it; and having finifhed the bufinefs of their embaffy, returned again into *Spain*, to render an account of their proceedings to their refpective mafters.

an

an interdict: then, for his fubjects eafe and his own, he parted with his wife Donna *Urraca* [e]; and about a year after, efpoufed Donna *Therefa*, the daughter, though fome hiftorians call her the widow, of Don *Nugno de Lara* [f]. This is more particularly mentioned, becaufe there is not the flighteft hint in any ancient hiftorian, that this monarch was in the leaft diffatisfied with his wife, or entertained any diftafte of his fon, but quite the contrary; fo that if there was any thing in this tranfaction repugnant to morality or the laws of God, it muft not be afcribed to the humour, appetite, or policy of Don *Ferdinand,* but to the Pope's abfolute will and pleafure, which, though a powerful and independant monarch, Don *Ferdinand* durft not refift.

Don *Alonfo,* king of *Caftile,* no fooner found himfelf freed from the war of *Navarre,* by the reference to the king of *England,* which had been accepted by all parties, than he refumed his former intention of imitating his illuftrious predeceffors, by turning his arms againft the infidels. With this view he caufed great magazines to be erected at *Toledo,* where, having affembled a numerous army, and amongft them the flower of the feveral orders of knighthood, he marched into the enemies country, and laid fiege to *Cuenca,* a place feated on the top of a hill, at the confluence of two little ftreams, which, after they have joined their waters, form the river *Xeucax.* Strong as this place was by fituation, the *Moors* had rendered it much more fo by labour and art; fo that it held out till provifions were fcarce in the Chriftian camp, and till the monarch of *Morocco* was apprifed of the fidelity as well as of the diftrefs of his fubjects, upon which, he directed levies to be made throughout all his dominions in *Spain,* for their relief [g]: the king of *Caftile,* in this fituation of things, thought it requifite for him to afk the affiftance of Chriftian princes, upon which, his old ally, the king of *Arragon,* marched with a body of good troops, and joined him before *Cuenca.* The *Moors* advanced with their forces in order to raife the fiege; but believing that too hazardous an undertaking, they made an irruption into the diftrict of *Toledo,* and marched directly towards that capital, as if they meant to befiege it. But the alcaydes Don *Gudiek* and Don *Alanfo* prevented this, by marching out with fuch forces as the city could raife, and giving them battle on the twenty-eighth of *July,* in which they obtained a glorious victory, or rather their fellow citizens,

King of Caftile takes Cuenca and beats the Moors who attempt its relief.

[e] Ferreras Hiftoria de Efpana, p. v. fec. xii. [f] Alphonsi, a Carthagena, reg. Hifp. Anacephalæofis, Roderic Santii Hift. Hifpan. Francisci Taraphæ de reg. Hifpaniæ. [g] Roderic Toletan Hift. Arabum.

for both those brave men fell in the field [h]. The garrison of *Cuenca*, notwithstanding they had been so long and so hard pressed, and that by this blow they were deprived of all hopes of relief, held out to the twenty-first of *September*, and did not even then surrender, but in consequence of a good capitulation [i]. The king of *Castile*, to manifest his just sense of the friendship and service rendered him by the king of *Arragon*, released him from the homage due to the crown of *Castile*, for the city of *Saragossa*, and all the territory on that side the *Ebro* lying next to his dominions [k].

A. D.
1177.

Forced by the king of Arragon to make peace with his uncle the king of Leon.

WE are told by some historians, that while the king, Don *Alonso*, was employed in the siege of *Cuenca*, his uncle Don *Ferdinand*, king of *Leon*, invaded and made himself master of some part of his dominions; which may be true, but is certainly very improbable. Upon this, the king of *Castile*, in conjunction with the king of *Portugal*, entered the dominions of *Leon*, and committed great outrages (D). The king, Don

[h] RODERIC TOLETAN de reb. Hispan. lib. vii. LUCÆ Tudensis Chron. 　[i] RODERIC TOLETAN de reb. Hispan. lib. vii. RODERIC TOLETAN Hist. Arabum. 　[k] Chron. var. antiq. [l] RODERIC TOLETAN de reb. Hispan. lib. vii.

(D) There is a passage related by *Mariana*, which happened during the siege of *Cuenca*, that well deserves the reader's notice. Don *Alonso*, king of *Castile*, finding the place hold out so much longer than he expected, left the king of *Arragon* before it with the army, and returned to *Burgos*, in order to hold an assembly of the states, his finances at that time being in much disorder. In this assembly, by the advice of Don *Diego de Haro*, who seems now to have gained an ascendancy in the king's favour, and whose sister was married to his uncle the king of *Leon*, he proposed, that since the people were already exhausted, and that if any tax was laid upon them it could not be levied so soon as the public exigence required, the nobility should for once, and without creating a precedent, consent to a small imposition upon themselves, which being immediately paid, might supply the demands of the army. The states were on the point of consenting to this proposition, when Don *Pedro de Lara* stood up, and declared he would defend the immunities of the nobles of *Castile* to the last drop of his blood, and that those would follow him who were of his opinion. Upon this he went out, attended by the majority of the assembly, by which the king's proposition was totally defeated; and it seems the nobility conceived this bold opposition so great and so well-timed a service, that they resolved to perpetuate the memory of the obligation they were under, by giving Don *Pedro* and his successors a splendid dinner annually upon the day

on

Don *Ferdinand,* engaged the Infant Don *Sancho,* of *Portugal,* who intended to have besieged *Ciudad Rodrigo,* and totally defeated his army, but discovered a great unwillingness to engage with his nephew, of whose proceedings he immediately complained to the king of *Arragon,* who had been guaranty of their last treaty, which surely he would not have done if himself had broke it. On the other hand, the king of *Arragon* sent two prelates, and a gentleman of his court, embassadors to *Castile,* in order to demand of the king the castle of *Ariza,* and to forbear all hostilities against the king of *Leon,* threatening that, if he did not, he would join with his own troops those of his uncle [m], which seems to render it certain that Don *Ferdinand* was not so much in the wrong as historians suppose him to be, and an additional proof seems to be furnished from the conduct of the king of *Castile,* who complied with his friends request, by which the peace of *Spain* was once more restored, at least among the Christian powers, at a very critical juncture [n].

A. D. 1178.

In order to strengthen that harmony which reigned at present between the two nations, Don *Ferdinand,* king of *Leon,* and Don *Alonso* of *Castile,* had an interview at *Tordesillas,* in order to remove all subjects of jealousy and dispute [o]. About this time died Donna *Theresa Lara,* queen of *Leon,* and soon after Donna *Tiennetta,* the wife of Don *Ferdinand de Castro,* by whom she had a son of the same name, commonly stiled Don *Ferdinand* the *Castilian* [p]; and the year following, Don *Ferdinand* espoused Donna *Urraca Lopez* [q], the daughter of the count Don *Lope de Haro,* one of the principal lords in the province of *Biscay;* and on the twentieth of *April* was born at *Burgos,* Don *Sancho,* son to Don *Alonso,* king of *Castile* [r]. That monarch made for several years together, incursions into

Don Ferdinand present at the glorious victory of Santaren.

A. D. 1181.

[m] Chron. var. antiq. [n] FERRERAS Historia de España, p. v. sec. xii. [o] RODERIC TOLETAN de reb. Hispan. lib. vii. LUCÆ Tudensis Chron. [p] ALPHONSI a Carthagena reg. Hisp. RODERIC SANTII Hist. Hispan. Anacephalæosis. FRANCISCI TARAPHÆ de reg. Hispan. [q] MARIANA Historia general de España, lib. xi. [r] LUCÆ Tudensis Chron. FERRERAS Historia de España, p. v. sec. xii.

on which this transaction happened. *Mariana* relates this story with great spirit, though he censures it as an indecency to the crown; other historians have perhaps expressed their sentiments more strongly by burying it in silence. We thought it inconsistent with our duty, either, to follow his example in deciding, or theirs in concealing, and have therefore stated the fact, and leave our readers to judge for themselves.

the

the territories of the *Moors,* with great success, and in one of
them he made himself master of *Alarcon,* by which *Cuenca*

A. D.
1184.
was so well covered, that he thought fit to erect it into a
bishop's fee [s]. About the same time Don *Ferdinand,* king of
Leon, besieged and took *Caceres* from the infidels, so that it
is evident, whenever the Christian princes were at peace
amongst themselves, they never failed to carry the terror of
their arms into the countries still subject to the *Moors* [t]. On
the twenty fourth of *July,* Don *Ferdinand* was likewise present, as an auxiliary to the king of *Portugal,* at the glorious
victory of *Santaren,* when the whole force of the *Moors,* commanded by their monarch *Joseph,* was totally routed without
fighting [u]. The death of that monarch by a fall from his
horse just as the battle began, intimidated his subjects to such
a degree, that they immediately quitted the field of battle to
place all their safety in flight, which afforded the Christians
an opportunity they did not neglect of quitting scores with the
Moors, for their recent severities [w].

Repeated   Don *Alonso* of *Castile* had the next year the misfortune to
expeditions be beaten by the *Moors,* in the neighbourhood of *Sotillo* in
of Don   *Estremadura* [x], which however did not hinder his taking the
Alonso of field again in the succeeding spring; and, after having enriched
Castile his troops with a great booty, he returned triumphant, and
against the went afterwards to an interview with the king of *Arragon,*
Moors in with whom he concerted the means of continuing the peace
Andalu- which had already lasted for some years amongst the Christian
sia. powers, and of prosecuting the war against the infidels, points

A. D.
1186.
which these two princes had equally at heart, and, by con-
curring therein, contributed greatly to their own reputation
and the good of their subjects [y]. The next year Don *Alonso*
was in the field again, and made himself master of some
small places; but his chief design seems to have been the security of his own dominions, by keeping the *Moors* in such a
state of apprehension and distraction, as might hinder them
A. D.
1187.
from undertaking any thing to the prejudice of his territories,
without which it would have been impossible for the people to
have enjoyed that degree of peace and safety, that was necessary
to cultivate and improve their lands.

[s] Chron. var. antiq.   [t] RODERIC TOLETAN Hist. Arabum.
[u] EMANUEL DE FARIA Y SOUSA, Epitome de las Historias Portuguesas, MAYERNE TURQUET, FERRERAS.   [w] RODERIC
TOLETAN Hist. Arabum.   [x] LUCÆ Tudensis Chron. Ro-
DERIC TOLETAN de reb. Hispan. lib. vii.   [y] Chron. var.
antiq.

IN

In the autumn of this year, Don *Ferdinand,* king of *Leon,* went to pay his devotions at the tomb of the apostle St. *James* [z], in the church of *Compostella* ; and at his return to *Benavente,* which is ten leagues from *Leon,* found himself extreamly indisposed : he lingered however through the remaining months of that year, and to the twenty-first day of *January* in the next, when he breathed his last, to the great regret of his subjects. *Mariana* says that he was fitter for the general of an army, than for the government of a kingdom [a] : but if we consider his actions, we may, with equal reason, believe that there have been very few kings fitter for both ; for he was a prince of great virtue and generosity, and as remarkable for piety as for valour. He left at his death three sons, Don *Alonso* by his first queen the Infanta of *Portugal,* with whom, as the reader has seen, the Pope forced him to part, and Don *Sancho* and Don *Garcia,* by Donna *Urraca,* who survived him [b]. *Mariana,* and after him other historians [c], have suggested, that at the time of his decease, Don *Alonso* was on the point of flying into *Portugal,* being weary of the continual ill usage of his mother in law, who reflected on him for his mother's misfortune, and pretended to treat him as a bastard ; but this is very improbable, since even these historians allow that his mother in law's hatred arose from his father's affection to him ; neither does it appear that the Pope pretended to bastardize the issue of those marriages, which they declared null on the score of consanguinity. The body of Don *Ferdinand* was buried in the cathedral of St. *James,* near that of his mother Donna *Berengara,* and of his grand-father Don *Raymond* [d]. His successor was present at the solemnity, and some days after went to pay a visit to his mother in law, with whom it appears that he was inclined to live at least upon fair terms, notwithstanding her intentions to have deprived him of the succession, to have placed her son Don *Sancho* on the throne of *Leon,* and to have bestowed the crown of *Galicia* on Don *Garcia,* are said to have been generally known ; so that the moderation of the young monarch deserved to be highly admired [e]. But as he was universally acceptable to the

The death of Don Ferdinand of Castile, and his posterity.

A. D. 1188.

---

[z] Hist. Compostel. Annal Compostel.   [a] RODERIC TOLETAN de reb. Hispan. lib. vii.   ALPHONSI a Carthagena reg. Hispan. Anacephalæosis FRANCISCI TARAPHÆ de reg. Hispan. RODERIC SANTII Hist. Hispan.   Historia general de Espana, lib. xi.   [b] RODERIC TOLETAN de reb. Hispan. lib. vii. LUCÆ Tudensis Chron.   [c] FERRERAS, MAYERNE TURQUET. [d] RODERIC SANTII Hist. Hispan.   LUCÆ Tudensis Chron. [e] Chron. var. antiq.

people, and sure of support from the crown of *Portugal,* there seems to be good reason to doubt whether the queen Donna *Urraca Lopez* could ever entertain such notions, more especially considering the age of her children, and her having no protector capable of affording her the least degree of assistance towards the execution of such a design. It is therefore more than likely that these conjectures took rise from succeeding events, with which, when the reader is acquainted, he will be enabled to form a better judgment.

Don Alon- THE king of *Castile* held this year the general assembly
so the of the states of his kingdom at *Carrion,* to which, through a
ninth, his desire of expressing his great affection for his cousin, and that,
son and according to the custom of those times, he might be made a
successor, knight by a monarch in so high reputation for wisdom, cou-
knighted rage, and all other royal virtues, the king of *Leon* resorted;
by the king and having in that assembly, purely from a spirit of politeness
of Castile. and complaisance, kissed the hand of the king of *Castile* as he took his seat, this was afterwards wrested into an act of solemn homage, and was the true cause of that distaste which quickly succeeded to this superabundant kindness between these princes [f]. The next year however they acted as confederates against the *Moors,* and with great success, recovered out of their hands abundance of places in *Estremadura*; not content with which they passed the *Sierra Morena,* and wasted all the territory of *Seville* with fire and sword to the sea side. One would have imagined that nothing could have contributed more than the issue of this campaign, to convince the monarch of *Castile* of the expediency of living upon good terms with his cousin of *Leon*; yet this was so far from being the case, that it proved the cause of a rupture between them; for though the latter had shared in the danger and fatigue, yet the former kept all the conquests, though some of them, from their situation, were very convenient for his cousin, and of little consequence to him. This was resented by Don *Alonso* of *Leon,* like a young man; for he immediately sought the friendship of the king of *Portugal,* with the same zeal that he shewed in embracing that of the king of *Castile,* and as the strongest proof of his sincerity, married the Infanta Donna *Theresa* [g], who was his cousin German, by the mother's side, without reflecting on what had happened to his father.

[f] RODERIC TOLETAN de reb. Hispan, lib. vii. LUCÆ Tudensis Chronicon. FERRERAS Historia de España, p. v. sec. xii. · [g] RODERIC TOLETAN Hist. Arabum, Annal Toletan. EMANUEL DE FARIA Y SOUSA, Epitome de las Historias Portuguesas.

AMONGST

·Amongst other circumstances that contributed to inspire *The in-* the king of *Castile* with unreasonable haughtiness, one was, *tended* that the emperor *Frederick Barbaroffa* had concluded a treaty *marriage* of marriage between his son prince *Conrad,* and the Infanta *between* Donna *Berengara,* daughter of the king of *Castile,* and had *the empe-* sent the young prince into *Spain,* that their nuptials might be *ror's son* celebrated at *Toledo*[h]. Don *Alonso* received him in that city *Conrad,* with the utmost magnificence, and with all the marks of *and the* respect he could desire, signed the contract of marriage which *Infanta* had been before subscribed by the emperor, and made his in- *Berenga-* tended son-in-law a knight. Yet after all this was done, the *ra, fails.* nuptials did not take place[i]. Most of the *Spanish* historians[k], for the honour of their country, ascribe this to the Infanta's terror of so long a journey, a distaste to the climate of *Ger-many,* and a prejudice against the manners of the people: but *Ferreras*[l] has assigned, if not a more certain, at least a much more probable cause: he observes, that Donna *Eleonora,* queen of *Castile,* was, during the stay of prince *Conrad,* brought to bed of the Infant Don *Ferdinand,* which entirely spoiled the scheme of the *German* prince, who, as the king of *Castile* had no male issue living, expected to have succeeded him in the throne, in consequence of his marriage; of which, perceiving that there was now little hopes, he took leave of the king, the queen, and the Infanta, and returned into *Germany*[m]. Soon after this, the monarch of *Castile* presum-ing on his cousin's youth and his own great power, committed acts of hostility in the kingdom of *Leon;* of this the king of *Arragon* was no sooner informed, than he made an irruption into *Castile;* upon which Don *Alonso* turned his arms against him, but with very indifferent success. By the interposition of the nobility and prelates of both kingdoms, the peace was quickly renewed, upon a[n] promise that the king of *Castile* should do nothing to the prejudice of his cousin of *Leon,* whom, because he had injured, he hated.

The Pope's legate in *Spain,* cardinal *Gregory,* who was *Don Alon-* sent to promote peace amongst the Christian princes, gave a *so, his* singular specimen of his abilities that way, by insinuating to *queen* the kings of *Leon* and *Portugal,* that the marriage of Don *Therefa,* *Alonso,* with the Infanta Donna *Therefa,* was void, and that *and four*

h Alphonsi a Carthagena reg. Hispan. Anacephalæosis Fran-cisci Taraphæ de reg. Hispaniæ. Annal Toletan. ¹ Ro-deric Toletan de reb. Hispan. lib. vii. k Mariana His-toria general de Espana, lib. xi. ¹ Historia de Espana, p. v. sec. xii. m Lucæ Tudensis Chron. Mayerne Turquet, Histoire general d'Espagne, liv. x. n Roderic Toletan, de reb. Hispan. lib. vii.

there-

prelates,
excommu-
nicated,
and his
marriage
null'd,

therefore they ought to part; but none of the parties inclin
to obey, he summoned a council at *Salamanca* [o], in whi
the point was determined as he would have it; but the bish
of *Leon, Astorga, Salamanca,* and *Zamora,* who did not affi
at this council, protested against the decree, alleging, th
marriages of this sort were not prohibited by the divine,
even by the ecclesiastical law, but by the civil, and for certa
political reasons; and that therefore princes, who had a pow
of establishing this law, must likewise have the power of d'
pensing with it.   The cardinal legate effectually refuted th
pernicious doctrine, by excommunicating the four prelate
and threatening both the kingdoms of *Leon* and *Portugal* wit
an interdict; and very soon after he carried his threats int
execution [p], which were attended with most dreadful conf
quences, the people in both kingdoms being extremely pr
voked at the obstinacy of the king of *Leon,* who, in spite
the express will and pleasure of the Pope, would needs li
with his wife.   That monarch in vain sent the bishop
Zamora to *Rome,* to prevail upon the Pope to remove the im-
pediment as to the legality of his marriage; the pontif would
hear nothing upon that head, but at the earnest suit of the
bishop took off his excommunication and the interdict, allowing divine service and the sacraments to be administered
every where, except in the presence of the king and queen
of *Leon* [q], who were left to the most desperate courses if their
own piety had not guarded them.

A. D.
1193.

Archbishop
of Tole-
do's expe-
dition
against
the Moors
excites a
dreadful
war.

Don *Alonso,* king of *Castile,* was all this while engaged in
continual expeditions against the Infidels; and this very year
had sent a potent army, under the command of Don *Martin,*
archbishop of *Toledo,* into *Andalusia,* where he had acted with
unexampled severity, destroying the corn and the vines, tearing the olive-trees up by the roots, putting multitudes of men,
women, and children in chains, sweeping away all the cattle;
and, to compleat this scene of destruction, laying every village
and open town he passed through, in ashes.   The reader
must not imagine that we are guilty of any exaggeration, for
we transcribe not only the fact, but the very words, from a
Spanish historian [r].   The report of this cruel proceeding was
no sooner brought to *Jacob Aben-Joseph,* king of *Morocco,*
than he wrote a letter to the king Don *Alonso,* in which he
expostulated on this new way of making war, in a manner
barbarous beyond all example; to which Don *Alonso* gave so

[o] Ferreras Historia de España, p. v. sec. xii.   [p] Chron.
var. antiq.   [q] Lucæ Tudensis Chron.   Roderic Toletan.
de reb. Hispan. lib. vii.   [r] Historia de España, p. v. sec. xii.

haughty

haughty an answer, that the *Moor* immediately published the *Gacia* [s], which answers to our croisade, and insures to every *Muffulman*, who either kills a Christian or is killed himself, a plenary absolution from all his sins, and an immediate entrance into Paradise. This called every man that was able to bear arms into the field, and the king of *Morocco* himself, coming over with a prodigious army from *Africa*, ordered a general rendezvous of the whole forces of his empire at *Seville* [t]. Don *Alonso* of *Castile*, upon this, condescended to ask the assistance of the kings of *Leon* and *Navarre*, representing it as a war of religion, and in which the common cause of all the Christians in *Spain* was at stake; as they were convinced of the truth of the fact, they did not enquire nicely into the cause, but readily promised him, not only all he asked, but that they would march with all the forces of their respective kingdoms, to join him at *Toledo*, and began immediately to make the necessary levies for that purpose, not doubting that this confederacy would secure both his and their own dominions.

JACOB ABEN-JOSEPH found his army so numerous, that he *The king of Castile obliged to ask succours, and fights imprudently before he received them.* was obliged to order part of them to rendezvous at *Cordova*, where having joined them with the rest of his forces from *Seville*, he entered the kingdom of *Toledo*, and encamped within sight of *Calatrava* and *Alarcos*, both places of great strength, and which might have found employment for some time, even for his prodigious army [u]. But the king of *Castile*, who had assembled all his forces, advanced, without waiting for his allies, within a small distance of the enemy. The principal officers of his army suggested to him that he ought either to retreat in time or fortify his camp, since both the kings of *Leon* and *Navarre* were within a few days march, and not adventure on a battle with such a vast disproportion of forces. But the king could not be brought to relish these wholesome counsels; he had treated the *Moor* with contempt, and to retire before him would be a perpetual disgrace: besides, he was unwilling to share the honour of a victory, and he looked upon his troops and himself as invincible. On the eighteenth of *July*, the two armies came in sight, at a small distance from the town of *Alarcas*, and the engagement quickly began. The Christians behaved with great intrepedity; but, after a warm and obstinate dispute, they were

[s] RODERIC TOLETAN Hist. Arabum. [t] RODERIC TOLETAN de reb. Hispan. lib. vii. MAYERNE TURQUET, Histoire general de Espagne, liv. x. [u] Annal Toletan. LUCÆ Tudensis Chronicon.

overborn

overborn by numbers [w]. Don *Alonſo* perceiving that they began to give way, and apprehending the loſs of that high reputation which he had acquired, grew perfectly furious, and would have thrown himſelf into the midſt of the enemy, but the nobility about his perſon reſtrained him, and carried him off by force [x]. The *Moors* upon this occaſion gained one of the completeſt victories that hiſtory records [y]. There fell upwards of twenty thouſand *Caſtilians* upon the ſpot, amongſt whom was the flower of the nobility : the military orders, their camp and their baggage fell likewiſe into the hands of the enemy, and the ſhattered remains of the army retreated with difficulty to *Toledo*, and ſhut themſelves up under cover of the extended fortifications.

Diſmal conſequences of his defeat at Alarcos, and inſolent behaviour afterwards.

A. D. 1195.

Don *Alonſo* had ſcarce entered this city, before the king of *Leon* arrived with a numerous army : he went immediately to viſit his couſin, and mildly expoſtulated with him the imprudence of his conduct [z]. The *Spaniſh* hiſtorians, for the honour of their country, have unanimouſly ſuppreſſed the anſwer of the monarch of *Caſtile* ; but it is nevertheleſs certain, that he endeavoured to throw that blame, which belonged wholly to himſelf, upon the two kings [a], and this in ſuch coarſe terms, that Don *Alonſo* of *Leon* immediately quitted *Toledo*, and returned into his own dominions, ravaging thoſe of *Caſtile* as he paſſed ; and the monarch of *Navarre* did the like [b]. Upon this, the king of *Caſtile*, having provided for the ſecurity of *Toledo*, repaired to *Burgos*, leaving *Jacob Aben-Joſeph* to make the beſt uſe of his victory, who reduced *Calatrava* and *Alarcos*, though with ſome difficulty, and afterwards made a furious irruption into *Portugal*, where he murdered all the *Monks* and eccleſiaſtics that fell in his way, and waſted all the country with inexpreſſible barbarity, as far as appears from the hiſtories of theſe times, in which Don *Roderic* [c] *de Ximenes*, then biſhop of *Siguenca*, and afterwards primate of *Toledo*, flouriſhed, he met with little or no reſiſtance ; for the Chriſtian princes were more intent on puniſhing the inſolence of the king of *Caſtile*, than cautious in protecting their own dominions, which, how groſs ſoever the provocation they had received might be, was beyond all doubt to the full as inexcuſable. At length they were awakened from their le-

[w] Roderic Toletan de reb. Hiſpan. lib. vii, [x] Roderic Toletan Hiſt. Arabum. Annal Toletan. [y] Mariana Hiſtoria general de Eſpana, lib. xi. Ferreras Hiſtoria de Eſpana, p. v. ſec. xii. Mayerne Turquet. [z] Rod. Tol. de reb. Hiſpan. lib. vii. [a] Chron. var. antiq. [b] Ferreras Hiſtoria de Eſpana, p. v. ſec. xii. [c] Rod. Tol. Hiſt. Arabum. Rod. Tol. de reb. Hiſpan. lib. vii.

thargy,

thargy, and began, though a little too late, to assemble their forces, and to provide for the chastisement of an enemy, who, in respect to them, had met with nothing that could justify the brutality of his behaviour.

THE kings Don *Alonso* of *Leon*, and Don *Sancho* of *Portugal*, no longer able to resist the importunities of their subjects, submitted to the papal decree, and the Infanta Donna *Theresa* of *Portugal*, queen of *Leon*, returned home to her father, leaving behind her the two princesses, her daughters; and there is reason to believe, that this event threw the affairs of that kingdom into great disorder. [d]. This induced the king of *Castile*, who had now collected a great body of forces, to fall with them into the kingdom of *Leon*; though the *Moors*, with the miramamolin at their head, had actually invaded his own dominions, penetrated as far as *Toledo*, and remained ten days before that city, which, however, they found so well fortified, and the people so much disposed to make a vigorous resistance, that at length, loaded with pillage, and sated with revenge, they thought fit to retreat [e]. In the mean time, Don *Alonso* of *Castile* took many places of small strength in the kingdom of *Leon*, ruined one of the suburbs belonging to the capital, which was inhabited by *Jews*, and at last besieged the city of *Astorga*, but without effect; which provoked him to such a degree, that he wasted all the open country with as little mercy as if he intended to copy, in his cousin's dominions, the dreadful lesson which had been set him by the infidels in his own [f]; and having done this, he returned to *Toledo*, with an army laden with spoils taken from their fellow Christians, through a country miserably ruined by the infidels, merely for want of that defence which it was his and their duty to afford g.

Invades the kingdom of Leon, while his own dominions are ravaged by the Moors.

A. D. 1196.

IT might be naturally apprehended that his own reflections, the advices of great and good men about him, joined to the clamours of the common people, which were loud, in proportion to the evils they had endured, must have wrought upon the mind of the king of *Castile*, and brought him back to a just sense of things. It happened however far otherwise; he spent the winter in negotiating with Don *Pedro*, king of *Arragon*, and prevailed upon him to send a strong corps of auxiliaries to assist in his next campaign, while the king of *Leon* on the other side was indefatigable in raising forces in *Galicia* to resist him; so that it looked as if the Christian princes had acted in concert with the *Moors*, and were bent

They over-run the kingdom of Toledo again, but at length retire into their own territories.

---

[d] ROD. TOL. de reb. Hispan. lib. vii. LUCÆ Tudensis Chron.
[e] Annal Toletan, MORALES.   [f] ROD. TOL. de reb. Hispan. lib. vii. LUCÆ Tudensis Chron.   g Annal Toletan.

upon

upon each other's deftruction [h]. In all probability this had been brought about, if the *Moorifh* emperor, *Jofeph*, had not taken the field with an army fo numerous, as to threaten the conqueft or deftruction of the king of *Caftile*'s dominions; which conftrained that monarch to fufpend his refentment againft his coufin, that he might prevent the lofs or total ruin of his own countries. He did not find himfelf in a condition, even with the fuccours of *Arragon*, to act offenfively againft the *Moors*; and experience had taught him not to hazard battles with a handful of troops againft thoufands. He did therefore what it became him to do; he put ftout garrifons into all the ftrong places in his territories, and kept himfelf in the mountains, with a flying camp, which prevented the *Moor* from taking any place of importance, though he attempted feveral; and at length, his army being much reduced by fatigues and ficknefs, was compelled to retire into *Andalufia*, with many flaves and much booty, but with diminifhed forces, and their reputation rather declining than increafed [i]. So little did he profit by his important victory.

A peace concluded between the two kings of Caftile *and* Leon.   As foon as his territories were delivered from the *Moor*, Don *Alonfo* of *Caftile*, having drawn out part of his garrifons, fell, with a potent army, into the dominions of *Leon*, where he took fome places of no great ftrength, and ruined all the open country [k]. The king of *Leon*, having an army not at all inferior to his, marched towards him, with a defign to give a check to his proceedings by a battle. The perfon upon whofe advice and abilities he chiefly relied, was his coufin, Don *Pedro Fernandez de Caftro*, the fon of that great hero of the fame name, who had commanded the forces of the king his father, who had ferved the *Moorifh* emperor *Jofeph*, and who, it is even more than probable, was at the head of a corps of *Mohammedan* auxiliaries at this very time, and by him he was diffuaded from fighting [l]. He obferved that the event of a battle was in all refpects uncertain, except one, which was the ruin of both parties, let the victory fall where it would, fince the *Moors* were ready and waited to take the advantage. He propofed therefore a treaty, to which, though the king was backward, he found the nobility and prelates of *Caftile* were unanimoufly inclined. He went therefore to *Valladolid*, in perfon, to negotiate with queen *Eleanor*, and having propofed a marriage between the Infanta Donna *Berengara*, and Don *Alonfo*, king of *Leon* [m], the

---

[h] Zurit. Annal Arragon.   [i] Annal Toletan.   [k] Rod.
Tol. de reb. Hifpan. lib. vii.   [l] Lucæ Tudenfis Chron.
[m] Rod. Tol. de reb. Hifpan. lib. vii.

treaty

treaty was quickly concluded, and the marriage soon after solemnized in the same place, though the king of *Castile* was not present; and shewed thereby, that what he did, he did with reluctance, against his own sense of things; for in his temper united qualities that rarely meet, hastiness and obstinacy.

At the entrance of the ensuing year, the king of *Castile* found himself freed from all apprehensions of the *Moors,* by an application from their monarch, either for a peace or a long truce; the reason of which was, that his affairs had taken a wrong turn in *Africa,* where several of his governors had revolted, and set up for themselves. The king of *Castile* was not ignorant of this; and yet he acted as if he had been so; and concluded a peace with the *Moorish* prince, upon the very same terms, that might have been prudently accepted when he was in the full career of his victories [a]: the reason of this was, that the king of *Castile* meditated, in conjunction with the king of *Arragon,* to over-run the territories of the king of *Navarre,* who, from the sense he had of the implacable enmity of these two monarchs, had suffered himself to be strangely deceived by the *Moorish* emperor, who pretended to give him his daughter in marriage, and with her all his dominions in *Spain* [o]. This war the two kings accordingly prosecuted, but with little success, though they had great superiority, as will be shewn in another place.

In the mean time, Pope Innocent the third, succeeding *Celestin* in the see of *Rome,* took umbrage at the marriage of the king of *Leon,* with his cousin the Infanta of *Castile,* and sent peremptory instructions to his nuncio to part them, and, if they refused to part, to put the kingdoms of *Castile* and *Leon* under the censures of the church; which the nuncio, less violent or more afraid than his master, was not inclined to do; but gave time for the two kings to send their ambassadors to *Rome,* in order to pacify, if possible, this haughty successor of St. *Peter* [p]; but notwithstanding this was attempted, with all imaginable humility, the Pope remained fixed to his point, and sent fresh orders for separating the king and queen, or for putting all the churches in *Castile* and *Leon* under an interdict; the very thoughts of which, it was well known, would terrify the common people almost to madness, and consequently expose the state to such dangers, as were most likely to fright, even crowned heads, into obedience [q]. The arms of *Castile* were this year more successful

The former concludes a peace also with the miramamolin of Africa.

A. D. 1197.

Pope Innocent III. insists upon the annulling the marriage of the king of Leon.

A. D. 1198.

<hr>

[a] LUCÆ Tudensis Chron.   [o] MORALES, FERRERAS.   [p] Epist.
Pap. INNOCENT III. lib. i.   [q] FERRERAS Historia de España,
p. v. sec. xii.

in *Navarre*, the king of that realm being absent in *Africa*, and had reduced the city of *Victoria*, and some other places of importance, to a state of such distress, that a kind of provisional capitulation was made, dependent upon the orders of the king of *Navarre* for their surrender, which orders soon after arrived, that monarch being at this time in no condition to vindicate his own rights, or to defend those of his subjects, which left it in the power of Don *Alonso* to gratify his ambition in a very extensive degree [r] : so that this ancient and once powerful kingdom was reduced within an hair's-breadth of destruction.

The Infanta Donna Blancha espouses prince Lewis of France.

THE satisfaction he derived from thence must have been very much heightened, by an honourable event, in respect to his family, which fell out soon after, and which, for some particular reasons, we are obliged to represent at large. *John*, king of *England*, finding himself under a necessity of making a disadvantageous peace with *Philip*, king of *France*, his mother, queen *Eleanor*, contrived to lessen the discredit of this transaction, by a very singular expedient, which she no sooner proposed, than it was by all parties very readily embraced [s]. According to her scheme, the places conquered by *France* were to be restored to her son, who was then to make a voluntary cession of them, as the dowry of his niece, the Infanta Donna *Blanca*, or, as the *French* call her, *Blanche*, who was to marry prince *Lewis*, heir apparent of the crown of *France*; and to carry all this into execution, she offered to go herself into *Spain*, to fetch the young princess [t]. Upon her arrival at the court of *Castile*, she was received by Don *Alonso*, her son-in-law, and by her daughter, queen *Eleanor*, with all possible marks of respect and affection, and her proposal readily accepted, the young princess put into her hands, whom she carried to her son, the king of *England*, in *Normandy*, where the peace being signed upon the twenty-second of *May*, the marriage was celebrated on the twenty-third, at a place called *Purmor*, in that dutchy, the ceremony being performed by the archbishop of *Bourdeaux*; the reason of which was, that the king having incurred the displeasure of the Pope by a divorce, the kingdom of *France* was then under an interdict [v]. The marriage thus concluded, the young princess was conducted to the court of her father-in-law, there to be brought up, till such time as herself and her spouse were of a fit age to consummate [w]; which circumstance seems to

A. D.
1200.

[r] P. MORET Investigaciones historicas de las antiquitades del Reyno de Navarra.   [s] ROG. HOVEDEN Annal.   [t] Nic. TRIVET. Annal, vol. i. p. 140.   [v] ROG. HOVEDEN Annal. [w] P. DANIEL Histoire de France, vol. iii. p. 481.

be

be a sufficient refutation of that notion, which passed for ages as a point of true history, that this Infanta was the eldest daughter of *Castile*, and with which some very eminent *French* writers seem at this day very unwilling to part [x], notwithstanding the clear proofs that may be brought of the contrary. But the following history will shew nothing like it was surmised in some ages after the event.

THE same year Don *Alonso*, king of *Leon*, had, by the Infanta Donna *Berengara*, his son *Ferdinand*; the day of his birth is no where recorded; but it is certain he was born before the month of *August*, and baptized with great solemnity in the cathedral church of *Leon*, to the great joy of both courts [y]. About this time, the disputes between the king of *Leon* and his mother-in-law produced a kind of rupture; for the late king *Ferdinand*, having bestowed upon her some fortresses of great importance to the safety of his dominions, Don *Alonso* did not think it consistent either with his dignity or interest, to leave them any longer in her hands, and therefore demanded them [z]. On the other hand, the queen dowager Donna *Urraca*, by the advice and with the assistance of her brother Don *Diego Lopez*, fortified them; and that nobleman also applied himself to the king of *Castile*, in hopes that he would have interposed with his son-in-law, to prevent things from coming to extremities. But that monarch, either judging the thing in itself unreasonable, or being unwilling to take part in any thing against his son-in-law, rejected this demand; and the places not long after were taken by the king of *Leon*, which so highly provoked Don *Diego Lopez*, that he retired to his own estates, exceedingly exasperated against both kings, and consequently disposed, whenever any occasion should offer, to sacrifice his duty to his resentment [a]. Such was the situation of things in *Spain*, at the opening of the thirteenth century, when the Christians were indeed become more potent than in former times, but were as little united as ever.

DON *Alonso* of *Castile* was extremely provoked at this haughty behaviour in one for whom he had done so much, and for whose sake he had disobliged so many; but his resentment, in some measure, received a justification from Don *Diego*'s wasting his country, as soon as he found himself safe in *Navarre*, with a considerable body of desperate people

Marginal notes:
Birth of St. Ferdinand, afterwards king of Castile and Leon.

Kings of Castile and Leon join their forces against Don Diego

[x] See the notes on the French translation of Mariana. [y] ROD. TOL. de reb. Hispan. lib. vii [z] Annal Toletan, LUCÆ Tudensis Chronicon, [a] ROD. TOLETAN de reb. Hispan. lib. vii. Chron. var. antiq.

who

who had followed his fortunes. His insurrection became in
a short time so formidable, that the king of *Castile* requested
the assistance of his son-in-law to reduce him ; accordingly
both princes took the field, at the head of a numerous army.
Don *Diego* had not forces sufficient to give them battle ; but,
having fortified *Estella* in *Biscay,* and provided it with all
things necessary to sustain a siege, after harrassing the royal
armies in the field, he gradually withdrew his forces thither.
The two kings invested the place, and battered it with great
fury, and as soon as the breaches were practicable, made repeated assaults, but to no purpose ; so that in the end they
were constrained to raise the siege [b]. About this time, the
kings of *Castile* and *Arragon* concluded a truce for three years
with the king of *Navarre,* in order more at leisure to negotiate a peace.

*The king
of* Leon
*obliged to
part with
his second
queen, by
the Pope.*

THE steadiness shewn by Don *Alonso,* king of *Leon,* in
keeping his queen, contrary to the decrees of Pope *Innocent*
the third, so provoked that zealous head of the church, as to
induce him to execute what he had threatened, by putting
the kingdom of *Leon* under an interdict, upon which a schism
arose, some of the bishops adhering to the king, and some to
the Pope [c]. But the king of *Castile* prevented this thunder
from falling on the heads of his subjects, by declaring that he
was ready to receive the Infanta, his daughter, whenever the
king of *Leon* should think fit to send her home. While things
continued in this state, queen *Eleanor* of *Castile* was brought
to bed of a son, on the 14th of *April* [d] ; and not long after
this, in pity to their subjects, and, so far as appears, without
any distaste or dispute between themselves, the king and queen
of *Leon* resolved to separate. The Pope, in consideration that
the marriage was entered into and consummated on both
sides with sincere and laudable intentions, declared the
children legitimate : these were the Infants *Ferdinand* and
Alonso, and the Infantas *Eleonora, Constantia,* and *Berengara.*
As for the dowry which had been settled by the king of *Leon,*
the Infanta *Berengara* generously gave it up. All these
great points being adjusted, *Alonso,* king of *Castile,* threw
in a proposition, too weighty and too reasonable to be rejected ; this was, that the Infant Don *Ferdinand,* and his daughter's eldest son, should (in case of his brother's demise) be
declared heir apparent of the kingdom of *Leon* [e]. An assem-

---

[b] P, MORET, Investigaciones historicas de las antiquitades del
Reyno de Navarra. [c] MORALES, RODERIC TOLETAN de reb.
Hispan. lib. vii. Chron. var. antiq. [d] Annal Toletan.
[e] RODERIC TOLETAN de reb. Hispan. lib. vii. LUCÆ Tudensis
Chron. Epist. INNOCENT III. et HONOR. III.

bly of the eſtates was accordingly called, who unanimouſly ſwore to the ſucceſſion; and this ceremony over, queen *Berengara* returned to her father's court, leaving all her children at that of the king her huſband [f]. Thus, through the pious application of the papal power, Don *Alonſo* was once more declared a ſingle man, though with two wives living, and ſix or ſeven children (E).

AT the time of the concluding the truce between the kings of *Caſtile*, *Arragon*, and *Navarre*, Don *Diego Lopez de Haro* was reſtored to his old maſter's favour, who alſo interceded for him with the king of *Leon*. The great military ſkill which he had ſhewn in defending *Eſtella*, had its merit even with thoſe monarchs, againſt whom he defended it; and they could not help eſteeming and admiring the courage and *Which, in ſpite of all precautions taken to prevent it, occaſions a war.*

[f] Lucæ Tudenſis Chronicon.

(E) It may not be amiſs to obſerve here, that, ſo long as the common people had amongſt them a real ſpirit of religion, the interdict was ſuch a weapon as no prince, however potent, could reſiſt. It was ſo called, becauſe it implied a prohibition of all public worſhip, and the adminiſtration of all ſacraments, ſo that, while it laſted, a whole Chriſtian nation was deprived of every kind of ſpiritual comfort. But by having recourſe to this violent remedy too often, the Popes very much weakened its force, and by degrees brought the people, not only to deſpiſe that, but to be very cold and indifferent even as to the eſſentials of religion, which is the neceſſary and inevitable conſequence of pious frauds and eccleſiaſtical tyranny. While the old *Gothic* church ſubſiſted, *Spain* was exempted from every thing of this kind; for, though the church made uſe of cenſures, and ſometimes excommunicated perſons of high rank, and ſome-times conſiderable bodies of people, yet this was always for their own offences; whereas the interdict puniſhed multitudes, for the crimes or the ſuppoſed crimes of individuals, contrary, not only to the practice of the primitive church, and to the whole current of the ſcriptures, but alſo to the common ſenſe of mankind. However, ſince they had ſubmitted to the papal authority, and were reſolved, at all events, to adhere to the ſpiritual monarchy, as it was ſtiled, of *Rome*, the *Spaniſh* kings found themſelves as much and as effectually ſubjects, or rather more ſo, than their people were to them; for theſe monarchs were by no means abſolute, they governed according to the laws and cuſtoms of their country; whereas the Pope governed without law, or, which came to the ſame thing, was believed to have a power of declaring thoſe laws, by which he would be pleaſed to govern.

conduct

conduct of this nobleman, though exerted against them. The case is singular enough to deserve notice; but besides this, it is necessary that we should have an idea of the character of Don *Diego.* It is uncertain whether he commanded in that war, which, at the sollicitation of *Philip Augustus* of *France,* Don *Alonso,* king of *Castile,* carried on in *Aquitaine* against king *John* of *England,* of the reality of which we cannot doubt, though passed over in silence by the *English* and *French* historians; since we find it recorded by two grave *Spanish* prelates, who lived in those times [g]. The birth of the Infant Don *Henry* might possibly lessen the respect which had been hitherto paid by Don *Alonso* of *Castile* to the king of *Leon;* and this was still more diminished upon his sending back his daughter, though with her own consent, and with great reluctance on the part of that king. That this was really the case, appears from the refusal of the *Castilian* governors to surrender the places assigned for the queen's dower, which she had relinquished by an act of her own, and this act confirmed by the Pope [h]. The king of *Leon* resenting this, at-

A. D.
1205. tempted to reduce them by force, which gave beginning to a war that lasted for three years, but with the interposition of some truces; and at this period, his affairs making it necessary, the king of *Castile* shewed a desire of peace, and that it might be well kept left the terms of it to the king of *Leon* [i]. This afforded that monarch an opportunity of shewing, that, when he parted with his queen, he did not part with his affections for her. He had stipulated the delivery of the places in question, and he had made a war to acquire them; now he was left to dictate the peace, he consented that the best part of them should remain in the condition they were, and

A. D.
1208. that the Infanta Donna *Berengara* should enjoy the revenue [k]. About this time, the king of *Castile* gave his second daughter Donna *Urraca* in marriage to the Infant Don *Alonso,* prince of *Portugal;* and at the request of Don *Roderic Ximenes,* the historian, founded a university at *Palencia,* which in the succeeding reign was, as some say, transferred to *Salamanca* [l].

This with some diffi-culty ended, THE truce was now on the point of expiring, which the king of *Castile* had concluded with the miramamolin, and it was this that made Don *Alonso* so extremely sollicitous to

[g] Roderic Toletan de reb. Hispan. lib. vii. Lucæ Tudensis Chron. [h] Chron. var. antiq. [i] Roderic Toletan de reb. Hispan. lib. vii. Lucæ Tudensis Chron. [k] Chron. var. antiq. [l] De reb. Hispan. liv. vii. Lucæ Tudensis Chron.

put an end, not only to the wars, but to the quarrels and dif- *and a new* ,
putes amongſt the Chriſtian princes in *Spain.* It was with *one breaks*
this view, that he prevailed once more with the kings of *out with*
Arragon and *Navarre* to meet him ; and the great generoſity *the* Moors.
he ſhewed in abandoning ſeveral places of great importance
to the laſt of theſe princes, had an extraordinary good effect ;
, ſo that at length they parted perfectly good friends, with
mutual promiſes of aſſiſtance and ſupport againſt the *Moors* [m].
Things being thus ſettled, Don *Roderic Diaz*, grand maſter
of the order of *Calatrava*, for ſo it was ſtill called, though
the place was in the hands of the *Moors*, made an irruption
into their territories, and by taking ſeveral places began the
war. The next year, the Infant Don *Ferdinand* received the   A. D.
order of knighthood with great ceremony, in the cathedral   1210.
church of *Burgos*, that he might be qualified, according to
the notions of thoſe times, to take the field [n] with his father,
againſt the infidels ; who, while they were preparing to reſiſt
the *Caſtilians*, found themſelves ſuddenly attacked by the king
of *Arragon*, who made this ſummer ſome conqueſts at their
expence. Don *Alonſo* of *Caſtile* did not take the field till
the following ſpring ; and then, with a numerous and gallant
army, advanced as far as *Alcala*, which place, when he had
reduced, he proceeded next to over-run the beſt part of the
kingdom of *Murcia*, in which he met with no conſiderable
reſiſtance, till the extreme heat of the ſeaſon obliged him to
retire [o]. *Mohammed*, then king of *Morocco*, had aſſembled
a numerous body of troops in *Andaluſia* ; and having paſſed
the *Sierra Morena*, inveſted *Salvatierra*, the reſidence for the
preſent of the knights of *Calatrava*. Though the town was
not very ſtrong, the knights defended it ſo well, that they had
time to give Don *Alonſo* notice of their diſtreſs, and that
without a ſpeedy relief it was impoſſible to preſerve the place.
Upon this the Infant Don *Ferdinand* was ſent with a very
ſtrong detachment to make an irruption into the *Mooriſh*
territories on the ſide of *Eſtremadura*, which he performed
very gallantly, but it did not produce what was expected, the
miramamolin perſiſting in the ſiege ; ſo that the prince returned to his father's camp in the month of *Auguſt*, and the
place having no other relief to expect, was ſurrendered in the
enſuing month [p]. This certainly chagrined the king of
Caſtile not a little ; but an event which followed ſoon after
affected him much more. The royal Infant, either over

[m] P. Moret, Inveſtigaciones hiſtoricas de las antiquitades del
Reyno de Navarra.   [n] Chron. var. antiq. Morales.   [o] Annal
Toletan. Roderic Toletan de reb. Hiſp. lib. vii.   [p] Lucæ
Tudenſis Chron. Annal Toletan.

M 4   fatigued

fatigued by the operations of the campaign, or from some other cause, fell ill of a fever soon after his return with his father to *Madrid*, of which he died there *October* 14, A. D. 1211, to the universal sorrow, not only of his royal parents and the court, but of the whole nation in general [q].

A prodigious army assembled by the miramamolin against the Christians. THE king could not allow himself much time to grieve, as he had certain and indisputable intelligence, that the miramamolin, having pacified the troubles in *Barbary*, had brought the whole force of his empire together, with an intention to conquer the kingdom of *Toledo*, at least. Being sensible from experience, that the power of *Castile* was by no means capable of supporting him against such an enemy, he sent the bishop elect of *Segovia* to *Rome*, the archbishop Don *Roderic* and other bishops into *France*, while himself managed a conference with the kings of *Arragon* and *Navarre*, in which he obtained from them all that he could desire or expect [r]. Don *Sancho*, king of *Portugal*, dying about this time, was succeeded by his son Don *Alonso* [s], who involving himself in some disputes with the king of *Leon*, the monarch of *Castile* could not promise himself much help from either of those princes, with the want of which, however, he might dispense, since multitudes inrolled themselves for this holy war in *France*, *Italy*, and *Germany*, the pontif at *Rome* using the same methods to excite Christians in all places to enter into the *Spanish* war, as in other croisades, and with better reason.

The monarchs of Spain have recourse to a croisade for their defence. THE rendezvous of the Christian troops was appointed at *Toledo*, about *Easter*; but it was a considerable time before so numerous an army, and that too composed of so many different nations and languages, could be brought into any tolerable order. Don *Pedro*, king of *Arragon*, with the forces under his command, arrived on *Trinity Sunday*; the foreigners in a short time after; and to prevent the inconveniences that must have happened, if they had been admitted into the city, all these forces were encamped in the field, as soon as they arrived, which did not, however, hinder the foreigners from falling upon the *Jews* in the suburbs, and committing many other irregularities, which cost the king of *Castile* a great deal of trouble to correct [u]. At last, on the twentieth of *June*, the army began to move, the Ultramontans or foreigners, from beyond the Pyrenees, had the van, composed of ten thousand horse, and forty thousand foot, under the command of Don *Diego Lopez de Hara*; the king of

A. D. 1212.

[q] RODERIC TOLETAN de reb. Hispan. lib. vii.   [r] Annal Toletan. Epist. INNOCENT III.   [s] ZURETA. Annal Arragon.   [t] ÈRANDAON.   [u] Chron. var. antiq.

Castile and the king of *Arragon* moved next, but in separate bodies, that they might not incommode each other; the rest of the army formed a rear-guard, and took post upon the frontiers [w]. The first place that felt the weight of their arms was *Malagon*, which the foreigners took by storm, and put all the *Mohammedans* therein to the sword. The next place they attempted was *Calatrava*, in which there was a very good garrison, commanded by the alcaydes *Abenaliz* and *Almoad*, officers of great reputation, and who lost none of it by their behaviour upon this occasion. The town notwithstanding, being attacked on all sides, was quickly taken by assault; but the *Moorish* generals retired into the citadel, which being strong and well supplied, they made a gallant defence; at length they offered a capitulation, in case they had leave to retire where they pleased, which the foreigners violently opposed, professing, that they meant to give no quarter to any infidels: but the kings of *Castile* and *Arragon* were of another mind: they knew the importance of the place, and of the magazines which were in it, and therefore they readily signed the capitulation; and Don *Diego Lopez de Haro*, with his own troops, escorted the *Moors* till such time as they arrived in a place of safety [x]. The strangers were so much offended at this instance of moderation, and the not giving up the place to be pillaged, that, pretending they were not able to endure the heats which began to come on, they decamped with their forces, in spite of all the sollicitations and prayers of the Christian monarchs, and marched back towards *Toledo*, the troops under *Arnold*, archbishop of *Narbonne*, and *Thibaud Blacon*, only excepted [y].

THIS loss, though it diminished, did not discourage, the Christian army, or the kings who commanded it, and who soon after attacked and reduced *Alarcos*, and other small places. While they were thus employed, the king of *Arragon* received a considerable reinforcement, which gave the army fresh spirits; and before their rejoicings on this subject were over, Don *Sanchez*, king of *Navarre*, with most of the nobility of his kingdom, and a very gallant corps of troops, joined them likewise; upon which, being again in motion, they advanced to *Salvatierra*, where they made a general review of the army, and resolved to march on towards the enemy, notwithstanding the desertion of the foreigners [z]. This resolution was indeed very gallant and heroic, but at the

Gain some small places in their march towards the Moorish army.

[w]. LUCÆ Tudensis Chron. Annal. Toletan.   [x] LUCÆ Tudensis Chron. Annal. Toletan.   [y] RODERIC TOLETAN de reb. Hispan. lib. viii. Chron. var. antiq. [z] ZURETA, P. MORET, Annal. Toletan.

same

same time extremely hazardous, as they had that rugged ridge of mountains, stiled the *Sierra Morena*, to pass, before they could reach the infidels, who they knew waited for them, and would be sure to give them all the trouble that was possible in their passage. The *Moorish* monarch *Mohammed*, who from his wearing a turbant of that colour, had acquired the surname of the *Green*, acted through this campaign like an able general, and an officer of great experience [a]. He had drawn together his forces early in the neighbourhood of *Jaen*, amounting to fourscore thousand excellent horse, and a body of troops so numerous, that no historian has ventured upon a calculation. He advanced slowly, as he heard of the progress of the Christians, resolved not to waste his forces in skirmishes, or to venture a general and decisive engagement, before the fatigue of the several sieges and the usual heats should have abated the ardour of the enemy. At length he took post at *Baeza* [b], marked out the field of battle at his leisure, and caused all the narrow passes in the mountains to be occupied by strong detachments, with express orders to his officers to maintain their respective posts as long as it was possible; so that, all things considered, it seemed almost an impracticable project for the Christian army to reach that of the *Moors*, and still more impracticable to defeat troops more numerous than their own, that had served long, and with great reputation, fresh, well supplied with every thing, and in posts of their own chusing, and of consequence very advantageous.

Pass the Sierra Morena by a route never till then known, and stiled the royal passage ever since.

THE Christian army arrived at the foot of the *Sierra*, on *Thursday* the 12th of *July*, when a small corps of troops, under the command of Don *Diego Lopez*, after a brisk dispute, possessed themselves of the pass of *Muradal*, and the next day, after an obstinate resistance, drove the *Moors* from some of the eminences about it; but perceiving that the pass was very narrow, of a considerable length, and the enemy in a condition to cut them off as fast as they appeared at the opening on the other side, they judged it impossible to pursue their design, and at the same time could not bear the thoughts of returning to *Toledo*, without seeing an enemy [c]. In this distressed situation, a person altogether unknown, but who from his appearance seemed to be a shepherd, desired to speak with the kings, and after some importunity was conducted into their presence. He proposed to shew them a passage hitherto very little known, and which never had been

[a] RODERIC TOLETAN de reb. Hispan. lib. viii. LUCÆ Tudensis Chron.   [b] Annal Toletan. LUCÆ Tudensis Chron.   [c] RODERIC TOLETAN de reb. Hispan. lib. vii.

passed

passed by any army, through which they might march without difficulty, and at the same time without being observed
by the *Moors*. The monarchs were very desirous of accepting so seasonable an offer; but at the same time afraid to
trust to a guide whom nobody knew. At length, Don *Diego
Lopez* and Don *Garcia Romero*, offered to follow him with a
corps of troops, and he led them according to his promise,
by a winding passage, which has ever since born the name of
the *Royal Passage* [d], to the summit of the mountains, where
they found a fair and spacious plain, where the whole army
might be ranged conveniently in order of battle.

On *Saturday* the 14th of *July*, the Christian army, in con- *The glori-*
sequence of this happy discovery, took possession of the plain *ous victory*
beforementioned, and disposed their troops in proper order: *of Tolosa,*
the *Moors* were infinitely surprised when they beheld them *which en-*
in so advantageous a situation; but as soon as they had re- *tirely*
covered themselves a little, neglected nothing that might *breaks the*
have provoked them to fight immediately; but in this they *power of*
were disappointed, for the Christians having secured the ad- *the* Moors.
vanced posts, and provided in the most effectual manner possible, in case of an attack, rested that day and the next,
which they spent in devotion, and preparing themselves, in a
Christian manner, for whatever event Providence might design them [e]. On the 16th, in the morning, the whole army
was disposed in order of battle, the right wing was commanded by the king of *Navarre*, who, besides his own forces,
had some battalions of *Castilian* troops, the foreigners under
the archbishop of *Narbonne*, and the volunteers; the king of
Arragon and his forces were on the left; Don *Alonso* of
Castile in the centre, his troops being divided into four bri-
gades, the first commanded by Don *Diego Lopez de Haro*,
the second by Don *Gonsalez de Lara*, in which were the
troops of the military orders, the third by Don *Roderic Diaz*,
composed of the flower of the *Castilian* nobility, the last, was
under the king in person, who had about him all the prelates, and the whole force of the kingdom of *Toledo* [f]. The
Moors were likewise disposed in very exact order, and in the
center the choicest troops were covered by a strong barricade
of iron chains; the miramamolin was there in person, dressed
in a rich robe, with the khoran in one hand and a sabre in
the other [g]. The battle was begun by Don *Diego Lopez de
Haro*, and soon after both the wings engaged. This attack

[d] Annal Toletan, Lucæ Tudensis Chron.   [e] Chron. var.
antiq.   [f] Roderic Toletan de reb. Hispan. lib. viii.
Lucæ Tudensis Chronicon.   Annal Toletan.   [g] Chron.
var. antiq.

was made with all imaginable vigour, and the *Moors* received them with the utmoft intrepidity. The difpute continued long, without any fenfible variation of fortune ; but the loffe of the *Moors* being continually fupplied with frefh troops, the Chriftians began to lofe ground in every part of the line [h]. The *Moors* perceiving this, made a great effort, which had a very fenfible impreffion, infomuch that Don *Alonfo* of *Caftile* cried out, that there was nothing now left, but to fe- cure the honour of the nation, by dying glorioufly ; and was on the very point of throwing himfelf into the thickeft of the enemy, if the archbifhop *Roderic* of *Toledo,* and Don *Ferdi- nand Garcia,* had not reftrained him [i]. The latter told him things were not yet defperate, if he did not make them fo, by precipitation, and advifed him to fupport his retiring troops by feafonable and well difpofed fupplies. This had its effect, and the Chriftians having recovered their fpirits, pufhed the infidels in their turn, broke them, and advanced to the bar- ricade of iron chains, where things were in danger of taking a new turn, the infantry being unable to do any thing. But the king of *Navarre,* at the head of his own cavalry, attack- ing them in full career, with a defperate refolution, leaped the barricade, and having driven the *Moors* from their firft pofts, opened a paffage for the *Caftilians* [k]. It was then no longer a battle, but a carnage. The miramamolin, by the perfuafion of his brother, quitted the field ; and the Chriftians purfuing their flying enemies, continued the flaughter till it was night: the army then took poffeffion of the enemies camp ; and the archbifhop of *Toledo,* affifted by all the bifhops and ecclefiafticks, fung *Te Deum* [l]. The next day, Don *Diego Lopez de Hara,* made a diftribution of the fpoils, and gave almoft the whole to the auxiliaries and ftrangers, telling the *Caftilians,* that they were fufficiently rewarded by the victory itfelf, fince all the advantages derived from it would be theirs ; and, which is not a little fingular, his conduct met with univerfal applaufe [m]. The *Moors* loft upon the field, and in the purfuit, 200,000 men ; the Chriftians, if you will believe archbifhop *Roderic,* but 25, and but 150 in the courfe of the whole campaign [n] (F).

AFTER

[h] Epift. Reg. ADEOPHONS ad Innocent III.   [i] RODERIC TOLETAN de reb. Hifpan. lib. viii. LUCÆ Tudenfis Chron. [k] Epift. Reg. ADEOPHONS ad Innocent III.   Annal Toletan. [l] RODERIC TOLETAN de reb. Hifpan. lib. viii. LUCÆ Tudenfis Chron. Epift. Reg. ADEOPHONS ad Innocent III.   [m] Chron. var. antiq.   [n] RODERIC TOLETAN de reb. Hifpan. lib. viii. LUCÆ Tudenfis Chron.

(F) The date of this battle is fixed with great certainty, by the unanimous confent of hif- torians, to *Monday, July* the 16th,

AFTER the army had rested three days, they resumed their progress, and reduced all the country as far as *Baeza*, which they found slighted and without inhabitants, except a number of infirm and aged people, who had taken shelter in the great mosque, to which they cruelly set fire °. They marched from thence to *Ubeda*, a place of strength, to which the re-

Conse-quences at-tending this me-morable battle

° Chron. var. antiq.

16th, *A. D.* 1212 ; as to the place, there is not, as we observed, the same concurrence ; and yet such as are well acquainted with the country, may possibly find that the differences about it are but of very little consequence. Some stile it the battle of *Muradal*, from the pass of that name, through the *Sierra Morena* ; others the battle of *Loça*, from a great rock of that name ; but it is most commonly known by the title of, the battle of *Tolosa*, from a little town of that name, in the open country, beyond the mountains. Some writers have reported, that, at the very beginning of the action, a most resplendent cross appeared in the heavens, a sure presage of victory to the Christians : but this is not to be found in the letter written by the king of *Castile* to the Pope, in that of *Arnold*, archbishop of *Narbonne*, or in the history of Don *Roderic*, archbishop of *Toledo* ; and is, therefore, justly suspected by *Mariana*, as well as *Ferreras*. But it is unanimously asserted, that *Dominic Paschal*, the archbishop of *Toledo*'s cross-bearer, and who, in process of time, became himself both dean and archbishop of the same diocese, passed several times through the enemy's line, without receiving any hurt. Some have attempted to assign a physical reason, why no blood appeared upon the field of battle; *viz.* from the heat of the weather and the dryness of the soil. Some have also corrected the numbers said to be slain in this battle, and instead of 25 Christians, would have us read 25000. This, however, is utterly irreconcileable to the archbishop of *Toledo*'s relation, who maintains the fact to be true, however incredible it may seem : he adds farther, that the quantity of spears, javelins, and arrows, found upon the field, was so great, that they served the Christian forces for two days, as fewel for dressing their provisions, though during that space they burnt nothing else. The value of the spoil was immense, as we may guess from the number of horses, which are said to have amounted to 35,000. But the most signal advantage of all was, the breaking the power of the miramamolin, which revived that spirit of independency natural to the *Spanish Moors*, put them upon revolting, setting up separate principalities, and destroying each other, which made their total expulsion a work much easier to the Christians than otherwise it would have been, and opened a way also to the declension of this dynasty in *Africa*, which weakened the *Mahammedan* power in general.

mains

and return mains of the *Moorish* army and most of the inhabitants of
of the *Baeza* had retired, and to which the Christians laid siege.
kings of They met there with a stubborn and obstinate resistance, yet
Arragon on the side of the *Arragonian* attack things were pushed so
and Na- far, that the besieged offered a million of crowns, by way of
varre. ransom P ; but the prelates persisting in opposing all capitula-
lations, the besieged found their safety in despair, behaving afterwards with such desperate resolution, that famine and
diseases breaking into the camp, all the three monarchs concurred in opinion, that the only proper step to be taken was,
to raise the siege, which they accordingly did ; and, having
put strong garrisons into their new conquests, repassed the
mountains, and continued their march to *Calatrava* q. There
they met the duke of *Austria*, with a great number of troops
coming to their assistance, who finding their campaign over,
joined his forces to those of the king of *Arragon*, who here
took leave of Don *Alonso* of *Castile*, in order to return into
his own dominions r. Don *Alonso*, accompanied by Don
Sanchez, king of *Navarre*, proceeded to *Toledo*, into which
city they entered in triumph ; and at the departure of the last
mentioned monarch, Don *Alonso*, as a mark of his gratitude
and esteem, restored to him fifteen of the most considerable
places that he had taken during the long war ; he also instituted an annual festival on the 16th of *July*, which was stiled
the triumph of the holy cross, and it was long kept with
great solemnity, through both the kingdoms of *Castile* and
Leon, in memory of an event which, in a great measure, determined the fate of the *Moors* in *Spain* s.

Don Alon- WHILE Don *Alonso* of *Castile* was employed in this im-
so's sacri- portant war, the troops of the king of *Leon*, under the com-
fices, in mand of Don *Pedro Fernandez*, recovered all the places
order to that had been conquered by the *Castilians* t. After this, the
settle a king of *Leon* turned his arms against *Portugal*, where the
lasting
peace with king, Don *Alonso*, was labouring to dispossess his sisters, one
the crown of which was Donna *Theresa*, once queen of *Leon*, of the
of Leon. places which his father had left them by his testament for
their subsistence. It was at the request of these distressed
princesses, that the king of *Leon* made a diversion in their
favour, offering, however, to retire, if Don *Alonso* of *Portugal* would desist from his enterprize. But that king, who
from his infancy hated his brothers and sisters, marched
against him with a superior army, and forced him to battle,
in which, however, the king of *Leon* was victorious, and

P ZURETA, Annal Arragon.   q Chron. var. antiq.   r ZU-
RETA, Annal Arragon.   s Annal Toletan.   t LUCÆ
Tudensis Chron.

would,

would, perhaps, have availed himself in another manner of his success, if the apprehensions of being attacked by the king of *Castile* had not withheld him [u]. Don *Alonso* of *Castile* behaved upon this occasion with great magnanimity; for, instead of committing any hostilities, he invited him to *Valladolid*, and there, in a personal conference, convinced him of the necessity of their living upon good terms, in order to which, he not only relinquished all the places he had taken, but gave him several others that he knew he much desired, together with the castles of *Carpio* and *Monreal*, in the territory of *Salamanca*, upon condition that they should be demolished, and a considerable town and district in *Asturias*, merely because it lay conveniently for him [w]; so that the king of *Leon* left him in sentiments of the most perfect friendship; and Don *Alonso* of *Castile* thought a secure peace very cheaply purchased by these sacrifices, being desirous only of extending his dominions at the expence of the *Moors*, and by making a proper use of the great advantage he had gained. It was in order to this, that he stipulated with the king of *Leon*, as an equivalent for the concessions he had made, that he should restore to the king of *Portugal* the places he had taken from him, and conclude a peace with that monarch, upon fair and equal terms [x]. Upon this peace, the Infant Don *Pedro* of *Portugal*, perceiving that he had no Christian court to which he could fly, and dreading the implacable disposition of the king his brother, retired to the miramamolin. On the other hand, that monarch, perceiving how much he was lessened in the opinion of his subjects by his late defeat, went over to *Africa*, where he passed the remainder of his days under that cloud which usually attend sovereigns that are unfortunate [y].

Don *Alonso* of *Castile* took the field again early the next year, with a competent army, and having reduced *Duegnos*, at the foot of the *Sierra Morena*, and some other places, though not without resistance, soon after invested *Alcares*, where the *Moors* had a good garrison, and flattered themselves that it was impregnable; but the king continued before it so long, and took such precautions for supplying his troops with provisions, that at length, on the 22d of *May*, the place was surrendered [z]. After putting a strong garrison into it, the king returned in triumph to *St. Torcaz*, where he met his queen, with the Infant Don *Henry*, his daughter queen *Berengara*,

A famine in Castile, *by which the people are reduced to very great distress.*

[u] Epist. INNOCENT III.   [w] RODERIC TOLETAN de reb. Hispan. lib. viii.   LUCÆ Tudensis Chron...   [x] Annal Toletan. [y] BRANDAON.   [z] Annal Toletan.

and

and her two sons Don *Ferdinand* and Don *Alonso*, and there kept his *Whitsuntide* [a]. Some other actions of less importance happened in this year, with different success; but the most remarkable event was, a great scarcity of provisions, arising from the excessive consumption made by the great armies the year before, and the people being also hindered, by the continuance of the war, from attending in a proper manner to the cultivation of their lands.

The Infant Don Ferdinand, heir of Leon, dies unexpectedly. As Don *Alonso* of *Leon* had made no diversion in favour of the king of *Castile* this campaign, and as, upon application to him the next year, he imputed his slowness to his defect of cavalry, Don *Diego Lopez de Haro* was sent to him with 600 excellent horse, and, by the assistance of these and his own infantry, he made himself master of *Alcantara* [b], and had taken some other places, if the extreme heat of the weather had not obliged him to put his troops into quarters of refreshment. This was a great disappointment to the king of *Castile*, who thereby lost the opportunity of taking *Baeza*,

A. D. 1214. which the *Moors* had repeopled and fortified, and which he besieged for three months, till sickness and famine obliged him to retire [c]. Soon after the return of the king of *Leon* from his campaign, his heir apparent, the Infant Don *Ferdinand*, whom he had by Donna *Theresa* of *Portugal*, died, and was buried in the cathedral church of St. *James* at *Compostella*, near the remains of Don *Ferdinand* of *Castile*, his grandfather [d]. This accident exceedingly afflicted his parents, and might well excuse the king, his father, for not making an autumn campaign. About this time, the archbishop *Roderic* of *Toledo* finished his fortress of *Milagro*, now known by the name of *Almagro*, the capital of one of the districts in the province of *La Mancha*, into which he put a competent garrison, to restrain the incursions of the *Moors*, which he had hardly done, before it was besieged by an army of 5000 horse and foot, under the command of a *Moorish* officer of great reputation; but the prelate, its founder, took such care to supply those within with all kinds of necessaries, that at length, not without great loss, the enemy found themselves obliged to raise the siege and to retire [e].

Death of Don Alonso, king of Castile, at THE king, Don *Alonso* of *Castile*, being still very sollicitous about the affairs of his cousin the king of *Leon*, and apprehensive that he did not clearly comprehend what considerable acquisitions might be made to his own territories, by entering

[a] RODERIC TOLETAN *de* reb. Hispan. lib. viii.   [b] Chron. var. antiq.   [c] Annal. Toletan. LUCÆ Tudensis Chron. [d] Annal. Toletan.   [e] RODERIC TOLETAN, de reb. Hispan. lib. viii. LUCÆ Tudensis Chron.

heartily

heartily into a war with the *Moors,* invited him to an inter- *a very cri-* view at *Placentia* [f]. This was as readily accepted as proposed; *tical con-* but in his journey thither, Don *Alonso* of *Castile* was attack- *juncture.* ed by a malignant fever, of which he died at a little village on the way, on the fifth or sixth of *August,* in the year 1214 [g]. He had the comfort of having his queen, and most of his children about him, as well as the archbishop Don *Roderic* and several other prelates, in his last moments; and by his will appointed the queen dowager. *Eleonora,* regent [h], during the minority of her son; but this provision, though very prudent, did not avail much, since she also died in the month of *October* the same year; in which also expired the two greatest men in *Castile* and *Leon,* Don *Diego Lopez de Haro,* and Don *Pedro Fernandez* [i]. Such a series of unexpected events had, as the reader will easily conceive, a very great effect on the minds of the people, and made way for those troubles and disturbances that very speedily ensued, and of which, if they had been under any settled form of government, and had acted with any proper degree of prudence, the *Moors* would certainly have availed themselves more than they did (G).

DON

[f] Annal Toletan. [g] RODERIC TOLETAN de reb. Hispan. lib. viii. LUCÆ Tudensis Chron. [h] Annal Toletan. [i] Annal Compostel. et Toletan.

(G) This great monarch was, to speak correctly, *Alonso* the third, of *Castile*; for though, after the union of the two kingdoms under his grandson, Don *Ferdinand,* the succeeding kings were reckoned in the order of those of *Leon,* so that his successor was stiled Don *Alonso* the tenth, and not Don *Alonso* the fourth, yet this manner of computing did not or could not take place before. He was, at the time of his demise, in the 59th year of his age, and in the 56th of his reign. It is true that the old historians differ about these dates, and that, even in the printed copies of Don *Roderic*'s history, it is said to have been but the 53d year of his reign;

yet we ought to consider that transcribers mistake in nothing so much as dates; and therefore we must not suffer ourselves to be misled by such slips of theirs, when visibly repugnant to the current of history. There is another difficulty that ought to be cleared, which relates to the occasion of that journey which cost the king his life; for, in the printed copies of the archbishop of *Toledo*'s history, it is said, that the king was going to an interview with the king of *Portugal,* his son-in-law, at *Placentia*; whereas *Ferreras,* whom we follow, asserts, that his design was to confer with the king of *Leon,* which seems to be much more probable,

Henry suc-
ceeds his
father in
that king-
dom in the
11th year
of his age.

Don *Henry*, the young king of *Castile*, was in the 11th year of his age; and having lost his mother in two months after his father, the regency, according to the direction of the king's testament, devolved on the queen Donna *Berengara*, with the general satisfaction of the whole kingdom; the counts of *Lara*, Don *Ferdinand*, Don *Alvaro*, and Don *Gonçales*, only excepted. They were desirous of getting the person of the king into their hands; and in a short time, by insinuations of various kinds, drew many of the nobility, from motives of interest, into their notions. The great difficulty was, how to bring their scheme to bear; and it was in the management of this that they shewed themselves consummate politicians. They corrupted a servant who was much in the confidence of that princess, who persuaded her, that the nobles in general were highly displeased that, since they had a child for their king, the care of that child should be confided solely to a woman; and that, therefore, out of respect to the king's safety and her own, the wisest thing she could possibly do was to call an assembly of the states, and leave the choice of a regent to them [k]. She did so, and by the intrigues of the faction, Don *Alvaro de Lara* was chosen

---

[k] Roderic Toletan, de reb. Hispan. lib. viii. Lucæ Tudensis Chronicon. Chron. S. Fernand.

---

bable, considering the place assigned for their interview, and the route the king took to go thither, notwithstanding that a modern historian tells us his disease was rendered mortal by his chagrin, on a message sent him by the king of *Portugal*, that he would not come out of his own dominions; which is exceedingly improbable, since we never hear that these monarchs had any difference; and the king of *Castile* had, but a very little before, given the king of *Leon* an equivalent out of his dominions, in order to induce him to restore to *Portugal* the places he had conquered. He is very highly commended by Don *Roderic Ximenes*, who knew him perfectly, and who, where there is occasion to mention them, has not dissembled his vices. We may, however, affirm, that he was much more indebted to experience than education; and that it may be very truly said of him, it was by reigning that he knew how to reign: perhaps, we may add to all this, that his misfortunes were the great instruments of his glory; that his being beaten put him into the road of victory; and that the close of his reign did honour to his memory, because it was very unlike the beginning. We are not, indeed, warranted to give him this character, from what is said of him in other histories, but we are led to it from facts; and truth is, of all other, the best authority in history.

under

under various reftrictions, which, when he had taken an oath punctually to obferve, the young king was delivered to his care, in order to his receiving a proper education. But no fooner was the affembly diffolved, than Don *Alvaro* broke through all the reftrictions, governed with a rod of iron, and not only trampled on the liberties of the laity, but infringed likewife on the immunities of the clergy [l]. His politicks were of a very extraordinary kind ; for, in this firft year of his regency, he contrived to fecure an influence over the king, for life, by marrying him to the Infanta Donna *Mafalda* of *Portugal*, and with this view, leaving the king to the care of fome of his friends in whom he could confide, he went, in perfon, to the court of *Portugal*, to negotiate this marriage. In this, fome writers fay, that he fucceeded ; and it is on all hands agreed, that the court of *Portugal* came into it, and that the young princefs was fent into *Spain* ; but the Pope interpofed, at the requeft of the nobility, and by his influence over the prelates caufed the Infanta to be fent back into *Portugal*, where fhe became a nun [m]. *Mariana* fays, that when the count Don *Alvaro* found it impoffible to make her a queen, he would have made a merit of his endeavours in order to have efpoufed her himfelf, but that the young princefs rejected his offer with contempt. [n]

A. D. 1215.

As ecclefiafticks generally bear ill treatment with lefs temper than other people, fo, upon Don *Alvaro*'s making free with the revenues of the church of *Toledo*, the dean of that cathedral, without ceremony, excommunicated him, which quickly obliged him to make fatisfaction[o]. In order to appeafe the nation in general, he called an affembly of the ftates at *Valladolid*, at which the king and his fifter Donna *Berengara* affifted ; but the difputes rofe quickly to fuch a height, and the behaviour of Don *Alvaro* was fo imperious, that the queen Donna *Berengara* thought proper to retire to the fortrefs of *Autillo*, and was followed thither by fome of the nobility of the firft families in *Caftile* [p]. The regent was very little concerned at this ; but when he afterwards underftood that the king himfelf was inclined to take the fame route, he carried the young prince, under pretence of vifiting his dominions, firft to *Segovia*, then to *Avila*, and at length to *Maquella*, in the kingdom of *Toledo*, where he kept him feveral

The regent Don Alvaro de Lara incurs univerfal hatred.

A. D. 1216.

[l] Annal Toletan.   [m] Chron. S. FERNAND. RODERIC TOLETAN de reb. Hifpan. lib. viii. LUCÆ Tudenfis Chron.   [n] Hiftoria general de Efpana, lib. xii.   [o] Annal Toletan.   [p] RODERIC TOLETAN de reb. Hifpan, lib. ix. LUCÆ Tudenfis Chron. Chron. S. FERNAND.

months,

months, and oppressed all the country in the neighbourhood to such a degree, that it was very near causing an insurrection, and, as it was, increased those clamours that had been loud enough before [q].

The young king Don Henry, killed by the fall of a tile upon his head. To stifle these, or at least to turn them from himself upon those who opposed him, Don *Alvaro* took a very bold step. He discovered that the queen Donna *Berengara* had sent a person very secretly to her brother, to enquire after his health, and to learn how he was used. This gentleman he seized, hanged him without any judicial process, and then produced a counterfeit letter from the queen, which he confidently insinuated contained instructions to poison the young king [r]. The scheme was well laid, though it did not take effect; for the archbishop of *Toledo*, and the people in general, instead of charging the queen with poisoning, charged him with forgery; and that so loudly, and with so little ceremony, that he found it necessary to shift his quarters, and to carry the king to *Hueta* [s]. He afterwards went from thence to *Valladolid*, where he assembled forces, and summoned Donna *Berengara* and the lords of her party to surrender all the places they held, upon pain of being treated as rebels. This put them under great difficulties; for though they were ready to defend themselves against the regent, and put him to the trouble of one siege, yet, when they found the king's person exposed in the army, they grew uneasy, and inclined rather to expose their own persons than his. The queen, in the mean time, applied to her husband, the king of *Leon*, and demanded either his assistance, or at least his interposition; but Don *Alvaro* was before-hand with her there, and proposed a match between the king and the Infanta Donna *Sancha*; so that, in all probability, he would either have carried his point, or a civil war must have broke out in *Castile*, if an unlooked for accident had not changed the face of affairs entirely [t]. The regent having carried the king to *Polentia*, lodged him in the episcopal palace; and as he endeavoured to gain his affection by indulging him in every thing, the young king was at play with some boys of his own age, in the court of the palace, when one of them throwing a stone upon the roof, dislodged a tile, which fell directly upon the king's head, and of this wound he died *June* the 6th, in the year 1217, in the third year of his reign [u].

---

[q] Chron. var. antiq. [r] Chron. S. FERNAND. [s] Annal Toletan et Compostell. [t] RODERIC TOLETAN de reb. Hispan. lib. ix. LUCÆ Tudensis Chron. [u] Annal Toletan Chron. S. FERNAND.

THE

THE regent would willingly have concealed the king's *Don Alva-*
death, but that was impossible; and the queen Donna *Be- ro the re-*
rengara was no sooner informed of it, than she sent Don *gent, still*
Lopez Haro and Don *Goncales Giron* to the king of *Leon, aims at*
to desire him to send her son, the Infant Don *Ferdinand, preserving*
under pretence that she longed very much to see him [w]. The *the sove-*
king made no difficulty; and the queen no sooner had him in *reignty in*
her power, than she quitted the fortress, and went directly *himself.*
to *Palentia*, where all the nobility and prelates, who composed
the late king's court, received her with all the duty and affection imaginable. She resolved from thence to go to *Vallado-*
lid; but first some overtures were made to Don *Alvaro de*
Lara, that he should return to his duty. He very modestly
proposed, that the queen should immediately put her son into
his hands, in which case he would be content to own him for
his king; but that proposition being rejected, the court proceeded to *Valladolid*, where the people testified their loyalty
and submission with all the joy imaginable [x]. The queen
intended to have carried her son next into *Estremadura*, and
had actually begun her journey; but the family of *Lara* had
so effectually corrupted the inhabitants of most of the great
towns, that they refused to open their gates; upon which, the
queen and her son returned to *Valladolid*, where having called
a general assembly of the states, and at the same time summoned every one of the places that were in the hands of the
faction to submit, on pain of being declared rebels by the
approaching assembly, which had its effect, the cities, upon
mature deliberation, opened their gates, returned to their duty,
and sent deputies to the diet [y].

THIS assembly was remarkably numerous, almost all the *Donna Be-*
prelates and nobility in *Castile* being present therein, when *rengara*
they solemnly acknowleged the Infanta *Berengara*, in her own *proclaimed*
right, queen of the two *Castiles*, after which they proclaimed *queen, who*
and swore fealty to her [z]. Her reign, however, was of very *resigns the*
short continuance; for, by the advice of the principal nobility, *crown to*
she caused a kind of theatre to be erected before one of the *her son,*
principal gates of the city, upon which the Infant Don *Fer-*
dinand appeared in his robes of state, and the queen, his
mother, at the head of a deputation of the prelates and nobility, having paid her respects and saluted him king, he was
carried, with the acclamations of all the spectators, to the

[w] RODERIC TOLETAN de reb. Hispan. lib. ix.   [x] Annal
Toletan. Chron. S. FERNAND.   [y] Chron. var. antiq.
Chron. S. FERNAND.   [z] RODERIC TOLETAN de reb. Hispan.
lib. vii.

cathedral church, and there solemnly inaugurated, *August* the 31st, 1217 [a]. This scene of joy was strangely discomposed, by the news that Don *Alonso*, king of *Leon*, at the head of a great army, had entered *Castile*, by the advice and in company with Don *Alvaro de Lara*, to revenge the signal affront he had received, in having his son made a king without asking his consent. The queen sent the bishops of *Burgos* and *Palentia* to intreat him not to injure the subjects of his son, nor to disturb the dawn of his reign ; but he would listen to no accommodation ; and believing that he should surprize the court without resistance, continued his march directly to *Burgos* ; but Don *Lopez de Haro*, having assembled a small body of good troops, threw himself into the city, and prepared every thing for a vigorous defence, upon which Don *Alonso* thought fit to retire into his dominions, expressing great indignation against such as had prevailed upon him to act in so unkingly and in so unnatural a manner [b]. This storm over, the queen sent to Don *Alvara*, to demand the body of her brother, which he had clandestinely withdrawn and concealed ; but which, with some shew of civility, he caused to be delivered to the bishops who brought the queen's message, and by whose orders it was interred with great solemnity at *Burgos* [c]. About this time, Pope *Honorius* the third wrote to the prelates in *Spain*, in regard to the *Jews*, in a manner becoming a Christian bishop. He permitted that some mark of distinction they should be obliged to wear; but desired that no force might be used to compel them to baptism ; that they should be permitted the free exercise of their religion ; and that the people should not be allowed to insult them when celebrating their feasts [d]. The knights of *Calatrava* finding the place in which they had fixed their residence very unwholsome, the grand master caused it to be removed to *Salvatierra* ; but notwithstanding this, their original title remained, as it still remains, exactly the same.

Don Alvaro de Lara taken prisoner by the king, through his own imprudence.

THE lords who were addicted to the faction of Don *Alvaro de Lara*, or rather who were desirous of exempting themselves from the power of their sovereign, continued still to yield but a kind of precarious obedience, which obliged the king and his mother to raise an army, in order, once for all, to put the king into full possession of his dominions. The great difficulty they met with arose from want of money, which in some measure the queen removed, by selling her jewels. In order to strike at the root, the king marched to *Herrera*, where Don

[a] LUCA Tudensis Chron. Chron. S. FERNAND.   [b] Annal Toletan. Chron. S. FERNAND.   [c] RODERIC TOLETAN de reb. Hispan. l.b. ix.   [d] Epist. Honor. III.

Alvaro

Alvaro himfelf was, with a ftrong garrifon. The king's troops were but raw, and, it may be, indifferently cloathed and armed. Don *Alvaro*, coming with a fmall body of horfe to view them at a little diftance, conceived fo contemptible an opinion of them, that he advanced nearer and nearer, on purpofe to infult them; but it coft him dear: for fome of the nobility about the perfon of the king, fuddenly charged and took him prifoner[e]. He was much better treated than he deferved; for the queen offered him his liberty, upon his caufing the places to be furrendered that were in the hands of himfelf and his dependents, which he accepted, and the agreement was punctually performed on both fides. After he recovered his liberty, he tried, for fome time, to live in quiet, but fpeedily relapfed into his old intrigues; of which the king having intelligence, he marched againft him inftantly, with a body of troops, and he thereupon quitted *Caftile*, and went to feek protection at the court of *Leon*[f].

A. D. 1218.

THE king Don *Alonfo* received him kindly; and, though he had been deceived by him once before, fuffered himfelf to be again feduced, and merely, from a perfuafion that the enterprife would be eafily accomplifhed, raifed a powerful army, in order to invade *Caftile*. His fon, king *Ferdinand*, affembled another ftill more powerful, with which he encamped in the neighbourhood of *Medina del Campo*, as being unwilling to act againft his father, if it might be avoided. Don *Alonfo*, lefs cautious, advanced into the territory of *Salamancha*, and invefted a place of no great confequence, where fome troops had taken poft. While he lay before the place, Don *Alvaro* fell fick, and, being unable to come into the king's prefence, the prelates laid hold of that opportunity to convince him of the injuftice of the war, which induced him to raife the fiege, and to retire into his own dominions[g]: a circumftance that broke the heart of Don *Alvaro de Lara*, who, upon the march of the army, died at *Toro*; expreffing, with his laft breath, a ftrong defire that his body fhould be cloathed in the habit of St. *James*, and interred at *Ucles*[h]. As he left nothing behind him to bury him with, this had very probably been omitted; but coming to the ear of the queen, Donna *Berengara*, fhe fent a rich robe for his body; and a fum of money for defraying the expences of his funeral; an example of Chriftian charity that deferves to be remembered[i]. As for his brother, Don *Ferdinand de Lara*, whofe conduct had been very equivocal

His flight to Leon, *author of a new war, and miferable death.*

[e] RODERIC TOLETAN de reb. Hifpan. lib. ix. Chron. S. FERNAND. [f] Chron. var. antiq. [g] Annal Toletan. [h] RODERIC TOLETAN de reb. Hifpan. lib. ix. Chron. S. FERNAND. [i] RODERIC TOLETAN de reb. Hifpan. lib. viii.

during

during these troubles, he purchased the king's leave to quit his country by surrendering the places he held, and then he retired to *Morocco*, where he died in obscurity [k].

Marriage of the king of Castile to the princess Beatrix of Suabia, daughter to the emperor.

THE archbishop, Don *Roderic* of *Toledo*, having procured from the pope a bull of croisade against the Infidels, caused it to be published throughout all *Spain*, and, by that means, assembled a great army in the neighbourhood of his city, with which he invaded the territory of the *Moors*, reduced some places of no great importance, and at length besieged *Requena*, which was strong both by art and nature, and had in it a numerous garrison : he persisted, however, in his design of taking it for more than two months, but, in the end, was compelled to rise from before it, with the loss of ten thousand men, to his great mortification [l]. The queen, Donna *Berengara*, had better success in the negotiation of a marriage for her son with the princess *Beatrix*, daughter to the deceased *Philip*, duke of *Suabia*, and emperor of *Germany*, who, in her passage through *France* into *Spain*, was kindly received and magnificently entertained by *Louis* the eighth and his queen *Blanche* [m], which is an additional proof that they never formed any claim upon the *Spanish* monarchy. The princess *Beatrix* was met at *Victoria* by the queen, Donna *Berengara*, and, being conducted to *Burgos*, she was married on the feast of St. *Andrew*, in the cathedral of that city, to the young king *Ferdinand*, in the presence of most of the prelates and nobles of *Castile*, with the universal acclamations of the people [n]. About this time the knights of the order of St. *Julian*, by the consent and approbation of Don *Alonso* of *Leon*, took possession of *Alcantara*, and at the same time received a grant of all such places as they could conquer from the Infidels, to be held as fiefs from the crown of *Leon* [o] (H).

A. D. 1219.

THE

---

[k] SALAZAR.   [l] RODERIC TOLETAN de reb. Hispan. lib. ix. Annal Toletan.   [m] LUCÆ Tudensis Chron. Chron. S. FERNAND.   [n] LUCÆ Tudensis Chron. RODERIC TOLETAN de reb. Hispan. lib. ix.   [o] Chron. var. antiq.

(H) In the time of the emperor *Trajan*, the several nations that inhabited the country then called *Lusitania*, contributed their proportions towards building a most superb bridge over the river *Tagus*, which still remains a monument of the skill and magnificence of those times: this bridge is elevated 200 foot above the level of the water, and though it consists but of six arches, it is 617 feet in length, and 28 in breadth. There were formerly four tables of stone, upon which were inscribed the names of those at whose expence this bridge was built; three of these time and accident have overwhelmed, the fourth has escaped,

THE province of *Rioja* had been committed to the government of Don *Roderic Diaz de los Cameros*, who oppreſſed the
people to ſuch a degree, that many complaints were brought
to the king, who thereupon ſent for him to *Valladolid*; and having ſignified to him that he was not at all ſatisfied with his defence, that nobleman retired privately from court, fortified
ſome of the ſtrongeſt places in his government, and put garriſons into them [p]. The king, Don *Ferdinand*, aſſembled an
army, with full intention to chaſtiſe him; but the queen his mother interpoſed, and put the king in mind, that, during all their
troubles, this nobleman had been faithful ; upon which, in
conſideration of a large ſum of money, he reſigned his government [q]. About this time the affairs of the *Moors* fell into
great confuſion, ſeveral alcaydes, or governors, revolting againſt
Zeit-Arax, the ſon and ſucceſſor of *Mohammed* in *Africa*, thoſe
in *Spain* thought themſelves at liberty to follow their example;
and accordingly *Aben-Hut*, who was deſcended from the kings
of *Saragoſſa*, poſſeſſed himſelf of the kingdom of *Murcia*, and
the beſt part of *Andaluzia* [r]; *Mohammed Aben Abdallah* ſeized
Baeza and the country round it; and the kingdom of *Valentia*
was all that remained to *Abuzeit*, the brother of *Mohammed*

---

[p] RODERIC TOLETAN de reb. Hiſpan. lib. ix.   [q] Chron.
S. FERNAND.   [r] RODERIC TOLETAN de reb. Hiſpan. lib. ix.

---

eſcaped, and we learn from
thence, the names of 13 of theſe
nations. The two inſcriptions
that fix the date of this building
to the emperor's ſixth conſulſhip
are yet entire. The *Moors*,
ſtruck with the beauty of this
elegant performance, as well as
with the fertility of the country
and the conveniency of its ſituation, built there a town, to
which they gave the name of
Al-Cantara, i. e. the bridge.
There are ſeveral other places of
this name in different parts of
Spain, which, upon a ſtrict examination, will be all found to
have derived that denomination
from ſome eminent bridge belonging to them; as for this in
Eſtremadura, which is by far
the moſt conſiderable, we are

told by *Mariana*, and all the
writers who follow him, that it
was given by Don *Alonſo* of *Leon*,
when taken from the *Moors*, to
the knights of *Calatrava*; but
more exact writers affirm, that
it was beſtowed on Don *Diego
Sanchez*, grand maſter of the
military order of St. *Julian de
Perraro*; but it is true that the
knights of *Alcantara* bear a
croſs, reſembling that of the
knights of *Calatrava*; viz. each
point ending in a *Flower de Luce*,
except that the croſs of *Alcantara* is green. At preſent the
order poſſeſſes 33 commanderies, three priories, and as many
alcaydias, which produce altogether a revenue of about 80000
ducats per annum.

Enazor.

A. D.
1280.

Eraxor [s]. Thus the very errors and mistakes of the Christians operated in their favour ; and while they seemed to neglect their true interest, by allowing the Infidels time to rest and recruit themselves, they employed that time more to their own prejudice than if the war had continued ; which seems, so far as the weak light of human understanding will permit us to judge, that Providence interposed in support of the faith professed, though very indifferently practised, by the *Spanish* Christians (I).

[s] Chron. var. antiq.

(I) We have given the reader several instances of men of very high quality, who, either out of ambition or resentment, or from terror or necessity, fled to the *Moors*. At this time there happened something still more extraordinary, which we have inserted in the notes, as it may serve to give the reader some kind of notion of the humour of the people in those times. The Infant Don *Sanchez* of *Leon*, younger brother of Don *Alonso* the ninth, and by his mother's side descended from the family of *Haro*, had given frequent marks of that sort of courage which is stiled ferocity, particularly in the battle of *Toloso*, where he served under the king of *Castile*, as a volunteer. He had some difference, though we know not upon what ground, with the king's brother, which filled his mind with so much rancour, that quitting his court he went to *Toledo*, giving out wherever he passed, that he had received very advantageous proposals from the miramamolin, that he had undertaken to carry him a numerous corps of brave fellows, and that such as would follow him, might be sure of large pay. He picked up by this means 40,000 men, with whom he marched to *Seville*, where he pretended they were to receive their levy money. But arriving in the neighbourhood of this place, he thought proper to withdraw, having in reality received no such invitation, and with a handful of desperate men, who were in his secret, seized upon *Cagnmero*, an old abandoned castle in the skirts of the *Sierra Morena*. The gross of his followers, when they found themselves cheated, got back again into *Portugal*, *Leon*, and *Castile*, as well as they could; and as for the Infant Don *Sanchez* and his associates, they plundered, without distinction, both Christians and *Moors*. On the 23d of *August*, in the year 1220, as he was hunting a bear, the creature suddenly turned upon the unfortunate Infant Don *Sanchez*, and tore him to pieces. His people, if they were so disposed, had not much time to regret his loss; for the very next day the alcayde of *Badojox* invested their fortress, attacked it without delay, carried the place by storm, and put every person they found in it to the sword.

THE

THE next year *James* king of *Arragon* married Donna
Eleonora, sister to the queen Donna *Berengara*, and aunt to
Don *Ferdinand*, king of *Castile* [t]. Amongst the numerous
sons of the house of *Lara* was the count Don *Goncales de Molina*, who hitherto had lived peaceably, but now, at the insti-
gation of another Don *Goncales*, of the same family, brother to
the late Don *Alvaro*, he took up arms, and was joined by that
old rebel, who had taken shelter among the *Moors* [u]. This
obliged the king to march against him with a numerous body
of forces; and the war, perhaps, had not been very quickly
finished, if the queen had not caused an intimation to be given
to Don *Goncales de Molina*, that she intended to have married
the Infant Don *Alonso* to his daughter. This effectually disarmed him : he constrained his cousin to quit the kingdom,
surrendered all his places into the king's hands, was restored
to them and to his favour, and soon after the royal Infant married his daughter [w]. On the twenty-third of *November* the
queen Donna *Beatrix* was delivered of the Infant Don *Alonso*, who succeeded his father in his dominions, and about three
months after his birth was acknowleged for his successor in
a general assembly of the states [x], the king being at that time
determined to enter into a war against the *Moors*. This design was, however, suspended, by the breaking out of a formidable rebellion in *Galicia*, for the suppressing of which, his father demanded of him a considerable body of troops, which he
very readily sent him, and by whose assistance the insurrection
was suppressed [y]. The king of *Leon*, in the succeeding year,
thought fit to establish an university at *Salamanca*.

DON *Ferdinand* of *Castile*, being informed that Don *Alvaro Perez*, who, on account of his having a share in the late
troubles, had retired amongst the *Moors*, was an excellent
officer, he caused it to be insinuated, that if he would return
home, he would not only pardon but employ him, which had
its effect ; and it was from him chiefly that he took his measures for the ensuing war [z]. His forces rendezvoused at *Toledo*, to which city he went ; and, after a general review, he
marched with them, attended by the archbishop Don *Roderic*,
into the territory of the *Moors* ; but, before he had advanced
far, he was met by *Abuzeit*, king of *Valentia*, who offered to
become his vassal, whom he received kindly, and sent back
with a promise that no hostilities should be committed against

Margin notes:
James, king of Arragon, espouses the Infanta Eleonora.

A. D. 1222.

John de Brienne, king of Jerusalem, espouses the Infanta Berengara.

---

[t] ZURITA Annal Arragon. [u] Annal Toletan. [w] Ro-
DERIC TOLETAN de reb. Hispan. lib. ix. [x] Chron. var.
antiq. [y] LUCÆ Tudensis Chron. [z] Chron. S. FERNAND.
RODERIC TOLETAN de reb. Hispan. lib. ix.

his subjects [a]. He then passed the *Sierra Morena*, ravaged the territory of *Baeza*, defeated a body of *Moors* who attempted to oppose his passage, and concluded the campaign by taking *Quezada*, which, with some other fortresses, he demolished. While the king was in the field, *John de Brienne*, king of *Jerusalem*, arrived in *Spain*, in order to perform a vow he had made to visit the shrine of the apostle St. *James*. After he had accomplished this, he visited the court at *Burgos*, and there concluded a marriage with Donna *Berengara*, the sister of king *Ferdinand*, and soon after set out with her for the court of *France* [c].

A. D.
1224.

Campaign of the king Don Ferdinand against the Moors.

THE king took the field early the next spring; but had scarce passed the *Sierra Morena*, before he was met by *Aben-Mohammed*, the son of *Aben-Abdallah*, descended from the miramamolins of *Africk*, who became his vassal, and agreed to pay him the fourth part of his revenues; for which, by way of security, he gave his son *Abdul-Menin* as a hostage, and put likewise into his hands the castles of *Baeza*, *Andujar*, and *Martos*, which put an end to the campaign [d]. Don *Alonso*, king of *Leon*, was, at the same time, in the field; and being met by a numerous army of *Moors*, under the command of *Aben-Hut*, king of *Seville*, a general engagement ensued; in which, after a warm and bloody dispute, the Christians were victorious, and Don *Alonso* returned into his own dominions, covered with glory, as his troops were laden with plunder [e]. The pope, towards the end of the year, sent a bull of croisade into *Spain*, to enable the kings of *Leon* and *Portugal* to carry on the war against the Infidels, in which they were engaged with the greater effect, for, as we have observed, the archbishop of *Toledo* had procured a bull of the same kind, on behalf of the king his master [f].

A. D.
1225.

He demands several fortresses from Mohammed, king of Baeza.

As soon as the season would permit, the young monarch was again in the field, with the troops of *Castile* and *Leon*, though it does not appear that his forces were very numerous; for his design was no other than to reduce the several places which the *Moors* still possessed, at the descent of the *Sierra Morena*, through the pass of *Muradal*; and having accomplished this, and thrown into them strong garrisons, he retired, and put his forces into quarters of refreshment, which delivered the *Moors* from their fears, and hindered them from acquiring any just idea of that important plan he had formed for extend-

---

[a] Annal Toletan.   [b] RODERIC TOLETAN de reb. Hispan. lib. ix. Chron. S. FERNAND.   [c] RODERIC TOLETAN de reb. Hispan. lib. ix. LUCÆ Tudensis Chron.   [d] Chron. var. antiq. [e] LUCÆ Tudensis Chron.   [f] Chron. S. FERNAND. RODERIC TOLETAN de reb. Hispan. lib. ix.

ing

ing his own dominions, and curtailing theirs [g]. The next
year he returned, with a more potent army, into *Andaluzia*,
and demanded of *Mohammed*, king of *Baeza*, the fortresses of
Bergamilar, *Salvatierra*, and *Capilla*. The reader will observe, that there were many places of the second name, and
there were also several of the third. That monarch, afraid of
a war with so enterprising a prince, whilst he was at the same
time in dread of all the rest of his neighbours, acquiesced under this demand; and sent his orders to the commandants of
the respective places, to put them into the hands of the king
of *Castile*; and, till this could be done, he put the castle of
Baeza into the king's hands, by way of security, who sent
Don *Goncales*, grand master of the order of *Calatrava*, to take
possession of it, with a competent garrison; upon which the
Moorish monarch, who could not, with any decency, live in
a city commanded by a Christian garrison, withdrew to *Cor-
doua*, which was also in his possession, till the fortresses he had
demanded were rendered to the king of *Castile* [h]. As for the
two first, they were evacuated by the *Moorish* garrisons without
any dispute; but the last, having been used as a place of arms,
and being consequently spacious, strong, and well supplied
with provisions and military stores, the governor, who was a
brave man, and had a numerous garrison, refused to obey his
master's orders; and, after some altercations, Don *Ferdinand*
found himself under the necessity of besieging the place in
form [i].

As the people are but bad politicians, so the *Moors* of *Cor-* *That un-*
doua, instead of attributing the complaisance of their monarch *fortunate*
to those which were in reality its proper motives, began to sus- *monarch*
pect him of holding a secret correspondence with the Chri- *murdered*
stians, which quickly increased into a confident opinion, that *for grant-*
he was himself a Christian in his heart, which determined *ing his re-*
them to put him out of the way, and submit themselves to *quest.*
Aben-Hut, king of *Seville*. A popular conspiracy can never
long be concealed; *Mohammed* therefore, having gained intelligence of their design, endeavoured to provide for his personal security, by retiring privately to a place of safety, in
which he miscarried; for, being pursued and taken upon the
road, the conspirators, in pursuance of their original scheme,
cut off his head [k]. The news of this revolution no sooner
reached *Baeza*, than the inhabitants took up arms and besieged the castle, which the grand master defended with all

[g] Chron. var. antiq.   [h] RODERIC TOLETAN de reb. Hispan.
lib. ix.   [i] Chron. S. FERNAND.   [k] RODERIC TOLETAN de
reb. Hispan. lib. ix.

the spirit and resolution that became a man of his rank. At the end of four months, Don *Ferdinand* took *Capilla* by storm, and put the whole *Moorish* garrison to the sword [l]. The grand master, and those under his command, were very near meeting with the same fate; but, upon signifying his distress to Don *Alvaro Perez*, he fixed a short day for the sending him such a reinforcement as should enable him to raise the siege; and accordingly, in the night preceding that day, Don *Lopez de Haro* entered the castle with a numerous detachment, and as soon as it was light, in conjunction with the grand master and his garrison, attacked the posts of the Infidels with such vigour, that in a few hours they were all forced, and the Christians became masters of the place. This was a conquest of great importance; the city anciently called *Votia*, standing on an eminence not far from the *Guadalquivir*, and it was thought very remarkable, the *Castilians* recovered it on the feast of St. *Andrew*, to whom its church, in antient times, was dedicated [m].

The pope declares null the marriage between the king and queen of Arragon.

A. D. 1228.

IN the beginning of the month of *March*, in the succeeding year, Don *Ferdinand* laid the first stone of the new cathedral in *Toledo*, which is the same magnificent structure that adorns this city in our times [n]. The archbishop Don *Roderic* had a large share in this important work; and the materials being in readiness before it was begun, the undertaking, though great, was sooner completed than could well be imagined [o]. The king made also a short campaign, in which he ravaged the country about *Jaen*, in order to facilitate an enterprize, which was to be the business of the ensuing year. We have before observed, that *James*, king of *Arragon*, had married Donna *Eleonora*, sister to Don *Ferdinand* of *Castile*, by whom he was the father of the Infant Don *Alonso*; but having at this time a legate from the pope at his court, that prelate discovered, or as some writers hint, had it discovered to him by the king, that this princess and he stood equally related to the emperor Don *Alonso*, upon which a council was called of the bishops of *Arragon* and *Castile*, by whom the marriage was declared null, which the king bore with great moderation; but the queen, it is said, discovered a little impatience: however, the legitimacy of her son was provided for, and she returned again to the court of *Burgos* [p]. Don *Alonso*, king of *Leon*, took the field in *Estremadura*, and made himself master of *Caceres*, a place of importance, which himself and his predecessors had more than once attempted in

[l] Annal Toletan.   [m] RODERIC TOLETAN *de reb. Hispan.* lib. ix: [n] Annal Toletan.   [o] RODERIC TOLETAN *de reb. Hispan.* lib. ix.   [p] ZURITA Annal Arragon.

vain.

vain. Some say that it was antiently called *Casa Cereris*, which has been corrupted into its present name [q]. Don *Ferdinand* of *Castile* was not so fortunate in the design he had been so long meditating; for, though he made a siege in form, and of some continuance, he failed in taking *Jaen*; but, by the advice of Don *Alvaro Perez*, he destroyed several places in its neighbourhood, and took such other steps as might make what he aimed at more practicable when attempted another time [r].

A. D. 1229.

Don *Alonso*, king of *Leon*, resolved to pursue the war against the Infidels with greater vigour than ever; as having nothing to fear from any of his neighbours, and cast his eyes upon *Merida*, a place of great strength and of great consequence, to the safety of which the *Moors* were very attentive; but, however, he attacked it so vigorously, that it fell into his hands before they were in a condition to relieve it [s]. He was scarce entered into possession, before *Aben-Hut*, the most powerful of the *Moorish* monarchs in *Spain*, appeared at the head of an army of 20,000 horse and 60,000 foot [t]. The troops of Don *Alonso* were much inferior in number, but as he had no choice to make, except fighting or being besieged in his new conquest, he judged the former preferable to the latter; and therefore, recommending himself to the intercession of the *Spanish* apostle and St. *Isidore*, he marched out and gave battle to the *Moors*, and after a long dispute, gained a complete victory, and in consequence of it several considerable conquests [u]. His son, Don *Ferdinand* of *Castile*, impatient at his former miscarriage, besieged *Jaen* again with a very formidable army; but the *Moors*, who knew the importance of the place, and who saw how fast their affairs were declining, had in every respect provided so effectually for its defence, that the king was prevailed upon by his officers, rather to raise the siege a second time, than ruin his army, which however he did with great reluctance [w].

Don Alonso of Leon gains a glorious victory over the Moors at Merida.

A. D. 1230.

Don *Alonso* of *Leon*, immediately after his glorious campaign was over, went to visit the shrine of St. *Isidore*, and to return thanks to God for the victory of *Merida*. He intended to have done the same at *Compostella*, according to the religious notions of those times; but, in his journey thither, he

Dies in his journey to the tomb of St. James, et

[q] Les Delices d'Espagne, tom. i. p. 137.   Chron. var. antiq.
[r] RODERIC TOLETAN de reb Hispan. lib. ix.   [s] Annal
Toletan et Compostel. LUCÆ Tudensis Chron.   [t] RODERIC
TOLETAN de reb. Hispan. lib. ix.   LUCÆ Tudensis Chron.
[u] Chron. var. antiq.   [w] RODERIC TOLETAN de reb. Hispan.
lib. ix.

was

192

Compof-
tella.

The History of Leon *and* Caftile. B. XIX.

was feized with the diftemper of which he died, at *Villa-nova de Serria*, on the 23d of *September*, in the year 1230 [x]. By his teftament, he directed that his body fhould be interred in the cathedral church of St. *James*, as near as might be to that of his father; and, which was very fingular, he declared the Infantas Donna *Sancha* and Donna *Dulcia*, whom he had by his firft wife the Infanta *Therefa* of *Portugal*, coheireffes of his dominions, requiring feveral of the prelates and moft confiderable of the nobility by name to fee his laft will punctually executed [y]. He was a prince endowed with great virtues; but, at the fame time, had great foibles; with refpect to the former he was chiefly diftinguifhed by the ftrictnefs of his government, in point of juftice, and his great mildnefs in levying his revenue, which made his fubjects rich, and himfelf exceedingly beloved. The inconftancy of his temper was his greateft failing, and in the courfe of his reign expofed him to many inconveniences. He was unfortunate in both his marriages, though a good hufband to both his wives; but the firft remained ever miftrefs of his affections (K) : and, it is very

[x] Chron. S. FERNAND. RODERIC SANTII Hift. Hifpan. FRANCISCI TARAPHÆ de reg. Hifpan. [y] Chron. S. FERNAND.

(K) This king, Don *Alonfo* the ninth, of *Leon*, died in the 43d year of his reign, and is very highly commended by the two great hiftorians of *Spain*, who were his contemporaries. The point which gained him the greateft credit, was his love of juftice, of which he had a very right conception; for it was his fentiment, that the king ought to fhew his regard by making the adminiftration of it both honourable and profitable, that fuch as were chofen to decide fuits, might be under no fort of influence, and have no kind of temptation. He therefore expected that his judges fhould hear nothing, but when both parties were prefent, and that they fhould not, under any pretence whatever, take fee or reward. This made him beloved by people, and feared by the nobility, who, though he had great faults, found it more difficult to raife difturbances againft him than any of his predeceffors; for the peafants, being frequently ill ufed by their lords, upon complaint in the king's courts, were certainly redreffed, and this made his caufe theirs. He was likewife much in the good graces of the clergy, and, with all his faults, he was fincerely pious; and though he difcovered great ambition, in twice attempting upon his fon's dominions, yet in this he was mifled by flatterers, who made him believe, for a time, things, of which he was afterwards afhamed. His laft ficknefs was very painful, and yet he

very remarkable, that though both marriages were declared unlawful by the *Roman* pontiff, yet, Donna *Sancha* by the first, and Don *Ferdinand* by the last, are both acknowleged saints by the church of *Rome* [z].

THE manner in which he disposed of his dominions by his will was very near producing a civil war. *Galicia*, and some part of *Leon*, declared for the Infantas; but the far greater part of the kingdom for Don *Ferdinand* of *Castile*, to whose succession the states had solemnly sworn. Queen *Theresa* left *Portugal* to support the party of her daughters, and took shelter with them under the protection of the great master of the order of St. *James* [a]. The queen Donna *Berengara*, as soon as she heard of her husband's death, set out with all her family, and was overtaken by the king Don *Ferdinand*, on the road to *Leon*, into which capital they were received with all imaginable marks of duty and loyalty, to confirm which dispositions in the people, the king published two edicts, one for remitting of taxes, and the other threatening with very severe punishment such as should persist in rebellion [b]; notwithstanding which, many persons of great distinction remained firm to the Infantas; and things at last had certainly come to extremities, if the two queens *Theresa* and *Berengara* had not settled them amicably, at an interview which they had for this purpose. There they agreed, that the king, Don *Ferdinand*, should give each of his sisters a large pension, in consideration of which they renounced their pretensions under Don *Alonso*'s will [c]; and this reconciliation was so cordial on both sides, that the two queens fixed a time in the ensuing year for a second interview, that the whole royal family of *Leon* might have an opportunity of meeting and embracing each other [d]. A circumstance so singular, as hardly any thing of the like kind is to be met with in history, and which brings us to the close of this section, since from the union of the two kingdoms of *Castile* and *Leon*, which was perfected by this agreement, they have never been divided,

margin note: Disputes about the succession amicably compromised.

[z] MARIANA, FERRERAS, MAYERNE TURQUET. [a] RODERIC TOLETAN de reb. Hispan. lib. ix. LUCÆ Tudensis Chron. [b] Chron. S. FERNAND. [c] RODERIC TOLETAN de reb. Hispan. lib. ix. LUCÆ Tudensis Chron. [d] Chron. S. FERNAND.

he bore it very patiently. Besides his legitimate offspring, he left behind him a natural son, Don *Alonso*, for whom he made a provision suitable to his rank, but without any prejudice to his lawful issue.

but have gradually drawn to them all the other sovereignties in *Spain* ; those of the Christians by inheritance or marriage, and those of the *Moors* by conquest, as in the succeeding sections it will be our business to explain.

SECT. VII.

The History of the Kingdoms of Castile *and* Leon, *from the Accession of St.* Ferdinand *to the Union of all the Christian Monarchies in* Spain *(except* Portugal) *in the Persons of their Catholic Majesties* Ferdinand *and* Isabella.

Interview between both branches of the royal family, and harmony between them.

THE conjunction of the kingdoms of *Leon* and *Castile* was an event not at all more agreeable or more glorious for the sovereign than it was advantageous to the people, which the wiser and better part of the nobility very well knew ; and therefore preferred the justice and the conveniency of the king of *Castile*'s title to the will of their late prince, who, contrary to reasons of state, his own solemn act, and the oaths of his states, would have disinherited his son, merely because he was a king in his life-time [a]. But though Don *Ferdinand* very well knew this disposition, and that he might, without any danger, have trusted the tranquility of his kingdom of *Leon* to the affection of his subjects, yet he very punctually kept the appointment made by his mother queen *Berengara*, and repaired to *Benevente* with his family, at the time fixed. Thither also came the queen dowager *Theresa*, and the two infantas ; and the mutual sincerity of the whole royal family appeared not only in exterior marks of kindness and respect, and in the king's confirmation of large annual pensions, which had been promised, but from their maintaining a perfect and good correspondence while they were together, and from the resolutions taken when they came to part [b].

Don Ferdinand of Castile confers with the king of Portugal, and con-

IT was then agreed, that the infanta Donna *Sancha* should be left behind with queen *Berengara*, and reside, for the future, in the court of *Castile* ; and that the king should accompany queen *Theresa* and the other Infanta, her daughter, into *Portugal*, which he accordingly did [c]. The king, Don *Sancho*, quitted his dominions to go and meet them, and the two kings had a long interview at *Sabugal* ; where Don *Ferdinand* took great pains to persuade Don *Sancho*, how much it was their

[a] RODERIC TOLETAN de reb. Hispan. lib. ix.   LUCÆ Tudensis Chron.   [b] Chron. S. FERNAND.   [c] RODERIC TOLETAN de reb. Hispan. lib. ix.

common

common interest to live in the strictest terms of friendship and peace, that they might carry on the war with greater success against their common enemy, the *Moors*; and, to convince him that this was the language of his heart, he restored the important fortress of St. *Stephen de Chaves*, which his father had taken from him [d]. At his return from this interview, Don *Ferdinand* marched with a good corps of troops into *Galicia*, where the lords, who pretended to espouse the cause of the Infantas, were endeavouring to render themselves independent, despising the youth and want of experience in their new king. He reduced some, punished others, and obliged the rest to quit their country. Amongst these was Don *Lorenzo Suarez*, who retired into the territory of the *Moors* [e]. Towards the close of the year arrived a bull from pope *Gregory* IX. ratifying the treaty between him and queen Donna *Theresa*, by which the settlement of the kingdom of *Leon* was rendered complete [f].

As the king's attention was, for the present, wholly employed about civil affairs, Don *Roderic*, archbishop of *Toledo*, was intrusted with the care of the frontiers; and his zeal induced him to carry on the war very briskly against the *Moors*, from whom he took several places, and some of the most considerable were, for this reason, granted by the crown to his diocese [g]. In order to comprehend the reason of this more clearly, it will not be amiss to observe, that it very frequently happened, when the monarchs of *Castile* recovered places on the frontiers which they could not immediately either fortify or repeople, the *Moors*, upon the retreat of the army, took advantage of this, and got them again into their power; to prevent which, no method could be found so effectual as granting them to a prelate, who, by his influence, filled them speedily with inhabitants, and, in consequence of annexing them to his see, preserved them to the kingdom.

THE next year, however, the Christian army on the frontiers was commanded by the Infant Don *Alonso*, the king's brother, and Don *Alvaro Perez*. The young prince, being desirous of signalizing his courage, marched into the territory of *Cordova*; and, having ravaged it without opposition, advanced into that of *Seville*, and passed the *Guadiana* at *Xerez*. The *Moorish* monarch, *Aben-Hut*, having certain intelligence of the small number of forces the Infant commanded, and hav-

Side notes:
cludes a treaty.

A. D. 1231.

Many places taken from the Moors granted to the archiepiscopal see of Toledo.

1232.

The royal Infant gains a glorious victory over Aben-Hut, king of Seville.

[d] BRANDAON. EMANUEL DE FARIA Y SOUSA de las Historias y Portuguesas. FERRERAS Historia de España, p. vi. §. xiii. [e] RODERIC TOLETAN de reb. Hispan. lib. ix. LUCÆ Tudensis Chron. [f] RINALDUS. FERRERAS Historia de España, p. vi. sec. xiii. [g] MORALES, MARIANA, FERRERAS.

ing

ing received a large reinforcement from *Africa*, under the command of a general who acted from no other motives than religious zeal, resolved to lay hold of so favourable an opportunity to give a check to the Christian power; and having accordingly taken his measures with as much secrecy as possible, he advanced, with a numerous army, in order to surprize the Christians: but, notwithstanding this, the Infant *Alonso* might have retired, if his piety and courage had not induced him to risque a battle, from a persuasion that, with the Divine assistance, many may be vanquished by few. His little army was ranged in two lines, the first commanded by Don *Alvaro Perez*, the second by the Infant in person; they both observed a close order, and received the charge of the *Moors* with great firmness and intrepidity. The battle was obstinate and bloody, but, in the end, the Christians were victorious, and the *Moorish* general from *Africa* slain upon the spot, by a young gentleman of *Toledo*, who had received the honour of knighthood that morning in the field [h]. A prodigious number of *Moors* were killed upon the spot and in their flight, *Aben-Hut* himself escaped with difficulty, and most of the *Spanish* historians [i] are themselves persuaded, and would persuade their readers, that St. *James* was visibly present in the battle, in which there fell but one man on the side of the Infant. The archbishop of *Toledo* is silent upon this head; and though the bishop of *Tuy* mentions the victory, and ascribes it to the wonderful power of God, yet he says nothing to the presence of St. *James* [k]. The care of the finances being about this time in the hands of the *Jews*, the pope wrote to the archbishop of *Compostella*, to remonstrate to the king against a method that subjected his Christian subjects to great inconveniencies, and put them too much under the power of their implacable enemies [l].

Death of Donna Beatrix, queen of Castile, and an account of her children.

AT the very opening of the ensuing year, Don *Ferdinand* took the field in person, having several points of importance in view. In the first place he ordered the bishop of *Placentia* to make himself master of *Truxillo*, a place of great consequence, at the distance of ten leagues from *Merida*, which he performed. He next charged Don *Pedro Goncales*, grand master of the order of St. *James*, to reduce *Montial*, with its district: this likewise being performed in time, the king appointed those detachments to join his army, at a certain place, and, when the *Moors* least expected it, invested *Ubeda*, a city which

[h] Annal Toletan. Chron. S. Fernand.　　[i] Ferreras Historia de Espana, p. vi. sec. xiii.　　[k] Chron. Mundi.　　[l] Rinaldus, Ferreras.

had

had been often attempted, but in vain, and which commanded a country as fertile in wine, corn, oil, and fruits, as any in
Spain. The *Moors* made a long and gallant defence, in
hopes the king of *Seville* would have relieved them ; but he
was fo humbled and fo difabled by his late defeat, that he could
do nothing ; fo that, on *Michaelmas* day, that valuable city
was furrendered [m]. While the king lay before this place, he
loft his dear confort Donna *Beatrix,* who died at *Toro,* and
left behind her fix fons ; viz. the Infants *Alonfo, Frederic,
Henry, Ferdinand, Philip,* and *Sancho* ; he had by her alfo
the Infanta *Maria,* but fhe died fome fmall time before the
queen her mother [n].

A. D.
1234.

THIS lofs feems to have affected the king fo much, that he
was not in the field all the next year, and there was but little
done for that reafon ; but a great defign was contrived, which
the next year was carried into execution. In the courfe of
various expeditions, the *Caftilians* had taken prifoners a confiderable number of thofe foldiers, who, by their own countrymen, were ftyled *Almogaraves, i. e.* Invalids, who were generally put into garrifons ; and this might probably be one reafon why their places were fo well defended. But no care being taken to ranfom them, thefe old men took it fo ill, that
they began to infinuate to fome of the Chriftian officers, that
the great city of *Cordova* had but a fmall garrifon, the care of
it being chiefly trufted to the inhabitants, who were very re-
mifs, and that confequently it might be eafily furprized. Meafures for this purpofe being concerted, a fmall body of horfe
and foot marched in a dark and rainy night, being that of the
eighth of *January,* fcaled the walls, and poffeffed themfelves
of one of the fuburbs, in which they barricaded themfelves,
and kept it in fpite of all that the *Moors* in the city could do,
notwithftanding they were often attacked [o]. Don *Alvara
Perez* no fooner received news of their fuccefs, than he
marched to relieve them, with all the troops under his command, which prevented the *Moors* from driving them out of
the pofts they had taken, but was of no confequence towards
reducing the city, which was both ftrong and populous [p].
The king, Don *Ferdinand,* apprized of their fituation, and of
the great importance of this bold attempt, fet out immediately from *Benevente,* with a few of the nobility that were about

*The great
fcheme
formed for
reducing
the city of
Cordova,
and its
confe-
quences.*

---

[m] Annal Toletan. Chron. S. FERNAND. [n] RODERIC
TOLETAN de reb. Hifpan. lib. ix. RODERIC SANTII Hift.
Hifpan. p. iii. FRANCISCI TARAPHÆ de reg. Hifpan. [o] Chron.
S. FERNAND. RODERIC SANTII Hift. Hifpan. p. iii. [p] Annal
Toletan. Annal Compoftell.

him,

him, ordering troops to be sent after him as fast as they could be raised, and took post at the bridge of *Alcala*.

Don Ferdinand enters Cordova in triumph, and causes the city to be re-peopled.

THE *Moors* in *Cordova*, having an exact account of these proceedings, sent deputies to *Aben-Hut*, requesting him to lose no time in marching to their relief, as the king's army was very inconsiderable, and that, upon his retreat, those in the suburbs must be obliged to surrender. This monarch, we knowing the value of *Cordova*, assembled the whole force of his dominions, and, if he had marched with them, must have done his business without striking a blow; but, by using too much caution, he lost this opportunity, and soon after his life q (A). As soon as the season would permit, the troops of the

q Chron. S. FERNAND. RODERIC TOLETAN de reb. Hispan. lib. ix. LUCÆ Tudensis Chronicon.

(A) This *Moorish* prince was an able statesman, and a good officer; but the situation of his affairs, at the time that the people of *Cordova* demanded his assistance, embarrassed him extremely. He could not conceive how so potent a monarch as the king of *Castile* could advance so far into an enemy's country, with so small a body of troops, and therefore he sent for Don *Lorenzo Suarez*, who had served him from the time that Don *Ferdinand* expelled him out of *Galicia*, and proposed to him that he should go and examine the Christian camp in the night, and bring him such an account as he could depend upon. Don *Lorenzo* accepted the proposal; went privately into the camp, and sent the king word that Don *Lorenzo Suarez* had somewhat of importance to communicate to him. He sent for him, and asked him sternly how he durst appear in his presence? Don *Lorenzo* answered, that he hoped the service he was about to render him, would cancel his

former faults. He then informed him what force *Aben-Hut* had about him, and to how great danger himself was exposed; promised to report his army much more numerous than it was, and advised him to keep a very strict guard for the future. On his return, *Aben-Hut* received very pressing letters from *Zaen*, king of *Valencia*, whose capital was on the point of falling into the hands of the king of *Arragon*. Upon the report therefore of Don *Lorenzo*, he chose to march first to the relief of this prince, and with the assistance of his forces, to attempt the relief of *Cordova*. In his march, he was invited by *Aben-Ramin* his favourite, whom he had made governor of *Almeria*, to honour that place with his presence. There he was splendidly feasted, after which, retiring to the bath, he was there stifled by *Aben-Ramin's* order. As soon as his death was known, the army disbanded, which gave Don *Lorenzo Suarez* an opportunity of going away

the prelates, nobles, and of the several military orders, gradually arrived in the camp of Don *Ferdinand*, by which he quickly found himself strong enough to quit the post he had taken, and to invest *Cordova*; the inhabitants of which city, finding themselves much straitened for provisions, intimidated by the death of king *Aben-Hut*, and having no succour to expect, at length desired a capitulation, and, upon being permitted to march out freely, and go where they pleased, surrendered on the feast of St. *Peter* and *Paul*, on the twenty-ninth of *June*, in the year one thousand two hundred and thirty-six [r] (B). The settling every thing that regarded this

important

[r] Annal Toletan.   Annal Compostel.   RODERIC TOLETAN. LUCÆ Tudensis Chron.   S. FERNAND.

away with his squadron of horse to the Christian army (1). The death of *Aben-Hut* at this juncture was attended with the most fatal consequences to the *Moors*, and seems to have been the principal cause of the heavy losses they sustained.

(B) Amongst other things found in *Cordova*, were the bells that had been carried away when *Almanzor* plundered *Compostella*, brought thither upon the shoulders of Christian captives, and which had been used as lamps in the *Turkish* mosque. These Don *Ferdinand* obliged his prisoners to carry back upon their shoulders, cleansed and purified that stately building, and caused divine service to be celebrated there, to the glory of God, and to the inexpressible joy, not only of his own subjects, but of all the Christians in *Spain* (2). The bishop of *Tuy*, who concludes his chronicle with this great event, assures us, that it was chiefly owing to the

activity and spirit of Don *Ferdinand*, who came thither at first with no more than 100 men; and finding that the city received continual supplies over the bridge, passed the rapid river of *Guadalquivir* with the utmost hazard of his person; and taking post on the other side, cut off those supplies. He likewise observes, that unusual rains falling in that season, raised the rivers and brooks so high, that the troops marching to his assistance from different parts of his dominions were exceedingly delayed; so that, as he very prudently remarks, it ought to be ascribed to the special Providence of God, that an enterprize, so well contrived and so vigorously executed, did not from these sinister accidents become abortive; which if it had, the consequences might have proved no less dangerous to the Christians, than as they fell out they proved destructive to the *Moors* (3). This prelate was a

(1) *Chron. S. Fernand. Mariana Historia general de Espana, lib.* xii. *c.* 18. *Ferreras, Historia de Espana, p.* vi. *sect.* xiii. *Mayerne Turquet, Histoire de Espagne, liv.* xi.   (2) *Annal Toletan. Chron. var. antiq.*   (3) *Chron. Mundi, ap Schot. Hispan. illustrat.*

important conqueſt, coſt the king ſo much time, that it was the month of *September* before he found himſelf at liberty to return to *Toledo,* where he found the good old archbiſhop *Roderic,* juſt arrived from *Rome,* where he had been to ſollicit the rights of his church againſt that of St. *James* of *Compoſtella,* the popes having very wiſely declined to determine the long depending ſuit between theſe ſees for the primacy ; which, as it ſerved to flatter the power, ſo it turned likewiſe to the profit, of theſe eccleſiaſtical ſovereigns; and therefore we need not wonder that they proceeded at leiſure, and would precipitate nothing in a matter of ſuch conſequence [s].

Marries a   THE queen mother, Donna *Berengara,* reflecting very pru-
ſecond time dently on the inconveniencies that might attend the king's
the daugh- remaining a widower in the prime of his age, by the advice
ter of the of her ſiſter the queen of *France,* negotiated a marriage for
count de him with the lady *Jane,* daughter to *Simon* count *de Ponthieu,*.
Ponthieu. merely on account of the great reputation ſhe was in for the
purity of her manners and the ſweetneſs of her temper [t]. This
marriage, which was celebrated at *Bourdeaux,* and the renewing the league with the king of *Navarre,* took up the whole
of this year, in which the forces of *Caſtile* remained in winter
quarters and garriſons, without undertaking any thing of importance, and this without any prejudice to the affairs of the
Chriſtians, thoſe of the *Moors* being fallen into ſuch confu-
A. D. ſion, that they were in no condition of ſeizing even a greater
1237. advantage [u] (C). The next year, in all probability, would
have

---

[s] Annal Toletan. Chron. S. FERNAND.   [t] RODERIC
TOLETAN de reb. Hiſpan. lib. ix.   [u] Chron. S. FERNAND.

---

man of ſincere piety, and of very extenſive learning, for the times in which lived : in his youth he had travelled through *Italy* and the *Holy Land*; and in the latter part of his life was highly eſteemed by that pious and prudent princeſs queen *Berengara,* at whoſe inſtance he compoſed ſeveral large works, and amongſt the reſt his chro-nicle (4), to which we have been ſo much obliged.

(C) The reſpite which the king of *Caſtile* gave to the

Moors, after the recovery of *Cordova,* turned almoſt as much to their diſadvantage as the blow given to their power by depriv-ing them of their place; but be-fore we explain this, it may not be improper to mention the rea-ſon which induced Don *Ferdinand* to make a tour into the northern parts of his dominions at this time. The biſhop of *Palencia,* it ſeems, had diſcover-ed certain hereticks in his dio-ceſe, proceeded againſt them with that violence which was

---

(4) *Mariana Hiſtoria de Eſpana, lib.* xii. *Cave Hiſt. Liter. tom.* ii. *p.* 237.

           juſt

have been remarkable for action, if a famine had not broke out at *Cordova*, which might have had fatal consequences, if the king, who kept his *Easter* at *Valladolid*, had not taken care to send a large supply of provisions, together with a considerable sum in ready money w. In the autumn he made a tour himself to *Toledo*, and from thence to the frontiers, from whence he made some excursions into the territory of *Jaen*, to which city, if he had not found it so strong, he intended to have laid siege.

AT the opening of the ensuing spring died Don *Alvaro Perez de Castro*, grandson of Don *Pedro Fernandez*, of the same family, who had been expelled *Castile* by Don *Alonso*;

1238.

Don Diego de Haro

---

w Chron. general de Espana, par FLORIAN DE OCAMPO.

---

just come into fashion, and condemned such as could not be frightened into dissimulation to the stake (5). This was thought a point of such importance, that the king was present; and, to shew his profound submission to the flaming zeal of the church, he condescended, as the *Spanish* historians say, to light the fire, by which they suffered, with his own hands; and for this, the only cruel action of his life, they pretend he was reputed a saint. But let us now return to the *Moors*. The death of king *Aben-Hut*, the loss of *Cordova* to the king of *Castile*, and *Valencia* to the king of *Arragon*, threw them into grievous confusions, as their being now detached from the *Moors* of *Africa* left them, in a manner, without resource. The inhabitants of *Seville* formed themselves into a republic, and appointed one *Tasar* for their chief magistrate; nor is there any thing improbable in supposing that other cities would have taken the same step, if *Mohammed Al-hamar*, by his superior abilities, had not prevented it (6). His history is inserted in its proper place; and therefore here we shall conclude, with observing, that the *Moors* had still strength enough to have made a great stand, and to have preserved the most fruitful and pleasant part of *Spain*, if they could have united under this prince; and, on the other hand, if he had remained only master of the town of *Aronja*, which was the place of his birth, and the first that he seized, they could never have made any stand at all, but must have been presently over-run by the armies of *Castile*, *Arragon*, and *Portugal*. The true, though concealed, source of their ruin, was the universal corruption of their manners, that spirit of ambition and perfidy which reigned amongst the great, and that giddiness among the people, which was diffused by the pernicious practices and base examples of their chiefs, who made no scruple of sacrificing the public interest to their private advantage.

---

(5) *Reinald, Ferreras Historia de Espan. part* vi. *sect.* xiii. *riana, Ferreras, Mayerne Turquet.*

(6) *Ma-*

and

and not long after him died Don *Lopez de Haro*, governor of *Baeza*, whose son, Don *Diego*, because the king did not give him his father's government, took up arms, was reconciled to the king by the Infant Don *Alonso* his son, broke out into rebellion again, and, being beat in the field by that young prince, and reduced to great straits, fled privately to the king, and threw himself at his feet, with such visible marks of sincere repentance, that the king restored him to his favour, and to his former employments, to which he added the government of *Alcaraz* [x]. There happened this year, on *Friday* the third of *June*, as all the antient chronicles of *Spain* agree, a great

eclipse of the sun [y]. The old archbishop of *Toledo* was in the field all the autumn, or at least the troops in his pay, who repelled the *Moors* that were attempting to creep into possession again of most of the places that prelate had taken. The next spring the king was early at *Cordova*, took the field with a numerous army, and made many conquests, but they were such as cost no blood; for the people, being afraid of his forces, and seeing none of the *Moorish* princes strong enough to defend them, submitted upon the promise of being well used, moderately taxed, and allowed the free exercise of their religion [z].

THE great extent of country which had been added to his dominions, in the space of a few years, obliged Don *Ferdinand* to act with great caution, and hindered him from being so alert in his expeditions as in times past. He saw that it was to no purpose to waste his troops in subduing places which he must be afterwards forced to abandon, and leave his successors subject to the trouble of taking them again; for which reason he laboured all that in him lay to preserve a line of regular fortifications, and, by the promise of lands, immunities, and other advantages, drew multitudes from all parts to settle in the towns and villages that were behind that line [a]. The *Moors*, during that space of time, in which he was thus employed, neglected nothing that might contribute to restore their affairs, except the only method that could have been effectual, which was a general confederacy. This was at length perceived by the king of *Granada*, who invited his neighbour the king of *Murcia* to enter into a league with him, offensive and defensive, which that king, however, declined; and gave this reason for it, that very probably this might incense the king of *Castile*, who was infinitely more able to conquer than the other was to protect his dominions; which answer, tho' well

---

[x] Chron. S. FERNAND.　[y] Annal Toletan. Annal Compostell.　[z] Chronica general de Espana par FLORIAN DE OCAMPO.　[a] Chron. S. FERNAND. Annal Toletan.

founded,

founded, gave such offence to the king of *Granada*, that he began to raise forces, and to think of making war upon the prince who had rejected his alliance; of which the sovereign of *Murcia* had no sooner intelligence, than he dispatched ambassadors to Don *Ferdinand*, and desired to be taken under his protection [b]. The king of *Castile* doubted of the sincerity of this proposition, and therefore ordered the ambassadors to return to their master, and to bring his final resolution to the young prince Don *Alonso*, who, with a corps of troops, should advance to the frontiers, to support him if there should be occasion. Upon their return and repeating the same demand, Don *Alonso* prosecuted his march into the kingdom of *Murcia*, of which and of the capital he took possession, in the name and on the behalf of his father, who assembled a good army at *Toledo*, where his son joined him as soon as this service was performed [c].

THEY returned early the next year to the field, the king repairing to the frontiers of *Andalusia*, and the Infant *Alonso* into *Murcia*. The king of *Granada* beat a corps of troops commanded by a *Castilian* officer, but was not able to prevent Don *Ferdinand* from ravaging all the country as far as his capital, to which he laid siege, but without effect; the *Moors* receiving a great supply from *Africa* [d]. The old archbishop *Roderic* went this year again to *Rome*, to solicit his suit. The city of *Jaen*, once the seat of a *Moorish* monarchy, but now dependent upon that of *Granada*, had been long the object of the king Don *Ferdinand*'s attention, which, though he laboured to disguise, could not, however, be hid from its present possessor, who always took care to keep it in a good state of defence, with a numerous garrison, and well supplied with provisions. The king of *Castile* ravaged all the country about it this spring, with a full resolution to besiege it before the close of the year. From this expedition he returned to *Cordova*, and from thence went to meet his mother queen *Berengara*, who came to confer with him on the affairs of *Castile* [e]. Upon her return to *Burgos*, the king went back to the frontiers; and as soon as his forces were assembled, in the autumn invested *Jaen*, and, contrary to the opinion of most of his generals, continued the siege through the winter.

That monarch, af-
ter laying
waste the
country
about it,
besieges the
city of
Jaen.
1244.

[b] Chronica general de Espana, par FLORIAN DE OCAMPO. Chron. S. FERNAND. [c] Annal Toletan. [d] Chronica general de Espana, par FLORIAN DE OCAMPO. Chron. S. FERNAND. Annal Toletan. [e] Chron. S. FERNAND. Annal Toletan. Chronica general de Espana, par FLORIAN DE OCAMPO.

THE

Moham-
med Al-
hamar,
king of
Granada,
becomes
his vaſſal.

THE place made a vigorous and obſtinate defence, and the king of *Granada* was often in the field with his forces, in order to relieve it ; but Don *Ferdinand* was ſo much upon his guard; and took care to have his army ſo well ſupplied, that the *Moor*, notwithſtanding all his vigilance, met with repeated diſappointments ; which, though he was a wiſe and brave prince, humbled him ſo much, that he came at length to a ſudden and ſtrange reſolution f. He ſent a perſon of diſtinction to the king, Don *Ferdinand*, and offered to become his vaſſal, in caſe they could agree upon the terms ; upon which he propoſed to confer with him in perſon, in caſe he would ſend him a ſafe-conduct. Don *Ferdinand* accepted the propoſition ; upon which the *Mooriſh* monarch, *Aben-Alhamar*, came to his camp, kiſſed his hand, which, according to the ceremonial of thoſe days, was a mark of vaſſalage, conſented to deliver up *Jaen*, to pay him an annual tribute of fifty thouſand pieces of gold, and to ſerve in his armies with a corps of auxiliaries, whenever it ſhould be required. On the other hand, the king of *Caſtile* ſtipulated his protection in all caſes, and againſt all perſons, together with the guarantee of whatever he poſſeſſed. Theſe articles ſettled, the city of *Jaen* was delivered into his hands : the king took poſſeſſion of it about the middle of *April*, after a ſiege of eight months g. This glorious ſucceſs of his arms excited in the monarch of *Caſtile* a fervent deſire, attended with a ſtrong hope, of reducing *Seville* ; an enterprize, however, of great difficulty, and which demanded therefore much circumſpection (D). In order to facilitate this, the
king

f Annal Toletan. Chronica general de Eſpana, par FLORIAN DE OCAMPO. g Chron. S. FERNAND. Annal Toletan.

(D) We propoſe in this note to ſay ſomewhat of that famous prelate, Don *Roderic Ximenes*, archbiſhop of *Toledo*, to whom all *Spain* was ſo much obliged while living, and whoſe writings will be a laſting monument to the glory of his countrymen, as long as any regard for hiſtory ſhall remain(7) He was by birth of a very noble family in the kingdom of *Navarre*, received, in conſequence of that, a liberal and learned education, which raiſed him to the archbiſhoprick of *Toledo*, A. D. 1208 (8). In his ſtation he acted with great dignity, piety, and firmneſs. He was often in the field againſt the *Moors*, particularly in the great battle of *Toloſa*. He was immoveably attached to the royal family, and exceedingly tenacious of the rights of his church,

(7) *Cave Hiſt. Lit. tom.* ii. p. 282, 283. (8) *Mariana Hiſt. Gen. de Eſpan. lib.* xi.

which

king took the field in the autumn, ravaged all the country adjacent to that city, and reduced several places, *Albamar* king of
Granada serving in his army.   At the close of the campaign
he had the melancholy news of the death of his mother Donna *Berengara*, which happened at *Burgos November* the eighth,
in the year one thousand two hundred forty-six, which gave
him very great and very just concern [h].

THE king being fully satisfied that treasure was as necessary *Don* Ferdi-
as troops in the execution of great projects, demanded of the nand *of*
pope a bull for levying the third of the tenths of his clergy Castile *re-*
throughout his dominions, for the carrying on this war against *solves to*
the Infidels, which he obtained [i].   He passed the interval of *form a con-*
time between the putting his troops into winter-quarters and *siderable*
bringing them again into the field at *Cordova*, in seeing all the *fleet.*
necessary preparations made under his eyes, and, amongst other
precautions, he took that most necessary step of having a good
fleet, at least for those times, without which he could have
done nothing.   This was built and equipped under the direction, and put to sea under the orders, of *Raymond Boniface*, an
officer of note in those times, and whom, for this purpose, the
king took into his pay [k].

THIS fleet of his, for so it might be well called in those *Besieges*
days, consisted of thirteen large ships, and of several of a small *the city of*
size, with which he repaired to the mouth of the river *Guadal-* Seville *by*
quivir, and found in the port of St. *Lucar* a stout fleet from *land, and*

[h] Chronica general de España, par FLORIAN DE OCAMPO. S.
FERNAND.   [i] RAINALD, MARIANA, FERRERAS.   [k] Chronica general de España, par FLORIAN DE OCAMPO.

which disposition is thought to
have hastened his death ; for, in
his contest with the archbishop of
Tarragona, for the primacy of
Spain, who went once so far as
to excommunicate him, he found
himself obliged to apply himself
to pope *Innocent* IV. in the council of *Lyons*, whither, though
bending under a load of years
and infirmities, he actually went;
but being seized with a grievous
distemper in his return, he died
on board a vessel that carried

him down the *Rhosne*, *August*
9, 1245 (9). His history of the
Spanish affairs, in nine books,
ends with the king's second marriage ; he wrote, besides the
history of the *Ostrogoths*, of the
Huns, Vandals, &c. the history
of the *Arabs*, from *A.D.* 570 to
1150 ; as also the history of the
Romans, from the reign of *Janus*
to the year A.U.C. 708 (10).
All of them in great esteem, but
more especially his history of
Spain and of the *Arabs* (11).

(9) *Annal Toletan. Mariana Hist. general de España, lib.* xiii.   (10) *All
his works were printed together in folio at Granada, an.* 1545.   (11) *Gaspar.
Oudin Commentar. tom.* iii. *p.* 184. *Du Pin, Hist. Ecclesiast. vol.* ii. *p.* 60.

Barbary,

Barbary, with supplies of all kinds on board. The king, Don Ferdinand, having a numerous army, part of which was composed of *Moorish* troops under *Alhamar*, was very active all this time by land, made himself master of several towns and fortresses, and had, by degrees, blocked up the place[l]. As soon as he heard, therefore, that his fleet was at the mouth of the river, he sent a strong detachment to facilitate its coming up ; but the *Moors* sallied with so superior a force, that the troops were obliged to return without attempting any thing. *Raymond Boniface*, trusting then entirely to his own strength, attacked the *African* fleet with great spirit and resolution, and having beat and destroyed them, entered the port, and passed up the river [m]. The king, Don *Ferdinand*, then disposed every thing to attack the *Moors* encamped upon the mole ; but they abandoned their posts, and retired into the place, which was compleatly invested. The king began the siege in form, on the twentieth of *August*, and it lasted all the winter, which shews how much the manner of making war was altered from what it had been ; for it is particularly recorded, that the army was so regularly disposed, so thoroughly secured from the injuries of weather, and so amply supplied with all sorts of provision, that it seemed rather the suburbs of a vast city, than the transitory station of troops in the field [n].

At the opening of the spring, the queen came to pay her husband a visit : in the month of *March* arrived the Infant Don *Alonso* his son, Don *Lopez de Haro*, with the flower of the troops of *Biscay*, and, last of all, the archbishop of *Compostella*, with the forces of *Galicia*, in excellent order[o]. On the first of *May* Don *Raymond Boniface* broke the bridge of boats between *Triana* and *Alfarach*, which cut off the communication they had with places on the other side of the river, as the king had before put an end to their communication through the mountains. On the twenty-third of *November* the place surrendered, upon condition that the people should retire out of it with all their effects ; and the king made his public entry with the Infant Don *Alonso*, his brother, on one hand, and the Infant Don *Alonso*, his son, on the other [p]. The remainder of that and part of the next year was spent in puri-

---

[l] Chron. S. Fernand.　[m] Chronica general de Espana, par Florian De Ocampo.　[n] Annales Ecclesiasticas y Seculares de la Ciudad de Sevilla, par D. Diego Ortiz De Zuniga. Chron. S. Fernand.　[o] Chronica general de Espana, par Florian De Ocampo. Annal Compostel.　[p] Annales Ecclesiasticas y Seculares de la Ciudad de Sevilla, par D. Diego Ortiz De Zuniga. Chronica general de Espana, par Florian De Ocampo. Annal Toletan. Annal Compostel.

fying the churches, repairing the city, and in all poffible endeavours to repeople it.   About this time alfo, it is probable,
that the Infant Don *Alonfo* efpoufed Donna *Yoland*, daughter
to the king of *Arragon*, and the progrefs of the war feemed to
have been fufpended q.

But in the fucceeding year, the king, though his health began to be impaired through a long feries of fatigues, caufed
his army to take the field early, and fwept all the places that
ftill remained to the *Moors*, between *Seville* and the fall of the
Guadalquivir into the fea ; which was not barely with a view
to extend his territories, but to facilitate a glorious enterprize
he meditated, and which, if it ever entered into the thoughts,
was never in the power, of his predeceffors.   This was no
lefs than a hoftile defcent upon the coaft of *Africk*, for which
Don *Raymond Boniface* had orders to augment the fleet, and
was fupplied with every thing neceffary for that purpofe r.
The Infant Don *Alonfo*, the king's eldeft fon, about this time,
took the crofs, on the news of St. *Lewis's* misfortunes in the
Holy Land, and this notwithftanding the king his father was
about to attack the Infidels in their own dominions s.   He
was fo much in earneft in this defign, that it appears from the
teftimony of an eminent *English* hiftorian, who quotes his own
letters, that he warmly follicited *Henry* the third to concur
with him in that expedition, which, he believed, would be
equally honourable for the Chriftian caufe, and for the *Spanish*
and *English* nations t.   His younger brother, the Infant Don
Sancho, with the confent of the pope, was this year chofen
archbifhop of *Toledo* u.   The preparations for the defigned
invafion were vigoroufly carried on, tho' the increafe of the
king's infirmities delayed the execution ; at length Don *Raymand* failed to reconnoitre the coaft of *Africk*, and in his paffage met the *Moorish* fleet that cruized upon the coaft, in order
to protect it, and, after a fmart engagement, in which there
was confiderable lofs on both fides, he funk feveral of the enemy's fhips, and obliged them to retire in diforder into their
own ports, for which, at his return, he was highly careffed
by the king, to whom this fuccefs at fea was particularly
pleafing w.

Marginal notes:

Don Fer-
dinand en-
tertains
thoughts of
invading
the con-
tinent of
Africa.

A. D.
1250.

1256.

q Chron. S. Fernand.   Roderic Santii Hift. Hifpan. part
iii. Alphonsi a Castro reg. Hifpan.   Anacephalæofis.
r Chron. S. Fernand.   Chronica general de Efpana, par Florian De Oçampo.   s Rainald.   Chronica general de
Efpana, par Florian De Ocampo.   Ferreras.   t Mat.
Paris.   u Annal Toletan.   w Chronica general de
Efpana, par Florian De Ocampo. Chron. S. Fernand.

But

But a dropfy carries him to his grave, while he meditated this defign.

But though the fatisfaction arifing from this victory might in fome meafure, calm the mind and raife the fpirits of the king, yet it could not cure the dropfy, under which he laboured, and which gradually brought him fo low, that he plainly perceived he was drawing towards his end ; for which he made fuch preparations as equally became a great king and a good Chriftian. He fettled all the affairs of ftate in the beft manner he was able ; recommended his queen, his brother, and his children, to the Infant Don *Alonfo* his fucceffor ; exhorted him to govern with moderation, and not to load his fubjects with taxes [x]. When he had done this, he ordered all enfigns of royalty to be removed, and commanded that he fhould be no longer treated as a king, but as an humbled Chriftian, employed in the great and neceffary work of making his peace with his Creator [y] ; and, in this excellent difpofition of mind, breathed his laft, on the thirtieth of *May*, in the year one thoufand two hundred and fifty-two. His body was foon after buried with great folemnity in the cathedral church of *Seville* [z]. He was, from the very time of his demife, confidered as a faint, and fo ftyled by the people of *Spain* in general, but was not canonized at *Rome* till the year one thoufand fix hundred and feventy-one, by pope *Clement* the tenth, at the earneft requeft of his catholic majefty, and the ftates of his feveral king-doms [a].

Don Alonfo X. furnamed the wife, fucceeds to all his father's dominions.

Don *Alonfo* the tenth, who, for his learning and love of learned men, was furnamed the *wife*, fucceeded his father, with the general approbation of the people, who confidered him as a prince of great qualities, and remarkable generofity [b]. *Aben-Alhamar*, king of *Granada*, and *Aben-Afon*, fovereign of *Niebla*, which lies at no great diftance from *Seville*, and is at prefent a place of little or no confequence, became his vaf-fals, and fent their embaffadors to do him homage [c]. He broke in the firft year of his reign with *Henry* the third of *England*, upon pretence of his having a better right than that prince to *Gafcony*, into which country he fent an army, under the command of Don *Gafcon*, count of *Berne*, who was excommuni-cated by the pope for troubling a prince who had already taken the crofs [d]. At the fame time Don *Alonfo* profecuted, at a

[x] Chronica general de Efpaña, par Florian De Ocampo. [y] Chron. S. Fernand. [z] Roderic Santii Hift. Hifpan. part iii. Alphonsi a Carthagena reg. Hifp. Anacephalæofis Francisci Taraphæ de reg. Hifpan. Chron. S. Fernand. [a] Ferreras Hiftoria de Efpaña, part vi. fect. xiii. [b] Chronica general de Efpaña, par Florian De Ocampo. Mariana. Ferreras. [c] Chronica del Rey Don Alphonfo el Sabio, &c. [d] Rainald. Mat. Paris.

large

large expence, that expedition which his father had in view against the *Moors* in *Barbary*, and these expences exhausted his coffers to such a degree, that he was obliged to debase his coin; which, as it usually happens, raised the price of all things to such a degree, as occasioned great murmuring amongst the people [e]. The next year king *Henry* of *England* sent the bishop of *Bath* and Dr. *John Mansell*, his chaplain, to negotiate a peace, which was soon after concluded, on condition that prince *Edward*, son and heir apparent of the king of *England*, should marry Donna *Eleonora*, the king of *Castile*'s sister, in consideration of which the king would recede for the future from his claim to *Gascony* [f]. The preparations for the expedition to *Barbary* still went on, and the pope, in order to facilitate it, granted a crusade, and the same bull for levying an aid upon the clergy which had been granted to his father [g] (E).

Don

[e] *Chronica del* Rey Don Alonso el Sabio, &c. [f] MAT. PARIS, p. 884. [g] RAINALD.

(E) The *Spanish* historians are ready enough to commend their princes; and it may be said of them in general, that they are at least content to do them justice: but however, there are some few instances of the contrary; and we find the author of the chronicle of this prince's reign, one of the most remarkable in that respect. He charges this monarch with an inclination to repudiate his queen, under colour of sterility, and with contracting a marriage with a princess of *Denmark*, who actually came to *Spain*, but just as she came, the queen proved with child; upon which, the king, to make the princess some amends, married her to his brother the Infant Don *Philip*, who had been archbishop of *Seville*; all which we have good reason to believe were downright calumnies. For it is certain, that the queen Donna *Yoland* had an Infanta before this time, which excludes all pretence of barrenness; that *Christopher* the first king of *Denmark* had no such daughter; and that the Infant Don *Philip* was archbishop, and unmarried *A.D.* 1257: the same author says, that the king Don *Alonso* had had disputes with his father-in-law, the king of *Navarre*, of which no traces are to be found elsewhere, and is repugnant to the current of history. To all this he adds, that he had in view the conquest of the kingdom of *Navarre*. This notion certainly arose from his marching troops through that kingdom, which, for want of knowing the occasion, this writer concluded a mark of hostility; whereas, in fact, the king of *Castile* demanded a passage for these forces into *Gascony*, where they were to act against the king of *England*, in support of Don *Alonso*'s claim to that country, which he afterwards relinquished, upon the marriage of prince *Edward* with the Infanta Donna *Eleonora*. These points, though important

A. D. Don *Alonso*, king of *Portugal*, having committed some hostili-
1253. ties against *Mohammed Aben-Afen*, king of *Niebla*, the monarch of *Castile* interposed on his behalf, and, in a short time
also, this quarrel was compromised.

Prince HITHERTO Don *Alonso* had continued in *Andalusia* and on
Edward of the frontiers, but he now thought proper to visit *Toledo*, where
England the king of *Granada* did him homage [h]; and, after conferring
espouses the great privileges on the university of *Salamanca*, he proceeded
princess to *Burgos*, where the marriage between prince *Edward of Eng-*
Eleonora, *land* and the Infanta Donna *Eleonora* was celebrated with all
Infanta of imaginable solemnity, and at a vast expence; and, at the same
Castile. time, he conferred on that young prince the order of knight-
1254. hood [i]. The king likewise bestowed in marriage his natural
daughter Donna *Beatrix de Guzman* on the king of *Portugal*,
and with her, by way of dowry, he gave the country of *Al-*
garve [k]. The *Moors* upon the frontiers shewed a general
inclination to revolt, but those who were intrusted with the
care of that country quickly reduced them. It was the misfortune of this king, that he was equally ready in forming
great enterprizes and slow in the execution of them. The
preparations for his *African* expedition went on, and with it
the diminishing of the coin, though it produced daily new
confusions; and though this was sufficient to embarrass the
monarch of *Castile*, yet he embarked soon after in schemes that
brought him into farther difficulties [l]. He was desirous of
availing himself of the claim derived from his mother to the
duchy of *Suabia*; and having, on this account, some negotiation with the princes of *Germany*, he was induced to aim at
the imperial dignity, in which he had for his competitor *Richard*
earl of *Cornwall*, brother to king *Henry* the third of *England*;
which vain pursuit of both princes cost them immense sums of
money, and involved them in endless scenes of trouble, without any other advantage than that of bearing the lofty title of
emperor amongst the princes of their own party [m].

[h] Chronica del Rey Don Alonso el Sabio, &c.   [i] Roderic Santii Hist. Hispan. part iv. Chronica del Rey Don Alonso el Sabio, &c.   [k] Emanuel de Faria y Sousa de las
Historias Portuguesas. Mariana. Ferreras.   [l] Chronica del Rey Don Alonso el Sabio, &c.   [m] Roderic
Santii Hist. Hispan. part iv. Mariana. Ferreras.

important enough in themselves, without due examination, found
would scarce have deserved no- a place in the general histories of
tice here, if they had not, upon *Spain*, and imposed thereby upon
the credit of this author, and posterity.

It was in prosecution of this quarrel that he postponed the
expedition to *Africa*, and turned his views to *Italy*, where, by
the help of that money for which he ransacked his subjects,
he had gained several princes and states to approve his title ;
but, after all his trouble and expence, this new expedition
was laid aside, on account of some domestic disturbances.
These at last rose to such a height, that the Infant Don *Henry*
took up arms against his brother, and drew in *Mohammed
Aben-Afen* to join with him ; but the Infant being defeated in
a battle by count *Nugnes de Lara*, found himself under a necessity of seeking refuge in *Africa*, where, for some years, he
remained at the court of the king of *Tunis* [n]. As for the little
king of *Niebla*, Don *Alonso* besieged him in his capital ; and,
though the place was very strong, and he made a long and obstinate defence, yet he was forced at length to have recourse
to a capitulation ; and, to preserve his liberty, parted with almost all his dominions [o].

*The Moor-
ish prince
of Niebla,
reduced by
Don Alon-
so, and
deprived.*

1257.

1259.

AMONGST other great and noble designs of the late Don
Ferdinand, there was one which remained incomplete at his
death ; and this was making a general collection of the laws
made by himself and his predecessors, and digesting them under
proper titles, which was completed by his son, and is that celebrated code, intituled, *Las Partidas* [p]. He also redressed that
confusion in law proceedings, which was occasioned by the in-
termixing *Latin* with the vulgar tongue ; which he corrected,
by obliging his subjects to use their own language in pieces of
that kind (F). His love for learning, and his desire of promoting

*The king's
care of
justice and
great af-
fection for
learning.*

[a] Chronica del Rey Don Alonso el Sabio, &c. [o] Ro-
DERIC SANTII Hist. Hispan. part iv. MARIANA. FERRERAS.
[p] Chronica del Rey Don Alonso el Sabio, &c.

(F) It is believed, that the
original design of the king Don
Ferdinand, in assembling so many persons learned in the laws in
his court, was with a view to this
great and important work ; neither is it at all improbable, that
the first notion of it might proceed from the excuses of inferior
judges, when questioned for
their decisions in superior courts,
that they proceeded according to
the customs established in their
province. For the reader, to
have a just idea of these regulations, must understand that,
before the institution of the royal audience at *Castile*, the chief
tribunals in every province received appeals from inferior ju-
risdictions. Upon the representation therefore of these superior courts, those able lawyers
might be summoned by Don
Ferdinand, and directed to frame
a body of laws ; and this being a work of time, might be
likewise charged to hear and decide

moting the science of astronomy, of which he was passionately fond, engaged him in an intercourse with the Soltan of *Egypt*, to whom he sent, and from whom he received, an embassador [q]. But while his thoughts were wholly occupied by things of this nature, and the prosecution of his claim to the empire, he found himself on a sudden involved in a scene of troubles, so much the more perplexing, as they were wholly unexpected; this was occasioned by the intrigues of the *Moors*, who, finding themselves under far greater hardships, and, at the same time, observing that measures were not conducted with that steadiness as in the former reign, meditated a general revolt. Though this required much deliberation, and extensive communication of councils, yet it was managed with so great secrecy, that Don *Alonso* had scarce any intelligence of this contrivance till it broke out [r].

Conspiracy of some princes of the blood and great lords supported by the Moors.

THE chiefs were *Mohammed Aben-Hut*, king of *Murcia*, and *Mohammed Alcadila Alhamar*, king of *Granada* : these had privately demanded the assistance of *Aben-Joseph*, king of *Fez* and *Morocco*, who willingly consented to their request, upon condition that some ports were put into his hands, for the security of the auxiliaries that he undertook to send [s]. The king of *Murcia* declared first, by making inroads into the Christian territories, and recovering most of his castles which were garrisoned on the behalf of the king of *Castile*; and soon after the monarch of *Granada* took his share in the war, which, though Don *Alonso* had great reason to resent, yet he laboured to reclaim him by negotiation, if it had been practicable; for he had still the *German* election at heart, which was the true source of all his misfortunes, and, for the sake of the empty title of king of the *Romans*, he would not take those vigorous measures that would have made him a great king in *Spain*. At length, however, having taken the necessary steps to engage his father-in-law, the king of *Arragon*, to concur in

[q] Annales Ecclesiasticos y Seculares de la Ciudad de Sevilla, par D. DIEGO ORTIZ DE ZUNIGA.   [r] RODERIC SANTII Hist. Hispan. part iv.   [s] Chronica del Rey Don Alonso el Sabio, &c.

cide appeals from the superior courts. At this time, though they were completed and received by Don *Alonso*, yet they had not the royal sanction, but some space was allowed for reviewing and considering them, that, in a matter of such vast consequence, there might be nothing of hurry, or any speedy necessity of amendment, which the king very prudently foresaw would destroy their credit, and defeat the end of this learned and laborious collection.

repressing

repreſſing the *Moors* ; and having diſpatched embaſſadors to ſollicit pope *Urban* the fourth on his darling point of the election, he ſet out for the frontiers ; and, having aſſembled a numerous army at *Alcala Real*, he fell into the kingdom of *Granada*, which he waſted with fire and ſword [t].

THIS obliged the two *Mooriſh* princes to join their forces, which, when they had done, they marched towards Don *Alonſo*, and gave him battle. But that prince, who wanted none of the qualities requiſite to adorn a crown, except ſteadineſs only, diſpoſed his forces with ſo much judgment, gave his orders with ſuch preſence of mind, and diſtinguiſhed himſelf with ſuch acts of perſonal courage, that the *Moors* were totally defeated, obliged to abandon the field, and ſhut themſelves up in their ſtrong places [u]. In the winter he appointed commiſſioners to ſettle with thoſe of the king of *Arragon* the limits between the two kingdoms, that no future grounds of diſpute might ariſe between themſelves or ſucceſſors [w]. This year the pope, in the plenitude of his power, thought fit to impoſe a heavy tax upon the clergy of *Spain*, for the ſupport of the emperor of *Conſtantinople* ; upon which they ſent an agent to *Rome* to let this ſucceſſor of St. *Peter* know, that, being engaged in a war with the *Mohammedans* at home, they deſired to be excuſed from ſo heavy and ſo extraordinary a burthen, with which the pontif was not a little diſpleaſed [x]. The next ſpring the king was early in the field, with an army ſuperior to that which he commanded the year before ; upon which the *Moors* ſent to *Aben-Joſeph* king of *Morocco*, to let him know, that if his ſuccours did not ſpeedily arrive, the *Mohammedans* in *Spain* were for ever undone ; upon which he ſent over immediately ten thouſand horſe ; which conſiderable ſupply did not, however, enable theſe princes to take the field to cover their own dominions, much leſs to act offenſively [y].

ON the contrary the king Don *Alonſo* inveſted *Xerez*, and after a long ſiege, upon intelligence that *Aben Joſeph* meant to come in perſon into *Spain*, with a prodigious army, the king granted them a favourable capitulation, to retire whereever they thought proper [z]. This capitulation being punctually performed, the inhabitants at *Bejar*, *Sidonia*, *Rota*, St. *Lucar*, *Lebrija*, and *Arcos*, ſaved the king the trouble of coming before them, and left all thoſe places empty, which in a

Marginal notes:
Don Alonſo defeats the Mooriſh monarchs and brings them very low.
1263.

Beſieges the town of Xerez, and after a gallant defence grants the people terms.

[t] RODERIC SANTII Hiſt. Hiſp. part iv.   [u] MARIANA. FERRERAS. MAYERNE TURQUET.   [w] ZURIT. Annal Arragon.   [x] RAINALD.   [y] Chronica del Rey Don Alonſo el Sabio, &c.   [z] FERRERAS Hiſtoria de Eſpana, p. vi. ſec. xiii.

manner

manner swallowed up the king's army, as it scarce suffice
to settle all these places and *Port St. Mary's*, which the kin
ordered to be repaired [a].   The next year the limits betwee
Castile and *Portugal* were adjusted, to which crown Don *Alon
so* yielded *Algarve* intirely, except reserving a band of fift
lances to be sent to his army whenever it took the field [b].

*The king
of Grana-
da submits
and offers
to renew
his homage
to Don
Alonso.*

As the *German* empire had suffered extremely (thoug
perhaps particular princes might be gainers) by its havin
nominally two heads, tho' being in effect without any, grea
pains was taken to engage them both to resign, which Do
Alonso would not endure, for the title of emperor had grea
charms for him, and notwithstanding all the money an
trouble it had cost, he would not hear of quitting it [c].   Th
two alcaydes of *Malaga* and *Guadix*, taking offence at th
great complaisance of the king of *Granada* to the officers wh
commanded the *African* troops, revolted, and put themselve
under the protection of the crown of *Castile*, and in con
junction with Don *Nugnez de Lara*, distressed their old mast
to such a degree, that he caused it to be intimated to Do
Alonso, that he was willing to return to his allegiance, if hi
submission might be received upon easy terms.   The king
sent him word, that if he was in earnest he should meet him
at *Alcala Real*; and which shews how high the character o
this prince stood; the *Moor*, upon his bare promise, notwithstanding all that had passed, went thither, and submitted to
the terms he prescribed, and abandoned his confederate the
king of *Murcia* [d].   In the mean time, the king of *Arragon*
made an absolute conquest of that kingdom, or at least of the
greatest part of it, not for himself, but on the behalf of hi
son-in-law, to whom he immediately gave advice of his success, and desired him to send thither a corps of troops sufficient
to secure it.   Don *Alonso* marched in person from *Sevilla*
with his army, and on the frontiers met the king of *Murcia*,
who threw himself upon his knees at his feet, and sued to him
for his pardon [e].   The king told him, that for his life or liberty
he had nothing to fear, but that he could not expect he should
put into his hands a second time the power of hurting him.

*All Mur-
cia reduced
and repeo-
pled by*

THE king then left the Infant Don *Manuel*, governor of *Murcia*, and obliging the *Moors* to quit all the strong places, repeopled them with subjects of his own, or with those of the king
of *Arragon*; and thus, in a short time, and with as little effu-

[a] Chronica del Rey Don Alonso el Sabio, &c.   [b] BRANDAON.
EMANUEL DE FARIA Y SOUSA. Chronica del Rey Don Alonso el
Sabio, &c.   [c] RAINALD. RODERIC SANTII Hist. Hisp. part
iv.   [d] Chronica del Rey Don Alonso el Sabio, &c.   [e] MA-
RIANA. FERRERAS. MAYERNE TURQUET.

fion of blood as poffible, he put an end, at leaft for the prefent, *Chriftians*
to a very formidable confpiracy, and might, if he would have *from dif-*
declined all thoughts of *Germany*, have recovered his former *ferent*
reputation, reftored the grandeur of his crown, and peace to *kingdoms.*
his fubjects [f]. The fame year, the Infant Don *Ferdinand* of   1266.
Caftile efpoufed, by proxy, the princefs *Blanche*, daughter to
St. *Lewis*, on the eighth of *September*, at St. *Germain en Laye* [g].
The caufe between the two kings of the *Romans* was ftill depending at *Rome*, where Don *Alonfo* laboured by every method poffible to fupport what he called his right, and this at a
vaft expence, notwithftanding that his embaffador, the bifhop
of *Silves*, had been murdered in his paffage by fome banditti,
who took his papers from him [h]; on the other hand, the princes
of *Germany*, fick of their own fchemes, and perceiving the
real neceffity of having a chief, had agreed with the king of
Bohemia to proceed to a new election; but this the pope,
who pretended a right to declare which of the two was the
true king of the *Romans*, vehemently oppofed [i]. The next
year was fignalized by the moft pompous marriage that till
then had been feen in *Spain*, prince *Philip*, heir apparent of
the crown of *France*, conducting his fifter the princefs *Blanche*
to *Burgos*, where fhe efpoufed the Infant Don *Ferdinand*, in   1268.
the prefence of all the royal family of *Spain* [k], the king of
Arragon, and, as fome fay, prince *Edward* of *England*, and
the emprefs of *Conftantinople*; but thofe who are beft acquainted with the hiftory will be perhaps of opinion, that thefe
great names are only brought to fill up the fcene [l].

THE Infant Don *Sancho* of *Arragon*, being confecrated arch- *The kings*
bifhop of *Toledo*, foon after celebrated his firft mafs with *of Caftile*
great ceremony, in the prefence of the two kings, his father, *and Arra-*
and his brother-in-law [m]. After thefe fine fhews, both mon- *gon form*
archs, as if it had been by concert, entered upon fchemes dia- *at the fame*
metrically oppofite to the prudence for which they were both *time, no-*
famous. The king of *Arragon*, though much in years, *tions of*
would needs go to the *Holy Land*, though Don *Alonfo* did all *travel-*
that was in his power to diffuade him. On the other hand, *ling.*
this monarch himfelf was as much bent upon a voyage to *Italy*
to as little purpofe; but in the end, both their fchemes proved
abortive. The king of *Arragon* met with a ftorm at fea, which
drove him to *France*, from whence he returned into his own

[f] Chronica del Rey Ron Alonfo el Sabio, &c.   [g] P. DA-
NIEL Hift. de France.   [h] RAINALD. MARIANA. FERRE-
RAS.   [i] RAINALD.   [k] Chronica general de Efpan,
par FLORIAN DE OCAMPO.   [l] FERRERAS Hiftoria de Efpana, part. vi. fec. xiii.   [m] ZURIT. Anaal Arragon.

dominions, and was content to stay there,[n]. As for Don Alonso, the states of *Castile* interposed, when he was ready to set out, and represented the inconveniences that would attend his leaving the kingdom at that juncture in so strong a light, that he wisely, though unwillingly, dropped his design[o]. He persisted, however, against all advice, in remitting, as some *Spanish* historians say, the homage due from the crown of *Portugal* to that of *Leon*, out of affection for his grandson, the Infant *Denis*, which excited, or at least gave a plausible colour to, those discontents that produced so many and so great troubles, and even shook the throne upon which he sat [p] (G).

A. D. 1269.

THE

---

[n] Chronica del Rey Don Alonso el Sabio, &c.   Zurit. Annal Arragon.   [o] Mariana. Ferreras. Mayerne Turquet.   [p] Roderic Santii Hist. Hispan. part iv. Chronica del Rey Don Alonso el Sabio, &c.

(G) This is one of those dark points in history which can never be so thoroughly settled as to leave an inquisitive and critical reader entirely free from doubts. It is admitted on both sides, that homage was due from the crown of *Portugal* to that of *Leon*, for the country of *Algarve*, which kingdom Don *Alonso* of *Castile* bestowed upon the monarch of *Portugal*, at the request, or at least with the consent, of pope *Innocent* the fourth, without considering that the princess was but twelve, and the king her husband upwards of forty, years of age. There was besides another untoward accident; the king of *Portugal* had another wife, *Matilda* countess of *Boloigne*, and children also by her, which, though overlooked by one pope, drew upon the king an excommunication from another. He would not, however, part with his young wife, by whom he had his successor the Infant *Denis*, who, at this time, repaired to his grand-

father, and begged of him a boon which he received. Here it is the historians differ. The *Portuguese* assert, that Don *Alonso* remitted the band of lances which he had reserved as a kind of homage for *Algarve*. On the other hand, the *Spaniards* as positively affirm, that this had been released before; and from thence infer, that the favour now done was relinquishing the homage due from the crown of *Portugal*, or at least that part of the kingdom which had been given to count *Henry*, who was the first sovereign of it. *Ferreras* urges it as a strong argument, and, in truth, so it seems to be, that this concession was the principal grievance alleged by, the malecontents, and therefore must have been a matter of great importance. To this the only answer that can be given is, that malecontents do not always speak the truth, and therefore might possibly exaggerate the king's concession, and charge him with giving, upon this oc-

casion,

THE king Don *Alonso* had still his voyage to *Italy* in his *A deep con-*
head, with a view to which he laboured, by every method he *spiracy*
could devise, to raise money; but when he imagined that he *secretly*
had at length brought all things to bear, he was informed *managed*
that many persons of the first rank, amongst whom were the *against*
Infant Don *Philip*, Don *Nugnez de Lara*, Don *Lopez de* *Don Alon-*
Haro, Don *Ferdinand de Castro*, Don *Lopez de Mendoza*, *so of Cas-*
and several others, had met together at the castle of *Lara*, in *tile.*
order to consider of grievances arising from his administration;
the king, still fond of his journey, from which one would have
imagined these news would have diverted him, instead of taking
measures to chastise the malecontents, sent to know their demands, and promised to comply with whatever should be reasonable q. Their answer was very artificial, and perfectly calculated to serve their purpose ; for, though they had laid the
scheme of their operations, they were in great want of money
to carry them into execution ; they therefore informed the
king that they had no intention to disturb his government or
depart from their duty, but that they met together to concert
the means for obtaining their appointments ; and, upon this,   A. D.
the king weakly imagining that this would make them   1270.
quiet, paid each of them the sum he demanded, which
money they no sooner received, than they employed it in levying troops r.

THE next thing they did, was to endeavour to engage the *Breaks out,*
king of *Navarre* to enter into their league, in which they *and the*
failed ; but Don *Nugnez de Lara* persuaded the king of *malecon-*
Granada to dispose all things for a rupture, and to demand *tents retire*
succours from the king of *Morocco*. *Alonso* being informed *to the*
of this, sent to them Don *Juan de Lara*, and the bishop of *Moors.*
Cuenca, to let them know that he meant to summon the
states at *Burgos*, and that if they had any complaints to make
they would do well to appear there. The confederate lords
accordingly met the king at *Lerma*, each at the head of his
troops ; but behaved towards him with all the exterior marks
of duty and respect, and accompanied him to *Burgos*, but
would not enter the city. There Don *Alonso* held the assem-   1271.
bly of the states, and made new propositions to them, which
they rejected, and, as the custom was in those times, demanded

---

q MARIANA. FERRERAS.   r Chronica del Rey Don Alonso
el Sabio, &c.

---

cation, what, perhaps, he had   briefly stated the merits on both
never claimed. This is all we   sides, he must decide for him-
can tell the reader; and, having   self.

leave to quit his dominions, which they accordingly received:
They then began to defile with their troops towards the king
dom of *Granada* ; and though the queen sent the Infants Do
Ferdinand and Don *Sancho* her sons, and the Infant Don *San
cho*, archbishop of *Toledo*, her brother, to persuade them to
desist from this strange enterprize, it was in vain, and the
continued their route ; the king of *Granada* attacked the two
governors of *Malaga* and *Guadix*, and Don *Alonso* decline
supporting them, being still in hopes of making peace [t]. His
competitor, *Richard*, earl of *Cornwall*, was dead, and his
mind ran as strongly as ever upon the empire, though then
was never less probability of his attaining it [u].

*Don Alon-
so calls an
assembly of
the states
at Alma-
gro, and
reduces
taxes.*

AT the request of the queen, he sent the grand master o
Calatrava once more to the malecontents, with an offer to
forget what was past, and to restore them to their employ
ments and his favour. To this they answered, that before
they could treat, he must do justice to their friend the king
of *Granada*, against his rebel governors. The king made a
short and cool reply, that subjects had no right to prescribe to
their sovereign whom he should protect [w]. In the mean
time, the king of *Granada* attacked and beat the two alcaydes;
upon which Don *Alonso* disposed all things for a war, and
having assembled the states at *Almagro*, he remitted some and
moderated other taxes, which disposed them to make such returns of submission and loyalty, as left him no room to doubt
that he should be able to do himself justice [x]. But at this
juncture, having intelligence that *Rodolph* of *Hapsburg* was
elected emperor of *Germany*, he suddenly changed his measures, and renewed the peace with the king of *Granada*, notwithstanding all that was passed [y].

*1273.
In the
mean time
the Chris-
tian male-
contents
make a
new king
of Gra-
nada.*

THE king of *Arragon* behaved upon this occasion like a
wise prince and a faithful ally. He ordered the prince, his
son, to assemble an army on the frontiers of *Murcia*, sent
the bishop of *Segorba* to advise the malecontents to return to
their duty, and to embrace the kind offers that had been made
them by their sovereign ; and upon their rejecting this proposition, he acquainted Don *Alonso*, that he would punctually
perform his treaties, and act against all his enemies [z]. In this
critical situation of things, died *Mohammed Abcadilla-Alba-
mar*, which had like to have produced disturbances in *Gra-*

[s] MARIANA. FERRERAS. MAYERNE TURQUET. [t] Chronica del Rey Don Alonso el Sabio, &c. [u] RAINALD. [w] Chronica del Rey Don Alonso el Sabio, &c. [x] SALAZAR, tom.
iv. p. 630. [y] Chronica del Rey Don Alonso el Sabio,
&c. [z] ZURIT. Annal Arragon.

nada ;

nada; but the Christian malecontents, and particularly Don *Lopez de Haro*, advanced his son *Mohammed Alhamir-Albadie* to the throne, and supported him, notwithstanding there was a strong faction formed against him in favour of one of his brothers [a]. Don *Alonso* was no sooner informed of this, than he sent a person of quality to make fresh propositions to the new king and to the malecontents, who received them civilly, and seemed to be out of countenance at the consideration of their own behaviour. The queen and the Infant *Ferdinand* being informed of this, invited them to a conference at *Alcala*, where all things were compromised, upon an assurance that the king would receive them kindly; and that, in consideration of a considerable sum of money, he would accept the new king of *Granada*, upon the same terms that his father had held the crown [b].

THIS agreement being signed on both sides, was transmitted to the king, who ratified it without difficulty; and the king of *Granada* going to pay his respects to him at *Seville*, he not only performed punctually all that had been stipulated, but likewise conferred on him the order of knighthood with his own hand, which was then esteemed the highest obligation [c]. At *Burgos* a general assembly was held of the states, where the Infant Don *Philip* and the malecontents were restored to favour; and at this time it was that the king caused the body of his predecessor *Wamba* to be removed from the obscure place where it was buried, and to be interred in a manner suitable to his rank, at *Toledo* [d]. But he had still the empire at heart; and this induced him to send embassadors to the pope and council at *Lyons*, to dissuade that assembly from confirming the election of the emperor *Rodolph*. This had no effect; on the contrary, the pope not only confirmed the election, but wrote to the king of *Castile* to desist from all farther disturbances about his title; and, by way of gilding this bitter pill, he sent the king at the same time a bull, by which he permitted him to take the third part of the tenths of his clergy for six years [e]. All this did not hinder the king from desiring an interview, which the pope could not now civilly decline, though he had done it before; and upon this, the king left his son the Infant Don *Ferdinand* regent, set out as soon as the assembly of the states separated for *France*, by the way of *Arragon*, and kept his *Christmas* at *Barcelona*, with the

The malecontents with much difficulty reconciled to the king Don Alonso.

A. D. 1274.

[a] *Chronica del Rey Don Alonso el Sabio, &c.*   [b] MARIANA. FERRERAS. MAYERNE TURQUET.   [c] *Chronica del Rey Don Alonso el Sabio, &c.*   [d] Annal Toletan. FERRERAS.   [e] RAINALD.

king

king his father-in-law, who received him with great affection, and paid him all imaginable honours f.

Mohammed, *king* *of* **Grana-** *da, invites* *the* Moors *over from* **Africa.** THE departure of Don *Alonso* was no sooner known, than Mohammed Alhamir-Alboadic sent to *Aben Joseph,* king of *Morocco,* a representation of the state of things, to shew how favourable an opportunity they had of recovering, at least, all *Andalusia* out of the hands of the Christians, since the king, who was incontestably the best officer in *Spain,* had withdrawn himself, which none of his predecessors ever did, conferring the regency on a young prince of no experience, and trusting the best fortresses in his kingdom in the hands of those who had been lately in rebellion, and in confederacy with him g. *Aben-Joseph,* who was zealous for his religion, willingly promised him all that he demanded, on condition that the ports of *Tariffa* and *Algeriza,* in the bay of *Gibraltar,* were put into his hands, directing him to dispose every thing for opening the campaign early, which he did with such profound dissimulation, availing himself therein of his former acquaintance with the *Castilian* officers, that the Christians had little or no suspicion of his design h.

Aben-Jo- *seph lands* *in* Spain, *and de-* *feats Don* **Nugnez** **de Lara,** *who is* *slain.* IN the spring, *Aben-Joseph* entered the bay of *Gibraltar* with his fleet, and 17,000 fine troops on board; and the king of *Granada's* alcaydes, according to the orders they had received, put the places that were promised him into his hands i. The troops were no sooner debarked, than *Joseph* sent a detachment to join the king of *Granada,* who immediately began his march towards *Jaen,* at the same time that the emperor of *Morocco* advanced to *Cordova.* Don *Nugnez de Lara* commanded in the little city of *Ecija,* from whence he dispatched a courier to the Infant Don *Ferdinand,* who was at *Burgos,* and at the same time drew together what forces he could, with whom he took the field; *Aben-Joseph* immediately attacked him, and having a great superiority, routed the handful of men under his command; but Don *Nugnez* himself, and most of the gentlemen who had followed his party in the late troubles, were killed upon the spot. The king having caused the body of Don *Nugnez* to be carefully sought out, cut off his head, and sent it in triumph to the king of *Granada,* who remembring his former friendship with that nobleman, and that to his assistance he owed the crown he wore, returned it to the Christians, that it might be buried with his body at

---

f ZURIT. Annal Arragon. RAINALD.   g Chronica del Rey Don Alonso el Sabio, &c.   h MARIANA Historia general de Espana, lib. xiii.   i Chronica del Rey Don Alonso el Sabio, &c.

Cordova.

Cordova [k]. But notwithstanding this victory, the king of *Morocco* found his troops so roughly handled, that he spent the rest of the campaign in ravaging the country about *Seville*, without undertaking any siege.

THE forces of the king of *Granada* were at this time em- *The troops* ployed in plundering the country about *Jaen*, and against these *of the king* marched the Infant Don *Sancho*, archbishop of *Toledo*, with the *of Grana-* bands of *Madrid*, *Talavera*, *Alcala*, *Guadalaxara*, *Hueta*, and *da, rout* *Cuenca*. On his arrival at *Martos*, he had intelligence that the *the Casti-* *Moors* were at no great distance; and that, though they were very *lians, and* numerous, they were excessively fatigued and embarrassed with *kill the* a great booty of cattle, which induced him to follow them with *archbishop* his cavalry, without waiting for Don *Lopez de Haro*, who *of To-* would have joined him the next day. This rashness cost him *ledo.* dear, his forces being defeated and himself killed [l]. Don *Lopez*, who followed him with all imaginable expedition, met and preserved the flying remains of his army, and with them and his own forces, attacked the *Moors*, and recovered the cross of the archbishop out of their hands, but with difficulty and so great loss, that he was able to undertake nothing more [m]. The Infant Don *Ferdinand* began his march from *Burgos* with a small body of troops, and proceeded slowly, that the nobility might have time to join him, till he received an account of what had befallen Don *Nugnez de Lara* and the Infant Don *Sancho*, upon which he marched so hastily to *Ciudad Real*, that he contracted a fever, of which he died in a few days, recommending to his favourite Don *Juan de Lara*, the princess *Blanche*, and his two sons Don *Alonso* and Don *Ferdinand de la Cerda*, both very young, with whom, and the body of their father, Don *Juan* returned to *Burgos* [n].

THE Infant Don *Sancho*, the king's second son, on the *A stop put* news of his brother's misfortune, repaired to *Ciudad Real*, did *to the suc-* all that could be expected from him to encourage the forces, *cefs of these* and was quickly joined by Don *Lopez de Haro*, to whom, in *Infidels by* the midst even of that confusion, he communicated the de- *the Infant* signs he had already formed of seizing the throne. He pro- *Don San-* ceeded from *Ciudad Real* to *Cordova*, from whence he dif- *cho.* patched Don *Lopez de Haro* to *Ecija*, and the grand masters of St. *James* and *Calatrava* to *Jaen*; then leaving a good garrison in *Cordova*, under Don *Ferdinand de Castro*, he marched in person with the rest of his forces to *Seville*, where he equipped a strong fleet, which cruizing in the streights of

[k] FERRERAS Historia de Espana, p. vi. sec. xiii.   [l] Chronica del Rey Don Alonso el Sabio, &c.   [m] MARIANA. FER-RERAS. MAYERNE TURQUET.   [n] Chronica del Rey Don Alonso el Sabio, &c.

Gibraltar,

Gibralter, so alarmed the king of *Morocco,* that he retired with
his army to *Algeriza* [o]. While things were in this state in
Spain, the king Don *Alonso* was treating with the pope at
Baucaire, where he endeavoured to persuade him that the
election of the emperor *Rodolph* was void; and that, as he was
ready to resign the kingdom of *Castile* to his son the Infant
Don *Ferdinand,* there was nothing to hinder his going directly to *Germany,* and taking upon him the government.
The pope being of quite another opinion, the king fell next
on his pretensions to the duchy of *Suobia,* in right of his
mother, to which the pontif was equally deaf. While the
negotiation was in this aukward condition, came the news of
the death of the two Infants, which so far awakened the king
from his dreams, that he resolved to return immediately into
Spain. He at the same time remitted money into *Italy,* for the
use of his partizans there, and wrote to the king of *Bohemia,*
and to the princes of *Germany,* desiring them to remain firm
to his interest, and to rest assured that he had no thoughts of
dropping his claim; and that, as soon as the affairs of *Castile*
were settled, they might depend upon his coming amongst
them; in which letters, he continued to use the imperial
stile [p]. This done, he returned with as much haste as possible into his dominions, by the same road he came into *France,*
having spent immense sums of money, and obtained
nothing.

A. D.
1275.
Don San-
cho *claims
the crown
against the
children of
his elder
brother.*

THE king, Don *Alonso,* being arrived at *Alcala de Henares,*
and hearing wherever he passed prodigious encomiums of the
Infant Don *Sancho,* sent for him from *Seville;* but that prince
excused himself, under pretence that the then state of affairs
made it improper for him to quit the frontiers; whereas, in
reality, he was negotiating, by the assistance of Don *Alonso de*
Guzman, a peace with the *Moors,* which he conceived abso-
lately necessary to the conducting his designs. Accordingly a
truce being concluded [q], he set out for *Toledo,* to which city
his father was come to meet him, and there the first proposal
was made, that he should be declared heir apparent to the
crown. It does not appear that Don *Alonso* was at all averse
to this; but foreseeing the miseries that must attend a divided
title, he was unwilling to act precipitately, or without good
advice; and therefore directed an assembly of the states to be
held at *Segovia,* to determine the right of succession, according to the laws of *Spain.* This assembly was accordingly held,
and upon mature deliberation, and with the advice of the best

[o] Annales Ecclesiasticos y Seculares de la Ciudad de Sevilla, par
D. DIEGO ORTIZ DE ZUNIGA.   [p] RAINALD.   [q] Chronica del Rey Don Alonso el Sabio, &c.

lawyers

lawyers of those times, the Infant Don *Emanuel*, the king's brother, pronounced the judgment of that assembly to be, that the Infant Don *Ferdinand*, dying in the life time of his father, the right of succession was clearly in the Infant Don *Sancho*[r].

THE king, Don *Alonso*, seems to have been passive in this matter, or at most did no more than acquiesce in the judgment of the states.   When that assembly broke up, he proceeded to *Burgos*, where he met with an ambassador from *Philip* the hardy, king of *France*, who demanded the restitution of the portion given with the princess *Blanche*, and that the right of her sons to the crown should be well secured. *The crown of* France *interposes in support of those children.*
To this Don *Alonso* made a short answer, that the princess should enjoy her portion and her dowry in *Castile*; that the states had adjudged the right of succession to the Infant Don *Sancho*; and that he did not conceive it by any means expedient, that the princess and her children should leave his dominions; on which the embassador departed in great discontent[s]. At his return to *France*, king *Philip* was so much offended at the report he made of his negotiation, that he began to dispose every thing for obtaining by the sword what had been refused to his intercession.   It happened very fortunately, that at this time cardinal *Julian*, a native of *Lisbon*, being elected pope, and assuming the name of *John* the twenty-first, interfered warmly between the two kings, and even threatened with excommunication and interdict the king and kingdom of *France*, in case that monarch committed hostilities on the king of *Castile*.   He also interposed with *Edward* the first, king of *England*, to whom *Philip* had sent an embassador to represent the injustice done to the Infants *Alonso* and *Ferdinand de la Cerda*; and it is agreed, that, by his means, the war was hindered from breaking out[t].   The king of *Castile* flattered himself with the hopes of great things in other respects, from this pontif, who had a great affection for *Spain*; but he was unfortunately killed by the fall of a new apartment built by his own direction, in the spring of the ensuing year, and so the king's hopes of favour at *Rome* vanished[u].

THE monarch of *France*, if we may credit the best of the historians of that country, resented so highly the ill usage and injustice done to the princess his daughter, and her children, that, without respecting any interpositions, he was for attacking the dominions of the king of *Castile* without delay; but *Castile*, *Donna* Yoland *or* Violante, *queen of* Castile,

    [r] MARIANA Historia general de Espana, lib. xiii.   FERRERAS Historia de España, part vi. sect. xii.   [s] GUL. DE NANGIS.
    [t] RAINALD. MARIANA. FERRERAS.   [u] MARTINUS POLONUS CHR. PTOLOM. LEUENSIS, Hist. Eccl. lib. xxiii. c. 24.

retires with Donna Beatrix and the Infants.

it seems his nobility and general officers were not so much inclined to a war, which, at its very entrance, would put them to greater labour in passing the *Pyrenees*, than any in which they had been engaged; and therefore, under colour of making the necessary preparations, they delayed things for many months [w]. In the mean time, Donna *Yoland*, or, as the *French* writers stile her, Donna *Violente* [x], queen of *Castile*, being very much offended with the setting aside of the children of Don *Ferdinand*, her eldest son, made an overture to the king of *Arragon*, her father, to receive her, together with her daughter-in-law and her grand children, into his protection; which he had no sooner promised, than, by the care and assistance of Don *Juan de Lara*, who remained unalterably fixed in his fidelity to his master's family, the queen of *Castile*, the princess *Blanche* her daughter-in-law, and the two young Infants, retired into the dominions of *Arragon* [y], which gave great displeasure to Don *Alonso*, and much more to the Infant Don *Sancho*, who finding that the Infant Don *Frederick* and Don *Simon Ruez de los Cameros* were not entirely ignorant of the queen's retreat, he caused the former, though his uncle, to be either strangled or beheaded, and the house of the latter

1277. being set on fire, he perished in the flames [z]. Before the close of the year war was declared between *France* and *Castile* in form [a].

Don Alonso, king of Castile, compelled by the pope to renew the war with the Moors.

POPE *Nicholas* the third was to the full as earnest as his predecessor, in his endeavours to compromise the difference between the crowns; in order to which he employed two cardinals, with the titles of legates; but finding a backwardness in the king of *Castile*, he proceeded with him in that round manner, which the notions of those times put in his power. He sent him word, that for the support of his wars against the Infidels, his predecessor had permitted him to levy a tax upon the clergy, for which reason he expected that he should immediately renew the war against the Infidels, or discontinue the tax [b]. Upon this, he was constrained to break the truce he had made, and to send an army commanded by his sons Don *Pedro* and Don *Alonso*, to besiege *Algeriza*, and he likewise fitted out a fleet with instructions to block up that place by sea [c]. The quarrel in the royal family was by this time composed, the queen consented to return to her husband,

---

[w] P. DANIEL Histoire de France. FERRERAS. [x] MEZE-RAY. [y] ZURITA Annal Arragon. [z] Chronica general de Espana. [a] Chronica del Rey Don Alonso el Sabio, &c. [b] RODERIC SANTII Hist. Hispan. part iv. Chronica general de Espana. [c] Chronica del Rey Don Alonso el Sabio, &c.

the

the princefs *Blanche* was allowed to go into *France*, and the two Infants were kept by the king of *Arragon* [d]. This, one would have imagined, muft have been attended with favourable circumftances, but it happened otherwife. The queen thought it beneath her to return into *Caftile*, without difcharging the debts fhe owed in *Arragon*; the king's finances were fo low, and the demands of the public upon him fo preffing, that he could not fpare her that fum; but the Infant Don *Sancho* went to *Seville*, feized upon a *Jew* who was treafurer at war to the army commanded by his brethren, and taking the fum requifite from him fent it to his mother [e]. This proved the ruin both of the army and the fleet. The former was exceedingly weakened by famine, the latter beat by the *Moors*, being but very indifferently fupplied; fo that *Aben-Jofeph*, king of *Morocco*, coming over, forced the two young princes to raife the fiege with great lofs; and obferving afterwards that their camp was in a much better fituation than that of the town, he caufed the place, which bears now the name of *Algeriza*, to be erected there, and directed the old one to be demolifhed [f]. Towards the clofe of the year, the king who had rejected *Thouloufe*, when propofed by the pope, for the place of a congrefs, in which the differences fubfifting with the crown of *France*, might be determined, becaufe it was in that prince's dominions, yet readily approved of *Bourdeaux*, which was in the hands of the king of *England*; and where, under the mediation of the pope, a negotiation was begun [g]. The *French*, notwithftanding this, began their march towards *Navarré*, upon notice of which, Don *Alonfo* fent an army into that country likewife, which advanced within three leagues of *Pampeluna*, but could not prevent the *French* from becoming mafters of that city, where, under various pretenfions, which will be mentioned in another place, they committed great exceffes.

THE conferences held at *Bourdeaux*, at the requeft and under the mediation of the pope, were opened on the firft of *May*, but without producing what was expected from them; for the *French* plenipotentiaries, infifting that the Infant Don *Alonfo de la Cerda*, fhould be declared heir apparent of the crown of *Caftile*, the commiffioners on the part of Don *Alonfo* alleged they had no powers to treat upon that point; and this ftopped all proceedings for the prefent [h]. In the

Terminated the war againft the king of Morocco, in order to attack the monarch of Granada.

[d] ZURIT. Annal Arragon. Chronica del Rey Don Alonfo el Sabio, &c.   [e] Chron. general de Efpana. FERRERAS Hiftoria de Efpana. part vi. fect. xiii.   [f] Chronica general de Efpana. Chronica del Rey Don Alonfo el Sabio, &c.   [g] Chron. var. antiq.   [h] Chronica del Rey Don Alonfo el Sabio, &c.

mean time Don *Alonso* prepared for chastising the king of *Granada*; antecedent to which, he found it necessary to settle all disputes between him and the king of *Morocco*, which he at last brought to bear, and a truce was actually concluded [i]. It grew from hence into a received opinion amongst his subjects, that he meant to leave the *Moors* in quiet; and therefore the clergy complained loudly of his applying the revenues of vacant sees, and of part of the tythes due to the clergy, to the uses of the state; upon which they applied themselves to the pope, who wrote in very strong terms to the king, and to the Infant Don *Sancho*, to forbear such practices, and not to violate the immunities of the church.

A. D. 1279.

However, the king and his son, knowing their own intentions best, proceeded notwithstanding; and having engaged the king of *Arragon* to remain strictly neutral, in respect to their differences with the crown of *France*, caused a very numerous army to assemble in that part of *Andalusia*, which was already subject to the crown of *Castile* [k].

Negotiations with the crown of France, *and secret alliance with that of* Arragon.

THE king, Don *Alonso*, early in the spring, repaired to *Seville*, and being afflicted with a distemper in his eyes, the Infant Don *Sancho* commanded the army this campaign against the *Moors*, but without any considerable success [l]. On the other hand, a proposition being made for a personal conference between the kings of *France* and *Castile*, at *Auch* in *Gascony*, Don *Alonso* began his journey through the kingdom of *Arragon*, where he had a long interview with the king; and, as some say, very important resolutions were formed, in consequence of what passed at these conferences [m] H). But however that may be, it is certain that the

---

[i] RODERIC SANTII Hist. Hispan. part iv. Chronica general de Espana.   [k] ZURIT. Annal Arragon. Chronica del Rey Don Alonso el Sabio, &c. Chron. general de Espana.   [l] Chronica del Rey Don Alonso el Sabio, &c.   [m] Chron. var. antiq.

(H) In respect to the secret history of this court and these times, it falls very little within our province; and yet without some little attention to it, what is delivered in the text will hardly be understood. Donna *Yoland*, or *Violente*, by which last name she is commonly mentioned in all but the *Spanish* historians, was a princess of none of the clearest characters (1). She had retired to the court of her brother the king of *Arragon* out of affection, as she pretended, to her daughter-in-law and her grand-children, which provoked the king, who was passionately

(1) *Mariana Historia general de Espana, lib.* xiv.

fond

the other interview did not take effect, for reasons that are no where clearly explained; but the negotiation between *France* and *Castile* went on; and, as some say, an agreement was at length concluded, by which the Infant Don *Alonso de la Cerda* was to have the kingdom of *Murcia* for himself and his heirs, for which, however, he was to do homage to the Infant Don *Sancho*, when he should become king of *Castile* [a]. About this time began those heart-burnings between the king and the Infant who was to succeed him, by which afterwards both the court and the kingdom suffered severely.

A. D. 1280.

THE war against *Granada* was prosecuted with much bloodshed, but little success. Don *Sancho*, who piqued himself upon an unreasonable and extravagant bravery, exposed

The Infant Don Sancho pres

[a] Chronica del Rey Don Alonfo el Sabio, &c.

fond of her, to the last degree; and it was from their having a share in her secrets, that the infant Don *Frederick* and Don *Simon de los Cameros* were put to death, some say by the king's order, others by the Infant Don *Sancho*'s (2): certain it is, that the latter charged the former with it, to make him odious to his subjects, as Don *Alonso* himself affirms, in the instrument by which he disinherited his son (3). Yet, after all this, there appears to have been very close connections between the Infant Don *Sancho* and his mother, and, through her intrigues, between the same Infant and her brother, Don *Pedro* of *Arragon* (4). It was in consequence of these that, under pretence of doing honour to his uncle, Don *Sancho* accompanied him back to *Terrosona*, from this interview, in which, as the two kings had stipulated to act in concert for the recovery of

Navarre out of the hands of the *French*, upon condition that it should be equally divided between them, the Infant went farther, and undertook, that when, by the death of his father, he should be in possession of the throne, he would relinquish the whole of *Navarre* to that monarch, and give him likewise the town of *Requena* and its dependencies, which extended on one side to the frontiers of *Murcia*, and on the other to the kingdom of *Valencia*; in consideration of which the king of *Arragon* was to keep the Infants *de la Cerda* closely confined in the castle of *Xativa*, so that they might not be able to give Don *Sancho* any trouble (5); which contrivances, as will be seen hereafter, proved altogether ineffectual, and therefore *Ferreras*, for the honour of his country, passed them over in silence.

(2) *Chronica del Rey Don Alonso el Sabio, &c.*
(3) *Zurita, Indices rerum ab Arragoniæ regibus gestarum, lib.* ii. p. 171.
(4) *Chronica del Rey Don Alonso el Sabio.*
(5) *Mariana Historia general de Espana, lib.* xiv. *Ferreras Historia de Espana, part* vi. *sect.* xiii. *Mayerne Turquet, P. d'Orleans. Abbé Vayrac.*

Q 2   himself

vents the himself during the campaign in such a manner, that if the
conclusion king had not sent him a timely reinforcement of cavalry, he
of a peace and those who were about him must have been either made
with the prisoners or cut to pieces; which rash and indiscreet conduct,
crown of instead of lessening, raised his credit with the army °. A ne-
Granada. gotiation followed the campaign, but to no effect; for Don
Sancho insisted upon such terms without a victory, as would
have been thought hard, if the king of *Granada* had been at
his mercy. Before the troops quitted the field, there happened
a very remarkable event. A considerable body of banditti,
1281. who had enriched themselves by their booty, intreated the
king to pardon them a little before the campaign, with which
the king complied, upon condition that they should serve all
that year at their own expence; but after doing this, and behaving gallantly, they demanded a compensation, and threatened if they had it not, they would return to their old trade.
Don *Alonso* temporized with them a little, till a body of horse
fell into their rear, and then caused them to be surrounded
and cut to pieces P.

Assembly   IN order to reduce the distracted state of his affairs into
of the some order, the king appointed an assembly of the states at
states at *Seville*, which was accordingly held, and was more numerous
Seville, *in* than usual. The king told them that he was sensible of the
which the heavy load of taxes under which they laboured; that, not-
nobility withstanding, money must be raised for reducing the king of
differ with *Granada*; and instead of an additional tax, he advised the
the king giving a currency to copper money, not as an eligible measure,
Don but as an expedient dictated by necessity. The states, though
Alonso. very unwilling, yielded their assent q. The king then opened
to them the agreement which he had concluded in respect to
the kingdom of *Murcia*, in order to put an end to the disputes
with *France*. Upon this, the Infant Don *Sancho* withdrew
with his dependents and the rest of the members, repenting
what they had done; and being cajoled by that ambitious
prince, who told them that age and infirmities had rendered
his father incapable of government, and that for the future
he would take the administration upon himself, withdrew
likewise r. In the next place, as if he had been already king,
he made a treaty with the monarch of *Granada*, and accepted
a sum of money instead of those hard terms which he had before prescribed. His brethren, the Infants *Juan* and *Pedro*,

° Chronica general de Espana. FERRERAS Historia de Espana,
part vi. sec. xiii. P Chronica del Rey Don Alonso el Sabio, &c. q Chronica general de Espana. Chronica del Rey
Don Alonso el Sabio, &c. r Chron. var. antiq. Chronica
del Rey Don Alonso el Sabio, &c.

concurred

concurred with him in theſe meaſures, and abandoned their
father in his old age °.

Don *Sancho* ſpent the winter in labouring by himſelf, his
brothers, and his adherents, to engage the people every where
in his party; and in this he ſucceeded ſo well, that in the
month of *April*, when the ſtates aſſembled at *Valladolid*, they
were inclined, upon the motion of Don *Emanuel* his uncle, in
the preſence of his mother, to give him the title of king; but
that, with great appearance of modeſty, he refuſed: however,
he made no difficulty of accepting the regal power with the title
of regent °. His brothers, either repenting what they had done,
or being diſappointed in their expectations, left him; and
though he could not but foreſee that troubles muſt enſue, he
engaged in a marriage that ſeemed calculated to excite them;
for he eſpouſed Donna *Maria*, the daughter of Don *Alonſo de
Molina* his great uncle, and then went in great ſtate to *Cordova* °. The king Don *Alonſo* was no ſooner acquainted with
what had paſſed at *Valladolid*, than he wrote to moſt of the
nobility and to the magiſtrates of all the great cities, to eſpouſe
his cauſe, and relinquiſh all connection with the Infant Don
Sancho. The town of *Badajos* ſingly paid that obedience which
was due to the orders of their ſovereign; who finding himſelf
abandoned by the kings of *France*, *Arragon*, and *Portugal*,
and not knowing which way to turn, demanded aſſiſtance
of the king of *Morocco*, who in a ſhort time came over with
an army into *Spain*, and joined Don *Alonſo* with the handful
of troops he had about him °. In the mean time the Infant
Don *Sancho* advanced with his forces towards *Badajos*, which
he ſummoned, but the inhabitants remained firm, and prepared for a ſiege: this, however, was prevented, by the appearance of Don *Alonſo* at the head of a numerous body of *Moors*.
The two kings beſieged *Cordova* without effect, after which
they returned to *Seville*, where *Aben Joſeph* took his leave of
the Chriſtian monarch, who in a tranſport of rage, by a ſolemn act dated *November* the 12th, diſinherited his ſon, and
bequeathed his curſe to him and all his adherents °.

The pope exerted all his influence in favour of the king,
and obliged the grand maſters of the military orders to declare
for him, and to ſecure all the places in their power; at the ſame
time he threatened the Infant Don *Sancho* on account of his

Marginal notes:
Declare the Infant Don San-cho re-gent, and deprive the king of his dignity.

A. D.
1282.

Aben Joſeph, king of Fez and

° Chronica general de Eſpana. Chronica del Rey Don Alonſo,
el Sabio, &c.   ° Chron. var. antiq. Chronica del Rey Don
Alonſo el Sabio, &c.   ° Roderic Santii, Hiſt. Hiſpan.
p. iv. Chronica general de Eſpana.   ° Chronica del Rey
Don Alonſo el Sabio, &c.   ° Chron. var. antiq. Chronica
del Rey Don Alonſo el Sabio, &c.

Morocco, marriage, which he declared null y. The Infant Don *Sancho*
comes from brought back his brother Don *Pedro*, partly by force, partly by
Africa *to* rewards. But he found all methods vain with respect to Don
the aid *Alvaro de Lara*, who seized the city of *Palencia*; and when
of Don the Infant demanded for whom he held it, answered plainly "for
Alonso. "Don *Alonso*, my master and yours." However, finding himself
pushed by a superior force, he offered to leave the kingdom;
which being accepted, he retired into *Portugal* with his followers; and, having increased their number considerably, he
repaired to Don *Alonso* at *Badajos* z. The Infant, Don
James, who had been always dutiful, seized some places on
the frontiers of *Navarre*; in which, however, he had been
forced, if Don *Juan de Lara*, who had followed the fortunes
of the Infants *de la Cerda*, and who was then in the *French*
service, had not marched to his relief a. The king of *Mo-*
rocco returned about this time with great forces; and having
conferred with Don *Alonso*, resolved to open the war by reducing the king of *Granada*. Upon this occasion the king
of *Castile* sent him a corps of about a thousand men, under the
command of Don *Ferdinand Perez*, who, because he would
not incorporate them with the *Moors*, was so much suspected
by *Aben-Joseph*, that he found it requisite to quit the camp,
and retire towards *Seville*. The people of *Cordova*, having in-
A. D. telligence of this, attempted to surprize and surround him;
1283. but Don *Ferdinand* and his forces behaved so gallantly, that
that they were totally routed, with very considerable loss, and
amongst them many persons of distinction were slain or taken.
This troubled Don *Sancho* very much, and, which is singular,
he thought fit to declare, that they had met with no more
than they deserved, for being wantonly the aggressors against
their king and his father; as if his own want of duty had not
excited theirs b.

The king THE whole Christian power in *Spain* was now involved in
by his last discord and confusion; in *Portugal*, the king was excommu-
will disin- nicated, and the kingdom threatened with an interdict; Don
herits the *Pedro*, king of *Arragon*, was engaged in a war with *France*,
Infant Don about *Navarre*, in which the *French* had the assistance of the
Sancho, partizans of Don *Alonso* of *Castile*, while the *Arragonese* were
and calls to supported by the royal Infant Don *Sancho*. This afforded the
the successi- *Moors* an opportunity of raising their heads, which, however,
on the they overlooked; for *Aben-Joseph*, having formed a scheme of
Infants de conquering *Granada*, and finding little assistance thereof from
la Cerda.

y Chronica general de Espana. RODERIC SANTII Hist. Hispan.
p. iv. z Chronica del Rey Don Alonso el Sabio, &c. BRAN-
DAON. a RODERIC SANTII Hist. Hispan. p. iv. FERRERAS.
b Chronica del Rey Don Alonso el Sabio, &c.

Don

Don *Alonso*, returned in difpleafure to *Africa* [c]. The old king of *Caftile*, finding himfelf indifpofed, confirmed on the eighth of *November* his laft will and teftament, by which he folemnly difinherited the Infant Don *Sancho*, for his ingratitude, and which was afterwards urged as the ftrongeft proof of his title, and called to the fucceffion, in his ftead, the Infants *de la Cerda*, and, failing their heirs, the kings of *France* [d]. In the mean time, the infant Don *Sancho* acted quite another part ; he affembled the nobility at *Palencia* ; and having reprefented to them, that what he had done he did by their advice ; that he meant to preferve and not to deftroy the kingdom ; that he now expected they would name a perfon to go to his father and let him know that rebellion was far from their hearts ; that therefore they defired he would preferve the kingdom entire, and fufpend his applications at *Rome*, where the pope was on the very point of launching againft them the thunders of the church. Accordingly Don *Gomez Fernandes*, a nobleman of great probity, and who had meddled very little in thefe affairs, was fent to *Seville*, with inftructions to fay and do every thing that could pacify the king, and engage him to forget, or at leaft to forgive, every thing that had paffed [e].

ABOUT the fame time that Don *Gomez Fernandes* arrived at *Seville*, Donna *Beatrix*, queen of *Portugal*, came thither, to comfort her father under his misfortunes, and Donna *Maria*, the confort of the Infant Don *Sancho*, who had always preferved her intereft with the king, had her agents there likewife. While thefe negotiations were going on, for both the princeffes concurred with Don *Gomez*, the king added a codicil to his will, on the 22d of *January*, by which he gave to the Infant Don *Juan* the kingdoms of *Seville* and *Badajos* [f]. Yet by degrees he began to be foftened ; and upon the arrival of news from *Salamanca*, that the Infant Don *Sancho* was fallen dangeroufly ill there, and profeffed the moft fincere grief for his conduct towards his father, it affected the old king fo much, that it brought him to his grave on *Tuefday* the 4th of *April*, in the year 1284, after he had pardoned his fon, and revoked all his curfes [g]. He had by his queen Donna

Is prevailed on to pardon the royal Infant, and finifhes his days at Seville,

---

[c] BRANDAON. EMANUEL DE FARIA Y SOUSA. ZURITA, Annal Arragon. Chronica general de Efpana. [d] Chronica del Rey Don Alonfo el Sabio, &c. RODERIC SANTII Hift. Hifpan. p. iv. RAINALD. Chronica general de Efpana. [e] Chronica del Rey Don Alonfo el Sabio, &c. BRANDAON. EMANUEL DE FARIA Y SOUSA. [f] Chronica del Rey Don Alonfo el Sabio, &c. [g] RODERIC SANTII Hift. Hifpan. p. iv. Chronica del Rey Don Alonfo el Sabio, &c.

Yoland or *Violente*, five fons, Don *Ferdinand* who died in his life time, Don *Sancho* his fuccefsor, Don *Juan*, Don *Pedre* who likewife died in his life time, and Don *Jaques* or *James*. By his miftrefs Donna *Maria* he had Donna *Beatrix*, at the time of his demife queen dowager of *Portugal*; by another miftrefs, Don *Alonfo* and fome other children, of whom however we have no diftinct accounts. He was buried in the cathedral of *Seville*, near St. *Ferdinand* and Donna *Beatrix*, and left behind him the character of being a learned man and a weak king [h] (I).

As

[h] Chron. var. antiq. FERRERAS.

(I) The character of this great monarch is very differently reprefented, according to the various tempers of thofe who have undertaken to tranfmit his memoirs to pofterity, and the feveral lights in which it might be confidered. He is reprefented by thofe who lived in his own time as of a grave and ferene afpect, majeftic air, and very well made in his perfon. Affable and polite in his converfation, and naturally of a chearful, open, and generous difpofition. His faults were only virtues in excefs. He was much too learned for a prince, his magnificence bordered upon profufion, his own candour mifled him into credulity. His fubjects, however, reaped fome great and lafting advantages even from thofe qualities in him, which were moft cenfured; he augmented the privileges, and corrected many of the errors in the ftatutes made at the foundation of the univerfity of *Salamanca*; he polifhed the *Caftilian* tongue, caufed a general hiftory of *Spain* to be compofed in that language; directed that body of laws to be compiled therein, which we have

mentioned in the text, that all ranks of people might be in a condition to underftand the terms upon which their obedience was expected. Under his aufpices alfo, and at an immenfe expence, thofe aftronomical tables were drawn up which bear his name. He wrote a book intitled, *The Treafure*, comprehending treatifes of rational philofophy, phyfics, and ethics. He is alfo faid to have been deep read in aftrology and chemiftry, in which laft fcience, we are told, there are two volumes of his yet remaining in his catholic majefty's library in cypher. He is, however, charged with profanenefs, and particularly with faying that he could have contrived the univerfe in a better method than that in which we find it. A certain hiftorian has given us a long account of the judgments brought upon him by this notorious act of impiety; but it does not appear that this account of his has met with much credit; and, if we may have leave to fpeak plainly, perhaps the fact on which it is founded deferves as little; for as there are pieces enough of

this

As foon as the Infant Don *Sancho* was recovered from his disposition, which had brought him to the very brink of the grave, and had an account of his father's death, he went to *Toledo*, where he was crowned by the archbifhop Don Gonçales [i]. He proceeded from thence to *Andalufia*, after having had a conference with his uncle Don *Pedro*, king of *Arragon*, at *Ucles*, where he renounced all claim to the town and fortrefs of *Albarracin*, of which Don *Juan de Lara* was then in pofseffion, and made frequent excurfions from thence, fometimes into the dominions of *Arragon*, and fometimes into thofe of *Caftile* [k]. On the arrival of the king at *Seville*, he found that his brother, the Infant Don *Juan*, had been labouring to engage the people to fupport his father's will, by which he was to hold that kingdom; but the nobility interpofing, he had been conftrained to defift; and perceiving that he could not take a wifer meafure, came and did homage to the king Don *Sancho*, who received him very kindly, and who fhewed a difpofition to gratify him in every thing, except that of making him a king [l]. While he was there, *Aben-Jofeph* fent an embaffador to him, whofe name was *Abdalac*, who told him that his commiffion was to afk a plain queftion, whether his mafter was to confider him as a friend or enemy? To this Don *Sancho* made none of the plaineft anfwers, he bid him tell the king of *Morocco*, that he held his bread in one hand and a good ftaff in the other. *Aben-Jofeph* looking upon this as an affront, began immediately to ravage the Chriftian frontiers. Don *Sancho* marched with an army to cover them, and with the affiftance of the *Genoefe*, fent a very formidable

Don Sancho enters into the poffeffion of all his father's dominions, notwithftanding his will.

[i] MARIANA, MAYERNE TURQUET, FERRERAS. [k] Chron. del Rey Don Sancho el Bravo. ZURITA. Annal Arragon. [l] RODERIC SANTII Hift. Hifpan. p. iv. FERRERAS.

this prince come down to pofterity, to prove inconteftably that he was a man of great parts, uncommon penetration, and very extenfive knowlege, we may reafonably doubt of his impiety, more efpecially when we confider the occafion of this expreffion; from whence indeed it is pretty evident, that it regarded the *Ptolemaic*, and not the Divine, fyftem; and was fo far from being an infult upon, that it was really a vindication of the divine wifdom, which, for all that, might be very fhocking to pious ears, in thofe ignorant times, but which ought not to leave a ftain upon his memory in ours. As to his political adminiftration, the reader will judge of it from the facts that are recorded; and we have not either room or inclination to enter into a difcuffion of thofe cenfures that have been paffed upon this monarch by many great writers of different nations, more efpecially as we cannot affirm them to be without ground, fince he was very unfortunate.

fleet

fleet to sea, by which the whole naval power of the *Moors* was thoroughly beaten, which induced *Aben-Joseph* to return into *Africa*, with a resolution however of being revenged as soon as it should be in his power [m]. In the winter the king held an assembly of the states at *Seville*, where he told them he was resolved to preserve the kingdom entire, to curtail as few of his father's concessions and other acts of generosity as was possible, and to endeavour, by the frugality of his administration, to remove the inconveniences introduced by the dissipation of his father's reign, of whose memory however he spoke very respectfully, intimating, that though his dominions were extensive, and his revenues large, yet they bore no proportion to the greatness of his mind [n].

Defeats the king of Morocco at sea, and afterwards concludes a peace with him. THE beginning of the new reign did not pass without some disturbances; but they were very soon suppressed, or rather torn up by the roots; for Don *Sancho*, who had acquired the surname of *el Bravo*, or *the Fierce*, punished with extraordinary severity, and rewarded with great generosity [o]. King *Philip* of *France* sent embassadors to desire that he would not assist the king of *Arragon* in the war between the two crowns. Don *Sancho* thereupon dispatched two prelates to the court of *France*, to let the king know, that, being engaged in a war with the *Moors*, it was not in his power to assist his uncle; but at the same time he directed those prelates to gain the clearest notions they could of the maxims and forces of that court, that he might be the better able to act when he should find it convenient [p]. In the mean time *Aben-Joseph* returned from *Africa* with a great fleet and a numerous army; and as soon as he had landed his forces, besieged the town of *Xerez de la Fronteira*. Don *Sancho* marched immediately with his forces from *Toledo* to *Seville*; and, when the *Moor* little expected it, the Christian fleet appeared in the streights of *Gibraltar*, consisting of a hundred sail: at the same time Don *Sancho*, with his army, advanced to the relief of *Xeres*, upon which *Aben-Joseph* raised the siege and retired in haste. The monarch of *Castile* would have pursued and forced him to a battle, but his brother the Infant Don *Juan* and Don *Lopez de Haro* opposed and hindered it [q]. The king then returned to *Seville*, to which city repaired embassadors from *Morocco* and *Granada*. Don *Juan* and Don *Lopez* were for concluding a peace with the former, and continuing the war against the latter; the rest

[m] Chronica del Rey Don Sancho el Bravo.   [n] Chronica general de Espana.   Chronica del Rey Don Sancho el Bravo. RODERIC SANTII Hist. Hispan. p. iv.   [o] Chronica del Rey Don Sancho el Bravo.   [p] P. DANIEL Histoire de France. FERRERAS.   [q] Chronica del Rey Don Sancho el Bravo.

of

the council were for a general peace. Don *Sancho* propofed
conference with *Aben-Jofeph*, where, for two millions of
dies in ready money, the king confented to withdraw
his fleet and fuffered them to return to *Africa*[r]. The queen
was delivered on the 6th of *December* at *Seville*, of her fon
the Infant Don *Ferdinand*, to the great joy of the king, who
received this news in his journey to the kingdom of *Leon*,
where, if he did not meet with the moft joyful reception, he
found at leaft perfect obedience, which to a monarch of his
difpofition was almoft as acceptable[s].

In the fpring of the next year, he fent for his young fon
from *Seville* to *Burgos*, and obliged the ftates of *Caftile* to own
him for heir apparent, though in his cradle[t]. He next fent
the archbifhop of *Toledo* and other embaffadors to *Bayonne*,
in hopes of concluding a folid peace with *France*; but the
plenipotentiaries of that power infinuated that the king's
marriage was void for want of the pope's approbation, and
that the firft ftep to a peace muft be his refolving to marry the
fifter of their king: *Sancho*, who was himfelf at St. *Se-
baftian*, was no fooner acquainted therewith than he ordered
his embaffadors to quit *Bayonne*, and to return into his own
dominions[u]. He then went in pilgrimage to St. *James*, at
Compoftella, and, under colour of devotion, regulated all the
affairs of *Galicia*; then paffing to the city of *Palencia*, he there
held an affembly of the ftates of *Caftile* and *Leon*, in which
many excellent laws were made for the benefit of his fubjects.
About this time it was, that king *Edward* the firft, of
England, offered his mediation to facilitate the conclufion of
a peace between the crowns of *France* and *Caftile*, to which
likewife the pope contributed as far as lay in his power, and
actually named two cardinals as his legates, to affift at the conferences[w]. The king, Don *Sancho*, endeavoured to prevail
upon the king, Don *Alonfo*, who had fucceeded his father
Don *Pedro* in the kingdom of *Arragon*, to deliver up to him
the Infants *de la Cerda*, which that king very wifely, though
very civilly declined.

As the kingdom of *Caftile* had been hitherto diftracted by
factions, fo the intrigues that now broke out amongft the
courtiers were attended with confequences no lefs fatal; Don
Goncales Garcia, bifhop of *Siguenca*, was the firft who had

Marginal notes:
A. D. 1285.

King Ed-
ward *the
firft, of
England,
offers his
mediation
between
France
and Caf-
tile.*

Don Lo-
pez de
Haro be-
comes fo

---

[r] Chronica general de Efpana.   Chronica del Rey Don Sancho
el Bravo.   [s] Roderic Santii Hift. Hifpan. p. iv.   [t] Chron.
del Rey Don Sancho el Bravo.   [u] Chronica general de Efpana.
P. Daniel Hiftoire de France.   Roderic Santii Hift. Hifpan.
p. iv.   [w] Chronica del Rey Don Sancho el Bravo.   Rainald.
Ferreras.

great, that the king is jealous of him. the king's confidence, and was entrufted with the direction of the finances, and had been employed in a negotiation with the crown of *France*; but upon the difcovery that it was he who fuggefted that the queen's marriage was illegal, the great employment he held was taken from him, and beftowed upon Don *Lopez de Haro*, who was now in as great credit with the queen as with the king; and being a man of boundlefs ambition, accumulated titles, pofts, and revenues, which rendered him firft envied by many, and then, through his own haughty behaviour, odious to all. He had the title of count, which had been for fometime difufed, was high treafurer and prime minifter, while his brother Don *Diego de Haro* had the command of the forces in *Andalufia*, and his daughter Donna *Maria*, married, by the king's confent, his brother the Infant Don *Juan* [x]. The haughtinefs of Don *Lopez*, to thofe who had been before his friends and equals, the loofe he gave to his refentment in refpect to fuch as he accounted his enemies, and that fpirit of rapine which tempted him to opprefs without diftinction, brought numberlefs complaints to the king's ear. As for Don *Alvaro de Lara*, his patience being wore out, he retired with fome of his friends into the dominions of *Portugal*, where he affociated with the Infant Don *Alonfo*, and other malecontents in that kingdom, and made fome inroads into *Caftile* [y]. This brought both monarchs into the field, who united their forces againft thefe malecontents; but in the courfe of the campaign, Don *Sancho* of *Caftile*, who piqued himfelf much upon his juftice, received fuch certain information of the ill ufage Don *Alvaro* had received, that, inftead of purfuing him to deftruction, as he might have done, he received him into his favour, which, however, he did not enjoy long, being carried off by a diftemper foon after this reconciliation; upon which Don *Sancho* privately intimated to Don *Juan de Lara*, who had been fo long an exile for acting againft him, that, if he would return home, he fhould not only enjoy his brother's eftates, but alfo his pofts and appointments, which he accepted [z]. The king having now a minifter he could truft, called an affembly of the ftates at *Toro*, where the Infant Don *Juan* and Don *Lopez* oppofed the king's meafures, and at laft retired from that affembly without concealing their difcontent, or the refolution they had taken of raifing difturbances, if it was in their power.

[x] Chronica general de Efpana. Roderic Santii Hift. Hifpan. p. iv. P. Daniel. Ferreras. [y] Brandaon. Chronica del Rey Don Sancho el Bravo. Chron. var. antiq. [z] Chron. del Rey Don Sancho el Bravo.

THE

THE king at first endeavoured to secure their persons, upon the Infant Don *Juan* retired towards *Portugal* with forces, as Don *Lopez de Haro* did into *Castile* [a]. The king did not think proper to march with an army against either, but sent for them both to come to him, promising them any satisfaction that was reasonable. The royal Infant rejected the proposition as unsafe, but Don *Lopez* came to the place appointed, with his friends in arms: upon his asking him what it was he aimed at, and by what authority he raised troops to disturb the public peace, he answered by his own, to redress the injuries which the Infant Don *Juan* and himself had received. After many attempts towards a reconciliation which ended in nothing, it was agreed, that the royal Infant and Don *Lopez* should meet the king at *Alfaro*, where all things were to be compromised. At this conference, when the king proposed that Don *Lopez* should evacuate all the fortresses which he had committed to his charge, that nobleman laid his hand upon his sword, as the Infant Don *Juan* likewise did. The nobility who were about the person of the king, seeing this, killed the one and arrested the other. This threw the whole kingdom into a flame, and Don *Diego de Haro* the brother, and Don *Diego* the son, of the late Don *Lopez*, retiring into *Arragon*, persuaded that monarch to set the Infant Don *Alonso de la Cerda* at liberty, whom they immediately proclaimed king of *Castile*: their adherents in several places engaged the people to acknowlege and arm in defence of his title; so that a second civil war was begun, with more alarming circumstances than the first [b] (K).

DON

The Infant Don Juan seized, and Don Lopez de Haro killed, in the king's presence.

A. D. 1288.

---

[a] EMANUEL DE FARIA Y SOUSA, de las Historias Portuguesas. RODERIC SANTII Hist. Hispan. p. iv. [b] Chronica del Rey Don Sancho el Bravo. ZURITA, Annal Arragon. Chron. var. antiq. FERRERAS Historia de España, p. vi. sec. xiii.

(K) We have a very large and circumstantial account of this affair in the *Spanish* histories, out of which it will be proper to give the reader a few particulars that are absolutely necessary to set it in a proper light. When the Infant Don *Juan* first departed so far from his duty as to ravage the country about *Salamanca*, Don *Lopez de Haro* was at court, to whom the king complained of it with astonishment; upon which Don *Lopez* told him that he was in the right; that what the Infant did was by his advice; and that, if the king would go to *Valladolid*, he would undertake Don *Juan* should come to *Sigales* with his troops, in order to let him know his grievances. The king, Don *Sancho*, accepted this proposition; he went to *Valladolid*, and Don *Juan*,

Don Alonso de la Cerda and the Arragoneſe who abet his title, forced to retire.

Don *Sancho*, king of *Caſtile*, in the midſt of theſe difficulties ſupported himſelf with great firmneſs: he had a conference with the king of *Portugal*, from whom he demanded and received ſuccours; but when he was about to have taken the field, he found himſelf preſſed by *Philip le Bel*, king of *France*, to meet and confer with him; and as it was a point of great conſequence to prevent a breach with that monarch at this juncture, he advanced with a ſtrong corps of troops, as far as St. *Sebaſtians*, leaving the command of his army to Don *Alonſo de Molina*, the queen's brother [c]. The king of *Arragon*, taking the advantage of Don *Sancho*'s abſence, entered the dominions of *Caſtile* with the Infant Don *Alonſo de la*

[c] P. Daniel Hiſtoire de France. Chronica del Rey Don Sancho el Bravo.

Juan, upon notice from his friend, came to him, as he had promiſed. At this interview the king behaved ſo mildly, and gratified the Infant in ſo many reſpects, that things ſeemed to be pacified. But afterwards, when they both attended the king, who went to confer with the monarch of *Arragon*, they diſappointed his views, by the intelligence they gave to, and the influence they had over, that prince. When Don *Sancho* came to *Alfaro* in his own dominions, and ſaw both the Infant Don *Juan* and Don *Lopez* there without their uſual attendants, he cauſed a great council to be held of the prelates and nobility, in which he told them, that, ſince he found they were perſons whom good uſage could not move, or the greateſt favours inſpire, with any gratitude, he was reſolved to diſmiſs them from his ſervice, and expected they ſhould render the places, that he had committed to their care, to ſuch noblemen as he then named. While the king was ſpeaking, Don *Lopez* laid his right hand upon his ſword, wrapped his cloak round his left arm, and having called him a cruel, perfidious, and ungrateful tyrant, ſuddenly drew, and advanced towards him; upon which one of the nobles cut off his right arm at a blow, and the reſt who were preſent pierced his body with a multitude of wounds. The Infant Don *Juan*, who had wounded ſeveral in defence of his father-in-law, when he ſaw him extended upon the floor, fled to the queen's chamber, to which the king followed him with his ſword drawn, and with an intention to have diſpatched him; but the queen, putting herſelf between them, throwing herſelf upon her knees, by her tears and prayers ſo wrought upon the king, that he ordered him to be conducted to priſon, with a deſign to proſecute him for this and other acts of treaſon, which did not hinder his living, as the reader will ſee, to owe his preſervation a ſecond time to the kind interpoſition of the ſame good princeſs.

Cerda,

Cerda, who now used the regal title, at the head of an army, which some say fell little short of 100,000 men [d]. Don *Alonso de Molina* advanced towards him, encamped advantageously, but declined fighting till the king should return. This he did sooner than was expected, for the king of *France* failed at the interview, and then proposed another, which the situation of Don *Sancho's* affairs would not permit him to expect. Upon his return therefore, and joining his own army with a numerous corps of troops, the king of *Arragon* retired into his own country, to quell some disturbances that broke out in his absence; and the king Don *Sancho* following him, wasted all the country as far as the *Ebro* [e]. For this fruitless attempt, Don *Alonso de la Cerda* made a cession to the king of *Arragon* of all *Murcia*; and, by a treaty of the like nature, gained the king of *Granada* to acknowlege his title [f]. Don *Diego de Haro*, the elder, was more fortunate, for he beat a body of the king of *Castile's* troops, and ravaged the country about *Cuenca* and *Alarcon* [g]. About this time the inhabitants of *Badajos* had a quarrel with the *Portuguese*, and Don *Sancho*, upon hearing the merits, decided in their favour. But when the king's edict came to be put in execution, a new quarrel arose, in which the *Portuguese* being unarmed were cut to pieces. The people at *Badajos* dreading the justice of their sovereign, seized upon the citadel and declared for Don *Alonso de la Cerda*. The city however was quickly invested by the king's troops, and though the inhabitants defended themselves obstinately, they were at last constrained to surrender at discretion; but the troops, without any respect to the capitulation, put all they found in the place to the sword, without mercy [h].

A. D. 1289.

THE beginning of the next year, the kings of *France* and *Castile* had an interview at *Bayonne*, when it was agreed, that the Infants *de la Cerda* should have the kingdom of *Murcia*, doing homage for it to the crown of *Castile*; that king *Philip* should use his interest at *Rome*, to engage the pope to confirm the king's marriage; and that both princes should continue the war against the king of *Arragon* [i]. In the mean time Don *Juan de Lara*, being deceived by an anonymous letter, retired from the king's service, and went over to the king of

The king receives great disturbance from the jealousies of Don Juan de Lara.

[d] ZURITA, Annal Arragon.   [e] Chronica del Rey Don Sancho el Bravo. RODERIC SANTII Hist. Hispan. p. iv. ZURIT. Annal Arragon.   [f] Chron. var. antiq. ZURITA, Annal Arragon.   [g] Chronica general de España. RODERIC SANTII Hist. Hispan. p. iv.   [h] Chronica del Rey Don Sancho el Bravo. BRANDAON.   [i] P. DANIEL Histoire de France. Chronica del Rey Don Sancho el Bravo.

Arragon,

Arragon, to whom he did great service. At length however the queen Donna *Maria* proposed to him the marriage of her niece, the heiress of *Molina*, for his son, and hostages for the security of his person ; and upon receiving these he was content to return to his duty [k]. Such at that time was the power of the nobility in *Spain*, and so feeble the authority of kings. In the space of a few months, notwithstanding all these assurances, and the marriage concluded with his son, Don *Juan de Lara* was again seized with new apprehensions. A nobleman of great rank came to him in the dead of the night in the royal palace at *Toledo*, and told him that a body of armed men had been secretly let in, and that he suspected there was some design against his liberty or life. Don *Juan* upon this, attempted with a few of his friends to make his escape ; but finding that impracticable, and having told them the source of his uneasiness, they advised him to apply to the queen ; and she disclosing it to the king, he sent for him, and upon a solemn promise that he would do him no hurt, drew from him

the name of the nobleman who had told him this story. The king did not indeed punish him, but he reproached him in the face of the whole court, told him he was a faithless knight and a lying traitor, which drew upon him such universal contempt, that he could never afterwards appear in public [l]. Don *Juan* relapsed soon after into fresh inquietudes ; and to draw him out of these, the king promised him, that his own son, the Infant Don *Alonso*, should marry his daughter, which made him quiet for a little time, and but for a little time ; so that the king was forced to release his brother the Infant Don *Juan*, that he might oppose one faction to another [m]. Affairs however went better abroad, for he not only concluded a new treaty with the king of *Granada*, but, Don *Alonso* being dead, *James* the new king of *Arragon* renewed the ancient treaty between the two crowns ; upon which Don *Juan de Lara*, seeing he had no resource left in *Spain*, retired into *France*, though the king omitted nothing to have delivered him from his jealousies, and the queen still continued her kindness and protection to his family [n].

ABEN-JOSEPH, king of *Morocco*, either considering the treaty which the king of *Castile* had made with the monarch of *Granada* as a breach of the peace made with him, or as preparatory to a war, began to assemble troops and shipping, of which the king of *Castile* had very early intelligence. Upon

[k] RODERIC SANTII Hist. Hispan. p. iv. ZURIT. Annal Arragon. [l] Chronica del Rey Don Sancho el Bravo. [m] Chron. var. antiq. RODERIC SANTII Hist. Hispan. p. iv. [n] Chronica del Rey Don Sancho el Bravo. ZURITA, Annal Arragon.

this,

This, he immediately took into his pay the famous *Benedict Zachary*, a *Genoese* admiral, who had commanded his fleet in the former war; and being supplied with a large sum of money by the states of his several kingdoms, and auxiliary squadrons from the kings of *Arragon* and *Portugal*, he attacked the *Moors* by sea and land. His admiral had the good fortune to dissipate the enemy's fleet, and to destroy a great part of it; and the king, after a long siege, reduced *Tarefa*, and put a strong garrison into it; he likewise concluded a peace in quality of mediator between the crowns of *Arragon* and *Naples*, to their reciprocal satisfaction, and received the strongest assurances from the crown of *France*, that the late treaty should be punctually complied with, and no encouragement whatever given to any of his malecontents [o]. Donna *Elizabeth*, the wife of Don *Juan de Lara* the younger, dying without issue, her husband became, from that circumstance only, one of the number.

A. D. 1292.

THE Infant Don *Juan*, forgetting the clemency with which the king had treated him, entered into fresh cabals; and having drawn Don *Juan de Lara* the younger into his party, they quickly assembled a great number of seditious and licentious persons, and with them broke out into open rebellion. The king marched against them with an army, and pressed them so hard, that the Infant was forced to take shelter in his town of *Valentia*, which from him is still called *Valentia*; Don *Juan* and his associate threw himself, with some troops, into *Castro-Torafa*, at no great distance [p]. The king was no sooner informed of it, than he came and encamped between those two places, without besieging either; but published an edict, forbidding any to supply them with provision, on pain of death. This quickly reduced Don *Juan de Lara*, and his people, to such distress, that he went to the king, and in the most humble manner desired his pardon; Don *Sancho* received him kindly, bid him remember his distress, how he came into it, and by whom he was delivered [q]. The news of this brought his father back, whom the king entrusted with the command of his army against the Infant Don *Juan*, who had made his escape into *Portugal* [r]. The Infant invited Don *Juan de Lara* to a conference, under pretence that he had a mind to submit to the king, and then, in breach of his faith, made him prisoner; but

The Infant Don Juan *falls first into discontent, and at length into rebellion.*

1293.

[o] Chronica del Rey Don Sancho el Bravo. ZURITA, Annal. Arragon. BRANDAON. P. DANIEL. [p] Chronica general de Espana. RODERIC SANTII Hist. Hispan. p. iv. [q] Chron. del Rey Don Sancho el Bravo. FERRERAS. [r] Chron. var. antiq. BRANDAON.

the king of *Portugal* set him immediately at liberty; up
which he returned into *Castile*, adhered steadily to the kin
and died the next year in his service *.

An enor- THE Infant Don *Henry*, son to St. *Ferdinand*, and uncle to
mous act of Don *Sancho*, returned this year from *Italy*, to revisit his native
perfidious country, after having run through a long series of strange ad-
and un- ventures. The king received him very kindly at *Burgos*, and
manly cru- granted him such a settlement as was suitable to his high rank
elty com- and near relation to him ᵗ (L). Upon his application to the
king

---

* Chronica general de Espana. BRANDAON. RODERIC SAN-
TII, Hist. Hispan. p. iii.   ᵗ Chronica del Rey Don Sancho
el Bravo.

(L) It is requisite to say something here concerning the Infant
Don *Henry*, because the course
of the history will oblige us to
say a great deal of him hereafter; he was the son of St. *Ferdinand* by Donna *Beatrix*, who,
as some writers say, was addicted
to judicial astrology, and in-
fected her children with a propensity to that superstition (1).
It is uncertain whether this was
the cause or not; for it is pretended that there was a pre-
diction that Don *Alonso* would
be deposed by a near relation,
that prompted him to take up
arms against his brother, in
hopes, perhaps, of fulfilling it
when he was defeated, as we
have shewn in the history; and,
being refused shelter by the king
of *Arragon* (2), fled to *Tunis*,
and lived for some years under
the protection of the *Moorish*
prince who then governed there;
though *Mariana* says that he
was but in a mean condition,
and that his misfortunes did not
contribute at all to his amendment, since he still maintained a

correspondence with the malecontents in *Castile*. At length,
growing weary of *Barbary*, he
went into *Italy*, where he embraced the part of prince *Con-
radin*, grandson of the emperor
Frederick, had a share in his
fortunes and misfortunes, and
made himself first considerable,
and then odious there, for reasons that will appear in another
place, and which brought upon
him excommunication and imprisonment, he was absolved
from the former, and released
from the latter, upon a most
humble submission to pope *Honorius* (3); and this afforded him
an opportunity of returning to
Spain, after an absence of twenty-
seven years. The king D
Sancho had no personal kno
lege of him; for his rebelli
against Don *Alonso* happened t
very year after Don *Sancho* w
born; but he knew and piti
his misfortunes, and thought
his duty to relieve him as
uncle (4). As to his characte
he was of a haughty, mutabl
and turbulent disposition, cruc

---

(1) *Mariana, Histoire general de Espana.*   (2) *Zurita, Annal Arrag*
(3) *Rainald, A. D.* 1236.   (4) *Chronica del Rey Don Alonso el Sabio.*

avariciou

king of *Portugal*, not to protect his brother, the Infant Don
Juan transported himself to *Morocco*, and finding *Jacob Aben-*
Joseph meditating a war, he offered, if he would give him
5000 horse, and some foot, to recover *Tarefa*, which his
brother had taken the year before. His proposal was accepted,
and having embarked his forces in *Andalusia*, he invested
Tarefa with a numerous army. The place was defended by
Don *Alonso Perez de Guzman*, with such spirit, that the *Moors*
began to be discouraged. The Infant Don *Juan* being informed that the governor had a little son at nurse in an adjacent village, he caused the child to be brought to him, and
then bid the *Castilian* advanced guard tell the governor, that,
if he did not immediately surrender the place, he would cut
the child's throat before his eyes. This occasioning some
commotion in the garrison, Don *Alonso* rose from dinner to
know what was the matter, and coming upon the walls, saw
Don *Juan* with his son in his hand, and heard him repeat his
threats. Don *Alonso* immediately drew out his sword, and
throwing it to the Infant, said, " If you who were born a
" prince, and educated a Christian, dare to commit so exe-
" crable a villany, know that I dare both keep the place and
" furnish you with a weapon." This, though it struck both
the *Moors* and the garrison with admiration, had no effect
upon the monster to whom it was addressed, since, in the
sight of both, he took up the sword and butchered the poor
Infant. The length of the siege gave Don *Sancho* time to
come to its relief, with a numerous army, upon which the
Moors raised the siege, and Don *Juan*, being afraid to go back
to *Morocco*, deserted them, and retired to the king of *Granada*,
to whom *Aben-Joseph* yielded *Algeriza*, the only place he had
left in *Spain*, that he might be rid of any connections with

the Infant committed by the Infant Don Juan.

A. D. 1294.

avaricious, and perfidious to the
last degree; mean in adversity,
insolent in prosperity; and with
a multitude of vices, had as few
good qualities as any man of
those times : but he had a sup-
pleness, and a kind of specious
address, that rendered him capable of doing much mischief;
and he would have done still
more if he had been endowed
with better talents (5). The
reader may possibly blame us for
giving him so bad a character,
but the sequel of the history will
acquaint him with facts that must
convince him that the Infant
Don *Henry* has been here very
gently dealt with.

(5) *Mariana, Ferreras, Mayerne Turquet.*

that country ª (M).   A resolution however to which himself and his successors did not always adhere.

The death of Don Sancho the Fierce, and the condition of the kingdom at his decease. In the beginning of the ensuing year, the king, whose health had been long declining, found himself so much worse, that he resolved to take the speediest and the properest method for settling his temporal and his spiritual concerns.   In order to this, he made his will, in the presence of the archbishop of *Toledo*, and of such other prelates and great lords as were near his person, by which he appointed the queen tutoress and regent of the Infant Don *Ferdinand*, his successor, to whom the Infant Don *Henry*, and all who were present, took the oath

---

ª BRANDAON.   RODERIC SANTII Hist. Hispan.   Chronica del Rey Don Sancho el Bravo.   FERRERAS Historia de España, p. vi. sec. xiii.

(M) We have in some circumstances a different account of this matter in *Mariana*.   He tells us, that this son of Don *Alonso Perez de Guzman*, was a youth grown up, and taken prisoner in a sally; that the governor was at dinner when the Infant brought him before the fortress, and threatened to put him to death.   Don *Alonso* being informed of it, threw the sword, and told him he had rather lose a hundred sons, than forfeit his fidelity to his sovereign; and having said this, went back to his house, and sat down to dinner, but was quickly roused by the cry of the soldiers, on the sight of the young gentleman's head being struck off by order of the Infant Don *Philip*.   Being told what it was that occasioned this emotion, he said, coldly, I thought the enemy had entered the town, went back to his house, and seated himself again at table.   A most wonderful instance of heroic courage, says our author, worthy the heroes of old; and than which antiquity proposes nothing greater to our imagination (6).   As soon as the king Don *Sancho* received the news of it, he wrote a letter with his own hand to the governor, in which, having highly commended his behaviour, he bestowed on him the surname of *Bueno*, or the *good*, desired him to come to him at *Alcala*, and assured him, if his health would permit, that he would come out to meet him; which letter is said to be preserved in the archives of the dukes of *Medina Sidonia* (7), who have more reason to be proud of their being descended from this man, than of being, as they are, the first dukes in *Castile* (8).

---

(6) *Mariana, Historia general de España, lib.* xiv.   (7) *Id. ibid. Mayerne Turquet Histoire generale d'Espagne.*   (8) *Etat present del' Espagne, par l'Abbe de Vayrac, tom.* iii. *p.* 169.

of

of fidelity [w]. He removed afterwards to *Toledo*, in hopes the change of air might have been serviceable to him; but in this he was deceived, for, soon after his arrival, he departed this life on the 25th of *April*, in the year 1295. He left by his queen, the Infants Don *Ferdinand* (Don *Alonso* died before him), Don *Pedro*, and Don *Philip*; and two Infantas, Donna *Elizabeth* and Donna *Beatrix* [x].

Don *Ferdinand* the fourth succeeded his father, in the tenth year of his age; and, as soon as Don *Sancho*'s funeral was over, received the homage of the nobility, and was inaugurated in the cathedral church of *Toledo*, with the greatest solemnity, and with the most universal applause [y]; and yet, in the compass of this year, there arose as great troubles as ever perplexed a court, the beginning, progress, and issue of which, within this period, we will state as briefly as possible. The Infant Don *Juan* claimed the whole succession, under pretence that the king's marriage was illegal, and he was the only right heir of Don *Alonso* the *wise*, according to the system maintained by his deceased brother, and in virtue of which he had enjoyed the kingdom. As strange a title as this was, it found some abettors; the *Moors* promised him their assistance, for their own interest, and upon the same motive the king of *Portugal* became his ally [z]. However, upon the queen's offering him the restitution of his honours and revenues, Don *Juan* came to court, and did homage to his nephew: Don *Denis*, king of *Portugal*, took up arms, to recover three towns which Don *Alonso* gave his mother; Donna *Beatrix*, the queen dowager, gave him those towns, and so there was an end of that quarrel [a]. Don *Diego Lopez de Haro* assembled forces, in order to recover the country of *Biscay*; the queen sent for Don *Juan* and Don *Goncales de Lara*, to whom the king in his last moments had particularly recommended her and his son, and having furnished them with a large sum of money, upon the strongest assurances of duty and fidelity, dispatched them to their own estates, in order to raise forces against Don *Diego*. They did accordingly raise the troops; but as soon as they were raised, they joined the rebels, against whom they were to have acted, and then sent a long list of demands

marginal note: Don Ferdinand the fourth proclaimed king of Castile, and owned by the states at ten years old.

[w] Chronica general de Espana. Chronica del Rey Don Sancho el Bravo.   [x] Mariana, Ferreras, Mayerne Turquet.   [y] Chronica del Rey Don Fernando IV. recopilada por Miguel de Herrera.   [z] Roderic Santii Hist. Hispan. p. iv. Chronica general de Espana. Brandaon. Chronica de los Moros de Espana.   [a] Chronica del Rey Don Fernando IV. recopilada por Miquel de Herrera. Emanuel de Faria y Sousa.

for

for themselves and for him to the court; and these being granted, they came to *Valladolid*, and did homage in the assembly of the states [b]. The Infant Don *Henry*, more modest than the rest, formed no pretensions against the king, but insisted upon having the government of the kingdom, with the title of regent, saving to the queen dowager the care of his person, and of his education, to which she was constrained to assent [c]; lastly, the king of *Granada* entered the frontiers of *Andalusia*, with a very numerous army, and wasted the country with fire and sword; Don *Rodrigo Ponce*, grand master of *Calatrava*, with the forces of the military orders, gave him battle, and, not without great loss, compelled him to retire. A few days after, Don *Rodrigo* himself died of his wounds, and was succeeded in his command on the frontier by Don *Alonso Perez de Guzman*, who so gallantly defended *Tarefa* [d].

Don Alonso de la Cerda assumes the same title, and makes an alliance with the king of Arragon. THE prospect which seemed to be grown in some measure serene, grew on a sudden as gloomy as before, and clouds began to gather on every side. *James*, king of *Arragon*, sent to the queen dowager, and desired she would take back the Infanta Donna *Elizabeth*, his mind being altered with respect to the marriage; upon which, anxious for the safety of that princess, she prevailed upon the regent to go and receive her on the frontiers. It was not long after this, that the whole scene of foreign and domestic treachery disclosed itself. Don *Alonso de la Cerda* returned out of *France* into *Arragon*, where, having confirmed the cession he made of the kingdom of *Murcia* to that monarch, he furnished him with an army to march into *Castile* [e]. The probability of his recovering that kingdom was indeed very great; the king of *Arragon* embarked the whole forces of his realm in his quarrel, the kings of *France*, *Portugal*, and *Granada*, were his allies; and, besides these foreign confederates, he had very good friends in the country to which he laid claim, such as the first queen dowager Donna *Yoland*, his grandmother, the Infant Don *Juan*, whom he had purchased with the promise of the kingdoms of *Leon* and *Galicia*, and Don *Juan de Lara*, who had formerly betrayed, and was now just reconciled to the queen

[b] Chronica general de Espana. Chronica del Rey Don Fernando IV. recopilada por MIGUEL DE HERRERA. RODERIO SANTII Hist. Hispan. p. iv. [c] Chronica del Rey Don Fernando IV. recopilada por MIGUEL DE HERRERA. [d] Chron. de los Moros de Espana. [e] ZURITA Annal Arragon. Roderic SANTII Hist. Hispan. p. iv. Chronica general de Espana.

and the regent[f]. As soon as they were ready to act, the Infant Don *Juan*, with the lords of his party, sent to give the king and his mother notice, that they renounced their fidelity, and so went to join his competitor.

THE first step was to put the Infant Don *Juan* in possession of the dominions promised him, which was performed without difficulty, and he proclaimed king at *Leon*[g]. The army of the allies, as it was called, then marched to *Sahagun*, where Don *Alonso* was proclaimed king of *Castile*[h]; the queen Donna *Maria*, in the absence of the regent, commanded Don *Diego Ramirez*, and Don *Garcia Fernandez de Soto* Major, to throw themselves with a body of good troops into the town of *Majorga*, which lies at the distance of five leagues from *Leon*. Don *Alonso de la Cerda* was for marching directly to *Burgos*, but the Infant Don *Juan* advised him not to leave *Majorga* behind him, upon which they laid siege to it. This advice was prudent, but it had a bad effect. The town was not well fortified, and therefore they attempted it by assault; failing in that, they were obliged to attack it in form[i]. In the mean time the regent Don *Henry* went to put himself at the head of the troops in *Andalusia*, in order to cover that country from the king of *Granada*, who entered it with a powerful army, beat, and would have taken him prisoner, if he had not been relieved by Don *Alonso Perez*. Upon this, the regent made a peace with the *Moors*, but on terms so bad, that the queen refused to ratify them[k]. Donna *Yoland* made an attempt upon *Valladolid*, which served only to shew her inclinations and her weakness; for the inhabitants shut their gates against her, and she was constrained to withdraw[l].

The confederates invade Castile, with numerous armies, but without effect.

AT length an epidemic disease, produced by the great heats, broke out in the army of the allies, and forced them to raise the siege of *Majorga*; the *Arragonese* retired into their own country, with the dead body of the Infant Don *Pedro*, who had commanded them, and Don *Alonso de la Cerda* went with them[m]. As for the Infant Don *Juan* and Don *Juan de Lara*, they retired to *Simancas*, where they joined the king of *Portugal*, who had taken some places in that neighbourhood.

Tarefa defended by Don Alonso Perez de Guzman, till the Moors raise the siege.

[f] ZURITA. Annal Arragon. P. DANIEL. BRANDAON. Chron. del Rey Don Fernando IV. recopilada por MIGUEL DE HERRERA. Chronica de los Moros de Espana. [g] Chronica general de Espana. FERRERAS. [h] RODERIC SANTII Hist. Hispan. p. iv. [i] Chronica del Rey Don Fernando IV. recopilada por MIGUEL DE HERRERA. [k] Chronica de los Moros de Espana. [l] Chronica general de Espana. RODERIC SANTII Hist. Hispan. p. iv. [m] Chronica del Rey Don Fernando IV. recopilada por MIGUEL DE HERRERA. ZURITA. Annal Arragon.

There a proposition was made to cut matters short, by beſieging the king and his mother in *Valladolid*. The project was plauſible and practicable; but Don *Juan de Lara* ſuddenly declared that neither he nor any that belonged to him ſhould act immediately againſt the perſons of the king and queen, which put an end to the ſcheme [n]. On the ſide of *Murcia*, the king of *Arragon* acted in perſon, and on his own behalf, which might perhaps be the reaſon that things took a different turn there; ſo that he reduced *Alicant*, and ſeveral of the moſt conſiderable places in that kingdom [o]. The king of *Granada*, extremely irritated at the queen's rejecting the peace he had concluded with the Infant Don *Henry*, came with a numerous army in the autumn before *Tarefa*, which, however, he was not able to reduce, neither could his good friend the Infant Don *Henry* prevail upon the ſtates, though he laboured it with great induſtry, to ſend their orders to Don *Alonſo Perez* to deliver it. The very propoſal hurt him with the *Caſtilians*, though he pretended to qualify the demand, by his deſire to abate their heavy taxes; and his deſiring the queen to give him the revenues of two conſiderable towns, ſoon after entirely deſtroyed his credit, and put it out of his power to do the miſchief that he intended [p].

Don Ferdinand, king of Caſtile, *makes a treaty with Don Denis king of* Portugal. ALL the true patriots who had the intereſt of their country, and that only at heart, ſtudied how to reſtore the public tranquility, and to deliver the ſtate and themſelves out of this diſtreſs. Don *Juan Fernandez de Limja* commanded on the frontier towards *Portugal*; and having framed in his mind a project which he thought might prove beneficial to both kingdoms, he deſired an interview with Don *Juan d'Albuquerque*, who was the king of *Portugal*'s favourite, to whom, when he had communicated his ſcheme, he promiſed to give it all the countenance that was in his power, which he executed with all the punctuality worthy of a man of his rank. The iſſue of this buſineſs was, that in an interview between the royal families at *Alcanizas*, a peace was concluded between the two crowns, upon condition that Don *Ferdinand* of *Caſtile* ſhould marry the Infanta Donna *Conſtantia* of *Portugal*, as ſoon as a diſpenſation could be obtained from *Rome*; that the prince of *Portugal*, Don *Alonfo*, ſhould eſpouſe the Infanta Donna *Beatrix* of *Caſtile*; and that, for certain reaſons expreſſed in the treaty, and which would have been better expreſſed by

[n] BRANDAON. EMANUEL DE FARIA Y SOUSA. FERRERAS Hiſtoria de Eſpana, p. vi ſec. xiii. [o] ZURITA. Annal Arragon [p] Chronica de los Moros de Eſpana. Chronica del Rey Don Fernando IV. recopilada por MIGUEL DE HERRERA.

the

the single word, *necessity*, several good towns, and a considerable district of country, should be yielded to the king of *Portugal*, who promised to assist Don *Ferdinand* with all his forces.   On the conclusion of the treaty the two Infantas were exchanged, and the queen dowager, Donna *Maria*, was in hopes that, by the assistance of the *Portuguese*, the war might have been carried on with greater vigour: but in this she promised herself too much, for those succours amounted to no more than 300 horse, under Don *Juan d'Albuquerque*, and they could not do much; indeed history does not inform us that they did any thing q.   The king of *Granada* was in the field some months, but we hear of no place that he took, except *Alcaudeta*, in the mountains, which was of no great consequence.

This measure fails of producing those great advantages expected from it.

THE queen dowager, Donna *Maria*, found means in the spring to obtain a considerable supply from the states at *Burgos*; and having a pretty good army in the field, directed them to lay siege to *Ampudia*, in which Don *Juan de Lara* was with a small garrison; the queen heard with surprize, that, although the place had been invested some days, the siege was not far advanced; upon which she went thither in person, suspecting, as the case really proved, that the fault was not in her forces, but in their generals.   Upon her arrival in the camp, Don *Juan* quitted the place in the night, which surrendered the next day r.   Don *Denis* of *Portugal*, in pursuance of the late treaty, and at the request of the states, came with a considerable army to her assistance; yet he refused to act against the Infant Don *Juan*; and entering into the intrigues of the Infant Don *Henry*, proposed to the states, that the kingdom of *Galicia* should be left to the Infant Don *Juan*; but the states, apprized of the true ground of this proposal, *viz.* that the Infant Don *Henry* might be always necessary, and *Castile* a less formidable neighbour to *Portugal*, they rejected it; upon which the king sent assistance to Don *Juan* s.   The king of *Granada* had a superior army in the field, with which he was very near taking *Jaen*, the suburbs of which he burnt; and having amassed a large booty, and reduced the town of *Quesada*, he retired t.

---

q BRANDAON. Chronica del Rey Don Fernando IV. recopilada por MIGUEL DE HERRERA.   r Chronica de los Moros de España.   Chronica general de España.   RODERIC SANTII Hist. Hispan. p. iv.   s EMANUEL DE FARIA Y SOUSA.   Chronica del Rey Don Fernando IV. recopilada por MIGUEL DE HERRERA.   t Chronica de los Moros de España.

Admirable conduct of the queen Donna Maria, by which the kingdom is preserved.

THE prudence of the queen had removed many difficulties, and had hitherto kept the crown on the head of Don *Ferdinand*, her son ; but so many new enemies arose, and the old ones continued so implacable, that it seemed scarce possible for her to proceed in the way she had hitherto done. She was, however, indefatigable ; and, with the greatest probity of mind, was so affable in her behaviour, and had such a dexterity in framing and in executing expedients, as rendered her superior to all the trials she met with. Some of her enemies insinuated that, her marriage being invalid, her children by the king were illegitimate. She took no notice of this at home, but directed the archbishop of *Toledo*, who was at *Rome*, to represent the matter to the pope in a proper light ; and he did this so effectually, that he procured a bull to confirm her marriage, and a cardinal's hat for himself. She found a very mercenary spirit amongst many of the nobility who had hitherto adhered to her, but were continually wanting rewards for their loyalty ; these she gratified as well as she was able, and returned them abundance of good words for their bad behaviour. But the Infant Don *Henry* exceeded them all in quality of regent; he was covetous and corrupt, he was, besides, very perfidious and very susceptible of offence. The queen behaved to him with great respect herself, and engaged her son to do the like ; but she took care that the people should know his true character ; and this made him less dangerous, though not less deceitful. She found money difficult to be got, and yet, by managing it frugally, and laying the accounts punctually before the states, she obtained whatever she thought proper to ask. But what gave her more trouble than any other, indeed than all the rest, was, the intelligence that the malecontents had in almost all the great towns in the king's dominions. To balance this, she visited many of them with him in person, and to those she suspected most, she sent her children, which fully answered her intention ; for the people, charmed with the confidence that the queen reposed in them, did, out of pride, what they ought to have done out of duty.

A. D. 1299.

Strange behaviour of the Infant Don Henry, in public and private life.

A GENERAL assembly of the states being held at *Valladolid*, the accounts given by the queen were so clear, and her necessities so pressing and so apparent, that they granted her thrice the usual sum at once, a great part of which the Infant Don *Henry* laid his hands upon, under pretence of going to take the command of the army against the *Moors*. The scheme of his campaign was to purchase a peace, by giving up *Tarefa*, that he might put most of this money in his pocket ; but the queen took care to apprize the officers of the army he was to command

command of his finister defigns, which they took care to defeat [u]. Don *Juan de Lara*, after making a journey to very little purpofe into *France*, returned into *Navarre*, and from thence made an expedition into *Caftile*, in which his troops were routed by Don *Juan Alonfo de Haro*, and himfelf taken prifoner, which happened well for the queen, and better for him [w]. Her army was then before *Palencuela*, into which he had thrown a garrifon; but thofe who commanded the queen's army were fo much his friends, that in all probability it had not been taken, if the queen had not fent for her prifoner into the camp, and prevailed upon him to give his orders for opening the gates. The Infant Don *Henry*, having thruft himfelf into this negotiation, was fo taken with the beauty of Don *Juan*'s daughter, whofe grandfather he might have been, that he would needs marry her; which ceremony the queen graced with her prefence, Don *Juan* being firft fet at liberty, who became once more the king's good fubject, and rendered all his places into the queen's hands. Towards the clofe of this year, the old queen dowager, Donna *Yoland*, died in her return from *Rome*, in the kingdom of *Navarre* [x] (N).

A. D. 1300.

THE

[u] RODERIC SANTII Hift. Hifpan. p. iv. Chron. var. antiq.
[w] Chronica general de Efpana.   [x] Chronica del Rey Don Fernando IV. recopilada por MIGUEL DE HERRERA. RODERIC SANTII Hift. Hifpan. p. iv, FERRERAS Hiftoria de Efpana, p. vi. fec. xiii.

(N) We have a very ftrong contraft in the characters of thefe two queen dowagers of *Spain*, than whom there could fcarce be any two women more unlike; for Donna *Violente* had a great hand in exciting all the troubles that difturbed her hufband's, her fon's, and her grandfon's reigns. A very judicious and well efteemed hiftorian has branded her for her gallantries, which, without doubt, he would not have done, if they had not been very notorious (9). She had a particular kindnefs for the Infant Don *Juan*; though, of all her children, he was un-doubtedly the moft unworthy; and there is great probability, that it was for his fake, rather than for that of her grandchildren, that fhe attempted to increafe the difturbances in *Caftile*, by folliciting the people to revolt from the fervice of the king and his mother (10). It appears, however, that fhe had very little intereft, and rather difcovered an inclination to do mifchief, than a capacity of doing it; though it is not impoffible that fhe might put her fon in poffeffion of thofe places that were left her for her dowry. Whether fhe refided afterwards

(9) *Zurita. Annal Arragon. Ferreras.*   (10) *Chronica del Rey Don Fernando IV.*

in

The king of Arragon, *in confequence of his intrigues with the Infant, invades* Castile.

THE king of *Portugal*, being very defirous to have the double marriage actually accomplished, defired an interview with the queen Donna *Maria*, to which fhe readily confented, and there all the meafures neceffary were concerted. Upon this, fhe fummoned an affembly of the ftates at *Valladolid*, where every thing paffed with fuch regularity, and fuch immenfe fums were granted for the fupport of the young king, that the Infant Don *Juan*, who hitherto had ftiled himfelf king of *Leon* and *Galicia*, and was actually in poffeffion of fome part of both countries, thought it moft for his intereft to renounce thofe titles, to which indeed he had no juft pretenfions, and to make the beft terms for himfelf he could; which, having done, he came to the affembly of the ftates, did homage to the king, and fwore to the eftablifhed fucceffion *y*.

y Chronica del Rey Don Fernando IV. recopilada por MIQUEL, DE HERRERA.

in that part of the kingdom of *Leon* that acknowleged the Infant Don *Juan*, or whether, notwithftanding what fhe had done, fhe returned again to the court of *Caftile*, is not very clear; but we have good reafon to believe that there was, at leaft, as much of difcontent as of devotion in her journey to *Rome*, where, however, fhe was well received by pope *Boniface* the eighth, who eftablifhed the jubilee, and countenanced, at leaft, an opinion, which nothing but the fuperftition of thofe times could have rendered credible, that whoever vifited the tombs of the apoftles *Peter* and *Paul*, might obtain full and free pardon for all their fins (11). In this refpect it may be the queen dowager Donna *Violente* might have her reafons, as well as other great perfonages who went thither the fame year: but in all probability, the fatigue of fuch a journey was too great for a

perfon fo far advanced in years, and might occafion her falling fick as fhe paffed the *Pyrenees* in her return, and after a fhort illnefs died at *Roncevaux*, where fhe was likewife interred, which is the reafon that her death is not mentioned by feveral of the *Spanifh* hiftorians. The celebrated *Bayle* (12), following *Mariana*, who was mifled by another hiftorian, upon whom the greateft blame ought to lie, has made fome fevere reflections on the king Don *Alonfo*'s character, as to the ufage of this princefs, which are not at all founded in truth, as we have fhewn in the text; and this is the more extraordinary, fince he might eafily have perceived the contradiction, even in his own account; for how is it poffible for a prince to ufe his wife unkindly, and defire to be rid of her, and be at the fame time uxorious to a ridiculous degree.

(11) *Rainald.* A. D. 1300. *Villani, Hift. Florent. lib.* viii. *c.* 36.   (12) *See the article of Alphonfo king of Caftile, in his dictionary.*

After all this, in conjunction with the Infant Don *Henry*, instead of obeying the queen's orders, he went to confer with the king of *Arragon*, with whom the two Infants made a secret and scandalous agreement, that, in consideration of his supporting them in their respective schemes, they would procure him the cession of the kingdom of *Murcia*[z]. In the mean time, the bishop of *Burgos*, whom the queen had sent to *Rome*, procured, but not without a vast expence, the bulls and dispensations for which he was sent, which, upon his return, were publickly read in the cathedral church of *Burgos*[a]. The king of *Arragon*, however, in pursuance of the intrigues between him and the two Infants, invaded *Castile*; and though the people and the army were perfectly disposed to do what was fit for them to have done for the service of the king and kingdom, yet the private views of the nobility spoiled all. While the army of *Arragon* besieged *Lorca*, that of *Castile* remained altogether inactive, and this notwithstanding all the pains the queen took to prevent it[b].

A. D.
1301.

AFTER a siege of many months, the governor of *Lorca* entered into an agreement, that, in case the place was not relieved in fifty days, he would deliver it to the king of *Arragon*. The queen pressed the Infants to march with the army to its relief, which they at first declined, and at last refused; upon this, she put herself at the head of the army, and the Infants were obliged to follow her, though very unwillingly. They had, however, scarce taken the field, before they had intelligence that *Lorca*, though the time was not expired, was through treachery surrendered[c]. This, though a very bad action, was much exceeded by the Infants Don *Juan* and Don *Henry*, who suffered the king of *Arragon* to retire when they had him much in their power. The queen knew, but could not prevent this act of infidelity. Providence soon after enabled her to return the injury in the same way; for, by countenancing the malecontents in *Arragon*, she brought that monarch, of his own accord, to offer to evacuate *Murcia*, if she would grant him the single town and fortress of *Alicant*, which she refused, from a firm persuasion that it would be very soon in her power to recover, for her son, all that had been lost during a minority full of confusion[d]. Don *Alonso de la Cerda*, perceiving how

Finds himself obliged to make proposals of peace, which are rejected by the queen.

---

[z] ZURIT. Annal Arragon. RODERIC SANTII Hist. Hispan. part iv.   [a] RAINALD. Chronica general de Espana.   [b] Chronica del Rey Don Fernando IV. recopilada por MIGUEL DE HERRERA. ZURIT. Annal Arragon.   [c] Chronica general de Espana. ZURIT. Annal Arragon. ROD. SANTII Hist. Hispan. part iv.   [d] ZURIT. Annal Arragon. Chronica del Rey Don Fernando IV. recopilada por MIGUEL DE HERRERA.

desperate

desperate his affairs were grown, left *Arragon*, in order to
solicit assistance in *France*, where he found it utterly out of the
king's power, how much soever it might be in his intention.
The affairs of the church being in great disorder, Don *Goncales
Diaz Palomec*, archbishop of *Toledo*, held a council of his
suffragans at *Penafiel*, in which many regulations were made,
and, amongst the rest, it was intimated to the Infant Don
Henry, that if he did not restore the places he had taken from
the church, they would proceed to excommunicate him, and
that they would do the same to any who should commit the
like outrages for the future [e].

The Infant Don Juan *and his associates prevail on the young king to leave his mother.*   As the Infant Don *Juan* loved to fish in troubled waters,
as he found a very ready associate in Don *Juan de Lara*, and
found no great difficulty in drawing the Infant Don *Henry* into
his projects, they, by the help of Don *Goncales Gomez de Cal-
delas*, who was of his bed-chamber, insinuated to the young
king, that he was too much a man to live under the restric-
tions of a nursery; and that, if he meant to make his subjects consider him, or desired to live, as a king, he ought to
leave his mother, and live as he liked.   The young king, like
most other young kings, listened to these plausible offers,
eloped, while the queen was gone to *Victoria*, to prevent, by
a conference with the *French* viceroy of *Navarre*, a war on
that side, and went to the lords [f].   It was not long before the
Infant Don *Henry* found that he had mistaken his man; and
that he had lost more by this revolution than the queen, to
whom he returned, and exclaimed bitterly against those who
had seduced their sovereign, and offered to have recourse to
arms, on his own and her majesty's behalf.   The queen, on
the other hand, behaved herself, and, at last, taught him to
behave, with moderation.   The favourites engaged the king
to celebrate his marriage with Donna *Constantia*, which the
queen would not permit, till the king of *Portugal* restored
those places he had taken from the kingdom of *Leon*, when
the solemnity was performed with great magnificence [g].   Thus
far things went well; but when an assembly of the states
came to be held at *Valladolid*, matters wore another aspect.
The people of the town were for shutting their gates, if the
queen had not prevented it; and the deputies refused to assist
without her consent.

1303.

[e] Rod. Santii Hist. Hispan. part iv.   Chronica general de
Espana.   [f] Chronica del Rey Don Fernando IV. recopilada
por Miguel de Herrera.   [g] Brandaon. Rod. Santii
Hist. Hispan. part iv.   Chronica general de Espana.

After

AFTER all this, the favourites attacked her conduct in that *Are obliged* assembly ; insisted upon the restitution of the late king's jew- *to court her* els, which she had given to the Infanta Donna *Elizabeth,* and *favour to* upon having a strict account of what had been expended in the *gain their* maintenance of her houshold ; she complied with both de- *demands in* mands, and, when all things were at a stand, procured, by *the assem-* her influence, a free gift of two millions of marvadies, and *bly of the* four subsidies [h]. Upon the dissolution of that assembly, and *states.* after holding the states of *Castile* at *Burgos,* where, by the like means, the like grants were obtained, the king went to *Palencia,* where Don *Alonso,* the son of the Infant Don *Juan,* married Donna *Teresa,* the sister of Don *Juan de Lara* [i]. After this he entered into a kind of league or confederacy with these great lords, which so exasperated Don *Henry,* that he insisted upon the queen's entering into a like confederacy with him and Don *Lopez de Haro,* with which measure, for her own sake, she was obliged to comply ; upon which the most considerable of the nobility resorted to her at *Valladolid,* from all quarters, to offer her their services [k]. This alarmed the favourites to such a degree, that they prevailed upon the king to go thither to try to pacify his mother. The queen received him with great kindness ; but spoke to him with the utmost freedom ; shewed him how much she had done for him, and how much he had done against himself ; and concluded with telling him, that he would do well to guard against the result of his own confederacy ; but that he had nothing to fear, with respect to his person or authority, from that of which his follies had compelled her to become the head [l].

His favourites, being still in fear, pressed Don *Ferdinand* to *Death of* confer with his father-in-law the king of *Portugal,* at *Badajor,* *the Infant* under pretence that he would give him a sum of money, by way *Don Hen-* of portion with the queen, which, at the conference, appeared *ry, and ge-* to have no foundation ; but however, the king, being ac- *nerous be-* quainted with his son-in-law's expectation, gave him a million *haviour of* of marvadies, to prevent any coldness arising between him *the queen-* and his queen [m]. This interview so alarmed the Infant Don *dowager.* *Henry* and Don *Diego de Haro,* that they made a treaty with the king of *Arragon,* into which they would have drawn the

[h] Chronica del Rey Don Fernando IV. recopilada por MIGUEL DE HERRERA.   [i] ROD. SANTII Hist. Hispan. part iv. Chronica general de España.   [k] Chronica del Rey Don Fernando IV. reeopilada por MIGUEL DE HERRERA.   [l] ROD. SANTII Hist. Hispan. part iv. Chronica del Rey Don Fernando IV. recopilada por MIGUEL DE HERRERA.   [m] BRAN-DAON. Chron. var. antiq.

queen-

queen-mother; but she not only refused, but gave notice of
to her son [n]. Immediately after the Infant Don *Henry*
died without heirs, and the king instantly seized on all his
estates; and so little care was taken of his body, that it had
scarce been decently interred, had it not been for the queen
who directed a funeral suitable to his rank as regent of the
kingdom, at which she assisted in person, saying, upon this
occasion, we ought to remember his birth, and forget his
faults [o]. By her endeavours Don *Diego de Haro* was detached from that league into which he had entered; and, if the
king would have followed her advice in all things, his affairs
might have been restored; but he resembled his grandfather
in the unsteadiness of his temper, and, by the advice of his
favourites, concluded an alliance with the new king of *Granada*, who took the advantage of these troubles, and, like a
wise prince, neglected nothing that might contribute to the
prosperity of his subjects, and the establishment of his own affairs [p].

Treaties with the king of Arragon and the Infants de la Cerda.

THE king of *Arragon*, perceiving how prejudicial this scene
of disturbance and confusion was to the interest of the Christians in *Spain*, proposed to the king of *Castile* concluding all
differences between them by a solid and equitable peace, to
which Don *Ferdinand* shewed himself very inclinable. Before any effectual measures could be taken on this head, Don
Diego de Haro, after a very free expostulation with the king,
by which, notwithstanding the interposition of the queen his
mother, he could obtain nothing, broke out into an open insurrection, in conjunction with Don *Roderic de Castro*, a nobleman of great power in *Galicia*; but the latter being killed
in one of his first exploits, the peace of the kingdom was, for
the present, restored [q]. The king then sent the Infant Don
John to regulate matters with the king of *Arragon*, and by
them it was agreed, that all differences should be referred to an
arbitrator on behalf of each of the kings, and an umpire, who
was to moderate things between the arbitrators. Upon this
plan the Infant Don *John* was to act for the king of *Castile*,
the bishop of *Saragossa* for the king of *Arragon*, and the king
of *Portugal* was to be the umpire; of all which Don *Ferdinand* gave notice to the queen his mother, desiring her consent,
which she declined; but promised him not to oppose it. In
consequence of this agreement, the king of *Portugal* came into *Castile*, and was received every-where with all possible magnificence: he then repaired to the place of conference, which

A. D.
1304.

[n] ZURIT. Annal Arragon.   Chronica general de Espana.
[o] FERRERAS Hist. de Espana, part vii. sect. xiv.   [p] Chronica de los Moros de Espana.   [q] Chron. var. antiq.

was

was *Campillo*, where things were quickly settled at the expence, as the queen dowager foresaw, of the king her son; for it was agreed, that the river *Segura* should be the common boundary between the dominions of the two monarchs in the kingdom of *Murcia*; so that not only the town and fortress of *Alicant*, but also several other places, and all the country on the north of that river, was yielded to the crown of *Arragon* [r]. This great affair decided, they proceeded to another, which was still of higher importance; for Don *Ferdinand* consented to refer the pretensions of the Infants *de la Cerda* to the kings of *Arragon* and *Portugal,* who determined that Don *Alonso de la Cerda* should have *Alba de Tormes, Bejar, Valdecarneja, Mançanares, Monçon, Gaton, Gibraeleon, Aljaba,* and other places, the revenue of which altogether was esteemed at four hundred thousand marvadies; that Don *Ferdinand de la Cerda,* his younger brother, should have the revenue of an Infant of *Spain*; and, on the other hand, the few places that Don *Alonso* still held were to be evacuated, and both brothers were to render homage to the king, previous to their reaping any benefit by this decision [s]. These great points over, all the three royal families met several times, feasted each other, and parted with all imaginable testimonies of the most perfect friendship.

A. D. 1305.

THE king, Don *Ferdinand*, began now to have a clearer notion of things, and to be able to form a better judgment of men; but he still had his favourites, though the Infant Don *John* and Don *Juan de Lara* were no longer such: he was also very desirous of power, though hitherto he had enjoyed but a very limited authority. In order to compass these points, he found it absolutely necessary to bring back Don *Diego de Haro* to his duty, for he began to perceive the truth of what his mother had often told him, that he was a person of greater honour, and more to be depended upon, than any of the rest. The point in difference was between him and Don *Juan,* who claimed to be the heir of *Biscay* in right of his wife, the daughter of Don *Lopez de Haro,* Don *Diego's* elder brother. On the other side, Don *Diego* insisted upon his right as the heir male, and also in virtue of an agreement made with the Infant Don *Juan* and his wife, by which an equivalent was stipulated, and to the strict performance of which they had sworn. For the decision of this dispute, an assembly of the states was called, but they rose without determining any

Don Ferdinand finds himself obliged to court Don Diego Lopez de Haro.

[r] ZURIT. Annal Arragon. Chronica del Rey Don Fernando IV. recopilada por MIGUEL DE HERRERA. BRANDAON.
[s] Chronica del Rey Don Fernando IV. recopilada por MIGUEL DE HERRERA. BRANDAON. ZURIT. Annal Arragon.

thing, Don *Diego* being in poffeffion of *Bifcay*, and fully
determined to keep it [t]. Don *Juan de Lara* alfo, being offended with the Infant Don *Juan*, for not taking care of his
interefts in the treaty with the king of *Arragon*, entered into a
clofe alliance with Don *Diego de Haro*, which offended the
king extremely, as through certain ftories that had been told
him, which, however, were falfe, he had conceived an extreme diflike to Don *Juan*, whom he feems to have fixed
upon already for an example to the reft of the nobility, that,
by his punifhment, they might be taught obedience.

1306.
Attempts
to reduce
Don Juan
de Lara
by force of
arms, in
which he
*fails.*THE king, Don *Ferdinand*, laboured firft to detach Don
Diego de Haro from that clofe alliance he had contracted with
Don *Juan de Lara*; in order to which, he propofed making
his fon, Don *Lopez de Haro*, mafter of his houfhold; which
poft his father did not hinder him from accepting, but refufed
entering into any engagements either to procure or preferve
it [u]. On the contrary, he brought Don *Juan de Lara*, after
this, to court, and laboured all in his power to reconcile him
to his mafter, which was alfo done in appearance. But, notwithftanding this agreement, the king, who could no longer
bridle his temper, marched with a body of his own troops,
and with another, commanded by the Infant Don *Juan*, tho'
his mother laboured all fhe could to prevent it, againft Don
Juan de Lara, at *Aranda*. He was very hard preffed; but
found means to efcape, and, which muft have aftonifhed the
monarch of *Caftile*, paffed through the midft of his camp with
an efcort of horfe, in order to join Don *Diego* and Don *Lopez de Haro*, who were come, with a great body of forces,
to his affiftance. The king marched againft them with his
army, being extremely provoked at a meffage from the two
lords, importing, that, as he made war upon them, he ought
to releafe their allegiance [w]. The king's army beginning to
crumble away, and thofe that remained acting rather according to their own notions than in obedience to orders, the Infant Don *Juan*, by the king's command, began to reprove
fome of the gentlemen who ferved therein; upon which they
told him, that it was not the king's quarrel, but his; and that,
fince he was become weary of their company, they were very
willing to leave him. As foon as the king obferved this, he
had recourfe again to negotiation, and, by the interpofition
of the queen his mother, all things were at laft adjufted upon
thefe terms, that Don *Diego de Haro* fhould hold *Bifcay* during his life, and that, upon his demife, that country, a very

1307.

---

[t] Chron. var. antiq.   [u] ROD. SANTII Hift. Hifpan.
part iv. FERRERAS.   [w] Chronica del Rey Don Fernando
IV. recopilada por MIGUEL DE HERRERA.

few

few places excepted, should belong to the Infant Don *Juan*
and his wife, or to their heirs [x].

THIS treaty, which had been made with a great deal of fe- *Detaches*
crecy, did not become public till the assembly of the states, held *from him*
in the month of *April*, at *Valladolid*, was called upon to ratify *Don Die-*
and confirm it.   This had such an effect on the temper of *go de Ha-*
Don *Juan de Lara*, who considered it as a scheme laid for *ro, and*
his destruction, that he quitted the place abruptly, after *makes an-*
giving some public testimonies of discontent [y].   The queen- *other at-*
mother was, for the first time, misled, and gave her son advice *tempt to no*
which he and she both had reason to repent; and this was, to *purpose.*
carry things to extremity against Don *Juan*, as the most effectual means to restore some lustre to the royal authority.   Don
Juan, having early intelligence of this, threw himself into the
fortress of *Torde humos*, with a small body of good troops:
the king quickly invested him, and, though he made a very
stout defence, brought him so low, that he was obliged to demand a conferrence with the Infant Don *Juan*. At this meeting
he put the Infant in mind of their former friendship; observed,
that though himself might be the first, it was not probable he
should be the last victim; and that it was very unnatural for
wife men to be the authors of their own destruction.   This
had its effect; the Infant Don *Juan* proposed very high terms
to the king, in the name of Don *Juan de Lara*, and, upon his
rejecting them, as he expected, insinuated to all the nobility, that the king was bent upon taking Don *Juan*'s life,
who, though a victim to justice in his eyes, ought to appear
a martyr in theirs; upon which they unanimously shewed an
inclination to change sides, Don *Diego de Haro* only excepted.   The king, seeing things in this situation, desired him
to interpose with Don *Juan*, and to advise him to come and
ask his pardon, which he very readily did; and the king,
having received him into favour, bent all his thoughts to the
humbling the Infant Don *Juan*, who had been the principal
author of all the disturbances during his reign [z]. About this time   1308.
the knights Templars, who were prosecuted throughout all
Europe, surrendered all their possessions in *Spain* to the Infant
Don *Philip*, till the suit against them should be determined;
and this involved him in a quarrel with the Infant Don *Juan*,
who pretended that some of his vassals had been oppressed and
injured by the Infant Don *Philip*, for the redress of which he
had recourse to arms.

[x] Chron. var. antiq.   [y] Chronica general de Espana.
ROD. SANTII Hist. Hispan. part iv.   [z] Chronica del Rey
Don Fernando IV. recopilada por MIGUEL DE HERRERA.

THE king, by the advice of his mother, neglected nothing that might engage that prince to return to his duty, which, however, was no very easy task; and, after a long negotiation, Don *Juan* prevailed, or, to speak with propriety, forced upon the king a change of measures and of ministers, whom he removed and replaced at his pleasure [a]. This done, the kings of *Castile* and *Arragon* had an interview at the monastery of *Huerta*, where it was agreed that prince *James* of *Arragon* should marry the Infanta *Leonora* of *Castile*; that both monarchs should make war on the *Moors*; and that they should send ambassadors to *Rome*, to procure such bulls from the pope as might, in some measure, supply the necessary expence [b]. In pursuance of these resolutions, the king of *Castile* took the field with a very numerous army, after he had dispatched Don *Juan de Lara* to *Rome* as his ambassador. He had also a good fleet at sea, which induced him to change the first plan of operation, and to besiege *Algeriza*, which was become exceeding strong, and was considered as one of the most important places that belonged to the king of *Granada*. While this siege was carried on, the king's army made various expeditions by detachments from before the place; in one of which they became masters of *Gibraltar*, then of no great consequence, and in another they lost Don *Alonso Perez de Guzman*, who had done so many and so great services to the crown of *Spain* [c]. They might also have taken *Algeriza*, if the Infant Don *Juan* had not abruptly quitted the siege, which induced many of the nobility to follow his example. Upon this the king of *Granada* offered Don *Ferdinand* a sum of money, together with *Quesada* and *Bedmar*, which had been recovered by the *Moors*, if he would conclude a separate peace, with which, finding himself unable to carry on the war, he complied [d].

THE king, in his return from this campaign, meditated a strange design, which he thought requisite to his own safety, and this was removing out of the world the Infant Don *Juan*, from whom he had received so much vexation. He began with attaching Don *Juan de Lara*, who was returned from his embassy, to his service, by bestowing upon him the important post of master of his household; tho' in order to do this, he was obliged to remove the Infant Don *Pedro* his

1309.

---

[a] Chron. var. antiq. [b] ZURIT. Annal Arragon. ROD. SANTII Hist. Hispan. part iv. [c] Chronica de los Moros de España. Chronica general de España. [d] Chronica de los Moros de España. Chronica del Rey Don Fernando IV. recopilada por MIGUEL DE HERRERA.

brother.

brother [e]. The marriage of his sister the Infanta Donna *Elizabeth* with *John* duke of *Bretagne*, which was to be celebrated at *Burgos*, seemed to offer the king a fair opportunity of executing a design that nothing could justify. The queen-mother invited the Infant Don *Juan* to that solemnity, who was so cautious as to demand a safe-conduct, which the queen readily granted: the king, notwithstanding this, directed those, who had his orders to kill the Infant, to post themselves in such a manner, as to surprize him in his return from visiting the queen-mother. The preparations for this black affair could not be so secretly managed, but that they came to the ear of this princess, who thought herself bound in honour to give notice of his danger to the Infant Don *Juan*, who fled privately out of the city, and was followed by many of the nobility, who did not know what designs might be formed against them [f]. This attempt upon the Infant Don *Juan* rendered him more powerful, and not at all less troublesome, than before; so that the king was obliged to have recourse to the pope, to whom he insinuated, that some of his seditious subjects hindered him from making war upon the Infidels, and therefore desired, that authority might be given to some ecclesiastics to restrain them from troubling his government, by threatening them with the censures of the church; which favour he obtained [g]. On the third of *August*, the queen, Donna *Constantia*, was delivered of her son the Infant Don *Alonso*; but the joy occasioned thereby was quickly clouded by the king's falling dangerously sick at *Palencia*, from which, however, he recovered, contrary to the opinion of his physicians [h]. The heavy accusations brought against the knights Templars being thoroughly examined, in a council held at *Salamanca* for that purpose, the order was acquitted, to the great honour of that assembly, which equally disregarded private views and popular clamour [i]. A revolution also happened in *Granada*, where the king *Mohammed Aben-Alhamar*, who was blind, was deposed, and thrust into prison, and his brother *Mohammed Aben Nazar* placed upon the throne [k].

THE kings of *Castile* and *Arragon*, having an interview at *Calatayud*, agreed upon another marriage between the Infant Don *Pedro*, the king's brother, and Dona *Maria*, daughter to the king of *Arragon* [l]. The queen-mother, Donna *Ma-*

Fresh disturbances break out, to the great

[e] ROD. SANTII Hist. Hispan.   [f] Chronica del Rey Don Fernando IV. ubi sup.   [g] RAINALD.   [h] Chronica general de Espana. ROD. SANTII Hist Hispan. part iv.   [i] FERRERAS Historia de Espana, part vii. sect xv.   [k] Chronica de los Moros de Espana.   [l] ZURIT. Annal Arragon. ROD. SANTII Hist. Hispan. part iv.

ria,

detriment ria, with the affistance of several prelates, brought about a re-
of the king conciliation between the king and the Infant Don *Juan* and
and king- his party, which had like to have proved fatal to this mon-
dom. arch ; for having invited them to a supper, and exceeding a
little in his usual course of diet, he was seized with a diftemper which, not without imminent danger, he escaped ᵐ. But,
notwithftanding this agreement, new disputes quickly arose,
and Don *Juan de Lara,* doubting of his safety, retired into
Portugal. The prudence of the queen-mother prevented this
1311.　flame from breaking out ; but, however, the meafures concerted with the king of *Arragon* for renewing the war againft
the *Moors,* was, for the prefent, hindered by thefe jealoufies
from being put in execution ⁿ. The king of *Caftile* reclaim-
ed from the king of *Portugal* the places given up, in his minority, by the Infant Don *Henry;* and the king his father-in-law,
to prevent difputes, offered to leave all the matters in difference to the king of *Arragon,* which was accepted ; but it
feems the great point of Don *Ferdinand* was to get a little money, to procure which he mortgaged to the crown of *Portugal*
Badajos and fome other places, as the *Portuguefe* hiftorians
inform us º.

Death of　THE factions and difturbances which had hitherto limited
Don Fer- the king's power and inclinations, being in fome meafure
dinand appeafed, the king laid before the ftates, at *Valladolid,* the ex-
IV. of pediency of renewing the war with the *Moors,* and propofed
Caftile, as to them a plan for that purpofe ; with which they were fo well
fome think, pleafed, as to take upon themfelves the whole expence of the
by Divine campaign ᵖ. The Infant Don *Pedro* was declared general
judgment. and commander in chief, and, in that quality, affembled the
forces on the frontiers of *Andalufia,* and in the beginning of
the mouth of *June* laid fiege to *Alcaudeta* in the mountains.
The king, Don *Ferdinand,* when the fiege was pretty far advanced, fet out for the army, and fixed his quarters at *Martos,* a place at a fmall diftance from the camp : here he found
Don *Pedro* and Don *Juan de Carvajal* prifoners, who were
charged with killing Don *Juan Alonfo de Benavides,* as he came
out of the royal apartments, one evening, at *Palencia* ꝗ. The
king was no fooner informed of this, than he ordered them
to be thrown over the rock, without any form of trial. The

ᵐ Chronica del Rey Don Fernando IV. recopilada por MIGUEL
DE HERRERA.　ⁿ Chronica general de Efpana.　EMANUEL
DE FARIA Y SOUSA. RODERIC SANTII Hift. Hifpan. part iv.
º EMANUEL DE FARIA Y SOUSA.　BRANDAON.　ᵖ Chronica del Rey Don Fernando IV. recopilada, par MIGUEL DE HER-
RERA.　ꝗ ROD. SANTII Hift. Hifpan. part iv. Chronica
general de Efpana.

tho

two brothers protested their innocence, of which they affirmed they could give the cleareft proofs, but to no purpofe. When they came to die, they fummoned the king to anfwer for this act of injuftice, at the tribunal of Almighty God, in thirty days [r]. The king went to the camp, where he found the fiege fo far advanced, that there could be no doubt of his becoming mafter of it very foon ; however, finding himfelf indifpofed, he thought proper to retire to *Jaen*, where he figned the capitulation on the fifth of *September*, and alfo a peace with the king of *Granada*, on certain conditions, with which he feemed very much pleafed, and he was thought to be out of danger [s]. But having taken fome refrefhment on the feventeenth, and falling afterwards afleep, his domeftics, when they came to wake him, perceived that he was dead ; and what *Ferreras* obferves was thought very remarkable by the old hiftorians : this was the thirtieth day from the death of the two brothers. He farther obferves, that we ought not from hence to pronounce rafhly concerning either his guilt or theirs (O). As his whole reign had been a feries of confu-fions,

A. D. 1312.

---

[r] Chron. var. antiq. Chronica del Rey Don Fernando IV. re-copilada por MIGUEL DE HERRERA. [s] FERRERAS Hiftoria de Efpana, part. vii. fect. xiv. Chronica del Rey Don Fernando IV. por HERRERA.

(O) We find this matter of Don *Ferdinand*'s death very cautioufly treated by *Mariana* (1), who, on the one hand, informs us, that the king was infirm ; that he was too much addicted to the pleafures of the table; that he had, more than once, ran the hazard of dying fuddenly before of fuch exceffes ; and that many, think he died of fuch an excefs now (2). Thefe facts are fairly collected from antient hiftories. On the other fide it appears, that, in the firft tranfports of his paffion, the king was exceedingly violent; and that fome of his courtiers knew well enough how to excite thefe tranfports,

and were wicked enough to avail themfelves of them againft fuch as they were willing to remove (3). There prevailed at that time a very ftrong opinion, arifing very probably from executions apparently unjuft, that fuch adjudications to the tribunal of God were anfwered by a particular interpofition of Providence ; and this, *Mariana* fays, was the common notion with refpect to pope *Clement* the fifth and *Philip* the *Fair* of *France*, whom the knights Templars fummoned to appear and anfwer before God for the crying acts of injuftice done to them in this world (4). But he ob-

---

(1) *Hiftoria de Efpana, lib.* xiv. (2) *Chronica del Rey Don Fernando* IV. (3) *Mariana Hiff. de Efpana, lib.* xv. (4) *Idem Ibid.*

ferved,

sions, so his death proved the cause of still greater mischiefs, as it made way for another minority, before those evils were in any degree removed that had been introduced during the last; and when there were many of those living who, from motives of ambition and private interest, had been the principal actors in the disorders of the two last reigns, and who, though farther advanced in years, were not at all better disposed towards each other, or towards the public, which gave those who had its safety and prosperity really at heart a most melancholy prospect.

A schism in the assembly of the states, and two regents thereupon chosen.

THE young king, Don *Alonso*, was scarce entered into the third year of his age, when the death of his father placed him upon the throne; and the prudence of his grandmother recommended him to the care of the bishop of *Avila,* and the inhabitants of that town, who were distinguished even in *Spain* for their unalterable affection to their sovereigns [t]. That princess having declined the regency, the two principal pretenders to that high office were the Infant Don *Pedro* and the Infant Don *Juan,* each of whom came with an army into the neighbourhood of *Palencia,* where the states were assembled, in order to fix their choice, which, notwithstanding the utmost pains taken by some true patriots, was found impracticable; so that one party retiring to the convent of St. *Francis,* voted the tutelage and regency to the queen-dowager, Donna *Maria,* and her son the Infant Don *Pedro*; while those who met at the convent of St. *Paul,* bestowed their suffrages on the queen-dowager Donna *Constantia,* and the Infant Don *Juan* [u]. Both parties had recourse to arms; and both endeavoured to

A. D.
1313.

[t] Chronica del Rey Don Alonso el Onzeno, por Don JUAN NUNEZ DE VILLASAN. Ferreras Historia de España, part vii. sect. xiv.   [u] Chron. var. antiq. Rod. SANTII Hist. Hispan. part iv.

serves, with regard to the fact before us, it admits of no doubt at all, that is to say, that two brothers certainly summoned the king, fixed the period of thirty days, on the last of which the king died (5); and from hence, in the old *Spanish* chronicles, he is called Don *Fernando el Emplazado* (6), that is Don *Ferdi-*

nand who was impleaded, or called to answer. In cases of this nature historians cannot be too precise, tho' at the same time this precision does not at all clear the doubt, whether the king died in an ordinary or extraordinary manner, but ascertains the fact only that he was summoned and did die on the thirtieth day (7).

(5) Roderic Santii Hist. Hispan. part iv. c. 10.   (6) Mariana Historia general de España, lib. xv.   (7) Chronica del Rey Don Fernando IV. Roderic Santii Hist. Hispan. part iv. c. 10. Mariana. Mayerne Turquet. Ferreras. P. d'Orleans. Abbé Vayrac.

get the person of the young king into their hands, in which, however, neither prevailed; but, towards the end of the year, the queen-dowager, Donna *Constantia,* dying suddenly, opened a prospect of accommodation; and the troubles that broke out amongst the *Moors* hindered them from reaping any advantage from those which at present distracted the Christians [w].

THE queen, having nothing at heart but the public tranquility, earnestly sollicited the two Infants to consent to some agreement for that purpose, which she at last brought to bear by her influence over Don *Juan;* and it was stipulated between them, that the custody of the king's person, and the care of his education, should be left intirely to the queen, and that the regents should exercise that authority respectively in the places by the votes of which they were chosen [x]. In the spring of the succeeding year, this agreement was solemnly confirmed by an assembly of the states at *Valladolid;* the people of *Avila* resigned the king's person to the care of the queen his grandmother, who carried him to *Toro* [y]. The Infant Don *Pedro* embarked in the civil-war of *Granada,* and behaved himself with great reputation [z]. In the month of *September* there was another assembly of the states at *Carrion,* where they obliged both the regents to give security for so much of the public money as should come to their hands, and for exhibiting, as often as required, a distinct and just account [a]. The Infant Don *Juan* saw, with envy and chagrin, the high reputation the Infant Don *Pedro* had obtained, and therefore hindered his drawing any troops out of the kingdom of *Leon,* and the rest of the provinces under his jurisdiction; which, however, did not prevent his making a campaign with as much, or rather more, honour than he had acquired by the last [b]. These successes were far from lessening the envy of the Infant Don *Juan,* who began to take umbrage at the expence. Don *Pedro* thereupon applied himself to pope *John* the twenty-second, who directed the archbishop of *Toledo,* and two other prelates, to publish the croisade, and to raise a large sum of money upon the clergy, for the support of the war; by which *Ishmael* king of *Granada* found himself so much pressed, that he demanded succours of the king of *Fez,* and, to facilitate the receiving them, put *Algeriza* and several other places into his hands, which gave the Christians much

The Infants Don Juan and DonPhilip assume the administration.

1314.

1315.

1316.

[w] *Chronica general de* España. [x] *Chronica del Rey Don* Alonso *el* Onzeno, *por Don* JUAN NUNEZ DE VILLASAN. [y] *Chron. var. antiq.* [z] *Chronica general de* España. [a] ROD. SANTII *Hist. Hispan. part* iv. *Chronica del Rey Don* Alonso *el* Onzeno. [b] *Chron. var. antiq.*

concern,

concern, and, it is probable, the Infant Don *Juan* some pleasure [c].

1317.
*The pope
sends over
a legate to
compose
the fac-
tious dif-
putes in
Spain.*

THE Infant Don *Juan*, who had hitherto troubled himself
no farther about the war, than to impede it, no sooner perceived that, in virtue of the pope's bull, it produced money,
than he demanded a share of it ; and this naturally excited
fresh disputes.   The queen-regent, however, and the pope's
nuncio, interposed with some effect.   An assembly of the
states being held at *Valladolid*, the two Infants assisted therein, and, to the surprize of most of the nobility, gave
unquestionable tokens of their being thoroughly reconciled :
upon which it was determined, that the pope's bull's being general, the tax upon the clergy should be levied throughout the
whole kingdom, and received by both regents, who, for the
future, should equally concur in the military service, as well as
in the direction of the civil government; which proposition

1318.
being chearfully accepted by the Infant Don *Juan*, he began
to raise forces throughout the whole extent of his government,
which, on the other hand, was highly agreeable to the Infant
Don *Pedro*, who found the *Moors*, in consequence of the supplies they had received from *Barbary*, much superior to any
troops that it was in his power to bring into the field [d].   A
circumstance that might have had very dangerous consequences to the common cause of the Christians.

*Christians
defeated by
the* Moors,
*and both
the In-
fants die
on the
spot.*

IN the spring of the succeeding year, the Infant Don *Pedro*
assembled his troops in the kingdom of *Jaen*, and made himself master of *Piscar*, in which, through some degree of ne-
gligence, the *Moors* had but a very small garrison ; and as
soon as he was informed that Don *Juan*, with the forces under his command, was arrived in *Andalusia*, he marched
without delay to join them at *Baena* [e].   They proceeded from
thence into the kingdom of *Granada* ; and, having taken
Mora, plundered all the country in the neighbourhood of the
capital, till the *Moorish* army, being completely assembled
under the command of *Ozmin*, a very brave and experienced
general, advanced towards them in order of battle, which the
Infants did not decline [f].   The two armies appeared in sight
of each other on the twenty-seventh of *June*.   The Infant
Don *Juan* was on the right, with the forces of *Leon* and *Galicia*, the military orders, and the troops of the archbishops of
Toledo and *Seville*; the Infant Don *Pedro* on the left, with

[c] Chronica general de Espana.   RAINALD.   [d] Chronica
del Rey Don Alonso el Ouzeno.   FERRERAS Historia de Espana,
part vii. sect. xiv.   [e] ROD. SANTII Hist. Hispan. part iv.
Chronica de los Moros de Espana.   [f] Chronica del Rey
Don Alonso el Ouzeno.

the veteran forces that had been accuftomed for fo many years to fight and conquer in thefe wars. The *Moors*, it is faid, made their principal effort againft Don *Juan*, upon a fuppofition that his troops were frefh raifed. But we can fcarce depend on what the *Spanifh* authors fay of this battle, which they acknowlege to have loft, but are unwilling to own that they were beat. They alfo admit that both the Infants died upon the fpot, but affert that neither of them were killed. Don *Juan*, fay they, finding his troops ready to give ground, fent to his collegue for a reinforcement, which the Infant Don *Pedro* immediately ordered ; but, the troops refuſing to obey, he rode from one corps to another, exhorted, menaced, befeeched, till, through paffion and fatigue, he fell dead from his horfe ; the news of which being carried to Don *Juan*, produced the like effect on him ; and upon this the army retired in the beft order they could, leaving, however, the body of Don *Juan* upon the field, which the *Moors*, on their requeft, permitted them to fearch out the next day, in order to its being interred ᵍ (P).

THIS

ᵍ Chronica de los Moros de Efpana. FERRERAS Hiftoria de Efpana, part vii. fect. xiv. MAYERNE TURQUET.

(P) The true circumftances of this battle, and of the manner in which the two infants loft their lives, are not eafy to be collected, more efpecially from the antient hiftorians (1). The moft probable relation, however, is that of *Mariana*'s (2), which the reader may compare with what is faid in the text, and which, therefore, we fhould have placed there, if that author had cited his authorities. He tells us, that when the Infant Don *Juan* joined the army, which was very numerous, fince there were no fewer than nine thoufand horfe in the field, he was refolved to advance into the neighbourhood of *Granada*, in order to attack the whole force

of the *Moors*, who, as he affures us, kept clofe within the place, and could not be provoked to fight on any terms. When the army had continued there all *Saturday* and *Sunday*, without performing any thing of confequence, and without being able to inveft the place, it was found requifite, or rather neceffary, on the *Monday*, to retire ; the Infant Don *Pedro*, who had hitherto commanded the rear, being now in the van, and Don *John*, who had been all along in the front, having the command of the rear. It was then that *Ozmin* marched out of *Granada*, with five thoufand horfe, and a proportionable body of infantry, not with any thoughts of fight-

(1) *Chronica del Rey Don Alonfo el Onzeno.* *Chronica de los Moros de Efpana.*
(2) *Hiftoria general de Efpana, lib. xv.*

ing

This cala-
mity re-
vives the
disputes
and in-
trigues
which had
been paci-
fied.

THIS disaster, for such it certainly was, and the victory plainly on the side of the *Moors*, had most terrible consequences; for the enemy made themselves masters of *Huusca* and several other places, ravaged the country about *Jaen*, and took the town but not the citadel of *Martos*, while those who ought to have been employed in the defence of their country were contending about the regency [h]. The number of these pretenders was greater than at the death of Don *Ferdinand* : of these the chief were the Infant Don *Philip*, uncle to the king, Don *Juan Emanuel*, who had the command of the frontier of *Murcia*, son to the Infant Don *Emanuel* and the Infanta Donna *Constantia* of *Arragon*, Don *Juan*, son to the Infant Don *Juan*, and Don *Ferdinand de la Cerda*, who was just reconciled to the court ; and each of these endeavoured to raise forces, in order to support his claim by

[h] Chronica del Rey Don Alonso el Ouzeno.

ing, or at least of coming to a general engagement, but with a view to harrass the Christians in their retreat. In order to do this the more effectually, *Ozmin* directed his march so, that the army of the Infants was obliged to move all day long without being able to come at any water, and this, as the weather was excessively hot, distressed them to the last degree ; which, when *Ozmin* perceived, and that the two Infants persisted in this precipitate retreat, he caused several small bodies of horse to approach very near, and even to attack them, but with express orders to retire as soon as the Christians put themselves in a posture of defence, by which method having tired them gradually, till they were scarce able to move; at length, when it was evening, he attacked the rear-guard, and threw them speedily into confusion. It was then that the Infant Don *Pedro* faced about, and would have engaged the troops

he commanded to march to their relief ; but they were so excessively fatigued, and withal so extremely provoked against the Infant Don *Juan*, whom they looked upon as the sole author of all their misfortunes, that they did not move ; which threw Don *Pedro* into such a passion as quite overcame his spirits, weakened by long travel, extreme heat, and great thirst, so that he fell from his horse, being either struck with death, or killed by the fall ; which fatal accident was the principal cause of that total route which followed, and that must naturally have been attended with a prodigious loss, and made way for the *Moors* recovering abundance of places that had been taken from them by the Christians but a little before, and which either were not fortified, or, upon the first news of this defeat, were abandoned, as was common enough on all sides in these wars (3).

(3) *Mayerne Turq. et Histoire general de Espana, liv.* xiii.

hint of arms [i]. Another ſingular event happened ſoon after, A. D. which was the marriage and divorce, on the ſame day, of the 1319. prince of *Arragon* and the Infanta *Leonora* ; for as ſoon as the ceremony was over, the prince declared that what he had done was to oblige his father, and to comply with the terms of the treaty between the two crowns : that he took no exception whatever to the princeſs ; but that, nevertheleſs, he was determined not to live with her ; and ſoon after this abrupt parting with his wife, he publicly relinquiſhed all right to the crown, which the ſtates of the kingdom ſecured to his younger brother [k].

THE diſturbances in *Caſtile* increaſed daily, and the calm- *The queen* neſs, moderation, and prudence of the queen, which had *makes uſe* formerly done ſo much, was now leſs effectual ; but how- *of various* ever, what little was done could be attributed to nothing elſe. *expedients* She granted many favours to Donna *Maria Diaz*, the wi- *with very* dow of the Infant Don *Juan*, and to his ſon, who was ſur- *little ſuc-* named the *deformed*, which induced them to aſk more ; ſo *ceſs.* that the queen was at length forced to refuſe, and afford them that pretence which they wanted for being ingrateful. She raiſed Don *Ferdinand de la Cerda* to the poſt of maſter of the king's houſhold ; for which, at the time, he was exceedingly thankful, but deſerted her ſoon after, though he ſtill kept his employment [l]. Don *Juan Emanuel* was ſo deſirous of being regent, that he took the title before it could be given him ; and his aſſuming it induced the Infant Don *Philip* to do the like ; which divided the beſt part of the kingdom, even to the frontiers, where *Cordova* declared for Don *Juan*, and the city of *Seville* for the Infant [m]. Don *Juan* the *deformed* had a 1320. great party in the ſtates of *Caſtile*, aſſembled at *Burgos*, and was for obliging both parties to lay aſide the title before a legal regent was elected, having great hopes that this would make way for himſelf ; but the queen, Donna *Maria*, ac- quainted this aſſembly, that it would be by far more ſafe to confirm thoſe who had taken the title of regents, than to augment the confuſion by declaring a third, to which they ac- quieſced [n].

BUT Don *Juan* the *deformed*, in conjunction with Don *A cardinal* *Ferdinand de la Cerda* and others, entered into a ſolemn con- *ſent from* federacy, and then ſent the queen word, that, if ſhe would *Rome to* not unite with them againſt her ſon the Infant Don *Philip*, *endeavour*

---

[i] ROD. SANTII Hiſt. Hiſpan. part iv. Chronica general de Eſpana. [k] Chron. del Rey Don Alonſo el Ouzeno. ZURIT. Annal Arragon. [l] Chron var. antiq. [m] ROD. SANTII Hiſt. Hiſpan. part iv. Chronica general de Eſpana. [n] Chron. del Rey Don Alonſo el Ouzeno.

they

a new re-
concilia-
tion.

1321.

The queen,
Donna
Maria,
dies, which
greatly
augments
the disturb-
ances in
Castile.

they would join unanimously with Don *Juan Emanuel* against her and the Infant both. The queen was so embarrassed, that she knew not which way to move; she had no great reliance upon Don *Juan Emanuel,* though he had treated her from the beginning with great civility and respect; and though the party of the Infant Don *Philip* was strong, yet by no means strong enough to act against all the rest. At length, to gain time and better advice, she sent the confederates word, that they should have her final answer by the mouth of the cardinal legate, whom the pope had sent on purpose to assist her in quieting these disorders; with which they were little satisfied [o]. In the mean time the Infant Don *Philip* concluded a truce with the king of *Granada,* for that part of *Andalusia* which acknowleged his authority, which left that monarch at liberty to besiege *Lorca.* The inhabitants, having no reason to hope for succours, defended themselves with that obstinacy, which despair only can inspire, and ruined the army of the *Moors* to such a degree, that the king was at length obliged to raise the siege, and retire into his own territories [p].

THE cardinal legate assured the confederates, on the part of the queen, that, since it was absolutely necessary to the peace of the kingdom, she would prevail upon the Infant Don *Philip* to desist from his pretensions to the regency, and, at the same time, the cardinal offered to use his utmost endeavours with Don *Juan Emanuel* to do the same. But when he entered upon this negotiation, he found little probability of success : at length, however, he prevailed, that nobleman being rather wearied than persuaded into a compliance [q]. This point gained, the cardinal called a council at *Valladolid,* to regulate the discipline of the church, which, as we may easily imagine, had suffered exceedingly in those times of confusion; and the cardinal was of opinion, that the clergy could have no weight, while their lives did no credit to their doctrine [r]. This council hindered the assembly of the states from being opened at *Palencia* so early as otherwise it might have been, and it was hardly opened, before the queen, Donna *Maria,* was seized by that distemper which carried her to her grave. She died, as she had lived, with firmness and tranquility of mind; pious without affectation, and supported her dignity by the lustre of her virtues. In her last moments she exhorted the nobility to be careful of the person, and attentive to the education, of their young monarch, and to have a just respect for his sister

[o] Rod. Santii Hist. Hispan. part iv. Rainald.   [p] Chron. de los Moros de Espana. Chron. general de Espana.   [q] Chron. del Rey Don Alonso el Onzeno.   [r] Conc. tom. ii. part ii. col. 1682. Card. d. Aguirra Conc. Hisp. tom. iii. p. 556.

the Infanta Donna *Leonora.* She breathed her last on the first
of *June,* when the affairs of the kingdom were in the utmost
confusion; and in this respect her demise was a favourable
event; for it affected all parties to such a degree, that the cardinal legate prevailed upon them to consent to a cessation of
hostilities for the remainder of the year [*].

A. D.
1322.

As soon as that term was expired, a civil-war broke out in
all quarters, with so much the more fury, as it had been check-
ed by this short restraint; Don *Juan Emanuel* shewed that
his cruelty was equal to his ambition, by the murder of some
persons of distinction in *Castile,* which rendered him universally hated, and gave great advantages to the Infant Don
Philip. To sustain himself after so flagrant an error, he was
constrained to join with Don *Juan* the *deformed* and Don *Ferdinand de la Cerda;* and this confederacy enabled him to bring
an army into the field, sufficient to look the Infant in the face,
but they did not judge it proper to fight [t]. The young king,
Don *Alonso,* seeing nothing but discord, confusion, and bloodshed, amongst his subjects, and his own influence scarce extending farther than his court, wrote to the principal magistrates in all the great cities, to put them in mind that he
should very soon be of age, and that they ought to reflect that
they could then have no other master [u].

*Infant
Don Phi-
lip and
Don Juan
Emanuel
act as re-
gents, and
against
each other.*

1323.

THESE letters had some little effect, and but a little:
however, he no sooner entered his fifteenth year, than he
made choice of a person of integrity and probity to go to the
city of *Seville,* in order to feel the pulse of the inhabitants.
He executed his commission so discreetly, that the citizens declared for the king, who lost no time in going thither. Upon
his arrival, he issued his letters for convoking a general assembly of the states at *Valladolid;* to which both the regents re-
forted, and laid down their authority [w]. This pacific disposition did not last long: Don *Juan Emanuel* quitted the court
in discontent, and projected a marriage between his daughter
and Don *Juan* the *deformed,* that he might attach him effectually to his interests. Those who were about the young
king's person, saw plainly the consequences that would attend
such an alliance, and insinuated to him, that the only way to
prevent it was to espouse Donna *Constantia* himself; and,
upon the first whisper of this, Don *Juan Emanuel* returned to

*Don Alon-
so begins to
take upon
himself the
govern-
ment, as
soon as
turned of
fourteen.*

[*] Chronica del Rey Don Alonso el Ouzeno. ROD. SANTII
Hist. Hispan. part iv. FERRERAS Hist. de Espana, part vii. sect.
xiv. [t] Chronica general de Espana. Chronica del Rey
Don Alonso el Ouzeno. [u] ROD. SANTII Hist. Hispan. p.
iv. [w] Chronica general de Espana. Chronica del Rey
Don Alonso el Ouzeno.

Valladolid,

Valladolid, in the highest transport of loyalty and affection for the king's service [x].

Acts with much severity, in order to recover some appearance of justice.

THE king, Don *Alonso*, when he had once taken possession, was resolved not to pass his days as his father had done, with the title of sovereign, and in a state of subjection. We may be thought to assume this hastily, considering his tender age, and that we ought rather to ascribe it to such as were about his person, and in his favour. However, as the king was the chief actor in all that was done, and as things of that kind could not have been done but by a person capable of contriving them, we take this for a convincing argument, that, young as he was, Don *Alonso* might listen to the advice, but not to the dictates, of his ministers. He formed a small corps of troops, which were constantly about his person, picked men, and thoroughly devoted to his service. With these he pursued a crew of banditti to the castle of *Valdenebra*, strong by situation, though but indifferently fortified. The king summoned the place in form ; but these desperate wretches refused to submit ; upon which he caused it to be attacked, and, being carried by storm, put every one of the malefactors to that kind of death he deserved [y] (Q). He pursued

[x] ROD. SANTII Hist. Hispan. part iv. FERRERAS.   [y] ROD. SANTII Hist. Hispan. part iv. Chronica general de Espana.

(Q) The chief persons about the young king were Don *Garcilasso de la Vega*, who had been lord lieutenant of *Castile*, strongly attached to the Infant Don *Pedro*, and, for that reason, extremely hated by the Infant Don *Juan*, and his son Don *Alvaro Nunez Osorio*, a young cavalier of a good family, much of the king's disposition, the companion of his diversions, and rather his favourite than his minister. We must add to these one *Joseph* a *Jew*, upon whom he chiefly relied in affairs relating to money, as had been long the custom in *Spain*, notwithstanding the clamour of the people, the complaints of the clergy, and the remonstrances of the pope (4). The first of these might possibly give the young king some useful information as to the state of his affairs ; but it is more likely that his grandmother instructed him in the capital maxims of government, and pointed out to him particularly the mischiefs arising from faction, and how much it was his interest to reduce the exorbitant power of those great lords who made no difficulty of opposing the royal authority, and who thought they had a right to oppress the people, while they were so lucky as to have vassals

(4) *Chronica del Rey Don Alonso* xi. *Mariana Historia general de Espana,* lib. xv.

ready

ſued the ſame conduct to the ſame ſort of people, where-ever they could be found, and this, in a few months, cleared all the great roads in *Spain* that had been, for many years, infeſted by theſe banditti, who retired to Don *Juan* the *deformed* for protection [z].

AT *Burgos* the king chaſtiſed ſeverely ſuch as had been guilty of cruelty and oppreſſion during his minority, but at the ſame time took a reſolution of gaining Don *Juan* the *deformed*, if it was practicable, by fair means, though he knew that he had been practiſing with the courts of *Arragon* and *Portugal* to raiſe freſh diſturbances, and had laboured to engage Don *Alonſo de la Cerda* to revive his claim to the crown. He came, at the king's command, to *Burgos*, attended by a ſtrong corps of troops, and by a ſtronger of banditti and murderers, and, in complaiſance to him, the king forbid his ſubjects to moleſt them. He then tried every method, and made all the offers poſſible, to engage Don *Juan* to return to his duty, and to give him proper aſſurances of it; but he refuſed, to which he was principally moved by an advertiſement from Don *Juan Emanuel*, that in becoming the king's father-in-law, he did not ceaſe to be his friend [a]. After parting in this manner, the king viſited the reſt of *Caſtile*, puniſhing malefactors where-ever he came with unrelenting ſeverity. On his arrival at *Toro*, and receiving advice of new intrigues between the two

Cauſes Don Juan *the deformed to be aſſaſſinated, and avows it to the people.*

---

[z] Chron. var. Antiq.   [a] Chronica del Rey Don Alonſo el Ouzeno, par Don JUAN NUNEZ VILLASAN.

---

ready to fight in defence of this extravagant power in their lords, and, which is ſtill more extraordinary, inclined to miſtake this power for liberty. But it is not at all probable that either the queen or his miniſters put any of the great things which he afterwards performed into this young prince's head, becauſe, in fact they wear the appearance of originals, and flow intirely from the ſame ſpirit which the king Don *Alonſo* exerted when he was certainly at liberty to follow the bent of his own diſpoſition (6). This attack of the caſtle of *Valdenebra*, the firſt of his exploits, affords a ſufficient proof of the truth of what we advanced; he was deſirous to eſtabliſh a reputation for juſtice, and to make the firſt inſtances of that ſeverity which he ſaw would be requiſite to reſtore the royal dignity and public peace altogether unexceptionable even to the wiſeſt, univerſally agreeable to the nation in general; and having by this ſtep formed the character, and made an impreſſion, we ſhall ſee him, through his whole reign, purſuing his firſt point, and laying the foundation of his own greatneſs, in the ruin of faction (7).

---

(6) *Ferreras Hiſtoria de Eſpan. tom* vii. *ſect.* xiv *Hiſt. Hiſpan. part* iv. *Frantiſci Taraphæ de reb. Hiſp.*

(7) *Roderic Santii*

Don *Juans,* he ordered his favourite Don *Alvaro Nuguez Oforio,* to engage Don *Juan* the deformed to come to him, under pretence that the king was inclined to give him the Infant Donna *Leonora;* with fome difficulty he was drawn thither, and received by the king, on the laft day of *October,* with all imaginable marks of kindnefs and favour [b]. The next day he was invited to a feaft, but as he entered the hall he was ftabbed, and two gentlemen with him, who, upon the

A. D. firft appearance of violence, had drawn in his defence [c]. The
1325. very next day the king appeared in public, and being feated on a throne of ftate, and having admitted perfons of all ranks into his prefence, he ftood up and told them that Don *Juan* was a traitor, whom the misfortunes of the times had rendered too big for the laws; that his crimes, which he enumerated, together with the proofs, made it neceffary to remove him, which had been done by his orders, to prevent a new civil war; that notwithftanding this, he meant to make the laws the meafure of his authority; and that none of his fubjects had reafon to fear, from what had happened to Don *Juan,* except thofe who meant to imitate his conduct. He proceeded next to feize all his eftates; and having given an equivalent in money to Donna *Maria Diaz,* the mother of the late Don *Juan,* he annexed the lordfhip of *Bifcay* to the crown [d]. Don *Juan Emanuel,* though he had juft gained a confiderable victory over the *Moors,* made a truce with the king of *Granada,* and retired to the caftle of *Chinchilla,* refolved not to truft his perfon in the hands of a prince capable of fuch fentiments and of fuch actions [e].

Archbifhop THE next year the king went to *Segovia,* and enquired into
of Toledo, a feditious tumult that had happened there two years before,
brother to in which fome blood had been fhed, and for which thofe who
Don Juan had been moft culpable were now feverely punifhed. Thence
Emanuel, he proceeded to *Toledo,* hearing the complaints of the people
removed wherever he came, enquiring diligently into the truth of the
from the facts, and punifhing, with equal feverity, fuch as had been
chancery. guilty of bad actions, and fuch as were either weak or wicked
1326. enough to bring falfe accufations [f]. While he refided there, the Infant Don *Philip* died on the fifth of *June,* much regretted by his nephew [g]. Upon certain intelligence that Don

[b] Chronica general de Efpana.   [c] Chronica del Rey Don Alonfo el Ouzeno.   [d] Rod. Santii Hift. Hifpan. part iv. Chronica general de Efpana. Chronica del Rey Don Alonfo el Ouzeno.   [e] Chronica de los Moros de Efpana. Chronica general de Efpana.   [f] Chronica del Rey Don Alonfo el Ouzeno.   [g] Ferreras. Mayerne Turquet.

Juan

Juan Emanuel was endeavouring to raise fresh troubles, the king removed his brother-in-law, the archbishop of *Toledo*, from the post of chancellor, with which that prelate was so offended, that he exchanged his see for that of *Tarragona* [h]. As for Don *Juan Emanuel*, no invitations or promises could induce him to quit his retreat, where he studied how to revive those troubles to which he owed his greatness, and issued his orders on all sides to his dependants, agreeable to these resolutions; of which the king being informed, he gave the government of the marches of the kingdom of *Murcia*, which Don *Juan* inherited from his father, to a nobleman upon whom he could more safely rely [i].

THE next year the king took the field against the *Moors*, with whom Don *Juan Emanuel* had entered into an alliance. The king ordered the admiral of *Castile* to clear the seas, who defeated a strong squadron from *Barbary*, with troops on board; and coming to pay his duty to the king at *Seville*, presented him with 300 slaves. The king laid siege to *Olbera*, and from thence made some expeditions, in which he was not very successful; however, he persisted in his design, and at length reduced that and several other places [k]. On the frontiers of *Murcia* there was an insurrection, excited by Don *Juan*, which had no great effect; however, the king, who would not be insulted without shewing his resentment, immediately gave away all his employments; and, which perhaps was not altogether so justifiable, put his daughter, Donna *Constantia*, who had born the title of queen, under a guard. Don *Juan*, upon this, sent him word that he renounced his allegiance, and that he looked upon himself as at liberty to take what measures he pleased [l]. He then addressed himself to the king of *Arragon*, representing how nearly his daughter was allied in blood to that crown, and how injurious the usage was that she had met with from the king of *Castile*. His complaints were held reasonable, and that monarch promised him all the assistance in his power, in hopes of which, Don *Juan*, with what forces he could collect, began to make inroads into *Castile*, which he wasted with fire and sword [m].

WE have already seen the great troubles and disturbances arising from ambition, resentment, and private interest; but nothing hitherto related comes near to those troubles that

Don Juan Emanuel revolts and renounces his allegiance to king Alonso.

1327.

In consequence of which the

[h] Rod. SANTII Hist. Hispan. part iv. [i] Chron. var. Antiq. [k] Chronica de los Moros de Espana. RODERIC SANTII Hist. Hisp. part iv. [l] Chronica del Rey Don Alonso el Onzeno. [m] Rod. SANTII Hist. Hispan. part iv. ZURIT. Annal Arragon. Chronica general de Espana.

disorders in were excited by Don *Juan Emanuel,* whose turbulent spirit
Castile be- was supported by abilities, that Providence, in compassion to
come much human society, very rarely bestows upon such men. A body
greater of troops from *Arragon* traversed the dominions of *Castile,* in
than ever. order to join him, and marked their route with fire and sword,
wherever they passed. The prior of St. *John,* who was very
closely connected with Don *Juan,* prevailed upon *Toro,*
Zamora, and some other places, to declare against the king,
under pretence that he was wholly governed by Don *Alvaro*
Nunez Osorio, whom the king had lately created count of
Trastamara ⁿ. The king, who had assembled a considerable
army near *Seville,* passed from thence to *Cordova,* where he
caused Don *Juan Ponce de Cabrera* to be beheaded for the
share he had in the sedition raised there, and put some other
persons to death on the same account ; and having found
means to engage the court of *Arragon,* where Don *Alonso* had
lately mounted the throne, to withdraw his countenance from
Don *Juan,* he caused *Escalona* to be invested, which was
one of the strongest places in Don *Juan's* possession °. In the
mean time, *Garcilasso de la Vega,* whom he had promoted to
the dignity of chancellor, being at *Soria* in *Castile,* and having
declared that he had the king's orders to provide, in the most
effectual manner, for the security of that kingdom, some secret
friends of Don *Juan* whispered it about, that he had private
orders to put some persons of distinction to death.   This gave
rise to a conspiracy, in consequence of which, the chancellor
was stabbed upon his knees at church, with twenty-four persons more, amongst whom were his son, and several of high
rank ᵖ. The king, having concluded a marriage with Donna
Maria, Infanta of *Portugal,* which he intended to celebrate
as soon as the campaign was over, sent for Donna *Leonora* his
sister from *Valladolid,* when, through the arts of Don *Juan,*
a rumour being spread that the king intended to marry her to
his favourite the count of *Trastamara,* the people revolted,
upon which the king was obliged to raise the siege of *Esca-*
lona, to march thither. The inhabitants of *Valladolid* shut
their gates, and held out a siege, which the king carried on
with such vigour, that the town must infallibly have been
taken, if the same arts that produced their revolt had not
raised a sedition in the king's camp, where several of the prin-

---

ⁿ Chronica del Rey Don Alonso el Ouzeno.   Zurit. Annal.
Arragon. Emanuel de Faria y Sousa.   ° Zurit. Annal.
Arragon. Chron. general de Espana. Ferreras Historia de
Espana, p. vii. sec. xiv.   ᵖ Chronica del Rey Don Alonso el
Ouzeno, &c.

cipal nobility told him plainly, that the only way to put an end to these disturbances was to disgrace the count Don *Alvaro*, which was presently done [q]. The count thereupon retired to his castle of *Belbar*, where he commenced rebel in his turn; but Don *Juan Ramirez*, with the king's consent, pretended to desert to him, and being kindly received by the count, took an opportunity to stab him; this put an end to all the insurrections in *Castile*: the king, towards the close of the year, celebrated his marriage with the Infanta of *Portugal*, and gave his sister, Donna *Eleonora*, in marriage to Don *Alonso*, king of *Arragon*; and thus an end was put to all troubles for the present [r].

A. D. 1328.

IN the beginning of the next year, the king having held an assembly of the states at *Burgos*, and conducted his sister, Donna *Leonora*, to the frontiers of *Arragon*, he concluded an alliance, offensive and defensive, with the monarch of that country, and with the king of *Portugal*, in order to prosecute the war against the *Moors* with effect [s]. The conferences for this purpose being over, the king went to *Soria*, where he made a strict inquisition into the murder of *Garcilasso de la Vega*, punished such of the principal persons with death as could be found, and seized the estates and effects of such as had concerted their security by a quick retreat [t]. Don *Juan Emanuel* in the mean time had projected several marriages, by the means of which he proposed to aggrandize Don *Ferdinand de la Cerda*, Don *Juan de Lara*, and to bind them to his party, of which, though the king had timely information, yet he made fresh offers to that potent lord, to engage him to return to his duty, and even went so far as to offer him to set his daughter at liberty, and to pay him a considerable sum of money, if, instead of disturbing the peace of his country, he would concur in making war against the *Moors* [u].

The king labours to bring Don JuanEmanuel back to his duty, but without effect.

1329.

DON *Alonso*, after conferring once more with the king of *Portugal*, proceeded to the frontiers, and finding his forces in excellent order, began the operations of the campaign with the siege of *Tebe*. *Ozmin*, who commanded the *Moorish* army, practised various stratagems in order to divide the *Christian* troops, but to no purpose: however, he encouraged the besieged to make a gallant defence, afforded them frequent succours, and spun out the campaign to the first of *August*, when

Makes a campaign against the Moors, and falls into an intrigue with Don-

[q] Chronica general de Espana. EMANUEL DE FARIA Y SOUSA. [r] ROD. SANTII Hist. Hispan. part iv. ZURIT. Annal Arragon. EMANUEL DE FARIA Y SOUSA. [s] ZURIT. Annal Arragon. Chronica del Rey Don Alonso el Onzeno, &c. EMANUEL DE FARIA Y SOUSA. [t] Chron. var. Antiq. [u] ROD. SANTII Hist. Hispan. part iv. Chronica general de Espana.

the place surrendered, and the *Moors* abandoned several little towns and castles in the neighbourhood ᵛ. Upon the king's return to *Seville*, he entered into an amour with Donna *Leonora de Guzman*, a lady of high quality, and great endowments of mind, by whom he had several children (R). There he received

ᵛ EMANUEL DE FARIA Y SOUSA. Chronica de los Moros de España.

(R) We are constrained, in order to render the current of our relation more intelligible, to enter a little into the secret history of this reign, which, tho' we are always unwilling to do, yet is sometimes requisite to be done. By comparing the *Spanish* and *Portuguese* historians one might be tempted to affirm that Don *Alonso* of *Castile* had at this time no less than three wives, or, to speak with propriety, who were, or whom he persuaded to think themselves such. The first was Donna *Maria* of *Portugal*, whom he married rather from a principle of policy than affection, and with whom he lived but indifferently, reproaching her with the want of issue, though they had not been long married, and which, some writers tell us, she took pains to wipe away (5). She was a prudent woman, and knew how to dissemble more passions than one. The second was Donna *Leonora de Guzman*, the daughter of Don *Pedro Nunez de Guzman*, and the widow of Don *Juan de Velasco*, lately deceased: her riches and her wit set off to great advantage a person so fine,

that she was esteemed the greatest beauty in *Spain*. The king, from the time he became enamoured of her, preserved no decency in his family or with the world, but behaved towards her in public as if she had been his queen, while Donna *Maria* had as little state about her as if she had been his mistress (6). The third was Donna *Constantia*, the daughter of Don *Juan Emanuel*, to whom the king had been contracted, and with whom he continued to hold a private correspondence by letters, in which he told her that she was the first mistress of his affections, and gave her hopes that, by the help of a divorce, she might one day become the partner of his bed and throne (7). Each had their political intrigues. The prior of St. *John*, who had excited the great revolt in *Castile*, was the queen's chancellor; and thro' him she corresponded with Don *Juan Emanuel* and Don *Juan de Lara*, in favour of whom she brought the king her father into a war with the king her husband (8). Donna *Leonora* had also a correspondence with Don *Juan Emanuel*, and with other great

(5) *Emanuel de Faria y Sousa, Epitome de las Historias Portuguesas, lib.* iii. *Mayerne Turquet Histoire general d'Espagne, lib.* xiv.   (6) *Chronica del Rey Don Alonso* XI. *Mariana, lib.* xv.   (7) *Faria y Sousa, Epitome de las Historias Portuguesas, lib.* iii. *Faria y Sousa. Ferreras.*   (8) *Mariana. Mayerne Turquet.*

ceived embassadors from the king of *Granada*, who offered to become his vassal, and to pay an annual tribute of twelve thousand pieces of gold, which was accepted, chiefly with a view of depriving Don *Juan Emanuel* of the protection of this prince [x].

THE king returning from *Seville* into *Castile*, was met in his passage, very unexpectedly, by Don *Alonso de la Cerda*, who told him, that being heartily weary of the life he had hitherto led, he was very desirous of passing the remainder of his days in peace; and that, forgetting past disputes, he hoped the monarch of *Castile* would consider him as a prince of his blood, and as his faithful subject. The king received him with the utmost affection, gave him an ample establishment, and assured him he might depend upon his favour and protection [y]. At his coronation the same year, at *Burgos*, Don *Alonso de la Cerda* assisted, and did him homage; and the feasts which attended this ceremony, were the most magnificent that ever had been seen in *Castile* [z]. Don *Juan Emanuel*, who for two years past had affected to live in such a manner as to give the king no umbrage, entered now into a treaty with Donna *Leonora de Guzman*, and offered, if she could prevail upon the king to repudiate the Infanta of *Portugal*, and to marry her, he would return to court, and depend upon her protection; but that lady generously answered, that if he would return to his duty, he might depend upon her favour; but that she did not either hope or desire to espouse the king [a]. About the same time, by a stroke of that policy which was

margin notes: 1330. *Receives Don Alonso de la Cerda into favour, and grants him an establishment.*

---

[x] Chronica del Rey Don Alonso el Ouzeno. Chronica de los Moros de Espana.   [y] ROD. SANTII Hist. Hispan. part iv. Chronica del Rey Don Alonso el Ouzeno.   [z] MARIANA. MAYERNE TURQUET. FERRERAS.   [a] Chron. var. Antiq.

---

persons about the court, who knew that to gain her was the only way to gain the king's favour. Donna *Constantia*, by her father's direction, managed a correspondence with the king with great dignity and decency; acknowleged that her hopes were once fixed upon him, reproached him with the ill usage of his queen; and intimated, that his mistress had other gallants (9). In a word, Donna *Leonora* knew how to govern the king, and was proud of it. The queen was able to govern herself, and, by doing so, triumphed in the end. Donna *Constantia*, by her address, maintained an interest in the king, till, by his consent, she espoused the prince of *Portugal*, of which country she became afterwards queen.

(9) *Faria y Sousa, Epitome de las Historias Portuguesas, lib.* iii.

natural to him, he cauſed it to be inſinuated to the king of *Portugal*, that the queen, his daughter, was very miſerable, that Donna *Leonora de Guzman* was in poſſeſſion of the king's affections, and that his own daughter, Donna *Conſtantia*, was a better match for the prince of *Portugal*, than the king's niece Donna *Blanca*, daughter to the Infant *Pedro*, who had many infirmities [b].

Inſtitutes the order of the Band, which is ſince grown into diſuſe.　THE king, who had intelligence of theſe proceedings, inſtituted a new order of knighthood, with a political view of attaching thoſe, upon whom it was conferred, in a more particular manner to his perſon, which, from the knights wearing a ribbon over their right ſhoulder, was ſtiled the order of the band. At firſt it was in very high eſteem, but by degrees grew into diſuſe [c]. The king of *Granada* made this year a voyage to *Africa*, in order to demand aſſiſtance from *Abul Aſſan*, king of *Morocco*, under pretence that Don *Alonſo* of *Caſtile* had nothing ſo much at heart as the utter extirpation of the *Mohammedans* in *Spain*, and having obtained from him the promiſe of powerful ſuccours, and a preſent ſupply of 7000 horſe, he returned very well ſatisfied into his own dominions, where he no ſooner arrived, than he renewed his intrigues with Don *Juan Emanuel*; who was employed in raiſing a new citadel at *Ucles*. He had engaged Don *Juan Nugnez de Lara*, and ſeveral other perſons of great diſtinction, in a confederacy; and it was agreed that they would be all ready to act at a convenient time [d]. The queen, Donna *Maria*, was brought to-bed of the Infant Don *Ferdinand*, and ſoon after Donna *Leonora Guzman* was delivered of Don *Sancho*, to whom the king gave the lordſhip of *Le Deſma* [e].

Abul-Malic, with an army, advances to Gibraltar, and forms the ſiege.　THE reinforcement from *Africa* arrived on board a fleet of tranſports from *Morocco* at *Algeriza*, under the command of *Abul Malic*, the ſon of *Abul Aſſan*; the Chriſtian fleet under the command of Don *Alonſo Tenorio*, having put to ſea with an intention to hinder them from debarking, but came too late [f]. The firſt ſervice the *African* troops performed, was beſieging *Gibraltar*, in which commanded Don *Vaſco Perez de Meyra*. Don *Alonſo* of *Caſtile*, upon advice of this ſiege, aſſembled a powerful army in order to relieve it, and in his march had a conference with Don *Juan Emanuel* and Don *Juan de Lara*, who pretended an inclination to ſubmit

[b] EMANUEL DE FARIA Y SOUSA. Chronica general de Eſpana. ROD. SANTII Hiſt. Hiſpan. part iv. [c] MARIANA. FERRERAS. [d] Chronica del Rey Don Alonſo el Ouzeno. Chronica de los Moros de Eſpana. [e] ROD. SANTII Hiſt. Hiſpan. part iv. MARIANA. FERRERAS. [f] Chronica del Rey Don Alonſo el Ouzeno. Chronica de los Moros de Eſpana.

themſelves,

themselves, and invited the king to dine with them in their castle of *Becerril*, which he accepted, and they promised to dine with him the next day, but, either through fear or falsehood, they broke their words, and the treaty came to nothing [g]. Not long after this, Don *Juan Emanuel* sent the king word, that if he would order his arrears to be paid, he would make a powerful diversion through the kingdom of *Jaen*, and prevent the kingdom of *Granada* from joining *Abul-Malic*. Don *Alonso*, like a great prince, complied with his demand; Don *Juan Emanuel* behaved also like himself, that is, he took the money, and broke his word [h]. The king, however, marched to the relief of *Gibraltar*, but when he was within sight of the place, he was informed that the governor had betrayed it.

Don *Alonso* continued to advance, invested that place and besieged it, but for want of provisions was forced to raise the siege; however, a supply arriving just as the army broke up, the king returned thither again [i]. The king of *Granada* having joined *Abul Malic*, marched with a numerous army to raise the siege. Don *Alonso*, as became a prudent officer, remained within his entrenchments, and could not be drawn out to fight. All his caution, however, proved ineffectual; for Don *Juan Emanuel*, Don *Juan de Lara*, and Don *Juan Alonso de Haro*, with the very money that the king had given them, had raised forces, and ravaged *Castile* in such a manner, that the king was obliged to conclude a truce with the *Moors*, and to march to the relief of his subjects; another motive which determined him to this measure, was the intelligence he had received, that several lords in the kingdom of *Jaen* were on the point of joining the *Moors*, for which he caused one of their heads to be struck off, when he arrived in those parts; but the rest executed their purpose, and fled to *Granada* [k]. The king's affairs, however, were in so perplexed a situation, that the king of *Morocco*, refusing to ratify the truce, unless the tribute of the king of *Granada* was remitted, he was obliged to comply, his subjects in *Castile* being so much distressed by the rebels, that they dispatched express upon express to hasten the king's march to their assistance, which, without doubt, afflicted him extremely, after all the pains he had taken to recover these noblemen to his service [l].

Don Juan Emanuel, and other malecontents, raise new troubles in the kingdom.
1333.

---

[g] Chronica del Rey Don Alonfo el Ouzeno. Rod. Santii Hist. Hispan. part iv. Ferreras.   [h] Chron. var. Antiq. [i] Chronica de los Moros de Espana.   [k] Chronica del Rey Don Alonfo el Ouzeno.   [l] Rod. Santii Hist. Hispan. Chronica general de Espana. Chronica de los Moros de Espana.

*The king
endea-
vours to
extinguish
factions by
extraordi-
nary acts
of severi-
ty.*
·But though the king was very impatient, and did all that
was in his power to comply with the requests of his subjects,
yet it was Lent before he was able to leave *Seville*. When he
came to *Ciudad Real*, a gentleman brought him a letter from
Don *Juan de Lara*, in which he told him that he quitted his
service for ever, and renounced his allegiance : the king having
read this epistle, said it came a little too late, that he wasted
his territories, and oppressed his people while he was yet in
his service, and his subject ; and therefore, said he, take
this honest gentleman, who has been in all his secrets, and
made no scruple of sharing in his rebellion, and strike off his
hands and feet, and then his head [m]. This struck a great
terror, and made people less inclined to have any correspondence with malecontents. The king prosecuted the war
against Don *Juan de Lara* with incredible diligence, and
hunted him very closely ; but not being able to take him, he
went into *Biscay*, which country he entirely reduced [n]. Upon
his return to *Burgos*, a man was seized with letters from Don
Juan Alonfo de Haro, to Don *Juan Emanuel* and Don *Juan
de Lara*, in which he pressed them not to submit to the king,
but to do him all the mischief they could, assuring them of
succours from the viceroy of *Navarre*. The king marched
immediately, and surprized Don *Juan de Haro* in his castle,
whom, after he had reproached with his perfidious behaviour,
he ordered to be put to death ; but he gave his lands to his
two brothers [o].

*His con-
duct is, in
some mea-
sure justi-
fied by
events.*
·After all this, Don *Juan de Lara* wrote to some persons near the king, that perceiving he was marked for destruction, he was desirous of knowing whether the king was
inexorable or not ; and if not, he was now ready to submit to
such terms as he should prescribe. The king sent him word to
render the two castles he then besieged, to renounce all title
to *Biscay*, and to put some of his best places into his hands
as pledges for his fidelity, with all which he immediately complied ; notwithstanding which, the king refused to see him [p].
The king having summoned the castle of *Rojas*, in which
Diego Gilles commanded for *Lopez Diaz*, he returned no other
answer than a shower of arrows and stones, though the persons were the king's immediate servants, After a short siege,
he desired leave to march out, which was given him ; but as

1334.

---

[m] Chronica del Rey Don Alonfo el Ouzeno.   [n] Chronica
general de Efpana.   Rod. Santii Hift. Hifpan. part iv.
[o] Chronica del Rey Don Alonfo el Ouzeno.   Mayerne Turquet. Ferreras.   [p] Chronica del Rey Don Alonfo el
Ouzeno.

soon as he and his garrison were in the field, the king caused him to be arrested, brought them to a court martial, by which the governor and officers were condemned to death. This severity had one good effect, for no gentleman would afterwards charge himself with the custody of a castle, without inserting, in the oath of fidelity to his lord, that he would defend it against all persons whatever, the king only excepted [q].

AT the opening of the ensuing year, Don *Juan Emanuel* addressed himself to the king, with an offer of entire submission, and informed him that Don *Pedro*, prince of *Portugal*, finding it impossible to marry his niece Donna *Blanca*, who was paralytic, was inclined to espouse his daughter Donna *Constantia*, if the king would be pleased to give his consent. Don *Alonso* answered, that, as to the first point, he was content to pardon all that was passed, if Don *Juan* would behave as a good subject for the time to come; and that as to the latter, he would consider of it, and give him an answer [r]. Soon after came embassadors from the crown of *Portugal* upon the same subject; and the king, Don *Alonso*, having sent persons into that kingdom to examine into the matter of fact, upon their report that Donna *Blanca* was really afflicted with the palsy, he declared that he would not oppose the marriage of the prince Don *Pedro* with Donna *Constantia*, in hopes that this condescension would entirely restore the tranquility of his dominions; and to demonstrate how welcome this would be to him, he celebrated *Whitsuntide* at *Valladolid*, with public feasts and a carousal, to which all the nobility were invited, and in which himself and his knights of the band opposed all comers.

Upon a short interval of quiet the king labours to divert his nobles with feasts.

1335.

BUT he had scarce begun to please himself with these hopes, than they were dissipated by an accident he could not foresee; for *Henry de Solis*, viceroy of *Navarre*, published a manifesto, in which he charged the *Castilians* with having injured the subjects of *Navarre* on the frontiers, and that he meant to do himself justice by arms. Don *Alonso* was so desirous of quiet, that he offered any satisfaction, but the viceroy would accept of none; and having a very powerful army, made an irruption into *Castile*, on the side of *Tudela*, wasting every thing before him with fire and sword [s]. Don *Alonso* assembled a body of troops for the defence of his dominions, and appointed Don *Juan de Lara* commander in chief, which

Viceroy of Navarre makes war on Castile, without cause or caution.

[q] Chron. var. Antiq.   [r] EMANUEL DE FARIA Y SOUSA. Chronica general de España. ROD. SANTII Hist. Hispan. part iv. [s] Chronica del Rey Don Alonso el Onzeno. MARIANA. MAYERNE TURQUET. FERRERAS.

he

he refufed, and the king thereupon declared *Martin Fernandez Portocarrero* mafter of his houfhold general [t]. Some of the principal nobility reprefented to the king, that he was by no means of a rank fit to command them; but that, to fhew how fenfible they were of the folly of private difputes, in a time of public danger, they thanked him for giving this opportunity of fhewing their obedience, as he had done his fagacity in appointing one of the beft officers in *Caftile* to his command.

Is feverely beaten, and forced to make peace on worfe terms than be might bave bad without a war.

MARTIN FERNANDEZ marched with his forces, and the viceroy of *Navarre* fent him a haughty meffage, that he intended the next day to reduce *Alfaro*, and plunder the country in the neighbourhood. *Martin Fernandez* marched towards the abby of *Futero*, which they had already taken, and the viceroy thereupon difpatched his cavalry, to cover his new conqueft. The viceroy feeming to perfift in his firft defign, drew out his whole army to fupport his horfe, of which *Martin Fernandez* having received intelligence, profecuted his march with great vigour, in order to give them battle. The difpute was fharp, but fhort, the army of *Navarre* being routed with great flaughter. He afterwards intercepted their cavalry in their retreat towards *Tudela*, and cut them off entirely, which put an end to the operations of the war, which was terminated afterwards by a peace, under the mediation of the crown of *France* [u]. At this time the court of *Caftile* appeared with unufual fplendour from the arrival of two great embaffies, one from the emperor of *Morocco*, and the other from *Edward* the third, king of *England*, whom Don *Alonfo* treated with great dignity and refpect [w]. At the clofe of the year, a council was held at *Salamanca*, in which fixteen canons were made, the great point in view being to extinguifh the cuftom which ftill prevailed amongft the *Spanifh* clergy of marrying, which, to render it odious, the court of *Rome* confounded, with keeping concubines [x].

The ftates declare againft Don Juan Emanuel and Don

WHEN the king Don *Alonfo* had made fuch difpofitions for war againft the *Moors*, who he had certain intelligence were meditating a general confederacy againft him, he difcovered a new contrivance for difturbing the peace of his people amongft his own nobility. Don *Juan Emanuel* and Don *Juan de Lara* were at the head of this; and what equally

[t] Hiftoire de Royaume de Navarre. ROD. SANTII Hift. Hifp. part iv. Chronica general de Efpana. [u] Chronica del Rey Don Alonfo el Ouzeno. Hiftoire de Royaume de Navarre. P. DANIEL Hiftoire de France. [w] ROD. SANTII Hift. Hifpan. Chronica general de Efpana. FERRERAS. [x] Card. D'AGUIRRE Conc. Hifp. tom. iii. p. 584.

amazed

amazed and chagrined him, Don *Pedro Fernandez de Castro*, John Nu-
and Don *Juan Alonso de Albuquerque*, for whom he had nez de La-
always testified the highest esteem, were engaged with them, ra, *and*
the whole confederacy being formed under the protection of *proscribe*
the king of *Portugal* y. Upon this discovery, he sent for *them.*
Don *Pedro de Castro*, who, though he was in one of his own
castles, made no scruple of obeying his order. He expostulated the matter with him freely; assured him that he was so
sensible of his past services, that having no other way to reward him, he had determined to marry his son the Infant
Don *Henry*, to his daughter; and that, if he had at any time
given him offence, he was willing to give him what satisfaction he pleased. Don *Pedro*, afflicted and ashamed, freely
confessed his fault, and promised to reclaim Don *Juan de Albuquerque*, which, when he had performed, the king called
together an assembly of the states, in which he fairly laid
before them his condition and their own, with the several
overtures he had made to Don *Juan Emanuel*, and Don *Juan
de Lara*. The states immediately voted them both traitors,
gave him five subsidies, and desired him to prosecute the war
against them both, to their utter destruction ᶻ.

Don *Juan Nunez de Lara* made several propositions, very *After a*
plausible in their nature, to prevent the storm which he saw *long siege*
ready to fall upon him, but the king rejected them all. In the *the latter*
month of *June*, the king took the field and invested *Lerma*, *surrenders*
in which Don *Juan de Lara* was with a numerous garrison *to the king,*
excellently well provided, and fortifications for those times in *is pardoned*
very good condition. Don *Juan Emanuel* made various at- *and pre-*
tempts to succour and relieve him, but was so closely pursued *ferred.*
by the king, whenever he was in the field, that he was at
length forced to consult his own safety, and retire into *Arragon*, having more than once very narrowly escaped falling into
the king's hands ᵃ; when the siege had continued for several
months, and the place was in apparent danger, the secret
friends of Don *Juan de Lara* practised every art to extricate
him from his difficulties. The king of *Portugal* claimed him
as his subject and vassal. Don *Alonso* answered he might be
so; but he was also his rebel, and as such he would punish
him. This produced a war between the two crowns, which,
however, could not oblige the king to raise the siege ᵇ.

ʸ Chronica del Rey Don Alonso el Ouzeno. Emanuel de
Faria y Sousa. ᶻ Rod. Santii Hist. Hispan. Paria
y Sousa. Chron. general de Espana. ᵃ Chronica del
Rey Don Alonso el Ouzeno. Zurit. Annal Arragon. Faria
y Sousa. ᵇ Chronica del Rey Don Alonso el Ouzeno.
Faria y Sousa.

The

The queen Donna *Maria* was then prevailed upon to go to the camp, and to interpose in his favour, but that also was without effect. At length, when it was towards *Christmas*, his escape was contrived through a common sewer, of which the king, having intelligence, surprized his friends at the mouth of it, and it was with some difficulty that he got back. This humbled him to such a degree, that he sent to the king to know what terms he would be pleased to prescribe. Don *Alonso* answered, that he would grant him and his people their lives, except three persons who had deserted from his camp [c]. Don *Juan*, having first provided for the escape of these three men, named a day for delivering the place; and though the king sent him a horse, yet he chose to meet him on foot, kissed his hand with great respect, and assured him that he would be from that moment his most faithful servant. The king ordered the fortification of *Lerma* to be demolished, carried Don *Juan* with him to *Valladolid*, restored him to his post of standard bearer of *Castile*, and made him several considerable presents; which had such an effect, that, during the remainder of his life, he was the most steady and the most affectionate servant the king had [d].

A truce with diffi-culty con-cluded be-tween the crowns of Castile and Portugal.
1337.

THE new year brought with it new disturbances. Don *Pedro*, who had succeeded his father Don *Alonso*, as king of *Arragon*, was upon extreme bad terms with his mother-in-law Donna *Leonora*, sister to the king of *Castile*, which induced him to favour Don *Juan Emanuel*; and, on the other hand, produced a civil war in his own dominions, several great lords declaring on the side of the queen dowager; but at length, through the interposition of Don *Juan de Lara*, these disputes were compromised [e]. The mother of that lord, who had a very great interest with the king, presumed upon it so far, as to deliver him a letter from Don *Juan Emanuel*, in which he made great professions of penitence, and of inclinations to return to the king's service: to which Don *Alonso* answered, it was entirely in his own power, and that whenever he was disposed to give him proofs of his obedience, he might depend upon his favour. Upon which Don *Juan Emanuel* submitted [f]. In regard to *Portugal*, the war went on; the fleet of *Castile* was victorious by sea, and the king rejected all terms of accommodation, notwithstanding the pope inter-

[c] Chronica general de Espana. ROD. SANTII Hist. Hispan. part iv. FARIA Y SOUSA.   [d] Chronica del Rey Don Alonso el Ouzeno. MARIANA. MAYERNE TURQUET. FERRERAS.
[e] ZURIT. Annal Arragon. Chronica del Rey Don Alonso el Ou-zeno.   [f] Chronica general de Espana. MARIANA. FER-RERAS.

posed; at length, however, the legate putting the king in mind that every step he took to gratify his resentment was destructive of his interest, since it was very well known that the *Moors* intended to attack them both, he was at length prevailed upon to listen to some accommodation with his father-in-law; but, however, the negotiation was not perfected till the beginning of the year following [g].

THE repeated advices he received from *Barbary*, left him no room to doubt that he should quickly find himself exposed to as great danger from the Infidels, as any that his ancestors had overcome. For the king of *Morocco*, *Jacob Abul-Assan* was providing a prodigious force by land and sea, and having reduced the little kingdoms of *Tunis* and *Tremecen*, was to the full as formidable as any of his predecessors. The king Don *Alonso* ratified the truce with *Portugal*, and perhaps had done it more readily, but that he was willing to make that monarch believe that he did not readily forgive any assistance given to his malecontents [h]. He afterwards held an assembly of the states of *Castile*, in which some excellent laws were made. Amongst the rest it was provided, that all fortresses should be considered as belonging of right to the king; and that none should presume to hold them against him; that no rank whatever should exempt men from the laws, or give them a title to do themselves justice; and that all persons should conform themselves in their garb and way of living to the condition of life they were in, so that none might be made poor by affecting a false shew of riches. These were published in the cathedral church of *Burgos*; for, in those rude days, they never expected that men should obey laws, unless they knew them [i].

Excellent laws made for the reformation of manners in the dominions of Castile.

THE king went from *Burgos* to the frontiers of *Arragon*, to confer with his sister the queen dowager, with whom he found Don *Juan de Lara*, and his mother. After this interview was over, Don *Juan* proposed to the king going to the castle of *Garcia-Munoz*, where he assured him that Don *Juan Emanuel* had given orders that he should be received with the utmost respect, and the place put into his hands. The king went and took possession of it, and upon his arrival at *Cuenca*, Don *Juan* himself came to pay his duty, and was so kindly and frankly received by the king, that he could not forbear telling him, that it should be the business of his life to remem-

Don Juan Emanuel submits, and is reconciled to the king Don Alonso.

[g] Chronica del Rey Don Alonso el Ouzeno. FARIA Y SOUSA. RAINALD. P. DANIEL Histoire de France. FERRERAS. [h] FARIA Y SOUSA. BRANDAON. Chronica general de Espana. ROD. SANTII Hist. Hispan. part iv. [i] Chronica del Rey Don Alonso el Ouzeno.

ber

ber the offences he had given him, and his study to make his majesty forget them. The king took this so well, that he confided to him the care of his interests at the court of *Arragon*, and sent him thither to manage them, which he did with great ability and equal integrity [k]. Pope *Benedict* the twelfth wrote about this time to the king, to thank him for the respect paid to his interposition in the affair of *Portugal*, and to exhort him to part with Donna *Leonora de Guzman*, and to lead a life worthy of a Christian prince [l].

A campaign against the Moors, *in which the king is successful and Abul-Malic slain.*

THE insinuations of Don *Juan Emanuel* had such an influence over the king of *Arragon*, that not content with accommodating every thing to the satisfaction of his mother-in-law, he resolved to enter into a close alliance with the king of *Castile*, as the only means for securing both kingdoms against the invasion of the *Moors*, which appeared every day more formidable; and having sent an embassador for that purpose, a treaty offensive and defensive was concluded, from which both princes promised not to depart, or to make any truce with the Infidels, but in conjunction [m]. Don *Alonso* proceeded then to the frontiers, and at *Seville* conferred the honour of knighthood on Don *Juan de Lara*, with his own hand [n]. He entered the enemy's territories with a numerous and complete army, and ravaged the country about *Ronda*, till, through want of provisions, they found themselves obliged to retire, which the *Moors* observing, thought it a very favourable opportunity to strike one of their great blows. Accordingly they issued out of the place with great fury, and fell upon the rear of the Christian army. Don *Juan Emanuel*, Don *Juan de Lara*, and the grand master of the order of St. *James*, who commanded there, repressed them but faintly, and restrained the ardour of the soldiers for some time; till at length, being at a great distance from the place, those three officers having conferred together, faced about at once, and charged the *Moors* so vigorously, that they fled to an adjacent mountain, which was of very difficult ascent. The *Castilian* cavalry, however, dismounted, and forced their passage up, though with difficulty and loss; but of this numerous detachment of the *Moors*, there did not escape a single man [o]. In the autumn, Don *Alonso de Guzman*, grand master of the order of St. *James*, beat the king of *Granada* before *Silos*. *Abul-*

[k] ZURIT. Annal Arragon. Chronica general de España. ROD. SANTII Hist. Hispan. part iv. [l] RAINALD. Epist. Benedict XII. [m] Chronica del Rey Don Alonso el Ouzeno. ZURIT. Annal Arragon. [n] ROD. SANTII Hist. Hispan. part iv. FERRERAS. [o] Chronica del Rey Don Alonso el Ouzeno. Chron. de los Moros de España. MARIANA. MAYERNE TURQUET. FERRERAS. FARIA Y SOUSA.

Malic;

Malic, with the army of *Morocco,* was still more unfortunate, for he was defeated by Don *Alonso's* generals, and killed in his retreat[p]. This year would have ended happily, if the grand master of the order of St. *James,* resenting too hastily some ill usage from Donna *Leonora de Guzman,* had not revolted against the king, notwithstanding that he used all possible means to bring him back to his duty, which he renounced so entirely, as when the king approached the walls of the fortress where he was, in order to expostulate with him, he caused him to be repulsed with arrows and stones, some of which fell on his shield, and others wounded his horse, for which, when it was reduced, the king caused him to be put to death[q].

A. D. 1339.

ABUL-ASSAN, king of *Morocco,* not at all discouraged by the defeats of the preceding year, or the loss of his son, prosecuted the war with a degree of fury, that sufficiently spoke his resentment. He assembled a great army, a vast quantity of military stores and provisions, and a fleet of 200 sail, exclusive of thirty gallies. Don *Alonso* did all that was possible to provide against the effects of this invasion, and, if possible, to prevent it; for, by the rudeness of the winter, he lost several of his ships, and by the unwholsomeness of the season, a great number of men, which put it out of the power of the admiral to hinder, with six ships and twenty seven gallies, the *Moors* from passing. Donna *Elvira,* the wife of the admiral, hearing what weak and improper judges said, wrote to her husband, that his fidelity was suspected, and that it was supposed he had received a vast sum of money to let the *Moors* pass; upon which the admiral, having received a reinforcement of six gallies, sailed with so inconsiderable a strength, and to wipe off this imaginary stain, sacrificed himself and the whole fleet, five gallies only excepted[r]. The king Don *Alonso* provided *Tarifa* for a long siege, and was forced to apply to the king of *Portugal,* his father-in-law, for assistance by sea; and in order to obtain it, had recourse to the queen Donna *Maria,* who wrote in the most pressing terms to the king her father, and sent it by the dean of *Toledo,* her chancellor; upon which he sent the fleet of *Portugal* to *Seville.*

The king of Morocco arms in order to revenge his son's death, and defeats the Castile fleet.

DON *Alonso* dispatched also a minister to *Genoa,* and Don *Juan Martinez* to expostulate with the king of *Arragon,* for not sending the vessels he had promised to his fleet. The king

A peace and alliance con-

[p] Chronica del Rey Don Alonso el Ouzeno. Chronica de los Moros de España. [q] MARIANA. FERRERAS. [r] Chronica general de España. Chronica del Rey Don Alonso el Ouzeno. Chronica de los Moros de España.

cluded be- anſwered plainly, that it was for want of money to equip
tween the them, otherwiſe he had ten gallies which he would have ſent.
crowns of Don *Juan* advanced the money neceſſary, and inſtead of ten,
Caſtile and the king ſent twelve [e]. The *Genoeſe* alſo ſold him their
Portugal. aſſiſtance, but ſold it dear. While the king was employed
in theſe precautions, the king of *Morocco* tranſported upwards
of ſixty thouſand men into *Spain*; and when the king of *Caſtile*
had notice of this, he ſent an embaſſy to Don *Alonſo*, king of
Portugal, to thank his father in-law for the ſuccours he had
given him, and to let him know that he was deſirous of
turning the truce, which they had concluded, into a ſolemn
peace, which was ſigned on the tenth of *July*. One of the
articles was, that the king ſhould permit Donna *Conſtantia*,
the daughter of Don *Juan Emanuel*, to go into *Portugal*, to
conſummate her marriage with the Infant Don *Pedro*, to
whom ſhe had been eſpouſed by proxy, ſome years before.
When Don *Alonſo* laid down the pen, after ſigning this treaty,
Don *Juan Emanuel* ſeized his hand, and kiſſed it with great
tranſport, aſſuring him he would never forget the obligation
conferred upon him by this favour; and the king, to heighten
it, gave him leave to conduct his daughter in perſon, and ſent
ſome of the greateſt men in the kingdom to accompany him,
and to be witneſſes of the marriage [f].

Abul-Aſ- ABUL-ASSAN, king of *Morocco*, arrived in the latter end
ſan inveſts of the ſummer; and having joined the army of the king of
Tarefa *Granada*, marched to inveſt *Tarefa*, in which was *Juan*
with a *Alonſo de Benavides*, and came before it on the 23d of *Sep-*
prodigious *tember*. He immediately gave the king notice of the ſituation
army, and things were in, and prepared to make as good a defence as
it joined by poſſible. The ſiege, however, was carried on with all ima-
the king of ginable vigour, and the place in great danger, when the
Granada. garriſon received freſh ſpirits from the appearance of the fleet
of *Caſtile*, under the command of the new admiral Don
Alonſo Ortiz, riding in the ſtreights, by whom the daily ſup-
plies of proviſions, which hitherto the *Moors* had received,
were intercepted, and the beſiegers reduced to the utmoſt
diſtreſs. The face of things was quickly changed, a tempeſt
diſperſed the Chriſtian fleet, and all, except three gallies,
were loſt, which plunged the garriſon once more into deep
diſtreſs. The king being informed of their circumſtances,
took a generous reſolution of hazarding all for their relief.

[e] BRANDAON. ROD. SANTII Hiſt. Hiſpan. part iv. FERRE-
RAS. [f] FARIA Y SOUSA. BRANDAON. Chronica de los
Moros de Eſpana. Chronica del Rey Don Alonſo el Onzeno.
FERRERAS.

He

He sent the queen into *Portugal*, to procure what succours she could from the king, her father; and that brave prince, as soon as the queen had informed him of the situation that her husband's affairs were in, resolved to march to his assistance with the whole force of his kingdom [u].

Don *Alonso* received him at *Seville* with all possible marks of gratitude, reverence, and friendship; and when the two armies had rested and refreshed themselves, they marched towards the enemy, being about eighteen or twenty thousand horse, and forty thousand foot. They arrived in sight of *Tarefa*, on *Sunday* the 29th of *October*, and held it for a good omen, that they received intelligence of Don *Pedro de Moncado's* arrival in the streights, with the fleet of *Arragon*. In the night, the king threw a reinforcement of one thousand horse and four thousand foot into *Tarefa*; and the next morning, having made the necessary dispositions, and sent a strong detachment to join the *Portuguese*, he advanced to attack the king of *Morocco*, while the king of *Portugal* did the same against the king of *Granada*. The dispute was long and obstinate, more especially on the side of the king of *Castile*, but at length the *Moors* were defeated, with the loss of near half their army, amounting to two hundred thousand men. The king of *Granada* retired into his own dominions, with the broken remains of his forces; the king of *Morocco* retired first to *Algerixa*, thence to *Gibraltar*, from whence he passed to *Ceuta* in the night; the two kings, after having provided for the security of *Tarefa*, went together to *Seville*, where prodigious rejoicings were made; the king of *Castile* offered his father-in-law all the prisoners and plunder that were taken, which he generously refused; and it was with great difficulty that he was brought to accept a few of the principal prisoners, some very rich arms, and a few jewels. His son-in-law accompanied him two days journey, in his march towards *Estremos*. The king of *Castile* from this time, as well out of gratitude as piety, conversed with Donna *Leonora de Guzman* no more, except in public, and as the mother of his children [w].

The king, Don *Alonso*, sent an embassador with his own standard, twenty-four horses richly caparisoned, and twenty-

The King of Castile and Portugal gain the glorious victory of Salsedo.

1340.

Don Alonso reduces

[u] BRANDAON. Chronica del Rey Don Alonso el Ouzeno, par Don JUAN NUNEZ DE VILLASAN. Chron. de los Moros de Espana. [w] EMANUEL DE FARIA Y SOUSA. ROD. SANTII Hist. Hispan. ZURIT. Annal Arragon. Chron. de los Moros de Espana. Chronica del Rey Don Alonso el Ouzeno. MARIANA. MAYERNE TURQUET. FERRERAS.

Alcala de four *Moors* to lead them, as a present to the pope at *Avignon* [x].
Benzayde, The king having summoned the states of his dominions, and
Moclin, having laid before them his wants, they, in consideration of
and seve- his late victory, and the zeal expressed for them, and the
ral other good of his subjects, made him a tender of a large free gift,
places. which he refused, and accepted only of a part, saying, that his
own necessities forced him to take that, and the sense he had
of theirs, to decline the rest. The king had formed a design
of investing *Alcala de Benzayde*, a place of great importance
to him, because the loss of it could not but be very sensible
to the king of *Granada*, since it opened a passage into the
heart of his dominions. By causing a report to be spread
that he intended to attack *Malaga*, and causing some of his
ships to appear before it, he drew the king of *Granada's* forces
on that side, which left him at liberty to invest *Alcala* without opposition. He had no sooner formed the siege, than Don
Gilles de Boccanegra, brother to the duke of *Genoa*, arrived
with a strong squadron of gallies in the streights, and prevented any troops passing from *Barbary*. The king of
Granada, however, was reinforced by the best part of that
corps, which his ally, the king of *Morocco*, had left at *Algeriza*, and with these and with his own army he attempted
to relieve *Alcala*, but in vain ; upon which Don *Alonso*, having offered the garrison that they should march out and be
escorted to whatever place they pleased, they very readily accepted these terms. While the king was employed in this
siege, some of his generals reduced the castle of *Moclin* ; and
after the surrender of *Alcala*, the king made himself master of
several places of less importance ; which so alarmed the *Moorish*
1341. prince, that he offered to become his vassal again, and to pay
him the accustomed tribute ; to which Don *Alonso* added, that
he should renounce his alliance with *Abul-Assan*, which he
rejected, and thus the negotiation ended [y].

The king THE king found great difficulty in raising the supplies for
at length the next year, and money was extremely necessary, as he
undertakes had the *Genoese* and other foreigners in his pay, and therefore
the very what he could not obtain from the states, he borrowed. The
important king of *Morocco* had made vast preparations, and seemed dif-
siege of Al- posed to return once more into *Spain*. Don *Gilles de Boccane-*
geriza. gra sunk, burned, and took twelve of his gallies that lay in
port ; and being afterwards joined by ten gallies from *Portugal*,

[x] RAINALD. EMANUEL DE FARIA Y SOUSA. ROD. SANTII
Hist. Hisp. part iv. MAYERNE TURQUET. [y] Chronica
del Rey Don Alonso el Onzeno. Chron. de los Moros de Espana.
MARIANA. FERRERAS.

and

and the squadron of *Arragon*, attacked and beat the whole *Moorish* fleet with great loss [z]. The king, notwithstanding he found some backwardness in the nobility, who were really tired out with the length and the hardships of the service, to rid himself once for all from the apprehensions he was under from *Barbary*, resolved to besiege *Algeriza*, which, as he was informed, was at that time but indifferently provided: this equally amazed and chagrined the king of *Granada*, who endeavoured and found several methods of conveying succours into the place, which kept Don *Alonso* before it all the rest of the year. The *Moor* attempted likewise its relief, by negotiation and by force, but without effect. He likewise commissioned a *Moor* to make an attempt upon the king of *Castile*'s person, which was happily discovered and prevented, the fellow, as he deserved, being put to death [a].

THERE are few instances in history of a more remarkable *Artillery* siege than this of *Algeriza*, in which, on both sides, there *used by the* was manifested all that human skill and courage could per- Moors *in* form; the king of *Morocco* raised another great army, and *the defence* assembled a vast fleet; but when he was ready to pass the *of that* streights, one of his sons revolted; and though he found *place* means to have him killed, yet one of his adherents personated *against* him and maintained a rebellion. The king of *Granada,* *the* Casti-having received a part of the succours which his ally had pro-*lians.* mised, under the command of prince *Aly*, another of his sons, attempted over and over again to raise the siege, and ventured several actions, in which they were defeated by Don *Juan de Lara.* The besieged thundered upon the king's camp with cannon, which were here first employed, as all the *Spanish* historians agree [b]. Besides this opposition from his enemies, Don *Alonso* found himself much straitened in other respects. He could not leave the siege to seek supplies, and his credit was gradually exhausted. At length he thought of a stratagem, which procured him those aids his subjects had refused to his fortitude in necessity. He sent his own plate, and that of the lords who were with him, to *Seville*, where he ordered it to be coined into pieces current, at a higher rate than the standard; of which the inhabitants in his great cities having notice, offered him a large free gift to desist from that expedient, which he willingly accepted [c].

[z] ZURIT. Annal Arragon. Chronica del Rey Don Alonso el Ouzeno. BRANDAON. [a] Chron. de los Moros de Espana. ROD. SANTII Hist. Hispan. part iv. FERRERAS. [b] Chronica del Rey Don Alonso el Ouzeno. Chron. de los Moros de Espana. MARIANA. MAYERNE TURQUET. FERRERAS. [c] ROD. SANTII Hist. Hispan. part iv. Chronica general de Espan.

Remarkable circumstances during this siege, which attracted the eyes of all Europe.

THE pope and the *French* king likewise sent him large sums [d]. The fame of this siege was so great, that Don *Philip,* king of *Navarre,* repaired thither with a great body of troops, and died in his return: several *English* and *French* men of quality, with considerable reinforcements, came thither, and served for a time; but the extream length of the siege tired out all the strangers, and brought the king into fresh distresses for money, the *Genoese* threatening to return or to revolt if they were not paid [e]. On the other hand, the king of *Granada* made a proposition to pay the whole expences of the war, if the king would raise the siege; and this, in effect, was a fresh distress, for his hungry troops importuned the king to close with these offers; but his good sense furnished him with an expedient to turn, even this, to his advantage; for he demanded three hundred thousand pistoles in gold, and granted a passport for a gally to go to *Ceuta* to receive them from the king of *Morocco.* This gally in her return, notwithstanding the king's passport, was attacked by the *Genoese,* but, however, escaped; but, instead of bringing the money, brought an order to hazard a battle, and to save the place at any rate. These orders were obeyed, and the *Moors* thoroughly beaten [f]. Still the place held out, notwithstanding the port was blocked up, not only by a strong squadron, but by a kind of dyke, in spite of which one *Muza,* a *Moorish* seaman, at stated times when the nights were dark, passed with fifty small vessels that drew little water, and carried supplies of provisions; so that, notwithstanding the king's information was true, that their magazines were low at the beginning, yet they were, by this means, supplied, and the place remained in the hands of the *Moors* all this year [g].

1343. *Algeziras at last rendered to Don Alonso by the kings of Morocco and Granada.*

AT the beginning of the next, the king discovered *Muza's* practice; and having made such alterations in his dyke, as rendered it impossible for the future, of which *Abul Assan* being informed, he directed the king of *Granada* to make the best terms for the garrison he could. That prince proposed to Don *Alonso,* that the troops and inhabitants should have free leave to march out; that he would acknowlege himself his vassal, and pay the usual tribute; and that a truce should subsist for fifteen years; the king, to maintain his dignity, reduced the truce to ten years; and upon these terms the capi-

[d] RAINALD: P. DANIEL Hist. de France. FERRERAS. [e] Historia de Royaume de Navarre. Chron. var. Antiq. P. DANIEL. FERRERAS. [f] Chronica del Rey Don Alonso el Onzeno. Chron. de los Moros de España. ALPHONSI a Cartagena reb. Hispan. Anacephalæosis. [g] ROD. SANTII Hist. Hispan. p. iv. Chronica de los Moros de España.

　　　　tulation

tulation was signed on the twenty-sixth of *March*, when the plenipotentiaries of the king of *Granada*, kissed Don *Alonso's* hand, in token of homage[h]. The place was evacuated the next day, and Don *Juan Emanuel* entered it with a corps of troops, and the banner of *Castile* displayed, to the immortal honour of this great prince, and of his faithful nobility; by whose constancy, expressed in expending vast sums for his service, and by exposing their persons, this great conquest was attained. As soon as the king came to *Seville*, he ordered that the princesses, daughters of *Abul-Assan*, who were taken in that monarch's camp, at the defeat of *Salsedo*, should be provided with most magnificent equipages, and sent them with a suitable train on board his own galleys to *Ceuta*, without ransom, and with all the rich jewels in their possession when taken. *Abul-Assan* was amazed at this act of generosity, and soon after sent an embassy to return the king of *Castile* thanks, and to testify his esteem by presents of jewels, rich arms, gold and silver stuffs, most exquisite balsams and perfumes, together with lions, tigers, ostriches, and a considerable number of camels and horses[i]. Soon after, Don *Alonso* received embassadors from *England* and from *Arragon*, the former in reference to a marriage, which he thought proper to defer, and the latter in regard to the alliance subsisting between the two crowns, which the king was content to renew for ten years[k].

A. D.
1344.

THE sovereignty of the *Canary* islands, held in vassalage from the holy see, by a tribute of four hundred pistoles a year, having been conferred by pope *Clement* the sixth on *Louis de la Cerda*, count of *Clermont* in *France*, son of Don *Alonso de la Cerda*, the king of *Castile*, at the request of the pope and of that young prince, desisted from his pretensions to them, as appears by his letters, dated *February* the eighteenth, which, however, proved of little service to this nominal monarch, notwithstanding that he procured the like renunciation from the king of *Portugal*[l]. The king indeed was entirely occupied in finding ways and means to discharge the vast debts he had contracted during the tedious siege of *Algeriza*, in pacifying the king of *Portugal*, who took it much amiss that he

The pope bestows the sovereignty of the Canary islands on Don Louis de la Cerda.

1345.

[h] Chronica del Rey Don Alonso el Onzeno. Chron. de los Moros de Espana. Rod. Santii Hist. Hispan. p. iv. Alphons, a Carthagena reg. Hispan. Anacephalæosis. Mariana. Maytene Turquet. Ferreras.   [i] Rod. Santii Hist. Hispan. p. iv. Chron. de los Moros de Espana. Chron. general de Espana. Rainald.   [k] Zurit. Annal Arragon. Rod. Santii Hist. Hispan. part iv.   [l] Brandaon. Chronica general de Espana. Rainald.

was not comprifed in the peace he made with the kings of *Morocco* and *Granada*, and in protecting his fifter the queen of *Arragon* [m]. The kingdom of *Caftile*, it is true, and the dominions annexed to it, enjoyed a profound peace, which, however, contributed very little to repair the loffes fuftained by the late war, fince the inhabitants were afflicted with a grievous plague and other calamities thefe diftreffes created; by which the king endeavoured to remedy to the utmoft of his power, by feveral wife regulations, and by fparing them in the point of fupplies as much as it was poffible. He would in all probability have purfued this method of acting, at leaft, to the expiration of his truce with the *Moors*, if his ambition had not been awakened by an unforefeen event, which feemed to promife himfelf and his fubjects very great advantages [n].

ONE of the fons of *Abul Affan*, forgetting the refpect due to him by the laws of nature as well as civil fociety, had taken up arms againft him, and thrown all that monarchy into confufion; of which Don *Alonfo* was no fooner informed, than he conceived in his mind a fcheme for turning thefe diffentions in *Barbary* to his advantage. He called, with this view, an affembly of the ftates at *Alcala de Henares*, where he laid before them the fituation things were in, the probability there was of his making himfelf mafter of *Gibraltar*, the only place that monarch held in *Spain*; and thereby removing all fear of leaving his fucceffors under the neceffities of fighting for their crowns, on terms as precarious as thofe upon which he fought the battle of *Salfedo*. This affembly clofed with the king's propofition, and granted him the fupplies that he demanded, which, however, was chiefly owing to his dexterity in managing fuch affemblies, an art in which he has hardly been excelled. Thefe points fettled, he fent to demand of the king of *Arragon* a fquadron of gallies, and embaffadors likewife to other foreign powers [o]. About the beginning of the month of *Auguft*, having intelligence that four *Arragonefe* gallies had joined his fleet, and that it was cruizing off *Gibraltar*, he traverfed *Andalufia* with a potent army, and invefted that place, round which he opened a large and deep trench.

THE fiege continued that whole year, notwithftanding the king was fo fortunate, at leaft in appearance, as to fee all his fchemes take effect; for his fleet effectually prevented fuccours

Side notes:

A. D. 1347.

1348.

Don Alonfo refolves to break the truce with the Moors, and befiege Gibraltar.

Dies of the plague before that

[m] ZURIT. Annal Arragon. P. DE ESPINOSA. ROD. SANTII Hift. Hifpan. part iv. [n] Chronica general de Efpana. FERRERAS ,Hiftoria de Efpana. MARIANA. MEYERNE TURQUET. [o] ZURIT. Annal Arragon. ROD. SANTII Hift. Hifpan. part iv. ALONSO MORGADO. Chronica de los Moros de Efpana.

coming

coming by fea; the king of *Granada* was afraid to attempt *place at* any thing openly, and the confufions in *Morocco* prevented that *the very* monarch from being able to do any thing for its relief. The *time it was* garrifon and inhabitants therefore being in want of provifions, *about to* and the fortifications in a manner ruined, began to think of a *capitulate.* capitulation, when the plague broke out in the camp[p]. The Infant (of *Arragon*) Don *Ferdinand*, his nephew Don *Juan Nunez de Lara*, who was always near his perfon, Don *Ferdinand Emanuel*, and other great lords, preffed him either to raife the fiege, or at leaft to retire himfelf; but it was in vain: he obferved to them that *Gibraltar* had been loft during his minority, that he was under a kind of obligation to recover it to his country, and that the plague might reach him in his court as well as in the camp. It may be, he had not confidered, that though this enterprize had been very maturely concerted, and executed with great circumfpection, yet it was a direct violation of the law of God, and of nature; and that, therefore, notwithftanding thefe favourable appearances, he had no reafon to flatter himfelf with fuccefs. However it was, the plague feized him at that critical juncture, and of it he died on *Good-Friday*, *March* the 26th, exceedingly regretted by the army, and by all his fubjects[q]. His nephew the Infant Don *Ferdinand*, Don *Juan Nunez de Lara*, Don *Ferdinand Emanuel*, and fome other noblemen, attended the king's body when it was removed from the camp; and the *Moors* in *Gibraltar* fhewed, upon this occafion, a politenefs that ought to have covered their enemies with confufion: they fufpended hoftilities that whole day, and refufed to take advantage of that forrow and confufion which reigned through the Chriftian camp. The king's body was carried firft to *Seville*, and depofited in the royal chapel till it could be removed to *Cordova*, where, by his laft teftament, he defired to be buried with his father[r].

The peace and glory of his country expired with Don *Don* Pedro *Alonfo*. His fucceffor, Don *Pedro*, furnamed the *cruel*, was *the cruel* the only furviving fon by the queen; for Don *Ferdinand* died *fucceeds his* in his infancy: but by Donna *Leonora de Guzman* he had *father*, *Sancho*, who was weak in his mind and infirm in his body; *and is go-* Henry *Frederick*, whom the *Spaniards* call *Fradrique Her- verned by* *nando* or *Ferdinand*, and *Tello*[s]. At the time of his demife, *his mother*

[p] Chron. var. antiq. Chronica de los Moros de Efpana. Ferreras. [q] Rod. Santii Hift. Hifpan. part iv. Chronica general de Efpana. Mariana. Mayerne Turquet. Ferreras. [r] Rod. Santii Hift. Hifpan. part iv. Ferreras. Mayerne Turquet. [s] Chronica del Rey Don Pedro primero, &c.

Don

and Don Juan de Albu-querque. Don *Pedro* was in his sixteenth year; and though not a legal minor, yet absolutely governed by the queen his mother, and her favourite Don *Juan Alonso de Albuquerque.* The siege of *Gibraltar* was carried on after the king's death, till orders could be received from court, and was then raised, though the place might have been easily taken [t]. But the spirit of government was lost, and the spirit of intrigue occupied the court. Donna *Leonora de Guzman* retired immediately to *Medina Sidonia,* which the king had given her, which was well provided and excellently fortified. She had intrusted it to the care of Don *Alonso Coronel,* an experienced officer, who had long enjoyed her protection, and who, as soon as the king expired, sought that of the queen. Many persons of great distinction, and most of the nobility of the illustrious house of *Guzman,* resorted to Donna *Leonora,* which filled the court with apprehensions: these, however, it was thought proper to dissemble; and upon the faith of Don *Juan de Albuquerque,* and Don *Juan de Lara,* Donna *Leonora* was prevailed upon to go to the court at *Seville,* where, without any ceremony or regard to their faith, she was clapped into prison [u]. Her sons, notwithstanding this were well received; and the king gave them to understand, that though he would not protect their mother, with whom he had no connections, yet he should always consider them as his brethren. They were permitted to visit Donna *Leonora,* who, in spite of the endeavours of the court, procured for Don *Henry,* Donna *Joanna,* the sister of Don *Ferdinand Emanuel;* which marriage so provoked the queen, that she gave orders for arresting Don *Henry,*
1350. but he made his escape into *Asturias* [w]. The king falling ill soon after, increased those jealousies that were but too high already; and upon his recovery, Don *Juan de Lara* and Don *Ferdinand Emanuel* retired from court, and died soon after, the former at *Burgos,* and the latter at *Valena* [x].

Consents, at their instigati-on, to the murder of Donna Leonora de Guzman. THE king Don *Pedro* removed in the beginning of the year from *Seville,* and carried with him Donna *Leonora,* under a guard. He visited, however, his brother Don *Frederick,* and feasted with him several days. After this, the court removed to *Talavera,* where, by the persuasion of his mother, the king consented to the death of the unfortunate Donna *Leonora,* the first stain on the annals of his reign, which were afterwards wrote in blood. This place belonged to the dowager, and to

[t] Chronica general de Espana. FERRERAS. [u] Chronica del Rey Don Pedro de Castilla. ROD. SANTII Hist. Hispan. [w] Chronica del Rey Don Pedro primero, &c. [x] ROD. SANTII Hist. Hispan. MARIANA. MAYERNE TURQUET. FERRERAS.

perpetuate

perpetuate the memory of this cruel act, is thought to have received the epithet of *Talavera de la Reyna*, which it still retains[y]. Upon the king's arrival at *Burgos*, which city had shewn some dislike to Don *Juan de Albuquerque*, he sent for *Garcilasso de la Vega*, the son of the late chancellor; and as soon as he came into his palace, caused him to be murdered, and his body thrown into the street: he attempted likewise to have got Don *Nunez de Lara*, the only son of Don *Juan*, and then a child, into his power, but without effect; however, he died soon after, and then he seized all the estates of that family[z]. Don *Carlos*, surnamed the *wicked*, king of *Navarre*, made him a visit at *Burgos*, where he was well received, and after he had remained there some time, the two kings parted perfectly pleased with each other[a]. The states of *Castile* assembled at *Valladolid*, were not very complaisant to the king, who, as soon as they rose, went with his mother to *Ciudad Rodrigo*, in order to confer with his grandfather the king of *Portugal*. That monarch gave them a great deal of good advice, and engaged, or rather obliged, the king to be reconciled to his brother Don *Henry* count of *Trastamara*[b], who had taken shelter in his dominions, and who, notwithstanding, had no great confidence in the king or his favourite.

THE tranquility of *Castile* could be of no long duration, under a prince so much hurried away by his passions. He prepared to reduce Don *Alonso Fernandes Coronel*, and having dropt some expressions that alarmed his brethren the counts Don *Henry* and Don *Tello*, they retired privately from court, and stood upon their defence, fully persuaded, that if the king had them once in his power, they should never have such an opportunity again[c]. The king Don *Pedro* followed them into *Biscay*, and took several places; and it was while he was thus employed, that Don *Juan Alonso de Albuquerque*, from a base ambition, and through an unworthy scheme of politics, plunged this unfortunate prince in that fatal amour, which brought upon him destruction and disgrace. He had observed that the king had expressed some emotion at the sight of *Maria de Padilla*, a young gentlewoman who lived as a companion with his own wife, and who being now grown somewhat older, was become a perfect beauty. By proposals of

Becomes enamoured of Donna Maria de Padilla, which proves the ruin of his affairs.

[y] Chronica del Rey Don Pedro de Castilla. Chronica general de España. FERRERAS.   [z] MARIANA. MAYERNE TURQUET.   [a] Histoire de Royaume de Navarre. Chronica del Rey Don Pedro primero, &c.   [b] BRANDAON. Chronica del Rey Don Pedro primero, &c. FERRERAS.   [c] FERRERAS Historia de España, p. vi. sec. xiii. Chronica del Rey Don Pedro de PED. LOPEZ de Ayala.

A. D.
1352.

promoting their intereſts, he drew her relations to conſent to his ſcheme of her becoming the king's miſtreſs, though he knew that the queen his mother was actually treating of a marriage for the king, with Donna *Blanca*, daughter to the duke of *Bourbon*. His ſcheme ſucceeded to his wiſh, the king ſaw Donna *Maria* at *Sahagun*, and became captivated to ſuch a degree, that the common people of thoſe times believed, and the bulk of the *Spaniſh* hiſtorians have reported, that he was bewitched by her[d] (S). An excuſe, which, however it might operate heretofore, will do nothing now.

Thiſ

---

[d] Mariana Hiſtoria general de Eſpana, lib. xvi. c. 18. Rainald. Rod. Santii Hiſt. Hiſpan. p. iv.

(S) We ſhall have occaſion to ſay ſo much of this lady, that it ſeems requiſite to give the reader ſome particulars relating to her in a note, that he may be acquainted with her more particularly. She was of a good, though not of a great, family, and is by ſome writers repreſented as if educated according to the cuſtom of thoſe times, in the houſe of Don *Juan de Albuquerque*, rather than as an attendant on his lady (1). She was a little woman, but exquiſitely beautiful, and was endowed with ſo many rare qualities, that it is ſaid, abating her criminal complaiſance for the king, ſhe was by no means unworthy of a crown (2). How far this complaiſance was criminal may, notwithſtanding, admit of ſome queſtion, ſince, after her demiſe, the king Don *Pedro* aſſerted that he was lawfully married to her, in the preſence of Don *Juan de Hineſtroſa* her brother, Don *Diego Garcia de Padilla* his own

chancellor, and his firſt chaplain (3). The two laſt were living at the time, and ſwore it to be truth. We ſhall hereafter ſee, that this monarch made no ſcruple of marrying at any time to gratify his deſires, and therefore might very poſſibly do it now, though it muſt be acknowleged that it was kept very ſecret; and when publiſhed by the king, and ſworn to, it was very far from meeting with entire credit (4). The reader may meet with ſome very judicious and moral remarks upon the conſequences of the king's ill conduct, in regard to this lady; the mean and low ſpirit of his courtiers, in paying her the moſt profound reſpect, and the generous freedom of cardinal *Albornoz*, who not only diſdained ſuch a behaviour, but both ſpoke and wrote freely to the king upon the ſubject, till he found himſelf in ſo great danger, that he thought it beſt to retire to *Avignon*, to be ſafe from the reſen-

(1) *Chronica del Rey Don Pedro de Pedro Lopez de Ayala. Hiſtoire d'Eſpagne, par Mayerne Turquett.* (2) *Hiſtoria general de Eſpana, par Mariana, lib.* xvi. (3) *Pedro Lopez de Ayala.* (4) *Hiſtoria de Eſpana, por Ferreras, part* viii. *ſect.* xiv.

THIS intrigue did not hinder the king from pursuing his *Espouses* revenge against Don *Alonso Fernandes Coronel*, whom he be-*Donna* sieged all the winter in his castle of *Aguilar*, took the place *Blanca,* by storm, in the beginning of the spring, and put that noble-*daughter* man and many of his relations to death [e]. In the month of *to Peter* *February*, Donna *Blanca* arrived in *Spain*, and was received *duke of* by the queen dowager Donna *Maria*, and by the queen *Bourbon,* Donna *Leonora*, the king's aunt [f]. Don *Juan de Albuquerque* *slights and* was at that time in *Portugal*, but returned upon the first news *sends, her* of it to court; and finding that the kindred of Donna *Maria* *to prison.* *de Padilla* began to supplant him in the king's good graces, he applied himself with all imaginable diligence, to persuade the king to go and consummate his marriage with Donna *Blanca* at *Valladolid*, in which he found more difficulty than he expected. But the relations of Donna *Maria de Padilla* prevailed upon him more easily to receive his brethren Don *Henry* and Don *Tello* into his favour, though each of them came attended with such a number of armed followers, as left them no reason to fear any thing from his displeasure. But as they gave out that they were not afraid of him, but of Don *Juan de Albuquerque*, he received this excuse, and behaved towards them very kindly [g]. At length, with much persuasion, he **1353.** went to *Valladolid*, and in the presence of the two queens, and of all the princes of the royal blood, he espoused Donna *Blanca*, but left her abruptly the next day, to return to his mistress [h]. Don *Juan de Albuquerque* retired in discontent

[e] Chronica del Rey Don Pedro de PED. LOPEZ de Ayala.
[f] ROD. SANTII, Hist. Hispan.   [g] Chron. del Don Pedro
de Castilla. FERRERAS.   [h] Chronica del Rey Don Pedro de PED. LOPEZ de Ayala.   MARIANA.   MAYERNE TUR-
QUET.

ment of a monarch whose hands were already dipped in blood (5). The learned Mr. *Bayle* has vouchsafed this lady an article in his dictionary, which is drawn from the historian last mentioned; and she also occupied the first place in a celebrated history of royal mistresses, where, if not accurately, her story is at least elegantly told (6). She was absolutely mistress of the king's heart for nine years; and he was so much afflicted with her death, that he had almost lost his senses (7). Her uncle became his principal favourite; and he committed acts of the greatest violence and injustice, in order to bestow upon her two brothers, Don *Diego* and Don *Juan*, the grand masterships of *Calatrava* and St. *James*.

(5) *Hist. gen. de Espana, por Mariana, lib.* xvi.   (6) *Historia des Fa-*
vourites, premiere partie.   (7) *Ayala, Mariana, Ferreras, &c.*

from

from court, and refused to go towards *Toledo*, as the king directed. As soon as Don *Pedro* was informed of this, he quitted that city, and returned to *Valladolid*, where he staid two days with the three queens, which was the last time he saw his consort Donna *Blanca*[i]. He proceeded from thence to *Olmedo*, to his mistress, and sent for Don *Juan de Albuquerque* thither, under pretence of a reconciliation; but, in reality, with a design to cut him off with his principal adherents. Donna *Maria de Padilla*, having some connections with these lords, gave them notice of the king's design, upon which, not without danger and difficulty, they retired into *Portugal*. The king was no sooner informed of this, than he shut up his queen Donna *Blanca* in prison, married his brother Don *Tello* to Donna *Joanna de Lara*, the heiress of that family, and removed from all their employments the creatures of Don *Juan de Albuquerque*[k]. And thus, for the present, the court of *Castile* received quite a new face.

Causes himself to be divorced, marries Donna Joanna Fernandez de Castro, and leaves her.

THE king, understanding that Don *Juan Nunez de Prada*, grand master of the order of *Calatrava*, was retired into *Arragon*, he wrote to him in the strongest terms, assuring him he had nothing to fear, upon which that lord returned into *Castile*. On his arrival at *Almagro*, the king caused him to be seized, and ordered him to renounce his dignity; and then compelled the knights to elect Don *Diego de Padilla*, brother of his mistress: but understanding that the knights were not mighty well satisfied with a renunciation, he, to prevent their restoring the old grand-master, directed him to be murdered; one of the foulest actions of his whole reign[l]. He next took it into his head to make his addresses to Donna *Joanna Fernandes de Castro*, the widow of Don *Diego de Haro*; and finding no other way to gratify his desires, he prevailed upon two of his bishops to declare his former marriage null, and then married Donna *Joanna* publickly. He left her, however, almost as soon as he had done his former queen; and

1354.

understanding that his two brothers had entered into a league with Don *Juan de Albuquerque*, he married Donna *Isabella*, younger sister to Donna *Joanna de Lara*, to Don *Juan of Arragon*, and declared him lord of *Biscay*, in prejudice to his brother Don *Tello*, who had married the eldest sister[m]. The king then ordered Donna *Blanca* to be removed to *Toledo*,

---

[l] FERRERAS. ROD. SANTII Hist. Hispan. part iv. [k] Chronica del Rey Don Pedro de PED. LOPEZ de Ayala. MARIANA. [l] ROD. SANTII Hist. Hispan. part iv. ZURITA, Annal Arragon. FERRERAS.   [m] Chronica del Rey Don Pedro de PED. Lopez de Ayala. Chronica general de Espana. ROD. SANTII Hist. Hispan. part iv.

where,

where, having humbly defired leave to perform her devotions
in the cathedral, fhe refufed to come out of it, and by a very
moving fpeech induced the inhabitants to revolt in her favour [n].
Don *Henry*, count *de Traſtamara*, with the reſt of the confederates, repaired thither, and began to take the beſt meafures they were able for reducing the king to reafon, in which
they were not a little difappointed by the death of Don *Juan
de Albuquerque*, who was poifoned by an *Italian* phyſician.
Their party, however, by degrees, became fo ſtrong, that
the king found himſelf obliged to come to them to *Toro*, where
he confented to all that they afked, and diſſembled with fuch
addreſs, that he deceived not only them, but the pope's legate; but having, in the mean time, by a fecret treaty, detached fome of the members of the league, he took the advantage of a thick fog, and withdrawing out of their hands,
retired to *Segovia* [o]; a circumſtance that alarmed thofe
whom he left behind, and who knew his implacable and fan-
guinary temper.

THE princes who remained firm in the confederacy, were *The city of*
the king's three brothers, Don *Henry* count of *Traſtamara*, Toledo,
the grand maſter Don *Frederick*, and Don *Tello*, lord of *Biſcay*, *which had*
in right of his wife, with Don *Ferdinand de Caſtro*, brother *declared*
to the lady whom the king had abufed, under pretence of *for queen*
marriage, and who had himſelf eſpouſed the fiſter of thofe *Blanca*,
princes. But the Infants of *Arragon*, who were likewiſe *reduced by*
of this league, now followed the king; who having artfully *the king.*
drawn from the ſtates at *Burgos* confiderable fupplies, took
the field with a good army, and upon various pretences cut
off feveral great lords, whom he fuſpected. At length he
made an attempt upon *Toro*, where the queen his mother was
under the protection of the count Don *Henry*, by whofe valour
and prudence the king's army was repulfed [p]. Don *Pedro*,
difappointed and provoked, marched with all poſſible diligence
towards *Toledo*, fending word before him, that, yielding to
the prayers of his people, he refolved to live with the queen
Donna *Blanca* as became him. The count Don *Henry*
marched thither alfo, with fuch expedition, that he got into
the city; yet the greater part of the inhabitants, confiding in
the king's promifes, received the king's troops alfo, and the
count finding himſelf obliged to retire, took his meafures with
fuch addreſs, that having feized and plundered the king's
camp, he returned with credit to *Talavera* [q]. The king no

[o] Chronica del Rey Don Pedro de PED. LOPEZ de Ayala.
FERRERAS.   [p] ROD. SANTII Hiſt. Hiſpan. part iv, MA-
RIANA. MAYERNE TURQUETT.   [q] Chronica del Rey
Don Pedro de PED. LOPEZ de Ayala.

fooner

ſooner found himſelf maſter of the place, than he ſent the queen Donna *Blanca* priſoner to *Siguenca*, cauſed ſeveral noblemen to be beheaded, and twenty-two of the principal inhabitants to be hanged. Amongſt other ſeverities, he thought fit to impriſon the biſhop of *Siguenca*; which ſo irritated the pope, that he ſent word to his legate to excommunicate him, and put all the places in his obedience under an interdict. Don *Pedro*, notwithſtanding, made another attempt upon *Toro*; and, after all that had paſſed, amuſed the cardinal legate with ſuch fair promiſes, that he abſolved him from the excommunication, and took off the interdict; but being quickly undeceived, he had recourſe to theſe eccleſiaſtical thunders again [r]. It does not appear, that, except their temporal conſequences, the king heeded them much.

THE king having reduced his mother, and thoſe who adhered to her in *Toro*, to great extremities, and having found means to draw off his brother the grand-maſter Don *Frederick*, became at length maſter of the place; the queen dowager Donna *Maria* retiring to the *Alcazal*, with Donna *Joanna*, the wife of Don *Henry* count *de Traſtamara*, and moſt of the nobility repaired thither likewiſe. As the place could not hold out long, ſhe ſent in the moſt humble manner to her ſon, to deſire he would promiſe life to her, and thoſe who were with her; which he refuſed, and they were compelled to ſurrender at diſcretion. They were no ſooner in the king's power, than he ordered moſt of the nobility to be put to death in the preſence of the queen dowager, who fainting at ſo barbarous a ſpectacle, was carried back ſenſeleſs to the palace [s]. Amongſt ſo many acts of cruelty, there was one which had an air of generoſity: there was in the place one *Martin Abarca*, a nobleman of *Arragon*, to whom the king Don *Alonſo* had committed the care of Don *Juan*, a ſon of his by *Leonora de Guzman*. He ſent to the king from the place where he was concealed, and deſired him to ſpare the life of Don *Juan*, and of himſelf. The king anſwered, that if he produced Don *Juan* immediately, that prince ſhould be ſaved; but that his own death was a thing ſettled. The generous old man brought his pupil inſtantly to the king, to whom, having recommended him in the moſt pathetic manner, he offered himſelf to die; upon which the king told him that it was his intention he ſhould live and enjoy his favour [t]. He thought fit, however, to proſcribe his brothers, Don

1356.

[r] RAINALD. MARIANA. FERRERAS.   [s] Chronica del Rey Don Pedro de PED. LOPEZ de Ayala. MARIANA. MATERNE TUQUET.   [t] Chronica del Rey Don Pedro de Caſtilla. FERRERAS.

Frederick

Frederick and Don *Tello*, and some attempts were made to affassinate them; but people were become now so much afraid of him, and trusted so little to his promises, that he was not able to accomplish his bloody purposes so easily as he had formerly done. He gave Don *Henry* count *de Trastamara* leave to retire to *France*, but posted murderers upon the roads through which he was to pass; but being well accompanied, he retired safely, though not without difficulty, out of his dominions. This year a war broke out between him and Don *Pedro* of *Arragon*, about a dispute at sea, which had very bad consequences u (T). By which we may discern how early princes began to be jealous of the slightest injuries offered to their dominion of the sea.

THE war with *Arragon* brought back the count of *Trasta-* *The wife* mara into that prince's dominions, who employed him in *of Don* his service, and gave him considerable appointments. Don *Henry* *Pedro* of *Castile*, however, gained some advantages this cam- *rescued,* paign, and might have obtained greater, if he had not laboured *and carri-* to corrupt the views of his two generals Don *Juan de la Cerda,* *ed to her.*

u Chronica del Rey Don Pedro de Ped. Lopez de Ayala Zu-rit. Annal Arragon. Mariana. Ferreras.

(T) The king, Don *Pedro*, having embarked at *Port St. Mary's*, was amusing himself with the fight of his subjects fishing for tunnies, when a squadron of ten gallies belonging to the king of *Arragon*, commanded by Don *Francisco Carrillos*, came upon the coast, and took two vessels under *Pisan* colours, but freighted by the *Genoese* with oil for *Alexandria*. As this was done in the very fight of the king, he sent two persons of distinction to let Don *Francisco* know, that those vessels were under his protection at the time they were taken, and that therefore he expected they should be discharged. Don *Francisco* answered, that, his master being at war with the *Genoese*, he took them to be good prizes, and therefore sold them without delay. Don *Pedro*, upon this, seized the effects of the *Catalan* merchants at *Seville*, by way of satisfaction. He sent also an ambassador to the king of *Arragon*, to demand that Don *Francisco* should be put to death, or sent prisoner into *Castile*. The king of *Arragon* answered very mildly, that he disapproved his admiral's conduct, and that he would call him to an account for it, upon his return. The ambassador of *Castile*, who, probably, had secret instructions, replied, that his master would take a proper satisfaction by force of arms. The monarch of *Arragon* told him, in return, that he saw no ground for a breach between the two crowns; but that, if he was attacked, he would repel force by force, and trust the decision of the cause to the supreme Being, who is the sovereign distributer of justice. Upon these grounds the war began, which *Mariana* describes as bringing desolation and destruction on both kingdoms.

husband, and Don *Alvaro Perez de Guzman,* which induced them to
by Pedro revolt; when the latter, being defeated and taken, the king
de Carillo. caused him to be presently put to death.   The pope's legate
obtained a truce, which the king of *Castile* speedily broke;
and, as if he had been afraid to leave a single good action upon
record, finding *Martin Abarca,* whom he had suffered to return home in one of the places he took, he caused him to be
put to death [w].   His brother Don *Henry,* being under continual apprehensions that he would put his wife Donna
Joanna Emanuel, whom he had taken at *Toro,* to death, one
Pedro Carillo, who had been long in his service, and unable
to bear his master's passionate complaints, left him, and went
to the king.   He told that prince that he had been extremely
ill used by the count, that he was well acquainted with many
others, who had personal resentments against him; and that
if he would give him leave to raise a troop of these, he
1357. would put his brother into his hands, either dead or alive.
The king accepted the proposition with joy; upon which
Pedro Carillo assembled at his expence a strong body of horse,
composed of gentlemen well affected to his master, with which
entering *Toro* suddenly, he took Donna *Joanna* out of prison, and carried her safe to her lord [x].   Don *Ferdinand,*
Infant of *Arragon,* about the same time reconciled himself
to his brother [y], so that Don *Pedro* had various causes of
The king chagrin.
causes his   As nothing irritated this prince so much as the escapes of
brother, those whom he had destined to destruction; so having still
Don Fre- about him Don *Juan* of *Arragon,* the brother of Don *Ferdi-*
derick, *nand,* and his own two brothers Don *Frederick* and Don *Tello,*
and his he resolved to dispatch them all by degrees, and to make use
cousin, Don of them in dispatching each other.   He resolved to begin with
Juan de his brother Don *Frederick,* the grand master, with which he
Arragon, acquainted the Infant Don *Juan* of *Arragon;* whom, in consi-
to be mur- deration of his assisting his designs, he promised to make lord
dered. of *Biscay.*   His brother was slain in his presence, on the 27th
of *May,* in the hall of his palace at *Seville,* and he afterwards
dined in the very room, before the body was removed [z].   He
directed also several other lords to be killed the same day; and
afterwards set out with his cousin Don *Juan* of *Arragon* for
the castle of *Aguilar,* where he had determined to treat his
brother Don *Tello* in the same manner; nor was he a little

[w] Zurit. Annal Arragon.   Chronica del Rey Don Pedro de
Ped. Lopez de Ayala. Rainald. Ferreras.   [x] Zurit.
Annal Arragon. Mariana. Mayerne Turquet.   [y] Chro-
nica general de Espana. Zurita. Annal Arragon. Chron. var.
Antiq.   [z] Chronica del Rey Don Pedro de Ped. Lopez
de Ayala. Mariana. Ferreras.

chagrined

chagrined at finding he was withdrawn; however, he secured his wife, and, to shew how much he was in earnest in this pursuit, understanding that his brother had fled by sea, he went on board a ship, in order to follow him, but a storm obliged him quickly to return [a]. He then proceeded in his journey to *Biscay*, and carried his cousin Don *Juan* with him, who, having acted in all things as the creature of his will, pressed him to perform his promise of making him lord of that country. The king gave him to understand that it was necessary to assemble the states of that country for that purpose; which being done, they resolved, according to the instructions they had received, that they would never have any other lord than the king himself. Don *Pedro* sent intelligence of this to his cousin, and assured him that he was very sorry for this disappointment. Don *Juan* understood him too well to pay any respect to this message, and therefore retired from court; yet he suffered himself to be deceived by a second, in which he gave him to understand, that he would endeavour to persuade the states to admit of his renunciation in his favour. Don *Juan* went to meet the king at *Bilboa*, where he then was; and as soon as he entered the audience chamber, and paid his respects to him, a person behind knocked him down, while those about him stabbed him in many places; some say the king gave him his mortal wound with a javelin. However this might be, the body was presently thrown out of a window, from whence the king looked out and insulted it, in the hearing of the people who gathered about it [b]. His aunt, queen *Leonora*, and the wife of Don *Tello*, he shut up in prison, seizing upon all they had; but in the mean time his brother the count Don *Henry*, with the army of *Arragon*, took several places upon the frontiers, while the king, in order to revenge himself, caused a potent fleet to be equipped at *Seville* [c], to ravage the coasts.

1358.

AT the opening of the ensuing year, the pope sent a legate into *Spain*, to accommodate these differences between the kings of *Castile* and *Arragon*. Don *Pedro* received that prelate with all the marks of deference and respect imaginable; complained of exceeding ill usage he had met with from the king his neighbour; notwithstanding which, out of pure regard to his holiness, he was ready to make peace upon the most moderate terms; such as, that the king of *Arragon* should

Poisons his aunt Donna Leonora and the widow of Don Juan.

---

[a] Chronica del Rey Don Pedro de Ped. Lopez de Ayala. Rod. Santii Hist. Hispan. part iv.   [b] Chronica del Rey Don Pedro de Ped. Lopez de Ayala. Mariana. Ferreras.   [c] Zurit. Annal Arragon. Chronica del Rey Don Pedro de Castilla.

X 2

deliver

deliver up to him Don *Francisco Perellos*, with whom he had reason to be offended ; should banish his brothers and all the *Castilians* in his service ; should restore *Alicant*, *Oribuela*, and other places that formerly belonged to *Castile*, and pay him half a million of pieces of gold for the expences of the war. The cardinal reported these terms to the king of *Arragon*, and laboured to soften their resentments against each other, but to very little purpose [d]. As soon as the fleet at *Seville* was ready, Don *Pedro*, to shew how much he was inclined to peace, proclaimed Don *Ferdinand*, Infant of *Arragon*, Don *Henry* count of *Trastamara*, and their adherents, traitors ; and that his resentment might not seem to be confined to words only, he ordered his aunt, the queen dowager of *Arragon*, Donna *Leonora*, to be put to death, and caused Donna *Isabella*, the widow of the Infant Don *John* of *Arragon*, to be poisoned [e]. He went afterwards to spread desolation with his fleets on the coast of *Catalonia* ; but while he was thus employed, his brother, the count Don *Henry*, made an irruption into his territories, gained a complete victory, and killed his favourite Don *Juan Fernandez Hinestrosa*, who was uncle to Donna *Maria de Padilla*, who was this year brought to-bed of her son Don *Alonso* [f], whom his father afterwards procured to be owned by the states for the lawful heir to the crown.

1359.

Other instances of the king's barbarous, vindictive and avaricious temper.

Don *Pedro*, though he could not repair the loss of the last battle, yet revenged it upon such of his subjects as were in the interests of his brethren, or whom he so much as suspected of being so. The many examples he made in this way, so frighted the most considerable persons in his dominions, that many, merely out of fear, went and joined the count Don *Henry*, and others retired into *Portugal*, where the king gave them a good reception ; but after having in vain endeavoured to reconcile his neighbours, at length took part with the king of *Arragon*, as the more reasonable [g]. The king Don *Pedro* had a good army in the field, which gave him an opportunity of gratifying his resentments, which he did in many instances ; but it happens fortunately for us, that the nature of this history does not oblige us to give an exact catalogue of his murders. We are, however, compelled to take notice, that in his march towards *Najara*, where his brother the count Don *Henry* was with his army, a priest very earnestly desired audience of him,

[d] RAINALD. ZURIT. Annal Arragon. FERRERAS. [e] Chronica del Rey Don Pedro de PED. LOPEZ de Ayala. ZURIT. Annal Arragon. MARIANA. MAYERNE TURQUET. [f] ROD. SANTII Hist. Hispan. part iv. Chronica del Rey Don Pedro de PED. LOPEZ de Ayala. [g] BRANDAON. ZURIT. Annal Arragon. FERRERAS.

which, when he had obtained, he told him that St. *Dominick* had commanded him in his sleep to admonish him to beware of his brother Don *Henry*, by whose hands he should certainly fall. The king was at first a little surprized ; but having re-collected himself, ordered the priest to be burnt alive, which was done; and soon after, the king lost the opportunity of reducing his brother, who had shut himself up in *Najara*, when it was actually in his power [b]. Towards the close of the year, he entered into a negotiation with the king of *Portugal*, whom he secretly advised, that as the persons who had taken shelter in his dominions were men who had given him great offence, he would, upon putting them into his power, deliver up those who had taken refuge in *Castile*, for putting to death *Agnes de Castro*, the king of *Portugal*'s wife, in his father's lifetime, and by his orders. This was soon accepted, and punctually performed on both sides ; in consequence of which, most dismal slaughters ensued : amongst these was *Samuel Levi*, a *Jew*, who had been his treasurer during the whole reign of Don *Pedro*. It does not appear that he suffered for any other crime than that of being rich ; and that the king might have an opportunity of possessing himself of about 160,000 pistoles in gold, and upwards of 4,000,000 in silver. It is probable he had obtained still more, if, in the midst of those tortures, employed to force from him a discovery, this miserable man had not died sooner than Don *Pedro* expected [i] ; at least this the king's unextinguished avarice tempted him to believe.

A. D. 1360.

MOHAMMED BARBAROSSA, who had raised himself to the throne of *Granada*, having, in consequence of a league made with the king of *Arragon*, invaded the territories of *Castile*, Don *Pedro*, whose passions made him frequently take sudden and strange resolutions, concluded, by the interposition of the pope's legate, a peace with the king of *Arragon*, that he might be at liberty to revenge himself upon the *Moors* of *Granada* [k]. About this time, the king, from what particular motive does not appear, ordered his beautiful, but unfortunate wife, Donna *Blanca*, to be put to death, in the fortress of *Xerez*, where she had been long confined (U). The governor

Puts the queen Donna Blanca to death, and aims at assassinating Don Henry.

[h] Chronica del Rey Don Pedro de PED. LOPEZ de Ayala. MARIANA. [i] EMANUEL DE FARIA Y SOUSA. Chronica general de Espana. FERRERAS. [k] RAINALD. • Chronica del Rey Don Pedro de PED. LOPEZ de Ayala. ZURITA, Annal Arragon.

(U) We are told by some historians, that the murder of the unhappy queen was the fruits of another extraordinary adventure. The king, Don *Pedro*, being one day hunting, a rustic,

governor excufed himfelf from obeying the order; but the king foon fent another perfon who fulfilled his intentions, as fome fay, by poifon [1]. In the mean time, Don *Henry*, count *de Traftamara*, and his affociates, found themfelves conftrained to retire once more into *France*, which they did, however, with the lefs regret, becaufe they difcovered that the king of *Arragon* had actually been taking meafures to raife his brother the Infant Don *Ferdinand* to the throne of *Caftile*, who, for that important fervice, was to make him a ceffion of the king-dom of *Murcia*. This treaty, however, was not extremely well performed on either fide; but as hoftilities ceafed, Don *Pedro* of *Caftile* made the ufe he intended of it, and engaged in a war with the *Moors* of *Granada*, which was managed with indifferent fuccefs. This year, and but a fmall time after the queen, deceafed Donna *Maria de Padilla*, leaving a

A. D. 1361.

[1] *Chronica del Rey Don Pedro de* PED. LOPEZ *de Ayala.*

ruftic, who made a moft rueful appearance, came up to him, and admonifhed him to defift from perfecuting fo religious and virtuous a princefs, and live with her as he ought to do, if he meant to efcape the heavy venge-ance of God. Upon this the king ordered the man to be feized, and thrown into a dun-geon, while fome of his creatures were ordered to make a ftrict enquiry, whether the queen had not fome hand in fending this meffenger; but, being fatisfied that this conjecture was ground-lefs, he ordered the peafant to be fet at liberty, whether from his imprifonment only, or from all the miferies of this life, is not very clear; for it is afferted that the man was never feen af-terwards: he judged from hence that his ill ufage of the queen, having raifed her many friends, and him as many enemies, the moft effectual method to pre-vent any future attempts in her favour was to remove her out of the world; and, having entruft-

ed a phyfician with this com-miffion, he went to the place where fhe was confined, and difpatched her with a dofe of poifon. The *Spanifh* hiftorians feem to make a point of render-ing that juftice to the queen which her hufband refufed her; they reprefent her as the beft princefs that ever fat upon the *Spanifh* throne; and the elo-quent *Mariana* is more eloquent than ufual in deploring her mif-fortunes, which he obferves be-gan with her marriage, and ended with her life. Donna *Maria de Padilla* did not furvive her many weeks; and the fon which the king had by her fol-lowed her to the grave foon af-ter. It may be, that authors are too bold in affirming thefe were the judgments of God upon the king for the unjuft treatment of fo good a princefs; but it may be very true hiftory, that this was the current opinion at the time, and in that light very well de-ferved to be recorded.

fon, Don *Alonfo*, and three daughters, Donna *Beatrix*, Donna
Conftantia, and Donna *Ifabella*, by the king Don *Pedro*,
who is faid to have expreffed great forrow for her death [m].
But his fubjects were far from looking upon this event as a
calamity.

In the month of *January*, the king of *Caftile* ordered the
grand mafter of *Calatrava*, accompanied by Don *Henry*
Henriquez, and fome other old officers, with 1000 horfe,
and 2000 foot, to furprize *Cadiz*, which, though a place of
fo great importance to the king of *Granada*, was according
to his intelligence but indifferently guarded.   Artifices of
this kind were familiar to the *Moors*; the army of *Caftile* advanced near the place without difcovering an enemy; a fmall
party was detached to the very fuburbs of the city to gain intelligence, a more confiderable body followed to fupport them;
the firft faw no troops, the latter retired from an apprehenfion
of an ambufcade, without being purfued.   This proceeding
was too fine for the Chriftian generals, they concluded the
city to be defencelefs and fecure, upon which, they fent off
detachments to plunder the country on every fide.   As foon
as thofe detachments were at a confiderable diftance, a fmall
detachment of *Moorifh* horfe came out of the city, and fkir-
mifhed with the like number of Chriftians, who paffed the
bridge for that purpofe.   By degrees the *Moors* grew ftronger,
the remains of the army under the command of the generals,
were obliged to engage to bring off their friends.   It was then
that they faw their ruin plainly, a great body of *Moors* having
paffed the river, attacked them in the rear, and the Chriftians
being furrounded, were very fpeedily defeated, the grand
mafter, Don *Henry*, and moft of the chief commanders taken
prifoners [n].   Guilt is never fecure : *Mohammed Barbaroffa*
had ufurped the crown of *Granada* from his mafter, who,
to fave his life, had retired to *Ronda*, and therefore this victory,
inftead of rejoicing, alarmed him.   He knew that the king of
Caftile was equally impetuous and obftinate; he was fenfible he
had provoked him, and he was confcious of his fuperiority.
He acted, however, very prudently in this critical fituation;
he underftood that the grand mafter and Don *Henry* were the
king's principal favourites; he fet them at liberty without ranfom, he fent by them magnificent prefents to Don *Pedro*, and
he defired them to mediate a peace [o].

His forces defeated by the Moors before the town of Cadiz, with great lofs.

[m] Zurit. Annal Arragon.   Chronica del Rey Don Pedro de
Ped. Lopez de Ayala.   Chron. de los Moros de Efpana.   Ferreras.   [n] Chronica del Rey Don Pedro de Ped. Lopez
de Ayala.   Chronica de los Moros de Efpana.   [o] Chronica
del Rey Don Pedro de Caftilla. Chronica de los Moros de Efpana.
Ferreras.

Moham-
med Bar-
baroffa,
king of
Granada,
murdered
by Don Pe-
dro of Caf-
tile.

ALL this, however, had no effect; Don *Pedro* carried on the war with such fiercenefs, that at length *Mohammed Barbaroffa* refolved to go in perfon to *Seville*, and fubmit himfelf to a prince, whom he found it not in his power to refift. He demanded and received a fafe conduct for this purpofe, and then executed his defign. Don *Pedro* received him with all the kindnefs and affability imaginable, and ordered one of the principal lords of his court to make a great feaft for his new vaffal. But being informed that *Mohammed* had brought with him great treafures, and that thofe who attended him had very rich jewels, he caufed them to be feized at that feaft; and having mounted the king of *Granada* upon an afs, fent them out into the moft public place with a herald, proclaiming before them, that the king of *Caftile* had condemned them to be put to death, as traitors againft their lawful fovereign P. Some fay that Don *Pedro* with his own hands gave the king of *Granada* a mortal wound, and afterwards cut off his head q. However that may be, it is univerfally confeffed, that this unfortunate monarch, with thirty-feven of the principal perfons in his court, were there flain, in breach of public faith, and fpoiled of all their wealth (W). After this, the head of *Mohammed*

P Chron. del Rey Don Pedro de PED. LOPEZ de Ayala. ROD. SANTII Hift. Hifpan. part iv.   q FERRERAS.

(W) The death of *Moham-med* king of *Granada* was attended with fo many aggravating circumftances, and carried in it fuch pregnant marks of barbarity, that one cannot eafily conceive Don *Pedro* could hope to ward off any part of the fhame that ought to attend fuch a glaring breach of hofpitality, and a violation fo apparent of public faith. Yet, in confequence of his being long practifed in fuch myfterious and bloody expedients, he formed a fcheme of fetting this atrocious act in fo plaufible a light, that fome well-meaning people have been deceived by it. He pretended that *Mohammend* had ufurped the crown of *Granada*, and therefore was a fit object for public juftice, which was executed upon him, and his adherents; not, indeed, according to the ordinary forms, to which ufurpers have no title, becaufe it would be unjuft to allow the benefit of laws to thofe who have taken the benefit of them from others. There would, indeed, have been great weight in this, if *Mohammed* had fallen into his hands as a prifoner of war; but as he knew who he was, and what he was, before he granted him a fafe conduct, as he had received his homage and his prefents, and taken him into his protection, thefe arguments were of no weight at all. Befides, avarice and cruelty were the natural vices of this monarch, both of which were gratified in this

foul

Mohammed Barbaroffa being fixed upon a pole, he sent it to *Mohammed Yago*, at *Ronda*, advising him to go back to *Granada*, and resume the government, which he accordingly did; the *Moors* being so terrified at this action, that they received him without hesitation [r].

THE king of *Castile* soon after called an assembly of the states at *Seville*, where he declared to them that he was lawfully married to Donna *Maria de Padilla*, before he espoused any other woman, in the presence of four witnesses, of whom her uncle *Hineftrofa* was deceased, but the rest were living, whom he accordingly produced; and these were the grand master of *Calatrava*, Donna *Maria*'s brother, his own chancellor, and his own chaplain, who swore what the king had said was true; upon which Don *Alonfo* was acknowleged for the king's successor, and his three sisters in case of his demise, according to the ordinary rules of succession [s]. He proceeded from thence to *Soria*, where he had sollicited Don *Carlos*, king of *Navarre*, to meet him. Don *Pedro* entertained that prince, not only with all the splendour and magnificence, but with all the kindness and respect imaginable. One day, however, after dinner, Don *Pedro* took the king of *Navarre* aside, and told him, that having revenged himself on the king of *Granada*, for hindering that vengeance he would otherwise have taken of the king of *Arragon*, he found himself now at liberty to chastise that monarch to the utmost, in which he hoped he would not refuse him his assistance. Instead of observing that the peace still continued, or that himself had no quarrel against that king, Don *Carlos* approved of all, and promised his concurrence; the fate of the king of *Granada* was fresh in his mind, and the sight of the king of *Castile*'s troops, of whom the town was full, would not suffer him to recollect any scruples, so that they parted very good friends [t]. The war began the same year, and being made by surprize, Don *Pedro* of *Castile* gained some considerable advantages; the king of *Arragon*, on the other hand, recalled

Obliges the states to acknowlege his children by Donna Maria de Padilla heirs to the crown.

1362.

---

[r] Chronica de los Moros de Espana. MARIANA. MAYERNE TURQUET.   [s] Chronica del Rey Don Pedro de PED. LOPEZ de Ayala.   [t] Histoire de Royaume de Navarre. Chronica del Rey Don Pedro de Castilla.

---

foul action; and therefore it is the duty of an impartial historian to discover the fallacy, and to shew that these pretended motives of justice were, in fact, the colours only which this cunning prince invented after the fact, to cover the most crying of all crimes.

the

the count of *Trastamara*, and the followers of his fortune [u]. On the eighth of *October* died Don *Alonso*, whom his father Don *Pedro* had declared his successor, upon which that monarch made his will, under an apprehension that his grief might cost him his life [w]; but at the same time he made all imaginable preparations for carrying on the next campaign with vigour. In order to this, he not only pressed the kings of *Portugal, Granada*, and *Navarre*, to send troops and ships to his assistance, but entered likewise into an alliance with *Edward* the third, of *England*, the terms of which were settled with his son *Edward* the black prince [x].

The Infant Don Ferdinand of Arragon cruelly murdered by his brother.　THE king of *Arragon*, though he paid great respect to Don *Henry*, count of *Trastamara*, yet he secretly revived his design of raising his brother, the Infant Don *Ferdinand*, to the throne of *Castile*; which coming to take air, most of the exiles quitted the count Don *Henry*, and adhered to the Infant; and amongst these deserters were his own brethren, which occasioned no little discord. It is not at all unlikely, that this scheme was divulged in order to promote a peace. Don *Pedro*, through the pope's legate, expressed himself not averse to it; and the plan, upon which he offered to treat, was this: he was willing to espouse Donna *Joanna*, the king of *Arragon*'s daughter, and to give his own daughter, Donna *Beatrix*, to the Infant Don *Juan*, son and heir of the king of *Arragon*; but previous to these measures and some others, he expected that the king of *Arragon* should oblige him so far as to put his own brother, together with three or four of his brethren, who were at the court of *Arragon*, to death, without delay [y]. At this, that monarch did not much hesitate, tho' it may be doubted whether he was in earnest or not; however, his brother Don *Ferdinand* being exceedingly alarmed, excited a mutiny among the *Castilians* who were about him, and Don *Henry*, count of *Trastamara*, desired leave to retire into *France*. In this confusion, the king of *Arragon* ordered his brother, the Infant Don *Ferdinand*, to be arrested, who, resenting this usage, and endeavouring to defend himself, was slain [z]. In the midst of these troubles, Don *Pedro* had a son

---

[u] ZURIT. Annal Arragon. FERRERAS.　[w] Chronica del Rey Don Pedro de PED. LOPEZ de Ayala.　[x] BRANES's Life of Edward III. BRANDAOR. Chronica de los Moros de Espana. Histoire du Royaume de Navarre. FERRERAS.　[y] RAINALD. ZURIT. Annal Arragon. Chronica del Rey Don Pedro de PED. LOPEZ de Ayala.　[z] ZURIT. Annal Arragon.

born by one of his miſtreſſes, whom, upon this event, he determined to marry, and therefore broke off the treaty [a].

ALL the *Caſtilians* who were in exile, uniting with zeal, under the count Don *Henry*, in whom lay all their hopes, the king of *Arragon* was forced to treat him with much reſpect. At the ſame time, advancing towards the frontiers of his dominions, he had a private interview with the king of *Navarre*, who had hitherto acted in favour of *Caſtile* from conſtraint. They agreed to ſet up the count Don *Henry*, and pull down his brother; but, at the ſame time, reſolved that the king of *Navarre* ſhould have *Biſcay* and *Caſtile* for his ſhare, the king of *Arragon* the realms of *Murcia* and *Toledo*, and that count *Henry* might keep the reſt if he could [b]. In order to bring this fine project to bear, a new interview was appointed at the caſtle of *Sos*, on the frontiers of *Navarre*, to which the count Don *Henry* was invited, in order to communicate to him ſo much of their ſcheme as might induce him to aſſiſt in the execution of it. The count conſented to the interview, but upon condition that the caſtle was put into the hands of Don *Juan Ramirez de Arellano*, as not caring to truſt himſelf to the good faith of thoſe monarchs. This was agreed to, Don *Juan* put into poſſeſſion of the place, which he garriſoned with his own vaſſals, and then the two kings and the count Don *Henry* repaired thither, with a very few domeſticks [c]. While the conference laſted, the monarchs of *Arragon* and *Navarre* propoſed to Don *Juan*, the maſſacreing the count Don *Henry* and all his forces, which that nobleman rejected with equal firmneſs and contempt; ſo that, in the end, they found it their intereſt to treat the count of *Traſtamara* on the footing of an equal, and as a prince whom they meant to aſſiſt in becoming king of *Caſtile*. That prince diſcovering ſoon after the plots that had been formed againſt him, took a ſudden reſolution to quit *Spain*; but the king of *Arragon*, with ſome difficulty, pacified him, and made a new treaty, to the performance of which both parties ſwore, in the preſence of the archbiſhop of *Tarragona* [d]. But it was, notwithſtanding, but indifferently kept.

THE next year was full of events of the ſame kind, and of treaſons and murders; which, relating more particularly to the affairs of *Arragon*, belong to another place. We muſt, however, take notice, that Don *Tello* betrayed his brother and

Marginal notes: Confederacy between the kings of Arragon, Navarre, and the count Don Henry.

1363.

An army brought out of France by

---

[a] ROD. SANTII Hiſt. Hiſpan. p. iv. RAINALD. du Royaume de Navarre. ZURIT. Annal Arragon. ANA. FERRERAS. MAYERNE TURQUET. Annal Arragon. Hiſtoire du Royaume de Navarre. Rey Don Pedro de Pao. LOPEZ de Ayala.

[b] Hiſt. [c] MARIANA. [d] ZURIT. Chronica del

Bertrand du Guesclin, *and others.*

1364.

the king of *Arragon* to the king of *Castile*, who still carried on the war with great vigour and success, both by land and sea [e]. As the king of *Arragon* saw clearly, that, in the course of this war, he was in great danger of losing his dominions, or at least a great part of them, unless the scheme of deposing Don *Pedro* of *Castile* actually took effect, he began the next year to turn his thoughts that way in earnest, and Providence furnished the means of chastizing that barbarous prince. There were at that time in *France* upwards of 20,000 veteran troops, who had served against the *English*, and, from being the defenders, were now become the terrors of that country.

1365.

These, by the assistance of the king of *Arragon*, the count Don *Henry* took into his pay. Under the command of the famous *Bertrand du Guesclin*, and *John de Bourbon*, count *de la Marche*, they began their march for *Catalonia*, and brought with them likewise some of their old enemies, the *English*, under several officers of note; for their common wants had made them very good friends, and their business in *Spain* was to get money [f].

The count Don Henry advances to Calahorra, and is proclaimed king of Castile.

These forces were no sooner arrived and reviewed, but Don *Henry*, count of *Trastamara*, entered *Castile*, and summoned the town of *Calahorra*, which immediately opened its gates. As soon as he was in the town, by the advice of *Bertrand du Guesclin*, he caused himself to be proclaimed king, and then began his march directly towards *Burgos*, where his brother Don *Pedro* then was [g]. The nobility and people sollicited that prince, who had a numerous army, not to stir, assuring him of their fidelity; but he told them that he knew his brother's inclinations and theirs better, and would therefore march to *Seville*, in order to secure his children and his treasures. The count Don *Henry* meeting with little opposition, came to *Burgos*, where, finding most of the nobility of *Castile*, they readily accepted him for their king, and he was solemnly inaugurated a few days after [h]. One of Don *Pedro's* creatures, to save his life, discovered an immense treasure in gold; and the *Jews*, who were ever in danger in such cases, made him a present of a vast sum of money [i]. *Henry*, who had hitherto known little but danger and distress, and who perhaps was made wise by his brother's misfortunes, resolved;

---

[e] Zurit. Annal Arragon. Chron. var. antiq.   [f] P. Daniel Histoire de France. Zurit. Annal Arragon. Emanuel de Faria y Sousa. Mariana. Ferreras.   [g] Chronica del Rey Don Henrique Segundo de Ped. Lopez de Ayala.   [h] Chronica del Rey Don Pedro. Chronica del Rey Don Henrique Segundo.   [i] Rod. Santii Hist. Hispan. p. iv. Ferreras.

by the actions of one day, to secure the crown to himself and his descendants. His politics were not deep or refined, but they were very sensible and solid. He had in the day of his calamity made many promises, which had been taken in current payment by those who had advanced him to the throne; he thought it would contribute to keep him firmly settled thereon, if he performed them punctually; and this he did the very day he was crowned king. The count *de Ribagorce*, who had married the heiress of Don *Juan Emanuel*, had all the estates of that family, with the title of marquis of *Villena*; to *Bertrand du Guesclin* he gave the lordship of *Molina*, and his own county of *Traslamara* to his brother Don *Tello*; the lordship of *Biscay* to another brother of his, Don *Sancho Albuquerque* and *LeDesma*; and, in short, to all who had rendered him service, he gave, if not to the value of their services, yet beyond their expectations [k].

Don *Lopez de Luna*, archbishop of *Saragossa*, upon the king's letter, conveyed the queen and her children to *Burgos* [l]. Soon after their arrival, the king marched towards *Toledo*, which opened its gates on his approach; while Don *Pedro* at *Seville*, who the year before had concluded a marriage for his daughter Donna *Beatrix*, with the Infant of *Portugal*, sent her thither with a vast fortune in ready money; and, having embarked his treasures on board his fleet, quitted that city with his army, which he still commanded in person, and marched into *Galicia* [m]. Don *Gilles de Bocqnegro* fitted out a small squadron, and seized the ship in which the king's treasures were, which fell into the hands of his brother *Henry*, and amounted to thirty-six quintals of gold, and a prodigious quantity of jewels, which he had been amassing all his reign [n]. Don *Pedro* changing his intentions, proceeded to the frontiers of *Portugal*, and gave notice of his arrival to the king, who sent him word, that he could not prevail upon his son to marry his daughter, whom he therefore thought fit to restore with all her fortune [o]; he went next to *Albuquerque*, where he proposed to leave his children: the inhabitants prevented that, by shutting their gates against him; this obliged him to demand a safe conduct through *Portugal*, into *Galicia*, where the people received him very chearfully, through the persuasion of the archbishop of *Compostella*, whom he rewarded very strangely; for, understanding that he was immensely rich, he murdered

The king retires into Portugal, and from thence into Guienne.

[k] Chronica del Rey Don Henrique Segundo. [l] Mari-ANA. Mayerne Turquet. [m] Chronica del Rey Don Pedro. Brandaon. [n] Chron. del Rey Don Henrique Segundo. [o] Brandaon. Emanuel de Faria y Sousa. Chronica del Rey Don Pedro.

him,

him, and seized all that he had [P] : then leaving the government of *Galicia* to Don *Ferdinand de Castro*, he marched to *Corunna*, and embarked his troops on board his fleet, with which he sailed to *Bayonne*, in order to demand assistance from the prince of *Wales* [q]. The king, Don *Henry*, after receiving the submission of all *Andalusia*, marched with an army into *Galicia*; and having fully satisfied his mercenaries, dismissed them, reserving only the forces of the count *de la Marche*, those of *Bertrand du Guesclin*, of *Hugh Corbelay*, whose *English* name, for he was an *Englishman*, was Sir *Hugh*

A. D. 1366.

Calverly, and some others [r]. Don *Ferdinand de Castro* shut himself up in *Lugo*, with a good garrison, which the king besieged; thinking his presence, however, necessary in *Castile*, he made an agreement with Don *Ferdinand*, that he should surrender all the places he held, if he was not relieved by Don *Pedro* before *Christmas*, in consideration of which he would bestow on him the lordship of *Castro de Xerez*; with the title of count, because it had belonged formerly to his ancestors. On the king's arrival at *Burgos*, he summoned an assembly of the states, who very chearfully gave him all that he could ask, for the defence of himself and his dominions [s].

Edward prince of Wales, surnamed the Black Prince, undertakes to restore him.

THE king, Don *Pedro*, who in his passage had touched at *St. Sebastians*, and received on board thirty-six thousand pistoles in gold, which he had there, brought so much wealth into *Guienne*, that he was extremely welcome to the *Black Prince*, and to all the great lords of that country, who very readily offered him their services, in consideration of his money [t]. After mature deliberation, it was resolved that the prince should go in person, with a numerous body of his victorious troops, to restore him to his dominions; which troops the king was to pay, and to bestow upon the prince the province of *Biscay*, and some other places. The constable of *Guienne* was to have the town of *Soria* and its district; and the king of *Navarre*, in consideration of a passage through his country, was to have the fortress of *Alfaro*, and all the country as far as *Navarette*; and, for the just performance of these promises, the king gave his children as hostages [u]. It was not long before king *Henry* obtained a pretty good account of these transactions, upon which he invited the king of *Navarre* to an interview, in which, having taken great pains to

[P] BRANDAON. Chronica del Rey Don Pedro. FERRERAS. [q] Chronica del Rey Don Pedro. [r] Chronica del Rey Don Henrique Segundo. [s] Chronica general de España. ROD. SANTII Hist. Hispan. part iv. FERRERAS. [t] BARNES's History of Edward III. Chronica del Rey Don Pedro. [u] Histoire du Royaume de Navarre. Chronica del Rey Don Pedro.

shew

shew him his own interests, and how easily he might prevent
Don *Pedro* and the prince of *Wales* from passing through his
country, concluded with him a treaty for that purpose, to the
due performance of which both kings were sworn, in the presence of the archbishops of *Toledo* and *Saragossa* ; king *Henry*
promising him *Logrono*, and giving him sixty thousand pistoles
in gold [w]. Don *Pedro* having notice of this, offered him, not
only the place before-mentioned, but *Victoria* also.

The king of *Navarre* concluded a treaty with him too; and, *Dexterous*
to shew what a royal politician he was, when the *English* forces *manage-*
arrived upon his frontiers, he sent for *Oliver de Mauny*, who *ment of*
was cousin to *Bertrand du Guesclin*, and desired him to seize *the king of*
upon his person, as he was hunting, and carry him prisoner *Navarre*
to a fort of which he was governor, for which service he *in deceiv-*
offered him a sum of money, and the castle of *Cherbourg* in *ing both*
Normandy, which *Oliver*, who was a soldier of fortune, ac- *parties.*
cepted; so that Don *Pedro* and the prince of *Wales* passed
through *Navarre* without any opposition [x]. Such *English* as
had hitherto served king *Henry*, left him upon the approach
of the *Black Prince* ; notwithstanding which, he resolved to
give the enemy battle, contrary to the opinion of *Bertrand du Guesclin*, and the foreign officers, who assured him
that the troops of the prince of *Wales* were invincible, while in
full health and vigour ; but that if he drew them farther into
the country, and exposed them but for a few weeks to the
rays of a *Spanish* sun, they would either retire of themselves,
or fall an easy conquest [y]. But Don *Henry*, knowing that his
brother had many partizans, and being diffident, even of some
of the troops in his own army, resolved to venture a battle,
which was accordingly fought on the sixth of *April*, between
Najara and *Navarette*, where, through the fault of Don
Tello, the king's brother, the left wing was quickly beat, which
brought on a total route, notwithstanding the king exposed
himself extremely to prevent it [z]. The loss was very great;
and, besides the numbers slain upon the spot, there were many
persons of distinction taken prisoners. The king, Don *Henry*,
made his escape with all possible diligence through *Arragon*;
into *France* ; his queen, with her children, went to *Saragossa* [a].

[w] Histoire du Royaume de Navarre. Chronica del Rey Don
Henrique Segundo. FERRERAS.   [x] Chronica del Rey Don
Pedro. Histoire du Royaume de Navarre.   [y] Chronica
del Rey Don Henrique Segundo.   [z] Chronica del Rey
Don Pedro. Chronica del Rey Don Henrique Segunda. MARI-
ANA. FERRERAS. MAYERNE TURQUET.   [a] Chronica
del Rey Don Henrique Segundo.

                                                    DON

The king,   Don *Pedro's* natural cruelty shewed itself, not only in the
Don Pedro, usage of the prisoners taken by his troops, but in causing a
feated   gentleman to be put to death, who fell into the hands of an
again upon English lord, which produced an expostulation on the part
the throne, of the prince of *Wales,* which, how much soever he disliked,
and again he thought fit to dissemble [b].   They proceeded together as far
endangered as *Burgos,* where the prince lodged in the monastery *De las*
by his *Huelgas,* and his brother *John* of *Gaunt,* duke of *Lancaster,*
vices. in the convent of *St. Dominick.*   The prince of *Wales* found
it necessary for his own safety to conclude a truce between
the crowns of *Castile* and *Arragon,* and a treaty for himself
with the last-mentioned crown and that of *Portugal,* by
which he stipulated the reciprocal assistance of each power in
the division of the states of *Castile,* in case Don *Pedro* broke
his faith with them, which they all suspected; and then,
taking leave of him, returned back into *Guienne,* moved
thereto chiefly by a sickness that broke out in his army [c].
Don *Pedro,* now left to himself, began to indulge, in a greater
degree than ever, that thirst of blood which rendered him
universally odious and terrible.   At *Burgos, Toledo,* and
Seville, some people of the first quality were put to death,
and numbers of inferior rank.   In this political inquisition,
even women did not escape [d].   The king, Don *Henry,* did
not suffer his spirits to be sunk through his misfortunes; but,
on the contrary, sollicited the count *de Foix,* who, out of mere
compassion, offered him a retreat in his country, the king of
France by letters, and pope *Urban* the fifth, who then resided
at *Avignon* in person.   He received from each of them, which
rarely happens in such cases, more than he could demand or
expect.   The count gave him leave to raise forces in his territories, and allowed his son to command them.   The pope received him kindly, freed him (if we can suppose that in his
power) from all blemish of illegitimacy, and dismissed him
from his presence as legal a monarch as he could, and as rich a
one as it was convenient to make him [e].   The king of *France*
exceeded both; for he ordered his brother, the duke of *Anjou,* to
give him a large sum of money, made him a present of a strong
fortress on the frontiers of *Navarre,* and allowed him to raise
what troops he could. In virtue of these assistances, he assembled
an army, with which he entered *Castile,* after having passed
through *Arragon,* without the leave of that monarch, in the

[b] Chronica del Rey Don Pedro. Ferreras.   [c] Brandaon.
Zurit. Annal Arragon. Chronica del Rey Don Pedro.   [d] Ma-
riana. Ferreras.   [e] P. Daniel Histoire de France.
Rain-ld. Chronica del Rey Don Henrique Segundo.

month

month of *September*, and, before the clofe of the year, was mafter of *Caftile* and the kingdom of *Toledo* [f].

THE generous manner in which he had behaved towards fuch as affifted him in his former expedition, had induced all, who were not murdered or imprifoned, to put themfelves in motion for his fervice. By the end of the month of *April*, he became mafter of the city of *Leon*, the beft part of that kingdom, and a great part of *Afturias* [g]. The city of *Toledo*, however, refufed to acknowlege him, though their archbifhop had accompanied him in his exile. The king, having in vain tried every method to perfuade them, at length invefted the city with a great army, being determined to reduce it by force [h]. At this time, Don *Pedro*, with the very fame intention, was before *Cordova*, with the king of *Granada*, who had brought fix thoufand horfe and thirty thoufand foot to his affiftance, and they pufhed this fiege with fo much vigour, that they became mafters of a great part of the city by ftorm ; yet the cries of the women, from the apprehenfions of Don *Pedro*'s cruelty, were fo loud and piercing, that the fight of their forrow banifhing all fenfe of danger, the men returned with fuch fury to the charge, that they difpoffeffed the *Moors* of all the places they had taken, and threw the greateft part of them over the walls. The next day the two kings attacked them again, and were repulfed with lofs; after which they raifed the fiege, and feparated their forces [i]. The people of *Toledo*, finding themfelves exceedingly diftreffed, fent to Don *Pedro* for fuccours ; and feveral towns on the frontiers of *Navarre*, having entered into an affociation for their own defence, and having a fmall body of regular troops, commanded by Don *Tello*, fent likewife to affure him of their fidelity, and to receive his orders, letting him know at the fame time, that, on the one hand, they were preffed by the king of *Navarre*, and on the other, by Don *Henry*. Don *Pedro* returned them for anfwer, that he was preparing to relieve *Toledo*, which might create a diverfion in their favour ; but if, notwithftanding they found themfelves obliged to yield, he chofe they fhould do it to his brother, and not to the king of *Navarre*. Yet Don *Tello* prevailed on them to take the contrary courfe, and to fubmit to the king of *Navarre* [k]. The king, Don *Henry*, in

Befieges, in conjunction with the king of Granada, the city of Cordova without effect.

1368.

[f] P. DANIEL. Hiftoire de France. Chronica del Rey Don Henrique Segundo. ZURIT. Annal. Arragon.　[g] Chronica del Rey Don Henrique Segundo.　[h] ROD. SANTII Hift. Hifpan. part iv. FERRERAS.　[i] Chronica del Rey Don Pedro. Chronica de los Moros de Efpana.　[k] Chronica del Rey Don Pedro. MARIANA.

the camp before *Toledo*, created Don *Bernard de Foix*, the son of his friend, a count, and gave him the town of *Medina Cæli*, from whom the noble family, bearing afterwards the title of dukes of the same place, descended [1].

The king, Don Henry marches to give his brother Don Pedro battle. A NEW war having broke out between the *French* and *English*, *Charles* the fifth sent his embassadors to the king, Don *Henry*, before *Toledo*, with whom he made a perpetual league for themselves, their heirs, and successors; and the *French* king, in virtue of his engagements, promised to send *Bertrand du Guesclin*, with six hundred lances to his assistance [m]. Don *Pedro* having drawn together all the troops he was able to assemble, in the neighbourhood of *Seville*, summoned his principal ally, the king of *Granada*, to send him fresh assistance, which he very readily did; and with these, and with the forces of the kingdom of *Murcia*, he resolved to attempt the relief of *Toledo*. As soon as Don *Henry* had intelligence of this, he left the archbishop with a sufficient corps of troops to invest the place; and with the flower of his nobility, and a well appointed army, marched to find out his brother. He looked on it as a good omen, that at the very time he took this resolution, *Bertrand du Guesclin* arrived with his six hundred lances that had been promised him from *France* [n]. On his march he was joined by the grand master of St. *James*, with the forces he had brought out of *Andalusia*; and thus strengthened he advanced into the plains of *Montiel*. The country people making fires in the neighbourhood to give notice to Don *Pedro*, he surmised that these troops came to his assistance; but, before it was day, the next morning his advanced guards brought him advice, that Don *Henry* was in full march with all his forces to give him battle.

Don Pedro defeated, and after-wards killed by his brother Don Henry at Montiel. Don *Pedro* made the best disposition he could, and behaved very gallantly, but his troops never recovered the surprize they were in on the first attack, and were quickly routed [o]. But Don *Pedro*, with a small body of foot, threw himself into the castle of *Montiel*, while Don *Martin Lopez de Cordova*, with eight hundred horse, and a thousand cross bows, retired into the strong fortress of *Carmona*, which the king had intended for his own retreat, and where he had left his children [p]. This battle was fought on the fourteenth of

[1] Chronica del Rey Don Henrique Segundo. [m] P. DANIEL Histoire de France. FERRERAS. [n] Chronica del Rey Don Pedro. Chronica de los Moros de España. Chronica del Rey Don Henrique Segundo. [o] MARIANA. FERRERAS. MAYERNE TURQUET. [p] Chronica del Rey Don Pedro.

March,

March; and the king, Don *Henry*, having confidered the place into which his brother had thrown himfelf, caufed a line to be drawn round it, well fortified and well guarded. Don *Pedro* foon found the place not tenable againft his brother's forces, and befides this, his garrifon were in great want of provifions; he therefore applied himfelf to *Bertrand du Guefclin*, and promifed him a large fum of money if he would fuffer him to pafs through his quarters. *Bertrand* having confulted his officers, difcovered this to the king, Don *Henry*, and, at his requeft, affigned an hour when Don *Pedro* might come to his tent, where Don *Henry*, followed by fome refolute perfons; rufhed in, and, having ftruck him firft in the face with his dagger, the reft fell upon him and put him to death on the twenty-third of *March*, when he was thirty-five years and feven months old [q]. This monarch was debauched, cruel, cunning, faithlefs, and covetous, in a fupreme degree. After all the loffes he had fuftained, he left behind him at *Seville*, *Almodava*, and other places, no lefs than one hundred and fifty millions in gold and filver, befides jewels and plate to an immenfe value [r]. Befides his children by Donna *Maria de Padilla*, he left a fon Don *Juan* by Donna *Joanna de Caftro*, and two other fons Don *Sancho* and Don *Diego* by Donna *Ifabella*, who had been governefs to his fon Don *Alonfo*. His two eldeft daughters, at the time of his death, were hoftages in *Guienne*, and the reft of his children in the caftle of *Carmona* [s]. He expired, therefore, with the moft dreadful profpect before his eyes, in refpect to all he held dear.

THE king, Don *Henry*, was far from remaining the peaceable poffeffor of his brother's dominions, by his death; but, upon his arrival at *Seville*, he acquired all his treafures, which put him into a condition of maintaining the war againft all his enemies, though they invaded his dominions almoft on every fide [t]. The firft thing he did was to offer good terms to Don *Martin*, who commanded in *Carmona*, which, when he rejected, he caufed the place to be blocked up. The towns of *Molina* and *Requina* declared for the king of *Arragon* [u]. *Ciudad Rodrigo*, *Le Defma*, *Alcantara*, *Zamora*, *Tuy*, *Corunna*, the city of St. *James*, *Lugo*, *Orenza*, and many other places,

The king of Portugal claims and affumes the title of king of Caftile and Leon.

[q] Chronica del Rey Don Henrique Segundo. Chronica del Rey Don Pedro. MARIANA. FERRERAS. [r] ROD. SANTII Hift. Hifpan. p. iv. Chronica del Rey Don Pedro. [s] MARIANA. FERRERAS. MAYERNE TURQUET. [t] Chronica del Rey Don Henrique Segundo. [u] ZURIT. Annal Arragon.

acknowleged

acknowleged Don *Ferdinand*, king of *Portugal*, who immediately coined money, with the arms of his own crown on one
fide, and thofe of *Caftile* on the other ". The king of
Granada likewife gave him a vaft deal of trouble; and the
king of *Arragon* entered into a league with the prince of
Wales and duke of *Lancafter*, for facilitating the conquefts he
meditated in *Caftile*; and he likewife entered into another
treaty with the king of *Portugal*, who, in fupport of his pretenfions, invaded *Galicia* ˣ. On the other hand, *Toledo* having furrendered to the archbifhop, and the queen and her
children being come thither, the king went to meet them ʸ.
He had not been long there, before he received the news of
the king of *Portugal*'s invading *Galicia* with a numerous
army, upon which he marched thither with the troops that
were about his perfon, with fuch celerity, that the king, Don
Ferdinand, who was unwilling to rifk a battle at fo great a
diftance from his own dominions, left his troops in *Corunna*,
A. D. and returned home by fea ᶻ. The king, Don *Henry*, was
1369. no fooner informed of this, than he directed his march into
Portugal, and having made himfelf mafter of the city of
Braga, defolated all the country round about with fire and
fword; upon which Don *Ferdinand* fent him a challenge, to
which Don *Henry* anfwered, that if he came with an army,
he knew where to find him; foon after which, having executed all that he defigned by this invafion, he difperfed his
troops into garrifons on the frontiers, and returned into
Caftile ᵃ.

Don Hen- AT this juncture, the enemies of the king Don *Henry*
ry defends were many, and the obftacles he had to overcome were great;
his domini- but his notions of government were clear, his temper mode-
ens againft rate, his application indefatigable. He had many things to
the kings of attend; he fuffered none of them to efcape his notice; he kept
Portugal his frontiers well guarded; *Carmona* and *Zamora* blocked up,
and Arra- and two or three flying armies in the field. In the affembly of
gon. the ftates at *Medina del Campo*, he ballanced accounts with
the officers of the foreign troops in his fervice, paid them their
whole demands, and gave them confiderable gratifications,
telling the ftates at the fame time, " to thefe ftrangers we
owe our prefent fafety; it is but juft, therefore, we fhould

ʷ BRANDAON. EMANUEL DE FARIA Y SOUSA. FERRERAS.
ˣ Chronica de los Moros de Efpana. BRANDAON. ZURIT. Annal Arragon. MARIANA. ʸ Chronica del Rey Don Henrique Segundo. ᶻ EMANUEL DE FARIA Y SOUSA. FER-
RERAS. ᵃ Chronica del Rey Don Henrique Segundo.
BRAND ON.

afford

afford them establishments; as for their posterity, they will be brave men and *Spaniards* [b]." The king of *Granada* had taken and rased *Algezira*, which gave the king great concern. He ordered his generals to lay waste the open country, which was extremely well cultivated, which forced the *Moors* to demand a truce, which his resentment did not hinder him from granting, because it was convenient for his affairs [c]. The *Portuguese* blocked up the river of *Seville* with a fleet; his admiral *Ambrose Bocanegra* broke through it, with seven stout gallies, having a large sum of money on board, with which he proceeded to *Biscay*, where he soon assembled a numerous squadron of large ships, well manned, with which he first beat the *Portuguese*, and then, by his master's orders, sailed to the assistance of the *French* monarch, and had the good fortune to defeat an *English* squadron, and to make the earl of *Pembroke* prisoner [d]. His brother, the Infant Don *Tello*, dying, he gave the lordship of *Biscay* to his own son, the Infant Don *Juan*, and by that means annexed it for ever to the crown [e]. On the frontiers of *Arragon* he kept a body of troops sufficient to defend his subjects, till his affairs were in such order as might enable him to recover what he had lost; and thus by degrees, and the happy management of events, the prospect began to clear on every side, and the mildness of his administration made him beloved at home, while his prudence and vigour rendered him respected abroad [f].

A. D. 1370.

IN the beginning of the year, the pope sent his legates into *Spain*, with letters directed to the kings of *Castile*, *Arragon*, and *Portugal*, to persuade them to a peace; and at the same time he wrote to the prelates of *Toledo*, *Seville*, *Saragossa*, and *Coinbra*, requiring them to give all the assistance in their power to this good work. Don *Henry* received them with great kindness and respect, but advised them not to lose time at his court, since he was already as well disposed in that respect as they could wish, upon which they departed for *Portugal* [g]. In the mean time the king went in person to the siege of *Carmona*, where, some say, his life was in great danger from a sally made by the besieged. His guards, however, attempted the place by scaling, and about forty of them got into the town; but before they could force their passage to a gate,

Becomes master of Carmona, and makes peace with the king of Portugal,

[b] Chronica general de Espana. ROD. SANTII Hist. Hispan. MARIANA.　　　[c] Chronica del Rey Don Henrique Segundo. Chronica de los Moros de Espana.　　[d] BRANDAON. P. DANIEL Histoire de France. FERRERAS.　　[e] Chronica del Rey Don Henrique Segundo.　　[f] MARIANA. FERRERAS. MAYERNE TURQUET.　　[g] RAINALD. FERRERAS.

　　　were

were surrounded and taken prisoners, and some days after, the governor ordered them to be put to death [h]. At length, famine and frequent losses compelled Don *Martin* to capitulate, when he offered to deliver up his master's treasures and children, provided he might be at liberty to go where he pleased. The king added he must likewise deliver up Don *Pedro's* chancellor, who had been the great instrument of his cruelties, to which he very readily agreed [i]. The king sent the treasures and the children of Don *Pedro* to *Toledo*, and ordered the chancellor and the governor to be put to death. The latter insisted that this was against public faith; but the king alleged the murder of the forty soldiers, which being likewise against public faith, left him, in the king's opinion, no title to it [k]. A severe judgment, but a good example. *Zamora*, and all the country of *Galicia*, quickly submitted; and the king of *Portugal* very wisely consented to a peace, and agreed to marry Donna *Leonora*, Infanta of *Castile*, with a portion of three hundred thousand crowns. Yet, soon after, falling in love with Donna *Leonora Tellez*, the wife of *John Lawrence de Acunha*, he sent embassadors to the king of *Castile*, to excuse his declining the marriage; and, having caused the lady to be divorced from her husband, secretly made her his wife. The king of *Castile* told the embassadors that he could always find a match for his daughter, and that though he wished him for his son-in law, he was very well content to esteem the king of *Portugal* his friend and ally [l]. Towards the close of the year, at the request of the pope's legate, he concluded a truce with the crown of *Navarre*, and another with that of *Arragon*; and the face of peace being thus universally restored, he sent the Infant Don *Juan* to take possession of *Biscay* [m].

A. D. 1371.

That monarch, notwithstanding, meditates new disturbances. As those who have done a great injury can seldom be brought to forgive sincerely, so the king of *Portugal*, apprehending the resentment of Don *Henry*, entered into a treaty with *John* of *Gaunt*, duke of *Lancaster*, who had married Donna *Constantia*, daughter to the king Don *Pedro*, invited him into his dominions, and promised to support his pretensions; upon which he assumed the title of king of *Castile* [n]. In confidence therefore of receiving these succours in due time, he made an irruption into *Galicia*, surprized *Tuy* and

[h] Chronica del Rey Don Henrique Segundo. [i] MARIAN. MAYERNE TURQUET. [k] Chronica del Rey Don Henrique Segundo. [l] BRANDAON. FERRERAS. [m] Hist. du Royaume de Navarre. RAINALD. ZURIT. Annal Arragon. [n] BRANDAON. Chronica del Rey Don Henrique Segundo.

some other places, which were speedily recovered by the king of *Castile*, who, when he once understood the bottom of the design, immediately undertook to cure the king of *Portugal* of a resolution to disturb him. In the first place, he sent a squadron of ships to the assistance of the *French*, that by finding employment for the *English* nearer home, he might be in the less danger of being troubled with them in *Portugal*; and at the same time he charged his admiral with negotiating the repurchase of those lands, which he had given to *Bertrand du Guesclin*; for, as he was now become constable of *France*, it was not at all probable he should ever think of returning into *Spain*, which proposal was readily accepted; and, for the sum of two hundred and seventy thousand crowns in gold, the king recovered all the places he had formerly granted him [o].

WHILE his fleet was thus employed, the king made an expedition into *Portugal*, and took several places; but, upon the application of the pope's legate, he consented to a short truce, and likewise renewed that with *Arragon* for eight months [p]. The truce being expired, Don *Henry*, in the very depth of winter, made himself master of *Viseo*, and from thence advanced towards *Coinbra*; but being informed that Donna *Leonora*, queen of *Portugal*, had retired thither to lie in, he sent her a compliment, importing that her presence was an invincible garrison [q]; upon which he moved towards the king of *Portugal*, who was encamped at *Santaren*; but finding that he would act only on the defensive, he proceeded to insult *Lisbon*, and, by the assistance of a squadron from *Seville*, he burnt part of the lower town, and some ships in the harbour [r]. This gave such weight to the endeavours of the pope's legates for obtaining a peace, that at length the preliminaries were settled, by which the king of *Portugal* engaged, that whenever king *Henry* sent a squadron to the assistance of *France*, he would likewise send five ships or gallies; that Don *Ferdinand de Castro*, and the rest of the exiles from *Castile* should be obliged to quit his dominions; and that Don *Sancho*, the king of *Castile*'s brother, should marry Donna *Beatrix*, sister to king *Ferdinand*; and, that Don *Alonso*, the natural son of king *Henry*, should marry Donna *Isabella*, the natural daughter of king *Ferdinand*, when they were of competent age: in consideration of which, the king, Don *Henry*,

Margin note: 1372. Don Henry compels both him and the king of Navarre, once more to demand peace.

---

[o] P. DANIEL Histoire de France. EMANUEL DE FARIA Y SOUSA. FERRERAS. [p] Chronica del Rey Don Henrique Segundo. RAINALD. ZURIT. Annal Arragon. [q] BRANDAON. Chronica del Rey Don Henrique Segundo. [r] BRANDAON. FERRERAS.

was to restore all the places he had taken. This treaty the two kings signed and swore to, in the presence of the legates; after which, the first of the two marriages was celebrated, and Donna *Isabella* was put into the hands of the king of *Castile* [r]. A peace was some months afterwards concluded with the king of *Navarre*, who took advantage from thence to sollicit the king of *Castile* to detach himself from *France*, and to make a league with the *English*, which the king absolutely refused, notwithstanding that the duke of *Lancaster* offered, in that case, to accept of a sum of money in lieu of his pretensions; to which, independant of the league, the king of *Castile* declared he had no objection: the truce with *Arragon* was also prolonged; and thus the peace of his dominions was once again restored [s], which enabled him to put his affairs into so good order, that he had no reason to fear any of his neighbours.

A. D.
1373.

Concludes at length a sincere and solid peace with the king of Arragon.

THE duke of *Lancaster* being extremely piqued at the refusal of the king of *Castile* to quit the party of the *French*, resolved to carry his threats into execution, and with this view levied forces, and entered into a treaty with the crown of *Arragon.* The king, Don *Henry*, assembled a great army in the neighbourhood of *Burgos*, where a quarrel happening amongst the soldiers on the 19th of *March*, his brother, Don *Sancho*, interposing, to prevent a mutiny, received a wound in his face with a lance, of which he died, leaving his wife, Donna *Beatrix*, with child of a daughter, named Donna *Leonora*, who was afterwards queen of *Arragon* [u]. The king was extremely afflicted, and, in the first transport of his passion, would have put to death all the soldiers that had any share in the quarrel; but the nobility pacified him; so that only a few of the most guilty were punished [w]. He then sent to the king of *Arragon*, to put him in mind of their former friendship; to press him to send his daughter Donna *Leonora* to espouse the Infant Don *Juan*, prince of *Castile*, as they had been passionately in love with each other from their very childhood; and to assure him, that he was content to give him any reasonable satisfaction in reference to the disputes between them. The king of *Arragon* demanded, in a peremptory manner, the kingdom of *Murcia*. The king of *Castile* answered that it was true he had promised him that kingdom for his assistance, but

---

[r] Chronica del Rey Don Henrique Segundo. BRANDAON.
FARIA Y SOUSA.   [t] Histoire du Royaume de Navarre.
Chronica del Rey Don Henrique Segundo. ZURIT. Annal Arragon.   [u] Chronica del Rey Don Henrique Segundo. ZURIT. Annal Arragon.   [w] Chronica del Rey Don Henrique Segundo.

that this promise was made void by his entering into a treaty with the prince of *Wales*, and the share he had in deposing him; that, notwithstanding this, he was unwilling to have recourse to arms, in order to recover those places which he had seized in times of public confusion. After much altercation, a treaty was concluded, and signed by the two kings, on the 12th of *April*, by which a perpetual peace was stipulated for themselves and successors, the time fixed for the marriage, and the sum of one hundred and eighty thousand pieces of gold fixed as an equivalent for the restitution of the places which the king of *Arragon* was to restore [x]. This treaty was ratified and sworn to on the 28th of *May*, to the great satisfaction of both nations. The same year, the king being informed that the *French* had obliged the duke of *Lancaster* to abandon his design of invading *Castile*, by harrassing his troops in such a manner, that they were unable to prosecute their march, he thought himself obliged to return this favour, by making an expedition, in person, into *Guienne*, and sending also a strong fleet to their assistance, which terminated the operations of this year [y].

A. D. 1374.

IN the spring, Don *Carlos*, prince of *Navarre*, came to *Soria*, and there espoused, on the 27th of *May*, the Infanta Donna *Leonora* of *Castile*, and on the 17th of *June* following, the Infanta *Leonora* of *Arragon* was married at the same place, to Don *Juan* Infant of *Castile* [z]. But Don *Alonso*, count of *Gijon*, the king's natural son, taking some distaste to the princess of *Portugal*, whom his father had chosen for his wife, fled out of his dominions; and after visiting the court of *France*, and that of the pope at *Avignon*, he at length thought proper to return, and to comply with his father's inclinations [a]. The engagements he had entered into with the duke of *Anjou*, brother to the *French* king, who claimed the kingdom of *Majorca* by donation, gave some umbrage to the king of *Arragon*, but not sufficient to create any rupture between the two crowns, because the monarch of *Arragon* saw clearly, that if the king of *Castile* had meant any thing more than was pretended by those treaties, he would have stipulated greater succours; and, therefore, he thought it best to pass by an offence that might be augmented by taking notice of it. This had a good effect; for the king of *Castile* gave him to understand, that though he could not refuse his assistance to

Enters into fresh engagements, and a treaty of marriage with the king of Portugal.

1375.

---

[x] ZURIT. Annal Arragon. MARIAN. FERRERAS [y] Chronica del Rey Don Henrique Segundo. P. DANIEL Histoire de France. [z] Histoire du Royaume de Navarre. ZURIT. Annal Arragon. FERRERAS. [a] Chronica del Rey Don Henrique Segundo.

the

the brother of the *French* monarch, yet he meant not to infringe the treaty that fubfifted between them [b]. The Infanta
Donna *Beatrix* of *Portugal*, being the apparent heirefs of that
kingdom, the king of *Caftile* propofed a match between her
and his fon Don *Frederick*, which the king of *Portugal* readily
accepted, though Don *Frederick* was a baftard; and the
children were accordingly married, with great folemnity, by
proxy; but, as we fhall fee hereafter, this marriage never
took effect. In the courfe of this year, died *Edward*, prince
of *Wales*, which was confidered as a favourable event in the
councils of *Caftile* [c].

*The king
of* Navarre
*attempts
to fur-
prize* Lo-
grono,
*and is fur-
prized in
his turn.*

THE king of *Navarre* having entered into a project for
exchanging the territories he poffeffed in *Normandy*, with the
crown of *England*, for lands of an equal value in *Gafcony*, it
was refolved to fend the prince Don *Carlos* to conclude and
execute this bargain. As Don *Carlos* had married the daughter
of the king of *Caftile*, it was natural for him to confult him
upon his journey, from which the king diffuaded him, as he
was to take the court of his uncle, the king of *France*, in his
way; where he muft either deal perfidioufly with that monarch,
or avow to him his father's defigns. The prince, notwithftanding, went with fome counfellors of his father's, but they
were arrefted at *Paris*, and his companions proceeded againft
and condemned as traitors. In the mean time, king *Edward*
the third, of *England*, died; notwithftanding which, the
king of *Navarre* continued his intrigues with his grandfon
Richard the fecond [d]. He forefaw that this would bring on a
war with the crown of *Caftile*, and therefore projected the
acquifition of *Logrono*, a place of great beauty and importance,
ftanding in the midft of a fair plain on the bank of the river
Ebro. The method he took was to corrupt Don *Pedro Manrique*, a nobleman of the niceft honour in *Caftile*, and the fum
he offered him was 20,000 pieces of gold. Don *Pedro* having
firft acquainted the king his mafter, clofed with the propofals,
received all the money at feveral payments, and, at the time
appointed, admitted fix hundred of the king of *Navarre's*
troops; but immediately after difarmed and made them prifoners of war, and was very near trapping the king himfelf [e].
Soon after, the Infant Don *Juan* of *Caftile* made an irruption
into *Navarre*, and advanced within fight of *Pampeluna*. At

[b] MARIAN. FERRERAS.   [c] Chronica del Rey Don
Henrique Segundo. BRANDAON. BARNES's Hiftory of Edward
III. FERRERAS.   [d] P. DANIEL Hiftoire de France. Hiff.
du Royaume de Navarre. Chronica del Rey Don Henrique Segundo.   [e] Hiftoire du Royaume de Navarre. Chronica
del Rey Don Henrique Segundo.

this time there was a schism in the church of *Rome*, occasioned by the election of *Urban* the sixth, and *Clement* the seventh, to the papal dignity; the *French* adhering to the former, and the *English* to the latter; but the kings of *Castile* and *Arragon* very wisely declined owning either; and this by the advice of the wisest of their prelates and great lords [f]. So that in such cases as these, we find those suing to be acknowleged to have any power, who, as soon as that was admitted, laid claim to all.

THE king thought fit to hold an assembly of all the prelates in his dominions, in the town of *Illescas*, where a resolution was taken to sequester the papal revenues, till it could be known to whom they belonged; for the discussion of which matter another assembly was held at *Burgos* [g]. There the king of *Navarre* applied himself to Don *Henry*, to obtain a peace, of which his affairs stood in great need. The king of *Castile* prescribed to him such terms as he thought fit, and amongst the rest, discharging the *English* and the *Gascon* troops that were in his pay, to which the king of *Navarre* objected that he had no money to give them, and they would not go without; upon which Don *Henry* lent him a considerable sum; and having taken the necessary securities for his observing the peace, restored all that he had taken during the war [h]. In a very short time after the conclusion of this treaty, the king fell ill of a slow consuming disease, which having gradually wasted his strength, brought him at last to the grave, on the 29th of *May*, as is reported by Don *Pedro Lopez de Ayala* [i]; though many other historians report, that *Mohammed Yago*, king of *Granada*, perceiving that he had at length accomplished his plan of settling a firm peace with all his neighbours, suspected that it must be with a view of attacking his dominions with his whole force, and therefore prevailed upon an old servant of his to seek shelter at the court of *Castile*, as if he had been ill treated by him, and to watch an opportunity of poisoning the king, which he is said to have effected by a present of a pair of beautiful buskins, which were scented with a venomous perfume [k]. *Ferreras* considers this as a vulgar report, which might take rise from the king's falling ill not long after this present was made him. Indeed, if we consider the propensity of the common people to attribute the deaths of princes to some extraordinary cause, and their

The death of Henry II. *of Castile, with strong suspicion of poison.*

[f] RAIN. FER. ZURIT. Annal Arragon. [g] Chronica del Rey Don Henrique Segundo. [h] Histoire du Royaume de Navarre. MARIAN. FER. [i] Chronica del Rey Don Henrique Segundo. [k] FER. MAYERNE TURQUET.

implacable

implacable hatred of the *Moors*, it will not appear at all improbable.

Don Juan succeeds the deceased king, and renews the truce with the king of Granada.

THE Infant Don *Juan* succeeded his father, and was crowned on the 25th of *July*, with his queen *Leonora*, at *Burgos*; and, on the 4th of *October* following, the queen was delivered, in the same city, of the Infant Don *Henry* [l]. About the same time arrived embassadors from *France*, to thank the king for the succours sent by his father and himself, which had done remarkable service. *Mohammed Yage*, king of *Granada*, dying, was succeeded by his son *Mohammed Guadix Abulhagen*, a prince of many virtues, and of a most pacific disposition, who immediately sent embassadors to felicitate the king Don *Juan* on his accession to the throne of *Castile*, and to renew the truce between the two crowns, during their reigns; which proposition was well received, and the embassadors returned highly satisfied with the civilities that were paid them [m]; and this, which seemed but a temporary expedient by the correspondence between their tempers, lasted all their reigns.

1379. Makes a treaty, and consents to another marriage with the crown of Portugal.

THE young king of *Castile* resembled his father extremely in his temper, and laboured nothing so much as to preserve peace, and to protect his subjects in the full enjoyment of it; with this view he sent embassadors into *Portugal*, where they were extremely well received by the king Don *Ferdinand*, who, with some great and many amiable qualities, was one of the most fickle and mutable princes of that age [n]. He desired, therefore, that the marriage formerly contracted between Don *Frederick*, the king's natural brother, and his daughter, the Infanta Donna *Beatrix*, should be cancelled, that she might be at liberty to marry the Infant Don *Henry*, who was not quite a year old. To this the king readily consented; and though there was something very whimsical, not to say ridiculous, in this affair, yet the treaty was managed with a great deal of ceremony; a very singular clause inserted, that if either of the parties should die without issue, the other should inherit the dominions of both, and was with great ceremony ratified by the states of both kingdoms [o]. The monarch of *Castile* having adjusted these points, and dispatched a squadron of twenty men of war to the assistance of the *French*, went to *Toledo*, in order to assist at his father's funeral; and afterwards held an assembly of the states at *Medino del Campo*, where,

[l] Chronica del Rey Don Juan el Primero.   [m] P. DA-
NIEL Histoire de France.   Chronica de los Moros de España.
[n] BRAND. Chronica del Rey Don Juan el Primero.   [o] FARIA
Y SOUSA. BRAND. MARIAN. FER.

after

after mature deliberation, it was resolved to acknowlege pope *Clement* the seventh P.   Before this assembly was dissolved, the king had intelligence, that in the midst of all that appearance of cordiality shewn by the king of *Portugal*, he was actually negotiating an alliance with *Richard* the second, of *England*, and with *John*, duke of *Lancaster*, who still continued to use the title of *Castile*, and whom Don *Ferdinand* had invited to come with a fleet and army to *Lisbon*.   Don *Juan*, instead of expostulating upon this subject, ordered his forces to assemble, and the principal places on his frontiers to be repaired; being thoroughly persuaded, that the best way to prevent a war is to prepare for and provide for it in time q.

A. D. 1380.

On the 25th of *May* deceased Donna *Joanna*, queen dowager of *Castile*, a woman, distinguished by virtues the most rare, as well as the most unaffected piety, whose firmness in adversity rendered her always respected, and whose humility in the time of her prosperity was universally admired r.   The king being informed that his brother Don *Alonso* held a private correspondence with the king of *Portugal*, endeavoured to surprize him, but he made his escape into *Asturias*, where he took shelter in his strong castle of *Gijon*; to which, when the king followed him, Don *Alonso* came out, assured him that he had been misrepresented, upon which they were presently reconciled s.   The king, Don *Juan*, then resolved to attack *Portugal*, both by land and sea, before the arrival of their auxiliaries from *England*; but Don *Ferdinand* spared him the labour, by sending a fleet of four ships and twenty gallies to insult the harbour of *Seville*.   In their passage they met the admiral of *Castile*, Don *Ferdinand de Tobar*, with twenty gallies, who at first declined fighting; but, perceiving that five of the *Portuguese* gallies were gone to take in water at a port upon the coast, he attacked the rest of the fleet with so much vigour, that he took sixteen gallies, and on board of one of them Don *Juan Alonso*, who was the queen's brother, and with these prizes returned in triumph to *Seville* t.   The king, Don *Juan*, besieged the castle of *Almeyda* and reduced it.   On the 18th of *July*, the *English* fleet arrived in the harbour of *Lisbon*, commanded by *Edmund*, earl of *Cambridge*, the eldest son of the duke of *York*, having with him a small army of between three and four thousand men, his countess, and his son *Edward*, afterwards duke of *York*, who was killed at the battle of *Agincourt*, then a child

That crown negotiates an alliance against him at the same time, and soon after commences war.

P RAINALD.   Chronica del Rey Don Juan el Primero.
q BRAND. FER.   r ROD. SANTII Hist. Hispan. part iv.
s Chronica del Rey Don Juan el Primero.   t MARIAN.
FER. MAYERNE TURQUET.

of

of fix years old; notwithftanding which, the firft thing done
was, to marry him to the Infanta *Beatrix*, and they were not
A. D.   only married, but bedded in public.   The good corref-
1381.   pondence, however, between the *Englifh* and *Portuguefe*, did
not laft long; there were great complaints, and very probably
not altogether without caufe, on both fides ; of which the king
of *Caftile* having notice, he refolved to fhut up the .port of
Lifbon againft frefh fuccours, and to deal with thofe who
were already arrived as well as he could u.

The king,   WHILE the king meditated certain important operations,
Don Juan, both by land and fea, his brother Don *Alonfo*, count *de Gijon*,
forces Por- actually quitted his dominions, and retired to *Braganza* in
tugal *to*   *Portugal*, with feveral lords who were attached to him.   The
conclude a king diffembled the offence againft him, continued his prepa-
fecret and rations, and fitted out a fleet, with which he gave great
feparate difturbance to the inhabitants of *Lifbon*, and obliged the king
peace.   of *Portugal* to remove his court from thence w.   As foon as
his army began to be in motion towards the enemies frontiers,
he fignified to his brother, who was ftill at *Braganza*, that he
fhould return without delay, upon which he repeated the
order ; Don *Alonfo* returned for anfwer, that if he would
fend him the Infant Don *Ferdinand*, his fecond fon, the fons
of fix of the principal nobility, and put a certain number of
caftles into his hands, for his fecurity, himfelf and his friends
would return.   Don *Juan*, without taking the leaft notice of
this propofition, fent a third order for him and his adherents
to return to their duty by a certain day, on pain of being declared traitors, and all their eftates confifcated; upon which
his friends retired without taking leave, and, after a few days,
he was conftrained to follow their example x.   The king of
Portugal having affembled all his forces, and feeming determined to give the *Caftilians* battle, the king created Don
Hernando Alvarez de Toledo, and Don *Pedro Ruys Sarmiento*,
marfhals of the field, which was the firft time that title had
been heard of in *Caftile* y.   The king of *Portugal*, to fhew he
would not be vanquifhed by titles, gave that of conftable to
Don *Alvaro Perez de Caftro*, and made *Vafquez de Azevedo*
marfhal z.   The two armies being in fight of each other, the
new conftable and marfhal advifed their mafter to make
peace, to which he readily liftened, and granted them full
powers for that purpofe, but defired they would treat it with
great fecrefy.   Upon this, they went in the night to the

u BRAND.   Chronica del Rey Don Juan el Primero.   w FA-
RIA Y SOUSA.   Chron. del Rey Don Juan el Primero.   FER.
x MARIAN. FER. BRAND.   y Chronica del Rey Don
Juan el Primero.   z BRAND.

camp

mp of *Castile*; where, having acquainted the king with their commiffion, he likewife named two plenipotentiaries, by whom the peace was prefently fettled on the following terms. The Infanta Donna *Beatrix* was to be once more married to the Infant Don *Ferdinand*, fon to the king of *Castile*, who was in the fecond year of his age; the *Portuguefe* admiral, with his gallies and men, were to be fet at liberty; and the king of *Castile* was to furnifh a fleet to carry the *English* home. Don *Juan* fcrupled this at firft; but the *Portuguefe* plenipotentiaries reprefented, that home they muft be fent, and they had no fleet; and, if they had, they were afraid of its being feized in *England*; fo that at length it was ratified [a]. As foon as this came to be divulged, the earl of *Cambridge* and his troops were extremely irritated; but the *Spanish* fleet arriving before the bay of *Lisbon*, and there being no remedy, they embarked, and were very fafely carried home. The joy which the king Don *Juan* conceived at the conclufion of this troublefome affair, was quickly turned into grief, by the death of his queen Donna *Leonora*, in childbed, exceedingly regetted, as fhe was univerfally beloved by his fubjeéts [b]. At the requeft of the king of *Navarre*, he interpofed with the *French* monarch, for the liberty of the prince Don *Carlos*, and *Charles* the fixth granted it, as a very particular mark of his efteem. Upon his return home, the king, his father, fent him to return thanks to the king of *Castile*, in perfon, who received him very kindly, and difmiffed him with rich prefents, by which he attached him moft cordially to his interefts [c].

A. D.
1382.

As foon as it was decent, or perhaps a little earlier, the king of *Portugal* fent one of his minifters to infinuate to Don *Juan* of *Castile*, that his daughter, the Infanta Donna *Beatrix*, being of a fit age to be married, he would be much better pleafed to have him for his fon-in-law, than that the Infanta fhould wait for the Infant Don *Ferdinand*. There was fome oppofition to this in the councils of *Castile*; but, as the king himfelf was inclined to the marriage, it was quickly concluded, upon condition that the children of the king and the Infanta fhould fucceed to the kingdom of *Portugal*; and that, in cafe the throne became vacant before fuch children were born, the queen-dowager fhould govern with the title of regent [d]. Donna *Leonora* accompanied her daughter to the frontiers: the

*By his
marriage
with the
Infanta
Donna
Beatrix he
acquires a
title to
Portugal.*

---

[a] Chronica del Rey Don Juan el Primero. BRAND.   [b] ROD. SANTII Hift. Hifpan. part iv.   [c] Hiftoire du Royaume de Navarre. Chronica del Rey Don Juan el Primero. P. DANIEL Hiftoire de France.   [d] BRAND. Chronica del Rey Don Juan el Primero.

king,

king, Don *Juan,* arrived at *Badajoz* on the first of *May,* from
whence he proceeded to *Yelves,* where he espoused the Infanta Donna *Beatrix,* brought her the same afternoon to *Badajoz,*
and the next day received the nuptial benediction in the cathedral church [e]. Soon after this his brother Don *Alonso* revolted the second time, or rather the third, and retired
to *Gijon,* whither the king followed and reduced him ; and,
though he did not deprive him of his liberty, yet he reprimanded him severely [f]. In the assembly of the states, held
soon after at *Segovia,* the old method of reckoning by the æra
of *Cæsar* was laid aside for that of our Lord, according to
Ferreras, in the year of that æra 1421 [g]. While the king
was employed in regulating the domestic concerns of his government, he had intelligence that his father-in-law, Don
Ferdinand, lay at the point of death ; upon which he sent
some persons, in whom he could confide, to *Lisbon,* and drew
himself nearer to the frontiers. On the 22d of *October* that
monarch departed this life, and left his dominions in almost
inexpressible confusion [h]. Donna *Beatrix* his only daughter,
had been acknowleged by the states as the legal heiress of the
throne. The people in general, however, inclined to Don
Juan the king's brother, who was son to Don *Pedro* by his
second wife, the famous *Agnes de Castro.* This Don *Juan,* a
few years before, falling in love with Donna *Maria Tellez,*
sister to *Leonora* queen of *Portugal,* married her ; which raised such a spirit of envy in the queen, that she caused it to be
insinuated to Don *Juan,* that her sister was false to his bed,
and that, if he was once free from so bad a wife, she was inclined to give him the Infanta Donna *Beatrix :* upon which,
transported with jealousy and ambition, he barbarously murdered the innocent lady [i]. But discovering, when it was too
late, the falshood of the queen's information, and of her promise, he retired into *Castile* ; where, upon the death of his
father-in-law, the king caused him to be arrested, together
with his brother the count Don *Alonso,* whom their father had
married against his will to a bastard daughter of the late king
of *Portugal,* in whose right, or rather in whose name, he attempted to form some pretensions [k]. The queen-dowager
had the title of regent ; and her daughter, the reigning queen
of *Castile,* was proclaimed queen of *Portugal :* but another
brother of the late king, whose name was likewise Don *Juan,*
but a bastard, being grand master of the military order of *Avis,*

---

[e] Rod. Santii Hist. Hispan. part iv. Marian. Fer.
[f] Chronica del Rey Don Juan el Primero. [g] Historia de Espana. [h] Brand. [i] Marian. Fer. [k] Chronica
del Rey Don Juan el Primero.

seized

seized up$\tilde{o}$n the government, partly by force, partly with the consent of the people, and assumed the title of protector [1].

THE more the king of *Castile* considered the affairs of *Portugal*, the more he found himself at a loss how to conduct himself therein. He was very desirous of complying with the engagements to which he had sworn at his marriage, and signified the same to the states of *Portugal*, assuring them that he was willing the queen-dowager should govern with the title of regent, during her life, and that he did not seek the crown for himself but for his posterity [m]. The queen *Leonora*, being constrained to quit *Lisbon*, retired to *Santaren*, and from thence intreated the king to come to her relief, as she had no other resource. Upon this Don *Juan* of *Castile* put himself at the head of his forces, and marched with them into *Portugal*. The grand master of *Avis* declared this a breach of the marriage treaty, and that he had forfeited all his rights thereby. At the same time he sent ambassadors into *England*, to make an alliance with king *Richard* the second, or rather with his uncles who governed him. The king of *Castile*, perceiving plainly that there was no hope of acquiring *Portugal* but by conquest, ordered his fleet from *Seville* to block up the port of *Lisbon*, and invited his brother-in-law Don *Carlos* prince of *Navarre*, to come to his assistance [n]. War was now carried on with great fury on both sides; several great towns, and many of the nobility, acknowleged Don *Juan* of *Castile* for their king; but the *Portuguese* nation in general adhered firmly to the protector [o]. Several actions happened with variety of success; sometimes the troops of *Castile* had the better, sometimes they were beaten by the *Portuguese*. This great confusion was increased by the king's discovering that the queen-dowager had entered into a new intrigue with Don *Pedro* Count of *Trastamara*, whom she proposed to marry, and to murder the king. Upon this he caused her to be arrested, and sent prisoner into *Castile* [p]. He then besieged *Lisbon*, took the fort of *Almeyda*, and, upon the arrival of Don *Carlos*, with a noble body of troops, his affairs began to wear a better appearance: but the scene was soon changed; the plague broke out in his army, and, though he persisted some time in carrying on the siege, yet at length, chiefly by the persuasion of the prince of *Navarre*, he decamped; and, having put strong garrisons into the places that had declared for him, retired with the rest of his army

*He takes
upon him
the regal
title, and
labours to
acquire
that coun-
try by
force.*

[1] BRAND.   [m] Chronica del Rey Don Juan el Primero.
[n] FAR. Y SOUSA. FER.   [o] Chronica del Rey Don Juan
el Primero. BRAND.   [p] Chronica del Rey Don Juan el
Primero. FAR. Y SOUSA.

A. D.
1384.

into his own dominions, not a little chagrined at the turn that things had taken [q].

Invades it with a very potent army, and is beaten by Don Juan, whom the Portuguese elected for their king.

THE king of *Caftile*, being informed that Don *Pedro de Caftro*, count of *Traftamara*, was in the camp of the protector of *Portugal*, sent to let him know, that if he would remove this dangerous enemy, he would reward it as a moft acceptable fervice. The count embraced this infamous propofition, and took his meafures with two other noblemen for the execution of it : but the protector arrefting two of their friends upon certain fufpicions, the confpirators imagined, tho' without any grounds, they were difcovered, and immediately confulted their fafety by flight [r]. This mortified the king Don *Juan* extremely ; nor was it long before he received another piece of news, which gave him ftill greater uneafinefs, which was, that the ftates of *Portugal* had taken upon them to elect and proclaim the protector king [s]. After mature deliberation, however, and a thorough perfuafion of his own title, and that the force of his dominions was infinitely fuperior to that of *Portugal*, he determined to invade it by land and fea. With this view he ordered a great fleet to be fitted out at *Seville*, as well as a ftrong fquadron from *Bifcay*, with a vaft quantity of provifions on board, for the fupport of his army, at the head of which he marched to the frontiers [t]. There, however, he held feveral councils of war, in order to fettle the operations of the campaign ; and fome of the ableft perfons about him diffuaded him from proceeding farther, at leaft in perfon, as he was very ill of an ague, as the new king of *Portugal* had obtained a confiderable victory at *Truncofo*, as the king had loft moft of his father's old officers by the plague the preceding year, and as the whole nation feemed determined to fucceed or perifh in fupport of their new king: but the young lords, who were about him, had their heads fo full of the glory of *Caftile*, and relied fo much on the fuperiority of their forces, that at length the king was perfuaded to profecute his defign ; and, after having in vain attempted to enter into a treaty, he refolved to ftake all upon a decifive action [u]. It is faid that the army of *Caftile* exceeded thirty thoufand men ; whereas thofe who carry things higheft acknowlege, that the king of *Portugal* had not above twelve thoufand, and the hiftorians of that country fay not above half

[q] Hiftoire du Royaume de Navarre. Chronica del Rey Don Juan el Primero. BRAND. [r] Chronica del Rey Don Juan el Primero. BRAND. [s] MARIAN. FER. MAYZINE TURQUET. [t] Chronica del Rey Don Juan el Primero. [u] ROD. SANTII, Hift. Hifpan. part iv. BRAND. FER.

that number. He did not, however, decline fighting, but chose an advantageous post, and declared his resolution to wait there for the army of *Castile.* When the king, Don *Juan,* was in sight of the enemy, he halted, in order to advise once more with his principal officers, amongst whom there were some who suggested that, as the enemy were posted between two morasses, it would be very imprudent to attack them, more especially that day, the army being fatigued, and having had scarce any refreshment: but the young officers insisted that it would be infamous, after looking the *Portuguese* in the face, not to attack them without delay. The king, being himself under great doubts, had recourse to M. *de Rie,* the *French* ambassador, a man of sixty years of age, who had spent his whole life in arms. He modestly told the king, that, a battle being resolved upon, the point was to gain a victory, and not to pique himself upon being hasty in attacking. In spite of this the young people prevailed; the *Portuguese* were immediately attacked in their advantageous post, and, in half an hour, the *Castilians* were routed. There fell upon the spot Don *Pedro de Arragon,* son to the marquis of *Villena,* the king's two nephews, Don *Juan,* son to count *Tello,* and Don *Ferdinand,* son to the count Don *Sancho,* with many other persons of great distinction, and a multitude of private men w. This, which is generally stiled the battle of *Aljubarrota,* was fought upon the fourteenth of *August,* about three in the afternoon: the king fled that night to *Santaren,* upon his mule, which is above thirty miles. There he embarked on board a tartane, which carried him to his fleet, and soon after he returned to *Seville* x. The just sorrow arising from so heavy a loss was not a little increased by the *Portuguese* invading *Castile,* and beating the grand masters of St. *James, Alcantara,* and *Calatrava,* with a superior army, the first of these great men being killed on the spot y. To repair these disasters, and to provide against the consequences of the duke of *Lancaster's* arriving in *Portugal,* with a numerous fleet and army from *England,* Don *Juan* dispatched ambassadors to pope *Clement* the seventh, at *Avignon,* and to king *Charles* the sixth of *France,* to desire their advice and assistance z. An employment his ambassadors had never exercised before.

A. D. 1385.

His ministers were received at *Paris* with all imaginable marks of kindness and respect, and were sent back with the strongest assurances that the king would second his professions

John of the Gaunt, duke of

w BRAND. EMANUEL FAR. Y SOUSA. FER.   x Chronica del Rey Don Juan el Primero.   y RAINALD. P. DANIEL Histoire de France. MARIAN.

Lancafter,
lands in
Galicia,
and takes
Compof-
tella.
of friendfhip, by marching two thoufand lances to his affiftance [a]. Don *Pedro,* the fon of Don *Frederick* the grand
mafter, who was the king's uncle, returned with thofe ambaffadors to *Caftile,* and was, in confideration of the *French*
king's letters, very kindly received by the king his coufin. As
for the pope, he had nothing to give but a little good advice,
which he fent him very freely [b]. At the opening of the fpring,
the king of *Portugal* fent a fleet of twelve fhips and fix gallies
to bring over the duke of *Lancafter* and his forces ; foon after
which he took the field, and befieged *Chaves,* which, after
a gallant defence, he reduced. In the month of *July* the duke
of *Lancafter* landed at *Padron,* in *Galicia,* with fifteen hundred lances, and the like number of crofs-bows. He marched
directly to the city of St. *James,* at *Compoftella,* which opened
her gates as to her fovereign, and there he was proclaimed
king of *Caftile* in right of his wife Donna *Conftantia,* who accompanied him, with their daughter Donna *Catalina,* and two
daughters that the duke had by his former wife, *Blanch,* heirefs
of the houfe of *Lancafter* [c]. The king of *Portugal* fent him a
prefent of twelve white mules ; the duke, in return, gave him
as many greyhounds and falcons : a treaty was, not long after,
concluded between them, in confequence of which that
monarch efpoufed Donna *Philippa,* one of the duke's daughters, the other, *Ifabella,* being already married to the earl of
Pembroke [d]. Within a fhort fpace after the conclufion of
this treaty, the duke of *Lancafter* fent a herald at arms to Don
Juan, requiring him to furrender the kingdom of *Caftile ;*
who thereupon fent *Juan Serrano* a clergyman, and two doctors of the civil law, to *Orenza,* where the duke then was, to
acquaint him with the grounds of his title, and they were
both patiently and publicly heard. But *Juan Serrano,* having
fought a private audience of the duke, told him, that his mafter was willing to put an end to the difference, by marrying
his fon and heir, the Infant Don *Henry,* to Donna *Catalina*
his daughter ; which the duke did not at all diflike, and which
his wife, Donna *Conftantia,* highly and heartily approved ;
but, for the prefent, the treaty with *Portugal* ftood in the
way, and the duke contented himfelf with giving them a civil
anfwer [e].

[a] Chronica del Rey Don Juan el Primero. P. DANIEL Hiftoire
de France.　[b] RAIN.　[c] ROD. SANTII Hift. Hifpan.
part iv. POLYD. VIRGIL. THOM. WALSINGH. in Richard II.
[d] BRAND. EMANUEL DE FAR. Y SOUSA.　[e] Chronica del
Rey Don Juan el Primero. THOM. WALSINGH. in Rich. II.
ROD. SANTII Hift. Hifpan. p. iv.

THE king, Don *Carlos* of *Navarre*, dying on the first day 1386.
of the succeeding year, and his son, the prince Don *Carlos*, *His claims*
being raised to the throne, his brother-in-law the king of *to the*
Castile, as a mark of his affection, remitted the twenty thou-*crown of*
sand pistoles that were due to him from that crown, and restored Castile
the castles that had been put into his hands to secure the re-*relinquish-*
payment of that sum [f]. In the summer the *Portuguese* and *ed upon a*
the *English* made an irruption into the territories of the king *marriage.*
of *Castile*, who, at that time, either had not an army sufficient
to give them battle, or, from motives of policy, sought to decline it. He therefore caused the country before them to be
laid waste, harrassed their troops upon every march, and gave
them so much disturbance in one or two sieges, that they
found it very expedient to retire into *Portugal*. Thither the
king of *Castile* sent some of his ministers again to the duke of
Lancaster, who, finding that the climate did not by any means
agree with his troops, resolved to return into *Gascony*, and
sent the king of *Castile* word he should be glad to receive his
ministers at *Bayonne* [g] (X). Thither, accordingly, repaired
the

[f] Histoire du Royaume de Navarre. FER. [g] Historia
Vitæ & Regni Ricardi II. Angliæ Regis, a Monacho quodam de
Eversham consignata. EMANUEL DE FAR. Y SOUSA. MA-
RIAN.

(X) The campaign complet-
ed the ruin of the *English* army,
which the winter had begun.
The climate of *Galicia* did by
no means agree with *English* con-
stitutions: the season proved
rainy and unwholsome; provisions were scarce, which tempted
the soldiers to plunder, and, in
revenge of this, the *Spaniards*
knocked them on the head. It
was with difficulty, therefore,
that he assembled a tolerable
force to join the *Portuguese*, and
when he did they could do but
little. The *Spanish* historians
relate all this but very modestly,
and without treating our countrymen with the least disrespect;
whereas our own historians, who
wrote in or near those times,
expose this expedition of the
duke's as very rashly undertak-

en, and very unskilfully conducted. One writer particularly assures us, that the duke's troops,
through famine, deserted in such
numbers, that the king of *Portugal* insisted upon giving the
enemy battle immediately; because in their present feeble
condition, the *English* deserters
would be a burthen to them;
whereas he dreaded the effects of
their valour, if they had time to
recover their strength: but the
duke is said to have dissuaded him
from this, being sensible that it was
not thro' disaffection that they
went over to the enemy, but
through downright want. Upon this our author assures us,
that the duke humbled himself
in a very extraordinary manner
before God; promised an a-
mendment of life, and made

A. D.
1387.

the king's confeffor and two doctors, who were of his privy council, met with a very gracious reception, and, in a very fhort time, concluded a decifive treaty ; by which it was fettled, that the duke's only daughter by Donna *Conftantia* fhould efpoufe, as foon as he was of an age to marry, the Infant Don *Henry :* and, in cafe he died before the confummation of the marriage, fhe fhould become the wife of his younger brother Don *Ferdinand:* that five good towns, with their territories, which were named, fhould be given as a dowry to Donna *Conftantia :* that the duke fhould receive fix hundred thoufand pieces of gold, for the expences of the war : that his duchefs fhould receive forty thoufand franks a year ; and that, in confideration of the due performance of thefe articles, the duke and duchefs fhould renounce for ever their rights to the crown of *Caftile.* All this was ratified and approved in an affembly of the ftates of the kingdom, as well as by the king Don *Juan :* but when it came to be ratified by the duke and duchefs, they did it with this provifo, that the heir apparent of the crown of *Caftile* fhould thenceforward bear the title of Prince of *Afturias* [h]. The princefs, Donna *Catalina* was conducted from *Fontarabia* to *Palentia,* and there, in the prefence of the king, efpoufed to the Infant Don *Henry ;* that prince being about nine years old, and

[h] Chronica del Rey Don Juan el Primero. ROD. SANTII Hift. Hifpan. part iv. Hiftoria Vitæ & Regni Ricardi II. WALSING. in Ric. II.

other vows, to which he attributes entirely the king of *Caftile*'s renewing the treaty, and offering an enemy in diftrefs all that he could have demanded if he had been victorious ; for the duke of *Lancafter*'s only view was to fee his daughter queen of *Caftile.* *Mariana* and this author likewife feem to be a little premature in affirming that the principal points of the agreement were fettled while the duke remained in *Portugal ;* whereas in reality he declined treating while within that kingdom, but gave the king Don *Juan* good reafons to believe that things would be amicably adjufted by permitting lord *John Holland,*

upon his arrival at *Lifbon* from *London,* to enroll as many of his men as were willing to go with him into *Gafcony ;* which very plainly intimated either a refolution in him to put an end to the war, or an abfolute inability to continue it. There is no doubt that the king of *Portugal* was not very well pleafed with this treaty, which he forefaw muft be concluded ; but his people were very weary of the company of foreigners ; fo that, upon the whole, he was well enough fatisfied to be rid of thofe who might do him a great deal of hurt, and who could do him but very little good if they would.

herfelf

herself about fourteen [i]. *Mariana* says the prince was ten
and the princess nineteen years of age; but this is clearly a
mistake, since it is very certain that the duke of *Lancaster* had
not been married to Donna *Constantia* above sixteen years [k].
Some short time after the duchess of *Lancaster* sent to let the
king know, that she was extremely desirous of seeing him and
her children the prince and princess of *Asturias*; upon which
he sent several persons of the first distinction to conduct her to
Medina del Campo, where he was; and, during her stay there,
she was treated with such respect and cordiality, that she presented the king with a crown of gold, that had been made
for her husband, and a vessel of the same precious metal, exquisitely wrought [l]. After a considerable stay at *Medina*, she
complied with the king's request of going to pass the winter at
Toledo, where she received the compliments of almost all the
nobility of the first rank in *Spain*, and where her conduct
was so prudent, as gained her the hearts of the king and
queen.

IN the spring the king accompanied the duchess of *Lancaster* to *Burgos*, with an intent to have proceeded to *Fontarabia*, that he might also confer with the duke her husband.
But, within a very short time after his arrival, he fell extremely ill; but, growing better, he set out with her again
for *Victoria*, where he was attacked with the same disease in
such a manner, that he was obliged to excuse himself from
proceeding farther northwards; and sent his compliments by
his ambassadors to the duke of *Lancaster*, with whom all
things were amicably adjusted: the large sum that had been
stipulated was paid, and hostages were given for the duchess's
annuity. The king of *Portugal* having, this year, gained some
advantages, the king of *Castile* took much pains, and sacrificed
some places that were still in his hands, to get the truce renewed. He appears to have been a most conscientious prince; for
he grudged every thing that came out of his subjects pockets:
and chose rather to suffer any disgrace, than to exhaust them, in
order to aggrandize his own family. He carried this so far,
that, when the states had imposed an extrordinary tribute, to
raise the money for the duke of *Lancaster*, understanding that in some places the people murmured at it, he sent
them word, that it was true he could not exempt them from
paying, because he was to pay it himself; but that he would
allow it in the ordinary revenues of the next year [m]. This

margin:
1388.
*The king
of* Castile*'s
tender and
laudable
affection
for his
subjects.*

---

[i] Chronica del Rey Don Juan el Primero.   [k] Historia
general de Espana, lib. xx.   [l] Chronica del Rey Don Juan,
el Primero. ROD. SANTII Hift. Hispan. part iv.   [m] Historia
Vitæ & Regni Ricardi II. ROD. SANTII Hift. Hispan. part iv.
Chronica del Rey Don Juan el Primero. FAR. Y SOUSA.

had two good effects ; it produced the money, and it put an end to all murmurs. Whether the expences of the war with *Portugal,* and the misfortunes attending it, had unavoidably exhausted his treasury, or whether there was really any fault in those who managed his affairs, so it was, that the king grew extremely melancholy at the remembrance of the flourishing state of things in the last years of his father's reign in comparison of his own ; which, at length, affected him so heavily, that he called an assembly of the states, to propose resigning the crown to his son, tho' a minor, and putting the government into the hands of a council, who, by their wisdom and application, might bring things into a better state. But this assembly very wisely remonstrated to the king, that such a

A. D. 1389. resolution might augment, but never could diminish, the mischiefs to which his subjects were exposed ; that as to the regulation of his revenue, they would take that upon themselves ; and that, in a little time, under the auspices of so good a prince, they did not in the least doubt, that all things might be brought into order [n].

Sudden and unhappy death of that great and good prince by a fall from his horse. THE king's spirits were in some measure raised, by the application of the king of *Granada* to renew the truce ; who, upon that occasion, sent a magnificent embassy, and very costly presents : but what pleased him still more was, that the king of *Portugal* sent likewise to prolong the truce, which was a thing that the king of *Castile* heartily desired, but was unwilling to ask [o]. In this flow of good fortune, he erected a new order of knighthood, which he stiled *of the Holy Ghost,* the badge of which was a collar of gold, to which was appendant the figure of a dove, surrounded with a glory [p]. At the time the *Moorish* ambassadors were at his court, he understood that there were many Christians of distinction, who, from time to time, had retired out of *Spain,* either through discontent or fear, and were settled in the city of *Morocco,* notwithstanding which they were exceedingly desirous of returning home ; but apprehended the double difficulty of procuring pardon on one side, and permission on the other. The king of *Castile,* sincerely touched with the misfortunes of these people, whom the *Spanish* writers stile (Y) *Farfanes,* applied

[n] Chronica del Rey Don Juan el Primero. ROD. SANTII Hist. Hispan. part iv. [o] Chronica de los Moros de Espa: a. BRAND. [p] MARIAN. FER.

(Y) The word *Farfan* signifies a Christian soldier, or rather a Christian cavalier in the pay of the *Moors.* There were many circumstances that concurred to furnish the *Moorish* monarchs in

applied himself with such earnestness to the king of *Morocco*, that he gave them leave to depart. Some of the first of them arrived a little before winter, and desired to have the honour of being admitted to the king's presence, that they might return him their thanks. Don *Juan*, who had heard that they were wonderfully expert in horsemanship, desired they would meet him at *Alcala*, on his road to *Andalusia*. Arriving in this city, and understanding that they were at hand, he mounted on horseback, on *Sunday*, *October* the 9th, attended by the archbishop of *Toledo*, and some other persons of the first distinction, with whom he proceeded thro' the gate leading to *Burgos* ; met these new comers, and was infinitely delighted with their exercise : but spurring an high-mettled *Barbary* horse he rode, the beast suddenly plunged, threw him over his head, and, falling upon him, crushed him to death upon the spot (Z). The archbishop of *Toledo* caused a tent to

A. D. 1390.

in *Spain* and in *Africa* with these soldiers. Sometimes it was the pure effects of the spirit of rambling, and that spirit of chivalry which was then so much in fashion. Sometimes it was owing to private disasters or disappointments, which rendered their own country disagreeable to them ; but the chief cause was being some way or other obnoxious to justice for acts of private resentment, or of public discontent ; but resting ever upon this foundation, that a gentleman's sword ought to carve him out a subsistence, and that it was beneath him to exert any other talent for his advancement than his courage. At this juncture, it seems, the *Moors* were more peaceably disposed than usual ; for otherwise they would not have parted with these mercenaries, for whom they had a great esteem It is also not at all improbable, that the king Don *Juan* had political reasons for recalling them, which might have appeared in time, if Providence had granted him a longer life : at all events, it was an

act of generous charity, that could not fail of raising his reputation.

(Z) This melancholy accident, which cost the king Don *Juan* his life, happened chiefly by his seeing this exercise performed on ploughed lands ; so that, upon spurring his horse, his fore feet fell into a deep furrow, by which means the king was thrown over his head. Surgeons were sent for, and processions ordered, that the people might have opportunities of praying for the king's recovery. But this was the effects of the archbishop of *Toledo*'s prudence, for the king gave not the least sign of life after his fall. The reason why this prelate thought these precautions necessary, was the uneasiness expressed by all ranks of people on the apprehensions of losing a prince in the prime of his years, for the king was but three and thirty, and the government's falling into the hands of a child, and he too of so weak a constitution, that they had already bestowed on him the surname of the *Sickly*.

In

to be pitched near the place, carried the king thither, and gave out that he was not dead, in order to gain the more time for the peaceable acceſſion of his ſon ; which being accompliſhed, his body was tranſported to *Toledo*, and buried there according to his own deſire q ; and afterwards with ſtill greater ſolemnity, by command of the king his ſon.

King Henry III. aſcends the throne, when juſt entered on the eleventh year of his age.

DON *Henry*, the third of that name, king of *Caſtile*, was but five days more than ten years old at the demiſe of his father, and ſucceeded him without any heſitation or diſturbance; tho' this, like all calms at court, more eſpecially in minorities, was of very ſhort duration r. The late king had a numerous family of women to maintain, and this charge deſcended upon his ſon. Theſe were Donna *Leonora*, queen-dowager of *Portugal* ; her daughter Donna *Beatrix*, queen-dowager of *Caſtile* ; another Donna *Leonora*, queen of *Navarre*, the late king's ſiſter, who, with her two daughters, had retired into *Caſtile*, under pretence that the air of *Navarre* would not agree with them, and would not return, though ſtrongly ſollicited by the king her huſband ; and the queen conſort, tho' as yet the marriage was not complete ; to which we may add Donna *Conſtantia*, ducheſs of *Lancaſter*, who had likewiſe a large annuity, though it was but indifferently paid s. In order to keep things quiet, it was found neceſſary to call the princes of the blood to court, and to gratify them with great places and penſions. Theſe were Don *Frederick*, duke of *Benavente*, the natural ſon of king *Henry* the ſecond, and uncle to the late king ; Don *Pedro* count of *Traſtamara*, who was the ſon of the Infant Don *Frederick*, grand maſter of the order of St. *James*, who had been barbarouſly murdered by the king Don *Pedro* ; Don *Alonſo de Arragon*, marquis *de Villena*,

q Chronica del Rey Don Juan el Primero. ROD. SANTII Hiſt. Hiſpan. p, iv. Chronica de los Moros de Eſpana. FERRERAS. r Chronica del Rey Don Henrique III. par Don PEDRO LOPEZ de Ayala. s ROD. SANTII Hiſt. Hiſpan. p. iv. FRANCISCI TARAPHÆ de reg. Hiſpan. Chronica del Rey Don Henrique III.

In the midſt of theſe diſaſters the caſe of the queen was moſt to be deplored, for in loſing the king her huſband ſhe loſt all : ſhe was already, in a manner, cut off from her own country, deprived of the crown to which ſhe was intitled by her birth, and left amongſt ſtrangers, without children, and without any

means except thoſe flowing from the prudence of her own conduct, to ſupport the precarious title of a queen, in a country where the ſeeds of faction were continually ſhooting up upon the ſmalleſt relaxation in government, and more eſpecially in minorities.

and

d Don *Alonso* count of *Gijon*, the king's uncle, then a
'foner, foon after releafed : to fay nothing of the children
the king Don *Pedro*, or of the Infant Don *Juan* of *Por-*
tal, who were likewife prifoners, and maintained at the
pence of the ftate [t]. The duke *de Benavente* was no fooner
court than he meditated a marriage which alarmed the
)ung king and his minifters very much. The lady upon
hom he fixed his eyes was alfo a princefs of the blood, Don-
Leonora, daughter of the Infant Don *Sancho*, and, by far,
e richeft heirefs in *Caftile*. The only method that could be
ought of to prevent this was to contract the countefs, with
r own confent, to the king's brother, the Infant Don *Fer-*
dinand ; with a provifo that, if the king fhould die before he
was of age to confummate his own marriage, the contract
fhould be void, and the Infant at liberty to efpoufe the queen [n].
Some difputes there were about fettling a regency : it was
furmifed that the king had left a will, and at length that will
was found : but the contents of it being difapproved, it was
ordered to be burnt, which was prevented by the archbifhop
of *Toledo*, on account of fome legacies that were given to his
church. At length a council of regency was formed by common confent, confifting of the duke *de Benavente*, the count
de Traftamara, the marquis *de Villena*, the archbifhops of
Toledo and *Compoftella*, the grand mafters of St. *James* and
Calatrava, and fixteen deputies from the principal towns :
though this regency was approved and eftablifhed by authority of the ftates ; yet, before the end of the year, the
archbifhop of *Toledo* withdrew from court, declared againft
them, and drew the duke *de Benavente* into his meafures [w]. So
foon are factions formed !

THE regents laboured all they could to bring this prelate *The duke*
into their meafures, but in vain ; upon which they removed *de Bena-*
the court to *Segovia*, and gave the title of conftable to Don *vente's in-*
Pedro count of *Traftamara* [x]. At length, through the medi- *trigues*
ation of the queen of *Navarre*, things were brought to an ac- *perplex the*
commodation ; and the ftates were affembled at *Burgos*, *queen and*
where the principles of the late king's will were adopted, a *the re-*
new regency framed, and a great deal of public money very *gency.*
prudently beftowed in penfions to preferve the public peace. A. D.
Though the duke *de Benavente* had all the reafon in the 1391,
world to be fatisfied, and a variety of alterations had been
made for that reafon folely, yet he ftill perfifted in his in-

[t] ALFONSI a Carthagena reg. Hifpan. Anacephalæofis. ROD.
SANTII Hift. Hifpan. part iv. [u] Chronica del Rey Don
Henrique III. [w] ROD. SANTII Hift. Hifpan. part iv. FER-
RERAS. [x] FRANCISCI TARAPHÆ de reg. Hifpan.

trigues ;

trigues; in confequence of which he formed a projeᵭ of marrying a natural daughter of the king of *Portugal*, with whom he was to have a large fum in ready money, and the proteᵭion of the king befides *y*. To balance this the council

A. D. of regency offered him the like fum of money to decline that 1392. marriage, and upon this the duke was brought to fufpend it.

Wearied This disjointed ftate of affairs in *Caſtile*, gave its neigh-
with per- bours many opportunities of behaving otherwife than they
petual con- were wont. The *Moors* of *Granada* made a fudden irruption, in
trivances breach of the truce which *Joſeph* the fon and fucceffor of *Ma-*
to diſturb *hammed* had made with the young king, and carried away a great
the regency booty; but the *Caſtilians* attacked them in their retreat fo judi-
the king cioufly, and with fo much vigour, that they recovered all they
aſſumes the had taken, and cured them of the defire of making fuch incur-
admini- fions for the future: this, together with fome quick meafures
ſtration. taken againſt the duke *de Benavente*, induced the king of *Por-*
tugal to let fall fome very haughty and unreafonable articles, upon which he had infifted in refpeᵭ to a truce, but which he at length thought proper to conclude for fifteen years, upon condition that fome of the principal lords would fign it within a limited time; and of thefe the duke de *Benavente*, the count of *Traſtamara*, and the count of *Gijon*, refufed *z*. The regency, fufpeᵭing the archbifhop of *Toledo* of a defign to ex-cite frefh troubles, caufed him to be arrefted; but, upon his giving them proper affurances, he was quickly releafed. *Charles* the fixth of *France* fent, about this time, ambaffa-dors to compliment the young king upon his acceffion, and to let him know that he heard that fome of his nobility were in-clined to create difturbances, which if true, he would give him what aid he defired; or, if it was requifite, march in per-fon, with the whole force of his dominions; the king thank-ed him in the warmeft terms for this noble inftance of his friendfhip, but did not demand his affiftance *a*. As he was now within two months of thirteen complete, and of a capa-city far beyond his age, Don *Henry* affumed the government, held an affembly of the ftates at *Madrid*, and, having con-firmed the privileges of *Biſcay*, and done other neceffary and popular aᵭs, he fet out for *Toledo*, where he caufed the ob-fequies of his father to be performed in his prefence with

y Chronica del Rey Don Henrique III.   Rod. Santii Hiſt. Hiſpan. part iv.   *z* Chronica de los Moros de Eſpana. Brandaon.   Ferreras.   *a* Chronica del Rey Don Henrique III.   P. Daniel Hiſtoire de France.

great

eat solemnity [b]. He next celebrated his marriage with the
incess *Catherine* of *Lancaster*, and his brother Don *Ferdi-
ınd*, at the same time, espoused the countess of *Albuquerque*.

hese salutary steps taken, he curtailed those exorbitant pensions which the regency had been obliged to give to the
princes and princesses of the royal family ; for he was tho- A. D.
roughly tinctured with his father's maxim, that kings were 1393.
to be the fathers of their people, and were not to impoverish a
nation to enrich their families [c].

BUT the princes and princesses of the blood were very un- *All the*
willing to learn this lesson, which they understood to be a *princes and*
most crying act of injustice with respect to them, retired to *princesses*
their respective estates, and began to cabal as usual. The *of the blood*
king, finding the archbishop of *Toledo* a very sensible man, *concur in*
and ready to give him good advice, when his own interests *opposing the*
were well secured, gratified him in that particular, and took *king's mea-*
him into his confidence [d]. He then sent the marshal of *Castile sures.*
to the queen of *Navarre,* the duke of *Benavente,* and the rest
of the malecontents, to let them know that what he had done
was by the advice of his states ; and that, when the times
were better, they might expect better provisions. This had
no great effect, for as yet they did not know the king, whom
a strange affair had drawn, in the midst of these disputes, from
Castile to the city of *Toledo* (A). By the midst of summer he
was

[b] ROD. SANTII Hist. Hispan. part iv. ALFONSI a Cartha-
gena reg. Hispan. Anacephalæosis. [c] Chronica del Rey Don
Henrique III. FRANCISCI TARAPHÆ de reg. Hispan. [d] ROD.
SANTII Hist. Hispan. part iv.

(A) The occasion of the king's
journey to *Toledo* would have
been too great a digression, if we
had given it a place in the text;
and yet it seems a point of too
great importance to be totally
neglected, for which reason we
have placed it here. Amongst the
lords of *Portugal,* who followed
the party of the king of *Castile,*
was Don *Martin Yanez de la
Barbuda,* who was treasurer of
the military order of *Avis* in
that kingdom, a person of great
courage, and esteemed one of
the ablest officers of his time.
The king, in reward of his fide-

lity, procured his election to the
office of grand master of *Alcantara,* which gave him at once,
title, rank, and a large revenue.
There dwelt not far from *Alcantara,* in a desert part of the
country, an hermit, whose name
was *Juan Sago,* who had acquired a reputation of sanctity ;
this man addressed himself to
the grand master, affirming, he
had a revelation, that if he
would attack the *Moors,* merely
as enemies to the Gospel, and
without any secular views, he
should drive them out of *Spain,*
and this without the loss of a
man.

was on his return, and the marquis *de Villena* met him at *Il-lefcas* with a hundred lances.   The king received him kindly
but

man. The grand mafter was weak enough to credit this, and fent two of his efquires to challenge the king of *Granada*, offering to fight him alone, or with any number of troops he would appoint, allowing him two to one, in defence of the Gofpel againft the *Koran*. The king of *Granada* rejected the propofition, and put the perfons who brought it into prifon. The king, Don *Henry*, hearing that he was raifing forces, fent for the grand mafter, to put him in mind of his duty, and of the truce that fubfifted between the two crowns. This had no effect, his hermit perfuaded him to affemble an army; and, upon a promife of their being invulnerable, this was eafily done; fo that in a fhort time he had a body of three thoufand, fome writers fay, five thoufand foot, and about three hundred lances, all men of family, and tried courage. Upon his arrival with thefe forces at *Cordova*, the inhabitants were inclined to have difputed the paffage of their bridge, which at length, however, they declined. On his arrival at *Alcala*, Don *Alonfo Fernandez de Cordova*, lord of *Aguilar*, with his brother Don *Diego*, met him, and ufed all poffible arguments to diffuade him from this rafh enterprize, but to no purpofe. When he entered the territory of *Granada* he attacked a fmall fort, where he loft three men, and was himfelf wounded in the hand; upon this he reproached the hermit, who retorted his reproaches, by

telling him, that the promife he made him did not regard pillaging fmall places, but rendering the truth of religion vifible by the defeat of the Infidels, in a decifive battle. Thefe altercations were hardly over, when the king of *Granada* appeared at the head of five thoufand horfe, and one hundred twenty thoufand foot.   T Chriftians were prefently furrounded, and the fight, or rather the flaughter, began. Some fay that the infantry were intimidated, and endeavoured to make their efcape; others, that they behaved bravely. About fifteen hundred returned, twelve hundred were made prifoners, and the reft killed. As for the three hundred lances, they had no thoughts of retreating, the grand mafter difpofed them in the beft order imaginable; gave the higheft proofs of his fkill and experience in the art of war; but, in the end, after wonderful inftances of valour, he fell, covered with wounds, and with him all that glorious body of cavalry, who were thus offered as victims to his credulity and their own. At the requeft of the Chriftians, the *Moors* permitted them to fearch for and carry away his body, which was buried in the church of our lady, at *Alcantara*, under a tomb, with this infcription, by his own order. *Hic fitus eft Martinus Yanius, in omni periculo experti timoris animo.* " Here lies Martin Yanez, on whofe mind the fight of the greateft danger could never imprefs a
fenfe

but infifted upon his fubfcribing the truce with *Portugal*, to
which he affented ᵉ.   The king proceeded to *Valladolid* with
an army about him; and underftanding that the malecontents had entered into a league, and were all armed, he proceeded with caution.

IT is very remarkable that this young king, forefeeing that *He perfifts*
whatever he did would be afcribed to the archbifhop of *Toledo*, *in his own*
if he was with him, left him behind, and this meafure was of *refolution,*
the utmoft confequence.   The archbifhop of *Campoftella*, *and tri-*
hearing that his competitor was abfent, came readily to the *umphs glo-*
king, and was reconciled.   The king then granted a fafe *riouſly over*
conduct to the duke *de Benavente*, who came, made a long *them all.*
defence, and fubmitted to the terms that the king prefcribed;
but he would not fuffer him to fubfcribe them there, requiring
him to return to his own fortrefs, and confider them for a
week, that he might not pretend to be forced ᶠ.   The king
then reviewed his forces, and difmiffed the greateft part of
them, the duke did the like.   The count *de Traftamara*
followed the duke's example, firft demanded a fafe conduct,
and then made his terms with the king.   He infifted upon
the reftitution of a place that had been taken from him by
the count of *Gijon*, and the king promifed him juftice.   The
name of this place was *Paredes de Nava*, to which the king
went and fequeftred it, allowing fixty days to the count *de
Gijon* to make out his title.   While the king was thus employed, the count *de Traftamara* went to vifit the queen of
Navarre, at her requeft, and by the advice of the duke of
Benavente, that they might take their meafures together.
The king being informed of this, after his arrival at *Burgos*,
caufed the duke to be arrefted, and feized all his places.   After
this, he reduced *Roa*, where the queen of *Navarre* had taken
fhelter, and made her a prifoner likewife.   He marched next
in perfon into the *Afturias*; and underftanding that the count

---

ᵉ Chronica del Rey Don Henrique III.   ᶠ ROD. SANTII
Hift. Hifpan. part iv.

---

fenfe of fear." When this hiftory was told the emperor,
Charles the fifth, he anfwered,
fmiling, and yet I dare fay this
grand mafter would not have
fnuffed out a lighted flambeaux
with his fingers.   It was this
unfortunate affair that brought
the king of *Caftile* to *Toledo*,
where he began to affemble his
troops, from an apprehenfion

that the *Moors* would attack his
dominions; but upon his acquainting the king of *Granada*
that it was an act of temerity in
a fingle man, which he could
not either forefee or prevent,
and ought not to be confidered
as a breach of the truce, that
monarch anfwered, that he was
of the fame fentiment; and fo
this affair was blown over.

of

of *Gijon* had taken possession of *Oviedo*, with a body of troops, he attacked and put the best part of them to the sword. He then invested *Gijon*, which the count had fortified with great industry, and in which he had a numerous garrison. While he remained there, he summoned the count *de Trastamara* to join him with his forces, who, though he was not without apprehensions, obeyed. The king received him kindly, pardoned all that was past, and gave him part of the lands of the duke of *Benavente*. The winter drawing on, the count *de Gijon*, offered to submit his dispute with king *Henry* to the king of *France*, which was accepted; but care was taken that no supplies should be put into the place ᵍ.

Resolves to enter into a war with Portugal with all his force.

THE king carried his aunt, the queen of *Navarre*, with the two princesses her daughters, to the frontiers of that kingdom; and, having taken her husband's oath that he should live kindly with her, sent her home ʰ. The marriage was now celebrated between the Infant Don *Ferdinand*, and *Leonora*, countess of *Albuquerque*.ⁱ. The *French* monarch having decided that *Alonso*, count of *Gijon*, had forfeited all his lands for rebellion, the king returned to the siege of the castle, which was defended by the countess, who offered to surrender, if the king would restore her son who was in his hands as a hostage. The king consented to this, and as soon as the castle was in his hands, demolished it ᵏ. He returned through *Castile*, to pass the winter at *Seville*, where he renewed the truce with the king of *Granada*, and suppressed the factions that disturbed the peace of the city and kingdom of *Murcia*; the *Portuguese*, having corrupted an officer intrusted with the care of one of the gates of *Badajoz*, surprized that place, and attempted *Albuquerque*, in which they failed. The king, Don *Henry*, resolved to revenge this affront, and made great preparations for that purpose by land and sea. The king of *Portugal* sent embassadors to pacify him, but he ordered them to depart his dominions, and prosecuted his resentment with great violence, which gave some of the *Portuguese* nobility, who were much disgusted with their king, an opportunity of retiring into *Castile* ˡ. *Joseph*, king of *Granada*, dying, *Mohammed*, his son and successor, went, as some

ᵍ ALPHONSI a Carthagena reg. Hispan. Anacephalæosis, Chronica del Rey Don Henrique III. ROD. SANTII Hist. Hispan. part iv. MARIANA. FERRERAS.   ʰ FRANCISCI TARAPHÆ de reg. Hispan. Chronica del Rey Don Henrique III.   ⁱ RoD. SANTII Hist. Hispan. part iv.   ᵏ P. DANIEL Histoire de France. Chronica del Rey Don Henrique III.   ˡ ORTIZ DE ZUNIGA. Chronica de los Moros de Espana. BRANDAON. Chronica del Rey Don Henrique III.

writers fay, in perfon, to the court of the king of *Caſtile*, and renewed the truce; the *Portugueſe* having recovered from their conſternation, made an irruption into *Caſtile*, with ſome effect; and, on the other hand, the *Caſtilians* beat the *Portugueſe* at ſea [m].

A. D.
1397.

THE king, Don *Henry*, being deſirous of determining this diſpute, levied a tax throughout his whole dominions, and began to make vaſt military preparations [n]. Being deſirous of putting an end to the ſchiſm which ſtill continued, he reſolved to withdraw his obedience from *Benedict* the thirteenth, who reſided at *Avignon*; but before pope *Boniface*, who governed at *Rome*, could be informed of this, he endeavoured to take advantage of the war with *Portugal*, pronounced the king a ſchiſmatic, fallen from his crown and dignity, and incapable of governing, and ſent a bull to this purpoſe to the archbiſhop of *Braga* [o]. The next year a negotiation was ſet on foot between the kings of *Caſtile* and *Portugal*, which ended in a truce for ten years; ſoon after died Don *Pedro Tenorio*, archbiſhop of *Toledo*, at the age of ſeventy-five, to whom the king was much indebted for his advice [p]. The corſairs of *Barbary* being extremely troubleſome, the king ordered the fleet that had been prepared againſt *Portugal* to clear the ſeas of thoſe robbers, which they did; and taking it to be a proper appendix to their commiſſion, undertook to clear the land a little alſo; with this view they landed their forces, and attacked *Tetuan*, of which they quickly became maſters, pillaged it, carried away all the inhabitants, and then burnt it to the ground [q]. There was this year a moſt violent and deſtructive plague in *Spain*, but more eſpecially in *Andaluſia*, inſomuch that the king was conſtrained to ſuſpend the law, which reſtrained widows from marrying within a year after the death of their huſbands. On the ſixth of *July*, this year, the firſt clock that was ever ſeen in *Spain* was erected at *Seville* [r].

Concludes
a ten year's
truce with
that
crown,
and humbles the
Corſairs of
Barbary.

1398.

1399.

1400.

THE king having called an aſſembly of the ſtates at *Tordeſillas*, made ſeveral laws there for the benefit of his ſubjects. As the great point he had in view, in withdrawing his obedience from pope *Benedict* the thirteenth, was to put an end to a ſchiſm, which, in the preſent ſituation of things, proved very detrimental to Chriſtendom in general, and to his own dominions in particular; and perceiving that this ſtep in-

Receives a
very reſpectful
embaſſy
from Timur or Tamerlan the
Great.

---

[m] FARIA Y SOUSA. Chronica de los Moros de Eſpana. ROD. SANTII Hiſt. Hiſpan. part iv.   [n] Chronica del Rey Don Henrique III.   [o] RAINALD.   [p] BRAND. FRANCISCI TARAPHÆ de reg. Hiſpan.   [q] ROD. SANTII Hiſt. Hiſpan. part iv.   [r] Chronica del Rey Don Henrique III. FER.

creased the latter, without diminishing the former inconve-, niency, he acknowleged the same pope again, who thereupon, took the advantage of naming his nephew, Don *Pedro de Luna,* to the archbishoprick of *Toledo,* upon the lapse of the, dean and chapter[s]. The same year the king having heard of, the great reputation of *Timur Bec,* whom the *Spanish* writers of those times call *Tamerlan,* he sent two embassadors to com-, pliment him, and to make him an offer of his friendship[t]. As under the reigns of the three last princes, the people in, general had been treated with great lenity and kindness, their, circumstances were much altered, more especially in the great, cities ; and this proved the source of factions, that were very detrimental to the public peace. In *Seville* and *Cordova* especially they were risen to such a height, that the king was forced to interpose, but he did it with such a spirit of equity, as left no room for complaints, and with an air of dignity, which shewed he was not to be moved by clamour[u]. The embassadors of *Castile* saluted the illustrious emperor of the *Tartars,* immediately after he had vanquished the whole power of the *Ottomans,* and taken *Bajazet* prisoner. He received them very kindly, expressed a proper sense of the compliment paid him, and sent an officer of his houshold, with rich presents into *Spain,* to return it. The name of this embassador was *Mohammed Acagi,* and he brought with him two young ladies, the daughters of an *Hungarian* count, who had been taken by *Bajazet,* at the fatal battle of *Nicapolis,* and were found amongst the spoils upon his defeat. These young ladies, who were exquisitely handsome, and whose names were Donna *Maria* and Donna *Angelina,* being thus set at liberty, were extremely acceptable to the king and queen, and were very soon happily married in *Spain*[w]. On the 14th of *November,* the queen was delivered of a daughter, named Donna *Maria,* to the great joy of the king, and of his subjects ; and, in the beginning of the next year, the states at *Toledo* acknowleged and swore to maintain her title, in case the king left no heir male[x]. The king sent a second embassy to *Tamerlan,* with letters of thanks, and presents of very considerable value. The Infant Don *Ferdinand,* out of reverence to the blessed virgin, instituted a new order of knighthood, which he called *de la Jarra,* that is of the *Jar,* or

A.D. 1401.

1402.

1403.

[s] Alphonsi a Carthagena reg. Hispan. Anacephalæosis. Rain. [t] Rod. Santii Hist. Hispan. part iv. Francisci Taraphæ de reg. Hispan. Fer. [u] Chronica del Rey Don Henrique III. [w] Rod. Santii Hist. Hispan. part iv. Marian. Fer. [x] Alphonsi a Carthagena reg. Hispan. Anacephalæosis. Francisci Taraphæ de reg. Hispan.

Vaſe, becauſe the device was a flower pot filled with white lilies [y].

As the kingdom enjoyed a profound peace, the monarch *The king's* of *Caſtile* thought it a proper time to put his plan in execu- *great frus-* tion. He ſaw, with regret, the fineſt country in *Spain* in *gality;* the hands of the *Moors;* and they growing infinitely more *founded on* ſtrong and powerful every day, by that ſpirit of induſtry and *the moſt* frugality that reigned amongſt them, he ſaw that a very long *generous* and expenſive war would be neceſſary to reduce them. He *motives.* knew, that how chearfully ſoever his people might begin ſuch a war, they would very ſoon grow weary of the taxes that were neceſſary to ſupport it; he determined therefore to reduce the expences of his government as much as poſſible, and, out of his own ſaving, to heap up a treaſure ſufficient for this purpoſe. The king of *Granada,* afraid of his great power, and perhaps not altogether ignorant of his ſcheme, ſent two of the principal perſons about his court to teſtify his reſpect for him, with very rich preſents, and, which he eſteemed the higheſt mark of reverence and regard, one of the fineſt women in his ſeraglio; the king of *Caſtile* received this *1404.* compliment and his preſents very politely, and made him a proper return; but there afterwards grew a ſuſpicion, that the principal end of this embaſſy was of a very dark nature, as hereafter will appear [z].

The king being at *Toro* in the ſpring, the queen was *After a* there delivered on the ſixth of *March,* of the Infant Don *very long* *Juan* [a]. He held, ſoon after, an aſſembly of the ſtates at *and tedious* *Madrid,* where ſome laws were made to moderate the exor- *illneſs, died* bitant uſury taken by the *Jews,* and to oblige them to wear a *at length* mark of diſtinction upon their garments, and at the ſame time *of a ſlow* the concubines of prieſts were forbid to appear in public, *poiſon.* without a piece of ſcarlet cloth or ribbon, tacked to their head dreſs [b]. The queen taking advantage of the extreme good humour the king was in, upon the birth of his ſon, prevailed upon him to ſet at liberty Don *Pedro* and Donna *Conſtantia,* the children of her uncle Don *Juan,* who died a little before, in the caſtle of *Soria,* upon a promiſe that Don *Pedro* ſhould enter into holy orders [c]. This year the king built *1405.* the royal palace of *Madrid,* which was burnt ſome time after. He likewiſe built the alcazal of *Murcia,* and was the founder of the pleaſant country villa, called *Pardo;* for he was na-

[y] Rod. Santii Hiſt. Hiſpan. part iv.   [z] Chronica del Rey Don Henrique III.   Chronica de los Moros de Eſpana.   [a] Al- phonſi a Carthagena de reg. Hiſpan.   Anacephalæoſis.   Fran- ciſci Tataphæ de reg. Hiſpan.   [b] Chronica del Rey Don enrique III.   [c] Rod. Santii Hiſt. Hiſpan. part iv.

turally very magnificent, and frugal only from a principle of public spirit [d]. His embassadors returned the next spring from the court of *Tamerlan,* and the king was extremely well pleased with the account they gave him of the reception they had met with. On the complaints of the common people, that provisions were grown scarce and dear, the king found it necessary to settle the prices of grain of all sorts, to prevent extortion [e]. The state of the king's health being better known at *Granada* than in *Castile,* the *Moors* began to break that truce which they had begged with so much seeming humility; Don *Henry* complained, by his embassadors, without obtaining redress, and then threatened to seek it by force of arms; by way of reply to which the king of *Granada* marched into the realm of *Jaen,* and on the fourth of *October* invested *Guezada,* with an army of four thousand horse, and twenty-five thousand foot: he was not, however, able to take the place; and in two actions that happened this year the Christians had the better [f]. The king, Don *Henry,* hoped the time was come to which Providence had fixed the subversion of the *Moorish* kingdom; and therefore he directed an assembly of the states to be held at *Toledo,* with a view to concert measures with them for pouring the whole force of *Spain* upon the kingdom of *Granada;* but when the states were assembled, he was too weak to assist there in person, and therefore sent his brother, the Infant Don *Ferdinand,* who opened to them at large the king's scheme. While the substance of it was under deliberation, Don *Henry* breathed his last, about nine in the morning, on *Christmas-day,* after a lingering tedious illness, which was discovered to be the effects of a slow poison, given him by a *Jew* physician. His obsequies were performed with all due solemnity, and his subjects in general, but more especially the common people, who rather loved and obeyed him as a parent than a prince, deplored him with tears [g] (B).

1406.

His

---

[d] Chron. del Rey Don Henrique III. Marian. Fer.　[e] Rod. Santii Hist. Hispan. part iv. Fer.　[f] Chronica de los Moros de Espana. Chronica del Rey Don Henrique III.　[g] Rod. Santii Hist. Hispan. part iv. Alphonsi a Carthagena reg. Hispan. Anacephalæosis. Francisci Taraphæ de reg. Hispan. Chronica del Rey Don Henrique III.

(B) This monarch was highly commended for the sweetness of his temper, and for his great affability to all ranks of people, in which, however, he lost no-

thing of his dignity, because it did not arise from any feebleness of mind, much less from timidity. There never was a king of *Castile,* of whom the nobility stood

His son, Don *Juan*, who was but fourteen months old, *Don* was recommended particularly to the care of his uncle, Don Juan II. *Ferdinand*, who, as soon as the royal funeral was over, went *succeeds,* into the assembly of the states, and, in a short speech, de- *under the* fired them to take proper measures for proclaiming their king: *tutelage of* many of the prelates, and some of the nobility, fearing a long *his mother* minority, and knowing the great abilities of Don *Ferdinand,* *and uncle.* put one of their number upon asking him what king he would have them proclaim? The royal Infant was thunderstruck at the insinuation; but quickly recollecting himself, he turned to the marshal, and said, It is impossible that my nephew should have any competitor; display the standard of the crown immediately for Don *Juan* the second, the only lawful king of *Castile* and *Leon* [h]. He afterwards caused the late king's will to be read, and then sent it to *Segovia,* to the queen. By this will the king nominated two gentlemen to have the care of his son's person and education; but the queen being determined not to part with him, caused the gates of *Segovia* to be shut against the Infant Don *Ferdinand,* from an apprehension that he was come to take away her son. But, upon his prevailing on those two persons to accept of a sum of money, and to make over their claim to the queen, she altered her sentiments, and consented that the young king

[h] Epitome de la Chronica del Rey Don Juan II. de Castilla, por JOSEPH MARTINEZ de la Puente. FER.

stood more in awe than this; because he was entirely beloved by the populace. On the other hand, this affection was not the fruit barely of his indulgence, but arose also from their respect and esteem, founded, in part, upon his strict justice, of which he gave a strong instance in the severity with which he punished the repeated disturbances occasioned by the two factions in the city of *Seville*; on account of which seditions, there were no less than a thousand persons put to death. Yet he was never suspected of cruelty; and tho' he amassed a much greater treasure than any of his predecessors, it was without any imputation of covetousness. His common

saying was, that he did not fear the hatred or the arms of his enemies, but the disaffection and curses of his subjects. The *Spaniards,* who often fancy their kings are poisoned upon very slight, and sometimes without any grounds at all, had no apprehension that this was the cause of Don *Henry's* death, because he had been infirm for many years; but some time after, certain *Jews,* who were executed at *Segovia,* for insults offered to the Christian religion, confessed, that long before he had received a slow poison 'from a physician of their religion, by which he gradually wasted to the time of his decease.

should be publickly inaugurated [1]. The states declared the queen and the royal Infant regents; and, to prevent all disputes, the dominions of *Castile* were divided between them [k]. Don *Ferdinand* carried on the war against the *Moors* with vigour, and in some great actions with success; though the king of *Granada*, which is almost incredible, brought, more than once, armies of fourscore thousand, and once of an hundred thousand, foot, into the field; the fleet of *Castile* likewise defeated the combined squadrons of *Tunis* and *Tremecen*, and prevented their landing any succours to the *Moors*

1407. in *Spain*; so that the campaign concluded both happily and honourably for the Christians [l]. The states granted very considerable supplies for the support of the war; but the king of *Granada* was early in the field, and undertook the siege of *Alcaudeta* with a very numerous army; but the garrison made so obstinate a defence, and the *Moors* were so much harrassed, that they were at length constrained to raise the siege with discredit; notwithstanding which, the states of *Castile* resolved, merely to save expence, to act only upon the defensive; and upon the king of *Granada*'s demanding a suspension of arms for eight months, the proposition was accepted. He did not survive long; and his brother *Joseph*, whom he had kept in prison during his whole reign, succeeded him [m]. Some of the queen's favourites, notwithstanding all he had done for her service, created a misunderstanding between that princess and

1408. the Infant Don *Ferdinand*, in which, however, the latter acted so prudently, that they were quickly reconciled [n].

The Infant Don Ferdinand's wife and upright administration.

THE grand master of *Alcantara* dying, the Infant Don *Ferdinand* procured that important office for his son, the Infant Don *Sancho*, at whose installation the queen and the whole court assisted [o]. The duke of *Austria* made a proposal of marriage to the queen-dowager Donna *Beatrix*, widow of the king Don *Juan*, but she modestly declined it, by saying that women of her rank married but once [p]. The *Moors*, after having committed hostilities more than once, desired, and were permitted, to renew the truce [q]. The queen, plainly perceiving that her confidence had been abused in respect to the umbrage she had taken against the Infant Don *Ferdinand*, very wisely resolved to connect their families more

[1] Histoire del Rey Don Juan II.   [k] Rod. Santii Hist. Hispan. part iv   [l] Chronica de los Moros de Espana. Galindez de Carvajal.   [m] Chronica del Rey Don Juan II. Chronica de los Moros de Espana.   [n] Historia del Rey Don Juan II   [o] Rod. Santii Hist. Hispan. part iv.   [p] Francisci Taraphæ de reg. Hispan. Fer.   [q] Chronica de los Moros de Espana. Historia del Rey Don Juan II.

closely, and with this view contracted her daughter Donna *Maria*, to his son Don *Alonso* [r]. The grand master of the order of St. *James* dying, that office, though with some difficulty, was procured for the Infant Don *Henry*, another son of the Infant Don *Ferdinand*, though he was then very young [s]. The war with the *Moors* broke out again, and great preparations were made for carrying it on, on both sides. The Infant Don *Ferdinand* prevailed upon the states to change their sentiments in regard to a defensive war, and to furnish the supplies early, so that he took the field with a numerous army, and invested *Antequera*, a large and well built town, within twelve leagues of *Granada*, defended by a strong citadel, and, from its situation, of very great importance. The king of *Granada* practised every method in his power for its relief, but without effect. He at last attempted a negotiation, with a view of corrupting some of the *Moorish* slaves in the Christian camp, to assist in a perfidious contrivance for the destruction of their masters; but a converted *Moor* discovering the plot in time, the conspirators were very severely punished, and not long after the place was taken by assault, and the citadel by capitulation [t]. This so humbled the *Moors*, that they demanded a truce of seventeen months. The Infant Don *Ferdinand* put in his claim to the kingdom of *Arragon*; and upon the demise of the king Don *Martin*, pushed his pretensions warmly by his embassadors, the queen giving him all the assistance in her power; notwithstanding which, the troubles in that country lasted a long time [u].

An assembly of the states was held at *Valladolid*, during which the Infant Don *Ferdinand* fell dangerously ill. Don *Frederick*, duke *de Benavente*, who had been many years prisoner in the castle of *Monreal*, murdered the governor of that place, and made his escape into *Navarre*, where, at the instance of the court of *Castile*, he was secured, though he was the queen of *Navarre*'s brother [w]. The states granted forty-eight millions of *Marvadies*, to be employed in the war against *Granada*, at the expiration of the truce. In compliance with the desires of the subjects of both nations, a peace was concluded between the crowns of *Castile* and *Portugal*. The Infant still continued to sollicit his claim to the crown of *Arragon*, which, as *Ferreras* rightly observes, must have pro-

Assisted by the queen and council of Castile, in his claim to the crown of Arragon.

[r] ALPH. a Cartagena de reg. Hispan. Anacephalæosis. [s] ROD. SANTII Hist. Hispan. part iv. [t] Chronica del Rey Don Juan II. Chronica de los Moros de Espana. GALINDEZ DE CARVAJAL. [u] ZURIT. Annal Arragon. ROD. SANTII Hist. Hispan. part iv. [w] Historia del Rey Don Juan II.

ceeded upon this foundation, that the junction of the two crowns was not to be admitted; for otherwise his nephew, the king of *Castile*, had a prior right; but it is plain that this was never infifted upon, and that the queen continued to do every thing that he could ask or defire [x]. The king of *Granada*, in the beginning of the enfuing year, defired to renew the truce, to which the queen confented. Don *Ferdinand*, finding that money was a very ufeful thing to a man in his fituation, earneftly defired to have the money that had been laid by for the war; the council were divided upon this, fome were for giving it him, but others obferved, that the queen and the Infant had fworn not to employ that money but in war; but this objection was eafily removed; pope *Benedict* the thirteenth abfolved them from their oaths, the Infant had the money, and by the help of it carried his point [y]. Donna *Leonora Lopez de Cordova*, who had been the queen's favourite and difgraced, applied herfelf to the Infant Don *Ferdinand*, to make her peace; but the queen wrote to him to banifh her into *Andalufia*, and immediately difgraced her brother, and all her relations. Towards the clofe of the year, the nine judges chofen by the ftates of *Arragon*, after long and

mature deliberations, declared the Infant Don *Ferdinand* king, who immediately repaired to *Saragoffa*, where he was proclaimed and crowned; notwithftanding which, he found himfelf engaged in a civil war, raifed by the count *de Urgel*, who was in poffeffion of many ftrong places, and had a numerous party at his devotion [z].

The deaths of the king Don Ferdinand, and of the queen Donna Catalina, regents.

THE king, Don *Ferdinand*, finding that his enemy had applied himfelf for fuccours to *Thomas*, duke of *Clarence*, fon to *Henry* the fourth of *England*, he judged it high time to make trial of the affection of the nobles of *Castile*; and, upon his fignifying his requeft by letters, they drew together fo great a force, and made fo expeditious a march to his relief, as not only aftonifhed his new fubjects, but placed him in quiet poffeffion of his dominions, after a fhort and fharp difpute, which ended in his competitor's furrendering himfelf at his difcretion; and the king, to fhew how much he relied upon his friends, fent him prifoner into *Spain* [a]. By his in-

terpofition, the king of *Navarre* was prevailed upon to deliver

---

[x] Chronica del Rey Don Juan II. ZURIT. Annal Arragon. BRAND. Hiftoria de Efpana.   [y] RAINALD. ROD. SANTII Hift. Hifpan. part iv. Hiftoria del Rey Don Juan II.   [z] ZURIT. Annal Arragon. ROD. SANTII Hift. Hifpan. part iv. Chronica del Rey Don Juan II. FER.   [a] ZURIT. Annal Arragon. ROD. SANTII Hift. Hifpan. part iv. FER.

up the duke of *Benavente*, who was carried back into *Castile*, and continued there a prisoner to his death [b]. In order to fix himself more effectually in his new dominions, and to strengthen that union which already reigned between the two crowns, the king pressed the marriage of his eldest son Don *Alonso*, with the Infanta Donna *Maria*, to which the queen-dowager of *Castile* very readily consented, and the ceremony was soon after performed with great solemnity [c]. This great point thus settled, the king was inclined to make a short tour to visit his sister, but a distemper, from which he had but lately recovered, surprized him again upon the road; and, after a short illness, carried him to his grave, on the second of *April* [d]. He left behind him Don *Alonso*, who succeeded him in the throne of *Arragon*, the Infant Don *Juan*, the Infant Don *Henry*, grand master of the order of St. *James*, and the Infant Don *Pedro*; as for Don *Sancho*, grand master of the order of *Alcantara*, he died a month before his father. By the demise of this brave and prudent prince, the regency of *Castile* devolved solely upon the queen, who, with the advice of the nobility, made choice of a council to assist her. The first act which distinguished their administration, was representing to the queen, that *Agnes de Torres*, one of the ladies of her court, was a busy intriguing woman, and ought therefore to be forbid the court, together with Don *Juan Alvarez Offorio*, who had great connections with her, to which the queen consented [e]. The king of *Granada* being desirous of renewing the truce, the queen regent consented to it, upon condition that he released one hundred Christian slaves; in this year also some historians place the expedition of *Jean de Bethencourt*, for the reduction of the *Canaries* [f]. In the council of *Constance*, which was held to put an end to the schism that had so long subsisted, the embassadors of the crown of *Arragon* disputed precedency with those of *Castile*, but without effect, the point being clearly decided in favour of the latter [g]. On the first of *June*, the queen regent was found dead in her bed [h]. The *Spanish* writers allow her to have been a modest, charitable, and religious princess; but they likewise say, that she listened too much to the women that were about her, and that she was addicted to wine, which they insinuate to have

[b] Histoire du Royaume de Navarre. Historia del Rey Don Juan II.   [c] Zurit. Annal Arragon. Franc. Taraphæ de reg. Hispan.   [d] Chronica del Rey Don Juan II. Zurit. Annal Arragon. Rod. Santii Hist. Hispan. part iv.   [e] Zurit. Annal Arragon. Historia del Rey Don Juan II.   [f] Chronica de los Moros de Espana. Fer.   [g] Hist. Conc. Gen.   [h] Chron. del Rey Don Juan II.

been

been the caufe of her death [l]. The archbifhop of *Toledo*, whofe name was Don *Sancho de Rojas,* Don *Henry,* Infant of *Arragon,* the amirante, the conftable, *Juan de Velafco, Pedro Manrique,* and other great lords, thought it beft to proclaim the king of full age, though he was fcarce thirteen, which they did; and on the 20th of *October,* that young prince, in the prefence of Donna *Leonora,* queen-dowager of *Arragon,* and the three Infants her fons, efpoufed Donna *Maria,* their fifter [k].

The Infant Don Henry of Arragon, feizes on the king's perfon.

A GENERAL affembly of the ftates being held at *Madrid* on the feventh of *March,* the king declared to them that he had affumed the government, and was complimented there-upon [l]. He renewed the truce with *Granada,* and received into his favour Don *Alvaro de Luna,* of whom we fhall have occafion to fpeak more at large [m]. The two Infants of *Arragon,* Don *Juan* and Don *Henry,* who were men of abilities, but not of the fame rectitude of intention with their father, had each of them a great defire to engrofs the perfon and favour of the young king of *Caftile,* and to govern his dominions in his name. Don *Juan* having negotiated a marriage with Donna *Blanca,* daughter to the king of *Navarre,* and prefumptive heirefs of that kingdom, went thither to conclude it, which gave his brother an opportunity he did not let flip, of feizing the king's perfon, which he did at *Tordefillas,* being fupported in that infolent action by the conftable, the bifhop of *Segovia,* and fome other perfons [n]. On the fourth of *Auguft,* the king being in his hands, married his fifter; and, in the affembly of the ftates of *Avila,* the king juftified and approved all that Don *Henry* had done, as being in his power; and difavowed the endeavours of the Infant Don *Juan* to raife forces for his deliverance. The Infant Don *Henry,* to maintain his power, was very defirous of efpoufing the princefs *Catherine,* the king's fifter, who de-clared her diflike, and, when he furprized the king, had fled to a cloifter, from whence fhe would not be drawn, till he had promifed, upon oath, not to force her inclinations; and yet, on the eighth of *November,* fhe 'married him [o]. This gave the king an opportunity of making his efcape, trufting the

1419.

[l] Hiftoria del Rey Don Juan II. FER.   [k] FRANC. TARA-PHÆ de reg Hifpan. Chronica del Rey Don Juan II. ROD. SAN-TII Hift. Hifpan. part iv.   [l] Hiftoria del Rey Don Juan II. [m] Chronica de los Moros de Efpana. Chronica de Don Alvaro de Luna Condeftable de Caftilla y de Leon y Maeftro de la Orden y Cavalleria de Sant Iago.   [n] Hiftoire du Royaume de Na-varre. Hiftoria del Rey Don Juan II.   [o] ROD. SANTII Hift. Hifpan. part iv, Chronica del Rey Don Juan II.

secret entirely to Don *Alvaro de Luna*, who made use of *Frederick*, count of *Trastamara*, and Don *Rodrigo Pimentel*, count of *Benavente*, to assist him therein. It was accomplished, but not without difficulty and hazard; so that, after crossing the river *Tagus* in an open boat, the king got to the castle of *Montalban*, in which he was besieged by the constable, and afterwards by the Infant Don *Henry*; but, the Infant Don *Juan* assembling great forces, they thought fit to retire, and leave the king at full liberty to go where he pleased P.

1420.

THE king, who was alike unwilling to put himself into the power of the Infant Don *Juan*, treated him with great civility, when he admitted him to his presence, but did not suffer him to remain long at court; and at length sent him a positive order to disband his troops, as his brother had done. It was not long, however, before the Infant Don *Henry* created new disturbances; for the king, while he was under constraint, having bestowed upon him, by way of portion with his sister, the country of *Villena*, with the title of a duchy, he thought this warrant sufficient to take possession of it, and began to do it without waiting any forms. The king, Don *Juan*, was not only displeased, but thought himself at liberty to retract that grant, and therefore forbid such as held lands in or of that duchy, to acknowlege the Infant for their lord ⁹. Don *Henry* persisted in his first scheme; but the king persisted likewise: they would both be obeyed; and, as that was impossible, the greater part of the people chose the greater lord, and adhered to the king. In the mean time, the consort of the Infant Don *Juan* was brought to-bed of a prince, who was named Don *Carlos*, whom his grandfather presently declared his successor ʳ. The truce with the *Moors* was renewed; and though he struggled hard, and gave the king a great deal of disturbance, yet, in the end, the Infant Don *Henry* was obliged to disband his troops, and to wear, at least, the appearance of submission, notwithstanding the king, Don *Juan*, refused to admit him to his presence.

His beha-viour ex-cites that monarch's indigna-tion in a very high degree.

THE troubles of *Castile* were but begun. The Infant Don *Henry* having parted with his troops, received the king's orders to come to court, which he was very unwilling to obey, insisting upon promises, and even upon hostages for his safety; the king would have given him some moderate satisfaction, but that would not content him. At length, suspecting the use his enemies might make of his contempt, he took a sudden

The In-fant Don Henry imprisoned, and the princess flies into Arragon.

P GALINDEZ DE CARVAJAL. Historia del Rey Don Juan II.
⁹ ROD. SANTII Hist. Hispan. part iv. Chronica del Rey Don Juan II.   ʳ Histoire du Royaume de Navarre. Historia del Rey Don Juan II.

resolution

reſolution of going to *Madrid* ; but Don *Ruez Lopez de Ava-
los*, the conſtable, and *Pedro Manrique*, refuſed to accompany
him, which, however, could not determine *Garcia Manrique*,
who followed him out of perſonal affection. The Infant came
to *Madrid* on the 13th of *June*, kiſſed the king's hand, and
would have ſpoke to him that day, but the king adviſed him to
go home and take his repoſe, and promiſed to ſend for him
the next day. He did ſo, and the Infant found himſelf in the
midſt of the king's council, where he was charged with being
privy to ſome letters written by the chancellor to the king of
Granada, exciting him to make war, that the preſence and
affiſtance of the Infant Don *Henry* might be more neceſſary to
the king :] the Infant denied the fact, though the letters were
ſhewn and read to him ; and *Garcia Manrique*, who was a
warm man, ſaid, that he was ready to prove with his ſword
that they were forgeries, as indeed they were, which, however, did not hinder their being both impriſoned : the Infanta,
though ſhe had married Don *Henry* unwillingly, would not
deſert his intereſts in his diſtreſs, but, putting herſelf under the
care of the conſtable, retired to the kingdom of *Valentia* [s]. The

1422. queen was this year delivered of the Infanta *Catalina* ; and
the archbiſhop of *Toledo*, who was an active and ambitious
prelate, departed this life [t]. The truce between the crowns
of *Caſtile* and *Portugal* was renewed for nineteen years, the
circumſtances of both nations making it equally acceptable to
their miniſters [u]. The king of *Caſtile* deprived the conſtable
of his dignity, which he gave to the count Don *Alvaro de
Luna* ; and diſtributed his eſtates, which were very conſiderable, amongſt the lords who were moſt in his favour [w]. In

1423. the month of *September*, the queen was delivered of another
daughter, named Donna *Eleonora* [x].

Troubles in   ALL the time the diſturbances ſubſiſted in *Caſtile*, Don
Caſtile   *Alonſo* of *Arragon* was in *Italy*, endeavouring to procure the
continue   kingdom of *Naples* ; but being obſtructed in that deſign, he
and in-   this year returned home, upon which the king of *Caſtile* ſent
creaſe to   embaſſadors to prevail upon him to deliver up the *Caſtilian*
the de-   lords, and the princeſs his ſiſter, who had taken ſhelter in his
ſtruction   dominions. The king of *Arragon* inſiſted that his were a
of the   free people ; and that, as they had obtained the protection of
kingdom: certain towns, it was not in his power to give them up. On

[s] Rod. Santii Hiſt. Hiſpan. Chronica de los Mores de
Eſpana. Chronica del Rey Don Juan II. Galindez Carvajal.
[t] Chronica del Rey Don Juan II. [u] Brand. Francisci
Taraphæ de reg. Hiſpan. [w] Chronica de Don Alvaro de
Luna Condeſtable de Caſtillla. [x] Alphonsi a Carthagena
reg. Hiſpan. Anacephalæoſis. Hiſtoria del Rey Don Juan II.

4   the

the other hand, he follicited the king of *Castile* to fet his brother, Don *Henry*, at liberty, which was refufed; and the mifunderftanding between the two crowns rofe fo high, that military preparations were made on both fides [y]. The Infanta Donna *Catalina*, of *Castile*, dying, to whom the ftates had fworn as the prefumptive heir of the crown, the king, Don *Juan*, thought it neceffary to take the fame precaution, with regard to her furviving fifter, Donna *Leonora* [z]. $\qquad$ 1424.

In the beginning of the fuceeeding year, this meafure, *The Infant* which had been thought fo neceffary for the fecurity of *Don* Juan the royal family, and the welfare of the nation, was fet afide *of* Arrä- by the queen's being delivered of a fon, on the fixth of *gon raised* *January*, who was named Don *Henry*, after his grandfather, *in right of* who, within a week after, was acknowleged for the heir appa- *his confort* rent of the dominions of *Castile* [a]. The difputes with the *to the* crown of *Arragon* continued in the fame fituation, or rather rofe *crown of* higher, as Don *Alonfo* declared his refolution to have recourfe *Navarre.* to arms, for the deliverance of his brother Don *Henry*. The ftates of *Castile*, at the inftance of their monarch, approved the commitment of that prince, and gave the king the fupplies neceffary for defending himfelf, in cafe he fhould be attacked; for which purpofe he raifed forces in all parts of his dominions. At the bottom, however, both monarchs were inclined to accomplifh, if poffible, their refpective ends, without having recourfe to arms [b]; the king of *Castile* being well informed, that many of his nobility hated his favourite Don *Alvaro*, and wanted only an opportunity to fhew it; and the king of *Arragon* having many affairs upon his hands, which rendered a war with *Castile* very improper at that feafon. To deliver himfelf from the perplexities he was under, and in order to be thoroughly informed of the fentiments of his antagonift, he fummoned his brother Don *Juan* to return home, which, though a prudent ftep in him, perplexed that prince extremely, who was equally unwilling to differ with either of thefe kings. Upon his application to Don *Juan* of *Castile*, he drew him out of this difficulty, by advifing him to comply with his brother's fummons, and gave him full powers to treat of a peace [c]. He went accordingly, and was extremely well received in the camp of *Arragon*, where he had fcarce began to treat with his brother, before Provi-

[y] Zurit, Annal Arragon. Chronica del Rey Don Juan II. [z] Rod. Santii Hift. Hifp. part iv. [a] Hiftoria del Rey Don Juan II. Marian. Fer. [b] Zurit. Annal Arragon. Chronica del Rey Don Juan II. [c] Rod. Santii Hift. Hifpan. part iv. Hiftoria del Rey Don Juan II. Zurit. Annal Arragon.

dence put it in his power to treat with him on the level, by the death of Don *Carlos*, the noble king of *Navarre* ; upon which Donna *Blanca*, the daughter of that monarch, and the wife of the Infant Don *Juan*, sent him the royal standard to the camp of *Arragon* [d]. Soon after, he concluded a treaty with his brother Don *Alonso*, by which it was agreed, that the Infant Don *Henry* should be set at liberty, and should take a new oath of fidelity to the king of *Castile*, and be restored to all that he possessed ; and that the king of *Arragon* should bear no ill will to those who advised his cousin to imprison the Infant [e].

1425.
King of
Castile
compelled
to banish
Don Alva-
ro de
Luna.

THE calm derived from this treaty was of no long continuance : factions never want pretences ; and those in *Castile* soon run as high as before, chiefly from the jealousy which the nobility had of the constable. The king, perhaps, by his advice, found a way to awe the king of *Arragon*, by ordering the count of *Urgel*, whom his father had sent prisoner into *Castile*, to be removed nearer the frontiers, and treated with great indulgence [f]. But Don *Alonso* was not a prince to be long restrained ; he sent his mother Donna *Leonora*, and his sister of the same name, to treat with the king of *Castile* ; and, under the shadow of this negotiation, dispatched an officer, upon whom he could depend, to corrupt the governor of the castle, in which the count of *Urgel* was confined, who carried him swiftly and secretly into the dominions of the king of *Arragon*, who confined him for the rest of his life to

1426.

the castle of *Xativa* [g]. The king, Don *Juan*, of *Navarre*, was not so much pleased with his new title as with the power he had in *Castile*, where all the nobility, who hated the constable, considered him as their protector and support. *Pedro Manrique*, encouraged by them, charged Don *Alvaro de Luna*, whether truly or falsly is a little uncertain, with very enormous offences. He suggested that he was enamoure of the queen ; and that, by the help of Donna *Maria Tellez*, he proposed to remove the king, and to administer public affairs at his pleasure, during a long minority. He charged him, on the other hand, with persuading the king, Don *Juan*, to part

1427.

with that princess, and to espouse an Infanta of *Portugal*. After much confusion, the king found himself obliged to cause his favourite to retire, though he shewed his resentment strongly against such as had compelled him to that measure,

---

[d] Histoire du Royaume de Navarre. Chronica del Rey Don Juan II. ZURIT. Annal Arragon. [e] Historia del Rey Don Juan II. [f] Chronica de Don Alvaro de Luna Condestable de Castilla. ROD. SANTII Hist. Hispan. part iv. [g] ZURIT. Annal Arragon. Historia del Rey Don Juan II.

and began to countenance the Infant Don *Henry*, who had little or no hand in it [h].

Success is often dangerous to a faction. The great lords, who had concurred in obliging the king to banish the constable, quickly fell out amongst themselves, and fearing no restraint, committed so many and so great excesses, as raised a universal clamour; insomuch that the far greater part, with the king of *Navarre* at their head, desired the king to recal him. Don *Juan* dissembled the pleasure he felt from this request, and, by a short delay, made the evil more conspicuous, and them more earnest in their follicitations [i]. About this time died Don *Ruez Lopez Avalez*, formerly constable of *Castile*, in very mean circumstances; but when he was in his grave, his illustrious friends prevailed upon the king to restore his fame, by reversing the proceedings against him : an odd instance of respect for a man's memory, whom they had suffered to want bread [k]. When the constable was again brought to court, he was introduced into the king's presence by the king of *Navarre*, and the Infant Don *Henry*, who first quarrelled with each other about his friendship, whom not long after, by his dextrous policy, he caused, upon honourable pretences, to be removed from court [l]. *Mohammed*, surnamed the *Little*, having dethroned *Mohammed* the *Left-handed*, king of *Granada*, who, for his own safety, was retired into *Africa*, was encouraged by the king of *Castile* to attempt the recovery of his own dominions; and some hostilities passed between the *Castilians* and the *Moors* [m].

Who is brought to court again in triumph by those who drove him thence.

1428.

The heart-burnings against the constable naturally revived, upon his being known to have more power at court than ever; the various arts he practised to maintain that power, increased the number. and the rage of his adversaries, amongst whom the king of *Navarre* and the Infant Don *Henry*, perceiving that they had been both his dupes, might be reckoned the chief. The king of *Arragon* adhered to them firmly, raised an army in their support; so that a new war was on the point of breaking out, and both armies took the field; but such was the zeal and the address of the queen-dowager of *Arragon*, and the cardinal *Foix*, the pope's legate, that the kings of *Arragon* and *Navarre* were prevailed on to retire, though the armies

War breaks out between the crowns of Castile *and* Arragon.

[h] Histoire du Royaume de Navarre. Chronica de Don Alvaro de Luna Condestable de Castilla. Rod. Santii Hist. Hispan. part iv.   [i] Chronica del Rey Don Juan II.   [k] Francisci Taraphæ de reg. Hispan. Historia del Rey Don Juan II.   [l] Chronica de Don Alvaro de Luna Condestable de Castilla. Chronica del Rey Don Juan II.   [m] Chronica de los Moros de Espana. Rod. Santii Hist. Hispan. part iv.

were

were within sight [n]. After the retreat of their forces, Don *Juan* finding his own army much strengthened, resolved to revenge the insult he had received, having first sent a herald to the king of *Arragon* to denounce war. This produced a great deal of trouble and bloodshed on both sides ; for, while the king, or rather the constable of *Castile*, plundered the dominions of *Arragon* on one side, the Infants Don *Henry* and Don *Pedro* did the like in *Castile*, and even carried their irruptions as far as *Toledo :* by degrees, however, the king Don *Juan*, and his loyal subjects, repressed the malecontents every where, gradually dispossessed the Infants of almost all their strong places ; and, at length, blocked them up in *Albuquerque*, which the Infant Don *Henry* had received from his

1429.   mother, whose hereditary estate it was [o]. The same year, *Mohammed*, surnamed the *Left-handed*, recovered the throne of *Granada*, and *Mohammed* the *Little*, who had usurped it, suffered death [p].

A peace concluded, and the king Don Juan turns his arms against the Moors.   In the beginning of the ensuing year, the king came with an army before *Albuquerque* ; and knowing what great advantages he might reap by dividing his adversaries, he had thoughts of treating the two Infants favourably : with this view, he advanced in person under the walls, where he ordered a general amnesty to be proclaimed to all who would accept it. Don *Henry* and Don *Pedro*, instead of accepting the king's mercy, answered with shot, stones, and arrows. The king retired upon this, and immediately proclaimed the king of *Navarre*, and the Infant Don *Henry* rebels, and gave away all their estates in *Castile*, to his followers ; and it was remarkable, that the nobility of all ranks put in for their share, only the constable *de Luna*, out of policy, refused any part of their spoils ; and a gentleman, whose name was *Dias*, to whom the king gave a handsome gratification, refused it upon a more generous motive ; he said he could take no joy in the acquisition of that, for the loss of which another man must lament [q]. The kings of *Arragon* and *Navarre* offered to submit all points in dispute to the judgment of the king of *Portugal*. The count *de Foix* offered his mediation ; but it was rejected, with so little ceremony, that he joined his forces with those of the two crowns. At length the king of *Castile*,

[n] Chronica de Don Alvaro de Luna Condestable de Castilla. Zurit. Annal Arragon. Historia del Rey Don Juan II. [o] Chronica del Rey Don Juan II. Zurit. Annal Arragon. Rod. Santii Hist. Hispan part iv. Chronica de Don Alvaro de Luna Condestable de Castilla. [p] Chronica de los Moros de España. [q] Chronica del Rey Don Juan II. Chronica de Don Alvaro de Luna Condestable de Castilla.

perceiving that the *Moors* began to be turbulent, made a truce with the kings of *Arragon* and *Navarre*, upon condition that the exiles and malecontents of both countries should remain where they were; that the Infants Don *Henry* and *Pedro* should deliver the town and castle of *Albuquerque* into the king's hands; and that, for all points in dispute, they should be left to the decision of a certain number of judges, to be chosen by both parties. This gave offence to the king of *Portugal*, who thought himself slighted[r]. Don *Juan* was now resolved to turn his arms upon the *Moors*; but first he sent an embassy to the king of *Tunis*, to signify that the king of *Granada*, notwithstanding the assistance he had given him to remount the throne, had with-held his tribute, given assistance to his enemies, and made an alliance with the king of *Arragon*. Upon this, the king of *Tunis* sent word to the monarch of *Granada*, that he had countermanded the succours he intended him, and that he had nothing to expect from him till he had given satisfaction to the king of *Castile*. The war that followed was very prejudicial to the *Moors*, the *Castilians* making incursions within sight of the walls of *Granada*[s].

THE king, Don *Juan*, kept so strict an eye upon such of the nobility as he suspected of having any intercourse with the Infants of *Arragon*, and harrassed them in such a manner, that they were afraid to stir. At the same time, under colour of the war against the *Moors*, he raised so formidable an army, as induced all his neighbours to behave towards him with great complaisance and respect. At length, after having secured one or two great men who had been intriguing, or were suspected, he proceeded into *Andalusia*, and put himself at the head of his troops, carrying with him the queen and the prince of *Asturias*; but, when the season for action approached, he sent the prince to *Madrid*, the queen to *Carmona*, and ordered his council to remain at *Cordova*[t]. On the 13th of *June*, he marched from that city for the plains of *Granada*, where, on the 25th of the same month, he came to an engagement with the whole force of the *Moors*, at a place called *Caveca de los Ginetes*; some writers say, that each of the armies consisted of upwards of one hundred thousand men; but that they were pretty near equal is, on all hands,

Marginal note: Gains a complete victory over them, and causes the king of Granada to be dethroned.

[r] ZURIT. Annal Arragon. Histoire du Royaume de Navarre. Historia del Rey Don Juan II. Chronica de Don Alvaro de Luna Condestable de Castilla. [s] Chronica de los Moros de Espana. Chronica del Rey Don Juan II. ROD. SANTII Hist. Hispan. part iv. [t] Chronica del Rey Don Juan II. ROD. SANTII Hist. Hispan. part iv.

agreed, as well as that, after a long difpute, the *Moors* were defeated, with the lofs of upwards of ten thoufand men in the field of battle, and near twice as many in the purfuit; their camp and baggage fell alfo into the power of the Chriftians; and Don *Alvaro de Luna*, perceiving a great body of troops who had taken a ftrong camp on the top of a mountain, he caufed it to be invefted, and obliged them to furrender pri-foners of war [u]. After this decifive victory, in which both the kings commanded in perfon, it was propofed, in the coun-cil of war held in the prefence of Don *Juan*, to feize this favourable opportunity, and to lay fiege to the city of *Gra-nada*; but, to this, many objections were made, and the king, following the advice of the majority of his officers, refolved to lay wafte all the adjacent country, and then to retire into his own dominions. The true motive to this refolution, as the moft unprejudiced hiftorians agree, was the fecret averfion of the nobility to the conftable, who therefore would not fuffer him to have the honour of delivering *Spain* from the *Moors*; but this ftep was no fooner taken, and the army upon its march towards *Cordova*, than they gave out pofitively, that he was the author of the retreat; and that, under colour of a prefent of figs, the king of *Granada* had fent him fifty thoufand doubloons in gold [w]. Before the end of the year, the king concluded a peace with *Portugal*, and completed his revenge on the king of *Granada*, by enabling *Jofeph Ben Muley*, grandfon of that king of *Granada* whom Don *Pedro* the *Cruel* put to death with his own hands, to dethrone *Mo-hammed* the *Left-banded*, who was forced to fly to *Malaga*, while the new king declared himfelf a vaffal of *Caftile*; upon which all hoftilities ceafed [x].

A. D.
1431.

*The trou-
bles of
Caftile
break out
afrefh, in
which the
king is
victorious.*　THE troubles of *Caftile*, which had been fufpended during the war, broke out again as foon as it was over; for Don *Juan de Soto Major*, grand mafter of *Alcantara*, whom the king had long in fufpicion, and who would never truft him-felf in his power, perceiving that his mafter was bent upon reducing him, as well as the count *de Caftro*, and others, who had purfued the fame meafures, followed the dictates of his ambition, and refolved to join himfelf to the Infants *Henry* and *Pedro*; in confequence of which he delivered the town and fortrefs of *Alcantara* to the latter, and retired with the former

[u] Chronica de los Moros de Efpana. Hiftoria del Rey Don Juan II. Chronica de Don Alvaro de Luna Condeftable de Caftilla.　[w] Rod. Santii Hift. Hifpan. part. iv. Chronica del Rey Don Juan II. Chronica de Don Alvaro de Luna Condeftable de Caftilla.　[x] Chronica de los Moros de Efpana. Brand. Hiftoria del Rey Don Juan II.

to *Albuquerque*, which was become the chief seat and rendez-vous of all the malecontents[y]. This affair took a very strange turn; for, at the time of the delivering the fortress, he made prisoner therein one Dr. *Franco*, whom the king had sent to treat with him, and seized all his effects, and sent his nephew Don *Guitterez de Soto Major*, with a strong detachment of horse, to pillage the king's subjects, for the benefit of the Infants. This Don *Guitterez*, who was commander of the order, and next in authority to his uncle, had, upon his return, a conference with Dr. *Franco*, who hinted to him, that it was in his power to repair the disgrace of his family, and to establish himself for ever; and pointed out to him how it might be done. This staggered the young man; who knowing the mutability of his uncle's temper, and finding that he did not return, suspected that the Infant Don *Henry*, to make sure of him, had confined him in the castle of *Albuquerque*. Having once taken this in his head, he surmised his own turn would be next; to prevent which, he took Dr. *Franco's* advice, arrested the Infant Don *Pedro*, and declared for the king[z]. This totally ruined the malecontents; for the king immediately ordered the uncle to be deposed as a traitor; and, upon his recommendation, the knights very willingly elected the nephew[a]. In the next place, the king threatened *Albuquerque* with a siege, and to bring Don *Pedro* to his trial. Upon this, his brother Don *Henry*, seeing no other remedy left, addressed himself to the king of *Portugal*, and desired him to propose to the king of *Castile*, that, upon evacuating all the places he held in his dominions, his brother should be released, which was readily accepted, and punctually performed on both sides[b]. *Joseph Ben Muley*, by the advice and with the assistance of the king of *Castile*, made great preparations for attacking *Mohammed* in the town of *Malaga*; but, when he was on the point of taking the field, he was seized with a distemper, which carried him off in a few days; in consequence of which, *Mohammed* the *Left-handed* was, for the third time, placed on the throne of *Granada*; and, joining his forces with those of his competitor, became, for the present, so formidable, that the king of *Castile* thought fit to dissemble his resentment, and conclude a short truce with him[c].

A. D. 1432.

[y] Rod. Santii Hist. Hispan. part iv. Alphonsi á Cartha-gena de reg. Hispan. Anacephalæosis.   [z] Chronica del Rey Don Juan II. Galindez de Carvajal.   [a] Historia del Rey Don Juan II.   [b] Rod. Santii Hist. Hispan. Chronica del Rey Don Juan II.   [c] Chronica de los Moros de Espana.

Becomes superior to all his enemies, and punishes some with great severity.

THE king having called an assembly of the states at *Madrid*, laid before them the necessity of renewing the war against the *Moors*; and having obtained the requisite supplies, ordered proper dispositions to be made for that purpose [d]. At this time, a very extraordinary treason was discovered. Don *Frederick* count *de Luna*, the natural son of Don *Martin* king of *Sicily*, had been one of the pretenders to the crown of *Arragon*; and, in the first disputes which the king of *Castile* had with his cousin Don *Alonso*, had taken up arms against that monarch, and adhered ever after to his benefactor the king of *Castile*, who bestowed upon him the duchy of *Arjona*, and several other places; which, being a man of boundless extravagance, he had sold, and consumed the money [e]. A man without principles, and in distress, is capable of any thing. He framed, in these circumstances, a design of surprizing *Seville*, of plundering the citizens and merchants, and then equipping a squadron to seek his fortunes elsewhere. Into this base design he had drawn some gentlemen, who very probably were in like circumstances with himself; and, upon its breaking out, they were all secured. **1433.** His accomplices were broke upon the wheel; but as for himself, his treason against the king of *Arragon* excused him from sharing their fate as he deserved, and he was only imprisoned for life [f]. The queen Donna *Maria* of *Castile*, touched with pity for Don *Diego*, son to Don *Pedro* the *Cruel*, who was grown grey in confinement, interceded with the king, her husband, on his behalf, who gave him the town of *Coca*, in *Castile*, for his prison, where he spent the remaining part of his days [g]. The war with the *Moors* was carried on with various success, only the *Castilians* had the good fortune to render themselves masters of the town of *Huesca*; but, to balance that, Don *Guitterez*, grand master of *Alcantara*, was defeated with a considerable loss [h]. The military expeditions of the succeeding year were of the same kind, without any thing decisive in favour of either side; but the king of *Castile* was, in one respect, very happy, since he was now entirely free from the disturbance which had been given him by the kings of *Arragon* and *Navarre*, and the other princes of that house, who were engaged in a troublesome and fruitless war in *Italy*. There, being defeated in a

[d] Historia del Rey Don Juan II.   [e] Zurit. Annal Arragon. Chronica del Rey Don Juan II.   [f] Ortiz de Zuniga. Rod. Santii Hist. Hispan. part iv.   [g] Chronica del Rey Don Juan II. [h] Chronica de los Moros de España. Historia del Rey Don Juan II.

sea

sea fight, they were, together with all the *Castilian* exiles
who had followed their fortunes, taken prisoners, which
could not fail of affording Don *Juan*, notwithstanding their
near relation to him, much satisfaction, at the same time that
it left their dominions almost at his mercy [i]. However, he
continued the truce, in consequence of the promise he had
made, some time before, to his sister Donna *Maria* queen of
Arragon, in an interview that he had with her at *Soria*. In   1435.
a short time after Don *Juan* king of *Navarre* obtained his
liberty, and returned into his own dominions ; and Donna
Leonora, queen-dowager of *Arragon*, mother to these princes,
died suddenly, perhaps of grief, at *Medina del Campo* [k].

THE next year was more fortunate for the *Castilians*, in *Concludes a*
respect to their war with the *Moors*, since several towns on *peace with*
the frontiers of the kingdom of *Granada* submitted themselves *the kings*
voluntarily to the king Don *Juan* ; but the most remarkable *of Arra-*
event of this year was the peace concluded between the *gon and*
crowns of *Castile*, *Arragon*, and *Navarre*, by which the tran- *Navarre*,
quility of the Christians in *Spain* was effectually secured [i].
The county of *Ampurias* falling to the crown of *Arragon*,
the king very generously gave it to his brother the Infant Don
Henry, and sent him home : it was this that induced the king
of *Castile* to push the conferences that had been opened for a
general peace to a speedy conclusion ; and it was accordingly
signed on the twenty-second of *September*. By this treaty the
prince of *Asturias* was to espouse Donna *Blanca*, daughter of
the king of *Navarre*, who was to enjoy the revenues of his
estates in *Castile* for four years, and after that an annual pension of ten thousand crowns, in lieu of all his pretensions.
The Infant Don *Henry* of *Arragon* was to have a like annuity
of five thousand crowns, and the sum of fifty thousand crowns
in ready money, in full satisfaction of the Infanta *Catalina*'s
portion. The *Castilians* who had embraced the interest of the
king of *Navarre* and the Infants were to be pardoned, and,
all the places taken on either side restored. The king of *Navarre* and the Infants his brethren were not, on any pretence,
to set foot in *Castile*, without the express leave of the king.
Don *Juan* ; and all memory of past misunderstandings was
to be buried in oblivion. To shew his sincerity, the king.
Don *Juan* immediately sent full powers to the king of *Navarre* for contracting the prince of *Asturias* and the Infanta

---

[i] ZURIT. Annal Arragon. Histoire du Royaume de Na-
varre. HERRERA.   [k] Chronica del Rey Don Juan II.
ZURIT. Annal Arragon.   [l] Historia del Rey Don Juan II.
Historia du Royaume de Navarre. ZURIT. Annal Arragon.

Donna *Blanca*, with a promise that the marriage should be celebrated as soon as the season would permit [m].

Causes   THE king, to the many marks of favour which he had al-
Don Pe- ready granted to the constable Don *Alvaro de Luna*, added
dro Man- the gift of the town of *Montalvan*, though it belonged to the
rique to be queen, and obliged her to accept of *Arevalo* in exchange [n].
arrested, The winter proved extremely hard, notwithstanding which
and there- the king advanced towards the frontiers himself, and sent the
by occasi- prince of *Asturias*, accompanied by the constable, the bishop
ons fresh of *Osma*, and a great train to *Alfaro*, where he espoused the
troubles. Infanta of *Navarre*, Donna *Blanca*, esteemed the most beautiful woman of her age in *Spain* [o]. In a short time after this
marriage, the king caused Don *Pedro Manrique* to be arrested
and put into the hands of the constable, which occasioned
great discontents. As soon as it was known to the amirante,
he began to fortify his places ; upon which the king sent for
him, and even granted him a safe-conduct. In this conference it was agreed, that, as the king was determined to shew
his resentment, *Pedro Manrique* should be confined for two
years in the castle of *Roja*, with leave to hunt sometimes, for
the benefit of his health, and that things should go no further.

1437.   The reader may discern from hence, that the kings of *Castile*
neither had nor claimed a power of imprisoning without crime,
or of treating as a criminal, any man who was not charged
with an offence [p]. The war with the *Moors* still subsisted :
the Christians were so fortunate as to surprize the town of
Huelma, and were very near losing it again by their imprudence. In another expedition of more importance, their
troops were not only beaten, but most of them cut off. The
king, having gone the winter before to the castle of *Roja*, *Pe-*
dro Manrique, who was confined there, with his wife and
two daughters, was removed from thence to another place,
and from thence, on the 20th of *August*, they all made their
escape ; but would have been presently retaken, if the
amirante and his friends had not taken up arms in their de-
1438.   fence [q]. After taking this step, they endeavoured to interest
the king of *Navarre* and the Infant Don *Henry* in their support, to whom *Pedro Manrique* had been formerly a great
friend, but, in respect to the treaty lately concluded, they re-

[m] Chronica del Rey Don Juan II. ZURIT. Annal Arragon.
Histoire du Royaume de Navarre.   [n] Chronica de Don Alvaro de Luna, Condestable de Luna.   [o] Histoire du Royaume
de Navarre. Chronica del Rey Don Juan II.   [p] ROD. SANTII
Hist. Hispan. part iv. Historia del Rey Don Juan II. FER.
[q] Chronica de los Moros de Espana. Chronica del Rey Don
Juan II.

                                          fused

fused to interfere, otherwise than by their good offices. The king, taking advantage of the war against the *Moors*, ordered the nobility to repair with their forces to the frontiers, early in the ensuing spring; and, as most of them testified great willingness to comply with the king's order, the constable advanced money to such as wanted it for their levies [r].

WHEN they came, however, to open the campaign, it *These grow to a greater height than ever, and the whole kingdom is in arms.* clearly appeared, that the king and his minister were totally mistaken in their measures; for a great part of the nobility, after having raised their troops, joined the malecontents. The king of *Navarre* and the Infant Don *Henry*, who had obtained a safe-conduct, on account of the marriage of the prince of *Asturias*, made use of it to enter *Castile* each with a great body of troops. The king sent to compliment them, and to know the meaning of this; to which they answered, that, in a country where every body was in arms, they thought it requisite, for their own safety, to go armed also [s]. The king Don *Juan* sent for them to join him, which the king of *Navarre* did, but the Infant Don *Henry* went to the malecontents [t]. After many conferences and much trouble, the king yielded to an accommodation, by which the king of *Navarre* and the Infant Don *Henry* were to be restored to their estates, and the constable was to be banished the court for six months. Yet, after a little time, the king went off from this agreement, and endeavoured to collect such 1439. a force as might reduce the malecontents to reason; but he found things strangely altered; and many of those who had formerly served him with the greatest fidelity going daily over to the malecontents [u]. While things were in this situation, he received a very long letter, or rather manifesto, subscribed by the king of *Navarre*, the Infant Don *Henry*, the amirante, and all the lords of their party; in which, after very warm professions of the utmost duty and respect, they told him, that it was not against him, but against Don *Alvaro de Luna*, that they had taken up arms; because that, without his knowlege, he had imposed taxes upon the people, taken away mens goods and estates at his pleasure, caused money to be coined below the standard, had prevailed upon the king

<hr>

[r] Chronica de Don Alvaro de Luna, Condestable de Castilla. [s] ROD. SANTII Hist. Hispan. part iv. Historia del Rey Don Juan II. GALINDEZ DE CARVAJAL. [t] Chronica del Rey Don Juan II. ALPHONSI a Carthagena de reg. Hispan. Anacephalæosis. [u] Chronica de Don Alvaro de Luna, Condestable de Castilla. Histoire du Royaume de Navarre. ROD. SANTII Hist. Hispan. part iv.

to ſeize perſons of diſtinction without cauſe, and then carried them to be murdered without his privity; that he diſpoſed of all civil offices at his pleaſure, threatened ſuch as were in the king's ſervice if they did not pay a ſervile complaiſance to his will; and that, at *Arevalo*, he had killed one man, and beat another in his majeſty's preſence; ſo that they could not look upon him as acting freely, or believe themſelves or the kingdom in ſafety, while ſuch a man remained about his perſon. The king did not much regard this letter; but found himſelf under a neceſſity of aſſembling the ſtates at *Valladolid*; and, previous to their meeting, he formed the houſhold of the prince of *Aſturias*; at the head of which he placed Don *Alvaro de Luna* [w]. One of the firſt things done at *Valladolid* was completing the marriage of the prince of *Aſturias* and Donna *Blanca*, as they were then both of age; which was done with great ſolemnity and at a vaſt expence [x], though, as it afterwards appeared, there was no conſummation. About this time Don *Pedro Manrique*, in whoſe quarrel theſe diſturbances began, deceaſed; and, in a ſhort time after, the prince of *Aſturias*, by the perſuaſion of his favourite Don *Juan Pacheco*, privately quitted the court, and retired to the malecontents [y].

1440.

The queen and the prince of Aſturias *concur with the malecontents.*

THE king of *Caſtile* received early the next year the mortifying news of the Infant Don *Henry's* having taken poſſeſſion of the city of *Toledo*. He marched thither with ſuch troops as he could aſſemble, in hopes of recovering it, but without effect: and though he proceeded to extremities, and iſſued various edicts and proclamations, yet they neither encouraged his own party, nor intimidated that of the malecontents. The conſtable, and his brother the archbiſhop of *Toledo*, had aſſembled a great ſtrength at *Eſcalona*, and their friends, in ſeveral ſmall actions, came off with great reputation; inſomuch, that they accepted a challenge of deciding all differences in a ſingle battle: but the king ſending an order in writing to both parties to forbear hoſtilities, on pain of being denounced rebels, he was obeyed [z]. Some fortunate attempts made by thoſe who adhered to him, encouraged the king ſo much, that he began to ſeize the eſtates of the principal perſons embarked in what was now called the league; but it gave

[w] Chronica del Rey Don Juan II. Chronica de Don Alvaro de Luna, Condeſtable de Luna. Rod. Santii Hiſt. Hiſpan. part iv. Francisci Taraphæ de reg. Hiſpan. [x] Hiſtoire du Royaume de Navarre. Alphonsi a Carthagena reg. Hiſpan. Anacephalæoſis. [y] Rod. Santii Hiſt. Hiſpan. part iv. [z] Chronica de Don Alvaro de Luna, Condeſtable de Caſtilla. Chronica del Rey Don Juan II.

him

him great concern to find both the queen and the prince of *Asturias* affecting to act as mediators between him and his subjects, while in reality they were in the interests of the malecontents : however he yielded nothing to their intercessions. He sent for the constable and all his forces to *Medina del Campo*, where, as some writers say, he was betrayed, but, as all agree, suprized, by the forces of the league, who entered the town in the night [a]. The first thing the king did, was to send to the constable and the archbishop to retire with their friends, and provide for their own safety ; whilst himself, with such as he could depend upon, formed in the square, and, by that disposition, hindered an immediate pursuit ; but as soon as the constable had forced a passage, the king sent the archbishop of *Seville* to the lords of the opposite party, to let them know he should be glad to see them. This passed on the 28th of *June* ; and the king, finding himself now intirely in the hands of those he esteemed his enemies, consented to whatever they asked, as appears from a long treaty of twenty-nine articles, which amount to no more than this, That the constable should be separated from the king one half of the year ; that he should give his son as a hostage, and also nine fortresses, by way of security, that he would submit to these terms ; and all forfeitures and all grants from the king were to be void [b]. He went, soon after this, to *Burgos*, and consented to call an assembly of the states, as they desired him ; but made choice of *Toro* instead of *Madrigal*, which they recommended : and, in the mean time, both sides carried on their intrigues [c].

1441.

THE king, instead of caressing Don *Juan* of *Navarre*, or his brother Don *Henry*, paid a great deal of respect to the amirante, with whom also the constable endeavoured to entertain a private correspondence, which, in all probability, had succeeded, but for the circumspection of the count *de Castro*, who, considering that Donna *Blanch*, queen of *Navarre*, and the Infanta *Catalina* of *Castile*, were both dead, advised the king, and the Infant Don *Ferdinand* his brother, to strengthen their interest by marriage ; proposing to the former Donna *Joanna*, daughter to the amirante, and Donna *Beatrix*, sister to the count de *Benavente*, to the latter ; and those marriages, being quickly settled, strengthened the league extremely [d]. At the assembly of the estates at *Toro*, the king

By which the king is compelled to yield to their requests.

---

[a] Rod. Santii Hist. Hispan. part iv. Historia del Rey Don Juan II. [b] Chronica de Don Alvaro de Luna, Condestable de Castilla. Chronica del Rey Don Juan II. Rod. Santii Hist. Hispan. part iv. [c] Historia del Rey Don Juan II. [d] Alphonsi a Carthagena de reg. Hispan. Anacephalæosis.

obtained

obtained a conſiderable ſupply, and had very probably done more, if it had not been diſcovered that the conſtable had procured the lodgings of the king of *Navarre* and the Infant Don *Henry* to be undermined, with an intent to have blown them up, which added not a little to that hatred that was already borne him ; but notwithſtanding this, a diſpute having happened in the order of *Calatrava*, in which ſome blood had been ſpilled, the king marched with the forces about him to put an end to the diſorder, reduced *Talavera* in his way, and then proceeded to *Toledo* [e]. In his route the conſtable Don *Alvaro* came to kiſs his hands, and had a private conference with the king of *Navarre* and the Infant Don *Henry*, after which he returned to *Eſcalona*, not a little chagrined at the loſs of his brother the archbiſhop of *Toledo* [f]. The king managed his affairs with great addreſs ; for, perceiving that factions were formed, and that ſeditions broke out in ſeveral parts of his dominions, he commiſſioned the principal lords of the league to reduce theſe diſturbers of the public quiet ; and actually engaged the Infant Don *Henry* to beſiege the new grand maſter of *Calatrava*, who had been choſe without the king's conſent, and who loſt his life in this diſpute [g]. But the conſtable giving the king notice that his wife was delivered of a daughter, the king and queen went to *Eſcalona*, and aſſiſted at the chriſtening, which piqued the league extremely [h]. The king coming to *Madrigal*, the prince of *Aſturias* repaired thither, and propoſed in the privy council that ſeveral perſons ſhould be removed from his father's preſence, and all the creatures of the conſtable diſmiſſed ; ſo that, in a ſhort time, from being a great king, Don *Juan* found himſelf very little better than a priſoner, and this with the bitter circumſtance of being thus treated by his ſon.

The biſhop of Avila prevails on the prince to attempt his father's releaſe.　AT the opening of this year the affairs of the king of *Caſtile* were in a moſt diſtreſſed condition ; the malecontents, and more eſpecially the amirante, being ſo jealous of him, that they appointed the brother of that lord, and another perſon in whom they could confide, to keep him conſtantly in view ; which, as ſoon as that prince perceived, it threw him into a deep melancholy. This affected the biſhop of *Avila* to ſuch a degree, that he addreſſed himſelf to Don *Juan Pacheco*, and aſked him how he could be guilty of ſuch ingratitude to Don *Alvaro de Luna*, who had made him every thing ? or how he

[e] Chronica del Rey Don Juan II. Chronica de Don Alvaro de Luna, Condeſtable de Caſtilla. [f] Hiſtoria del Rey Don Juan II. Rod. Santii Hiſt. Hiſpan. part iv. [g] Chronica del Rey Don Juan II. [h] Roderic Santii Hiſt. Hiſpan. part iv.

durſt

durst inspire the prince his master with sentiments of disloyalty to his father? *Pacheco* gave him to understand, that the prince needed no tutors in an affair of that kind, and that himself was sick at that time; but that he was willing to bring his master off from the league; in which he was as good as his word [i]. The prince then made a treaty with the constable Don *Alvaro*, and stipulated certain terms for himself and his favourite, on which he was willing to attempt his father's release. In managing this affair he acted with the most profound dissimulation and deceit, till the bishop of *Avila* had engaged the count *de Haro*, and many other great lords, to take up arms in the cause of their sovereign [k]. The prince of *Asturias* then put himself at their head; upon which the league took the king from *Tordesillas*, and sent him to the fortress of *Portillo*, under the care of the count *de Castro*, and then marched with all their forces to give the prince battle. While they were in the field, the king, by the assistance of cardinal *Cervantes*, made his escape, and, by his own authority, quickly raised another army; so that the king of *Navarre* and his partizans had now the prince in their front, and the king in their rear; which struck them with such a panic, that many daily deserted them. At length, their army breaking up, the king of *Navarre* retired into the territories of *Arragon*, and the Infant Don *Henry*, losing all *Andalusia*, the king, who, at the beginning, was a close prisoner, found himself, before the close of the year, at least as much a monarch as he had ever been [l].

A. D. 1444.

THE king of *Navarre* was not long before he collected fresh forces, and gave notice to all his partisans to dispose things in the best manner they could to join him; and if they found that impracticable, to repair to his brother Don *Henry*, who, with infinite hazard and diligence, drew together the broken remains of the league [m]. The king, having the prince his son, the constable, and a considerable body of troops about him, endeavoured to hinder the brothers from joining, but without effect; so that they brought their whole strength together at *Almedo*, before which place the king soon presented himself with his forces. On the 19th of *May* in the morning, the prince of *Asturias*, at the head of two hundred horse, went to reconnoitre the place; upon which Don *Ro-*

A new civil war breaks out, in which the king is compleatly victorious.

---

[i] Historia del Rey Don Juan II. Chronica de Don Alvaro de Luna, Condestable de Castilla. [k] ROD. SANTII Hist. Hispan. part iv. Chronica del Rey Don Juan II. [l] ZURIT. Annal. Arragon. Histoire du Royaume de Navarre. [m] ROD. SANTII Hist. Hispan. part iv.

drigo Manrique iffued out with a fuperior body of cavalry, and drove him into his father's camp. The king, provoked and aftonifhed at this infolence, ordered his ftandard to be difplayed, and advanced towards the town in order of battle, and kept his troops under arms till it was within two hours of night, by which time the king of *Navarre* drew out his forces in exact order, and an obftinate engagement enfued. The king's forces had the advantage from the beginning, when, a little before night, the malecontents were entirely routed, the amirante, with Don *Henry* his brother, the count *de Caftro* and his fon, and many other perfons of diftinction, were made prifoners. The king of *Navarre*, and his brother the Infant Don *Henry*, who was wounded in the hand, retired firft to *Almedo*, and from thence in the night towards the frontiers of *Arragon*; where, when they arrived, the Infant Don *Henry* died of his wound [n]. The king, by the advice of the conftable, gave a loofe to his refentment, put fome of the prifoners to death, and granted away the eftates of moft of thofe who had been in arms. This difgufted the prince of *Afturias*, who, with his favourite Don *Juan de Pacheco*, retired to *Segovia*; and the amirante, having made his efcape, joined fuch of his friends as had retired to *Andalufia*; and, having drawn together a confiderable body of men, fought to make his retreat out of the kingdom [o]. The king went on, reducing the places belonging to the malecontents, and to that lord in particular; in which, however, he met with fome obftruction; the prince very roundly declaring, that he had taken the amirante and his family under his protection [p]. In the mean time, the conftable of *Portugal* entered *Caftile* with a body of troops, which the king, by the advice of Don *Alvaro de Luna*, had demanded, contrary to the opinion of the reft of the nobility, who forefaw that they would come too late. However, he gave them a good reception; and Don *Alvaro* had feveral private conferences with the conftable [q]. The queen Donna *Maria* of *Caftile*, fifter to the kings of *Arragon* and *Navarre*, died in the beginning of the year, not without fufpicion of being poifoned, by the contrivance of Don *Alvaro*; and that ambitious favourite, without fo much as faying a word to his mafter, concluded with the conftable

[n] Chronica del Rey Don Juan II. Zurit. Annal Arragon. Chronica de Don Alvaro de Luna, Condeftable de Caftilla. Hift. de Royaume de Navarre. Marian. Fer.   [o] Alphonsi a Carthagena de reg. Anecephalæofis. Francisci Teraphæ de reg. Hifpon.   [p] Rod. Santii Hift. Hifp. part iv. [q] Chronica del Rey Don Juan II.

of *Portugal* a marriage for that prince with Donna *Isabella*, daughter to the Infant Don *Juan* of *Portugal*[r]. When the strangers were departed, he acquainted the king with what he had done, and the advantages he proposed from the match, with which Don *Juan* was exceedingly offended, as he proposed to have married a daughter of *France* : but Don *Alvaro* had such an ascendency over him, that he consented to the match [s]. He was soon after obliged to disgest another disagreeable proposition from the prince of *Asturias*, which was the pardoning the amirante and the count of *Benavente* ; at the same time he made Don *Lopez de Mendoza* marquis of *Santillana*, and Don *Juan Pacheco* marquis of *Villena*. He procured likewise Don *Alvaro de Luna* to be elected grand master of the order of St. *James* ; and, having deposed Don *Alonso*, the natural son of the king of *Navarre*, from the office of grand master of *Calatrava*, Don *Pedro Gironne* was placed therein, tho' not without difficulty, to oblige the prince, who was still out of humour, and to whom he was obliged to give the town of *Caceres*, as he did the important town of *Albuquerque*, with all its dependencies, to the grand master Don *Alvaro* [t]. But, at the close of the year, deposing *Pedro Lopez de Ayala* from the government of *Toledo*, and ordering his process to be made for numberless crimes, the prince of *Asturias* took fresh offence thereat, and the king his father was obliged to promise him satisfaction in this and in every thing else [u]. There happened this year a revolution in the kingdom of *Granada*, where *Mohammed ben Osman*, the nephew of *Mohammed ben Nacer*, at this time upon the throne, having intelligence at *Almeria* where he lived of great heartburnings in the court, he came secretly to *Granada*, and causing a tumult to be raised by his partisans, proceeded suddenly to the *Alhambra*, or palace, where he seized his uncle, and, having confined him to a prison, mounted the throne. As this was conducted by the populace, and by a few inferior officers, *Abdilbar*, who was the chief magistrate, retired to *Monte Frio*, on the frontiers of the kingdom of *Jaen*, and, with others of the nobility, invited *Ishmael*, a prince of the blood, then in the service of Don *Juan* of *Castile*, to come to them, with a promise of using their endeavours to make him king; in which he had also some assistance from the monarch of *Castile*, but not enough

---

[r] Rod. Santii Hist. Hispan. part iv.   [s] Historia del Rey Don Juan II.   Chronica de Don Alvaro de Luna, Condestable de Castilla.   [t] Chronica del Rey Don Juan II. Francisci Taraphæ de reg. Hispan.   [u] Historia del Rey Don Juan II.

to carrry his point, though his partisans adhered to him with great fidelity [w].

The prince of Asturias raises fresh disturbances, and offers his father battle.

THE misunderstanding between the king Don *Juan* of Castile and his son the prince of *Asturias* rose higher, and grew much more public than ever; insomuch, that it was no secret to the people, that, under colour of repressing the insolence of the grand master Don *Alvaro,* he really meant to take the crown from his father's head, and to place it upon his own. Don *Juan,* being apprised of this, and having more steadiness in his temper than his son, thought the sooner this was decided the better; and therefore, hearing the prince was in the field, he marched against him with pretty near the same force [x]. The two armies met between *Arevalo* and *Madrigal;* but the clergy and people of discretion, who were about the king and prince, prevailed upon them to spare their subjects blood in so unnatural a quarrel; upon which it was agreed to leave the discussion of their respective grievances to the real authors of them, Don *Alvaro de Luna* and Don *Juan Pacheco,* who, for the present, patched up an agreement to their own satisfaction, who were to be the only gainers by it, which was subscribed on the eleventh of *May* [y]. The king Don *Juan* then turned his arms against his cousin of *Navarre,* and endeavoured to reduce the few strong places he had left; but while he was thus employed, Don *Juan Pacheco* revived in the prince's mind a desire of obliging the king to banish the grand master, who was become his own enemy: the king knew this well enough, and had no dislike at all to the thing, for he knew him to be a bad man, and hated him as a great one. Don *Alvaro* was not at all ignorant of this; but he shewed the king so clearly that it was by his power and abilities that he was himself kept on the throne, that he rendered him more steady to him through timidity than he had ever been through affection. By his advice the king wrote to the amirante and to the count de *Benavente,* to whom he knew that his son had made propositions, assuring them that he would make fidelity more their interest than treason. A more miserable nation than this, unconquered by a foreign force, was never seen; and yet into this miserable condition must every nation come, where factions long prevail [z]. The king of *Navarre,* to be revenged on the monarch of *Castile,* procured

---

[w] Chron. de los Moros de Espana.
Don Juan II. GALINDEZ DE CARVAJAL.
de Don Alvaro de Luna, Condestable de Castilla. ROD. SANTII
Hist. Hispan. p. iv.   [z] FRANC. TARAPHÆ. ALPHONSI a
Carthagena, & auct. sup. citat.   [x] Chron. del Rey
[y] Chronica

a great

a great body of *Gascons*, hungry and out of pay, to make a quick march through his own dominions, and take up their winter quarters in *Castile*, where, to all the untoward consequences of civil broils, they added every difmal misfortune that could offend a barbarous invader. To heighten the horrors of this fcene, the king of *Granada*, having first reconciled *Ifhmael*, made feveral incurfions into the territories of *Castile*, in quality of confederate to the king of *Navarre*, burnt feveral places, and drove multitudes into flavery ; while, to give the finishing touch to the piece, the prince of *Asturias*, who commanded on the frontiers, forbid any fuccours being fent to the places attacked, from the wicked defire of rendering his father more odious, and his administration more contemptible, as the most effectual method of compelling him to a refignation [a].

IT was not possible for any prince to have a truer or a fharper fenfe of his condition than Don *Juan* of *Castile* ; but, for many reasons, he was obliged to diffemble ; and, if that is to be efteemed, as fome fay it is, a royal quality, he poffeffed it in a fupreme degree. Don *Juan*, king of *Navarre*, bearing continually in his mind what noble eftates he once had in *Castile*, meditated every method possible for recovering them, and found none more promifing for the prefent than to complete the marriage with Donna *Joanna Henriques*, daughter to the amirante, which he had contracted fome time before; the brother of that lady being acquainted with his intentions, conveyed her privately to the frontiers of *Arragon*, where that monarch met and efpoufed her [b]. This alliance prompted him to raife new troubles in *Castile* ; but his fon the prince of *Viana* interpofed, and, by his great influence with the ftates of *Navarre* and *Arragon*, prevented him from doing what he propofed [c]. Don *Juan* of *Castile* married alfo a fecond time Donna *Ifabella*, daughter to the Infant Don *Juan* of *Portugal*, who, in a very fhort fpace of time, acquired his affection. to fuch a degree, that he intrufted her with his great fecret, which was, that he mortally hated, and was extremely defirous of being rid of, Don *Alvaro*, who had been fo long his favourite, for which he affigned many motives, but, in all probability, fuppreffed one, which was none of the leaft, that he. had obliged him to marry this very princefs against his incli-

The king of Castile espouses the daughter of Don Juan, Infant of Portugal.

---

[a] Chron. del Rey Don Juan II. de Castilla. HERNANDO PEREZ DE GUZMAN. [b] ZURIT. Annal Arragon. [c] Hiftoire du Royaume de Navarre.

nation.

A. D.
1447.

nation [d] (C). The king of *Granada*, in quality still of ally to the king of *Navarre*, made himself master of several places that lay very conveniently for him, and which the prince of *Asturias* might easily have prevented, but for the reason that has been before assigned ; which, though the worst in the

---

[d] BRAND. Chron. del Rey Don Juan el Segundo, por ALVAR GARCIA DE SANT. MARIA. JUAN DE MENA. HERNANDO PEREZ DE GUZMAN, y GOMEZ CARRILLO.

(C) This great favourite Don *Alvaro de Luna*, having maintained himself so many years in the possession of power, by studying the king's temper, and complying with it, saw plainly enough that he could not long remain a widower ; and that it was of the last importance to his safety that he should receive a wife from his hand. It was this that induced him to set on foot a secret negotiation with the crown of *Portugal*, or rather with the regent and his family, that in case of any revolution in *Castile*, which he had always to fear, he might have some neighbouring country, from which he might expect succours, or into which he might retire in case of necessity. Donna *Isabella*, in all probability, came to the court of *Castile*, with sentiments of respect and gratitude for Don *Alvaro*; but when she found the easiness of Don *Juan's* temper, and that Don *Alvaro* had lost his inclinations, though he preserved his influence over his master, she conceived a design of making herself, what he had formerly been, the sole oracle of the king, and the absolute mistress of his affairs. In order to this, there was no other way than to enter into the king's secret, and to

manage the destruction of her benefactor ; which, though she had a very good will, the king wanted capacity to bring about. For this, the *Spanish* historians, and it is no wonder, load her memory with the strongest imputations of ingratitude, and even cruelty ; since the king relented at last, and, if it had not been for the queen, would have preserved this great man's life. The vanity of oblique policy is evident in the pains that Don *Alvaro* took to bring about his own destruction, while, in his own opinion, he was taking the most effectual means to support his power, or at least to preserve his person. On the other hand, the folly of female intrigues is no less apparent from the queen's behaviour, who, by sacrificing Don *Alvaro*, exposed herself to all that contempt, ill usage, and severe treatment, which she met with in the succeeding reign. They had both of them great address in turning circumstances and events to the facilitating of their private views ; both of them triumph'd in their turns by these sinister contrivances ; and both of them perished in the end by the success of their own arts.

world,

world, continued to be the rule of his conduct [e] : or, if that be any apology for his conduct, it was the maxim of Don *Juan Pacheco*, who then and ever after governed him at his pleasure.

THE grand master Don *Alvaro de Luna*, perceiving that the greater part of the nobility of *Castile* inclined to the party of the king of *Navarre*, judged it absolutely necessary, for his own safety, that the king and the prince should be reconciled ; and this he brought about, as he had often done before, by gaining Don *Juan de Pacheco*. In order to this reconciliation, an interview was to be had between the father and the son, to which they came with an equal number of guards; and at which the king caused the count *de Benavente*, Don *Henry Henriquez*, and Don *Suero de Quinones*, to be arrested ; and the prince, on his side, did the same, with regard to the count *Alba de Tormes* and Don *Pedro de Quinones*, persons who had given umbrage to their respective favourites [f]. This, as might have been easily foreseen, augmented the troubles, which were already but too great, and obliged many of the nobility to unite more strictly to the king of *Navarre*. The *Moors* also renewed their incursions ; and though the prince, as a proof of his reconciliation, sent *Alonso Tellez* against them with a small body of forces, yet this served only to increase the evil ; since, thro' his own ill conduct, most of his troops were cut to pieces [g]. The count of *Benavente*, having made his escape, took up arms against the king, and gave him a great deal of trouble. The grand master Don *Alvaro*, having the king's order to protect the frontiers against the *Moors*, first went to *Toledo*, in order to borrow a sum of money ; which so irritated the citizens, that they revolted, and made *Pedro Sarmiento*, who was governor of the castle, their chief. He defended the city against the king, whom he treated with the utmost insolence ; and, when he found himself hard pressed, offered to declare for the prince, who thereupon required the king his father to raise the siege, as he had taken *Toledo* and all its inhabitants under his protection ; which, to avoid a new civil war, the king was constrained to do [h]. For these good services *Pedro Sarmiento* thought it reasonable to pay himself, by stripping most of the rich citizens of all that they were worth, which he did, with all the circumstances of oppression and barbarity that can be imagined. The prince, being informed of this, went thither and turned him out ; but suffered him to carry away all

An interview between the king of Castile and his son.

1448.

[e] Chron. de los Moros de España. [f] HERNANDO PE-REZ DE GUZMAN. Chronica de Don Alvaro de Luna, Condestable de Castilla. [g] Chronica del Rey Don Juan II. de Castilla. [h] Vid. auct. supra citat.

1449.
The Moors
renew
their in-
cursions.

his ill-got wealth, with which he retired into *Arragon* [i]. The Moors continued their incursions, and took several places upon the frontiers. The king of *Castile*, growing old and weary of continual disturbances, and becoming more and more uneasy at the power which the grand master Don *Alvaro* assumed, though he shewed him as great marks of favour as ever, resolved to reconcile himself, once for all, to the king of *Navarre* and the malecontents. While he was engaged in a negotiation for this purpose, the prince of *Asturias* fell into the like distaste of his favourite Don *Juan Pacheco*, marquis of *Villena*; but, as he could never keep a secret, the design he had laid to seize him miscarried, and he was forced to give him leave to quit his court, which he did, and retired to one of the fortresses in his own possession; yet, in a short time after, this quarrel was composed, and the marquis restored to the prince's good graces [k]; who, though a weaker man, was a better master than his father.

1450.
Reconcilia-
tion be-
tween the
king and
his son.

THE pope being fully acquainted with the sad and strange situation of affairs in *Castile*, which gave the *Moors* an opportunity not only of enriching themselves, by their annual excursions, but likewise to strengthen and enlarge their dominion, sent a bull, addressed to most of the prelates in *Spain*, requiring them to excommunicate such as refused to submit to their sovereign, and, by perplexing his affairs, gave such an advantage to the Infidels. This bull being published, had a great effect; insomuch, that the prince of *Asturias* found himself obliged to submit himself in earnest to his father; and, to take away all grounds of suspicion, took an oath, which was administered to him by the archbishop of *Toledo*, to remain inviolably attached to him for the future. In consequence of this, *Toledo* returned to the king's obedience [l]. Several of the adherents and instruments of *Pedro Sarmiento* were seized, convicted, and suffered cruel deaths. He was also condemned as a traitor, and his estates confiscated; but the king suffered him to live privately with his family, which, however, did not exempt him from the heavier sentence of another tribunal; for, falling into a violent illness, he suffered for a long time most excruciating tortures, and ended his days in the most deplorable manner [m]. The prince, in virtue of his reconciliation with the king, prevailed upon him to make war with *Navarre*; which, however, was soon compromised, by the prince of *Viana's* repairing to the king's camp, and af-

[i] ZURIT. Annal Arragon. Historia del Rey Don Juan II.
[k] HERNANDO PEREZ DE GUZMAN. Chron. de los Moros de Espana.　[l] RAINALD.　[m] Chronica del Rey Don Juan II.

suring him that he took no share in his father's measures; the truth of which quickly after appeared by the breaking out of a war between them. On the 23d of *April* this year, the queen was brought to bed, some say at *Madrid*, others at *Madrigal*, of the Infanta Donna *Isabella*, who, in process of time, became queen of all *Spain* [n].

A. D. 1451.

THE queen continued incessantly to irritate the king against the grand master Don *Alvaro*, to which she herself was chiefly instigated by the treasurer Don *Alonso Perez de Vivero*, a man of address and abilities; who, at the same time, owed all his preferments to the man whom he thus laboured to destroy, and by whom, at this time, he was entertained as a bosom friend. The king had it several times in his mind to cause him to be arrested; but the sense of continual danger had taught the grand master such an habitual caution, that every attempt of this kind was found impracticable. Yet he who, without knowing their schemes, could defend himself against others, facilitated his own ruin by the methods he took to accomplish theirs. He persuaded the king to attack his old enemy the count *de Placentia*, or rather to lend him the concurrence of his person and authority to despoil that nobleman of his estates; which the king, who no longer considered every man as his enemy that was so to his favourite, refused [o]. Of this project *Vivero* gave that nobleman a full account; who thereupon framed the scheme of a general confederacy for the grand master's destruction, which he sent to the prince of *Asturias*, and to several of the nobility. The prince, at that time, was not very clear, whether the destruction of the grand master was his interest or not, and therefore sent a loose and inconclusive answer; but the count *de Haro*, the marquis *de Santillan*, and the count *de Benavente*, entered into the confederacy, and promised to support it at the hazard of their lives and fortunes, and it was this that brought the grand master to his ruin [p]. The king and the prince of *Asturias* concurred in supporting Don *Carlos*, prince of *Viana*, against his father, and indeed he had all the plausible pretences that could be offered for such a proceeding. But Don *Juan* of *Navarre* was another sort of a man than Don *Juan* of *Castile*, and not to be frighted by appearances. His son took the field against him with a superior army, and endeavoured to force him to a battle; but, before the quarrel came to be decided by the sword, he offered him peace, upon such

---

[n] HERNANDO PEREZ DE GUZMAN.   [o] Chronica de Don Alvaro de Luna, Condestable de Castilla. Chronica del Rey Don Juan II.   [p] Historia del Rey Don Juan II. HERNANDO PEREZ DE GUZMAN.

Battle be- terms as he thought fit to prescribe. The king of *Navarre,*
tween the who looked upon the loss of his honour, and authority as a far
king of greater misfortune than the loss of life, rejected those terms,
Navarre and upon this an engagement ensued; in which, if the prince
and his would have been content with victory, he might have had it;
own son. but attacking the king's guards, and putting his father's per-
1452. son in danger, his brother Don *Alonso* exerted himself with
such passion for the preservation of him who had given him
being, that the prince's party were not only defeated, but he
was forced to deliver up his sword into his brother's hands,
and so became his father's prisoner, who treated him sternly
indeed, but not with cruelty q.

THE king of *Caftile* had a conference with the prince of
Asturias at *Madrigal,* to concert measures for procuring the
prince of *Viana's* liberty; and in this conference Don *Alonso*
Perez de Vivero engaged the prince to concur with his father
in the destruction of the grand master, for arresting of whom
some plots were laid, but without effect r. This did not hinder the king's accepting an invitation from the grand master to
go with the queen and the whole court to *Tordesillas,* where
they were splendidly entertained at his expence; and it was
in the midst of these diversions, that, by an accident, the grand
master discovered the intrigues and correspondences of *Vivero;*
upon which he first thought of destroying him, but referred it
to another occasion, when he might withdraw himself from
court, and stand upon his defence; but, considering that he
had always a gallant company of guards, commanded by a
natural son of his, Don *Pedro de Luna,* he rejected that likewise as beneath him s. He went therefore with the king to
Valladolid; but, when his master proposed going to *Burgos,*
he demanded a safe-conduct, which was granted him. When
the court arrived there, the king sent a person of confidence to
the count of *Placentia,* with orders to arrest the grand master;
but the count suspecting this was no more than an artifice to
entrap him, declined the commission, which, however, he
chearfully accepted, upon the king's writing him a letter with
his own hand. But, being confined to his bed by the gout, he
committed the direction of this difficult affair to his son Don
Alvaro de Zuniga, who, with a small body of determined men,
went privately to *Burgos* in order to effect it t. This design,
though conducted with all the art and all the spirit possible, .

q Chronica del Rey Don Juan II. Histoire du Royaume de
Navarre. HERNANDO PEREZ DE GUZMAN. FER. r ROD.
SANTII Hist. Hispan: part iv. s Chronica de Don Alvaro
de Luna, Condestable de Castilla. t ALPHONSI a Carthagena reg. Hispan, Anacephalæosis.

was

was attended with such difficulties, that the king once sent that young nobleman orders to desist ; but, upon his undertaking for the success, he renewed his command to proceed. The grand master, though he had no distinct intelligence of the measures pursued, knew in general that something was brewing against him ; and therefore, upon *Good Friday*, called a council of his particular friends to concert the properest means for securing his safety, to which, amongst the rest, Don *Alonso Perez de Vivero* was invited. The place where this consultation was held was the top of the tower of the palace in which he lodged ; and, having first shewn Don *Alonso* his own letters and the king's, which he could not deny, he then turned his back upon him ; on which signal two of his friends caught up Don *Alonso,* and threw him over the tower, by which his brains were beat out in the street [u]. Upon this they set up a great cry, as if it had happened by accident ; which, however it deceived the people, could not deceive the king, who, by this action, was determined in his measures. At length Don *Alvaro de Zuniga* invested his house, and would have forced it, but the king sent an order to the grand master to submit himself prisoner, which he offered to do, provided he had the king's promise that nothing should be attempted against his life or honour : this he accordingly received, though some say the words of that promise were, nothing should be *unjustly* attempted [w]. However upon this he submitted. His castle of *Portilla* being soon after reduced, the king ordered him to be sent thither, and directed a commission to twelve lawyers and lords of the council to form his process, and to proceed to judgment, which they did, and unanimously pronounced sentence of death on him [x]. He was transferred from thence to *Valladolid,* by Don *Diego de Zuniga,* who had the custody of him, where he suffered death on a scaffold, on the seventh of *June,* as *Ferreras* says [y], though *Mariana* and other writers affirm, on the 5th of *July* [z]. He died with great steadiness and courage ; and it is said that the king, if he had not been with-held by the queen, would have preserved him even on the morning of his execution (D).

The grand master of St. Jago suffers death upon a scaffold at Valladolid. This

[u] HERNANDO PEREZ DE GUZMAN. Chronica del Rey Don Juan II. [w] FER. [x] Chronica de Don Alvaro de Luna, Condestable de Castilla. ROD. SANTII Hist. Hispan. part iv. [y] Historia de España, part ix. sect. xv. Historia general de España, part ix. sect. xv.

(D) It was contrived by those who were about the king of *Castile,* that this sacrifice of the great master of St. *James,* and high

This action has been considered by different authors in very different lights; for some regard him as a criminal who met
with

high conftable, Don *Alvaro de Luna*, fhould be accompanied with all the pomp and folemnity poffible, that it might make the greater impreffion on the people. The fcaffold was erected in one of the moft public places in *Valladolid*; there ftood upon it a table covered with black velvet, upon which was a crofs, between two flambeaux of white wax lighted; to which, as foon as he came upon the fcaffold, he made a profound reverence. Upon the reading of his fentence, he faid, My fins have deferved not only this, but a much heavier punifhment. He then gave his hat and his ring to one of his pages, faying, Thefe are the laft favours I have to beftow; upon which the youth burft out into fuch a paffion of tears, as affected all the fpectators. He caft his eyes next on the mafter of the horfe to the prince of *Afturias*; *Baraxa*, faid he, tell your mafter from me, that he will do well not to follow his father's example in the rewarding of his old fervants. Obferving a very high poft with an iron hook upon the top of it, he faid to the executioner, My friend, what is that for? It is, returned the executioner, to place your head on when I fhall have fevered it from your body. Don *Alvaro*, without the leaft emotion, replied, when I am dead, you may do with my remains what you pleafe; no death can be fhameful, which is fupported with courage and intrepidity, or untimely, after a man has for many

years been at the head of affairs, and conducted all things with dignity and reputation. He then laid himfelf along upon the cloth prepared for that purpofe, for in *Spain* they do not behead, but cut the throats of perfons condemned for high treafon, and afterwards feparate the head from the body. Immediately before he lay down, the executioner would have tied his hands behind him with a cord; but Don *Alvaro* putting his hand into his bofom, pulled out a riband, which he gave him for that purpofe. As foon as he was proftrate the executioner ftruck his long knife into his throat, and prefently after divided his head from his body, which, after it had been expofed to the people, was placed upon the pole before-mentioned, and remained there nine days, tho' the body lay on the fcaffold but three. A bafon was placed near it, to receive the alms of charitably difpofed people, to defray the expence of burying, fays *Mariana*, a man, who in power and wealth, but a few days before, was equal to fome fovereign princes. Others, with more probability, fay this money was beftowed to procure maffes for his foul. He was at firft interred at St. *Andrews*, where malefactors were ufually buried; but leave was afterwards procured to remove his body to the church of St. *Francis*, in *Valladolid*: fome years after, with the king's permiffion, it was transferred to *Toledo*, and finally buried with great pomp

with no worse usage than he deserved, while others represent him as a victim of state, whose only crime was being a very able minister to a very weak prince (E). In this, however, most historians agree, that the king regretted the loss of him when it was too late, and when experience taught him that faction was not buried in the grave of the grand master, but that the powers of repressing it were much lessened by his death. He enriched himself exceedingly by the forfeitures, and by seizing the treasures of that great minister; though, by a kind of composition, he left much wealth to his widow and children On the 15th of *November* the queen was delivered of the Infant Don *Alonso*, at *Tordesillas* [d]. About the same time a revolution happened in the kingdom of *Granada*, where *Ishmael* at length found means to set himself on the throne, at least he was proclaimed king, though not without a rival, as will be seen hereafter [e]. The king of *Navarre*, at the request *The king* of the states of that kingdom and of *Arragon*, released the *of* Naprince Don *Carlos*, upon certain terms; neither ought we to varre *sets* omit that the prince of *Asturias* was separated from his prin- *his son at* cess Donna *Blanca*, daughter to the king of *Navarre*, and *liberty.* sister to Don *Carlos*, on account of a reciprocal frigidity to- 1453. wards each other; a cause which then, and ever since, has been considered in a proper, that is, in a ridiculous, light [f].

THE king Don *Juan* having now learned from experience, the proper mistress of such kind of men, that the only way to be safe, after a reign like his, was to be armed, kept eight thousand lances about his person, which had a good effect [g]. The intelligence he received of the discoveries made by the king of *Portugal*, and the great advantages that he was like to reap from them, chagrined him so much, who, during a very long reign, had gained no advantage at all to his people, that, surmising these discoveries to be inconsistent

---

[d] Rod. Santii Hist. Hispan. part iv. l'Histoire de Granada. Nando Perez de Guzman. Juan II.

[e] Pedraza [f] Zurit. Annal Arragon. Hernando [g] Chronica del Rey Don Juan II.

pomp in the chapel of St. *James* belonging to the cathedral in that city, which was of his own foundation. This was the end of him who had served his master forty-five years, thirty of which he had governed at his pleasure both the king and kingdom.

(E) We might expect to find some distinct account of the

crimes of which he was convicted in the sentence that was read to him upon the scaffold, in the hearing of the people; but upon the perusal of the sentence, it will appear that it consists only of general suggestions, and seems to ground the opinion of the king's justice upon the notoriety of his offences.

with the grant which his predecessors had obtained from the pope of the *Canary Islands*, and whatever depended upon them, he threatened *Portugal* with a war, if the king did not defist from all thoughts of discovery ; but that monarch having made him a general promise, not to invade his rights, pursued them without any regard to the threats of Don *Juan* [h]. His sister the queen Donna *Maria* of *Arragon*, being come into *Castile* on purpose to confer with him, he went, though he was ill of a fever, from *Avila* towards *Medina del Campo* to meet her, but was taken so extremely ill upon the road, that those about him thought he was dead ; yet, upon exhibiting a proper cordial, he recovered so much strength as to be carried to *Medina del Campo*, and from thence to *Valladolid*, where he relapsed, and, with great patience and resignation, breathed his last, on the twenty-first of *July* [i]. By his testament he devised to the queen Donna *Isabella* the towns of *Soria*, *Arevalo*, and *Madrigal*, with all their dependencies ; to the Infant Don *Alonso* the administration of the grand mastership of St. *James*, and to the Infanta Donna *Isabella* the town of *Cuellar*, with its revenues and territory. He recommended in the strongest terms to the prince of *Asturias* unanimity in the royal family, and a proper regard in him for his mother-in-law, and for his brother and sister ; of which, however, it does not appear he had any great hopes (F). His demise was not much regretted by his

Death of Don Juan king of Castile, who is succeeded by his son Henry IV.

---

[h] Perez de Guzman. Santii Hist. Hispan. part iv.　　　[i] Zurit. Annal Arragon. Rod.

(F) We are told by *Mariana* that this unfortunate prince died on the twentieth, instead of the twenty-first, of *June*, in 1454 ; and he assures us, that though, by his last will and testament, he assigned the great offices of grand master and constable to the Infant Don *Alonso*, it was much less than he designed, and yet even that was more than was in his power. The truth, in the opinion of this and of other historians was, that he meant to have disinherited the prince of *Asturias*, as incapable and unworthy of the royal dignity, and one who had forfeited his right to it by his frequent rebellions. *Ferreras* takes no notice of this, and yet he seems to confirm the truth of it, by observing, that, in the fit which the king had a little before his death, one of his principal ministers sent immediately for the prince Don *Henry*, from an apprehension that some of the nobility might get the person of the Infant Don *Alonso* into their hands, in order to create new troubles. This is scarce intelligible, unless some such intention of the king his father was known ; and allowing this, it will enable us to understand and account for many things that would otherwise appear very strange at least, if not altogether incredible, in the succeeding part of the history.

subjects,

subjects, and perhaps it would have excited still less sorrow if they had not been so well acquainted with his successor [k].

As soon as the obsequies of the late king were performed, his son, Don *Henry* the fourth, took possession of the kingdom, at *Valladolid*, with great ceremony, the principal nobility and prelates of the realm repairing thither to pay their allegiance, and testify their regard for the new king [l]. Upon this occasion Don *Henry* affected, by his behaviour as a king, to efface all memory of the strange things that had been done by the prince of *Asturias*. He caused Don *Diego Manrique*, count of *Trevino*, whom he had, for some time, kept in prison, to be set at liberty; and he did the like with respect to Don *Hernando Alvarez de Toledo*, count of *Alba*, who had been restrained for a much longer time; which acts of grace were very acceptable [m]. Soon after he sent ambassadors to renew the antient alliance with the crown of *France*; and, within as short a space as could be expected, he regulated with Donna *Maria*, queen of *Arragon*, the treaty of accommodation which had been begun by his father [n]. This settled and extinguished all the pretensions of the king of *Navarre* and his family, as well as their adherents. That monarch, his son Don *Alonso*, and his nephew Don *Henry*, had each of them a large annuity as a satisfaction for their estates; and for their partizans they were, a few only excepted, restored to their titles, dignities, and possessions, without being liable to any enquiry for what was past; the intire settlement of so perplexed an affair being referred to a congress [o]. As to the affairs of *Arragon*, the king Don *Henry* thought fit to settle these by an embassy sent for that purpose to king Don *Alonso* in *Italy*; and, this being in a fair train, he called an assembly of the three estates of the kingdom, in which his design of attacking the *Moors* was highly approved, and a liberal supply granted him for that purpose. He likewise negotiated a marriage with Donna *Joanna* Infanta of *Portugal*, which was concluded, though that princess was no stranger to the suspicions created by the dissolution of his former marriage with the Infanta of *Navarre* [p], which indeed were the common topics of discourse through *Spain*.

[k] Alphonsi a Carthagena reg. Hispan. Anacephalæosis. Hernando Perez de Guzman. [l] Chronica del Rey Don Henrique Quarto, de Alonso de Palencia. [m] Chronica del Rey Don Henrique Quarto, de Diego Enriques del Castillo. [n] Zurit. Annal Arragon. P. Daniel Histoire de France. [o] Vide auct. sup. citat. [p] Emanuel Faria y Sousa, Abarca.

1454.
Makes war upon the Moors.

In the congrefs held at *Agreda* all the points in difference between the crowns of *Caftile* and *Navarre*, and their allies and adherents on both fides, were very happily terminated, on the conditions that have been already mentioned. The war with the *Moors* was undertaken in the fpring with a great force, but with no great effect, fince the king only ravaged the open country about *Granada*. This difpleafed fome of the nobility; who, perceiving that the king was as much held in leading-ftrings by the marquis *de Villena*, as his father had ever been by Don *Alvaro de Luna*, refolved to feize on the perfon of their monarch, and then to make fuch alterations as they fhould think convenient. But this defign was difcovered and prevented [q]. He went afterwards to *Cordova*, where he efpoufed Donna *Joanna* of *Portugal* [r]. In the autumn he made a new irruption into the territories of *Granada*, where he did infinite mifchief; infomuch, that *Ifhmael* king of *Granada* entered into a negotiation, which, however, was attended with no effect; and at length, the feafon being fpent, the Chriftian army retired [s]. The grand mafterfhips of St. *James* and *Alcantara* being vacant, the king took their revenues to his own ufe; but the marquis *de Villena* was fecretly ambitious of attaining the firft. In this he was traverfed by *Michael Luc*, whom the king had lately taken into his good graces, and who, though a man of very mean birth, was fupported by the duke *de Medina Sidonia*, the bifhop of *Cuenca*, and others of the nobility, out of fpleen to the marquis; though the people in general bore an equal hatred to them both [t]: but, of the two, Don *Michael* had a better character, and deferved it.

1455.

The late treaty of peace concluded at *Agreda* appeared to the king of *Caftile* of fo great confequence, that he refolved to fend ambaffadors to the king of *Arragon*, then at *Naples*, in order to have his concurrence, in which he met with all the fuccefs he could defire. In the war with the *Moors* it was otherwife; he gave them, indeed, a great deal of difturbance, deftroyed their country, and took fome places of little importance, but there happened nothing decifive; and it was of very ill confequence to let the Infidels fee armies of forty or fifty thoufand men entering their territories in a hoftile manner, and quitting them again in a few weeks [u]. After his fummer expedition was over, the king had a ftrong inclination

[q] Chronica del Rey Don Henrique Quarto, de Diego Enriques del Caftillo.   [r] Faria y Sousa.   [s] Chron. de los Moros de Efpana.   [t] Chronica de los Reyes Catholicos, &c. Ferreras.   [u] Cartas del Bachiller Fernand. Gomez de Ciudad Real.

to visit all the sea coast as far as *Gibraltar*, which he accordingly did, under the protection of a proper escorte. There having
a sight of the opposite continent of *Africa*, upon the invitation
of the governor of *Ceuta*, he took a resolution of going thither, *Makes an*
and that in a small vessel, and with a few persons, which *excursion*
alarmed the principal persons about him exceedingly. The *to the coast*
king, persisting in his own scheme, traversed the streight of *of Barba-*
Gibraltar, and, after a few days amusement at *Ceuta*, where *ry.*
the governor omitted nothing that could give him pleasure, he
returned safely, though not without some difficulty and danger, to *Tarefa*; and there he was so unlucky as to hear that
the bishop of *Jaen*, and the count of *Castenada*, being defeated
in a battle against the *Moors*, were carried prisoners to *Granada* w. Towards the close of the year, he sent the marquis
de Villena to regulate with the chief justice of *Arragon* the
disputes that still subsisted in reference to the commanderies
of the order of St. *James* in that kingdom, which were to
have been restored in virtue of the late treaty, and which,
notwithstanding, remained in the hands of those to whom the
king of *Arragon* had given them. The marquis, instead of
executing this commission as he ought, took occasion from
thence to enter into engagements of quite another kind. He
suggested to the chief justice, *Lanuza*, that, very possibly,
there might come a time when he might be as much perse-
cuted in *Castile* as the grand master Don *Alvaro*; in which
case he was desirous of being sure of the king of *Arragon's*
protection: with this view he offered, and actually took, an
oath of fidelity to that monarch, which was administered to
him by the chief justice *Lanuza*: and thus, without taking
any care of his master's business, he returned to the court of
Castile, very well satisfied with what he had done in his own x.
The whole country of *Biscay* being in commotion, through
the disturbance excited by the factions of the *Gamboas* and
the *Otanez*, the king found himself under the necessity of going thither : arriving at *St. Sebastians*, he embarked there
on board a small vessel, that he might, with greater facility,
examine the sea coast : and, having ordered several small
castles to be demolished, as serving only for retreats to such as
were disposed to trouble the peace of the country, visited most
of the great towns, and quieted the whole province. He appointed Don *Juan Hurtado de Mendosa* governor of *Biscay*, and

---

w *Chronica de los Moros de Espana.* *Chronica del Rey Don
Henrique Quarto, de Alonso de Palencia.* x *Zurita
Annal Arragon.*

prepared

prepared to return into *Castile* [y]. Before he could put this in execution, he received an unexpected account of a new confederacy, into which the archbishop of *Toledo*, the amirante, the count *de Haro*, the marquis *de Santillan*, the count *de Alba*, the count *de Benaventé*, and several other noblemen had entered, in order to procure a reformation in the government. They represented to the king, that, through his indolence and inattention, the laws had lost their vigour, industry was almost every-where ceased ; that, jealous of his nobility, he gave up a great part of his private life to persons unworthy of his conversation ; that, from hence, the civil administration was contemned, his military expeditions had no effect; and, while he governed, as it were, at random, and without any system, things were every-where declining into ruin and confusion. The king was exceedingly chagrined at this news ; but, by the advice of the archbishop of *Seville* and the marquis *de Villena*, he resolved to have an interview with the king of *Navarre*, in order to prevent his giving any countenance to this new confederacy : they met accordingly on the frontiers, where it was agreed, that the Infant Don *Alonso* of *Castile* should espouse the Infanta of *Navarre*, and that the Infant Don *Hernando*, or *Ferdinand*, of *Navarre*, should espouse the Infanta *Isabella* of *Castile* [z]. These points settled, the king went to *Segovia*, and, having acquainted the lords of the confederacy, that, after the campaign was over, he would call an assembly of the states, in which all the grievances they had enumerated should be redressed, he desired them not to impede the progress of the war, which was of so great consequence to religion and the public welfare. With this they seemed to have acquiesced, since the king took the field against the *Moors* with a great army, and yet there passed nothing of more importance than the year before ; at length the king of *Granada* proposed to acknowlege himself the vassal of *Castile*, and to pay a large annual tribute, to which Don *Henry* listened ; but hostilities, notwithstanding, continued to the close

of the year [a]. The rebellion of Don *Alonso Fijardo* in *Murcia*, which had broke out about seven years before, continued still to give the king a great deal of trouble, in consequence of the support which, from time to time, he received from the *Moors*. He laboured this year, by an embassy sent expressly for that purpose, to reconcile the *French* king *Charles* the seventh to his son the Dauphin, tho' without effect [b].

---

[y] Chronica de los Reyes Catholicos, &c.　　[z] Zurit. Annal Arragon. Chron. del Rey Don Henrique Quarto.　　[a] Chron. de los Moros de España.　　[b] P. Daniel Histoire de France.

HISTORIANS agree that it was not without foundation this monarch of *Castile* was suspected of impotence, notwithstanding which he had several mistresses, for the sake of one of which, of the noble family of *Castro*, he treated the queen extremely ill. The disorders of his family, tho' they might resemble, were by no means comparable to those in his government; for, knowing that he was hated by many, he suspected most of his nobility, and laboured to secure himself from the effects of their resentment by raising up new families, supposing that gratitude must naturally follow favours. With this view he made *Michael Luc* his secretary constable, and gave him several towns that belonged to the crown ; which places, however, refused to acknowlege him for their lord. The mastership of *Alcantara* he bestowed on *Gomez de Solis*, a gentleman of good family indeed, but very poor. Don *Juan de Valencuela* he made grand prior of St. *John*, and *Bernard de la Cueva* master of his houshold [c]. The deaths of the marquis of *Santillan* and of the count *de Triveno* were favourable to the king, as they proved the cause of some disputes amongst their relations. The rebellion of *Fijardo* was entirely suppressed, and the war with the *Moors* carried on with various success, that is, with various losses to both nations. This year died Don *Alonso* king of *Arragon* and *Naples*, in the last-mentioned city, leaving all his dominions in *Spain* to his brother Don *Juan* king of *Navarre*, who became now a very potent, as he had been always a very active, prince [d]. The former league amongst the nobility being in some measure broken, was again renewed, by the industry of the archbishop of *Toledo*; upon which the king surprized some of their places, and amongst the rest deprived the unfortunate house of *Luna* of the best part of their estates, though they had given him no sort of provocation. The marquis *de Villena* was sometimes in full possession of his master's favour, and at others under a cloud. His brother Don *Pedro Giron*, master of *Calatrava*, who had been a malecontent from the beginning of the king's reign, was, by his brother's interest, restored to the good graces of his sovereign, about the end of this year, or the beginning of the next [e].

THE confederate lords transmitted to the king, by the hands of *Diego de Quinones*, a memorial, in which they exhorted him to observe the laws of the kingdom, which he had sworn to at the time of his accession, and not to violate the

---

[c] Chronica de los Reys Catholicos de HERNANDO del Pulgar. [d] ZURIT. Annal Arragon. [e] Chronica del Rey Don Henrique Quarto, &c.

liberties

liberties of the church, the nobility, or the people; to cause exact and impartial justice to be every-where administered; to dismiss the *Moors* that were about his court; to reform his houshold, to carry on the war against the king of *Granada* with effect, in virtue of the great supplies he had received.; to cause the Infant Don *Alonso* and the Infanta *Isabella* to be educated in a manner suitable to their rank; and to declare the former his successor to the throne, since he had no posterity of his own. The king answered, that he would consult of those things with the lords of his council [f]. Don *Bernard de la Cueva* was now become his principal favourite; and, being very desirous of making his fortune, he proposed to the marquis of *Santillan* that he should marry his youngest daughter, in which he prevailed. By restoring him to his estates, and giving the title of count to his son-in-law, Don *Bertrand*, he detached him from the confederacy : but what gave him the greatest uneasiness was, the knowlege he had that Don *Juan* king of *Arragon* and *Navarre* had deserted his alliance, and subscribed the confederacy; to shew his resentment for which, he entered into a secret negotiation with the prince Don *Carlos*, and offered him his sister the Infanta Donna *Isabella*, in breach of his former agreement with the king his father [g]. The next year was a scene of strange confusions; Don *Henry* took the *Catalans* under his protection who had revolted from their sovereign, on behalf of the prince Don *Carlos*; he invaded *Navarre*, and took some places there, reconciled himself to most of the malecontents, and, to gratify them, made various alterations in his government; brought the Infant and Infanta to court; so that there was a seeming harmony beyond any thing that had appeared during his reign. There was, however, much deceit and falshood on both sides. The king trusted these great lords by force, and there was abundance of fraud in their service; for, in the midst of the war they carried on against the king of *Arragon*, they held a private correspondence with that prince, as did also the marquis of *Villena*, and some others of the favourites. By these intrigues a new treaty was made between the two crowns with such secrecy, that the prince Don *Carlos* could learn nothing of its contents; and this raising many suspicions in his mind, threw him into a fever which cost him his life [h].

In the beginning of the year the queen Donna *Joanna* of *Castile* was delivered of a daughter, stiled the Infanta Donna

1460.

Death of the Infant Don Carlos.

---

[f] Chronica del Rey Don Henrique Quarto, de Alonso de Palencia. [g] Zurit. Annal Arragon. [h] Cartes del Bachiller Fern. Gomez de Ciudad Real.

Joanna,

Johanna, on account of which vaft rejoicings were made [i]. *The queen* The king had treated her, during the courfe of her pregnancy, *is deliver-* not only with the utmoft tendernefs, but with all poffible *ed of a* marks of affection, and even of fondnefs, with a defign to *daughter.* perfuade his fubjects that this was his daughter as well as the queen's ; which, notwithftanding all the pains he could take, very few or none believed.   However, fhe was folemnly bap- tized ; the marquis of *Armagnac*, a *French* nobleman of the firft rank, and ambaffador from that crown, the marquis *de Villena*, and the Infanta Donna *Ifabella*, being fponfors ; the archbifhop of *Toledo* performed the ceremony ; and two months after the king caufed her to be acknowleged heirefs of the crown, the Infant Don *Alonfo* and the Infanta Donna *Ifabella* being the firft who fwore to the fucceffion [k].   Yet fome of the nobility privately protefted againft this prepofter- ous proceeding ; and the whole nation was fo thoroughly per- fuaded that the child was not the king's, but the daughter of Don *Bertrand de la Cueva*, that they beftowed upon her the furname of *Bertraneja* [l].   The archbifhop of *Toledo*, fupport- ed by the reft of the fecret friends of the king of *Arragon*, pre- vailed upon the king Don *Henry* to make a tour to *Alfaro*, while the monarch before-mentioned was at *Tudela*, that, be- ing fo near each other, all the little points that were ftill un- adjufted might be the fooner fettled.   But, while the king of *Caftile* was thus employed, the queen, whom he had left at *Aranda*, mifcarried, by an unlucky accident, of a fon, upon which he went immediately away to comfort her, and fent the marquis *de Villena* to *Saragoffa* in order to conclude and fign the treaty with the king of *Arragon* and *Navarre*, which he accordingly did. Upon his return to the court, then held at *Ma- drid*, he met with a very gracious reception from the king his mafter ; notwithftanding which he could not help envying the credit of the count of *Ledefma* both with the king and queen [m]. The war with the *Moors* was ftill continued, through the per- fidious behaviour of the king of *Granada* ; and as the king trufted the war to his favourites, and fupplied them abundant- ly, it was carried on in fuch a manner as drove the Infidels to the greateft diftrefs, and at length excited a mutiny in the city of *Granada* [n].   The moft glorious event, however, of *Gibraltar* the campaign, was the reduction of *Gibraltar*, with which the *reduced.*

---

[i] Chronica del Rey Don Henrique Quarto, de ALONSO de Palencia.   [k] P. DANIEL Hiftoire de France. Chronica del Rey Don Henrique Quarto, de DIEGO ENRIQUES del Caftillo. [l] FERRERAS.   [m] ABARCA.   [n] Chronica de los Moros de Efpana.

king

king was highly and justly pleased (G). Such, however, was the inconstancy of this prince's temper, that, notwithstanding the

(G) The recovery of this important fortress was so much the more acceptable, as it was altogether singular and unexpected, since these were times in which it was infinitely more probable that the Christians should lose than that they should gain any thing from the *Mohammedans* (1). It happened in this manner : there dwelt in the town of *Gibraltar* a *Moor*, whose name was *Ali el Zurro*, who was desirous of becoming a Christian. With this view he retired to *Tarefa*, and disclosed his sentiments in that respect to *Alonso de Arcos*, who was then alcayde, and who, approving his design, caused him to be baptized by the name of, *Diego Zurro*. He then told him that it would be no difficult matter for the Christians to recover the place from which he came, since, upon the breaking out of a civil war at *Granada*, the whole garrison was marched thither to support one of the competitors to the crown. Don *Alonso* was too well acquainted with the *Moors* to give hasty credit to such a piece of intelligence ; he sent therefore a detachment of eighty horse and one hundred and fifty foot, with orders to seize some of the inhabitants, which they executed, and from them he understood, that *Diego* had told him no more than the truth : upon this he assembled some troops belonging to the count *d'Arcos*, the duke *de Me*-

dina Sidonia, and of the governors of the adjacent places, with which he invested *Gibraltar* very unexpectedly. The inhabitants, however, made a very gallant defence ; insomuch, that many were inclined to raise the siege ; but *Diego Zurro* exerted himself in such a manner, and sollicited with such vehemency, that they remained before the place. They were daily joined by fresh troops ; and Don *Rodrigo*, the son of the count *d'Arcos*, actually possessed himself of a great part of the town, and might have had the rest by capitulation, if the duke *de Medina Sidonia* had not sent to desire that he might have a share in the glory. He arrived accordingly with his forces, and the very same night entered into a private treaty with the *Moors*, who delivered up the place to him the next day. This sinister behaviour produced a feud between the families of *Medina Sidonia* and *Arcos*, which lasted many years, and cost a great deal of blood (2). The king was no sooner acquainted with this unexpected piece of good fortune, than he named Don *Pedro de Porras* governor of the place, and ordered the duke *de Medina Sidonia* to put it into his hands under the severest penalties, which he immediately obeyed. As a farther proof of his satisfaction, he ordered the title of king of *Gibraltar* to be added

(1) *Mariana. Mayerne Turquet. Ferreras. Henrique* IV. *de Alonso de Palencia.*

(2) *Chronica del Rey Don*

the peace lately concluded with *Arragon*, he entered into new intrigues with the *Catalans*, who pretended to prove from an old genealogy that he was their legal master; and, upon his *The king of* sending a body of troops to their affistance, they proclaimed Castile him their sovereign on the thirteenth of *November* in the *proclaimed* city of *Barcelona* °; not out of affection to him, but to obtain *sovereign* affistance against the king of *Arragon*. *of* Catalo-

As the step which the king had taken, in relation to the nia. principality of *Catalonia*, was altogether inconsistent with the 1462. notions of his favourites, they endeavoured to persuade him to refer all points in dispute to the arbitration of *Lewis* the eleventh king of *France*, which, by a piece of very dextrous management, they brought about P. All things, however, had like to have been overturned again, by the arrival of fresh deputies from *Catalonia*, whose propositions the king would needs heat himself in council. They began with shewing, that, by several notorious breaches of the constitution, the king Don *Juan* had lost all right to the realms of *Arragon* and *Valentia*, to which he might form just pretensions, which most of the nobility would willingly support: and as to the principality of *Catalonia*, as the king, by his own consent, had been proclaimed their sovereign, they had the same claim to his protection as the rest of his subjects. In the council, however, the archbishop of *Toledo* and the marquis of *Villena* alleged, that the *Catalans* were naturally a mutable, restless, and rebellious people, whom it was impossible to content; and that, besides, having referred all things to the decision of the king of *France*, nothing ought to be undertaken till that was known; in which, though against his own opinion, the king acquiesced q. It was afterwards agreed, that the two monarchs of *France* and *Spain* should have an interview on the frontiers, and that, in the mean time, hostilities should cease between the crowns of *Arragon* and *Castile*. It was not long after that the *French* monarch, as umpire of the disputes between the two crowns, made his award to this effect; That the king of *Castile* should quit all pretensions to the sovereignty of *Catalonia*, and withdraw his troops immediately out of

---

° Chronica de los Reyes Catholicos de HERNANDO del Pulgar. ROD. SANTII Hist. Hispan. part iv. P Chron. del Rey Don Henrique Quarto, de ALONSO de Palencia. q ROD. SANTII Hist. Hispan. p. iv.

to his titles; following therein *Moorish* monarch, who had done the example of *Abu Malic*, a the same thing long before (3).

(3) *Historia general de España, por Mariana, lib. xxii.*

Arragon and *Navarre* ; and, on the other hand, that the king Don *Juan* should yield to his cousin of *Castile* the town of *Estella,* with all its dependencies, and pay him likewise the sum of fifty thousand florins in gold, for the expences of the war : it was also settled that the queen of *Arragon* should remain as a hostage in the hands of the archbishop of *Toledo,* till this sentence should be complied with in all points [r]. The king

Interview between this king and Lewis XI. of France. of *Castile* had afterwards an interview with *Lewis* the eleventh on the river of *Bidassoa,* which was very short, but they parted with a thorough hatred and contempt of each other; the king of *Castile* having about him a great number of his favourites, but particularly the count of *Ledesma,* most richly dressed, and, in a manner, covered with jewels : whereas the duke of *Burgundy,* the marshal (there was then but one) and the admiral of *France,* in compliance with the king's humour, were very modestly dressed, and *Lewis* himself so plain, that it was impossible, by any exterior mark, to know the king [s]. Don *Henry* of *Castile* and Don *Juan* of *Arragon* were equally dissatisfied with his sentence. The former had lost much, the latter was to lose something, and the humour of kings is to part with nothing. The king of *Arragon* hoped to effect this by chicane ; for, instead of delivering up *Estella,* he put a strong garrison into it, and, on the complaint of the marquis of *Villena,* threw the fault upon the states of *Navarre,* declaring that he would take no umbrage at seeing the place reduced by force. In a little time a new negotiation was set on foot ; and the marquis, after having brought the king his master into *Navarre,* with so poor an army that he was able to do nothing, accepted a few inconsiderable places as an equivalent for *Estella*; upon notice of which the archbishop of *Toledo* released the queen of *Arragon,* as if the treaty had been fully executed [t]. By this the king of *Castile*'s eyes were opened, and he not only refused to approve of this convention, but dismissed the prelate from his councils, and threatened the marquis with his resentment. In the autumn the king marched with a numerous army against the *Moors* ; but, being on the frontiers of the kingdom of *Granada,* that monarch sent his tribute and very rich presents besides; upon which the king dismissed his troops, and went to pass his *Christmas* at

1463. *Seville* [u].

[r] P. Daniel Histoire de France. Zurit. Annal Arragon.
[s] Chron. del Rey Don Henrique Quarto, de Diego Henriques del Castillo. P. Daniel Histoire de France. [t] Abarca. Rod. Santii Hist. Hispan. part iv. Ferreras. [u] Ortiz de Zuniga. Chron. de los Moros de Espana.

In

IN the beginning of the enfuing year, the king, for his *Another*
amufement, made a tour to *Gibraltar*, the recovery of which *powerful*
he confidered as the great glory of his reign. On his arrival *league*
there, he heard that the king of *Portugal* was at *Ceuta*, upon *formed a-*
which he fent him a civil invitation to come to *Gibraltar*, *gainst the*
which was accepted : but, while he was employed in concert- *king of*
ing fome fchemes with that prince, to whom he promifed his *Castile, by*
fifter *Ifabella*, and renewing the truce with the *Moors*, things *the arch-*
had taken a very wrong turn in *Castile* [w]. The archbifhop of *bifhop of*
Toledo and the marquis *de Villena*, finding that they were totally *Toledo*
fhut out of the government, refolved to put themfelves once *and divers*
more at the head of a confederacy, in which the amirante, *noblemen.*
the counts of *Placentia, Benavente, Paredes, Miranda*, and
Offorne, the archbifhop of *Compoſtella*, the grand mafters of
Calatrava and *Alcantara*, very readily entered ; fo that this
league became more formidable than any that had been hitherto made [x]. The king being informed of this by the
queen, refolved to return, without delay, into *Castile*, where
he found the great affair of the peace of *Arragon* fet upon an
equitable foundation, through the fear that the archbifhop, the
marquis, and even the king of *Arragon* himfelf, were under,
that their contrivances fhould reach the ear of *Lewis* the
eleventh, who, in that cafe, would not fail to enter *Arragon :*
the king, therefore, feeing no reafon to refufe it, ratified the
peace, not without hopes that this might pacify the malecontents : he carried the queen alfo to an interview with the
Portuguefe monarch at *Guadalupe*, where he again promifed
him his fifter Donna *Ifabella*, and really meant to keep his
word ; but, when he mentioned it to the Infanta, fhe fhewed
no inclination to become queen of *Portugal*, but pretended
that a princefs of *Castile* could not marry without leave of the
ftates, to whom, therefore, the king engaged to propofe it [y].
As he perfuaded himfelf that he had ſtill a great influence over
the marquis of *Villena*, he had a mind to confer with him, in
hopes of diffipating the league ; to which, after hoftages given,
the marquis confented, as having an inclination to detach
the archbifhop of *Seville*, the moft able man the king had
about him, and to bring him over to the malecontents. At
this conference, therefore, he told the king, that the archbifhop was the principal object of his own apprehenfions, and of
thofe of his affociates ; and that, if he would arreft and keep
him confined, he made no queftion of bringing all the lords

[w] FARIA Y SOUSA. ROD. SANTII Hiſt. Hiſpan. part iv.
[x] Chron. del Rey Don Henrique Quarto, de DIEGO HENRIQUEs
del Caſtillo. [y] ZURIT. Annal Arragon. BRAND. Chronica
del Rey Don Henrique Quarto, de ALONSO de Palencia.

back

back to his service. The king very readily consented ; and the marquis no sooner left him, than he sent a domestic to inform the archbishop of the danger he was in ; upon which that prelate, knowing no other way to be safe, went immediately to the count *de Placentia,* one of the league, and to whom he had been the greatest enemy, to demand his protection [z]. The count received him with open arms ;. the detachment of the king's guard, sent to secure him, returned without their prisoner ; and thus the marquis *de Villena,* not satisfied with betraying the king, contrived to make him an instrument in betraying himself [a]. The success attending this enterprize, encouraged him to form one still more extraordinary ; and this was, to surprize the king at *Madrid,* to deliver the Infant and Infanta out of his custody, and to bring away the count of *Ledesma* ; but, though it was well laid and well conducted, this scheme miscarried, and the king threatened him with the utmost weight of his resentment [b]. This did not deter him from a bolder enterprize than the last : he prevailed upon Donna *Maria de Padilla,* the wife of *Ferdinand Carillo,* who lay in the room contiguous to their majesties bed-chamber, to admit his adherents in the night ; and, by this means, he hoped to secure the persons both of the king and queen ; in which, also, he very narrowly failed [c]. After all this, he engaged the king to promise an interview with some of the malecontents, to which, as he was on the road, he had intelligence of their having assembled a great force in order to seize him and those who were about him, upon which he thought proper to retire, which, if he had not done with great precipitation, would have been to no purpose [d]. To shew in a particular manner how much he was piqued at the marquis, he with great solemnity invested Don *Bertrand de la Cueva,* grand master of the order of St. *James,* which he knew was the principal object of the other's ambition [e]. The king of *Arragon* and *Navarre* having entered into the league, the confederates held a general assembly at *Burgos,* where, upon the twenty-ninth of *September,* they subscribed an instrument, comprehending the reasons of their revolt, and their plan of regulating public affairs, to which they not only subscribed, but solemnly swore to adhere inviolably to each other, till every point of it was accomplished ; and this league they

[z] Rod. Santii Hist Hispan. part iv. Fer. [a] Cartas del Bachiller Fernan Gomez de Cuida Real. Marian. [b] Chronica del Rey Don Henrique Quarto, de Diego Henriques del Castillo. [c] Rod. Santii Hist. Hispan. part iv. Fer. [d] Chronica del Rey Don Henrique Quarto, de Alonso de Palencia. [e] Rod. Santii Hist. Hispan. part iv.

caused

caused to be transmitted to *Rome*, to prevent the king's obtaining any bulls from pope *Paul* the second against them [f]. In the mean time, the king being informed that one of the principal points of the confederacy turned upon his impotency, and compelling the nobility to swear to a suppositious child, he pretended to establish his capacity by judicial proofs, and the testimony of his physician, which served only to lessen and debase his character. Yet, before the end of the year, without the participation of his council, he ventured upon another private interview with the marquis of *Villena*, at which he concluded an agreement with the malecontents, *His agreement with the malecontents.* upon the following terms ; that he should deliver the Infant Don *Alonso* to the marquis, and acknowlege him for his heir and successor; that Don *Bertrand de la Cueva* should renounce the grand mastership of St. *James*, and the pope be desired to confer it, by a bull, upon the Infant Don *Alonso*, agreeable to his father's will ; that the regulation of public affairs in general should be left to four lords, two of which should be named by the king, and two by the league, and, if they could not agree, the judgment of *Alonso de Oropesa*, prior of the order of St. *Jerom*, was to be decisive : for the due performance of all which Don *Bertrand de la Cueva* was to constitute himself prisoner in the fortress of *Portillo*, under the care of *Goncalez de Sahavedra*, and the count *de Benavente* was to do the like in the fortress of *Mucientes*, in the hands of the count of St. *Martha*, by which the king hoped to secure his own quiet and that of his subjects [g]. 1464.

WHEN the contents of this convention were known, several of the king's faithful subjects laboured to shew him how much he had been deceived, and that the sole aim of the confederates was to get the Infant Don *Alonso* into their hands, with a design to place him at their head, and perhaps to make him king. This alarmed Don *Henry* extremely ; but his secretary Don *Alvaro Gomez*, who was the creature of the marquis *de Villena*, terrified him so much with the thoughts of reviving all past disturbances, if he did not execute punctually every article of his treaty, that he no sooner understood the marquis of *Villena* was come to *Sepulveda* to receive the Infant, than he carried him thither, and put him into his hands [h]. He afterwards repaired to *Cabezon*, where he gave audience to all the confederates in a body, and after each of them had kissed his hand, Don *Alonso* was declared his suc-

---

[f] ZURIT. Annal Arragon. Chronica del Rey Don Henrique Quarto de ALONSO de Palencia. [g] ABARCA, Chronica del Rey Don Henrique Quarto, de DIEGO HENRIQUEZ del Castillo. [h] ROD. SANTII Hist. Hispan. part iv. F§R.

cessor

cessor to his dominions, and promised to espouse Donna
Joanna[i]. Don *Bertran* count of *Ledesma*, being present,
they summoned him to resign the grand mastership of St.
James, the most honourable and most beneficial office in the
kingdom. I will do it, answered Don *Bertrand de la Cueva*,
with much greater pleasure than I received it, because it is to
render a service to that most gracious monarch, to whose favour I owe that and all that I have, and am glad of affording a
testimony to his subjects, that he has raised at least one man of
fidelity and merit. This answer astonished the whole league,
and made the marquis of *Villena* blush[k]. The king rewarded
him bountifully, gave him the town of *Albuquerque*, with the
title of duke, four other lordships, with a pension of three
million and a half of marvadies[l]. They proceeded next to
name commissioners; the king chose Don *Pedro de Velasco*,
eldest son to the count *de Haro*, and *Goncalez de Sahavedra*;
and the league appointed the count of *Placentia* and the marquis *de Villena*. The marquis in a little time corrupted the
king's commissioners, so that he carried every thing at his
pleasure, and without being obliged to consult *Alonso de Orof-
pesa*, a person of incorruptible integrity, whom the confederates
named for umpire, merely to give a lustre to their cause[m].
The king having discovered the defection of his commissioners,
and the treachery of his secretary, the marquis *de Villena* had
recourse to a new artifice; he prevailed upon the archbishop of
Toledo, and the amirante, to make a shew of quitting the confederacy, and going over to the king. Don *Henry* received
them so graciously, and trusted them so entirely, that they
began to be in earnest on his side, when the marchioness of
Villena came to *Madrid*; and, by her arts, recovered them to
the league; and, which was more extraordinary, persuaded
the king that her husband was still loyal in his heart, and
would take an opportunity of doing his majesty good service[n].

His refusal to perform articles. By the advice of the archbishop of *Toledo* and the amirante,
the king annulled all that had been done by the commissioners,
summoned the confederates to restore to him his brother, and
threatened to declare them traitors if they did not. Upon
this they called a general assembly at *Placentia*, and soon
after, another at *Seville*, where it was publicly debated, whether
they should depose the king, and advance the Infant Don

[i] Francisci Taraphæ de reg. Hispan. Marian. Fer.
[k] Chronica del Rey Don Henrique Quarto, de Alonso de Palencia. [l] Rod. Santii Hist. Hispan. part iv. [m] Cartas
del Bachiller Fernan Gomez de Ciuda Real. Fer. [n] Chron.
del Rey Don Henrique Quarto, de Alonso de Palenc.

Alonso

Alonſo to the throne? The agent of the archbiſhop of *Toledo* ⟨*The con-*⟩ argued warmly for the affirmative, which was as warmly op- ⟨*federates*⟩ poſed by the marquis *de Villena*; but at length, after taking ⟨*depoſe him,*⟩ the opinion of ſome lawyers, they agreed that the king ſhould ⟨*and declare*⟩ be depoſed °. The king was at this time preparing to reduce ⟨*for the In-*⟩ *Salamanca,* and the count of *Alba de Tormes* was the firſt ⟨*fant Don*⟩ nobleman in *Spain* who declared for him. The archbiſhop ⟨*Alonſo.*⟩ of *Toledo* and the amirante attended him upon this occaſion; and, by their advice, he reſolved next to beſiege *Arevalo,* upon which they took their leaves, and promiſed to repair thither with their forces, receiving each of them money from the king for that purpoſe. The king waited for them long, and ſent to them often; at length the prelate ſent him word not to tire him with any more meſſages, for that he would quickly let him ſee who was the true king of *Caſtile* ; and, at the ſame time, the amirante ſeized *Valladolid,* and declared for the Infant Don *Alonſo* ᴾ. The king, amazed at this behaviour, retired ſorrowfully to *Salamanca,* and had ſunk under his misfortunes, but for the prudent counſels of his ſiſter Donna *Iſabella.* As for the confederates they went roundly to work, and having depoſed the king Don *Henry,* with great ſolemnity (H), they declared the Infant Don *Alonſo* king, and raſed

---

° Rod. Santii Hiſt. Hiſpan. part iv. Ortiz de Zuniga. Chronica del Rey Don Henrique Quarto, de Diego Henriques del Caſtillo. ᴾ Chronica de los Reyes Catholicos de Hernando del Pulgar. Fer.

(H) There is not any event in the *Spaniſh,* or, to ſay the truth, in any other hiſtory, the record of any tranſaction more extraordinary or more extravagant than this ; the malecontents cauſed a theatre of vaſt extent, in the great plain that lies on one ſide of the town of *Avila,* to be erected, ſo that all the multitude reſorting thither might ſee and hear every thing that was ſaid or done (4) ; upon this a magnificent throne was placed, upon which was ſeated the figure of the king Don *Henry,* with the crown upon his head, the ſceptre in his hand, the ſword by his ſide, the royal robe on his ſhoulders; and, in a word, with every other enſign of majeſty then in uſe. A herald then mounted the theatre, and read with a loud voice, a declaration, containing the motives which appeared to them ſufficient for depoſing and depriving him of the royal dignity. At the ſame time that he began to read, the archbiſhop of *Toledo,* the marquis of *Villena,* the count *de Placentia,* the grand maſter of

---

(4) *Chronica de los Reyes Catbolicos de Hernando del Pulgar.*

raised an army to make him so[q]. The archbishop of *Toledo,* who had the best head and the worst heart in the whole assembly, proposed marching, without loss of time, to crush the king at *Salamanca,* which he shewed them plainly might be done both safely and speedily. The marquis *de Villena* raised many difficulties, and in the end diverted that motion. At the same time he gave notice to the king to be upon his guard[r]. His sole view was to keep the world in storm, as not knowing how to steer in calm weather. The confederates marched with their forces, and besieged *Simencas.* The king was, for once, the better of the marquis's advice, and wrote to the nobility in pressing terms to come to his assistance. The count *Alba de Tormes* was again the first, the duke *de Albuquerque,* the count *de Trastamara,* the marquis *de Santillan,* the count *de Medina Cœli,* soon after joined him. By this time, the archbishop of *Toledo* began to grow jealous of the

[q] Rod. Santii Hist. Hispan. part iv. Ortiz de Zuniga. Zurit. Annal Arragon.   [r] Chronica del Rey Don Henrique Quarto, de Alonso de Palencia.

Alcantara, the counts of *Benavente* and *Paredas,* went up to the figure, and as he read, the archbishop took off the crown, the marquis *de Villena* took away the sceptre, the grand master pulled off the sword, and the other three stripped away the rest of the ornaments; after which they kicked the figure away from the throne with their feet, adding the most abusive and insulting language to these actions, which the populace beheld in profound silence, except that here and there some burst into tears (5). Then the Infant *Alonso* mounted the theatre, and being carried on the shoulders of those who were present, was at length seated on the throne; after which, all the prelates, noblemen, and persons of rank and property, who were present, did homage to him, and the trumpets sounding, the standards were displayed in his name; those who assisted in this strange scene crying, according to the custom of those times, "*Castile!* "*Castile!* Long live the king "Don *Alonso* of *Castile, Leon,* "&c. (6)." Besides those who were actually concerned in this act of deposition, the amirante, the grand master of *Calatrava,* the counts of *Luna, Castro, Castaneda, Osforno,* St. *Martha,* and many others, concurred in approving and applauding this subversion of the constitution, and pretended to own for their king, a child hurried about by a faction, who assumed a power of deposing their king for those acts of prodigality, to which they were indebted for their titles and splendour (7).

(5) *Diego Henriquez de' Castillo. Alonso de Palencia, &c.*   (6) *Zuniga,* *Pulgar, Palencia.*   (7) *Mariana, &c.*

marquis *de Villena*; but that subtle politician had the address
to deceive him again into a better opinion of him than ever.
He feigned himself indisposed, grew in a few days dangerously
ill, and having received those spiritual comforts that are only
given at the point of death, he made a will, by which he recommended his widow and children to the care, and left all
his estates to the direction, of the archbishop, who, being
thoroughly convinced by this of his friendship, rejoiced very
sincerely at his recovery [s]. This prelate having taken several
places in person, repaired with all his forces to *Simencas*, to
the relief of which the king advanced, with an army so much
superior to the malecontents, that they retired with some precipitation, and if the king had pursued them, and prosecuted
the war with vigour, he might have reduced them and reigned
the rest of his days in peace; but, by a most unaccountable
fit of credulity, he consented to an interview with the marquis
de Villena, who engaged him to consent to a suspension of *Suspension*
arms, and to dismiss his forces, which he accordingly did, *of arms be-*
after paying them punctually, and assuring them that he would *tween the*
reward them for their services, as he afterwards did very li- *king and*
berally, bestowing *Carpio* and some other places on the count *the male-*
of *Alba*; *Astorga*, with the title of marquis, on the count of *contents.*
Trastamara; *Agreda* and its territory he gave to the count
of *Medina Cœli*; and the county of *Gijon*, with the title of
duke, to the count of *Valentia:* neither was he unmindful or
ungrateful with regard to persons of less distinction [t]. This
year died *Ishmael*, king of *Granada*, and was succeeded by   1465.
his son *Albohacen*, a prince of a generous and martial
spirit [u].

In the beginning of the year, the archbishop of *Toledo* sent
some of the clergy, who were his creatures, to *Rome*, in
order to persuade the pope, that himself and his partizans had
done nothing amiss in solemnly deposing their king; but, on
the other side, the king sent the dean of *Salamanca* thither, to
espouse his cause; which he did so effectually, that the pope
would give no countenance to the rebels in *Spain* [w]. The city
of *Valladolid* declared for the king, who, though he had
been so often betrayed by him, would have gone from thence
to meet the marquis of *Villena*, if he had not been with-
held by the nobility about him [x]. The king, however,

[s] Rod. Santii Hist. Hispan. part iv. Marian. Ferreras.
[t] Chron. del Rey Don Henrique Quarto, de Diego Henriques
del Castillo.   [u] Chronica de los Moros de España. Francisci Taraphæ de reg. Hispan.   [w] Rainald. Fer.
[x] Chronica del Rey Don Henrique Quarto, de Alonso de
Palencia.

received

received the archbiſhop of. *Seville*, who came from him, and
liſtened to one of the ſtrangeſt projects that was ever deviſed.
He propoſed that Don *Pedro Giron*, grand maſter of *Calatrava*, and brother to the marquis *de Villena*, ſhould marry
the Infanta Donna *Iſabella*; upon which the archbiſhop of
Toledo, the grand maſter, the marquis, and all their dependants, would become once more good ſubjects, give the king
a large ſum in ready money, and ſacrifice the Infant Don
Alonſo; but all this the king was deſired to keep a profound
ſecret, and in the mean time to diſmiſs from the court the
biſhop of *Calahorra*, and the duke of *Albuquerque*, who they
knew were men not to be impoſed upon by ſuch artifices.
The king conſented to all this, the biſhop and the duke retired,
the grand maſter reſigned his dignity to his third ſon, and the
moſt pompous preparations were made for the wedding, tho'
the Infanta declared from the beginning that ſhe would never
give her conſent. But when all things were ready, and the
king diſpoſed to force his ſiſter, Don *Pedro* fell ſick upon the
road of a fever, and died in a few days y. The archbiſhop
and the marquis returned immediately to the party of the Infant Don *Alonſo*, who received them very graciouſly, becauſe
Fruitleſs he was afraid of them. The reſt of the year was ſpent in war,
negotia- without any other effect than that of ruining and deſtroying
tions for a the people, and in treaties that came to nothing, through the
peace. artifices of the marquis *de Villena*, notwithſtanding all the pains
1466. the pope's legate could take, which rendered the marquis as
odious to the malecontents, as he ought to have been to the
king, who, notwithſtanding, could never diveſt himſelf of
that affection for him, which he ſo little deſerved z.

THE weakneſs of this prince was ſuch, that even his beſt
as well as his worſt ſubjects, were driven into rebellion. The
archbiſhop of *Seville*, in the beginning of this year, had prevailed upon him to go and confer with the malecontents at
Bejar, where a ſcheme was laid to ſeize his perſon, All re-
preſentations to prevent this falſe ſtep were to no purpoſe; ſo
that the inhabitants of *Madrid* were forced to take up arms to
keep the king in his palace, from whence, when he had laid
aſide all thoughts of going to *Bejar*, he proceeded to *Segovia* a. In the mean while, the Infant Don *Alonſo* went to
Toledo, where ſome commotions had happened in favour of
the king, where he was joyfully received, publicly proclaimed,

---

y ROD. SANTII Hiſt. Hiſpan. part iv. FER.　　z Chron. del
Rey Don Henrique Quarto, de ALONS. de Palenc.　　a Cartas del
Bachiller. FERNAN GOMEZ de Ciuda Real.　ROD. SANTII Hiſt.
Hiſpan. part iv.

and

and treated with all royal honours [b]. The king, perceiving
that the rebels were reducing one place after another, and
that many of the nobility grew cold in their affections for his
service, resolved, while he had yet sufficient strength, to put
the issue of things to a battle, and accordingly advanced for
the relief of *Medina del Campo.* The rebels resolved to wait *Battle of*
for him there : when the two armies were very near, the Medina
archbishop of *Toledo* sent to give the duke of *Albuquerque* del Cam-
notice that forty persons had sworn not to suffer him to return po.
alive, if he appeared in the field ; and therefore advised him to
take care of himself. The duke, suspecting the truth of this
intelligence, invited a soldier of the enemy's advanced guard
to come and speak with him, and sent him a passport ; the
man came accordingly, and being asked if this intelligence
was true, he assured him it was, and that every body knew it
in the camp : why then, says the duke, tell those forty men
that I shall be in the field to-morrow, armed in such a manner, and with a scarf of such a colour, and dismissed him with
a reward [c]. This action happened on the 20th of *August* ;
the Infant Don *Alonso* was there, in person, having the archbishop of *Toledo* by his side, who wore over his robe a crimson
scarf, embroidered with white crosses. The king, at the instance of the constable of *Navarre,* retired, with thirty horse,
to a place at some distance ; his army consisted of eight hundred lances, seven hundred light horse, and two thousand foot ;
that of the rebels was of much the same strength ; the engagement began in the afternoon, and did not end but with the
light. It was far from being decisive, though there might
be about five hundred men slain on both sides, the king ordered his standard to remain in his camp, being unwilling to
display it against his people, and by that accident it was
taken. Both sides claimed and made rejoicings for their
victory, which belonged to neither [d]. The town of *Segovia*
was shortly after betrayed to the Infant, who by that means
got his sister, the Infanta *Isabella,* into his custody, but the
Alcazar, in which were the king's treasures, was preserved [e].
The king, notwithstanding this, was prevailed upon to go
thither, to confer with the malecontents, to whom he spoke
better than his friends expected. He told them he would say
little either of or for himself ; he could not govern so great a
country, but by his ministers and magistrates ; that these he

[b] Chronica del Rey Don Henrique Quarto, de DIEGO HEN-
RIQUES del Castillo.   [c] FER. Histoire de Espana. p. ix. sec. xv.
[d] ROD. SANTII Hist. Hispan. part iv. MARIAN. FERRERAS.
[e] Chronica del Rey Don Henrique Quarto, de ALONSO de
Palencia.

had

had often changed; and notwithstanding, had been generally
abused; if they knew where to find him better, he was willing
to employ them.   But what he had chiefly at heart, and what
he wished at theirs, was the misery and distress of the poor
people, the innocent victims of their passions and follies.   He
said it was plain that he was not accountable for this, either to
God or man, as they had left him no power to protect them;
but, forgetting what was passed, if they would yet take measures to make his subjects happy, and restore him to his authority, he would exert it for that purpose.   They promised
to consider of the matter, and the king delivered his queen
into the hands of the archbishop of *Seville*, as a hostage for

The male-
contents
excommu-
nicated by
the pope's
legate.
his making good his promises.   The true design of this conference, was to cheat the king out of the *Alcazar*, which they
could not so easily reduce, and to engage him to confirm to
the marquis of *Villena* the grand mastership of St. *James*,
which he had obliged the Infant Don *Alonso* to resign in his
favour.   This he very willingly did; and in return, the marquis hindered any peace from being made, to which most of
the lords of his party were inclined, and for which the bishop
of *Leon*, the pope's legate, after severe reproaches, excommunicated them all [f].

Death of
the Infant
Don A-
lonso..
     As the rebels found themselves not a little hurt by these ec-
clesiastical censures, they sent two of their party to *Rome*, to
make an apology to the pope, from whom they received a
very bad reception, who told them they were rebels to their
king, and tyrants to their fellow subjects, bidding them go
home, and pacify these troubles; and, as the *Spanish* historians say, telling them, if they did not, God would speedily
call the Infant, whose name they abused, and who was no
more than an image in their hands, to another life, and leave
them to answer for their own offences [g].   While they were
thus employed, the king Don *Henry* went in person to
assist in the execution of an enterprize for the recovery of
Toledo, in which he narrowly escaped with his life; for tho'
his party received him privately into the city, yet the populace no sooner understood that he was in the cathedral church,
than they attacked it with the utmost fury, and it was with
great hazard that he escaped.   A few days after, the populace
changed their minds, and, by the help of a little persuasion,
drove out the partizans of the royal Infant, and invited the
king back, who went thither, and was received with the
loudest acclamations by those who, but a little before, had

---

[f] RAINALD. ROD. SANTIL Hist. Hispan. part iv.   FERRERAS.
[g] RAINALD. Chron. del Rey Don Henrique Quarto, de ALONSO
de Palencia.   MARIAN. FER.

thruſt him out of the ſame place [h]. The Infant Don *Alonſo*
was then at *Arevalo* ; and his party being aſtoniſhed at the
news, thought it proper that he ſhould go to *Avila*. On the
road he dined with his ſiſter at *Cardenoſa*, and retiring afterwards to ſleep, was, in the ſpace of an hour, found dead upon
his bed, or at leaſt ſenſeleſs and dying [i]. This happened on
the 5th of *July*, when that prince was about fifteen (I). The
archbiſhop

[h] Chronica de los Reyes Catholicos de Hernando del
Pulgar.   [i] Francisci Taraphæ de reg. Hiſpan.
Rod. Santii Hiſt. Hiſpan. part iv. Zurit. Annal Arragon.

(I) Amongſt all the obſcure
paſſages in the hiſtory of theſe
diſtracted times, there is none
darker than the death of the
Infant Don *Alonſo* : an author,
indeed, who wrote expreſsly
the hiſtory of his reign, as he
was pleaſed to call it, does not
heſitate in the leaſt in declaring
that he was poiſoned by eating
a trout, that made part of his
dinner ; and with the like freedom he tells us, that the author
of this execrable action was the
marquis of *Villena* (1). *Mariana*
ſeems to doubt of the truth of
this, but he aſſigns no better
reaſon than this, that it is hard
to conceive how a nobleman,
like him, could be guilty of ſo
baſe an action (2) ; and, perhaps, the reader will wonder
how he could conceive this objection, after having enumerated
ſo many baſe actions that this
unworthy nobleman had done.
Other writers incline to think
he died of poiſon, without fix-
ing the blame any where (3).
Some have aſcribed his death
to a ſtroke of the apoplexy ;

and others allege that he died
of the plague (4). In what
manner or by whoſe hands he
received his death, muſt therefore remain, in ſome meaſure,
undecided. In two points, the
Spaniſh hiſtorians agree, though
no inference can be drawn from
it ; the firſt is, that his death
was predicted by pope *Paul* the
ſecond ; the other, that he expired within a few miles of the
place where the theatre had
been erected for his brother's
depoſition, and for his own election (5). He was a youth of
very pregnant parts, and had
given ſome inſtances of firmneſs,
and a love for juſtice, which
could not be very acceptable to
ſome about him, who might
poſſibly apprehend that the time
was approaching, when, from being treated and called, he might
think and act like a king (6).
The ſetting up therefore of the
Infanta Donna *Iſabella* would
have anſwered their purpoſes
as well, without expoſing them
for the preſent to the like
fears (7). But ſhe very pru-

(1) *Alonſo de Palencia.*   (2) *Hiſtoria general de Eſpana por Mariana,*
lib. xxiii. (3) *Diego Henriquez del Caſtillo. Chronica de los Reyes Catholicos, &c.*
(4) *Mariana, Mayerne Turquet, &c.*   (5) *Diego Henriquez del Caſtillo, Alonſo*
de Palencia, Hernando del Pulgar.   (6) *Alonſo de Palencia, Alcocer,*
Ferreras.   (7) *Mariana, Ferreras, Mayerne Turquet, &c.*

archbishop of *Toledo*, and the grand master of St. *James*, conducted the Infanta Donna *Isabella* to *Avila*, where, at the desire of the party, the archbishop began to dispose her to take
the title of queen, to which she answered very modestly, that
she was much obliged to them for their good affections, but
that the crown of *Castile* did not belong to them to bestow,
but was held from God by the laws. Yet, if they would interpose with the king, her brother, that she might be declared
the presumptive heir of the crown, which she took to be her
right, she would be thankful ; neither was she moved from
this resolution, when she heard that at *Seville* and several other
places they had proclaimed her [k]. The archbishop acquiesced,
The succes- and in a short time the accommodation was made. On the
sion settled 19th of *September*, the king, and his sister the Infanta, met the
on the In- pope's legate, released the lords from the oaths they had
fanta Isa- taken to the princess *Joanna* ; after which, they swore to the
bella. succession of the Infanta *Isabella* ; and the king, at the same
time, undertook to send the queen and her daughter into *Portugal* [l]. The marquis *de Castellan*, who had served the king
with great fidelity, thinking those services less considered than
they ought to have been ; and having Donna *Joanna* confided
to his care, sollicited the queen to come to him, also promising
at all times, and at all events, to defend her, and to support
her daughter's title ; the queen joyfully accepted this offer, and,
at the hazard of her life, made her escape from the archbishop
of *Seville*. Being let down by cords out of the window of her
apartment in the castle of *Alaejos*, she mounted behind Don
Lewis Hurtado, and retired to the marquis [m]. Yet some writers
say, that she found a gallant there, and that this gallant was
the archbishop's nephew, which others treat as a calumny.
The states were ordered to assemble at *Ocana*; but there were
very few of the deputies came thither ; and the king believing
his affairs to be in a better situation than they had been, did

    [k] Chronica del Rey Don Henrique Quarto, de ALONSO de Pa-
lencia.   [l] ROD. SANTII Hist. Hispan. part iv. RAINALD.
FER.   [m] Cartas del Bachiller FERNAN GOMEZ de Ciuda
Real. Chronica del Rey Don Henrique Quarto, de DIEGO HEN-
RIQUES del Castillo.

dently declined it; and, as some   serve her own rights, she was by
writers say, alleged the death   no means inclined to invade
of her brother, as the reasons of   those of her brother, but would
her declining it, intimating that   repose herself on Providence,
Providence did not seem to fa-   and contentedly wait the disposi-
vour these kind of counsels, and   tion of things, without creating
that, though she wished to pre-   any discord or disturbance.

not treat with much complaifance thofe that did come; fo that the affembly was quickly prorogued to the next year[n]. The marriage of the prefumptive fucceffor was now the great point in view, upon which it was very evident that the fecurity of the crown and the happinefs of the people muft, in a great meafure, depend; the old king of *Arragon*, Don *Juan*, never loft fight of his firft purpofe of procuring that princefs for his fon the Infant Don *Ferdinand*; and, the better to qualify him for fo great a match, he gave him the title of king of *Sicily*, which ifland was then a part of his dominions[o]. In order to bring this important defign to bear, he fent his agents into *Caftile*, with inftructions to apply themfelves to his old friend the archbifhop of *Toledo*, to his father-in-law the amirante, to the counts of *Medina Cæli, Triveno*, and other great lords. At the head of thefe agents was the conftable of *Navarre*; and, befides excellent inftructions how to manage the affair, they had blanks filled with promifes, with the king's fignature and feal, to be addreffed to fuch perfons as they fhould find it neceffary to gain, and what was like, perhaps, to go farther than all their inftructions and credentials, they had a very large fum in ready money, with full powers to difpofe of it as they thought fit[p]. The conftable of *Navarre* found, on his arrival at the court of *Caftile*, the archbifhop of *Toledo* perfectly well inclined to the bufinefs; and by his and the amirante's affiftance, many of the chief nobility were gained; and the gold, and the king's letters, being properly diftributed amongft the Infanta's domeftics, brought them to prefer the king of *Sicily* to all the princes upon earth[q]. The grand mafter, now in more favour with the king than ever, was exceedingly difturbed at this, and engaged many of the old malecontents, more efpecially fuch as had been enriched by the forfeitures of the houfe of *Arragon*, to concur with him in oppofing a marriage fo prejudicial to their intereft. To augment the ftrength of this party he devifed a new intrigue, which indeed was his great talent; for he ftruck in with the marquis *de Santillan*, and propofed to the king, with his confent, that Donna *Ifabella*, his fifter, fhould be given in marriage to the king of *Portugal*, and Donna *Joanna*, whom he owned for his daughter, to the Infant of *Portugal*. With this fcheme the poor king was highly

[n] Rod. Santii Hift. Hifpan. part iv. Fer. [o] Zurit. Annal Arragon. [p] Chronica del Rey Don Henrique Quarto de Alonso de Palencia. Zurit. Annal Arragon. [q] Rod. Santii Hift. Hifpan. part iv. Abarca.

pleafed,

pleased, and assured them of his concurrence [r]. The grand master founded next the archbishop of *Toledo*; but that prelate gave him a very round answer; he said, his ambition and his artifices had already cost his country too dear; that for himself he was confident that he was now on the right side, from which nothing should ever move him to depart. The monarch of *Portugal*, at the request of Don *Henry* and his ministers, sent the archbishop of *Lisbon* to demand the Infanta *Isabella*, who very decently, but at the same time very peremptorily, refused her consent [s]. The grand master, who foresaw this, had provided another match, and procured a *French* embassador soon afterwards to make the like demand, in favour of the duke of *Berry*, the king's brother; but he also met with a refusal, which, though very civilly expressed, he bore but very impatiently [t]. The grand master directed his bosom friend, the archbishop of *Seville*, to post several bodies of troops in such a manner about *Madrigal*, where the Infanta *Isabella* then was, that she found herself, in a manner, imprisoned; but the archbishop of *Toledo* and the amirante quickly delivered her, and carried her to *Valladolid*. She had not been long there before the archbishop of *Toledo* and the lords of his party determined, that it was fittest for her safety and theirs to conclude and solemnize this marriage without delay. Don *Ferdinand* had notice of this; having first signed such articles of marriage as that prelate had drawn (K), set out privately for *Castile*, and being safely conducted

Who espouses Ferdinand king of Sicily, son and heir of the king of Arragon.

---

[r] Chronica del Rey Don Henrique Quarto, de Diego Henriques del Castillo. [s] Brand. Faria y Sousa. Chron. de los Reyes Catholicos de Hernando del Pulgar. [t] P. Daniel Histoire de France.

(K) These articles, to the punctual performance of which the king Don *Ferdinand* was sworn in the presence of Don *Gomez Manrique,* who was sent into *Arragon* for that purpose, were in substance as follows: 1. He shall always acknowlege the pope for head of the church, and maintain all the ecclesiastical immunities. 2 He shall have all possible respect for the king Don *Henry,* his brother-in-law, and shall permit him to reign in perfect tranquility, conforming himself in all things to the accommodation that was made when he acknowleged that princess for his heir. 3. He shall administer justice impartially; and shall not infringe, in any respect, the laws, usages, prerogatives, and privileges, of any of the cities, towns, places, or persons, in his dominions, agreeable to the oath taken by the kings of *Castile* at their accession. 4. He shall not alienate

ducted to *Valladolid*, secretly espoused and afterwards publicly married the Infanta, in the cathedral of that city, on the 25th

alienate any town, place, or fortress, without the consent of the princess. 5. That all the royal orders shall be signed by them jointly, and that he shall not put into the council, governments, or any other officers of state, any but natives of *Castile.* 6. That all dignities, ecclesiastical and civil, shall be at the nomination of the princess. 7. That he shall grant a general amnesty, with respect to all things that may have happened in the former civil wars, and shall never set up any claim or pretensions to those lands and estates, which his father possessed in *Castile,* and which have been given away by the crown, and are in the hands of several of the nobility. 8. That the archbishops of *Toledo* and *Seville,* and the grand master of St. *James,* shall ever enjoy their ranks and pre-eminencies in the government of the monarchy, as shall also all the other lords and knights who have steadily adhered to the princess's party, and have contributed to secure to her the succession of the crown. 9. That the king Don *Ferdinand* shall come and reside in the dominions of *Castile,* and shall make war against the *Moors* as soon as it is in his power, but otherwise shall not take up arms against any, without the consent of his consort; in case, however, that any civil war should break out in *Castile,* he shall

furnish, as long as it lasts, a thousand lances from *Arragon,* to remain, during that space, in the pay of that crown. 10. That, over and above the sum of one hundred thousand florins of gold, the princess shall have and enjoy the towns of *Borja, Magalon, Elcha,* and *Cervellen,* in the kingdoms of *Arragon* and *Valentia;* and *Siracuse* and *Catanea,* in the kingdom of *Sicily* (1). It is true that *Mariana* omits some of these articles, and interprets others in a stricter sense, so as to leave the king no other share in the government than his consort should be inclined to allow him (2); but our readers will hereafter learn upon what motives we have preferred the authority of the *Arragonian* writers. As they stand here, they sufficiently shew the prudence and public spirit of the prelate, by whom they were drawn, and it must give every man of conscience and honour, no small uneasiness, to reflect, that with so great parts, and with such a perfect knowlege of the constitution of his country, this great prelate was frequently led by his passions and private views to act with the utmost violence against his principles; so that it may be truly said, there was hardly any good or any hurt done to his country in his time, of which he was not the author, or in which he was not an actor (3).

---

(1) *Annales de la Corona de Arragon por Geron. Zurita.*   (2) *Historia general de Espana por Mariana, lib.* xxiv. *Mayerne Turquet, Belligarde, &c.*   (3) *Mariana, Ferreras, Mayerne Turquet.*

A. D.
1469.

of *October* [u]. The king was extremely offended at the news; and though, upon the receiving a letter from the princess at *Truxillo*, he seemed to be in a better temper, yet he gave no ahswer to it, but pursued his secret intrigues for altering the succession in favour of Donna *Joanna*, according to the advice of the grand master and his adherents, who, for the present, were wonderfully attached to that princess [w].

The In-
fanta Jú-
anna is
betrothed
to the duke
of Berry,
and de-
clared
heiress to
the crown
of Castile.

ALL imaginable pains were taken by the archbishop of *Toledo* and the amirante, as well as by Don *Ferdinand* and the Infanta *Isabella,* to dispose the king in their favour, but he remained absolutely silent; and if at any time he gave an answer, it was, that he would consult the grand master of St. *James,* and other great lords. This favourite, in the mean time, was labouring and endeavouring to procure an embassy from the *French* monarch, to demand Donna *Joanna* for the duke of *Berry,* whom the Infanta *Isabella* had rejected, which at length he obtained; and the person sent upon this occasion was cardinal *Albi,* the same who had shewn himself so much piqued upon the former occasion. While the two courts were thus employed, there was a civil war carrying on in almost every province in the kingdom; in some, between such as adhered to the king, against those who were attached to the king of *Sicily* and the Infanta; in others between noblemen, who, setting the laws at defiance, decided the quarrels that arose between them by open force, and, in some popular factions, raised disturbances in almost every great town; so that peace was scarce any-where to be found. The king Don *Henry* was extremely pleased upon the arrival of the *French* embassador, paid him all the honours, and laboured to give him all the satisfaction imaginable; he also issued an edict, annulling all that he had said or sworn upon the treaty of accommodation with the Infanta *Isabella,* declaring the right of succession to be, as it always was, in the Infanta *Joanna,* his and the queen's lawful daughter [x]. The *French* cardinal, however, expected farther proofs, which the king resolved to give accordingly on a day fixed, which was the 20th of *October*; the king held a great assembly in the plain of *Lozoia,* to which, by his command, the marquis of *Santillan* brought the queen and her daughter: there the edict was publicly read in the king's presence; and all who were there took their oaths to

[u] ZURIT. Annal Arragon. FRANCISCI TARAPHÆ de reg. Hispan. MARIANA. FER. [w] Chronica del Rey Don Henrique Quarto, de ALONSO de Palencia. [x] ZURIT. Annal Arragon. P. DANIEL Histoire de France. Chronica del Rey Don Henrique Quarto, de DIEGO HENRIQUES del Castillo.

the Infanta Donna *Joanna*, except the marquis *de Santillan* and his family, who excused themselves, by saying they had taken that oath before; the cardinal then insisted that the queen should swear, as she did, that the princess was the issue of her body by the king; the king likewise swore that he verily believed her to be his own daughter; after which the count of *Boulogne* espoused her, with great solemnity, in the name of the *French* prince [y]. The king, as soon as this ceremony was over, issued his letters to all the towns in the kingdom, to inform them of this great event; and, on the other hand, Don *Ferdinand* and Donna *Isabella* emitted a manifesto, setting forth and insisting upon their rights, which they required all the people in the kingdoms of *Castile*, *Leon*, *Toledo*, &c. to maintain and defend, which only served to increase those disorders, by which these unhappy countries were but too much distracted and distressed [z]. The king Don *Henry* having procured two briefs from the pope; one against the bishop of *Segovia*, and the other against the archbishop of *Toledo*, caused them to be signified to both these prelates. This had some effect upon the former, but none at all upon the latter; who, on the contrary, wrote to the king, as he had often done before, that his misfortunes were the effects of his credulity and irresolution; that he (the bishop) had nothing in view but the general good of his subjects; and that he would do well to think of his own oath, and the concessions he had made in the treaty of pacification [a]. Don *Henry*, in the fury of his resentment, sent for four canons of the church of *Toledo*, pursuant to the pope's brief; and, having admitted them into his privy council, formed a process against the archbishop for high treason. The grand master of St. *James*, however, interposed in behalf of his uncle, the archbishop, and advised his master to have recourse to milder measures. An offer was thereupon made him of an immense sum of money, large grants in favour of his church, and still greater to his two sons; but all without effect: that prelate giving for answer, that as he was at length on the right side he would remain there, and stand or fall with it, let the pope or the king do what they please [b]. As a proof that he was in earnest, he seized three of the four canons in their return to *Toledo*; but the king making reprisals upon some of his domestics, they were at length discharged. The disturbances throughout the king-

Which is harrassed by domestic broils.

---

[y] P. DANIEL Histoire de France. MARIAN. FER. [z] ZURIT. Annal Arragon. Chronica del Rey Don Henrique Quarto, de ALONSO de Palencia. [a] RAINALD. FER. [b] Chronica del Rey Don Henrique Quarto, de DIEGO HENRIQUES del Castillo.

dom rather increafed than diminifhed; and, to heighten the
miferies of the people, the *Moors,* with impunity, made an
irruption into and plundered the frontiers [c]. Towards the
clofe of the year, the king, attended by the grand mafter, had
an interview with the king of *Portugal,* to whom he offered
the Infanta Donna *Joanna*; but that monarch looked upon
things to be then in fo unfettled a ftate, that he declined the
propofition ; and the king Don *Henry* and his favourite retired
exceedingly diffatisfied [d].

*A fcheme
fet on foot
for marry-
ing the In-
fanta* Jo-
anna *to
Don Hen-
ry of* Ar-
ragon.

THE grand mafter was feldom at a lofs for expedients; and
though his addrefs had failed him upon this occafion, yet he
quickly devifed a new fcheme, more plaufible and more likely
to be attended with fuccefs than the former. This new contrivance was to bring about a marriage between Don *Henry*
of *Arragon,* fon to the Infant Don *Henry,* who had formerly
created fo many and great difturbances in *Caftile,* and the Infanta Donna *Joanna,* whom the king acknowleged. His
mafter approved this expedient exceedingly, affured him of
his full confent, and defired him to leave no ftep untaken for
the fpeedy accomplifhment of this important negotiation [e].
The grand mafter faw, without any fign of pity, civil war
raging in all parts of the kingdom, but he could not hear,
without emotion, all thefe mifchiefs attributed to himfelf.
He perceived that the far greater part of the nobility envied
and hated him; and that, by the common people throughout
his mafter's dominions, he was held in perfect execration ;
which induced or rather obliged him to labour with the utmoft diligence in bringing this bufinefs to perfection, which,
with very good reafon, he confidered as the king's bufinefs
and his own. With this view he refolved to gain, if it was
poffible, the marquis *de Santillan,* and the potent family of
Mendoza, of which he was at the head. He propofed,
therefore, an interview with that nobleman and his friends,
which was accepted, and there he explained the many advantages that would refult from the marriage which he had
projected ; he obferved that it was the higheft mark of
gratitude they could give to the king and to his family; that
Don *Henry* was of the royal blood of *Caftile* ; that his marriage with the Infanta would divide the houfe of *Arragon*; that
it would infallibly gain the count of *Benavente,* who was Don
Henry's uncle by the mother's fide ; and that it would protect
them from the refentments of Don *Ferdinand,* and the Infanta

[c] Chronica de los Moros de Efpana. FERRERAS. [d] FARIA
Y SOUSA. MARIANA. [e] Chronica del Rey Don Henrique
Quarto, de DIEGO HENRIQUES del Caftillo.

Donna

Donna *Isabella*, from whom they had all things to fear. These arguments made a great impression upon the assembly; and the grand master, that he might absolutely determine them to a concurrence in this scheme, offered, as he was lately become a widower, to marry a lady of the house of *Mendoza*; but, as there was no such lady to give him, the confederates proposed that he should espouse Donna *Maria de Velasco*, the daughter of the count *de Haro*, which he accepted, and the marriage was soon after celebrated in the king's presence with great solemnity,[f]. The prince Don *Ferdinand*, in the mean time, made a tour into his father's dominions, where he met with the cardinal Don *Roderic de Borgia*, legate from pope *Sixtus* the fourth, who presented him with a dispensation that was necessary to render his marriage valid; and the extraordinary honours that prince and his father rendered to the cardinal, attached him entirely to their interest, in the support of which he was afterwards very serviceable [g]. At the same time Don *Ferdinand* acquainted the king Don *Juan* with the new scheme the grand master had formed of marrying Donna *Joanna* to Don *Henry* his nephew, to prevent which, his advice was to secure the person of Don *Henry*, which was in his power; but the king, who had always treated him as his son, could not be prevailed upon to take so harsh a step, as he persuaded himself that he would do nothing in an affair of such consequence without his consent, of which also he received the strongest assurances from Donna *Beatrix Pimentel*, his mother [h]. It appeared, however, from the event, that Don *Ferdinand* had formed a better judgment of the young man's disposition; for his thoughts were so elevated with the prospect of a crown, that he went privately into *Castile*, in order to complete the marriage. He was received there with all possible respect, and treated in so magnificent a manner, that he began to consider himself as the presumptive heir to the crown, and behaved himself with so much haughtiness towards the nobility, as lessened his interest with his friends; at the same time, that, by offering to decide all differences with Don *Ferdinand* in a single combat, and saying, rashly, that he would give the city of *Toledo* if his competitor would accept the challenge, he provoked the house of *Arragon* to an irreconcileable enmity. Before we conclude this year, it is necessary to observe, that, amongst other disturbances, there happened one at *Toledo*, which occasioned a great deal of blood to be spilt [i].

A. D. 1472.

[f] Francisci Tarapha de reg. Hispan. Rer. [g] Zurit. Annal Arragon. [h] Chronica del Rey Don Henrique Quarto, de Alonso de Palencia. Zurit. Annal Arragon. [i] Chron. del Rey Don Henrique Quarto, de Diego Henriquez del Castillo.

THE arrival of the pope's legate in *Castile* was very acceptable to the king, upon account of that deference and respect which had been always expressed towards him by the court of *Rome*; so that, at his first audience, he treated him with much kindness and esteem. But when the king and his ministers found that this cardinal was entirely in the interest of the princes, and that he approved the conduct of the archbishop of *Toledo*, they were much chagrined. He was suffered, however, to hold a general assembly of the clergy at *Segovia*, where he made many useful regulations, and obtained a subsidy for carrying on the war against the *Turks*, which was his principal business; and which, as soon as he had obtained, he returned into *Arragon* [k]. The seditions and disturbances in all parts of *Spain* were as frequent as ever. The nobility brought armies of several thousands into the field in their private quarrels; towns were sometimes taken by them after regular sieges, but more frequently they revolted or were surprized. In some places the people fell upon the *Jews* upon various pretences; but in many more places the new converts, or, as they are called in *Spain*, the new Christians, were exposed to the worst treatment imaginable, both in their persons and properties. In a sedition of this kind at *Jaen*, the constable Don *Michael Luc* was killed by a shot from a cross-bow, as he was hearing mass in the cathedral; with which, when the king was acquainted, he bestowed that high office upon the count *de Haro*, whose daughter the grand master had married [l]. The duke *de Medina Sidonia* and the marquis of *Cadiz* had made war against each other in *Andalusia* for some years, as if they had been independent princes; but the former, that he might have some colour of authority, thought fit to declare, about this time, for the prince Don *Ferdinand* and the Infanta Donna *Isabella* [m]. While things were in this state, Don *Henry* of *Arragon* expressed great impatience that the match was so long delayed; but the grand master, who perceived this young prince wanted a tutor more than the king, but was of a temper quite opposite to his, resolved to frustrate the match; in order to which, he told the king, that the only way to secure the crown to his daughter was to marry her to a crowned head; that the sending for Don *Henry*, contrary to his expectations, had strengthened the party of the princes, and that therefore the most prudent step he could take, was to delay the

Wars maintained by private noblemen against each other.

[k] RAINALD. ZURIT. Annal Arragon.   [l] MARIANA. FERRERAS.   [m] Chronica del Rey Don Henrique Quarto, de ALONSO de Palencia.

marriage,

marriage, and, if possible, to renew the negotiation with the
king of *Portugal.* Other kings were not more accustomed to
command than Don *Henry* to obey; he therefore pacified
Don *Henry* and his friends as well as he could, by promising
them to propose the marriage in the next assembly of the states,
which was to be held in a little time, and, during this interval, the grand master convinced his partizans that Don *Henry*
was like to give them more trouble than Don *Ferdinand,* and
that therefore they must find such a husband for Donna *Joanna*
as, with their assistance, might be able to clear the kingdom of
both; with which they were well enough satisfied[a].

THE treasures of the king Don *Henry,* which were still very
considerable, remained in the *Alcazar* at *Segovia,* of which he
had given the command to Don *Andres de Cabrera,* a very
brave man, and his faithful servant. The grand master was very
desirous of having this place, which was indeed the best, if not
the only, thing the king had to give; but finding him more
tenacious in this respect than in any other, and not being able
to obtain more than half a promise, he resolved to supply the
other half by force. He had observed that a great many of
the inhabitants of *Segovia* were new Christians; his emissaries
were employed to instigate the other inhabitants to fall upon
them; and when this disturbance was at the greatest height,
the grand master was to come in with a body of regular troops
to the assistance of the old Christians, and so make himself
master of the place. This scheme was very closely laid, and
very briskly executed, but without effect; for *Cabrera* had
taken care to arm all those new Christians, and, when the
insurrection was highest, issued from the castle, with a numerous body of horse and foot; upon which the grand master retired, much disappointed, to *Escalona*[b]. In the assembly of the states few things were regulated; and the king,
having obtained a free-gift, gave himself little trouble about
the marriage, notwithstanding that the count *de Benavente*
had quarrelled with the grand master upon that head. The
whole court, in the mean time, being very much alarmed at
the great cities declaring gradually for the princes, this increase of danger made the favourite more and more uneasy
about the fortress of *Segovia*; so that at length he teazed the
king into giving an order to Don *Andres de Cabrera* to put it
into his hands; which being signified to that old officer, he answered, that his loyalty and affection to the king would not

The grand master at-
tempts to
surprize
the castle
of Segovia.

[a] ZURIT. Annal Arragon. Chronica del Rey Don Henrique
Quarto, de DIEGO HENRIQUEZ del Castillo. [b] MARIAN.
FERRERAS.

suffer

suffer him to comply with an order which it was not fit for the king to give P. Under this dilemma, the grand master prevailed upon the king to go in person to *Segovia*, and try to persuade Don *Andres de Cabrera* out of the fortress. The king went, and was received with all the duty and submission possible; but when Don *Andres*, and his wife, Donna *Beatrix de Bobadilla*, who had been long about the person of the Infanta *Isabella*, had him by this means to themselves, they very boldly laid before him the true state of his affairs. They told him, that Don *Juan de Pacheco* was a very little gentleman, till the breath of his majesty's favour had swelled him into a great lord; that he had repaid this favour with ingratitude; had displayed his colours in the field against his majesty's royal standard; had assisted in the ceremony when his majesty was deposed, and had placed his sceptre in the hands of the royal Infant; that he had offered the crown to the Infanta *Isabella*, to whose generous refusal his majesty owed the return of his favourite, and that he still wore that crown upon his head. They advised him, therefore, to disgrace a man who had so often sacrificed him to his interest, and to consent to a reconciliation with Don *Ferdinand* and Donna *Isabella*, which would restore a legal government to his subjects, and secure to his majesty the peaceable possession of his crown, which, otherwise, he could never expect q. The king heard them without any token of displeasure, and at length seemed well enough pleased with the expedient. Donna *Beatrix* went to acquaint her mistress, in the disguise of a peasant; and the Infanta Donna *Isabella*, by the advice of the archbishop of *Toledo*, resolved to put herself upon the fidelity of *Cabrera*, and accordingly, on the 27th of *December*, she came to *Segovia*; upon the first news of which the marquis of *Villena*, son to the grand master, fled out of the town r. The king saw her at his return from hunting, and behaved towards her with great civility and respect. He made her a visit the next afternoon in the *Alcazar*, and was so well pleased with her company, that he stayed and supped; the third day they walked together publicly in the streets; and, on the fourth, the king, having presented most of the nobility about him to his sister, obliged her to go out of the *Alcazar* on horseback at the head of them, himself on foot holding the bridle s. Such was the strange temper of this

Reconciliation between the king and the Infanta Donna Isabella.

1473.

P Chronica del Rey Don Henrique Quarto, de ALONSO de Palencia.   q MARIANA. ‑FERR.   r Chronica del Rey Don Henrique Quarto, de DIEGO HENRIQUES del Castillo.   s Chronica del Rey Don Henrique Quarto, de ALONSO de Palencia.

monarch,

monarch, and such an ascendency over him had all who knew how to comply with his humours while they were about him.

THIS ample and unexpected reconciliation was speedily made known by the Infanta to her husband Don *Ferdinand*, whom she invited to *Segovia*, and, by the advice of the lords who were about him, he went thither, and was well received by the king[t]. The lords who attended that monarch thought that a more public testimony of the perfect harmony that reigned amongst the royal family was requisite; and therefore the king, the Infant, and the Infanta, went publicly to the cathedral on the feast of the *Epiphany*; afterwards they dined together in public: but, towards evening, the king complained of a violent pain in his side, and was carried to his palace in a very feeble condition; upon which there wanted not many who said he was poisoned [u]. The prince Don *Ferdinand* and the Infanta Donna *Isabella* visited him every day, during his illness. In that space their friends sollicited Don *Henry* to renew the declaration he had formerly made in favour of his sister as to the succession: but, tho' this was very artfully and assiduously managed, the king could never be brought to give any other than an evasive answer [w]. As soon as he began to recover, he resumed his private correspondence with the grand-master, who had lately compromised all differences, and entered into a strict league with the duke of *Albuquerque* and the count of *Benavente*. The next thing he did was to contrive, as closely as possible, to send troops into the town, to hide them in the church towers, and to dispose every thing for surprizing the princess, together with Don *Andres Cabrera* and his wife Donna *Maria*, in the *Alcazar*. But Don *Andres* perceiving some motions, easily guessed at the rest, and took his precautions so speedily and so effectually, that the grand master was forced to drop this project [x]. However, by the advice of the Infanta Donna *Isabella*, Don *Ferdinand* left *Segovia*, under pretence of paying a visit to the amirante: as the archbishop of *Toledo* was the only member of the king's council who openly espoused the cause of the princess, he took it amiss that they seemed to have a greater confidence in cardinal *Mendoza*, who was also of the king's council, and of

He afterwards endeavours to apprehend her and her husband Don Ferdinand.

---

[t] ZURIT. Annal Arragon. MARIANA. FERRERAS.   [u] Chronica del Rey Don Henrique Quarto, de DIEGO HENRIQUES del Castillo. ZURIT. Annal Arragon.   [w] Chronica del Rey Don Henrique Quarto, de ALONSO de Palencia.   [x] ZURIT. Annal Arragon. MARIANA. FERRERAS.

their

their party, but secretly. The archbishop wrote his sentiments upon this to Don *Juan* king of *Arragon,* and, after expostulating the matter freely, desired to withdraw from their
service. The king, and afterwards the princes, did all in their
power to satisfy him; and Don *Ferdinand,* having a mind to
see the Infanta, desired his opinion whether it was safe for him
to come to *Segovia* ; to which the prelate answered, he might
be safe for three days, but not longer [y]. He went thither accordingly, retired at the the time prescribed, and afterwards
assisted the marquis *de Santillan* in taking *Carrion* from the
count of *Benavente,* which, upon the interposition of the king,
was done by treaty. About this time the ambassadors of the
duke of *Burgundy* came to pay their respects to Don *Ferdinand,* and to invest him, by their master's command, with the
order of the Golden Fleece : after receiving which he went
to pay the Infanta another visit, but made a very short stay [z].
He not long after surprized *Tordesillas,* which was in the
hands of one of the king's favourites, who used the people
most cruelly : but tho' he took care to represent this to that
monarch in the fullest light possible, Don *Henry* could not help
shewing that he was extremely offended with that action, the
news of which he received at *Madrid;* having left the Infanta
at *Segovia,* to which place Don *Ferdinand* went for a little
time, and then, the affairs of that kingdom requiring his presence, he set out for *Arragon* [a].

It was the great object of the grand master's politics, and
consequently of the king's, to keep the princes from the succession, from a very strong apprehension that the lofty structure of his greatness would quickly be demolished, if they were
once seated on the throne. To prevent this, he judged two
things absolutely necessary ; first a great and well-conducted
strength at home, and next a powerful foreign support. The
shortest way to obtain the former appeared to be uniting in
his own hands the three grand masterships : as that of *Alcantara* was then in dispute, he ordered his bastard son Don
Alonso Pacheco to reduce, with a good body of troops, most of
the places belonging to the order, and to take himself the title
of grand master ; not doubting that his favour with the king,
and his money at *Rome,* would bear him out. To bring
about the latter, he engaged the king in a hunting party towards the frontiers of *Portugal,* and, being now reconciled to

[y] Zurit. Annal Arragon.   [z] Mariana. Ferreras.
[a] Zurit. Annal Arragon. Chronica del Rey Don Henrique,
Quarto, de Alonso de Palencia.

5   the

the duke of *Albuquerque*, whose large estate, as well as his own, was derived from the prodigality of the king, he confided him to his care, while he went to press the *Portuguese* monarch to marry the Infanta Donna *Joanna*, which would have rendered his system complete. He managed this as he did every thing of the same kind, with great dexterity and address, and at length brought the king of *Portugal* to promise, that he would take the matter into his serious consideration, and accept the proposition, if he could dispose things so as to afford them a probability of success. When he made a report of this, at his return, to the king Don *Henry*, it did not afford him that satisfaction which he expected ; for, finding his health daily decaying, he foresaw that he should not live to receive any benefit from the expedient. He resolved, however, to go to *Madrid*, the air of which was more favourable to him than that of any other place, and, at the pressing instance of his favourite, gave orders to the governor of *Truxillo* to surrender that place into his hands. This order was no sooner received, than the grand master marched with a body of forces to *Santa Cruz*, at a small distance from *Truxillo*, to enforce it; but, finding this method would be equally tedious and uncertain, he laboured to corrupt the governor, in which, at length, he succeeded. Yet, before the bargain was completed, he was suddenly attacked with a sharp pain in the throat, occasioned by an abscess, which quickly brought him, and all his great designs, to an end, on the 4th of *October*. Those who were about his person, and in his secrets, concealed his death till such time as *Truxillo* was surrendered, and then his body was transferred to *Segovia*, and buried there, pursuant to the directions he had given in his illness [b]. *Death of the grand master.*

THE news of the grand master's death gave infinitely more disquiet to the king than to any of his subjects : to shew that he not only lived but died in the full possession of his favour, he replaced him immediately by Don *Diego Lopez Pacheco*, marquis *de Villena*, his eldest son, whom he confirmed in the possession of all his father's estates, and requested of the pope a bull that might invest him likewise with the dignity of grand master of St *James* [c]. But as there were other noblemen who were ambitious of that high dignity, they pressed the knights to hold a chapter immediately, in order to secure to themselves a free election. This, however, was attended

[b] EMANUEL DE FARIA Y SOUSA. MARIANA. FERRERAS.
[c] Chronica de los Reys Catholicos de HERNANDO del Pulgar. FERRERAS.

with

with an unexpected inconveniency; the knights of the province of *Caſtile* met at *Tarrancon*, and choſe Don *Roderic Manrique*, count of *Paredes*, while thoſe of the province of *Leon* aſſembled likewiſe, and choſe Don *Alonſo de Cardenas* [d]. The marquis *de Villena* applied himſelf to the count *de Oſſorno*, brother to Don *Roderic Manrique*, in hopes of bringing him to a treaty; and, going to make him a viſit, the count took care to be out of the way; but having given proper inſtructions to the counteſs, ſhe cauſed the marquis to be arreſted. This outrage was highly reſented by the king, who, by the advice of the archbiſhop of *Toledo*, cauſed the fortreſs in which he was detained to be immediately inveſted, and, in a ſhort time, the marquis was releaſed upon a treaty, by which he obliged himſelf to deliver a place which his father had formerly promiſed to the count *de Oſſorno*, but which, notwithſtanding, he could never be brought to ſurrender [e]. The recovery of his favourite's liberty was the laſt conſiderable action of the king's life; for, very ſoon after his return to *Madrid*, the phyſicians who attended the king declared, that, from the rigour of the ſeaſon, the gradual diminution of the king's ſtrength, and the return of his vomitings and pain in the ſide, he could not laſt long; and that therefore they would do well to put him in mind of departing this world in a manner ſuitable to his rank as a king, and his hopes as a Chriſtian. Cardinal *Mendoza*, the count *de Benavente*, and the marquis *de Villena*, went accordingly to carry this melancholy piece of news; and the king, having called for the prayer of St. *Jerom*, confeſſed, and received the ſacrament. The prior then aſked him whom he declared heir to the crown, who were the executors of his teſtament, and where he deſired to be interred. The king anſwered, that the Infanta Donna *Joanna* was his ſole heir; that the executors named in his will were cardinal *Mendoza*, the counts of *Placentia* and *Benavente*, and the marquis *de Villena*; and that he deſired his remains ſhould be depoſited near thoſe of his mother, in the convent of *Guadalupe*. He fell ſoon after into an agony, and expired in the middle of the night of the twelfth of *December*. His body was depoſited in the convent of St. *Jerom*, at *Madrid*, where his obſequies were celebrated with great pomp, and afterwards cardinal *Mendoza* cauſed his body to be tranſported to *Guadalupe*, where, in gratitude for the favours he had received from him, he cauſed a magnificent monu-

The king dies at Madrid.

---

[d] Chronica del Rey Don Henrique Quarto, de Alonſo de Palencia.   [e] Marian. Ferreras.

ment

ment to be raifed, on the right hand of the high altar, to the memory of that prince, at his own expence [f].

THUS died *Henry* the fourth, king of *Caftile* and *Leon*, with all the dependencies on thofe crowns, after fitting many years on the throne, without having ever ruled. The *Spanish* writers fay, that he was pious and religious, which muft be underftood of exterior acts of devotion ; for his behaviour towards his father, and that indolence and want of application which rendered him contemptible while he wore the crown, were furely no teftimonies either of piety or religion. He made the fortunes of a few of his minions, while he ruined thofe of his fubjects: he was not, perhaps, cruel in his nature, and yet he caufed rivers of blood to be fhed through his indifcretion. It may be, he wifhed to make a better king; but hiftory has recorded no proofs of his having endeavoured it. He wanted firmnefs in oppofing his brother's ufurpation; he wanted gratitude to his fifter, who refufed a crown, that he might wear it ; he wanted fpirit, juftice, and common fenfe, in preferring Donna *Joanna* to the Infanta *Ifabella*, if he was confcious of his own impotence, as the *Spanish* writers affirm. But in this we agree with *Ferreras*, that if, in the reigns of his predeceffors, kings may difcover what qualities they ought to acquire, and what methods they muft take, to render their fubjects happy, and themfelves beloved, this reign alone will be a fufficient mirrour for them to contemplate whatever they ought to decline or defpife. Thefe reflections are due to juftice and to truth, and with thefe we fhall conclude a period, fertile in great and glorious events, though, from the errors of this weak and unhappy prince, it ended meanly; for which, however, the fplendour of the enfuing reign made full amends.

[f] Chronica del Rey Don Henrique Quarto, de ALONSO de Palencia. FRANCISCI TARAPHÆ de reg. Hifpan. ZURITA. Annal Arragon. Chronica del Rey Don Henrique Quarto, de DIEGO HENRIQUES del Caftillo. EMANUEL DE FARIA Y SOUSA. MARIAN. FERRERAS. MAYERNE TURQUET.

SECT.

SECT. VIII.

A general Description of the Kingdom of Arragon, *its Situation, Extent, Produce, and Inhabitants, &c.*

The great power and extensive dominions of the crowns of Arragon at the time of its union with Castile.

THE method we have hitherto pursued of treating the kingdoms erected in *Spain*, after the expulsion of the *Moors*, separately, obliges us, in this section, to give the reader as clear and as concise an account as it is possible of the kingdom of *Arragon*, which, in consequence of the marriage of Don *Ferdinand* king of *Sicily*, heir, and afterwards king, of *Arragon*, became united to the crowns of *Castile* and *Leon*, and the great dominions annexed to them, by the courage and conduct of the monarchs who had governed those realms. At the time this union was made, *Arragon* was one of the most potent sovereignties in *Europe*, and little, if at all, inferior to *Castile*; for, besides the principality of *Catalonia*, and the kingdom of *Valentia*, which had been long united to this crown, the kingdom of *Navarre* belonged to it likewise (in what manner will be hereafter explained), together with the kingdom of *Majorca*, including that island and *Minorca*, and those dependant upon them, as also the kingdom of *Sicily* [a]. So that, in point of territory, of commerce, and maritime power, it was, as we have said, very considerable. Some have carried this so far as to assert, that, till this union, the monarchy of *Spain* was hardly known beyond the limits of the mountains and seas by which it was bounded [b]; which, however, is carrying things much too far; since, as we have already seen, the monarchies both of *Castile* and *Arragon* had a very apparent influence on the affairs of *Europe*; and therefore those who say this, seem rather to reflect on the ignorance of their own nations, than on the crowns for which they express so unjust a contempt [c].

[a] CLUVER. Introduct. Geograph. lib. ii. cap. v. LUYTS Introduct. ad Geograph. sect. ii. cap. viii. Geographie Moderne, par ABRAHAM DU BOIS, part i. chap. iii. art. xiii. [b] THUAN. Hist. sui Temporis. HEYLIN's Geography, book i. [c] MARIAN. FERRERAS. Abbé DE VAYRAC, &c.

THE kingdom of *Arragon*, properly so called, is bounded *A general*
on the north by the *Pyrenean* mountains, on the west by the *description*
kingdoms of *Navarre*, *Old* and part of *New Castile*, on the *of the*
south by the kingdom of *Valentia*, and on the east by part of *kingdom*
the same kingdom, and the principality of *Catalonia.* In an- *of Arra-*
tient times it was inhabited by the *Celtiberians*, the *Jaecetans,* *gon, its*
and the *Sedetans* [d]. In length, from north to south, it con- *situation,*
tains about fourscore leagues, and its greatest breadth is about *extent,*
fifty. The common opinion is, that it derives its name from *and pro-*
the river *Arragon* ; but whoever considers the smallness of *duce.*
that river, in comparison of several others, but more especially
with the *Ebro*, or, as the ancients called it, *Ibèrus*, will scarce
be satisfied with that account, and perhaps will think it more
probable, that the denomination of *Arragon* arose from the
corruption of *Tarraconensis*, the name of the *Roman* province,
by striking off the first letter [e]. Besides the great river,
that is, the *Ebro*, which runs from north-west to south-east,
and divides this country almost into two equal parts, it is watered by some other streams that are pretty considerable ; such
as, on the north of the *Ebro*, the *Cirea*, antiently *Cinga*, the
Gallego, antiently *Gallicus*, and the *Isuela* ; on the south side
of that great river, the *Xalon*, antiently *Salo*, and the *Xiloca.*
We may add to these some that are still less, such as the *Ar-*
ragon, Riguelo, Guerva, Rio de Aguas, Rio Martin, Guada-
lope, Guadalaviar, and the *Alhambra* [f]. But, after all, this
country, if we take it in general, is but dry and barren, the soil
generally sandy, and, where it is not mountainous and stony,
in some parts it is very nitrous, and every-where naturally
hard and dry. In the vallies, however, where they have the advantage of rivers or rivulets, and in the plains where the want
of these can be supplied by canals, it is very pleasant, and tole-
rably fertile, producing corn, wine, oil, flax, fruits of different sorts, and in some places saffron [g]. The mountainous
country is at present as wild and desert as can be imagined,
and consequently useless and poor. It was not, however, always in this condition; for, in antient times, these mountains,
that are now so despicable, were rich in gold and silver mines,
and it is more than probable may be so still ; but here, as in
other parts of *Spain*, industry is extinct.

[d] CELLAR. Geograph. Antiq. lib. i. cap. 1. CLUVER. Introduct. Geograph. lib. ii. cap. 5. LUYTS Introduct. ad Geograph.
sect. ii. c. 8. Geograph. Moderne, par ABRAHAM DU BOIS, part
i. c. 3. art. xiii. Ætat present de l'Espagne, liv. i.   [e] AN-
TON. NEBRIX. JOAN. VASÆI Annal.   [f] CLUVER. LUYTS.
DU BOIS.   [g] Ætat present de l'Espagne, liv. i. Tour thro'
Spain and Portugal by UDAL AP RHYS, p. 236.

WE

The genius and dispo-sitions of the antient inhabit-ants, and the reasons why, in a long course of time, they were so little changed.

WE have already obferved that the principal inhabitants of this country, in antient times, were the *Celtiberians*; but concerning the origin of this nation, the moft learned authors are very much divided [h]. Some fay that the *Celtes* from *Gaul*, having fettled on the other fide of the *Iberus*, joined the name of that river to their own, and called themfelves, or were called by others, *Celtiberians* [i]. But it is at leaft equally probable that the *Celtæ* were feated on the north, and the *Iberians* on the fouth, fide; and we are told that, after they had for many years wafted each other by obftinate and bloody wars, they at length concluded a peace, and very wifely contrived, in order to render it more lafting, to blend both nations into one by continual intermarriages; and from thence the *Celtes* and *Iberians*, being both loft, this new nation was ftiled *Celtiberians* [k]. This feems to be the account hinted at by the poet *Lucan*, who might be well fuppofed to be thoroughly acquainted with its antiquity, being himfelf a native of this country. We have been the more particular with refpect to this nation, becaufe they were always famous for a kind of fupercilious haughtinefs, that made them look upon their neighbours with an eye of contempt, which, whatever difadvantages it might be attended with, kept them pure and unmixed; fo that their characters anfwered, for many ages, very exactly to what was recorded of them by the *Latin* writers [l]. They were active, hardy, enterprizing, enthufiaftically fond of liberty, very magnificent, but withal very induftrious. *Marcellus*, after a fhort war, taxed them at fix hundred talents of gold [m]. Thefe difpofitions were little, if at all, altered by their falling under the dominion of the *Goths*, from whom they fometimes revolted, and with whom they had continual ftruggles for the prefervation of their liberties, which never any nation better deferved, fince they were never by any nation either longer or better defended [n].

In what manner the people of Arragon provided for the prefervation of their reli-

WE may, therefore, juftly prefume, that when the reft of *Spain* was overborne by that dreadful inundation of *Moors*, thefe generous people retired in great numbers into their mountains and other inacceffible places, where they might enjoy that freedom which was to them felicity [o]. It is alfo not at all improbable, that the diftricts which are ftill diftinguifhed by the name of the county of *Arragon*, the principahty of *Sobrarve*, and the county of *Ribagorca*, of which we fhall

---

[h] Strab. Geograph. lib. iii. Plin. Hift. Nat. lib. iii. Ptolem. Geogr. lib. ii. [i] Lucan. [k] Appian in Ibericis. [l] Epift. Liv. lib. xlviii. Plin. Hift. Nat. lib. iii. Appian in Ibericis. [m] Zurit. Abarca. Moret. [n] Marian. Fer. [o] Zurit. Indic. Rer. ab Arragon. Reg. geft. lib. i.

take occasion to speak more particularly, were the countries *gion and* to which these brave men retired, and in which, for their own *liberties on* security, they, by common consent, erected such a form of *the irrup-* government, as least diminished their freedom P. But to en- *tion of the* ter into the long and intricate dispute; which has embarrassed Moors. the most judicious *Spanish* antiquaries, whether the kings of *Sobrarve* were more ancient than those of *Navarre*, would be fatiguing our readers and ourselves to very little purpose ; and, if it is to be discussed at all, it belongs more properly to the history of *Navarre*, where we shall take occasion to resume it q. At present it shall suffice to say, that, however this controversy may be determined, it is generally allowed that Don *Sancho the Great*, king of *Navarre*, was also count or earl of *Arragon*, in his own right, and master also of the other two little countries, now esteemed but provinces of this king- dom, as he became afterwards earl of *Castile* by succession, and consequently was the sole sovereign of what the Christians possessed in *Spain*, the kingdom of *Leon* and the earldom of *Barcelona* only excepted r. He it was who, by dividing his dominions amongst his four sons, erected three new kingdoms; of one of which, that is, *Castile*, we have already given the reader a long history : our present business is to gratify his curiosity in the like manner with respect to the other two, and this as succinctly as perspicuity will allow.

WE have elsewhere shewn that this potent prince died in the *Arragon* month of *February*, 1035 ; and we have likewise mentioned *erected into* the fable of his eldest son's charging the queen his mother *a kingdom* with adultery, and of the spirit with which his natural son vin- *in favour* dicated her innocence s. Without recapitulating, therefore, *of his son* these tales, which have been so fully refuted t, let us proceed *Don Ra-* to facts that admit of no dispute. The kingdom of *Navarre*, *miro, by* with the principality of *Biscay*, and the province of *Rioja*, he *Don San-* left to his eldest son Don *Garcia*; to Don *Ferdinand* he gave *cho the* the county of *Castile*, which he erected into a kingdom; to Don *Great,* *Goncales* he gave the counties of *Sobrarve* and *Ribagorca*, with *king of* the regal title also u. These three were his children by Don- *Navarre.* na *Munia Major*, daughter to the count of *Castile* : but, be- sides these, he had another son by a mistress of his, as most writers say, tho' a learned writer of the history of *Navarre* has, with great warmth, vindicated his legitimacy. The name of this son was Don *Ramiro*, and upon him he bestowed

P HIERON. BLANCÆ Arragonenf. rerum Comment. q Etat present de l'Espagne, liv. i. r MARIAN. ZURIT. MORET. s Historia general de Espana. por MAR. lib. viii. t P. Mo- RET Inveftigaciones de las antiquitades del Reyno de Navarra, lib. viii. u MONACH SILON. PET. MARSIL. FERRERAS.

Arragon, of which country, if he was not the first independent prince, he was, undoubtedly, the first king [w]. But, before we proceed to the history of him and his succeffors, it will be neceffary to fhew precifely, or at leaft as exactly as we can, what the territories were, which he and his brother Don *Gonçales* poffeffed, in virtue of their father's will [x].

WHAT now affumed the name of the kingdom [y], muft have been, in fact, a country very little, if at all, more extenfive, than that which now bears the title of the county of *Arragon* [z], having the *Pyrenean* mountains on the north, the kingdom of *Navarre* on the weft, the territories of the little *Moorifh* prince of *Huefca* on the fouth, and the country of *Sobrarva* on the eaft [a]. In this little tract there are feveral fruitful and pleafant vallies, which were, in thofe days, thoroughly peopled, and exceedingly well cultivated. The city of *Jaca* was its capital, feated very pleafantly on the river *Arragon*, in the midft of a fmall plain, at the foot of the *Pyrenees*, abounding with corn and fruits, famous for its fheep paftures, and plentifully ftocked with wild fowl [b]; a place of great antiquity, and celebrated in thofe earlier ages for being the capital of the *Jaccitani* [c]. It is for want of this diftinction between the bounds of the kingdom of *Arragon*, at the time of its firft erection, and thofe under which it is now comprehended, that many, indeed moft, of the hiftories of that crown are, in a manner, unintelligible, more efpecially to ftrangers. But when we remember that the kingdom given to Don *Ramiro* was not above an eighth part of what we now call *Arragon*, the fubfequent narration will be, in all refpects, confiftent and perfpicuous.

THE country of *Sobrarva* lies eaft from the kingdom of *Arragon*, as we have juft now defined it, having the *Pyrenees* on the north, the country of *Ribagorca* on the eaft, and the territories of fome *Moorifh* princes to the fouth [d]. The capital is the town of *Anifa*, upon the river *Ara*, not far from the angle which it makes in falling into the *Cinca* [e]. The country of *Ribagorca* has the *Pyrenees* on the north, *Sobrarva* on the weft, the territory of the *Moorifh* prince of *Huefca* on the fouth, and *Catalonia* on the eaft, from which it is divided

[w] Los Reyes de Arragon en Anales Hiftoricos diftribuidos por PEDRO ABARCA, l. i.   [x] ROD. SANTII Hift. Hifpan. part i.   [y] ZURIT. ABARC. MAR. &c.   [z] Delices de l'Efpagne par Don JUAN ALVAREZ de Colemenar, p. 666. [a] CLUVER. LUYTS. DU BOIS.   [b] Delices de l'Efpagne, p. 666.   [c] STRABO Geog. l. iii. PLIN. Hift. Nat. lib. iii. P. DE MARCA, M. H. lib. ii.   [d] CLUVER. LUYTS. DU BOIS. [e] Delices de l'Efpagne.

by a river called *Noguera Ribogorzana* : the whole territory
is about fifteen leagues in length, and fix in breadth, compofed of many rugged mountains, and fome few pleafant vallies [f]. Thefe countries taken together, and which were not
either much bigger or lefs than the kingdom of *Arragon*,
formed the new kingdom that was now erected in favour of
Don *Goncales* [g].

Don *Ramiro*, the year after he was fettled in the kingdom
of *Arragon*, efpoufed *Gifberga*, or *Ermifenda*, for we find her
called by both names by cotemporary writers, the daughter of
Bernardo Rogerio, count of *Vigorra*; a princefs much celebrated for her beauty. About two years after, Don *Goncales*
paffing over the bridge of *Monclus*, as he was hunting, was
affaffinated by a domeftic of his, whofe name was *Ramonet*,
who ftruck him to the heart with his javelin, but for what
caufe we no-where find [i]. As he died without iffue, the people thought fit to proclaim Don *Ramiro*, who, by this means,
added the countries of *Sobrarva* and *Ribagorca* to his own, fo
that now he was mafter of half that part of the kingdom of
Arragon which lies on the north of the *Ebro*. By this acceffion of territory he was become fo formidable, that, for fear
of a rupture with him, the *Moorish* princes of *Saragoffa*, *Huefca*, and *Tudela*, paid him each of them an annual penfion, by
way of tribute ; and the firft of thefe princes confented, at
his requeft, to the eftablifhment of a bifhop in his capital, to
fuperintend the ecclefiaftical affairs of his Chriftian fubjects [k].
This fuccefs had, as it too often happens, a bad effect on the
mind of this prince ; who, forgetting the ties of blood, and
the refpect due to juftice, made, in conjunction with the Infi-
del monarchs before-mentioned, an irruption into the territories of his brother, Don *Garcia* king of *Navarre*, and laid
fiege to the town of *Tafalla*. The inhabitants of that place
making a gallant defence, gave the king Don *Garcia* time to
affemble his troops, with whom, in the midft of a dark night,
he fell upon his enemies fo unexpectedly, and with fuch vigour,
that the beft part of their forces were cut in pieces, Don *Ramiro* himfelf narrowly efcaping upon a horfe without bridle or
faddle [l]. Don *Garcia*, purfuing his blow, entered the kingdom of *Arragon* with an army, and reducing a great part of
the country, forced his brother to retire into the mountains
of *Sobrarva*. On his fubmiffion, however, and the interpo-

Marginal notes: Don Ra- efpoufes Gifberga, daughter of the count of Vigorra. 1036. — Invades the territories of his brother Don Garcia king of Navarre.

[f] Geographie Moderne, par Du Bois, part i. chap. 3. art. xiii.
[g] Hieron. Blancæ Arragonenf. Rerum Comment.   [i] Chron.
Monach. Pennat.   [k] Rod. Tolet. rer. Hifpan. Lucæ
Tudenfis. Ferreras.   [l] Roderic Tolet. rer. Hifpan.
Lucæ Tudenfis. Mar.

sition of some of the clergy, Don *Garcia* consented to a peace, and restored the places he had taken [m]. This harmony subsisted between them during the remainder of their lives; and the great power of Don *Ferdinand* king of *Leon*, being equally formidable to Don *Ramiro* of *Arragon* and to Don *Sancho* the son and successor of Don *Garcia*, in the kingdom of *Navarre*, they concluded a defensive alliance, for their mutual security [n]. About two years after, the king of *Arragon*, being advanced in years, having first settled the affairs of his kingdom and family by his will, made war upon the Infidels, from a principle of devotion, and took from them the town of *Loharia*, which lies about four leagues from *Huesca* [o].

1060. The very next year he held the famous assembly of *Jacca*, at which assisted several prelates from the Christian states in this neighbourhood, in which assembly *Jacca* was made a bishop's see, and endowed with very considerable revenues. The king established very strict ecclesiastical discipline throughout his dominions, and, as far as he was able, bound his successors to maintain and support what at this time was established [p].

1063. Three years after, finding the king of *Castile* engaged in a war with the *Moors*, he judged it a favourable opportunity to fall upon them likewise; upon which, with a formidable army, he laid siege to *Grao*, which belonged to the king of *Saragossa*. This obliged the *Moorish* prince to demand the protection of the king of *Castile*, to whom he had been for some time tributary. Don *Ferdinand* was at that time in the southern parts of his dominions; but his son Don *Sancho*, at the head of a small body of chosen troops, having the famous *Cid* for his lieutenant, came to the assistance of the *Moors*; *Is slain in a battle with the king of Castile.* and, having surprized the army of *Arragon*, defeated it entirely, made a great number of prisoners, and a dreadful slaughter, the king himself being among the number of the slain [q]. This was the end of Don *Ramiro*, on whom, some say, pope *Gregory* the seventh conferred the title of *Most Christian* [r], when he had governed his realm twenty-eight years. His body was interred in the monastery of *St. Juan de la Pena*; and he left behind him two sons, Don *Sancho* and Don *Garcia*, and two daughters, Donna *Sancha* and Donna *Theresa*. He had also a natural son Don *Sancho*, to whom he gave the county of *Ribagorca*, but he died without issue [s].

[m] RODERIC TOLET. rerum Hispan. lib. iii.   LUCÆ TUD.
[n] MONACH PENNAT.   [o] Chron. antiq. de rebus Arragon.
[p] Chron. MONACH. PENNAT.   [q] ZURIT. ABARCA. MARIAN. FERRERAS. MAYERNE TURQUET.   [r] HIERON.
BLANCÆ Arragonens. Commentarii.   [s] ZURIT. BLANCA.
ABARCA. MAR. FER.

DON

Don *Sancho Ramirez* succeeded his father, with the general acclamations of his subjects [t]. We are told by *Mariana* that he was eighteen years old at the time of his accession, which he places near five years too late, and consequently he could have been but thirteen at the time of his father's de- mise: but, as he married that very year, this must appear improbable; and, if what a learned historian asserts be true, it is utterly impossible. He says that this was not his first marriage; but that the name of the lady, whose death made way for the princess he now espoused, was Donna *Beatrix,* whereas she to whom he was married in the first year of his reign was Donna, *Felicia,* daughter to *Hilduin* count *de Robey,* though many of the *Spanish* historians say she was the daughter of the count of *Urgel,* which very possibly may arise from his first wife's being the daughter of that count; for of this marriage they take no notice [u]. It is also said, that he abrogated the old *Gothic* code of laws, and introduced those of the empire, which, however, is not very certain. He was a prince of great parts, as well as of a martial disposition; and therefore, having provided for the domestic security of his king- dom, in conjunction with the count of *Urgel,* he undertook an expedition against the *Moors;* in which that count, having gained two victories, was slain [w]. The king Don *Sancho* was, at that time, before the town of *Balbastro,* a place of import- ance, situated on the little river *Vero,* not far from its conflu- ence with the *Cinca,* the territory of which, being well wa- tered, is very fruitful, in olive trees especially, of which they make very good oil, and in pretty large quantities. The *Moors* made a long and brave defence, but at length the place surrendered, and the king caused it to be strongly fortified, making it also a bishop's see, by transferring the episcopal chair from *Rhoda* [x]. Some years after he would have turned his arms against the *Moorish* prince of *Saragossa;* but, when he was ready to take the field, that prince very wisely put himself under the protection of Don *Sancho* king of *Navarre,* in respect to whom the king of *Arragon* dropped his design for that time. Upon the assassination of this good prince, his brother Don *Raymond,* about three years after, at the inter- cession of the greatest part of his subjects, called Don *Sancho* of *Arragon* to the throne of *Navarre,* tho', at the same time, there was a strong party formed, as hath been already shewn in another place, in favour of the king of *Castile* and *Leon,* which, it was feared, would have produced a war between the

[t] Chron. Monach. Pennat. Zurit. Abarc. [u] Hier. Blancæ Arragonens. Commentarii. [w] Zurit. Abarc. Marian. [x] Chron. antiq. de reb. Arragon.

two crowns; but by the great prudence and moderation of Don
Sancho of *Arragon*, it was prevented, and he was left in the
quiet poffeffion of that part of *Navarre* that lay on the fame
fide of the river *Ebro* with his own hereditary dominions [y].
At this juncture pope *Gregory* was extremely preffing upon
both monarchs to acknowlege themfelves feudatories of the
holy fee ; to which end he employed a perfon of great capacity as his legate, but with no effect : for, being born kings,
they could not be brought to become fubjects [z]. His power
being now much augmented, it was not long before he took
feveral places from the *Moors* of *Saragoffa* and *Huefca*, who
applied themfelves thereupon to all their neighbours, reprefenting it as a religious war, by which they were foon enabled
to affemble a numerous army, and to offer Don *Sancho* battle,
which he did not decline ; and, having gained a complete victory, contented himfelf with fecuring the places he had taken,
by which he extended and ftrengthened his frontier [a]. The
next year he took the field again, befieged the town of *Bohea*,
and took it by affault. In the fummer following he took
Grao, and repeopled and fortified feveral places on the con-
fines ; to prevent which, the *Moors* ventured another battle
at *Piedro Pifida*, in which they were again defeated, and the
king Don *Sancho* left at liberty to accomplifh all he had undertaken [b].

As foon as he had perfected his barrier in fuch a manner
as to cover his country from the infults of the Infidels, he began to think of acting again offenfively. While he meditated this irruption, the queen Donna *Felicia* died, on the
24th of *April*, which, however did not hinder the king's taking the field and invefting *Monçon*, a place very ftrong both
by art and nature, fituated on the flope of a hill, and commanding a confiderable diftrict round it [c]. The enterprize
was difficult : but, being conducted with courage and caution, the king at length became mafter of it, and rendered it
one of the principal fortreffes in his territories. Thefe facts,
however, fhew us plainly, that thofe authors are probably in
the wrong who affirm that he was prefent this year at the taking of *Toledo*. After allowing his fubjects fome years of
repofe, and caufing feveral places to be repaired in *Navarre*,
he once more affembled a puiffant army, with a defign to
make a complete conqueft of the little principality of *Huefca* ;
but the *Moors*, difcerning his fuperiority, offered to become

Marginal notes:

1083. *His exploits againft the* Moors.

1084.

1085.

1092.

---

[y] Zurit. Abarc. Fer.   [z] Chron. antiq. de reb. Arragon. Fer.   [a] Zurit. Abarc. Mayerne Turquet.
Fer.   [b] Hieron. Blancæ Arragonenfium Rerum Commentarii.   [c] Chron. var. antiq.

his

his vaffals, and to pay him a large annual tribute, which he accepted, refolving to turn his arms againft *Saragoffa* ᵉ. It was with this view that he caufed a ftrong place, to which he gave the name of *Caftellar*, to be erected on the frontier, as near as poffible to that city, by which it was, in a manner, always blocked up, and which might at any time be converted into a place of arms, as foon as he found himfelf ftrong enough to befiege that important place. As this had a very good effect, he proceeded foon after to take the fame method in regard to *Huefca*, which quickly created fome difturbances, and thefe furnifhed the occafion which he fought of declaring war ᶠ. His mind beind extremely fet upon this conqueft, it is faid that he fent his fon Don *Ramiro* into *France*, to take the habit of St. *Benedict*, in hopes this might procure him the Divine affiftance in this great and hazardous enterprize ᵍ. The prince of *Huefca*, being thoroughly apprized of his defign, had put the place into an excellent ftate of defence, raifed very large magazines, and drawn numbers of brave men from different parts of *Spain*, to augment his garrifon, and had befides a confiderable body of auxiliaries from his neighbour of *Saragoffa*. This did not hinder Don *Sancho* from executing his defign; and fitting down before the city, with a very numerous and well appointed army, he carried on the fiege with fuch vigour, that the place had ftood more than one affault, when, in bringing up a body of troops that had been repulfed, the king was, as he extended his arm in giving orders, mortally wounded by an arrow from the wall. Being carried to his tent, he expired, as fome fay, on the firft of *June* ʰ, or, as others affert, on the fourth of that month ⁱ, in the year of our Lord one thoufand and ninety-four, and in the thirty-fecond year of his reign, leaving behind him three fons, Don *Pedro*, Don *Alonfo*, and Don *Ramiro*. The two eldeft were with him in the camp; and, before he died, he caufed them to be fworn in his prefence, never to abandon the defign of reducing *Huefca*, which he looked upon as the firft ftep towards driving the *Moors* out of that part of *Spain* ᵏ.

Is mortally wounded at the fiege of Huefca.

THE Infant Don *Pedro* was immediately proclaimed king by the army; and, having caufed his father's body to be removed to the monaftery of *Jefus of Nazareth*, at *Mont Arragon*, he turned the fiege into a blockade, pofting a ftrong body of troops in the caftle of *Luna*, which the king his father had

1094. Don Pedro proclaimed king.

ᵉ ZURIT. MONACH. PENNAT.   ᶠ HIERON. BLANCÆ.
ᵍ ZURIT. MONACH. PENNAT.   ʰ ROD. TOLET. de reb.
Hifpan.   ⁱ Annal Compoftel. HIERONYMI BLANCÆ.
ᵏ ZURIT. MARIAN. FER.

built

built in a very proper fituation for that purpofe[1]. We are told by fome writers, that Don *Pedro* bore the title of king of *Sobrarva* before his father's death; and that, having efpoufed a lady whofe name was *Bearta*, he had by her a fon of his own name, and a daughter Donna *Ifabella*[m]. He was in the prime of his life, and not at all inferior to his father either in conduct or in courage; and therefore he laboured affiduoufly, though with as little ftir as poffible, to draw together an army numerous enough to return to the fiege. *Abdaramen* the *Moorifh* chief of *Huefca*, fufpecting this, repaired his fortifications, and fent to all his neighbours and allies to demand affiftance; affuring them that he was but the firft facrifice, and that all the little princes of the *Moors* were in danger of being gradually deftroyed; he likewife fent to the king of *Caftile*, putting him in mind that, as he paid him an annual tribute, it was but juft that he fhould protect him in the day of his diftrefs. That monarch did not refufe him, but fent a confiderable corps, under the command of Don *Garcia* count *de Najera*, and *Albocamen* king of *Saragoffa* marched with almoft all the troops he had, to his relief[n]. Don *Pedro* of *Arragon*, perceiving the enemy in full march towards him, refolved to leave but a fmall body before the place, and to advance with the reft of his army into the plain of *Alcaraz*, that the *Moors* might fee he had no inclination to decline *Defeats* fighting. Both fides, therefore, being much in earneft, they *the* Moors came to a decifive engagement on the 28th of *November*, in *in the* which, though the *Moors* and their auxiliaries did all that *plain of* could be expected from men of determined courage, yet, after *Alcaraz.* a very obftinate difpute, which lafted many hours, they were totally defeated, with the lofs of forty thoufand men killed, and the count Don *Garcia*, and moft of the forces he commanded, were made prifoners. This was, certainly, one of the moft important and moft fignal victories obtained over the Infidels, and, according to the humour of thofe times, it was afcribed to St. *George*, the patron of *Arragon*, who was reported to have fought in the firft ranks, mounted on a white horfe, having on his left arm a broad fhield with a bloody crofs; whence, though it is not very clear when they were affumed, the arms of *Arragon* are faid to have been taken; viz. On a field, argent, a crofs of St. *George*, gules, with four *Moors* heads proper[o]. As the price of this victory *Huefca* was furrendered

---

[1] Rod. Tolet. de reb. Hifpan. Chron. Monach. Annal Compoft.　[m] Iidem ibid.　[n] Rod. Tol. Hift. Arabum. Luc. Tudenfis Chron.　[o] Diploma Reg. Arragon. Annal Complut. Mar. Hiftoria general de Efpana. lib. x.

on the 15th, and the great mosque, being cleansed and purifi-   1096.
ed, was consecrated on the 17th of *December*, when the bi- *He takes*
shop of *Jacca* took possession of it ᴾ.   This city, which stands Huesca. _
on the bank of the river *Isuela*, at the distance of thirty leagues
north-east from *Saragossa*, is, after that, the fairest and finest
in *Arragon*, situate in a fertile plain, well cultivated, and producing the best wine that is made in this country ; and the
remains of its old fortifications, which are still preserved,
shew, that, at the time it fell into the hands of the Christians,
its walls were flanked with ninety-nine towers.   After this
happy success, the king caused his father's body to be carried to the royal monastery of St. *Juan de la Pena*, and to
be in interred near the body of his consort Donna *Felicia*, under
a stately tomb �۹.

  THE settling things in the territory of such an important
conquest took up some time.   This once accomplished, we
find the active and victorious prince in the field again, sweep-   1098.
ing several places of less consequence from the *Moors*, and at
length depriving them of the castle of *Calesans*, after a very
stubborn defence, which gave him an opportunity of extending his dominions, and securing his frontiers ʳ.   He also ap-   1101.
plied himself to pope *Paschal* the second, in order to obtain a
bull for transferring the see of *Rhoda* to *Balbastro*, which was
his father's conquest, though most of the historians of this
kingdom ascribe it also to him ; in which, if there be any truth,
the *Moors* must have surprized it again, of which there is not
the least hint to be found ˢ.   After this the king Don *Pedro*
seems to have applied himself chiefly to the arts of peace, and
to the establishing and improving that extent of country, which,
by the blessing of Providence on his own and his predecessor's
arms, had been recovered from the Infidels : but the satisfaction he enjoyed from those princely labours was sadly interrupted by the loss of both his children, in the month of
August, which, partly through grief, and partly through dif-
ease, brought himself to the grave, on the 28th of *September*,
in the year of our Lord one thousand one hundred and four, *His death,*
in the eleventh year of his reign.   His body was interred near   1104.
those of his father and mother, in the monastery of St. *Juan
de la Pena* ᵗ.

ᴾ Indices Rerum ab Arragoniæ Regibus Gestarum, P. MORET
Investigaciónes Historicas de las antiquitades del Reyno de Navarra. ABARC. FER. ᵠ ۹ ROD. TOLET. de reb. Hispan.
ZURIT. ʳ Annal Complut. Annal Toletan. ˢ Chron.
var. antiq. HIERONYM. BLANCÆ Arragonens. Rerum Comment.
ᵗ MONACH. PENNAT.

HE

His bro-   He was succeeded in the kingdoms of *Navarre* and *Arra-*
ther Don   *gon* by his brother Don *Alonso* [u], who, by the active display of
Alonso   his martial virtues, obtained the surname of *il Guerrero*; that
succeeds to is, *the warrior.* He was esteemed, at the time of his accession,
the throne. one of the handsomest and bravest princes of his time, which
           induced Don *Alonso* the sixth of *Castile,* who had caused
           himself to be solemnly crowned emperor of the *Spains,* to cast
           his eyes upon him, for the second husband of his daughter
           and heiress Donna *Urraca,* which took place in the second
1109.   year of his reign [w]; and, considering himself as the successor
Marries   of that prince, in right of his wife, he stiled himself *Alonso* the
Donna   seventh, king of *Castile* and *Leon,* and sometimes also em-
Urraca   peror [x] : the conclusion of this marriage seemed to promise as
daughter   great advantages, as, in its consequences, it produced miseries
to the em- and mischiefs to the Christians in *Spain.* The present pos-
peror of   sessor of *Castile,* and all the extensive territories lately annexed
the Spains. to it, was a woman, and her heir apparent a child; by which
           they were grievously exposed to the impressions of the Infidels,
           more vigilant then than in former times, through the losses
           they had sustained, the revolutions that had happened in their
           governments, and several other causes. The marriage of
           Donna *Urraca* to Don *Alonso* not only repaired the loss of
           the deceased emperor, and furnished the young heir of *Castile*
           of the same name with a powerful protector, but created, at
           the same time, a new and unexperienced authority, which
           threatened the *Moors* with immediate expulsion; since, ex-
           cept the two counties of *Barcelona* and *Portugal,* this Don
           Alonso was master, in his own and his wife's right, of all the
           states that the Christians possessed in *Spain,* and so able to
           bring into the field more numerous and potent armies than
           hitherto had been ever employed against the common enemy.
           Besides, it seemed a most happy and effectual provision against
           those factions that commonly arise in all monarchies, when
           the throne is occupied either by women or children. But so
           uncertain are all events in this sublunary state, and so short-
           sighted is human policy, that the hopes of the Christians and
1110.   the apprehensions of the *Moors* were equally disappointed;
           and this, almost as soon as they were excited : for, in a few
           months after the marriage was concluded, those differences
1111.   broke out between the king and queen, which could never

---

[u] HIERON. BLANCÆ Arragonens. Rerum Comment. Indices
Rerum ab Arrag. Regibus Gestarum. ROD. TOLET. de reb.
Hispan.   [w] LUCÆ Tudens. Chron. Chron. Adefons Im-
perat. FER.   [x] ROD. TOLET. de reb. Hispan.

afterwar

afterwards be reconciled; and which, almost as soon as they broke out, threw every thing into confusion; so that through their inteftine difcords, or rather through the appointment of divine Providence, if the Infidels had not been wanting to themselves, they might have had a fair opportunity of restoring their power, and of recovering a great part, at least, of those countries that the Christians had lately taken from them. But as we have given a full account of those matters in another place, we shall content ourselves with obferving here, that, after a great deal of confusion and bloodfhed, the marriage between Don *Alonfo* and Donna *Urraca* was declared null, in the council of *Palentia*; and the king, thereupon, turned his thoughts entirely to the care of his own hereditary dominions [y].

THE glory his father had acquired by his victories over the *Moors*, and the reputation raifed by his brother by the conqueft of *Huefca*, joined to fome infults and provocations which himself had received from the *Moors* of *Saragoffa*, inflamed the king Don *Alonfo* with the defire of adding that noble city to his dominions. He forefaw that this would be a difficult and hazardous enterprize, and, by a policy peculiar to a prince of his difpofition, he contrived to obtain the means of carrying it into execution by divulging his project, which had all the effect he propofed, fince it brought many of the *French* nobility, eager to obtain honour in a religious war, to his affiftance, particularly *Gafton* lord of *Bearn*, *Rotrou* count of *Perche*, the count of *Comminges*, the vifcount of *Gavardan*, and the bifhop of *Lefcar* [z]. He had quickly a fpecimen of their great military fkill, as well as of their bold and enterprizing difpofitions; for his troops being continually harraffed, and their convoys cut off by excurfions from *Tudela*, which the *Moors* were likewife in poffeffion of, he detached *Rotrou* count of *Perche*, with a confiderable body of troops, to reftrain thofe people. The count made a fudden and filent march into the neighbourhood of that city, and having pofted his forces in fuch a manner, as that they could not be difcerned, he ordered a fmall party of horfe to advance within fight of the place; upon which the *Moors*, fuppofing them to be the rear guard of a convoy, iffued out with their whole force, and upon their retiring, according to their inftructions, purfued them beyond the place where the count lay with his forces, who thereupon attacked them in flank, and having

(margin: 1114.)
(margin: Reduces Tudela.)

[y] LUCÆ Tuden. Chron. HIERON. BLANCÆ Arragonenf. Rerum Comment. ROD. TOLET. de reb. Hifpan. Indices Rerum ab Arragoniæ Regibus Geftarum.   [z] Chron. MONACH. PENNAT. P. DANIEL Hiftoire de France. FER.

gained

gained an eaſy victory, purſued them with ſuch vigour, that part of his troops entered with them into the town, and having ſeized an advantageous poſt, ſupported themſelves while he arrived with the reſt of his infantry, and carried the place by aſſault, to the no ſmall aſtoniſhment both of the *Moors* and the Chriſtians[a]. But the king, notwithſtanding this unexpected ſucceſs, being informed that the *Moors* in *Saragoſſa* had received numerous ſuccours, thought fit to ſuſpend his expedition, in order to make the neceſſary preparations for rendering it effectual, which took up the remaining part of this and all the ſucceeding year.

Obtains a victory over the Moors, and takes poſſeſſion of Saragoſſa. THE meaſure upon which the king principally relied, was diſturbing and diſtreſſing the inhabitants of that city, from the fortreſs of *Caſtellar*, which ſtood upon the *Ebro*, and gave the Chriſtians an opportunity of diſturbing all communication between that city, either by land or water. After many months wearying and harraſſing them in this manner, which ſerved only to keep his own troops in breath, and gave him leiſure to repair and fortify all the places he had taken, he brought a numerous army into the field, and beſieged the ſtrongeſt fortreſs of *Almadobar*, which, as it in ſome meaſure covered *Saragoſſa*, the *Moors* had provided with a ſtout garriſon, and with all things neceſſary for a good defence[b]. This he took after a brave reſiſtance, and then turned his arms againſt *Salici*, *Robles*, *Gurrea*, and *Zucra*, all of which he obliged to ſurrender. Having thus cleared that ſide of the river, and eſtabliſhed a free communication between his own camp and the kingdoms of *Arragon* and *Navarre*, he at length inveſted *Saragoſſa*[c]. The ſiege was very tedious, the beſieged made frequent ſallies, and the beſiegers were repulſed in more than one aſſault. This diſguſted the *French* lords, who loved to be upon the wing; and therefore, except the lord of *Bearne* and the count of *Perche*, they quitted the camp. The king, Don *Alonſo*, upon this, drew his forces nearer the place, and proſecuted the ſiege with greater vigour than before; however, the inhabitants found means to preſs the *Moors* of *Tortoſa*, *Merida*, and *Valentia*, to come to their aſſiſtance, aſſuring them that the Chriſtian army was much inferior to what it had been. Accordingly they aſſembled a very numerous army, under the command of *Temin*, and marched ſpeedily to their relief. The king Don *Alonſo* was no ſooner informed of this, than foreſeeing the diſadvantages that muſt attend his

[a] Rod. Tolet. Hiſt. Arabum. Hieron. Blancæ Arragonenſ. Rerum Comment.   [b] Chron. var. antiq.   [c] Rod. Tolet. Hiſt. Arabum. Luc. Tudenſ. Chron.

being

being attacked in his lines, left a small body of troops before the place, and marched with the rest of his forces to give the enemy battle, whom he entirely defeated, killed a great number upon the spot, and made a multitude prisoners, amongst whom was their general.   This had the consequence that was expected from it ; the place began immediately to capitulate, **A. D.** and on the 18th. of *December* the king took possession of it **1118.** with great solemnity [d]. As this was beyond comparison the finest place in his possession, and indeed one of the best built cities in *Spain*, he not only restored it to its ancient honour of being an episcopal see, but made it also the capital of his dominions.   Having rewarded generously those strangers who had assisted in reducing it, he caused it to be repeopled with Christians, and then demolished the fortifications, declaring that the seat of his monarchy should have no other defence than the force and courage of its inhabitants [e]. While he was thus employed, he had intelligence that numbers of people began to retire out of *Tarracona*, and other places ; upon which, resolving to make a right use of the consternation the *Moors* were in, he marched thither with his army : though a place of strength and consequence, he reduced it with very little trouble, and concluded this glorious campaign with the taking of *Borja*, *Alagon*, and other places on the banks of the river *Galeco* [f].   The next year, while the places he had **1119.** reduced were repairing, he made another expedition, in which *Takes di-* he swept the river *Xalon*, made himself master of the ancient *vers strong* town of *Calatayud*, and took several places of less importance *places* from the Infidels. He found it convenient after this, to remain *from the* for some time quiet in his own dominions, in order to provide *Moors.* effectually for their security, notwithstanding the many thou- **1120.** sands of *Moors* that were now become his subjects [g].

THESE precautions taken, he again assembled his forces ; *And de-* and having signified to the nobility of *France*, how well *feats them* pleased he should be to have them again for his companions *in a pitch-* in arms, they very readily accepted his summons, and joined *ed battle* his troops by that time they were in a state of action. The *near Al-* king Don *Alonso* first ravaged the territory of *Lerida*, after- *caraz.* wards invaded *Valentia*, and at length penetrated as far as the kingdom of *Murcia*, acquiring vast reputation to himself, and

[d] Annal Toletan. Annal Compostel. Annal Complut. ROD. TOLET. de reb. Hispan. MONACH. PENNAT. FER. [e] Indices Rerum ab Arragoniæ Regibus Gestarum. MARIANA, FERRERAS.   [f] ROD. TOLET. Hist. Arabum. HIERON, BLANCÆ Arragonens. Rerum Comment. ABARCA. ZURITA. [g] ROD. TOLET.

immense

immenfe riches to thofe who ferved under him [h]. The *Moors* had been hitherto fo much aftonifhed at the boldnefs of this enterprize, that they made little or no refiftance ; but, perceiving that his army was not very numerous, that he was at a great diftance from his own dominions, in the very centre of theirs, and that it was impoffible for any of his forces to efcape, in cafe of a defeat, they began to recover their fpirits, and eleven of their alcaydes having joined the ftrength of their refpective governments, advanced to give him battle near the city of *Alcaraz.* Don *Alonfo,* according to his ufual cuftom, placed all hopes of fafety in a frank declaration to his people, that if they were beat they were undone ; the fenfe of which operated fo powerfully, that, notwithftanding the inequality of the conteft, they gained a very decifive and glorious victory ; after which he took winter quarters in the enemy's country, and kept his *Chriftmas* at *Alcaraz* [i].

In the fpring of the enfuing year, when the *Moors* expected that he would have begun his retreat, he made a frefh irruption into the plains of *Cordova,* and having ravaged all the open country, threw himfelf next into the territories of *Jaen* and *Granada,* where he committed the like devaftation. But after all this fuccefs, it is very doubtful how this campaign might have ended, if he had not received an unexpected and almoft miraculous fuccour, which enabled him to return in triumph to *Saragoffa* [k]. While his army continued in the field, ten thoufand Chriftian families came down from the *Alpujarros,* and the mountains of *Alcaraz,* where they had maintained themfelves from the days of Don *Rodrigo* ; and having demanded and obtained his protection, returned with him into *Arragon,* where, having reduced *Molina, Ariza,* and fome other places, he fettled them to their fatisfaction, and. having difmiffed his army, began to apply himfelf to the arts of peace [l].

The Infidels lofe another great battle. At the clofe of the laft war, fome difference had arifen between the king and the *French* lords, who had ferved in his army, whom he had rewarded lefs liberally than formerly, on account of the number of *Mozarabic* Chriftians, for whom he was obliged to provide ; and in this difcontented humour the *French* returned home [m]. The *Moors* having intelligence of this, and having received prodigious fuccours from *Morocco,*

[h] HIERON. BLANCÆ Arragonenf. Rerum Comment. P. DANIEL. FERRERAS ZURITA. ABARCA. LUCÆ Tudenf. Chron. [m] Chron. var. antiq.
[i] ROD. TOLET. Hift. Arabum. [k] ROD. TOLET. de reb. Hifpan. [l] ZURITA. ABARCA. FEL.

eager

eager to revenge their paſt loſſes, reſolved to invade his domi‑
nions, and aſſembled a very powerful army for that purpoſe.
The king, on the firſt intelligence of their deſign, compromiſed
all matters in diſpute with his old friends, and engaged the
count of *Perche*, the viſcount of *Bearne*, and other lords, to
join him with their forces, which, with his own troops,
enabled him to ſecure his frontiers in ſuch a manner as totally
diſappointed the views of the Infidels [n]. The next ſpring he
made an irruption into the kingdom of *Valentia*, which not
only added to the reputation of his arms, but furniſhed an
immenſe booty to his troops. *Amorga*, the *Moorish* general,
endeavoured to give ſome check to his progreſs; but the at‑
tempt was only fatal to his own troops. However, *Albamin*,
at the head of a numerous army, having joined *Amorga*, and
having ſeized the paſſages in the mountains, the king Don
Alonſo found it impoſſible to recover his own territories, being
in a manner beſieged in the midſt of a wild and uncouth
country, where it was impoſſible to ſubſiſt, and from which
it was equally impoſſible to remove. In this critical ſituation
he ordered three days of ſolemn humiliation, to implore the
favour of heaven; and on the fourth, which was the ſixteenth
of *Auguſt*, he cauſed his proviſions to be equally diſtributed,
and when his army were thoroughly refreſhed, he attacked
the *Moors* with great fury. The action laſted many hours,
was very obſtinately fought, and the victory gained by the
king, at laſt, was eſteemed one of the moſt conſiderable that
the Chriſtians ever obtained, and, in conſequence of which,
he marched without any moleſtation home [o]. He was en‑
gaged the next year in a war with Don *Alonſo*, king of *Caſtile*,
which was quickly compromiſed, as we have ſhewn in ano‑
ther place; as another rupture of the ſame kind was, about two
years after, in which the king of *Arragon* was the aggreſſor;
but being perſuaded by his prelates that a war muſt be un‑
proſperous that was unjuſt, he retired in time.

A. D.
1126.

THE cloſe connections which the king of *Arragon* had en‑
tered into with the *French* lords, his neighbours, engaged him
in a war on that ſide, the particular cauſe of which is no
where explained: all we know of the matter is, that he made
a deſcent, with a well appointed army, into *Gaſcony*, where
he inveſted and beſieged *Bayonne*. While he was thus em‑
ployed, the *Moors* of *Lerida*, *Tortoſa*, and *Valentia*, taking
advantage of his abſence, made incurſions into his dominions,
againſt whom the biſhop of *Hueſca* and the viſcount of *Bearne*,

Reduces
Bayonne.

---

[n] HIERON. BLANCÆ. ZURITA. ABARCA.   [o] Annal
Complut. HIERON. BLANCÆ Arragonenſ. Comment. ROD.
TOLET. de reb. Hiſpan. FER.

marched

marched with a ſmall body of troops ; but engaging with a ſuperior force, were defeated and killed P. The king Don *Alonſo,* notwithſtanding this, continued the ſiege of *Bayonne* with that vigour and obſtinacy which were natural to him ; and, having at laſt taken it, returned with his forces into his own dominions q. The diſturbances his ſubjects received from the *Mooriſh* pirates, who came in ſmall veſſels up the Ebro, and the miſchiefs that were done by a numerous garriſon they had in the old town of *Mequinenca,* at the confluence of the *Segro* and the *Ebro,* determined him to beſiege that place, though covered by a fortreſs that hitherto had been eſteemed impregnable. He attacked it with great vigour ; and though the *Moors* made a gallant defence, he at length carried it by aſſault, and put the whole garriſon to the ſword r. This ſucceſs encouraged him to inveſt *Fraga,* which derives that name from the corruption of *Flavia Gallica,* by which it was known in the time of the *Romans.* It ſtands upon an eminence on the left ſide of the *Cinca,* three leagues from *Lerida,* on the frontiers of *Catalonia,* ſtrong by its ſituation in the midſt of mountains, having the river beforementioned in front, the banks of which are inacceſſible, and covered behind by a craggy mountain, on which there was a good fortreſs. It was at this time the capital of a *Mooriſh* government, full of a hardy and martial race of people, well fortified for thoſe days, and, tho' ſeated in the moſt ſterile parts of *Arragon,* plentifully ſupplied with proviſions. The king remained before it all the remainder of this year, and the beginning of the next ; and, as he was not accuſtomed to deſiſt from his enterprizes, the *French* lords, his confederates, and ſeveral of his own prelates, brought him great reinforcements early in the ſpring. On the other hand, *Aben Gama,* governor of *Valentia,* aſſembled all the forces of that province, and made two attempts to raiſe the ſiege, but without effect, being as often repulſed by Don *Alonſo* with great loſs.

The people of *Fraga,* finding themſelves extremely preſſed, much diminiſhed in their numbers, and without hopes of relief, offered to ſurrender the place, provided he would ſuffer them to march out, and retire where they thought proper, which he refuſed, inſiſting upon their ſubmitting at diſcretion. In the mean time, the forces of *Seville, Cordova,* and *Granada,* were advanced into *Valentia,* where *Aben-Gama* had likewiſe received a reinforcement of ten thouſand men

A. D.
1133.

And beſieges the capital of a Mooriſh government.

P HIBRON. BLANCÆ Arragonenſ. Rerum Comment. ZURITA. ABARCA. FER. q ROD. TOLET. de reb. Hiſpan. LUC. Tudenſ. Chron, r Indices Rerum ab Arragoniæ regibus Geſtarum.

from

from *Texefin Ben Hali*, king of *Morocco*, and with this numerous and potent army he advanced a third time to the fuccour of *Fraga*. It happened unfortunately, that, at this
juncture, the king Don *Alonfo* had detached a corps of his
beft troops, to fecure a great convoy of provifions, fo that the
difpute was extremely unequal. However, upon the approach
of the Infidels, the king quitted his camp, and, having made
the beft difpofition he was able, advanced to give them
battle. His forces behaved with great intrepidity, and him-*But is de-*
felf, and the nobility about him, exerted all the fkill and *feated in a*
courage that could be expected from perfons grown old in *great bat-*
arms, and enured to victory. But at length, being abfolutely *tle, and*
overpowered by numbers, the army was defeated, the greateft *dies of*
part flain upon the fpot, and amongft them the bifhops of *grief.*
Huefca and *Roda*, moft of the *French* nobility who ferved as
auxiliaries, and many alfo of the lords of *Navarre* and
Arragon [s]. The king Don *Alonfo* feing all loft, made a great
effort with feven hundred men, and having penetrated thro'
the *Moorifh* army, continued his route, having paffed by
Saragoffa, to the monaftery of St. *Juan de la Pena*, where he
arrived with ten of his great lords, amongft whom was Don
Garcia Ramirez; and, falling there into a deep melancholy,
died eight days after of pure grief [t]. His body was interred
with thofe of his anceftors, but without any tomb erected to
his memory; which, with the concealing of this melancholy
event for fome days, gave occafion to many ftrange reports,
which, on no better foundation than vulgar tradition, have
found a place in fome otherwife efteemed hiftories.

THIS monarch is juftly and univerfally acknowleged to *His cha-*
have been, in all refpects, one of the greateft princes of this *racter.*
age. He was, though moft confpicuous for his military exploits, one of the mildeft and moft courteous princes that ever
fat on a throne; and it was this that gained him, almoft at
firft fight, the efteem and affection of all the *Caftilian* nobility, who had the profperity of their country at heart, and
were not bent upon raifing fortunes by fcandalous intrigues,
or bafe complacencies at the court of queen *Urraca*. He
was very religious, according to the notions of that age in
which he lived, and very liberal to the clergy, which renders
very improbable what the *Caftilian* writers fay of his plundering the churches during the war in that country. He added

[s] ROD. TOLET. de reb. Hifpan.   LUCÆ Tudenfis Chron.
HIERON. BLANCÆ Arragonenf. Rerum Comment. Indices Rerum
ab Arragoniæ regibus Geftarum.   ABARCA.   MARIANA.   FER.
MAYERNE TURQUET.   [t] ROD. SANTII Hift. Hifpan. LUC.
Tudenfis Chron.   ZURIT.

to his hereditary kingdom of *Arragon, Saragoſſa, Tudela, Tarrazona, Calatayud, Daroca,* and a great extent of country on the ſouth ſide of the *Ebro*; ſo that he may, with propriety, be ſtiled the founder of the modern kingdom of *Arragon,* ſince he rendered it by his victories, and left it at his death, two thirds larger than when it deſcended to him. Some ancient writers ſay, that the battle of *Fraga* was the twenty-ninth he had fought againſt the *Moors,* to whom he was an implacable and terrible enemy [u]. It is certain that this monarch left his dominions in very great confuſion; but, tho' it is generally reported, *Mariana* makes no ſcruple of recording it as a fact out of diſpute, that, by a will made at the ſiege of *Bayonne,* he diſpoſed of all his territories to the knights templars, the knights of St. *John,* and the guardians of the holy ſepulchre at *Jeruſalem* [w]. Yet the ſtory has ſuch an air of fable, that it has been juſtly rejected by the beſt judges of hiſtory, as being to the full as improbable as the tale of his going privately to *Jeruſalem,* after the battle of *Fraga,* and performing great exploits againſt the Infidels in the *Holy Land.*

Separation between the kingdoms of Arragon *and* Navarre.

IT is however certain, that, whatever will he made, or was made for him (ſince forgery was not unknown in thoſe times) his ſubjects took not the leaſt notice of it; but as ſoon as they were recovered a little from that conſternation into which they were thrown by the irruption of the Infidels after their late victory, they began to conſider how to repair this loſs, by ſetting a new prince upon the throne. It is generally agreed, that a meeting for this purpoſe was held at *Borja,* on the frontiers of both kingdoms, for the electing a king of *Arragon* and *Navarre;* where diſagreeing, the former adjourned to *Hueſca,* and the latter to *Pampeluna.* But, all circumſtances ſtrictly weighed, it ſeems at leaſt as probable, that Don *Ramiro,* brother to the two laſt kings, and who was a monk in the monaſtery of St. *Pons de Tomiers,* in the dioceſe of *Narbonne,* was proclaimed king at *Hueſca;* and that the people of *Navarre* took this opportunity of ſhaking off a yoke which they had born but very impatiently, and ſetting up Don *Garcia Ramirez,* who was a direct deſcendant from their ancient kings. By this means theſe monarchies were again ſeparated; and this with circumſtances which excited great heart-burning and jealouſy between the two nations.

Don Ra-miro, bro-

AT the time of his acceſſion to the throne, it is very clear that Don *Ramiro* the ſecond had been forty-one years a

---

[u] Chron. var. antiq. ZURIT. ABARÇA, FER.   [w] Hiſtoria general de Eſpana, lib. x.

monk:

monk [x] : some writers affert, that he had been abbot of *Sa-* *ther to the* *bagun*, afterwards bifhop of *Burgos*, then of *Pampeluna*, and *late king,* at this time of *Balbaftro*; but of this there are no clear *afcends the* proofs [y]. He was no fooner feated on the throne, than it was *throne of* judged expedient that he fhould have a wife, and application Arragon. for this purpofe was likewife made to *Anacletus*, who then affumed the title of pope at *Avignon*; and, in virtue of a difpenfation from him, the king efpoufed Donna *Ines*, or *Agnes*, fifter to *William*, duke of *Aquitaine*, who, it appears, from the *French* hiftorians, was a widow [z]. It is fomewhat *Don* Alon- doubtful whether, before or after the celebration of this mar- *fo, king* riage, Don *Alonfo*, king of *Caftile*, entered the frontiers of *of* Caftile, *Arragon*, and advanced towards *Saragoffa*. Some authors *enters* Ar- fay, that Don *Ramiro* was fo much amazed at the approach ragon *as a* of a force which it was not at all in his power to refift, that *friend, and* he retired immediately into the impenetrable mountains and *leaves a* forefts of *Sobralva*; but the hiftorians of *Caftile*, who lived *garrifon in* neareft thefe times, affirm quite the contrary; and their ac- Saragoffa. count deferves the more credit, as it is perfectly natural and probable. They fay, that Don *Alonfo* declared, that he did not enter *Arragon* as an enemy, or as forming any pretenfions to the crown; but that, on the contrary, refpecting the memory of their late king, whom he had been formerly accuftomed to ftile father, he came to protect them againft the *Moors*, and to prevent their making any lafting advantage of their late good fortune; which act of friendfhip was very kindly taken, and his offer, fo generoufly made, very thankfully accepted [a]. Upon which Don *Alonfo* put a ftrong garrifon into the city of *Saragoffa*, and then retired. At firft fight, this may feem to have been no more than a political feint to get poffeffion of fo confiderable a place; but, if we confider the fituation things were in, the danger to which the kingdom was expofed from the confequences of domeftic troubles, and the efforts of a foreign enemy, and that, as foon as the people of *Arragon* were in a condition to keep and defend it, *Saragoffa* was again put into their hands, we fhall fee plainly that Don *Alonfo* of *Caftile* acted like a wife and great prince, and upon motives much more noble than thofe of a conqueror. It did him great honour to have fuccoured and protected a neighbouring prince, which was alfo his intereft, for the fake of his own do-

[x] HIERON. BLANCÆ Arragonenf. Rerum Comment. ZURITA. ABARCA. [y] Chron. var. antiq. [z] P. DANIEL Hiftoire de France. HIERON. BLANCÆ. ROD. TOLET. ZURITA. [a] ROD. TOL. de reb. Hifpan. LUC. Tudenf. Chron. ABARCA. FERRERAS.

minions;

minions ; and it reflected no difcredit on Don *Ramiro*, that he was very grateful for fo high a favour, and received his benefactor with all poffible marks of deference and efteem. This was certainly a more prudent and a more royal manner of proceeding than hiding himfelf in woods and caverns, and abandoning his country and his fubjects to the mercy of a ftranger, who, if this had been his conduct, would probably not have treated him fo well [b].

THE diftafte which had arifen between the two nations, rofe in a fhort time fo high, that it was very near producing a rupture between the crowns of *Arragon* and *Navarre*, tho' againft all the rules of policy, and without any juft caufe on either fide ; but, by the interpofition of the prelates, this difference was compromifed, the kings were each of them to hold their refpective dominions, to which Don *Ramiro* confented, becaufe he knew himfelf unable to conquer *Navarre*; and, on the other hand, Don *Garcia* was willing to do homage to Don *Ramiro*, as well on account of his being the brother of his late fovereign and much his fuperior in age, as becaufe he was in hopes, on his demife without children, he might fucceed him in the throne [c]. They were both difap-

A. D. 1135.

pointed in their views, for this was far from producing a fettled peace ; and, towards the end of this year, or the beginning of the next, the queen of *Arragon* was delivered of a daughter, who was ftiled the Infanta *Petronilla* [d]. We have feen that, notwithftanding his claim of right, the acceffion of Don *Ramiro* to the crown of *Arragon* was, in a great meafure, owing to the affection of his people ; but, as there is nothing more common than for them to grow quickly fick of their own choice, fo it feems Don *Ramiro* very fpeedily experienced the truth of this obfervation. Some very ancient chronicles report, with circumftances that render it probable this report was not without fome foundation, that he took a very fingular method of recovering the refpect due to his authority. In order to this, he directed an affembly of the ftates at *Huefca*, where he fuddenly feized and put to death the moft turbulent of the nobility [e]. It is added, according to the cuftom of this age, that having fent to the abbot of St. *Pons de Tomiers* for his advice, he carried his meffengers into the garden of the convent, and with a fcymitar cut off the

The king of Arragon caufes fome of his feditious nobles to be put to death.

---

[b] MARIANA Hiftoria general de Efpana, lib. x. FERRERAS. MAYERNE TURQUET.   [c] Indices Rerum ab Arragoniæ regibus Geftarum. HIERON. BLANCÆ. ROD. TOL. de reb. Hifpan.   [d] LUC. Tudenf. Chron. ZURITA. ABARCA. [e] Chron. var. antiq.

tops of the higheft plants, bidding them report to the king
what they had feen him do, from whence Don *Ramiro* took
the hint, as indeed it might be eafily taken, of this rigorous
proceeding. As this circumftance feems to have been invented, or rather copied, for the amufement of the great
vulgar, fo there was another contrived for the amufement of
groffer underftandings: the king is faid to have given out before this affembly, that he would caufe a bell to be made, the
found of which fhould be heard throughout his dominions:
in order to keep his word, he caufed the heads of fifteen of
the moft feditious to be nailed round the bottom of a wooden
bell frame, and, having fhewn this fhocking fight to their
neareft relations, told them this was the bell he meant, and
that he would toll it at their expence, if they had not wit
enough to change their conduct from this example. As this
tradition of the bell of *Huefca* fubfifts to this hour, and as
fome very ancient writers report, not only the fact of the
king's putting the chief of the nobility to death, but mention
alfo their names, and affure us, that there were five of the
noble family of *Luna*, though it is eafy to conceive the
circumftances fabulous, it is very hard to believe the whole a
fiction [f].

IT is, however, a glaring miftake that fome have committed,
who have reported that this bold action had its effect; and
that, as before no prince could be more contemned, fo afterwards none was ever better obeyed. The truth, however,
is directly the reverfe; for either this or fome other act of that
unfortunate prince, or the whole ftrain of his adminiftration,
loft him the affections of his people to fuch a degree, that he
took a fudden, and, in his fituation, a wife refolution of re-
figning the government, which, in all probability, he heartily
repented he had ever undertaken. The method he took in
doing this was fo proper and fo prudent, that we may reafonably conclude it was the effects of mature deliberation.

When he had digefted his defign in his own mind, he called
an affembly of the ftates at *Balbaftro*, where, on the 11th of
Auguft, he acquainted them with the refolution he had taken
of giving his daughter and heirefs *Petronilla*, in marriage to
Don *Raymond*, count of *Barcelona*, in cafe fhe fhould live to
an age fit to become his wife; that in cafe of her deceafe before that time, it was his defire that he fhould enjoy the kingdom; and that, for the prefent, as he was defirous of leading
a life of repofe, he would put the adminiftration into his
hands, with the title of count or prince, which, with the

1137.
He refigns
the admi-
niftration
to Don
Raymond,
count of
Barcelona,
and retires
to a con-
vent.

[f] ZURITA. ABARCA. FER. MAYERNE TURQUET.

confent

consent of that assembly, he did, and then retired to *Huesca*, where he lived privately with the clergy belonging to the church of St. *Peter*, for the space of ten years (within five days), without ever shewing the least inclination to recover that diadem which he had so willingly quitted ᵍ. Those therefore who have described this prince as a weak or wicked man, seem not to have considered his history attentively. He was a king but three years, and could not in that short space do much to the prejudice of his subjects. He found that a palace was no fit habitation for one who had spent forty years in a convent; a weak man would hardly have found this out. He executed his purpose, which required no small degree of fortitude; and he knew how to set a just value on that quiet, for the sake of which he resigned a crown. If from these circumstances, which is all that we know of his conduct, they can collect that he was either wicked or weak, they must have more penetration than we pretend to. However, leaving this to the reader's reflection, we shall proceed with our history.

Rupture between Don Raymond and the king of Navarre.

Don *Raymond*, upon whom the king devolved his whole authority, with the consent of his people, assumed the title of prince of *Arragon* ʰ, preserving also that of count of *Barcelona*, which was his own title. As the emperor, Don *Alonso* of *Castile*, had married his sister, and as, in his own right, he possessed dominions little if at all inferior to those of *Arragon*, it does not appear, that, either with regard to himself or his subjects, the old king could have made a better choice. But, from the moment he assumed the government, he had Don *Garcia Ramirez*, king of *Navarre*, for his determined enemy; it may be on account of his having promised himself the good fortune at which Don *Raymond* was arrived. However that may be, their disputes quickly produced a rupture, in consequence of which, the king of *Arragon* entered into a league with Don *Alonso* of *Castile*, and the king of *Navarre* with Don *Alonso* of *Portugal* ⁱ. The emperor, to shew his affection for his brother-in-law, and to bring the war to as speedy an issue as possible, made an irruption into *Navarre*, and penetrated as far as *Pampeluna*, which he invested. This might possibly have had its intended effect, if in the mean time Don *Garcia* of *Navarre* had not defeated the prince of *Arragon* on the frontiers, with considerable loss, which constrained the

---

ᵍ Indices Rerum ab Arragoniæ regibus Gestarum. Hieron. Blancæ Arragonens. Rerum Comment. Rod. Tol. de reb. Hispan. Luc. Tuden. Chron. Abarca. Mariana. Fer. Mayerne Turquet. ʰ Rod. Santii Hist. Hispan. P. Moret. Zurita. ⁱ Luc. Tuden. Chron.

emperor

emperor to raife the fiege, in order to march to Don *Ray-mond's* affiftance [k]. Before the close of the year, thefe two princes concluded a treaty, and Don *Raymond* was left to take what care he could of himfelf; he had already a war with *Navarre,* and another with the *Moors,* upon his hands, when another crofs accident happened, which gave him a good deal of trouble. Certain agents from the knights templars came into *Arragon* to claim the benefit of the late Don *Alonfo's* teftament, which the prince of *Arragon,* by his prudence and dexterity, converted to his own advantage. He told them that fuch of the knights templars as were willing to repair thither fhould be amply provided for; and, as a proof that he meant to make good his promife, he gave them the town of *Calatayud,* where they erected the church of the holy fepulchre. This agreement was ratified by the pope and the patriarch of *Jerufalem* [l]. Some time after, he held an affembly of the ftates at *Giron,* where, with the confent of the nobles and prelates, he made a ceffion to thofe knights of fix ftrong caftles, with large revenues, upon condition that they fhould defend his frontier againft the Infidels in his wars, with whom he was very fuccefsful; but while he was thus employed, the king of *Navarre* took from him *Tarrazona* and fome other places of lefs importance [m].

At the requeft of the prince Don *Raymond,* the emperor once more interpofed with the king of *Navarre;* and finding that monarch more ftubborn than he expected, had recourfe to arms; but he being a widower, and propofing to marry the emperor's natural daughter, that offer was accepted, and a truce only concluded between the crowns of *Arragon* and *Navarre* [n]. This was indeed a meafure abfolutely requifite, fince Don *Raymond Berenger,* count of *Provence,* brother to the prince of *Arragon,* had been traiteroufly killed in his own dominions, it was requifite for the prince Don *Raymond* to go thither to preferve the fucceffion to his nephew, which he happily performed [o]. The truce was prolonged to another year, on account of the prince of *Arragon's* affifting the emperor in the famous fiege of *Almeria,* at which he was prefent, and likewife furnifhed a confiderable naval force [p]. On the 6th of *Auguft,* this year, died Don *Ramiro* the fecond [q], by

[k] Hieron. Blancæ Arragonenf. Rerum Comment. Zurit. Rod. Tolet. de reb. Hifpan. [l] Chron. var. antiq. [m] Indices Rerum ab Arragoniæ Regibus Geftarum. [n] Zurit. Abarca. [o] Chron. var. antiq. [p] Lucæ Tudenfis Chron. Mariana. Fer. [q] Zurita. Hieron. Blancæ. Mayerne Turquet.

which

which his daughter, who was yet a child, became queen in her own right. In the next, the prince Don *Raymond* executed the scheme he had formed at the siege of *Almeria*, for depriving the *Mohammedans* of the strong city and convenient port of *Tortosa*, in order to which he had demanded the assistance of the count of *Montpellier*, the republic of *Genoa*, and other maritime powers; which great design he so happily conducted, that on the last day of the year he became master of the place, and very honourably fulfilled the promises he had made to all his allies, giving the *Genoese* and the count of *Montpellier* each a third part of the revenues of the place, and reserving no more to himself[r]. The next year he pushed the war against the *Moors* with such success, that he made himself master of *Fraga* and of *Lérida*, to which last city he restored the episcopal see that had been placed at *Roda*, then in *Balbastro*, while this place remained in the hands of the Infidels; and soon after, by a pragmatic sanction, secured the sees in his dominions from being impoverished·by himself or successors[s].

Don Raymond reduces Tortosa, and obtains several other advantages over the Moors.

1149.

As Donna *Petronilla*, heiress of *Arragon*, was now in her fifteenth year, Don *Raymond*, pursuant to the will of her father, married her with great solemnity at *Lerida*[t], in the presence of the principal nobility and prelates of *Arragon* and *Catalonia*: at the same time he resettled the episcopal see at *Tortosa*, and marked out the ancient boundaries of its diocese[u]. On occasion of the emperor's nuptials, and those of Don *Sancho*, king of *Navarre*, the prince of *Arragon* went to *Soria*, and concluded a truce with that monarch upon his marriage with his niece[w]. This gave him an opportunity of making an irruption into the territory of the *Moors*, where he took several places, and amongst the rest the castle of *Mirabet*, by assault, which he afterwards put into the hands of the knights templars[x]. He also took the *Moorish* king of *Valentia* and *Murcia* under his protection. ·When the truce was expired, which he had made with the king of *Navarre*, he attacked that kingdom with some degree of success; and having concluded an alliance with the emperor, in virtue of which his young son Don *Alonso*, who was yet in his cradle, was to marry the Infanta Donna *Sancha* of *Castile*, he prevailed upon that prince to join with him once more against *Navarre*; the

Espouses Donna Petronilla, daughter to the late king.

1151.

1153.

[r] Rod. Tolet. de reb. Hispan. Indices Rerum ab Arragoniæ regibus Gestarum. Mariana. Fer. [s] Hieron. Blancæ Arragonens. Rerum Comment. Zurita. Abarca. Fer, [t] Ron. Tol. de reb. Hispan. [u] Luc. Tudens. Chron. [w] Zurita. [x] Rod. Tol. Hist. Arabum.

4

hopes,

hopes, however, which he had from thence, were speedily dissipated by the death of that monarchy. This event produced another, which the prince of *Arragon* did not at all expect. Don *Sancho*, king of *Navarre*, had a numerous *Concludes* army in the field, with which he had already recovered the *a solid* valley of *Rancal*, which Don *Raymond* had taken from *peace with* him; but, on a sudden changing his measures, he repre- *the king of* sented to the prince of *Arragon* the folly of their proceed- Navarre. ings, offered to bury in oblivion all former grudges, and to 1157. restore the city of *Tarrazona*, in order to obtain a solid and lasting peace, to which, as it was all he ever sought, Don *Raymond* readily agreed: and thus this war, which with little intermission had lasted from the separation of the two crowns, was happily concluded to their mutual satisfaction [z].

In a short time after the death of the emperor, his son Don *Sancho*, king of *Castile*, entered into a close alliance with the prince of *Arragon*, his uncle, in which, however, the homage was reserved to the crown of *Castile*, which it is fit we should explain [a]. It is certain that it did not regard the 1158. ancient kingdom of *Arragon*, which never had any dependance upon *Castile*, but arose from that transaction which we have before mentioned of the emperor's taking the city of *Saragossa*, and the country on the south side of the *Ebra*, into his protection; for which, according to the custom of that age, he thought fit to exact homage. We shall hereafter have occasion to shew when and how this homage was remitted.

As Don *Raymond* had considerable dominions in *France*, *Interview* which made it requisite for him to be on good terms with *between* *Henry* the second of *England*, who, in right of his wife, *the kings* was become duke of *Aquitaine*, he accepted an invitation *of Arra-* given him by that monarch, which produced an interview *gon and* at the castle of *Blaye*; and, in consequence of that, a *England,* strict alliance between the two princes: amongst other *at the* things, it was agreed, that the king's younger son *Richard*, *castle of* who, by the death of his elder brother *Henry*, became af- Blaye. terwards his successor, should espouse Donna *Berengara*, 1159. daughter to count *Raymond*, and should be declared duke

[y] Chron. Adefons Imperat. FERRERAS. [z] Indices Rerum ab Aragoniæ regibus Gestarum. HIERON. BLANCÆ Arragonenf. Rerum Commentarii. P. MORET Investigaciones Historicas de las antiquitades del Reyno de Navarre. [a] RODERIC TOLETAN de reb. Hispan. LUCÆ Tudensis Chron. ABARCA.

of

of *Aquitaine* [b]. A war breaking out the next year between the king of *England*, as duke of *Aquitaine*, and *Raymond*, count of *Thouloufe*, the prince of *Arragon* went, in perfon, at the head of a confiderable body of troops to the affiftance of his allies. The year following he made another campaign in fupport of his nephew *Raymond*, count of *Provence*; and, upon this occafion, he had an interview with the emperor *Frederic*, with whom he entered into a clofe alliance [c]. That monarch having formed a defign of depofing pope *Alexander* the third, paffed into *Italy* for that purpofe, and held a kind of congrefs at *Turin*, to which repaired all the princes of his party. Amongft the reft, Don *Raymond*, prince of *Arragon*, intending to be prefent, made a journey into *Italy*, but falling fick upon the road, he was carried to a place called *Dalmace*, not far from *Turin*, where he breathed his laft, *Auguft* the fifteenth, one thoufand one hundred and fixty-two. His body was carried back into *Spain*, and buried with his anceftors, in the convent of the *Benedictines*, at *Ripol* [d].

Dies in Piedmont. 1162.

As foon as the funeral honours to her hufband were over, the queen Donna *Petronilla* affembled the ftates at *Huefca*, and there, agreeable to the declaration of the prince Don *Raymond* upon his death bed, fhe affigned to their eldeft fon the kingdom of *Arragon*, and the county of *Barcelona*; to their fecond fon Don *Pedro* fhe gave the county of *Cerdagne*, and all that he poffeffed befides in *France*, fubftituting his younger brother Don *Sancho* to that fucceffion, in cafe he fhould die without heirs male [e]. She referved to herfelf the tutelage of her eldeft fon, and the government of the kingdom of *Arragon*: fhe committed the adminiftration of *Catalonia* to Don *Raymond Berengera*, count of *Provence*; and recommended her two younger fons to the protection of king *Henry* the fecond of *England*: at the fame time fhe renewed the treaty with Don *Sancho* king of *Navarre* [f]. The peace of *Arragon*, notwithftanding all thefe precautions, was quickly interrupted, by the appearance of an impoftor,

An impoftor pretends to be Don Alonfo who died after the battle of Fraga.

[b] Rod. Tolet. de reb. Hifpan. Lucæ Tudenfis Chron. [c] Rod. Toletan de reb. Hifpan. Zurita. Hieron. Blancæ. Fer. [d] Rod. Santii Hift. Hifpan. Indices Rerum ab Arragoniæ regibus Geftarum. Abarca. [e] Hieron. Blancæ Arragonenf. Rerum Commentarii. Rod. Tol. de reb. Hifpan. Mariana. Mayerne Turquet. [f] Indices Rerum ab Arragoniæ regibus Geftarum. Luc. Tuden. Chron. Abarca.

who

who took upon him the name of the king Don *Alonso*, pretending, that, after the battle of *Fraga*, he had passed over to *Syria*, had served in the *Holy Land* against the Infidels, and was now returned to govern his own dominions. Some resemblance of person, a steady assurance, and other circumstances, enabled him to gain some credit with the vulgar; but the queen, causing him to be apprehended at *Saragossa*, put him publicly to death, and thereby restored the peace of the kingdom g. One sees nothing of weakness or folly in the conduct of this princess, whom it is certain that the historians of *Arragon* treat with great respect and esteem; notwithstanding which, *Mariana* will have it, that, through her want of capacity to administer the government, a resolution was taken to place her son upon the throne. It is certain that such a resolution was taken; but other writers affirm, that it was thro' the queen's free choice, who was desirous of seeing her son acknowleged and fixed on the throne of *Arragon* in her life-time h.

It was with this view that she caused an assembly of the states to be held at *Barcelona*, where, on the fourteenth of *June*, she made a free resignation in favour of the prince her son, whom she carried afterwards, for the same purpose, to *Saragossa*; upon which occasion public proclamation was made by the states, that such lords as held either castles or fortresses from the crown, should immediately resign their governments into the hands of the king, on pain of being deprived of their dignities, having their estates confiscated, and their persons banished: and all persons were forbid to violate the treaties subsisting with neighbouring princes, under pain of death, and the confiscation of their estates i. It may not be amiss to observe here, that, according to most historians, this young prince was baptized by, and during his father's lifetime bore, the name of *Raymond*, which he now changed for that of *Alonso*, as more acceptable to the people of *Arragon* k. It is likewise probable, that his sister, whom most of the historians call Donna *Dulcia*, was likewise called *Berengara*; and, besides her, it will appear that he had another sister, whose name was

The queen Petronilla resigns the government in favour of her eldest son Don Alonso.

g HIERON. BLANCÆ. ZURITA. P. MORET.   h RODERIC TOLETAN de reb. Hispan. Historia general de España, lib. x. ABARCA. Arragonensium Rerum Commentarii.   i HIERONYMI BLANCÆ Indices Rerum ab Arragoniæ regibus Gestarum. FER.   k ZURITA. ABARCA. MARIANA.

Donna

Donna *Leonora*[1].   We may fee, from their want of accuracy in matters of this nature, that the ancient memoirs of *Arragon* were very fhort and imperfect; fo that much of thofe ample hiftories that are now extant, muft have been fupplied from conjecture, and from comparifon with other *Spanifh* hiftories.

Subject of the next section.   WE have now completed this fection, and have therein traced thofe acceffions, by which, from a very flender beginning, the realm of *Arragon* grew to be what it now is. The reader likewife fees how, in virtue of the marriage between the count of *Barcelona* and the heirefs of this monarchy, the noble country of *Catalonia* was annexed to this crown; and, from the acceffion of power arifing from thence, *Abenlope*, the *Moorifh* prince of *Valentia*, came to feek the protection, and to own himfelf the vaffal, of the prince of *Arragon*, which afforded the monarchs of *Arragon* the firft pretenfions to that fruitful kingdom. The making thefe matters plain, fo that the original, the augmentation, and the conjunction of ftates, may be truly known, and clearly underftood, is one principal point of Univerfal Hiftory. It is therefore, in the prefent cafe, to render that as complete as poffible, we propofe, in the next fection, to give a fuccinct hiftory of the principality of *Catalonia*; or, which will be found to amount to the fame thing, to trace out the fucceffion of the counts of *Barcelona*, and their gradual acquifitions of power and territory, by which it will be rendered evident what a vaft advantage enfued to the crown of *Arragon*, from the annexing of this maritime province to its dominions, which, in procefs of time, led to far greater things, and enabled thefe monarchs to make the figure they did; whereas if they had continued to be circumfcribed within the bounds of their inland territories, they could have been very little known to the reft of *Europe*.

---

[1] ROD. TOLET. de reb. Hifpan. MARIANA. FER. MAYERNE TURQUET.

SECT. IX.

The History of the County of Barcelona, *and the County of* Catalonia, *from the Time of the erecting of that County, at the Beginning of the Ninth Century, to its Conjunction with the Realm of* Arragon, *by the Marriage of the Count Don* Raymond *the Fifth with the Infanta Donna* Petronilla, *Heiress of that Kingdom, the Children of which Marriage enjoyed both Sovereignties.*

THE descriptions in this part of our work are suited to the *Descripti-* history, and are only inserted to render it intelligible. *on of the* As for example; The country of *Catalonia,* of which we are *old county* going to speak, is precisely that which the count Don *Ray-* *of Catalo-* mond the fifth annexed to the kingdom of *Arragon,* which *nia.* was not only far greater than the antient county of *Barcelona,* the original patrimony of his anceftors, but also considerably more extensive than the principality of *Catalonia,* as it now stands ; comprehending in it, besides *Catalonia,* or, as the *Spaniards* always write it, *Cataluna,* the countries of *Rouf-* *fillon* and *Cerdana,* or *Cerdagna,* best part of which are now in the hands of the *French* [a]. This country, as it then ftood, had *Languedoc* on the north, the *Pyrenees,* the country of *Ri-* *bagorca,* and the kingdom of *Arragon,* on the west, a corner of the same kingdom, and a part of that of *Valentia,* to the south, with the *Medditerranean* on the east, ftretching about seventy leagues from south to north, and, where broadest, not much less from west to east : the air is, generally speaking, pure and wholsome ; the climate perfectly pleasant, and not so very hot in the middle of summer as in most other provinces in *Spain.* The greatest part of this country is mountainous ; but there are several large and beautiful plains, and more especially those of *Urgel, Cerdagna, Vic Gironne, Tara-* *gona,* and *Panades.* The mountains themselves are far from being barren, fince they are every-where covered with forests of excellent timber, are not deftitute of fruit trees, and abound with odoriferous fhrubs and medicinal herbs. There are few countries better watered, though none of its rivers are very large. It is plentifully furnifhed with edible roots, wine fruit, and corn, as also flax and hemp. There are in it many

---

[a] CELLAR. Geogr. Antiq. lib. i, Geogr. Moderne, par Du Bois, part i. c. 3.

inexhauftible quarries of marble of all forts, fuch as alabafter, &c. and as to ftones of higher value, jafper, amethifts, *lapis Lazuli*, and the *Hematites*, or blood ftone, are found here in confiderable quantities [b]. Heretofore, it is faid, there were mines of gold and filver; and of the former of thefe precious metals, there are ftill fome grains found in the fand of the *Segro*, and fome other rivers; but there are ftill mines of tin, lead, iron, allom, vitriol, and falt; and on the coaft, which is near ninety leagues in extent, there is a very valuable coral fifhery [c].

As to the antient inhabitants of this province, they were the *Caftellani*, *Auxitani*, *Indigites*, *Cofitani*, with part of the *Ibercones* and *Jaccitani* [d]. Some have conceived that it derived its name from the firft of thefe people [e]; others again think it more probable [f], that it derived its name from the *Catelauni*, an antient people in *Gaul*; but the moft probable account of the matter is this: upon the decline of the *Roman* empire, the *Alani* feized the beft part of this province, of which they were, in fome meafure, difpoffeffed by the *Goths*; and at length mixing together and becoming one people, they came to be called *Gothalani*, and their country *Gothalonia*, which, by degrees, was foftened into *Catalonia* [g]. The *Moors* pufhed their conquefts hither in the beginning of the eighth century, but they had at beft but an unquiet poffeffion; and the potent emperor *Charlemagne* attacked them frequently, and with fo much vigour, that the *Moorifh* governors in moft of the confiderable places were content to acknowlege themfelves his vaffals [h]. This, however, as it arofe from conftraint, feldom lafted longer than there was a force at hand to keep them within bounds; and in their repeated revolts they were guilty of fuch exceffes, that at length *Lewis the Mild* determined to make an abfolute conqueft, and to leave therein fuch a competent force as might effectually fecure this frontier againft the Infidels [i].

At the opening of the ninth century, the *Moors*, who were in poffeffion of *Barcelona*, were under the government of *Zade*, who had more than once abufed the clemency of *Charlemagne*, and at length fo irritated, by his perfidious behaviour, *Lewis* king of *Aquitaine*, fon of that conqueror, that he gave orders to his generals to inveft *Barcelona*, and not to rife from before it

[b] Delices de l'Efpagne, par Don Juan Alvarez de Colemenar. [c] Dictionaire de Commerce, tom. ii. [d] Strab. Geogr. lib. iii. Plin. Nat. Hift. lib. ili. [e] Heylin's Cofmography, l. i. [f] Cellar. Geogr. Antiq. l. i. [g] Delices de l'Efpagne, par Don Juan Alvarez de Colemenar. [h] Rod. Tol. de reb. Hifpan. [i] Vit. Ludovic. Annal Rivipul.

till

till they had put *Zade* into his hands.   The *Moor*, comprehending his danger, made a moſt obſtinate reſiſtance, ſo that
the ſiege laſted many months; at length, finding it impoſſible to
preſerve the city any longer, and that it was in vain to expect
any relief, he determined, or rather was compelled by the inhabitants, to go to the Chriſtian camp, and implore the emperor's mercy ; where he no ſooner arrived, than he was arreſted, and ſent priſoner to *Charlemagne*, who condemned him
to perpetual exile [k]. The people of *Barcelona* gaining nothing
by this expedient, continued to hold out for ſix weeks longer,
when the king of *Aquitaine*, having joined his army, took the
command of the ſiege, to whom they made a propoſal, that, if
he would permit them to march out, and retire whither they
pleaſed, they would ſurrender the place: to this propoſal having
given his conſent, he made his public entry into *Barcelona*,
where he formed a project of extending the bounds of his
father's empire as far as the *Ebro* ; but, being recalled before he could put this deſign in execution, he appointed
Bera count of *Barcelona*, and inſtructed him in the meaſures neceſſary to be taken for the perfecting his plan [l].

right margin: Barcelona *beſieged and taken by Lewis king of Aquitaine.* 801.

THIS count *Bera* held his government about eighteen
years, and in the beginning acted with great vigour and ſucceſs againſt the *Moors*, which encouraged the governors of
Hueſca and *Saragoſſa* to throw off the yoke of *Albacan* king
of *Cordova*, and to put themſelves under the protection of
Charlemagne, which, however, did not ſcreen them from the
reſentment of their old maſter [m]. After the death of *Charlemagne*, the emperor *Lewis* committed his conqueſts in *Spain*
to the care of his ſon *Lothaire* ; and finding that a peace with
the *Moors* was more prejudicial than war, broke it ; ſoon after
which count *Bera* was recalled, upon a diſcovery that, in imitation of the *Mooriſh* governors, he was carrying on ſecret in-
tigues to render himſelf independent [n]. *Sanila*, a conſiderable
officer under him, who brought this charge againſt him, offered, according to the cuſtom of thoſe times, to make it good
by combat. They fought accordingly on horſeback ; and *Bera*, being overcome, forfeited his life, according to the laws
then in force: but the emperor, naturally compaſſionate,
commuted his puniſhment, and baniſhed him to *Roan* during
his life [o].

right margin: *Bera firſt count of* Barcelona *baniſhed for life to* Roan. 820.

[k]. Chron. Barcinon.   Rod. Tol. *de* reb. Hiſpan.   [l] Vit.
Ludovic.   Chron. Barcinon.   [m] Vit. Ludovic. Annal Rivipul.   [n] Vit. Ludovic.   [o] Hiſtoire de Languedoc,
lib. ix.

He was succeeded in his government by count *Bernard*, son to *William* duke of *Thoulouse*, who carried on the war against the Infidels with great vigour, which raised him so high in his master's favour, that he made him his lord high chamberlain, and, as some say, his prime minister [P]. This had a bad effect ; for he began, immediately after, to oppress the clergy in his government, and had a great hand in the disturbances which broke out in the emperor's family, who thereupon deprived him of his dignities [q]. In resentment of this he induced the people of *Burgundy* to revolt in favour of *Pepin*, and soon after seized *Thoulouse*, depending on the protection of *Pepin*, who, by his advice, declared himself soon after king of *Aquitaine* [r]. On the death, however, of the emperor *Lewis*, he reconciled himself to his successor *Charles the Bald* ; but, as he still continued his intrigues, that monarch became jealous of him, and summoned him to repair to an assembly of the states, which was held in the neighbourhood of *Thoulouse*. The count, finding he had not strength enough to execute his design, went boldly thither, in hopes of pacifying that monarch by a feigned submission. But, when he came into his presence, and fell upon his knees to do him homage, the emperor, as he attempted to rise, caught hold of him with his left hand, and, with his right, drawing a dagger out of his bosom, stabbed him to the heart [s]. His son *William* attempted to make some disturbances, and entered, according to his father's example, into a close correspondence with the *Moors* [t].

ALEDRAN was declared count of *Barcelona* by the emperor, and kept possession of it for four years [u] ; at the end of which space *William*, by the help of his intrigues, formed a strong party there ; and, by the assistance of *Abderaman*, king of *Cordova*, made himself master of the place; and of a great part of *Catalonia*, his competitor making his escape with some difficulty [w]. As for count *William*, having procured a strong reinforcement of *Moors*, he undertook the conquest of all that the *French* possessed in those parts, and was at first so fortunate as to seize the counts *Ademare* and *Isembard*, whom he carried prisoners to *Barcelona*, and afterwards, with a potent army, besieged *Gironne* ; but miscarrying in

A. D.
828.

Bernard
the second
count,
stabbed
with a
dagger by
the empe-
ror Charles
the Bald.
844.

848.

[P] PETR. DE MARCA. Marca Hispanica five limes Hispanicus, i. e. Zeographica & Historica Descriptio Catalaunicæ ; a STEPH. BALUZIO, edita. Paris, 1688, fol. Vitæ Ludovic. [q] Chron. var. antiq. Vitæ Ludovic. [r] Histoire de Languedoc. [s] Annal S. Bertin. [t] Chron. var. antiq. [u] Marca Hispanica. [w] Annal S. Bertin.

this enterprize, and, returning to *Barcelona*, the two counts *His son* his prisoners found means to excite a tumult, in which *His son* count *William* was killed, and the place thereupon returned to William, the obedience of the emperor [x]. Things, however, were so *the third* ill managed, and so little care was taken of so important a *count, slain* place, that, two years after, it was taken and plundered by the *in a tu-* famous *Moorish* general *Musa*, governor of *Sarogossa*, who *mult. 850.* might have kept it, if he had not, at that time, meditated a revolt, which induced him to return into his own government [y]. After this we find one *Sunifred* there, with the title of viscount, which implies that he was the deputy of another lord, to whom the government was committed, and who, very probably, was the person we find next mentioned in history with the title of count of *Barcelona* [z].

THIS person was *Hunfrid*, or *Wifrid*, who, it is said, had also the title of marquis of *Gotia*, and duke of *Septimania*; which implies, that, besides *Barcelona*, he was intrusted with the administration of all that belonged to the empire in these parts; so that a considerable district in the southern provinces of *France*, with part of *Navarre*, *Arragon*, and *Catalonia*, were under his jurisdiction [a]: yet, it seems, he was not satisfied, because king *Charles*, surnamed *the Bald*, had bestowed *Thoulouse*, and the places adjacent, upon count *Raymond*, and of which, notwithstanding, he despoiled him, upon *863.* pretence that they belonged to his government. This so provoked the king, that he removed *Wifrid* from his employment, in the succeeding year, or at least divided this large government into two, restraining him to the countries on the other side of the *Alps*; which, it seems, he considered as a great injustice [b]. At this time one count *Solomon* was intrusted with *Cerdagna*, but under the orders of *Wifrid*. This count, *Count Wi-* whether prompted by duty or resentment is not very clear, *frid mur-* accused him of *Barcelona* of certain crimes, which occasioned *dered by* his being summoned to *Narbonne*; where, being insulted in a *the popu-* tumult, and a man having had the boldness to pull him by *lace of* the beard, he, in the first transport of his choler, killed him *Nar-* upon the spot; and endeavouring afterwards to force a pas- *bonne.* sage for his escape, was cut to pieces by those who seized him *872.* for the murder [c]. His son, who was of the same name, was conducted prisoner to king *Charles*, who expressed great concern for his father's misfortune; and, promising him his pro-

[x] Chron. var. antiq.   [y] Annal S. Bertin.   [z] AMON. Annal S. Bertin.   [a] Chron. five Histor. Com. Barcimon a MONACH. Rivipul. Script.   [b] FRANCISCO DIAGO Historica de los antiquos Condes Barcelona. Barcelona 1603. fol. [c] Marca Hispanica.

tection, sent him into *Flanders*, to be brought up under the care of that monarch's own sister, who had a great respect for him [d].

His son of his own name succeeds as count of Barcelona.
874.

THE county of *Barcelona* was, for the present, bestowed upon *Solomon*, the informer; of whose administration there is not the smallest circumstance to be found; nor does it appear whether he died, or was removed to make way for count *Wifrid* the second, son of *Wifrid* the first; who proving a person of great virtue and piety, as well as of singular charity, was very soon restored to his father's employment, and is considered as the first count of *Barcelona* who had any share of sovereign authority; inasmuch, as he did homage for this city and country, and was to hold it as a fief from the kings of *France*, for himself and his heirs [e].

885.

WIFRID II. surnamed *Velloso,* that is, the *Hairy,* and also *the Warlike,* taking advantage of the dissentions amongst the *Moors,* began to extend his dominions, making himself master of *Solsona* and *Cordona,* both of which he fortified, and established his affairs on so solid a foundation, that he had little to fear from the Infidels; who, though they attempted to invade his territories with a great army, were constrained to retire with a considerable loss, and soon after they sued to him for peace [f]. He was the founder of the *Benedictine* monastery of *Ripol:* himself, and his countess *Vinilda,* were present at the consecration, on the twenty-fifth of *July,* and one of his sons became a monk in that house, which was ever after much favoured by the princes of his family [g]. He ruled in *Catalonia* thirty-seven years with great reputation, and had by his countess before-mentioned four sons, *Ranulpho,* who became a monk, *Wifrid,* who died in the life-time of his father, *Miron,* who succeeded him, and *Seniofredo,* upon whom he bestowed the county of *Urgel.* His countess dying before him, he espoused a second time a lady, who survived him, and whose name was *Garsinda,* and, by his own direction, was interred in the monastery of *Ripol,* which became thenceforward the burying place of the counts of *Barcelona* [h].

890.
He rules with reputation, and dies in peace.

911.

His son Miron proves an inactive prince.

MIRON, count of *Barcelona,* appears to have been an inactive prince, since we find little or nothing recorded of him in history, though he enjoyed this principality seventeen years; neither do we know whom he married; but at his demise he left behind him three sons, *Seniofredo,* who succeeded him,

[d] Chron. Rivipul. DIAGO.   [e] Marca Hispan. ZURIT. Indices Rerum ab Arragoniæ regibus Gestarum.   [f] DIAGO. Marca Hispanica.   [g] Chron. Rivipul. ZURITA,   [h] DIAGO.

Olivia,

Oliva, to whom he gave the county of *Cerdagna*, and *Mira*, upon whom he bestowed that of *Gironne*, though, in his catalogue, *Mariana* makes him bishop of that place: as these children were in their nonage, at the time of his deceafe, their uncle, the count of *Urgel*, took the administration during their minority [i].

SENIOFRED, count of *Barcelona*, was put in possession of his dominions by his uncle, who governed them with great prudence and fidelity, and took the same care of his brethren [k]. This young count married the daughter of Don *Sanchez Abarca*, king of *Navarre* [l], by whom he had no issue, and, after a long reign, in which he did little, deceased, and was buried in the monastery of *Ripol* [m]. Both his brothers were living at the time of his death, and yet he was succeeded by

BORELO, his cousin, son to *Seniofredo*, count of *Urgel* [n]; but by what colour of right, or whether by force, as *Mariana* suggests [o], or by procuring the investiture from the crown of *France*, as *Ferreras* [p] conjectures, is not very clear. This prince made a journey to *Rome*, in order to settle the ecclefiaftical jurifdiction in his dominions; for, the city of *Taragona* being in the hands of the *Moors*, all the bishops in his territories were under the jurifdiction of the bishop of *Narbonne*, which was attended with such inconveniencies, that the pope, at his request, declared the bishop of *Offona* metropolitan of *Catalonia*, till such time as *Tarragona* should be recovered out of the hands of the Infidels [q]. But as the count had not taken the precaution to apply first to his lord paramount, the the king of *France*, this regulation did not take effect [r]. He was very affiduous in improving, fortifying, and adorning, the chief towns in his territories, and very fortunate in the defence of them against the *Moors*, till *Mohammed Almanzar*, who conceived some particular dislike to this prince, made an irruption into *Catalonia*, with a prodigious army, in which he committed most horrid depredations. Count *Borelo*, who could not bear to see the miseries of his subjects, advanced, with such an army as he was able to raise, to *Moncada*, where he gave the enemy battle, and where he had the misfortune to be so totally defeated, that, in all probability, no part of his army would have been preserved, if the adjacent moun-

Side notes:
928.

Is succeeded by his fon Seniofred. 967.

972. *Count Borelo is defeated by Mohammed Almanzar;*

---

[i] Marca Hispanica. ZURITA.   [k] Chron. Rivipul.
[l] P. MORET Inveftigaciones Hiftoricas de los antiquitades del Reyno de Navarra.   [m] DIAGO.   [n] Chron. Rivipul. ZURIT.   [o] Hiftoria general de Efpana.   [p] Hiftoria de Efpana.   [q] DIAGO.   [r] Chron. Rivipul. Marca Hifpanica.

tains

who takes Barcelona by assault.

tains and forests had not secured them from the pursuit of a barbarous and implacable enemy[s]. *Mohammed Almanzar* proceeded directly to *Barcelona*, and, finding but a small garrison, attacked and carried it by assault. A great part of the inhabitants was put to the sword; he carried away most of the rest; and, having left a body of troops in the fortress, set fire to the city, in which all the archives, records, and titles, public and private, were consumed, which is the true reason that the history of this principality is so imperfect[t]. Count *Borelo* in this distress, applied for assistance to *Lewis* the fourth of *France*; to whom he represented, that what the Infidels aimed at was to make a road through *Catalonia* into his dominions: upon which suggestion a great corps of troops was immediately sent to his assistance; with whom, having joined the remains of his own army, he returned immediately to

985.
But this city is regained by count Borelo, who dies in the year 993.

Barcelona, which he attacked and carried sword in hand; and, having destroyed all the *Mohammedans* he found therein, applied himself, with the utmost diligence, to repair and repeople the place[u]. The rest of his reign was spent in cultivating the arts of peace, and in fortifying his frontier in such a manner, as to prevent his subjects from suffering any misfortune of the like kind in time to come. He deceased in the month of *October*, in the year of our Lord nine hundred and ninety-three[w], and left several children, but of these we have no distinct account.

Don *Raymond* his son succeeded at the age of twenty-one, and proved a prince of great virtue and valour[x]. The *Moors*, with a prodigious army, attempted to invade his country; but Don *Raymond*, assisted by his brother-in-law, Don *Ermengild*, count of *Urgel*, gave them such a reception, that they were glad to retire: upon which the two counts fell upon their frontiers, and returned with a great booty[y].

1003.

Things were now so well settled in *Catalonia*, that the count held an assembly of the states, which is mentioned here, because it seems to be the first which had been held at *Barcelona*, since it was recovered by the Christians[z]; and the fame of Don *Raymond* was so great, that both by the Christians and *Moors* he was equally respected. *Mohammed Almahadi*, being dispossessed of the kingdom of *Cordova* by *Zulima*, applied himself, by the advice of his prime minister *Albamer*, to the count of *Barcelona*, for his assistance, promising to give him some places that lay very conveniently, in

---

[s] Diago.　　　[t] Marian. Fer.　　　[u] Marca Hispanica. Zurit.　　　[w] Diago.　　　[x] Chron. Ripul.　　　[y] Diago.　　　[z] Marca Hispanica. Marian. Ferreras.

case

case he would enable him to remount the throne. The count Don *Raymond*, having consulted his nobility and prelates, accepted this proposition ; and, having assembled the whole force of his dominions, he joined the *Moorish* army, and directed their march towards *Cordova* [a]. On the road they were surprized by *Zulima*, who attacked them so vigorously, while they were in disorder, that he killed great numbers, and amongst them *Ermengild* count of *Urgel*, *Aetius* bishop of *Barcelona*, *Arnulph* bishop of *Vich*, and *Otho* bishop of *Gironne* [b]. Don *Raymond* himself was in the rear, with a good number of his own forces, behind whom he rallied, and formed the flying remains of the broken army ; and, when *Zulima* thought there was nothing left but a pursuit, charged him so roughly, that, after a short dispute, he deprived him of that victory which he thought secure, and pushed his success so briskly, that he conducted *Mohammed Almahadi* in triumph to *Cordova*, and seated him again upon the throne [c]. After this he governed his dominions in splendour and peace, till at length he departed this life, in the year of our Lord one thousand and seventeen, leaving his dominions to his son Don *Berenger*, an infant, under the tutelage of the countess *Ermisenda* his mother [d].

margin: 1009. His son Don Raymond obtains a signal victory over the Moors

margin: 1017. Dies and leaves his territories to his son

DON *Berenger*, count of *Barcelona*, being arrived at full age, and, having assumed the government [e], married Donna *Sancha*, daughter, as some say, of the count of *Castile* ; but, as *Moret* [g] and *Salazar* assure us, the daughter of Don *Sancho* count of *Gascony*. He seems to have been a prince of a very pacific spirit, for which reason none of the *Spanish* historians have given themselves the trouble of recording his actions : all we know of them is, that he deceased in the year of our Lord one thousand and thirty-five, and that he was interred in the monastery of *Ripol* [i]. He left behind him three sons, *Raymond* his successor, *Guillormo* count of *Manreso*, and *Sancho*, who, in process of time, enjoyed the same county.

margin: Berenger, an infant, who dies in the year 1035.

DON *Raymond* the second was a prince of great parts and piety [k], and not at all inclined to pass his days in the same obscurity that his father had done : he espoused at first Donna *Beatrix*, and afterwards Donna *Almari*, the daughter of the count of *Limoges*; held various assemblies of his states at *Barcelona*, in which he regulated the civil and ecclesiastical dominions ; in one of which he amicably compromised some

margin: Succeeded by his son Don Raymond II.

[a] DIAGO. [b] Chron. Rivipul. ZURIT. [c] Marca Hispanica. Chron. Rivipul. [d] DIAGO. [e] Marca Hispanica. [g] Investigaciones Historicas de los antiquitades del Reyno de Navarra. [i] Chron. Rivipul. [k] DiAGO.

differences

differences that had arisen between him and his grandmother the countess *Ermisenda*, and gave her, in lieu of the places she held, one thousand ounces of gold [l]. He took from the *Moorish* king of *Saragossa Manresa*, and several other places [m]. The cathedral church of *Barcelona* being old and decayed, the count Don *Raymond* rebuilt it entirely, and caused it to be consecrated with great solemnity on the eighth of *November*, at which time the *Moor Ali*, king of *Denia*, *Majorca*, *Minorca*, and *Ivica*, confirmed to the bishop of *Barcelona* his spiritual jurisdiction over the Christians in his dominions [n]. Ten years after this he held a famous council at *Gironne*, in which were present the pope's legate, the archbishop of *Narbonne*, in quality of metropolitan, and all the bishops in his dominions, and in which various canons were made. It was this prince who introduced into his dominions the titles of viscount, baron, and vavasor; and, by several other wise regulations, rendered himself rich and potent, and his people secure and happy: he was by much the most eminent of the princes of this family; and, dying full of years and glory, *May* the twenty-fifth, one thousand and seventy five, was buried in the new church of *Barcelona*, which was of his own foundation [p].

1056.

a wife and pacific prince, who quitted this life in the year 1075.

His sons Don *Berenger* and Don *Raymond* succeeded, by the express will of their father, jointly [q], in the county of *Barcelona*; in which his affection as a father certainly prevailed over that great prudence which he had shewn in the government of his dominions. In a short time after his demise, the brothers, as might have been easily foreseen, fell out; upon which pope *Gregory* the seventh sent a legate into *Catalonia*, to try what might be done towards reconciling them, in which, however, he was not very successful [r]: but these disputes did not rise to such a height as to create any considerable disorders in the government; for Don *Raymond*, by the consent of the people, resided at *Barcelona*, and gratified his brother Don *Berenger* with the subsidies that he received from the king of *Saragossa*, and otherwise, so as to afford him a considerable revenue [s]. This Don *Raymond* espoused *Almodia*, or *Matilda*, a lady of the *Norman* race, by whom he had a son *Raymond Arnaldo* [t]. He had not governed his principality above five years before he was unfortunately murdered, at a place called *Pertica-de-Ostor*, by certain banditti [u]. Some historians assure us, that these assassins were employed by his brother Don *Berenger*, who, as he was the eldest of the

The government devolves to his two sons Berenger and Raymond;

which last is murdered by banditti.

---

[l] ZURIT. var. antiq. [m] Marca Hispanica. [n] Chron.
[q] DIAGO. [p] Marca Hispanica. Chron. Rivipul.
[t] DIAGO. [r] ZURITA. [s] Marca Hispanica.
[u] ZURITA.

two

two brothers, was exceedingly offended that his father and the people in general preferred his younger brother *Raymond*, and, while they intrusted him with the government, thought a penfion a fufficient equivalent for his pretenfions [w]. *Mariana* goes much farther; for he affirms that Don *Berenger*, being univerfally hated and defpifed, was thruft out of all that had been affigned him ; and, not being able to endure the continual reproaches he met with at home, chofe to retire out of *Catalonia*, and, in the end, out of *Spain*, under colour of taking upon him the crufade, and fighting againft the Infidels in the *Holy Land*. Arriving at *Jerufalem* he was ftruck dumb, and in that woeful ftate paffed the remainder of his days, in folitude, indigence, and contempt [x]. Yet one of the moft learned, diligent, and accurate writers of the affairs of *Catalonia*, has taken great pains to fhew that all this is the pure invention of later writers ; and that, though the brothers had not lived in the ftricteft harmony, yet Don *Berenger* was fo far from having any hand in his brother's murder, or from reaping any benefit by it, that he became the tutor and protector of his nephew, who was then in his cradle, and who, under his care, became as able, and, in procefs of time, as fortunate as any of the counts of *Barcelona* [y].

1082.

Don *Raymond Arnaldo*, or Don *Raymond* the fourth, became the heir of Don *Bernard* count of *Befalu*, in virtue of an agreement made between them, during their life-times, which added to his dominions and his territories [z]. He efpoufed Donna *Aldonça*, or *Dulce*, the daughter of *Gilbert* count of *Provence*, and the heirefs of that noble country [a]. Two years after this he entered into a league with *Aymer* vifcount of *Narbonne*, *William* count of *Montpellier*, and other neighbouring princes, againft the *Moors* in *Majorca*, who were continually pillaging their coafts, and more efpecially thofe of *Catalonia*. When they came to execute their fcheme, they found that nothing could be done without a naval force, and they could not altogether mufter up fo much as a fmall fquadron. By the interpofition of pope *Pafchal* the fecond, they prevailed upon the *Pifans* to furnifh them with a fleet, on board of which they put as many troops as the veffels of which it was compofed could tranfport, and, being debarked in *Majorca*, took and deftroyed that neft of pirates ; and it is highly probable that this firft put thofe princes upon aiming at a naval force, which they afterwards accomplifhed [b]. Don *Bernard* count of *Cerdagna*, dying

His fon Don Raymond IV. *fucceeds as count of* Barcelona. 1112.

[w] Ferr. ago. var. antiq.   [x] Hiftoria general de Efpana. [z] Marca Hifpanica. Zurit.   [b] Marca Hifpanica.   [y] Diago.   [a] Chron.

without

1117.

without issue, left his dominions to the count Don *Raymond*[c];
and *Mariana* says, that, after some disputes, and even a war,
with the count of *Thoulouse*, all differences were terminated,
by the two counts reciprocally adopting each other, which,
in its issue, brought that county into this family. At length,

At his death the title is inherited by his son Don Raymond V. **1131.**

having lived long, acquired great reputation, and many fair
seignories, he deceased, having first taken the habit of a knight
templar: his remains, according to his own order, were interred in the monastery of *Ripol*[d]. He had two sons, Don
Raymond who succeeded him, and Don *Raymond* who inherited the county of *Prevence*; and two daughters, Donna
Berengara, who married the emperor Don *Alonso* of *Castile*[e],
and Donna *Cecilia* who married the count *de Foix*[f].

DON *Raymond* the fifth, count of *Barcelona*, entered on
the government of this principality with great reputation g.
His alliance to the emperor Don *Alonso* made him extremely
considerable; and it was upon his doing homage to that
prince that Don *Alonso* count of *Thoulouse* was prevailed upon to take the same step[h]. He incorporated the county of
Cerdagna, to which there were some pretenders, into his
own dominions[i]; and was very useful to many of his neighbours, particularly in negotiatiating that alliance between
the crowns of *Castile* and *Arragon*, which saved the latter from
the *Moors*, after the unfortunate battle of *Fraga*, of which
Don *Ramiro the Monk* was so sensible, that he immediately
cast his eyes upon him for his son-in-law and successor[k]. Don

Who, marrying the daughter of Don Ramiro the Monk, united Catalonia to the kingdom of Arragon.

Raymond no sooner found himself presumptive heir to the
crown of *Arragon*, than he judged it a convenient season to
throw off all marks of dependency in *Catalonia*; in pursuance
of which he forbad his subjects to date any longer, as hitherto
they had done, by the years of the reigns of the *French*
monarchs[l]: which was in plain terms avowing he would be
their vassal no longer; tho' in reason and in law this could
have no force without the consent of the lord, that is, of the
crown of *France*, to whom these countries belonged, in right
of conquest; and, as we shall see hereafter, this, at another
favourable opportunity, was procured by his marriage with
Donna *Petronilla*, heiress of *Arragon*, when that kingdom and
the county of *Barcelona* came to be united in the person of the
same sovereign, but without any incorporation of territories;

[c] Chron. Rivipul.   [d] Historia general de Espana.
Chron. Rivipul.   [e] Chron. Adefons Imperat.   [f] Marca
Hispanica.   [g] DIAGO.   [h] Chron. Adefons Im-
perat   [i] DIAGO.   [k] ZURIT. HIERONYMI BLANCÆ
Arragonensium rerum Commentarii.   [l] DIAGO.

the

the *Catalans* and the *Arragonians* being equally inflexible in that particular, and looking upon their respective privileges as invaluable in themselves, and not to be communicated on any consideration [m] ; so that it may be truly said the princes of this family reigned over two of the proudest. nations upon the earth ; and the reader therefore need not wonder, that they did not always reign in quiet.

[m] ZURIT. Marça Hispanica. DIAGO. FER.

END *of the* TWENTIETH VOLUME.

Lightning Source UK Ltd.
Milton Keynes UK
UKHW020610110119
335177UK00005B/320/P